W9-BXG-761

ANTITRUST IN JAPAN

# ANTITRUST IN JAPAN

財閥解体と系列

by Eleanor M. Hadley

PRINCETON UNIVERSITY PRESS
PRINCETON, NEW JERSEY
1970

L.C. Card: 68-56312
S.B.N. 691-04194-6

Title page calligraphy by Miss Uwano Moto

Printed in the United States of America
by Princeton University Press, Princeton, New Jersey

*For*
M S H
*and*
*in memory*
H M H

# Contents

# Preface

THIS BOOK might be said to represent the unforeseen consequences of a bureaucratic argument. I became involved with the *zaibatsu* and the question of U.S. policy toward those giant combines in the World War II period when I was "borrowed" by the International Business Practices Branch of the State Department from the Office of Strategic Services to work on a research-policy paper on this matter. In the dispute within State as to which division would prepare the paper, the economists won the argument, but winning, discovered they had no one with familiarity with Japan. Subsequently I transferred to the Department, then in April 1946 left to join MacArthur's headquarters in Tokyo, where I was a member of General Whitney's Government Section for the next year and a half. In September 1947 I returned to Radcliffe College to take up a pending fellowship from the American Association of University Women.

Having become bureaucratically involved with Japan's giant business, I made the *zaibatsu* the subject of my doctoral dissertation, *Concentrated Business Power in Japan*, in 1949. I did not return to the subject of industrial organization in Japan until 1962 when I was in Japan as a Fulbright Research Scholar to observe the consequences of the Occupation's deconcentration policy.

The book is divided into two parts. Part I is an account of what was done in the Occupation toward breaking up concentrated business, and the reasons for doing so. Part II is an analysis of the current scene in Japan. Those familiar with the field may wonder why I decided to include Part I, inasmuch as Professor T. A. Bisson's study, *Zaibatsu Dissolution in Japan*, is available. My primary reason is the much fuller information available than when Professor Bisson wrote his study, although differences in interpretation and analysis likewise entered into the decision.

For a foreigner to undertake a study of Japan's economy and social change presents both weaknesses and strengths. Obviously I cannot bring to the subject the familiarity with the literature that a Japanese scholar would bring. On the other hand, the very lack of such familiarity provides an opportunity for freshness of perception. Also, the study of Japan's social structure has provided me with insights into the social structure of the United States.

Indebtedness to mentors and colleagues is extensive. Ariga Michiko, now a Commissioner of the Fair Trade Commission, whose leadership has been an important element in antitrust taking root in Japan, is one to whom very special acknowledgment is due. Throughout my research on the contemporary scene she has "opened doors." In a quite literal sense Part II of this book is "owing to her honorable shadow." Professor Wakimura, emeritus of Tokyo University, was kind enough to chair what I came to call my criticizing seminar made up of a group of Japanese scholars who gave me the benefit of their judgment on the small first draft of this book. Active members of the seminar, which was made possible by a grant from the Asia Foundation, were: Mrs. Ariga, Fair Trade Commission; Professor Shoda, Keio University; Professor Sakane, Hitotsubashi University; Professor Nakagawa, Tokyo University; Professor Togai, Senshu University; and Professor Hirono, Seikei University who also acted as executive secretary.

Royama Shoichi, then a graduate student and now on the faculty of Tokyo University as a research assistant, introduced me to pertinent scholarly sources and helped me through language problems, written and oral. His contribution to this study is substantial.

The number of other scholars, business executives, government officials, and friends who took time to discuss various matters with me is too large to be able to name individually. To all of these persons I again express my grateful appreciation.

Among scholars in the United States I am especially indebted to those who generously read key chapters or whole subsequent drafts. Professor Edward S. Mason and Professor Corwin D. Edwards read the draft which I brought back from Japan; Professor John Maki, Professor George Kakiuchi, and the other members of the Asian Faculty Seminar at the University of Washington read "Zaibatsu Yesterday; Business Groupings Today"; Professor Edwin O. Reischauer, Professor W. Geoffrey Shepard, Professor Dan F. Henderson and Professor Henry Rosovsky read the final draft.

Librarians and libraries play a key role in any such undertaking. I am indebted to Kuwabara Makoto of the National Diet Library, Tokyo, as I am to the librarians of the Smith College Library and the U.S. Tariff Commission, and I gratefully acknowledge the use of the library of the Economics Department of Tokyo University as well as the University of Washington Library.

Anyone engaged in writing understands the very real contribution that typists make to getting a study done and out. Royama Shimako of Tokyo typed the first draft used in the Japanese criticizing seminar. Betty Ann Best of Seattle handled the many subsequent drafts through which the study went, including all of the tables. Her speed, accuracy, and good judgment were invaluable additives to this project.

Some years ago, in installing a president at Mt. Holyoke College, a panel was organized on the theme: words are responsibilities. The words that follow are my responsibilities. I have endeavored to select them with care.

Eleanor M. Hadley
*Washington, D.C.*
*July 2, 1969*

# Part I

# 財閥解体

*The . . . truth is that the liberty of a democracy is not safe if the people tolerate the growth of private power to a point where it becomes stronger than their democratic state itself.*

*Government can deal and should deal with blindly selfish men. But that is a comparatively small part—the easier part—of the problem. The larger, more important and more difficult part of our problem is to deal with men who are not selfish and who are good citizens, but who cannot see the social and economic consequences of their actions in a modern economically interdependent community.*

—Franklin D. Roosevelt, The White House, April 29, 1938. From the Message to the Congress calling for an investigation of concentrated economic power in the United States.

# 1.

## Japan's Combines, Target of Occupation Reform

World War II differed radically from previous wars in the terms imposed by the victors on the defeated. Previously exactions had been limited to territorial changes, restrictions on the military establishment, and reparations. World War II, representing for the first time "total" warfare, extended to the peace conditions "total" peace, with demands for change in the political and economic structure of the defeated powers. In both Germany and Japan the victors attempted to revamp the social structure, to establish democracy. In the words of one descriptive title, the Germans and the Japanese were "forced to be free."[1] In the Allied view, Germany had started three major conflicts within a century; Japan, following its emergence from self-imposed isolation, had pursued a pattern of unremitting territorial expansion—Formosa, Korea, Manchuria, China, and Southeast Asia. Allied leaders saw the expansionist foreign policy of Germany and Japan as the product of their undemocratic governments, and believed that the future security interests of their own countries required nothing less than the social reconstruction of these two nations. By themselves, proscription of army-navy-air force, along with territorial adjustments, were insufficient. Nothing less than basic social reconstruction was needed if democracy, which would be peaceable, were to take root.

But not in all parts of the world has democracy been so closely associated with peaceful foreign policy as it was in official Allied thinking. Many Asians and Africans might have wondered what such analysis did with the facts of empire, with colonial Asia, with colonial Africa, perpetrated by metropolitan powers, the majority of which had democratic governments. In the Western view these colonial holdings were not the consequence of deliberate glorying in war; rather they came about almost as a by-product of the enormous increase in productivity of certain national economies at a time when the industrial and scientific revolutions began shrinking the world. By contrast, German and Japanese territorial expansion was

[1] John D. Montgomery, *Forced to be Free: The Artificial Revolution in Germany and Japan*, Chicago, 1957.

seen as the product of deliberate exaltation of war, of a philosophy which held the battlefield to be the testing ground of men.

Colonialism is a contradiction to democratic beliefs, as the postwar period has demonstrated. There was, however, no contradiction between German and Japanese political beliefs and territorial expansion. Regarding themselves as "chosen people," both peoples believed in the theory of a master race. Denying civil liberty at home, they openly professed subjugating others. The more extravagant Japanese imperialists called for the entire world to be under Japanese domination. "Hakko ichiu" was their cry: "Eight corners of the world under one roof."[2] The Allies believed that governments that tended to respect the rights of citizens at home were more likely to respect the rights of others abroad. Thus it was that the Allies undertook their experiment in democratizing.

The programs for democratization in Germany and Japan were essentially similar. In both instances they called for a new constitution, new leadership, and change in the structure of the economy. Economic change was demanded for political reasons. The Allies believed that a democratic constitution would be meaningless unless the key pressure groups of the nation supported its ideology. In both Germany and Japan concentrated business was seen as one of the most powerful pressure groups, and because German and Japanese concentrated business was not considered to support democracy but rather oligarchy, it became a target of Occupation reform.

The Allied assumption in the case of both countries was that giant enterprises, benefiting greatly by a policy of foreign aggression, had supported the leadership directing the foreign aggression, except when military projects seemed unduly risky. But more fundamentally, the charge was that the political climate that suited such giant structures was not equality but hierarchy, not individual rights and liberties but their suppression. If there was to be an effort to develop a different philosophy of values in Germany and Japan and the pyramided structure of business were ignored, the chance of success would be a great deal smaller than if the structure of business enterprise were changed.

That Allied thinking was highly critical of giant enterprise reflected American New Deal views.[3] In the Roosevelt New Deal period, long-

[2] Actually, "hakko ichiu" is an ancient Chinese expression emphasizing the unity of mankind, which early came into Japan. The expression was adopted by the Japanese militarists in order to give their overseas operations a more pleasing sound. I am indebted to Uramatsu Samitaro for this point.

[3] New Deal views on concentrated business are particularly evident in President Roosevelt's 1938 message to Congress, calling for an investigation of concentrated

standing American distrust of big business came together with massive malperformance of the American economy. The first two Roosevelt terms were periods of idle men and idle machines. The consequent criticism of big business had a sharpness to it which it would not have had if American capitalism had been performing well. On top of this, it became apparent with the outbreak of war in Europe that large German corporations had been actively and closely involved with the hated Third Reich. In the eyes of the Allies German big business was not as concerned with the historic bourgeois values of civil liberties and the diffusion of power, as it was a willing collaborator in their overthrow. It turned out that German private business arrangements with foreign firms in the form of cartels and patent agreements had been drawn to the national advantage of the Third Reich and the injury of nations opposing its policies.[4]

Thus to those in Washington it appeared of utmost importance to remake the character of enterprise in Germany and Japan if democracy were to be realized. Accordingly it seemed essential to break up the I. G. Farbens and the Krupps, the Mitsuis and Mitsubishis, into competitive enterprises.[5] Because of the scale of the American contribution to the Allied effort, American views were predominant,

---

business power in the United States and in the recommendation of the Temporary National Economic Committee (TNEC). Excerpts of the former are reproduced in Appendix I. These materials are offered to underscore the point that business deconcentration in Germany and Japan was not undertaken in a spirit of revenge or with the intention to weaken these economies, but rather as an outgrowth of thinking first developed toward the American economy, the action program of which was interrupted by the war.

This same approach to concentrated business is revealed in the abortive International Trade Organization, which was conceived to be the third great international institution alongside the International Monetary Fund and International Bank for Reconstruction and Development. Here the thinking is to be found in an organization which it was hoped the victorious Allies would join, as well as those defeated in the war.

[4] Cf., for example, G. W. Stockings and M. W. Watkins, *Cartels in Action*, New York 1946; Corwin D. Edwards, *Economic and Political Aspects of International Cartels*, Monograph No. 1, Senate Committee on Military Affairs, 78th Congress, 2nd Sess., Washington, D.C., 1946.

[5] In Japan, where concentration took the conglomerate path, "competitive" is used for the most part not in the sense of changing the number of members in markets but as cutting the ties which bound the major of one market to affiliates in other markets. That is, "competitive" is used in the sense of cutting the ties which made Mitsui Trading, Mitsui Banking, Mitsui Mining, Mitsui Shipbuilding, Mitsui Chemical, Mitsui Steamship, Toyo Rayon, Mitsui Warehouse, into a single business operation. Thus entry was to be promoted not by eliminating monopolistic positions—there were very few of them—but by making the members of a conglomerate combine separate and independent businesses.

and so were born the two greatest experiments in trust-busting the world has seen.

The extent, successes, and consequences of the Japanese experiment form the subject of this book. The entire arduous and contradictory episode is strewn with lessons about Japan, about what antitrust action can hope to accomplish, and about American views on competition.

### *"'Dissolve' Large Industrial and Banking Combinations"*

Because U.S. policy on the Japanese Occupation was still incomplete at the time of surrender, MacArthur was instructed on U.S. policy in two separate documents, a presidential statement of September 6, 1945 and the Basic Directive of November 1, 1945. The presidential statement represented the key portions of the Basic Directive. While the statement was sent by President Truman and the Basic Directive by the Joint Chiefs of Staff, both documents were in fact the product of the State, War, Navy Coordinating Committee, frequently abbreviated SWINCC (with the "I" for pronunciation only). In the presidential statement MacArthur was told that,

> Encouragement shall be given and favor shown to the development of organizations in labor, industry, and agriculture, organized on a democratic basis. Policies shall be favored which permit a wide distribution of income and of the ownership of the means of production and trade. . . . .
>
> To this end it shall be the policy of the Supreme Commander: . . . To favor a program for the dissolution of the large industrial and banking combinations which have exercised control of a great part of Japan's trade and industry.[6]

In the more detailed Directive, which carried the Joint Chiefs of Staff number JCS 1380/15 ("15" representing the number of successive versions), MacArthur was informed: ". . . you will require the Japanese to establish a public agency responsible for reorganizing Japanese business in accordance with the military and economic objectives of your government. You will require this agency to submit, for approval by you, plans for dissolving large Japanese industrial and banking combines or other large concentrations of private business control."[7]

[6] Reproduced in various publications. The quotation is from T. A. Bisson, *Zaibatsu Dissolution in Japan*, Berkeley, 1954, p. 239.

[7] The quotation is taken from Edwin M. Martin, *The Allied Occupation of Japan*, New York, 1948, pp. 139-40.

So much nonsense has been spoken and written in Japan about the origins of these instructions that it will be worthwhile to look in detail at how, in fact, MacArthur came to receive them. The first and most fundamental point is the indebtedness the Basic Directive for Japan, JCS 1380/15, owed the German Occupation document, JCS 1067. Policy for Germany and Japan was conceived in essentially similar terms, but because events were happening faster in the European theater than in the Pacific, American policy was developed for Germany first. At the Potsdam Conference in July 1945, in an understanding entitled "Principles to Govern the Treatment of Germany in the Initial Control Period,"[8] Truman, Stalin, and Atlee agreed that, "At the earliest practicable date, the German economy shall be decentralized for the purpose of eliminating the present excessive concentration of economic power as exemplified in particular by cartels, syndicates, trusts and other monopolistic arrangements."

In the United States document governing U.S. policy in the American sector of Germany, it is stated in Part II, Economic:[9]

> You will prohibit all cartels or other private business arrangements and cartel-like organizations, including those of a public or quasi-public character. . . .
>
> It is the policy of your Government to effect a dispersion of the ownership and control of German industry. . . .

In Part III, Finance, it is stated:

> You will make full application in the financial field of the principles stated elsewhere in this directive.

And in Part I, General and Political, it is stated under Denazification:

> All members of the Nazi Party who have been more than nominal participants in its activities, all active supporters and all other persons hostile to Allied purposes will be removed and excluded from public office and from positions of importance in quasi-public and private enterprises. . . .

The companion Japanese document to JCS 1067 was "Basic Initial Post-Surrender Directive to Supreme Commander for the Allied

[8] For one of several sources cf. U.S. Department of State, *Germany, 1947-1949; The Story in Documents*, Washington, D.C., 1950, pp. 47-57, for the full document.

[9] *Ibid.* The paragraphs quoted are Parts II, 36 and 37, III, 44, I, 6c. For the full document cf. pp. 23-33.

Powers for the Occupation and Control of Japan," JCS 1380.[10] Under Part II, Economic, of the document it is stated:

> It is the intent of the United States Government to encourage and show favor to: a) Policies which permit a wide distribution of income and ownership of the means of production and trade; b) The development of organizations in labor, industry and agriculture organized on a democratic basis. Accordingly, you will:
> 1) Require the Japanese to establish a public agency [which] . . . will . . . submit for approval by you plans for dissolving large Japanese industrial and banking combines or other large concentrations of private control. . . .
> 3) Dissolve the Control Associations. . . .
> 4) Abrogate all legislative or administrative measures which limit free entry of firms into industries to be reorganized where the purpose or effect of such measures is to foster and strengthen private monopoly.
> 5) Terminate and prohibit all Japanese participation in private international cartels or other restrictive private international contracts or arrangements. . . .

Part III, Financial:

> In the financial field you will make full application of the principles stated elsewhere in this directive. . . .

And Part I, General and Political:

> . . . in no circumstances will persons be allowed to hold public office or any other positions of responsibility or influence in public or important private enterprise who have been active exponents of militant nationalism and aggression, who have been influential members of any Japanese ultranationalistic, terroristic, or secret patriotic society, its agencies or affiliates, who have been influential in the activities of the other organizations enumerated . . . below, or who manifest hostility to the objectives of the military occupation.

Although the document for Japan was the product of SWINCC and the Germany document of the Informal Policy Committee on Germany (IPCOG) made up of representatives from State, War, Navy, and Treasury, the indebtedness of the former document to the latter is abundantly clear. In fact, an officer with drafting responsibility for the Japan document within the War Department commented to

[10] Martin, *Allied Occupation of Japan*, pp. 122-50. The paragraphs quoted are Parts II, 25, III, 34, I, 5b.

this writer that when he attempted to take a fresh approach to the Japan document he was told by his superior officer to abandon such efforts and proceed on the basis of the Germany document.

The Germany document clearly established a policy of economic deconcentration, but there had been differences of view within the State Department as to the merits of applying this policy to Japan. The argument was concentrated at the Japan desk and in one of the newly created economic divisions, the International Business Practices Branch of the Commodities Division. Officers at the Japan desk tended to see in Japan's combines political liberalism of the Western variety; officers of the economic division asserted that such giant aggregations of business power were "by definition" antidemocratic, that businesses employing hundreds of thousands of workers and covering the gamut of the modern sector of the economy could not help but represent quite different values than those found in free, competitive enterprise. Some estimates at the end of the war have put Mitsubishi employees at one million, and Mitsui employees within Japan at 1.8 million and in the whole of the Far East at two to three million.[11]

Japan-desk officers tended to interpret pre-Pearl Harbor Japanese history as a contest between the military and business elements, in which the military won out; officers of the economic division were not long on Japanese history, but, arguing analytically, they asserted that the scale of the combine investments in heavy industry, where the military were the chief consumers, made it impossible that there could be basic differences between the two. Further, the economists were impressed by the manner in which the combines gained business advantages in the areas falling under Japanese military control. In any event, the policy toward giant business in Japan followed that for Germany.

It has been said that American policy toward the combines was the handiwork of one or two subordinate persons in the State Department. To anyone with sophistication in government-policy matters, such a notion is inherently ridiculous; American governmental machinery simply does not work that way. As in all other matters, Amer-

[11] Eleanor M. Hadley, "Concentrated Business Power in Japan," unpub. ph.d. diss., Radcliffe College, 1949, p. 265a (hereafter cited as "Concentrated Business Power"), on the basis of private information. In the judgment of certain knowledgeable Japanese observers, these estimates are too high. If figures for the size of subsidiary networks were more reliable, one could be more confident of employee projections. It would be my guess that the Mitsui figure for the Far East includes, in addition to subsidiary employees, employees, for example, of firms and mines operated by Mitsui for the Japanese Army.

ican policy for Japan's combines was the product of many officers working together, officers representing three different departments whose work was reviewed as policy proposals moved from the "working level" to enunciation by responsible spokesmen as formal United States policy. At the working level drafting sessions on the economic section of the Japan document, in which I participated as a State Department member, it is my recollection that the meetings consisted of some 25 to 30 officers from the three departments. Proposals from these sessions were reviewed by intermediate-level committees before going to the State, War, Navy Coordinating Committee itself made up of assistant secretaries from the three departments for formal adoption.

### *The Allied Position*

The foregoing is an explanation of the development of American policy with respect to Japan; the Occupation, at least ostensibly, was Allied. Where did the voices of Allied representatives enter policy formulation? By and large, they did not enter at all. Allied policy machinery was almost entirely overtaken by events. Understandably, the United States government was insistent on avoiding the pattern of a divided occupation, as in Germany; the 11-nation Far Eastern Commission as the policy organ for Japan was the compromise. But while it was the official policy organ of the Occupation, it was not created until the Moscow Conference of December 1945, and it transmitted its reworking of the United States' Initial Post-Surrender Directive to MacArthur on June 26, 1947, 22 *months* after the start of the Occupation![12] If policy is to be effective, it must be enunciated while events are in the making.

There was no difference of opinion among the Allies about the desirability of economic deconcentration in Japan. Differences concerned only what should replace Japan's system of private collectivism. The United States wanted free private competitive enterprise, and under the circumstances, this policy prevailed. Most broadly put, the United States position, which became the Allied position, called for removal of the *zaibatsu* families from their position of business power and severing the ties—ownership, personnel, credit, contracts—which bound the component corporations into combine structures. Proposed, but essentially abandoned, was an effort to split up cer-

[12] For an authoritative and comprehensive account of the operations of the Far Eastern Commission and its preceding organization, the Far Eastern Advisory Commission, cf. U.S. Department of State, *The Far Eastern Commission*, prepared by George H. Blakeslee. Dept. of State Publication, 5138, Far Eastern Series 60, Washington, D.C., December 1953.

tain of the giant operating companies of the combines. This way, the Allies sought to achieve free competitive enterprise in the modern sector of the economy.

Some observers construed the Allied aim to have been one of establishing atomistic competition in the modern sector, a sort of industrial Morganthau plan. This interpretation is quite mistaken. In calling for a competitive structure to replace concentrated business in Japan, the Allies were attempting to create a situation in which there would be reasonable opportunity for entry into the markets of the modern sector of the economy and in which ownership of the means of production in that sector would be widespread, rather than concentrated under the control of a handful of business families. They were in no sense proposing to atomize Japanese industry along textbook lines.

Large numbers of Japanese, however, viewed dissolution of the combines and the subsequent antitrust legislation and labor standards laws not as a necessary condition to the establishment of democratic government, but as a device to weaken Japan, to destroy its ability to give vigorous competition to American and European business. A 1958 report, published by a Restrictive Trade Practices Study Team of the Japan Productivity Center, stated, "There are many who profess, and in all appearance honestly believe, that the Antimonopoly Law, along with the Standards of Labor Law, was forced by the victors upon the defeated nation for the covert purpose of keeping down her economy in a weak condition."[13] Yoshida Shigeru, writing in his Memoirs of the deconcentration effort, including the purges, said, ". . . it was the aim of Allied policy to democratize Japan; but, together with other Occupation measures such as the disintegration of major financial groups and the punishment of war criminals, the 'purges' were also the expression of a desire on the part of the Allied Powers to retaliate on the leaders of the nation they had defeated. . . ."[14]

Conservative spokesmen, intellectuals, and labor leaders were critical of the program. Many intellectuals and spokesmen for labor, influenced by the Marxian ideology so prevalent then and now in Japan, saw the program as a neat design of American "monopoly capital" to expand its market. The breakup of Japan's great combines had been called for so that General Motors, General Electric, International Business Machines, duPont, and others might have richer opportunities in the Japan market in the years ahead.

[13] Restrictive Trade Practices Study Team, Japan Productivity Center, *Control of Restrictive Trade Practices in Japan*, mimeographed, Tokyo, 1958, pp. 8-9.
[14] Yoshida Shigeru, *The Yoshida Memoirs*, London, 1961, p. 147.

The program for dissolving Japan's combines was not, however, completely without support in Japan. There were sophisticated intellectuals of liberal spirit who saw the development of more democratic forms of business to be essential if political democracy was to emerge. These intellectuals did not concentrate their attention on the historical factors contributing to the emergence of the *zaibatsu*; rather, they looked at the Japanese economy in the year 1945 and concluded that such concentrated forms of business were not necessary, leaving aside the historical question as to whether they had been necessary in earlier stages of the country's development. Illustrative of their thinking is the following:

> That the Zaibatsu obstructed the democratization of [the] Japanese economy is an undeniable fact. It was . . . only natural that one of the targets of the Potsdam Declaration for removing militarism and establishing democracy in Japan was directed toward the liquidation of the Zaibatsu. . . .
>
> With this Allied policy toward Japan as the warp and the Japanese people's ideal and fervor for the democratization of Japanese economy as the weft, the program for the liquidation of the Zaibatsu has been steadily put into shape.[15]

In addition to such intellectuals, there were large numbers of ordinary Japanese who gave the program warm support as evidenced by the letters received at headquarters by persons charged with carrying out the program.[16] Further, many smaller businessmen openly supported the effort.

*Background to the Japanese Reaction*

Part of the Japanese misinterpretation of the intent of the program stems from the weight of the Marxist tradition which permeates virtually all sectors of the country. It was close to inconceivable to large numbers of Japanese that the major Allied governments, dominated as they were conceived to be by "monopoly capital," would not use the occasion to promote their business interests. But the misunderstanding goes deeper. And it has to do with differences in other aspects of economic and political tradition.

The English-speaking tradition in economics has its roots in Adam Smith and the other classical and neo-classical writers. It is permeated

[15] Holding Company Liquidation Commission, *Laws, Rules and Regulations Concerning the Reconstruction and Democratization of Japanese Economy*, Tokyo, 1949, p. 9.

[16] As a member of the Government Section GHQ-SCAP, I, for example, received letters commending the headquarters' actions.

with the idea of economic laws, economic truths that hold regardless of time and place. Thus competition is not put forward as a market structure suitable for particular settings at particular times, but instead as the market form to be desired everywhere and at all times. The English-speaking tradition in economics has been overwhelmingly one of static analysis, abstracted from national or cultural details, an analysis which accentuates the idea of universal applicability.

The Japanese tradition in economics has been a mixture of the German historical school and Marxism. Its hallmark is dynamic analysis, with great attention to the temporal features of the setting. In this tradition one sees economic phenomena as an evolutionary process; what is true of one stage of development is by no means necessarily true of another.

Accordingly, part of the dismay with which the breakup of Japan's combines was viewed by many Japanese was the product of the very different tradition in political economy on the two sides of the Pacific Ocean. Americans have believed, at least in doctrine, that competitive markets were good at all times and in all places. The Japanese have not regarded competition as the best way of advancing economic development for a country wishing to come abreast of more developed economies. To paraphrase Joseph Schumpeter, Americans have concentrated attention on economic performance as of a given point in time;[17] Japanese have concentrated attention on performance over time, emphasizing the evolutionary nature of an economy and that an emerging economy represents different problems from those of a mature economy.[18]

There is more to the intellectual heritage. While the English-speaking tradition asserts that competitive markets are the most efficient markets—that is, they give the greatest output for the least input, not to mention their admired distributive performance—they also are desired for their political quality. They automatically diffuse power. And English-speaking persons, as do many others in the European tradition, in a heritage dating from the Greeks,

[17] Schumpeter, *Capitalism, Socialism and Democracy*, 2nd edn., New York, 1947 p. 83.

[18] Cf., for example, the review by Muto Masaaki of the Bank of Japan, of Edna E. Ehrlich's *The Role of Banking in Japan's Economic Development*, unpub. ph.d. diss., New School for Social Research, 1960, "Ehrlich joshi (no) 'Nihon Keizai Hatten Katei ni okeru, Ginko no Yakuwari' ni tsuite," *Banking*, September 1961, p. 104. While there is no consensus among Japanese writers as to what the stages are, there is consensus that there *are* stages. And while there is no consensus what is appropriate policy for a given stage, there is consensus that policy will differ according to the stage.

worry about the problem of power. Educated Englishmen and Americans have been reared in the philosophy that "power corrupts, and absolute power corrupts absolutely." Accordingly, the diffusion of power that competitive markets bring about is seen as a further virtue of a thoroughly competitive market system.

In Japan, however, with its Confucian heritage, power is not something distrusted or feared. Power is moral,[19] moral, that is, until lost by successful challenge. The concern Americans feel about power is expressed in popular and learned discussions of Big Government, Big Business, Big Labor, always in an accusative tone. One does not find a counterpart of this in Japanese discussions. Nowhere in the literature of Japan's combines today will one find a study paralleling the whole stream of American studies on the role of corporate power in a democratic society.[20] In Japan, power is not viewed as a problem.

### *Competition and Japanese Mores*

Yet among certain American students of Japan there was an uneasiness with the American antitrust solution that became the Allied position. The longtime and discerning student of Japanese affairs, T. A. Bisson, said of the American attempt to create competitive enterprise in the modern sector of the economy:

> In its choice of dissolution as the method of dealing with the combines, involving replacement of the Zaibatsu system by a free enterprise economy, the occupation policy hewed closely to the line of American ideology and experience. In the wider field, it equated democracy with the individualism characteristic of the American tradition. . . .
>
> No account, seemingly was taken of the roots of these American concepts, no question raised in regard to the congeniality of the soil into which they were being transplanted. . . .
>
> One did not necessarily have to make the counter assumption that the Japanese could not become individualists or could not operate in individualistic patterns. Given time and the proper circum-

[19] I am indebted to a discussion with Professor Albert Craig on this point.

[20] Cf., for example, Adolf A. Berle, Jr. and Gardiner C. Means, *The Modern Corporation and Private Property*, New York, 1933; Clair Wilcox, *Public Policies Toward Business*, Chicago, 1955; Edward S. Mason, ed., *The Corporation in Modern Society*, Cambridge, Mass., 1959. In his introduction, Professor Mason comments: "What . . . [we] are afraid of is that this powerful corporate machine, which so successfully grinds out the goods we want, seems to be running without any discernible controls."

stances or training, they might learn to do so. It was true, however, that the Japanese had not customarily so acted. . . .

Group cooperation, under leadership and discipline, was much more akin to Japanese habits of thought and action. . . .

The occupation officials who worked on the dissolution program soon learned that Japan "had no real tradition or experience in the basic aspects of democratic capitalism." . . . A competitive economy, regulated by government to maintain competition, Japan did not know. No favoring climate of opinion existed; the occupation would have to create it.[21]

An American foreign service officer with experience in Japan, Robert A. Fearey, wrote as follows[22]:

. . . Contrary to a rather widespread assumption abroad, the Japanese, with no real experience of the advantages of the competitive alternative, felt little or no resentment or animosity toward the Zaibatsu before the war,[23] and feel little or no gratification now at their destruction. . . .

Why has so little support been achieved? In part the answer lies simply in the unfamiliarity of the people with either the practices or the benefits of competition. Japan's experience throughout the formative period of its industrialization was with cartels on the German scale. . . .[24]

A second factor is that certain features of the nation's social and economic structure have in the past worked, and . . . continue to work, against a growth of the competitive system. . . .

There can be no question also . . . that the Japanese character is in many ways better adapted to a collaborative, hierarchical system of industrial organization than to a competitive one. . . . The typical businessman in prewar years welcomed the opportunity to link up with one of the Zaibatsu interests where an assured income

[21] Bisson, *Zaibatsu Dissolution in Japan*, Berkeley, 1954, pp. 39-41.

[22] Fearey, *The Occupation of Japan, Second Phase: 1948-1950*, New York, 1950, pp. 69-71.

[23] Mr. Fearey was evidently not recalling the outbursts of popular resentment against the *zaibatsu* in the thirties which claimed the life of Mitsui's *banto*, Baron Dan, in 1932 (cf. Chapter 3 for a brief discussion), nor the various propitiatory practices adopted by the *zaibatsu* to try to regain popular esteem. For one of several such studies cf. Mitsubishi Economic Research Institute, *Capital Acquisition and Control in the Mitsubishi Zaibatsu* (Mitsubishi Keizai Kenkyujo, *Mitsubishi Zaibatsu ni okeru, Shikin Chotatsu to Shihai*), published by the Economic Planning Agency (Keizai Kikaku Cho), Tokyo, 1958, pp. 124-27.

[24] Cf. Chapter 15 for an account of Japan's cartel history.

and opportunity for regular advancement awaited him. . . .[25] These traits of character and ways of doing things are deeply ingrained and hamper the introduction of a competitive system.

However, what these observers overlooked and what many Japanese observers like them disregarded was the fact that competitive enterprise was and is far from an unknown entity in Japan. Medium and small enterprise, which was and is highly competitive, accounts even today for some two-thirds of employment in manufacturing. While no doubt a sizable portion of medium-sized small enterprise in manufacturing is satellite to large enterprise as component parts producer or as product-finisher, this is not to say that the proprietors do not assume risk or that they are removed from competitive pressures. Table 1 provides data in manufacturing on the extraordinary pervasiveness of medium and small enterprise in Japan. Table 2 presents comparative information on other economies.

To concentrate attention on the capital-intensive sector of the economy, and to argue that the value patterns seen in it represent the value patterns of Japanese culture (not the patterns resulting from the cumulation of business power and most unusual market organization) is to ignore the larger part of manufacturing when the measure is employment. The pervasiveness of medium and small enterprise in Japan indicates to me that it was factors other than the value patterns of Japanese society that inhibited competitive conduct. As

25 The *Report* of the Mission on Japanese Combines suggests a rather different explanation for this phenomenon:

> From the questioning of a . . . [number] of experienced employee-executives of zaibatsu concerns, it became evident that four general reasons satisfactorily cover the reluctance of many Japanese to engage in independent business of sufficient size to attract zaibatsu attention. The first of these is that the control of banks and other financial institutions by the zaibatsu is sufficiently complete to block any new financing which may be desired or to prevent the granting of financial aid in an emergency. The second factor is that the scope of zaibatsu interests is such as to make interference with, or cutting off of, raw materials and supplies to a small competitor entirely possible. The third reason is another facet of the second, in that the same scope of zaibatsu interests, particularly in general trading, makes the selling of finished goods outside of a strictly local market largely dependent upon zaibatsu cooperation or at least toleration. The provision of Japanese law permitting exclusive dealing contracts is a useful instrument in interfering with or preventing small concerns from securing supplies and disposing of their finished products. The fourth reason is that zaibatsu interests are able to cripple a small firm by pirating its key employees and skilled workmen. Employment by a large and well-known concern is commonly considered by Japanese to add to personal "face," and this intangible factor is an element in the selection of employment.

*Report of the Mission on Japanese Combines*, Part I, a report to the Department of State and the War Department, Washington, D.C. 1946, p. 14.

Table 1-1: SHARE OF SMALL ENTERPRISE EMPLOYMENT IN MANUFACTURING INDUSTRIES, 1961 (in percent)

| Industry | Share of industry's employment in total manufacturing | Percent of Employees in various sized plants | | | |
|---|---|---|---|---|---|
| | | 1-49 | 50-99 | 100-199 | Total 1-199 |
| Manufacturing industry | 100.0 | 41.1 | 11.1 | 9.9 | 62.1 |
| Foodstuff processing | 10.7 | 62.6 | 10.0 | 10.2 | 82.8 |
| Spinning and weaving | 14.5 | 46.1 | 10.9 | 10.1 | 67.1 |
| Clothing and personal articles | 2.5 | 64.2 | 15.5 | 10.9 | 90.6 |
| Lumber and woodworking | 5.8 | 78.9 | 10.6 | 5.4 | 94.9 |
| Furniture and fixtures | 2.3 | 74.1 | 10.1 | 7.1 | 91.3 |
| Paper goods | 3.2 | 40.2 | 13.0 | 12.0 | 65.2 |
| Printing and publishing | 3.6 | 49.5 | 13.9 | 9.2 | 72.6 |
| Chemical industry | 5.3 | 13.9 | 8.0 | 8.7 | 30.6 |
| Petroleum and coal-processing | 0.4 | 27.5 | 13.9 | 11.6 | 53.0 |
| Rubber goods | 1.6 | 17.8 | 7.0 | 9.6 | 34.4 |
| Hide, leather, and their products | 0.6 | 69.2 | 12.0 | 6.4 | 87.6 |
| Glassware, stoneware, etc. | 5.0 | 42.8 | 13.2 | 12.8 | 68.8 |
| Iron and steel industry | 5.5 | 16.8 | 8.3 | 7.8 | 32.9 |
| Primary metal products (except iron and steel) | 2.0 | 18.7 | 8.0 | 8.0 | 34.7 |
| Metalware | 6.0 | 55.1 | 16.1 | 11.5 | 82.7 |
| Machinery | 9.7 | 33.6 | 12.7 | 12.4 | 58.7 |
| Electrical appliances | 8.8 | 16.4 | 9.8 | 10.3 | 36.5 |
| Transportation facilities | 6.3 | 18.0 | 8.2 | 8.6 | 34.8 |
| Medical, chemical, physical, and optical supplies, cameras, watches | 1.9 | 31.6 | 12.0 | 10.0 | 53.6 |
| Others | 4.3 | 72.7 | 12.4 | 9.7 | 94.8 |

Source and notes: Percentage entries calculated from absolute figures in Ministry of International Trade and Industry, *Industrial Statistics* (*Kogyo Tokei Hyo*), December 25, 1963, pp. 130-221. Employees are defined as "nontemporary" workers and include "masters" and family workers. The unit for scale is plant, not firm.

Table 1-2: AN INTERNATIONAL COMPARISON OF EMPLOYMENT IN MANUFACTURING ACCORDING TO SCALE

| | 1-19 | 20-49 | 50-99 | 100-199 | 200-999 | 1,000 & above | Total |
|---|---|---|---|---|---|---|---|
| Japan (1955) | 33.6% | 17.0% | 9.6% | 8.2% | 17.1% | 14.6% | 100 |
| America (1947) | 7.2 | 8.7 | 9.1 | (100-249) 15.6 | (250-999) 26.6 | 32.8 | 100 |
| England (1949) | (1-10) 5.0 | (11-49) 11.3 | 10.1 | 13.0 | 32.5 | 28.1 | 100 |

Source: *Economic White Paper* (*Keizai Hakusho*), 1957, p. 140, Table 65(2). A breakdown using different employment categories and providing more recent data for Japan and the United States will be found in The Japan Development Bank, *Facts and Figures on the Japanese Economy, 1964*, Tokyo, 1964, p. 122. Also, for additional countries, cf. D. L. McLachlan and D. Swann, *Competition Policy in the European Community*, London, 1967, p. 229.

will be seen in Part II of this book, the absence in the postwar period of top-holding company controls over the "majors" has resulted in far more competitive behavior in the "modern" sector, behavior which the Japanese government characteristically describes as "excessive competition."

Historically, what inhibited competition among the "majors" was not cultural values but the highly unusual situation of the oligopolists being the same oligopolists in market after market after market. Whatever the line of business examined, the top names were likely to be Mitsui, Mitsubishi, Sumitomo. Through top-holding companies, operations in markets as diverse as banking, coal mining, shipbuilding, electrical equipment, trading, were integrated into single wholes. The result was a live-and-let-live relationship among the great *zaibatsu*. Mitsui did not challenge Mitsubishi in markets of Mitsui's strength—so the writer would hypothesize—because Mitsui faced Mitsubishi in markets of Mitsubishi's strength.[26] For example, Mitsui through its subsidiary, Mitsui Mining, was much stronger in coal than Mitsubishi through its subsidiary, Mitsubishi Mining. However, in shipbuilding the positions were reversed; Mitsubishi, through its subsidiary, Mitsubishi Heavy Industries, was far

[26] Hadley, "Concentrated Business Power," p. 13, where indebtedness is expressed for a discussion with E. S. Mason on this point.

stronger than Mitsui through its subsidiary, Mitsui Shipbuilding. Expressed generically, one might say that oligopolist A did not challenge oligopolist B in markets of A's strength because it also faced oligopolist B in markets of B's strength. The result was "cordial oligopoly." If concentration is of an order of magnitude to prevent entry of newcomers through domination of credit sources, purchasing, and selling outlets, through price discrimination and the like, then the problem is permissible institutional arrangements rather than cultural values.

In recent years much has been written of "countervailing power" in the American economy, bigness on one side of the market breeding bigness on the other side of the market.[27] There was no countervailing power on the Japan scene. The odds were simply too great. The combines did not breed big unions. They prevented the development of a viable labor movement.[28]

The aim of the Allied economic deconcentration program was to give all Japanese businessmen the opportunity to engage in the modern sector of the economy, that is, to remove those conditions which preserved this sector for the chosen few, those conditions which in fact made it a private collectivism. The aim was to broaden the basis of ownership in the modern sector from a handful of business families of giant fortunes to ownership by the many. These were the goals of the Occupation. They were conceived not in idealism but because political democracy in Japan was regarded as essential to the security interests of the Allies, and because political democracy and economic democracy were viewed as inextricably related.

[27] J. K. Galbraith, *American Capitalism, The Concept of Countervailing Power*, Cambridge, Mass., 1952.

[28] For a brief sketch of prewar unionism cf. Solomon B. Levine, *Industrial Relations in Postwar Japan*, pp. 59-66.

# 2.

## Combine Enterprise in Japan

MacArthur's instructions were to "'dissolve' large industrial and banking *combines*," yet the agency of the Japanese government set up to carry out his orders was the *Holding Company* Liquidation Commission and the principal report which this agency issued was entitled, *Japan's Zaibatsu and their Dissolution* (*Nihon no Zaibatsu to Sono Kaitai*).[1] It will be helpful to clarify the relationship between "combines" and "holding companies" and "*zaibatsu*."

"Combine" refers to a complex of corporations displaying unified business strategy arising primarily out of an ownership base. The head organ of a combine will likely be a "holding company," a corporation which exists not for the production of goods and services but to control other corporations. If it is a "pure" holding company, it will only hold stock; if the adjective "pure" is not applied, its principal function will be to hold stock but it will have operating activities as well.[2] It may be asked, how does a combine differ from a corporation with a large number of subsidiaries? The difference is primarily that of scale. The principal subsidiaries of a combine will be "majors" in their own right, and because of this scale the control center will tend to spend full or close to full time on coordination, and little if any on operations.

The term "*zaibatsu*," by contrast, is a political expression referring to the estate of wealth, and by extension, to the source of this wealth, the combines. But in Japanese usage, not all combines are *zaibatsu*. In the vocabulary of many Japanese, only family-dominated combines are *zaibatsu*, though frequently such persons do not consist-

1 Holding Company Liquidation Commission, *Japan's Zaibatsu and their Dissolution* (Mochikabu Kaisha Seiri Iinkai, *Nihon Zaibatsu to Sono Kaitai*), Tokyo, is in two volumes. The textual volume was published in 1951, the data volume, 1950. Hereafter cited as HCLC, *Zaibatsu Dissolution*.

2 In the publication of the Organization for Economic Cooperation and Development (OECD) entitled, *Glossary of Terms Relating to Restrictive Business Practices*, Paris, 1965, a different usage will be found. There a "pure" holding company is defined as one holding for "investment reasons without interfering with or influencing the business activities of the other enterprises" (p. 23). Definitions inescapably have an arbitrary element and the definition employed here is in accordance with usage in the Japanese context.

ently abide by their own usage. The members of the Holding Company Liquidation Commission (hereafter the HCLC) maintained this view,[3] but then proceeded to name Nissan as one of the 10 designated *zaibatsu* (which they could scarcely escape doing, given its size), even though Nissan at no point had been family dominated. Although large numbers of Japanese subscribe to the family ingredient of "*zaibatsu*" when used in the sense of "combine," one finds many Japanese today speaking of a *zaibatsu* revival in spite of the fact that not a single one of the business groupings is family-dominated.

*Combine* is a broader term than *holding company.* It embraces the total complex of corporations in contrast to the command center alone. Thus in speaking of combine-dissolution, one would be referring to the entire range of controls used to achieve unity of action, as opposed to those controls emanating solely from the holding company. For example, in the case of Japan's combines, there were large, direct family holdings in addition to the holdings by the top-holding company. There were also horizontal ownership ties, or inter-subsidiary ownership. Further, there were contractual agreements between the subsidiaries, as well as credit controls.

To many Japanese, *zaibatsu* not only carries the connotation of a family-dominated combine but also has a time dimension. In contrast to the Western usage of this Japanese term, Japanese persons hold that the *zaibatsu* developed following World War I.[4] They maintain this even though Mitsui and Sumitomo, which were key Tokugawa merchant houses, began their strategic role in the modernization of Japan from the beginning of the Meiji period (1868-1912), and even though Mitsubishi and Yasuda began and rapidly flourished early in the Meiji period. Given the key role of these business groups in the Meiji period; given the Japanese conviction that the *zaibatsu* emerged in latter Taisho (1912-26); and given the fact that the expression is basically political, the writer cannot but wonder if this Japanese dating does not unconsciously reflect the introduction of

[3] When I asked a former HCLC Commissioner why the Japan Nitrogenous Fertilizer Company (Nippon Chisso Hiryo) had not been included, he replied that inasmuch as its founder had died in 1944 it was no longer a family-dominated combine.

[4] Illustrative of a *zaibatsu* expression of the view that *zaibatsu* business structures did not emerge until the World War I period is the following taken from Mitsubishi Economic Research Institute, *Mitsui, Mitsubishi, Sumitomo,* Tokyo, 1955, p. 11: "Maintaining control of their industries through holding organizations, this control developed to an indirect industrial controlling system, by which their associated companies controlled others through the ownership of shares. *This control network appeared roughly about the time of World War I* and expanded remarkably under the semi-war and war conditions after 1937." Italics added.

Marxism into Japan after World War I.[5] That is, the *zaibatsu* did not exist earlier because Japanese persons earlier did not think in terms of an "estate of wealth" or "monopoly capital."

How one counts the number of "large industrial and banking combines" in Japan at war's end depends on whether one uses "combine" in the Western sense of the word, in the sense of "*zaibatsu*," whether one is consistent in such usage, and where one chooses to draw the bottom line. In anyone's count there were the big four—Mitsui, Mitsubishi, Sumitomo, Yasuda—but here consensus stops. Although initially an additional 10 combines were named for *zaibatsu* dissolution, four were subsequently excluded on the grounds of their smaller size. The six that remained were Nissan, Asano, Furukawa, Okura, Nakajima, and Nomura; the four dropped were Shibusawa (Daiichi Bank), Matsushita, Kawasaki, and Okochi (Riken, an actonym for Rikagaku Kenkyujo, Physical-Chemical Research Institute).[6] The Commission explained that it made its designation of combines for *zaibatsu* dissolution on the basis of families categorized as "designated persons,"[7] though undoubtedly combine size was a major factor in deciding which families to designate as "designated persons."

While the Commission named 10 combines for *zaibatsu* dissolution on the basis of families designated as "designated persons," it named 83 holding companies for "holding-company" dissolution.[8] Holding companies came to number 83 by adding to the top-holding

[5] The literature in English on the historical development of the business groupings is not extensive. Among the studies are the following: Charles David Sheldon, *The Rise of the Merchant Class in Tokugawa Japan*, Locust Valley, N.Y., 1958; Thomas C. Smith, *Political Change and Industrial Development in Japan: 1868-1880*, Stanford, 1955; Johannes Hirschmeier, *The Origins of Entrepreneurship in Meiji Japan*, Cambridge, Mass., 1964; Oland D. Russell, *The House of Mitsui*, Boston, 1939; Mitsui Gomei Kaisha, *The House of Mitsui*, Tokyo, 1933. A few brief historical notes will be found on the Big Three in Mitsubishi Economic Research Institute, *Mitsui, Mitsubishi, Sumitomo*, Tokyo, 1955; on 12 of the major combines in State-War Mission on Japanese Combines, *Report*, Part I, Washington, D.C., 1946. In Hadley, "Concentrated Business Power," there is a chapter on Mitsui's historical development, as well as a few notes on the development of the Mitsubishi, Sumitomo, and Japan Nitrogenous Fertilizer Company. For a comprehensive bibliography on the *zaibatsu* up to 1951—their development, operation, dissolution—cf. HCLC, *Zaibatsu Dissolution*, data volume, where in Section 21 several hundred entries will be found. The large majority are, of course, Japanese-language works, but foreign-language material is also included.

[6] For the designations cf. HCLC, *Zaibatsu Dissolution* data volume, pp. 2-3, where they are listed by family groups; for those dropped cf. T. A. Bisson, *Zaibatsu Dissolution in Japan*, Berkeley, 1954, p. 92.

[7] *HCLC, Zaibatsu Dissolution*, data volume, explanatory notes to Table 14, note 2, unnumbered page preceding p. 468.

[8] Cf. Appendix IV for a listing of these.

companies of the 10 designated combines certain of the second-level holding companies of these combines, and by including the holding companies of combines not designated for *zaibatsu* dissolution, as well as the holding functions of certain very large operating companies. The distinction between undergoing *zaibatsu* dissolution and undergoing holding-company dissolution was not in the dissolution procedures but rather, because of the character of the principal shareholders, in the form in which compensation was received. The principal shareholders of companies named for *zaibatsu* dissolution were "designated persons," the *zaibatsu* families. *Zaibatsu* persons received their compensation in illiquid form, in 10-year nonnegotiable government bonds. The principal shareholders in other companies and minority shareholders in both received their compensation in negotiable form. It is noteworthy that nowhere in the deconcentration program was property confiscated. In all instances there was compensation, though the inflation which developed greatly lessened the value of the debt instruments in which the *zaibatsu* compensation occurred.

### *Organization of Combine Enterprise*

Whether one spoke of "combine," "holding company," or "*zaibatsu*" (in the sense of business structure), the organization was the same. Regardless of the nomenclature the arrangement represented a means of extending control far beyond the controller's corporate (or partnership) limits, to deny independence of action to businesses within the networks. Companies of a combine or *zaibatsu* were not operated for their individual advantage but collectively for the advantage of the top-holding company.

In the West, combines have been built on one industry or a group of closely related industries, with a view to achieving a monopolistic position. It was not so in Japan. The older (and the larger) of Japan's combines were all conglomerate, only some were more conglomerate than others. The goal was not high-market occupancy of a few related markets, but oligopolistic positions running the gamut of the modern sector of the economy.[9] The largest, the Mitsui combine, carried on operations in coal and metals mining, in shipbuilding, ordnance, aircraft, heavy and light electrical equipment, and in diverse other fields of manufacturing, in commercial banking and insurance, and in trading. A series of oligopolistic positions—frequently in the 10-20 percent range of market output—was the foundation

[9] See Tables 14-1 and 14-2 for a presentation of concentration ratios that vividly points up the truth of this observation.

for most exceptional business power and wealth. The returns from these business arrangements were sufficient for those who held the shares of the top-holding companies to produce an "estate of wealth," to create *zaibatsu* families.

Whether one speaks of the nerve center of these organizations, the holding company, or the larger whole, the combine or *zaibatsu*, he is speaking of a business arrangement for amplifying the power of capital. Through the capital of the top-holding company, control was extended over an entire network of companies. The underlying principle of this is of course quite simple. Inasmuch as a corporation can be controlled through 51 percent of its stock, a holding company can be used to control companies roughly twice the holding company's size, and these in turn can be used to control others twice *their* size, and so on. In the case of the *zaibatsu* families, this magnification of the power of capital was, until nearly the 1930s, not used extensively, so far as the *core* subsidiaries of their networks were concerned. The families not only provided the entire capital of the top-holding company, but in addition they insisted the key subsidiaries be held at close to 100 percent by the top-holding company alone or by the top-holding company in conjunction with direct family investments and some cross-ties. In contrast, the network of subsidiaries of the core companies and subsidiaries that were not core companies was held at much lower ownership levels, exemplifying control from a partial ownership base.

So long as it was possible, the families excluded outsiders from sharing in their key subsidiaries. However, out of the expansion of the industrial sector of the economy, resulting from the war in Manchuria, then China, and in preparation for the Pacific War, family capital became manifestly insufficient. Outside capital had to be admitted.[10] The Mitsubishi Economic Research Institute provides the following information on the opening of stock in certain key Mitsubishi companies.[11] It must be kept in mind, however, that "opening"

[10] One can see the aggregate increase in fixed private investment in these years in Table 17-4.

[11] Mitsubishi Economic Research Institute, *Capital Accumulation and Control in the Mitsubishi Zaibatsu* (Mitsubishi Keizai Kenkyujo, *Mitsubishi Zaibatsu ni okeru Shikin Chotatsu to Shihai*), published by the Economic Planning Agency (Keizai Kikakucho), Tokyo, 1958. References to the opening of stock will be found for the following companies on the following pages: Mining, pp. 49, 117, Trust, 117, Banking, 49, 117, Heavy Industries, 123, 140 (both 1934 and 1935 are given), Trading, 169-70, the top-holding company, 123. Year dates for establishment in corporate form are taken from Securities Underwriting Control Association, *Corporation Yearbook, 1943* (Shiken Hikiuke Kaisha Toseikai, *Kabushiki Kaisha Nenkan, Showa 18*), Tokyo.

did not refer to opening all of the stock of a company, but instead to some of the stock.

| | *Year established in corporate form* | *Year stock opened* |
|---|---|---|
| Mitsubishi Mining | 1918 | 1920 |
| Mitsubishi Trust | 1927 | 1927 |
| Mitsubishi Bank | 1919 | 1929 |
| Mitsubishi Heavy Industries | 1917 | 1934 (1935) |
| Mitsubishi Trading | 1918 | 1938 |
| Mitsubishi Top-holding Company | 1937 | 1940 |

Illustrative of the public's desire to share in the ownership of the *zaibatsu* subsidiaries is the report in this study that at the time 400,000 shares of Mitsubishi Heavy Industries were offered for sale in 1935, 250,000 were made available to the "public." 45,580 people applied to buy 6,777,170 shares, roughly 27 times the number offered![12]

Two features of the Japan scene increased the normal expansion attaching to the holding-company technique: stock did not have to be equally paid up;[13] and as the power of the larger combines increased it was possible to control more and more with less and less. Inasmuch as stock did not have to be equally paid-up, the way was opened for the families and the top-holding company to increase the "stretch" of their capital. It was possible for their stock to be paid up at a lower proportion than other stock, though carrying full voting powers, thus enabling them to spread their capital more widely.

Further, the position the *zaibatsu* families and their top-holding companies attained was such that control was possible at well under majority positions. As will be seen in Chapter 4, where ownership ties are examined more closely, there were a number of instances of core companies at war's end which were held well under majority control. If combine ownership is taken to include top-holding com-

[12] Mitsubishi Economic Research Institute, *Capital Accumulation*, pp. 140-41.

[13] T.F.M. Adams, *A Financial History of Modern Japan*, Tokyo, 1964, p. 197. Mr. Adams points out that a revision of the Commercial Code, July 12, 1948, "made it obligatory to have all issued shares fully paid-up. . . ." Study of the statistical information on *zaibatsu* holdings given in HCLC, *Zaibatsu Dissolution*, data volume, Section 12, not infrequently indicates a discrepancy in position, depending whether holdings are stated in terms of issued shares or paid-up shares. For example, the Mitsui Holding Co. at war's end accounted for 11.9 percent of the paid-up capital of Nippon Kinzoku Kogyo (Japan Metal Manufacturing), yet it held 16.8 percent of the issued shares. Conversely, in the case of Mitsui Trust, the holding company accounted for 15.4 percent of the paid-up capital and only 7.7 percent of the issued shares. This would seem clearly to indicate that shares were not equally paid-up.

pany ownership, direct-family holdings plus cross-subsidiary ties, there were at war's end 5 of the 22 core companies in the Mitsui combine held under majority control, 9 of the 19 core companies in the Mitsubishi combine under majority control, and 8 of the 20 Sumitomo companies. (For details cf. Tables 4-1, 4-2, and 4-3.)

That the larger combines came to believe that their will should prevail, regardless of their actual ownership position, was unwittingly revealed at the time of the merger of the Mitsui Bank and Daiichi Bank to form the Teikoku Bank. Stock in the new bank was evenly divided between the Mitsui and Shibusawa interests. In the merger agreement dated December 28, 1942 and signed in the presence of Bank of Japan officials, it was provided: "The Mitsuis shall make no objection whatever to any resolution that may be *passed* by the Board of Directors of the new bank. . . ."[14]

*Subsidiary Numbers*

The HCLC compiled information on the number of subsidiaries within each of the 10 combines designated for "*zaibatsu* dissolution." As presented in its *Zaibatsu Dissolution* report, the figures are:[15]

| | | | |
|---|---|---|---|
| Mitsui | 294 | Nissan | 179 |
| Mitsubishi | 241 | Asano | 59 |
| Sumitomo | 166 | Furukawa | 53 |
| Yasuda | 60 | Okura | 58 |
| The Big Four | 761 | Nakajima | 68 |
| | | Nomura | 19 |
| | | The Other Six | 436 |
| Total | 1,197 | | |

That Yasuda belonged to the Big Four and Nissan, with close to three times the number of subsidiaries, to the Other Six reveals the limitations of a count of mere numbers. The Yasuda combine centered in banking, and banking carries power far beyond its own field. Further, Yasuda, developing early in the Meiji years, had more solid ties than Nissan, which began around the World War I period; in addition, Yasuda was organized around a family, with the strength of loyalty which that implies.

[14] Filed with GHQ-SCAP, Tokyo, and cited in Hadley, "Concentrated Business Power," p. 209. Italics added.

[15] HCLC, *Zaibatsu Dissolution*, data volume, pp. 346-95. For different figures developed by the same agency, see Table 5-5, wherein the Mitsui total is given as 405 companies, and the total for these 10 combines is listed as 1,682.

*The Control Structure*

Given the number of companies in the larger of these networks—Mitsui close to 300, Mitsubishi close to 250—one might well wonder how all the control devices in the world could knit them into effective wholes, especially when it is remembered that the subsidiaries in question showed scant market-relatedness. Unity was achieved by focusing top-holding company coordination on the subsidiaries of greatest importance to the combine, the core companies; in this way tight control was achieved over what amounted almost to market-breadth of the combine. Through the controls, which these tightly held subsidiaries in turn exercised over other subsidiaries in conjunction with the market positions they held, other parts of the combine could effectively be brought into line.

Typically the combines had "designated subsidiaries" (which were often divided into "first-line designated subsidiaries" and "second-line designated subsidiaries"), "ordinary subsidiaries" of the top-holding company, and subsidiaries of the "designated subsidiaries." Exclusive of the subsidiary network attaching to Tokyo Shibaura Electric, which the HCLC put at 104, the Mitsui combine at war's end, according to information submitted by Mitsui to GHQ-SCAP, looked as follows:[16]

| | |
|---|---|
| Top-holding Company | 1 |
| Designated subsidiaries ("first-line" and "second-line") of top-holding company | 22 |
| Ordinary subsidiaries of top-holding company | 50 |
| Subsidiaries of designated subsidiaries, except Trading and Mining | 81 |
| Subsidiaries of Trading | 60 |
| Subsidiaries of Mining | 31 |
| Subsidiaries of ordinary subsidiaries of top-holding company | 27 |
| TOTAL | 272 |

It will be noted that the total given is somewhat smaller than that shown under "Subsidiary Numbers," the SCAP figure of 272 compar-

[16] Essentially in the form given, this is taken from Bisson, *Zaibatsu Dissolution in Japan*, p. 25, but Mr. Bisson took the data for his presentation from tables in Hadley, "Concentrated Business Power," which were based on document information submitted to SCAP; cf. pp. 191-92, 193-96, 204-206, 207-208, 220-29, 257-58. The major difference in presentation is in the size of Trading's subsidiary network. The figure of 126 Bisson used relates to both subsidiaries and investments.

ing to the HCLC figure of 294. If, however, the subsidiaries of the Tokyo Shibaura Electric had been included, then the total, 376, would have been appreciably larger than the HCLC figure of 294. It is difficult to be confident of any of these statistics, for they all differ. The most one can hope to gain is an "order of magnitude" impression. Later, in connection with other legislation, the Zaibatsu Appointee's Law, when the HCLC was again compiling information on the number of subsidiaries of the 10 combines, the total figure reported was almost 50 percent higher than that given in the *Zaibatsu Dissolution* report.[17]

### *Control Techniques*

The four key devices on which the top-holding company relied for control of the core companies, and by extension to the other subsidiaries, were ownership, personnel, credit, and centralized buying and selling. One would scarcely speak of the role of the families as representing a "control device," yet the families performed a peculiarly integrating function for the combines. Let us briefly note these in turn.

The basic control device was, of course, direct ownership. The top-holding company held large blocks of stock in the key subsidiaries, to which were frequently added direct holdings by the family, as well as cross-ownership holdings between subsidiaries. The result, as will be seen in detail in Chapter 4, was ownership well above 50 percent in the majority of the key subsidiaries, though, as previously noted, there were also instances among the vitally important core companies where the combined ownership was under 50 percent.

Regardless, however, of the combine ownership-position in the key subsidiaries, the top-holding company either directly appointed all of the officers of these corporations, or, after handpicking a chairman, let him nominate the other officers, subject to top-holding company approval. Appointment or review of officers of the key subsidiaries was done to make the management of these companies fully express top-holding company views. Because the management was to think in terms of the combine as a whole and not merely of the company out of which such persons came, it was customary in all cases to provide numerous management interlocks. Typically the core subsidiaries were extensively represented on the board of the top-holding company, the top-holding company among the core subsidiaries, with many cross core-subsidiary ties.

[17] Cf. Table 5-5.

Not content with the controls achieved out of appointment or review of the management of the core companies and the numerous officers interlocks, the combines not infrequently resorted to contractual agreements whereby subsidiary officers agreed in writing to refer a wide array of subjects to the top-holding company for "guidance" before speaking to them in their own board meetings. Under Japan's Commercial Code, officers of corporations were supposed to possess certain rights, but it was understood and contracted that the officers of the key subsidiaries would not exercise theirs. In Chapter 5 these personnel control measures are taken up in some detail.

In addition to the foregoing, coordination was further strengthened in the largest of the combines through their possession of financial institutions and trading companies. Where a combine possessed financial institutions, financing (pre-1945 style) was done mainly on an intracombine basis, which gave the top-holding company further checks on company activity. By reviewing both short-term and long-term applications for credit, the combine bank and its affiliated financial institutions could also check on subsidiary activities. Not infrequently, to enhance its control, the top-holding company borrowed from the bank and itself lent to the key subsidiaries. (Financial institutions are discussed in Chapter 8.)

There was a still further, very powerful control which was used—centralized buying and selling. Much as in a cartel that has a sales agency, key subsidiaries were denied the right to buy and sell on their own. Through sole-agency agreements, they contracted to buy and sell through the combine's trading company. This not only gave an additional highly effective control device to the top-holding company through its trading subsidiary, but at the same time assured that the weight of the entire combine would be brought to bear on each buying and selling negotiation. The business power of the combines showed most clearly in their trading companies. With preferential terms to their own companies and terms of whatever they chose to make to outsiders, it is understandable how it was that there were few new faces on the Japan scene until the 1930s. The terms and conditions of these sole-agency contracts are examined more fully in Chapter 8.

Among all the controls which the top-holding companies employed to weld their corporate complexes into single wholes, the integrating role of the family was of extraordinary importance. The great conglomerate structures were pervaded by a feudalistic loyalty to the family at the top. Any combine decision by definition will mean greater advantage to certain of the subsidiaries than to others. In fact, some combine decisions may mean severe sacrifice to one or more subsidiaries. The vital role of the families was in providing "legitimacy" to these actions.

The families relied on the political pattern they knew best: the relationship of knight to lord. A knight does not question his lord's decisions; likewise, no officer or employee was to question the family's decisions. He was to serve the family on the basis of unquestioning loyalty. This pattern of organization recalls Thorstein Veblen's essay on "The Opportunity of Japan."[18] For a limited period Veblen saw Japan occupying two worlds, institutionally its traditional world and technologically the modern world. The technology of the combines was Western, the corporate form was Western, but that which infused the combines and gave them their being was feudalistic. Clearly this arrangement gave Japan from the start of its modernization a remarkably disciplined executive and labor class, but it came at a high price politically. To this day one still senses the difference in the pattern of human relationships in those firms that were formerly part of the great combine groupings and those outside or new. In the former, employees, regardless of how well they know the answers, are far more self-deprecating in replying to questions than in the latter. In Japanese it is customary to make replies in probable rather than definite form, but employees of the older combines are, as it were, hesitant to express themselves even in probable form. The difference between employees' speech in the former combine firms and those outside is clearly noticeable to observers who know the language well.

Among the so-called newer combines which came into prominence in the thirties, the family role was either minor or virtually nonexistent. Japanese writers of the period were much given to describing these structures as "democratic." This reflected both the different pattern of employer-employee relations and the fact that the public was permitted to purchase shares of these corporations.

The foregoing serves to suggest how it was that vast complexes of corporations having few market ties among them could operate as monolithic wholes. Ownership, personnel, credit, centralized buying and selling, and the inculcation of feudal-like loyalty on the part of officers and employees to the business families at the top all combined to produce a situation where there was unity of purpose and action to these business groups.

[18] Veblen, *Essays in our Changing Order*, New York, 1943.

*Other Observers on Combine Controls*

Not all observers, however, have seen such unity in the zaibatsu complexes. Professor G. C. Allen, writing shortly before the outbreak of the Pacific War, commented,

> At first sight it seems perhaps surprising that competitive conditions should flourish in a country where the large scale trades are dominated by a few groups and where the State has had historically a large role, yet if the true nature of Japan's political and economic system is appreciated the apparent inconsistency disappears. For the State has not exercised dictatorial powers, nor in the great business groups has all power flowed out from a few strong personalities. On the contrary, political authority rests with groups whose relationship one to another is always changing and policy results from the interplay of rivalries and compromises among these groups. This, as we have already seen, is true of the great business houses also. . . . Thus, it would be wrong to suppose that Japan's political and social organization creates in industry conditions that are hostile to competition. Quite the contrary has been the case.[19]

The Mitsubishi Economic Research Institute's comments on the presurrender structure of the *zaibatsu* indicate not only awareness of the discipline and coordination with which matters moved, but candor. The most that this research group could say for autonomy is that the "controlled companies could and did operate independently in coordination with the top holding company"! Such, perhaps, might be labeled "independence in restriction." The quotation continues: ". . . but [controlled companies] generally cooperated in management, industrial planning, capital investment, funds provision, supply of raw materials and equipment, the introduction of techniques, rationalization of production and management, collective sales, custody and transportation of commodities, supply of services, and so on."[20] In short, in meeting the key subsidiaries, the "core" companies, one was meeting the policies of the top-holding company.

[19] Allen, in E. B. Schumpeter, ed., *The Industrialization of Japan and Manchukuo*, New York, pp. 682-83.

[20] Mitsubishi Economic Research Institute, *Mitsui, Mitsubishi, Sumitomo*, p. 11.

# 3.

# Japanese-developed *Zaibatsu*

MANY FACTORS contributed to the development of Japan's giant business complexes, the largest of which controlled up to one-tenth of the incorporated and partnership business of the nation: the hierarchical value system of the nation; the peculiar role of the government in the economy; the cumulative power of capital; the effective lobbying for privilege.

## *A Contrast in Value Systems*

In the West it was the power of the bourgeoisie which upset the hierarchical value system that prevailed until the emergence of the bourgeoisie in the 17th and 18th centuries.[1] While there are democratic elements in Christian thought, democratic ideology did not translate into constitutions and political practice until the nascent capitalist class put forward the revolutionary doctrine of equal rights as a means of arguing itself into a share of political power. The doctrine of equal rights was advanced so capitalists could join the aristocracy, the landed property interests, and the church in determining national policy—not for a moment, of course, so that those below them could also participate. But having cast their argument as they did, having succeeded in enshrining it in various political creeds, the bourgeoisie found it impossible to escape the consequences. In time, much later, labor came to use the doctrine as a means of gaining political participation.[2] And people colonized by capitalist powers began to use it extensively as a means of demanding their independence.[3] Democratic thought spread internally and internationally.

Japan was not a part of this Western movement.[4] In the 17th and 18th centuries Japan likewise had a rising merchant class, but while

[1] Among a host of sources cf. Karl Polanyi, *The Great Transformation*, New York, 1944.

[2] It is interesting to speculate what the views of Karl Marx (1818-83) might have been had his dates been a half-century later.

[3] While this was the cry of the 13 American colonies, widespread application has been in the post-World War II period.

[4] Cf. entries cited in Chapter 2, note 5.

merchants may have chafed at their low position and the restrictions placed on their activities, they did not attempt to overthrow the system which made them the lowest class in society. The Tokugawa who ruled Japan under a system of centralized feudalism from 1603 to 1868 were not overthrown by the rising bourgeoisie but by the rival feudal groups of Satsuma, Choshu and Tosa.[5]

Few principles other than diversification of risk are discernible in the conduct of the leading merchant houses during the last years of the Tokugawa Bakafu (literally tent, i.e., military, government, distinct from the Imperial Court). Let us note the activities of one of the largest of the Tokugawa merchant houses, which developed into the largest of the combines, the House of Mitsui.

> As late as 1866, in their role as loyal supporters of the Bakafu, the Mitsuis made a five-hundred-thousand-*ryo* forced loan to the Tokugawas. Further, in August 1867, just two months prior to the resignation of the last of the shoguns [head of the feudal government], they became official exchange agent for the introduction of the Bakafu's gold notes. . . . Their concurrent clandestine relations with the anti-Bakafu forces, however, led in October 1867 to their becoming chief quartermaster to those forces.[6]

Robert N. Bellah, in his study of social values in Tokugawa society, emphasizes the absence of conflict between merchant and feudal elements.

> The merchants were basically loyal to the old government or the new. They were hard working, frugal, and in most cases honest, but . . . they were oriented to receiving directions from the rulers, to whom they relegated policy-determining functions. The fact that the merchants were not the spearhead for change and were not oriented to taking initiative in new and challenging circumstances is of the first importance in understanding the process of modernization in Japan. If the merchants were not so, certainly neither were the farmers or the artisans. Only one class was in a position to lead the nation in breaking new ground: the samurai class. From the nature of its situation, its locus of strength was the polity, not the economy. I am insistent on this point because the tendency to regard economic development as "basic"

[5] Among a number of sources cf. E. H. Norman, *Japan's Emergence as a Modern State*, New York, 1940; Albert M. Craig, *Choshu in the Meiji Restoration*, Cambridge, Mass., 1961.

[6] Tsuchiya Takao, "Development of the Mitsui Zaibatsu" (Mitsui Zaibatsu no Hatten), *Chuo Koron*, in three parts, August, September, October 1947. The quotation is from the September issue, p. 59.

and political development as "superstructure" is by no means confined to Marxist circles but permeates most current thinking on such matters.[7]

Why capitalist development in Japan was so different from that of Europe is a tantalizing question. Some economic historians have suggested it may have been a consequence of the Tokugawa ban on foreign intercourse for more than some 200 years.[8] At a time when European commercial capitalists were ranging the world accumulating capital, Japan's had to be content with domestic trade only. However, in assessing such a view it is important to bear in mind that China, which had no policy of seclusion, did not produce as much of a bourgeois class as did Japan.[9] The Far Eastern value system may have had more to do with it.

The Far Eastern value system historically is Confucian. In the Confucian world there are no equals, only superiors and inferiors. While Christianity may have produced no democratic governments, it nevertheless provided social sanction for the doctrine of equality. There was no comparable equalitarian element in Japanese society.

Japan's early capitalists did not stand for any injection of fresh thinking into the hierarchical world which they entered. They organized their businesses on the hierarchical institution of the "house,"[10] and externally expected to operate as superiors and inferiors, as those favored and not favored. It might be countered that in its very nature business enterprise is necessarily organized hierarchically, and this would be quite true. But in the ideological development of the West, business hierarchy is a hierarchy of equals, a 9-to-5 affair among persons who believe themselves equal. The hierarchy of Japan's great business houses was vastly different. It was a paternalistic hierarchy of people taught to think in terms of superiors and inferiors.[11] As for external relations among businesses,

[7] Robert N. Bellah, *Tokugawa Religion: The Values of the Pre-Industrial Japan*, Glencoe, Ill., 1957, pp. 184-85.

[8] This was called to my attention by Nakagawa Keiichiro in a discussion of the first draft of this study in a seminar of Japanese scholars.

[9] Marion J. Levy, "Contrasting Factors in the Modernization of China and Japan," in Simon Kuznets et al., eds., *Economic Growth: Brazil, India, Japan*, Durham, 1952, pp. 496-536.

[10] For a discussion of house law, under which business was organized before the introduction of western forms of enterprise, cf. Hozumi Nobushige, *Lectures on the New Japanese Civil Code*, Tokyo, 1912, *passim*; also Nakano Takashi, "Structure & Function of Merchant's *Ie* in the Tokugawa & Post Tokugawa Periods," mimeog.; paper presented at Symposium 48, Social and Cultural Basis for Japan's Modernization, 11th Pacific Science Congress, Aug. 1966, Tokyo.

[11] For personnel relations within the combines, cf. the discussion in Chapter 5.

there were no voices to suggest that all should have an equal chance, that businesses should be treated equally. In other words, there was no Adam Smith, for there was no John Locke. There was no public policy of competition, for competition is a democratic doctrine. Competition radically asserts, "let all compete and may the best man win." Among Japan's bureaucrats, as among Japan's political leadership, the ideology was that of superior and inferior.

It should surprise no one that Mitsui, Mitsubishi, Sumitomo, and Yasuda were the superiors of Japan's business world. To those administering public policy it seemed perfectly appropriate for government policy to favor certain businesses. Frequently among democratic governments there is a marked difference between profession and practice, but no one in the Japanese government professed treating businesses equally. The superiority of the superiors was importantly influenced by the government's disposal of industrial and mining property in the 1880s.[12]

A few historical examples will indicate the spirit of government-business relations and suggest the consequences of such public policy. The Miike coal mine, the richest in Japan, came into government hands as part of the transferred Tokugawa properties. Ito Hirobumi, Minister of Public Works at the time, was concerned about arranging for effective disposal of the mined coal. Writing of the Mitsui acquisition of an exclusive-agency contract for sale of Miike coal, Masuda, who became managing director of the about to be formed Mitsui Trading Company, described the circumstances as follows: "At that time Mr. Ito . . . said to me, 'Masuda, since you are establishing the Mitsui Trading Company to engage in foreign trade, it would be good if you handled the coal from the Miike colliery. If you are willing to undertake this, we will not be tight. You can acquire the coal at cost price and get started on it directly.' "[13] What were the implications of the contract? Elsewhere the writer gave the following assessment:

> Acquisition of this contract [which Mitsui Trading held until 1888 when the government sold the mine outright to the Mitsuis and the contract was renegotiated between Mining and Trading] was of basic importance to the company. Profits from the arrangement were unusually large, while perhaps even greater significance attached to the fact that it led the company into valuable contact with British business. Though not top grade for industrial purposes,

[12] For one of several accounts in English, cf. Thomas C. Smith, *Political Change and Industrial Development.*

[13] Quoted in Tsuchiya, *Chuo Koron,* September 1947, p. 66.

> Miike coal was excellent for bunkering. British steamers active in the Far Eastern trade found it the best coal in the Far East for their purposes. Accordingly, it was not long before Trading established branch offices in Shanghai and Hongkong. A Singapore branch followed soon, as well as branches in India. The London branch of Trading was also a direct outcome of transactions in Miike coal.[14]

So began the company which in 1940 accounted for 22 percent of Japan's total imports and 10 percent of its total exports.[15] And so were laid two of the three cornerstones on which the Mitsui organization was built—Mining and Trading. If we were to explore the third—Banking—we would, according to Japanese scholarship, find comparable government favoritism.[16]

Not surprisingly, the favored businesses did not rely solely on the climate of opinion to provide for their interests; they promoted these interests. Illustrative of how this was done was Mitsui's request to the prominent Meiji statesman, Inouye Kaoru, to become their top adviser.[17] The following quotation is from my earlier study.

> Formalizing a relationship that had begun in 1871-72, when Inouye Kaoru was in the finance office, the Mitsuis asked him in 1891 to become the highest adviser to their organization. . . . Although Inouye continued his direct participation in the Govern-

[14] Hadley, "Concentrated Business Power," p. 141. Various sources list the Miike Mine as coming into Mitsui hands one or two years later, and cite H. Sasaki as the one to whom the mine was sold. Cf., for example, Hirschmeier, *The Origins of Entrepreneurship*, Cambridge, Mass., 1964 (who lists Sasaki as Sakaki), p. 243; Japan Productivity Center, *Control of Restrictive Practices*, p. 1. The confusion has come about from a lack of awareness that Sasaki was the proxy representative for the Mitsuis in the bidding.

[15] Cf. Table 8-1, "Mitsui Trading's Position in the Export and Import Trade of Japan Proper, 1936-1945."

[16] For example, for the first six years of the Meiji period the government delegated to the three leading merchant houses—Mitsui, Ono, and Shimada—the operational aspects of the collection, storage, and expenditure of tax funds. Initially no security was demanded; later, security was raised to 25 and to 33 percent. Suddenly in 1874 the provision fixing the rate of security was changed to read, "an equivalent of the amount." Popular rumor, quoted by scholars, has it that the Mitsuis were saved from the bankruptcy which befell their two rivals by news of the decision being leaked to them in advance by Inouye Kaoru. The circumstance served to give the entire exchequer business to the Mitsuis until 1882, when the Bank of Japan was established. Further, through Inouye, who was mint master, the Mitsuis managed to have themselves initially designated as sole agents of the mint. Cf. Mitsui Bank, *The Mitsui Bank, A Brief History*, Tokyo, 1926, pp. 20-30; Tsudiya, *Chuo Koron*, September 1947, p. 64. Tsuchiya, Hadley, "Concentrated Business Power," pp. 119-22.

[17] *Ibid.*, p. 133. Inouye's letter to Prince Yamagata and Prince Matsukata is quoted by Tsuchiya, *Chuo Koron*, October 1947, p. 67.

ment until 1898, one would not have expected him to see anything contradictory in concurrently holding government and private office. His remarks to the Princes Yamagata and Matsukata on his assumption of the formal post of top adviser to the Mitsuis provide the classic formulation of his view of the identity of Mitsui and national interests. He observed, "The Mitsuis and our economy are very closely related; if failure were to overtake the Mitsuis, the repercussions on our economy would not be small. Therefore, although their request to become top adviser is burdensome to me, I do not believe that I have any alternative but to accept. I am seeking your views in this matter. If you endorse my action, I trust that I may in the future count on your strong support."

The consequences of a government policy that deliberately favored certain businesses would not have been so widespread had the government not played a directing role in the economy. While Japan's modernization occurred in the format of capitalism, it was the format only, not its spirit. Laissez-faire is not suitable to forced development.

Initially Japan's development was forced for the most basic of all motives, self-protection. Throughout virtually all of Asia at this time one saw only Asian subordination to European metropolitan powers. Japan was independent and sought to remain so. Its answer to the fate of India, Burma, Indonesia, Indo-China, China, to the superiority of Western technology, was to adopt Western technology. Speed was of overriding importance. But no sooner was the crisis of independence passed than there were fresh reasons for forced development out of Japan's own foreign expansion. Forced development in a crisis framework makes an exceptionally strong basis for government direction.

But even without crises the role of government in forced economic development is necessarily greater than in ordinary development, inasmuch as high growth requires that the acquisition of technology and investments be programmed. There is need of the broad overview and consistent application, minimally, in terms of current phrasing, of *planification indicativ*. The marketplace is not set up to provide such an overview. It reflects consumer moods. It operates by assorted judgments which, when decisions are essentially of the more-or-less variety, are tied into an effective whole by market price. Market price does not steer when the issue in field after field in the economy is whether to adopt altogether new modes of production. It is government which is in a position to steer, and Japanese governments since Meiji have steered.

In addition to the matter of overview, there is a further deficiency to the market system if left to itself in times of accelerated development, namely, that consumer choice tends to be weighted to today's consumers! In accelerated development, one is by definition concerned with tomorrow's world. Few Japanese appear to think of the object of production as consumption, but however the matter is conceived and phrased, consumers "voting" with their purchasing power are going to weight their "votes" to the present over the future. Japanese governments from Meiji to close to the present have met this problem by actively encouraging an ethic of frugality.

The role of government in an economy operating in the format of the market system in times of accelerated development is different for still another reason. Inasmuch as the market system operates on the prospect of gain, private undertakings are not prospective where risk is pervasively high; this is what it is in the early stages of widespread adoption of new technology. It is necessary for government to reduce risk by pioneering certain of the new technologies, by offering subsidies, by providing generous tariff protection, and so on.[18] But this sets in motion favors and return favors, making it difficult to keep a sense of what is properly public and what is properly private. For many Meiji statesmen, and for statesmen in succeeding years, it has been difficult to distinguish between public and private interest. The combines' strength was regarded as national strength but their profits were seen as private property.

The older combines continued in their position of superiority without effective challenge until the 1930s, when the world depression brought about change in Japan, as it did elsewhere. The agents of change in Japan, however, were neither other elements in the business community nor labor (the police had assured that labor was politically impotent), but the "younger officers" of the army. Hugh Byas wrote in 1942: "The story of a disciplined army driven forward by its young officers is a strange one."[19] And it was strange indeed. Obviously only with the at least tacit sanction of senior officers could such a movement have occurred. During the spring of 1932 there

[18] This statement is made even though in the case of Japan complete tariff autonomy was not regained until 1911. Under 30-year treaties signed in 1858 and 1866, Japan was bound to a maximum tariff of 5 percent ad valorem on a wide range of items. Autonomy was largely regained on the expiration of these agreements in the 1890s, but there were still restrictions. Full independence in tariff matters did not come until 1911. Among various sources see James Murdoch, *A History of Japan*, London, 1926, Vol. 3, pp. 759-60; William W. Lockwood, *The Economic Development of Japan*, Princeton, 1954, pp. 539-40; Takeuchi Tatsuji, *War and Diplomacy in the Japanese Empire*, London, 1936, pp. 91-108.

[19] Byas, *Government by Assassination*, New York, 1942, p. 74.

were three assassinations in monthly succession—a finance minister, the chairman of the board of the Mitsui Holding Company, and a prime minister.[20] The first two were carried out by young country patriots, the murder of the prime minister by army and navy officers, as part of a wider plot. Some of the strategically placed senior army and navy officers felt uncomfortably restricted by disarmament conferences, the level of appropriations for their ministries, and with the balance of power between themselves and the leaders of the business community—the *zaibatsu* and the politicians who were thought to be in their pockets. The senior officers saw the younger officers' movement, which ideologically was a strange mishmash of patriotism and social protest—protest at an economic system which produced a few enormously wealthy family groups and an impoverished countryside—as a vehicle which might be used to their advantage. The protest movement came to be known as the "Showa Restoration," after what will be Emperor Hirohito's posthumous name, and reached a climax in 1936 with the "February 26th Incident" in an orgy of assassinations. At the time of the February 26th uprising the young leaders issued a "manifesto," of which the following excerpts will suggest a confused logic:

> The essence of the Japanese nation consists in the fact that [it has been reigned over by an] Emperor . . . from time immemorial. . . . This has been the glory of Japan. Now is the time to bring about an expansion of the power and prestige of Japan.
>
> In recent years many persons have made their chief purpose in life the amassment of wealth regardless of the general welfare and prosperity of the people, with the result that the majesty of the Empire has been impaired. . . .
>
> The Elder Statesmen, the financial magnates, the government officials, and the political parties are responsible. The London naval agreement and the unhappy events which have occurred in the Japanese army in recent years prove this statement. . . .
>
> Those incidents [past assassinations], however, have failed to remind men of their responsibility. The recent strained relations between Japan and the other powers are due to our statemen's failure to take appropriate measures. . . . It is our duty to take proper steps to safeguard our fatherland by killing those responsible. On the eve of our departure to Manchuria we have risen in revolt to attain our aims by direct action.[21]

[20] For a brief discussion of the three assassinations, and other assassinations, see *ibid., passim.*

[21] *Ibid.*, p. 123. I have taken the liberty of making a few tense and singular-and-plural changes in the Japanese-English given in the source.

The scale of the February 26th Incident—1,400 men were involved[22] —made it abundantly clear to the senior officers of the army and navy that they were playing a very dangerous game that was far too dangerous for their own welfare, and the whole matter of young officers leading revolts came to an abrupt halt.

The rise of the newer combines, in particular Nissan, headed by Aikawa, was tied in with the young officers' revolt. The leadership in the Kwantung Army, which seized Manchuria in September 1931, was critical of Mitsui, Mitsubishi, Sumitomo, and Yasuda, and favored putting the economic development of Manchuria into other hands, specifically Aikawa's. This did not mean the exclusion of the older combines from Manchuria,[23] as many Japanese, including knowledgeable ones, appear to believe, but it did mean favoritism to Aikawa, the sort of favoritism under which the older combines had prospered for the past many decades.

The interpretation that the older combines represented "liberal" forces and that it was the newer combines which joined hands with the "militarists" stems from this highly abnormal five-year period. (The "liberalism" of the leadership of the older combines was their unenthusiasm about being assassinated by military fanatics, but in no sense was the whole of the Japanese army and navy fanatic.) To interpret the split between the older combines and the younger officers as representative of relations between the combines and the military, that is, between the *zaibatsu* and the *gumbatsu*[24] is to generalize from an inadequate base.

There was no split at all between the older combines and the majority of the senior officers of the army and navy. Both groups deeply believed in oligarchy, both groups found democratic thinking close

[22] *Ibid.*, p. 119.

[23] Exclusion is hardly consonant with such corporation names as the following, taken from the lists of firms developed for the administration of the "Law for the Termination of Zaibatsu Family Control": Manchurian Synthetic Fuel (Mitsui); Manchurian Mitsubishi Machinery Co., Mitsubishi Kwantung Magnesium Co.; Antung Light Metal (Sumitomo), Manchurian Sumitomo Metal Industries. Cf. HCLC, *Laws, Rules, Regulations Concerning the Reconstruction and Democratization of the Japanese Economy*, Tokyo, 1949, pp. 102-16. Neither is exclusion consonant with Mitsui Trading's several subsidiaries in Manchuria, exclusive of holdings in control companies there. For names, capitalization, head office location, and so forth, of these subsidiaries, cf. Hadley, "Concentrated Business Power," p. 223.

[24] As is evident, there are coordinate terms to "*zaibatsu*" which divides into "zai" which is "wealth," and "batsu," which is "estate," "group," "clique." "Gumbatsu" is "gun," "military" (under a phonetic change occasioned by the second half of the compound the "n" becomes "m"), and "batsu," "group," "clique." Similarly, "kambatsu" ("kan" plus "batsu") is bureaucratic group or clique; "gakubatsu" is university group or clique.

to, if not in fact, "un-Japanese," and both groups found the divinity of the emperor an unchallengeable weapon in silencing opposition.

What chapter and verse can be put forward to substantiate close ties between the older combines and the military? Various "references." The strained relations induced by the "Showa Restoration" movement do not mean that Mitsui Trading failed to carry on its enormous operations with the army and navy, nor Mitsubishi, nor Sumitomo. It is noteworthy that all sales of aircraft by that newer combine, Nakajima Aircraft, to the army and navy were until 1937 and 1940, respectively, made through Mitsui Trading. Nakajima Aircraft and Mitsubishi Heavy Industries were the two leading producers of aircraft in Japan, with nearly the entire output of Nakajima Aircraft going to the services. However, no sales were made by it directly until the dates under discussion. Mitsui Trading acquired its sole-agency contract with Nakajima at the time of its establishment in 1920,[25] and until the indicated years handled all sales to the military.

It frequently happened that the Japanese army and navy turned industrial and mining installations in areas coming under Japanese jurisdiction over to Mitsui, Mitsubishi, or Sumitomo to operate. Thus, for example, as the Mitsubishi group wrote of itself: "The [Mitsubishi Heavy Industries] Company was entrusted by the Japanese Navy with the management and operation of the Kiang-Nan Shipyard and Engine Works in Shanghai in 1938 and with the Shonan Shipyard and Engine Works in Singapore in 1942."[26]

Further, as we shall shortly see in the tables presented below, the Big Four doubled their position in the economy in the years 1941 to 1945. They increased their position from 12 percent of total corporate and partnership capital to 24 percent in that four-year period. And in addition, the Big Four made comparable gains in their position outside Japan. While at the outbreak of the Pacific War, Nissan with its enormous investments in Manchuria represented three-quarters of overseas investments among the eight largest combines, it was down to six percent by war's end and Mitsui and Mitsubishi were up to 60 percent. It is customary to describe the Japanese government during World War II as being under the control of the militarists. What kind of cleavage between militarists and "liberal"

[25] Information presented in Hadley, "Concentrated Business Power," pp. 236-38, based on summaries of the 1920, 1923, 1932, 1934 contracts and a copy of the 1940 contract filed with GHQ-SCAP.

[26] Mitsubishi Economic Research Institute, *Mitsui, Mitsubishi, Sumitomo*, Tokyo, 1955, p. 196.

business elements can there be when the "liberal" business elements fared so handsomely? Rewards don't follow cleavages; they follow fundamental similarity. There were no real cleavages between the military and the views of the older combines. Other bits of information corroborating the similarity of *zaibatsu-gumbatsu* interests lie scattered about.

From conversations in Paris after the war, I learned that Mitsui Trading's French affiliate, S. A. Française Bussan, had been highly commended for the intelligence activities it had been carrying on up to the fall of the Vichy government. In fact, Française Bussan was in receipt of a memorandum from the Imperial Japanese War Ministry informing . . . [it] that the reporting job it was doing was superior even to that of the Japanese Embassy in Paris.[27]

One sees political indication in appointments. Under the *zaibatsu* system, all political work was handled from the top-holding company. There was no such thing as a subsidiary making direct political contributions, as one sees today, or engaging in political dialogue on its own. In the Mitsui combine the political work was carried on in the "research department" of the top-holding company. The research of this department was political maneuvering—with cabinet ministers, army and navy officials, bureaucrats, Diet members. Who did the House of Mitsui pick for its last appointment to this most sensitive post?—an ardent admirer of Nazi Germany. Elsewhere I remarked,

> The finances of the research department were handled on a cash basis for which no records were kept. The department was headed for a number of years by Sasaki Shiro, a favorite of Takakimi [head of the 11-family House of Mitsui], who in 1941 became concurrently president of Real Estate. Sasaki, who was an enthusiastic collaborator of Hitler Germany under the Berlin-Rome-Tokyo Axis, managed all political arrangements of the entire Mitsui combine. Under "normal" conditions the post was peculiarly important because of the extremely close relations between the major combines and government in Japan; under the war economy where informal combine-government collaboration gave way to legalized forms, the position was of even greater significance.[28]

When I interviewed Mitsui Takakimi in August 1947, at a time when severe inflation was threatening the economy and output in the second postwar year was little above the preceding year, Taka-

[27] Hadley, "Concentrated Business Power," p. 253.
[28] *Ibid.*, p. 187.

kimi's concerns were not with these problems but with Communism and international Jewry. He was fearful of domestic Communists spreading Communism within Japan. But it is not clear what he imagined about Jews. It is worth noting that at the time practically the only Jews in Japan were members of the Allied Occupation forces.

To suppose that the older combines represented liberalism of the Western type is to misread Japanese history. Nothing in their origins, in their structure, in their operations would suggest bourgeois thinking. Yet naturally such a supposition appealed to the conservative political groups who took over the government of Japan following its surrender. Mr. Yoshida, four-time prime minister of postwar Japan and a master politician, wrote in his *Memoirs* of a press conference he held shortly after the start of the Occupation:

> As was the case within GHQ, foreigners . . . in Japan in those days entertained feelings of animosity toward our financial leaders and there was already much talk among them of the coming disintegration of the trading "empires" which had been built up. So it came as no surprise when, at a press conference with foreign correspondents held shortly after the formation of the Shidehara Cabinet in October 1945 with myself as Foreign Minister, I was confronted with the kind of questions one might expect. The general purport was that since the financiers had been behind the war, the strictest measures should be taken against them. I answered that it would be a great mistake to regard Japan's financial leaders as a bunch of criminals, that the nation's economic structure had been built by such old established and major financial concerns as Mitsui and Mitsubishi, and that modern Japan owed her prosperity to their endeavors, so that it was most doubtful whether the Japanese people would benefit from the disintegration of these concerns.
>
> I explained further that the so-called Zaibatsu had never worked solely for their own profit, but often at a loss, as for instance during the war when they continued to produce ships and planes on Government orders regardless of the sacrifices involved; that the people who had actually joined hands with the militarists and profited from the war were not the established financial groups, but the new rich who were alone permitted by the military to conduct business in Manchuria and other occupied territories to the detriment of the old established concerns; and that those who had most heartily welcomed the termination of the Pacific conflict

were the leaders of these old established concerns that had laid the foundations of their prosperity in time of peace and had never felt at ease in their relations with the military clique who had become the masters of the nation for the duration of the war.[29]

It is colorful and lively to equate criticism of a system of enterprise which gave great opportunity and great wealth to a handful of families with "Japan's financial leaders a bunch of criminals," but it is scarcely descriptive. Obviously neither the *zaibatsu* families nor their hand-picked officers were a bunch of criminals. They were for the most part talented and able persons whom the political-economic system favored in enterprise and income to the disregard of all other Japanese persons. As quoted at the outset of this study, President Roosevelt, in his 1938 message to Congress, calling for an investigation of concentrated economic power in the United States, observed: "Governments can deal and should deal with blindly selfish men. But that is a comparatively small part—the easier part—of our problem. The larger, more important and more difficult part of our problem is to deal with men who are not selfish and who are good citizens, but who cannot see the social and economic consequences of their actions in a modern economically interdependent community."[30] The sin of the *zaibatsu* was that they and their political spokesmen, such as Prime Minister Yoshida, could not see the social and economic consequences of a system of enterprise which did not permit Japan to outgrow the duality of its economy,[31] which denied

[29] Yoshida Shigeru, *The Yoshida Memoirs*, London, 1961, pp. 150-51.

[30] As reproduced in Temporary National Economic Committee, *Final Report and Recommendations*, Senate Document 35, 77th Cong., 1st Sess., p. 16.

[31] In any economy one finds a wide range in scale of enterprise, but in advanced economies small and medium enterprise is competitive with large; that is, the productivity of small-medium enterprise is comparable with the productivity of large enterprise. In the early stages of modernization it is to be expected that there will be sharp differences in productivity between the new capital-intensive undertakings and those organized along more traditional lines, but the hallmark of the Japanese economy has been the continuation of this distinction. For example, in Japan in 1955, workers in plants employing 20-49 workers had only 40 percent of the productivity of those in establishments of 1,000 and above. On the other hand, in the United States in 1949, workers in plants employing 25-49 workers had 93 per cent of the productivity of plants employing 1,000 and above. For a statistical presentation of productivity by size of plant in Japan, the United States, and England, cf. Economic Planning Agency, *Economic White Paper* (Keizai Kikakucho, *Keizai Hakusho*), 1957, p. 146. For a discussion of duality in the Japanese economy cf., among numerous sources, Edna E. Ehrlich, *The Role of Banking in Japan's Economic Development*, esp. pp. 450-90; also Ohkawa Kazushi and Henry Rosovsky, "A Century of Growth,"

it a viable labor movement, failed to provide any real labor-standards legislation, and which stunted the consumer market. To their minds what was good for the *zaibatsu* was good for Japan, but of course the interests of 56 persons and the interests of 72 million persons are likely to be different.

### *The Role of the* Zaibatsu *in the Economy*

The nearest approximation to "facts" on the role, individual and collective, of the *zaibatsu* in the economy comes from data prepared by the HCLC and published largely in its two-volume (textual and data) Japanese-language report, *Japan's Zaibatsu and Their Dissolution* (*Nihon Zaibatsu to Sono Kaitai*). The commission also prepared a brief English-language report, *Final Report on Zaibatsu Dissolution.* The facts in the two reports do not always agree.

To indicate the importance of the *zaibatsu* in the economy, the commission sought a measure that would transcend market positions, and chose for this purpose the measure most commonly used in Japan—paid-in capital. Inasmuch as individual combines spread across the markets of the modern sector, frequently holding positions of 10-25 percent of output, an aggregate measure was clearly indicated. While assets are the most commonly employed measure in the United States for such a purpose, paid-in capital is the measure used in Japan.

Summarized, the findings from the Japanese-language report are that the four combines, the Big Four, in 1946 accounted for just under 25 percent of total paid-in capital, and that the Other Six represented an additional 10 percent, bringing the total of the 10 designated combines to 35 percent. The commission found one-third of the business enterprise of Japan to be in the hands of 10 business groupings. Individually, the findings (p. 46) were:

The percentage figures for the individual combines have been obtained by totaling the paid-in capital of the subsidiaries within the individual combine networks and dividing this by the total of paid-in capital for the nation. To develop such figures the commission was

---

in W. W. Lockwood, ed., *The State and Economic Enterprise in Japan*, Princeton, 1965, esp. pp. 77-83.

Dr. Ehrlich sees banking policy as highly responsible for the continued duality. She observes: "The orientation of bank credit in Japan . . . has contributed to a sharp polarization of Japanese industry. On the one hand there have developed a relatively small number of very large-scale enterprises with modern equipment and high productivity. On the other hand there have arisen multitudes of small-scale firms with very limited mechanical equipment at their disposal, and consequently low productivity." (p. 232).

| Combine | Percentage, total capital | Combine | Percentage, total capital |
|---|---|---|---|
| Mitsui | 9.4 | Nissan | 5.3 |
| Mitsubishi | 8.3 | Asano | 1.8 |
| Sumitomo | 5.2 | Furukawa | 1.5 |
| Yasuda | 1.6 | Okura | 1.0 |
| | | Nakajima | 0.6 |
| The Big Four | 24.5 | Nomura | 0.5 |
| | | The Other Six | 10.7 |

obliged, however, to reach decisions at both "ends": it had to decide on the number of subsidiaries within individual combines, and decide on which of the three official figures on total paid-in capital of the nation it would use. As has already been observed, the commission compiled the number of subsidiaries within individual combines at different times, which resulted in differing totals. Neither were the totals for aggregate paid-in capital for the nation compiled by three different agencies of the government. For 1946 the Ministry of Commerce and Industry reported a total paid-in capital for the nation of Y32 billion,[32] the Ministry of Finance, Y43 billion,[33] and the Bank of Japan, Y48 billion.[34] HCLC used the Ministry of Commerce and Industry figure as the divisor in obtaining the percentage figures; in its English-language report the Commission made no mention of this figure and referred instead to the Ministry of Finance total.[35] A divisor —in this case, Y32 or Y43 or Y48 billion—has a good deal to do with percentage findings; it would have been most helpful had the commission explained why it chose the Ministry of Commerce and Industry figure for its Japanese-language report yet made no mention of it in its English-language report.

The detailed information on the role of the *zaibatsu* in Japan's economy in 1946, 1941, and in 1937, presented in Tables 3-1, 3-2, and 3-3 which follow, is reproduced from the Japanese-language report. In order to assess the findings shown in these tables it is necessary to bear in mind that the divisor for the 1946 table is the Ministry of Commerce and Industry figure and presumably likewise for the 1941 and 1937 tables. While findings for the position of the *zaibatsu* in

[32] HCLC, *Zaibatsu Dissolution*, data volume. The figure is shown on p. 469, and it is explained in note 1 of the explanatory notes to the tables that it comes from the Ministry of Commerce and Industry.

[33] HCLC, *Final Report on Zaibatsu Dissolution*, Tokyo, 1951, p. 67.

[34] Bank of Japan, *Historical Statistics of Japanese Economy*, Tokyo, 1962, p. 21.

[35] HCLC, *Final Report*, p. 67.

the economy for points in time will clearly depend on which agency's total is used for the divisor, if it is assumed that disparities among the three agencies remain essentially consistent, intertemporal comparisons should hold, that is, "growth rates" should prove roughly the same regardless of the divisor. In addition, a further consideration needs to be kept in mind in evaluating the material of the tables. Capital tends to show a somewhat higher measure of concentration in Japan than other aggregate measures[36] so that these tables show the *zaibatsu* with a stronger position than if they had been calculated in terms of assets, sales, or employment.

With the foregoing qualifications in mind, let us note the material on the position of the *zaibatsu* in the economy—at war's end, in 1941, and in 1937—as presented in the tables. A study of Table 3-1 indicates that in 1946 the companies of the Big Four controlled 24.5% of the paid-up capital of all incorporated businesses, including partnerships, in Japan proper. The companies of the Other Six (representing two "newer" combines, Nissan and Nakajima, and 4 smaller, older ones) added another 10.7%, bringing the 10 to a total of 35.2% of the paid-up capitalization of Japan. It is instructive to look at the industrial positions of the Big Four and the Other Six. The Big Four accounted for 49.7% of finance, 32.4% of heavy industry, 10.7% of light industry, and 12.9% of "other." The position of the Other Six was 3.3% in finance, 16.6% in heavy industry, 6.1% in light industry, and 2.6% in "other." It will accordingly be noted that the Big Four were twice as important in heavy industry as the Other Six. The older combines, "those who built Japan," to use the former prime minister's phrase, were by the criterion employed here far more significant than the "new rich," than those "who had . . . joined hands with the militarists and profited from the war."

Part B of Table 3-1 shows the relative position of eight leading combines in areas outside Japan proper. Eight combines have been used in this table rather than the foregoing 10 because 2 of the 10, Nakajima and Nomura, had only negligible holdings outside Japan. This table, however, is not as informative as the preceding one, because the divisor for gaining percentage position is merely the sum of the investments of these 8 combines, not total paid-up capital invested outside Japan.[37] Further, by using these 8 combines only,

[36] Cf. the discussion of capital as an aggregate measure in Chapter 14.

[37] This is not explained in the notes to the tables, but study of the figures indicates it to be true. The divisor for all percentage positions is the sum of investments by the 8 outside of Japan, that is, the sum of Y1,114,109 and Y276,510, or Y1,390,619. Thus, for example, the 18 percent position of the Big Four in mining represents the proportion of investments by the Big Four

Table 3-1: THE ROLE OF THE ZAIBATSU IN JAPAN'S ECONOMY AT WAR'S END IN TERMS OF PAID-UP CAPITAL

Part A: Japan Proper (Unit: 1,000 Yen)

| Industry | Mitsui | Mitsubishi | Sumitomo | Yasuda | The Big Four | Percentage of National Total | Aikaw |
|---|---|---|---|---|---|---|---|
| *Financial* | | | | | | | |
| Banking | 148,125 | 87,675 | 53,675 | 193,361 | 482,836 | 48.0 | - |
| Trust | 15,000 | 7,500 | 5,000 | 7,500 | 35,000 | 85.4 | - |
| Insurance | 6,250 | 64,700 | 6,750 | 8,550 | 86,250 | 51.2 | 4,65 |
| Subtotal | 169,375 | 159,875 | 65,425 | 209,411 | 604,086 | 49.7 | 4,65 |
| *Heavy Industry* | | | | | | | |
| Mining | 481,300 | 274,275 | 111,150 | 1,000 | 867,725 | 28.3 | 565,46 |
| Metal Manufacturing | 270,005 | 185,000 | 550,200 | 4,150 | 1,009,355 | 26.4 | 18,90 |
| Machine Tool | 838,567 | 1,207,655 | 638,660 | 95,183 | 2,780,065 | 46.2 | 760,52 |
| Shipbuilding | 58,125 | 11,647 | 1,600 | 10,000 | 81,372 | 5.0 | 111,75 |
| Chemical | 566,169 | 187,455 | 167,850 | 9,080 | 930,554 | 31.4 | 101,41 |
| Subtotal | 2,214,166 | 1,866,032 | 1,469,460 | 119,413 | 5,669,071 | 32.4 | 1,558,06 |
| *Light Industries* | | | | | | | |
| Paper | 4,131 | 10,980 | - | 9,000 | 24,111 | 4.5 | - |
| Ceramics (inc. cement) | 63,496 | 14,750 | 11,230 | - | 89,476 | 28.4 | 2,85 |
| Textiles | 125,273 | 10,900 | 2,000 | 85,946 | 224,119 | 17.4 | - |
| Agr., Forestry, Food, Marine Products | 24,113 | 6,800 | 1,322 | - | 32,235 | 2.7 | 78,22 |
| Miscellaneous | 56,685 | 29,600 | 14,760 | 22,017 | 123,062 | 9.7 | 21,80 |
| Subtotal | 273,698 | 73,030 | 29,312 | 116,963 | 493,003 | 10.7 | 102,87 |
| *Others* | | | | | | | |
| Electric Power, Gas | - | - | 20,000 | - | 20,000 | 0.5 | 1,2 |
| Land Transportation | 18,682 | 13,254 | 1,075 | 12,600 | 45,611 | 4.9 | 5.2 |
| Marine Transportation | 179,127 | 399,922 | 6,525 | 17,500 | 603,074 | 60.8 | 1,1 |
| Real Estate, Construction, Warehousing | 48,937 | 40,000 | 16,680 | 30,647 | 136,264 | 22.7 | 5,5 |
| Commerce and Trade | 157,145 | 151,400 | 58,205 | 3,000 | 369,750 | 13.6 | 24,7 |
| Subtotal | 403,891 | 604,576 | 102,485 | 63,747 | 1,174,699 | 12.9 | 37,8 |
| TOTAL | 3,061,130 | 2,703,513 | 1,666,682 | 509,534 | 7,940,859 | 24.5 | 1,703,4 |
| National Percentage | 9.4 | 8.3 | 5.2 | 1.6 | 24.5 | | 5 |

Source: Holding Company Liquidation Commission, *Japan's Zaibatsu and Their Dissolution*, Data volume, pp. 468-469.

Explanatory notes to this table will be found in Appendix II.

| ano | Furukawa | Okura | Nakashima | Nomura | The Other Six | Percent-age of National Total | The Ten | Percent-age of National Total | National Total |
|---|---|---|---|---|---|---|---|---|---|
| - | - | - | - | 24,750 | 24,750 | 2.4 | 507,586 | 50.4 | 1,006,831 |
| - | - | - | - | - | - | - | 35,000 | 85.4 | 41,000 |
| - | 3,750 | 6,050 | - | 900 | 15,350 | 9.1 | 101,600 | 60.3 | 168,312 |
| - | 3,750 | 6,050 | - | 25,650 | 40,100 | 3.3 | 644,186 | 53.0 | 1,216,143 |
| | | | | | | | | | |
| ,700 | 16,400 | 26,362 | 13,750 | 18,750 | 683,428 | 22.2 | 1,551,153 | 50.5 | 3,070,750 |
| ,338 | 208,883 | - | 3,730 | 18,500 | 589,351 | 15.4 | 1,598,706 | 41.8 | 3,829,681 |
| ,618 | 203,863 | 143,345 | 167,400 | 11,500 | 1,306,255 | 21.7 | 4,086,320 | 67.9 | 6,018,598 |
| ,000 | - | - | - | - | 121,750 | 7.5 | 203,122 | 12.5 | 1,613,811 |
| ,200 | 50,162 | 48,000 | 3,400 | 1,500 | 211,678 | 7.1 | 1,142,232 | 38.5 | 2,968,529 |
| ,856 | 479,308 | 217,707 | 188,280 | 50,250 | 2,912,462 | 16.6 | 8,581,533 | 49.0 | 17,501,369 |
| | | | | | | | | | |
| - | - | - | 1,280 | - | 1,280 | 0.2 | 25,391 | 4.7 | 535,144 |
| 708 | - | - | - | - | 86,558 | 27.4 | 176,034 | 55.8 | 315,486 |
| - | - | 500 | 17,125 | 900 | 18,525 | 1.4 | 242,644 | 18.8 | 1,288,869 |
| 150 | - | 8,000 | 5,160 | - | 91,532 | 7.7 | 123,767 | 10.4 | 1,182,641 |
| 000 | 3,180 | 25,750 | 45 | 26,200 | 81,975 | 6.5 | 205,037 | 16.2 | 1,265,722 |
| 858 | 3,180 | 34,250 | 23,610 | 27,100 | 279,870 | 6.1 | 772,873 | 16.8 | 4,587,862 |
| | | | | | | | | | |
| - | - | - | - | - | 1,252 | 0.03 | 21,252 | 0.5 | 3,825,574 |
| 400 | 50 | - | - | - | 6,675 | 0.7 | 52,286 | 5.6 | 933,090 |
| 200 | - | 1,000 | - | - | 6,345 | 0.6 | 609,419 | 61.4 | 992,080 |
| 800 | 180 | 9,234 | - | 10,400 | 40,164 | 6.7 | 176,428 | 29.4 | 599,602 |
| 795 | 4,013 | 45,290 | 778 | 52,000 | 182,576 | 6.7 | 552,326 | 20.3 | 2,723,796 |
| 195 | 4,243 | 55,524 | 788 | 62,400 | 237,012 | 2.6 | 1,411,711 | 15.5 | 9,074,142 |
| 909 | 490,481 | 313,531 | 212,688 | 165,400 | 3,469,444 | 10.7 | 11,410,303 | 35.2 | 32,379,516 |
| 1.8 | 1.5 | 1.0 | 0.6 | 0.5 | 10.7 | | 35.2 | | 100.0 |

Table 3-1: THE ROLE OF THE ZAIBATSU IN JAPAN'S ECONOMY AT WAR'S END IN TERMS OF PAID-UP CAPITAL

(Part B: Outside Japan (Unit: 1,000 Yen)

| Industry | Mitsui | Mitsubishi | Sumitomo | Yasuda | The Big Four |
|---|---|---|---|---|---|
| *Financial* | | | | | |
| Banking | - | - | - | - | - |
| Trust | 3,000 | - | - | - | 3,000 |
| Insurance | - | - | - | - | - |
| Subtotal | 3,000 | - | - | - | 3,000 |
| *Heavy Industry* | | | | | |
| Mining | 63,223 | 171,648 | 21,200 | - | 256,071 |
| Metal Manufacturing | 50,500 | 6,250 | 176,000 | 5,000 | 237,750 |
| Machine Tool | 17,000 | 32,000 | 53,000 | 2,000 | 104,000 |
| Shipbuilding | - | 5,000 | - | - | 5,000 |
| Chemicals | 172,500 | 63,550 | 4,500 | - | 240,550 |
| Subtotal | 303,223 | 278,448 | 254,700 | 7,000 | 843,371 |
| *Light Industries* | | | | | |
| Paper | - | 125 | - | - | 125 |
| Ceramics (inc. cement) | 10,000 | - | - | - | 10,000 |
| Textiles | 19,700 | 12,000 | - | - | 31,700 |
| Agr., Forestry, Food, Marine Products | 6,785 | 17,100 | - | - | 23,885 |
| Miscellaneous | 65,640 | 13,395 | 450 | - | 79,485 |
| Subtotal | 102,125 | 42,620 | 450 | - | 145,195 |
| *Others* | | | | | |
| Electric Power, Gas | - | - | - | - | - |
| Land Transportation | 1,500 | 14,200 | - | - | 15,700 |
| Marine Transportation | 190 | 26,750 | - | - | 26,940 |
| Real Estate, Construction, Warehousing | - | 4,200 | - | 1,250 | 5,450 |
| Commerce and Trade | 27,453 | 47,000 | - | - | 74,453 |
| Subtotal | 29,143 | 92,150 | - | 1,250 | 122,543 |
| TOTAL | 437,491 | 413,218 | 255,150 | 8,250 | 1,114,109 |
| Percentage of Eight Combines' Investments | 31.5 | 29.7 | 18.3 | 0.6 | 80.1 |

Source: Holding Company Liquidation Commission, *Japan's Zaibatsu and Their Dissolution*, Data volume, pp. 468-69.

Explanatory notes to this table will be found in Appendix II.

| Percent-age | Aikawa | Asano | Furukawa | Okura | The Other Four | Percentage | Investments by the Eight Combines |
|---|---|---|---|---|---|---|---|
| - | - | - | - | - | - | - | - |
| 0.2 | - | - | - | - | - | - | 3,000 |
| - | - | - | - | - | - | - | - |
| 0.2 | - | - | - | - | - | - | 3,000 |
| 18.4 | 18,850 | 5,000 | - | 8,800 | 32,650 | 2.3 | 288,721 |
| 17.1 | 2,000 | - | 18,000 | - | 20,000 | 1.4 | 257,750 |
| 7.5 | 23,550 | - | 53,950 | - | 77,500 | 5.6 | 181,500 |
| 0.4 | - | - | - | - | - | - | 5,000 |
| 17.3 | 37,235 | - | - | - | 37,235 | 2.7 | 277,785 |
| 60.7 | 81,635 | 5,000 | 71,950 | 8,800 | 167,385 | 12.0 | 1,010,756 |
| 0.0 | - | - | - | - | - | - | 125 |
| 0.7 | - | - | - | - | - | - | 10,000 |
| 2.3 | - | - | - | - | - | - | 31,700 |
| 1.7 | 3,275 | - | - | - | 3,275 | 0.3 | 27,160 |
| 5.7 | 200 | 4,500 | - | 1,200 | 5,900 | 0.4 | 85,385 |
| 10.4 | 3,475 | 4,500 | - | 1,200 | 9,175 | 0.7 | 154,370 |
| - | - | - | - | - | - | - | - |
| 1.1 | 600 | - | - | - | 600 | 0.04 | 16,300 |
| 1.9 | - | - | - | - | - | - | 26,940 |
| 0.4 | - | - | - | 350 | 350 | 0.02 | 5,800 |
| 5.4 | 2,500 | - | - | 96,500 | 99,000 | 7.1 | 173,453 |
| 8.8 | 3,100 | - | - | 96,850 | 99,950 | 7.2 | 222,493 |
| 80.1 | 88,210 | 9,500 | 71,950 | 106,850 | 276,510 | 19.9 | 1,390,619 |
|  | 6.3 | .7 | 5.2 | 7.2 | 19.9 | 100 |  |

Table 3-2: THE ROLE OF THE ZAIBATSU IN JAPAN'S ECONOMY IN 1941 IN TERMS OF PAID-UP CAPITAL

(Unit: 1,000 Yen)

| Industry | Mitsui | Mitsubishi | Sumitomo | Yasuda | "Big Four" | Percent-age of National Total | Aikawa |
|---|---|---|---|---|---|---|---|
| *Financial* | | | | | | | |
| Banking | 60,000 | 62,500 | 50,000 | 126,931 | 299,431 | 21.9 | - |
| Trust | 7,500 | 7,500 | 5,000 | 7,500 | 27,500 | 43.3 | - |
| Insurance | 3,000 | 57,000 | 3,250 | 8,825 | 72,075 | 46.5 | 2,750 |
| Subtotal | 70,500 | 127,000 | 58,250 | 143,256 | 399,006 | 25.2 | 2,750 |
| *Heavy Industry* | | | | | | | |
| Mining | (34,087)<br>326,069 | (27,500)<br>244,120 | 34,150 | - | (61,587)<br>604,309 | 22.9 | (573,922<br>249,650 |
| Metal Manufacturing | 72,875 | 45,000 | (20,000)<br>184,350 | - | (20,000<br>302,225 | 12.3 | (280,000<br>- |
| Machine Tool | (8,000)<br>287,695 | 294,500 | (16,975)<br>123,150 | 52,000 | (24,975)<br>757,345 | 22.9 | (112,500<br>411,619 |
| Shipbuilding | 10,000 | - | - | - | 10,000 | 1.7 | - |
| Chemical | (5,800)<br>187,500 | (11,000)<br>97,250 | 62,050 | 6,750 | (16,800)<br>353,550 | 15.4 | (21,657)<br>172,735 |
| Subtotal | (47,887)<br>884,109 | (38,500)<br>680,870 | (36,975)<br>403,700 | 58,750 | (123,362)<br>2,027,429 | 18.0 | (988,079<br>834,004 |
| *Light Industries* | | | | | | | |
| Paper | - | 10,000 | - | 9,000 | 19,000 | 3.5 | - |
| Ceramics (inc. cement) | 40,388 | (1,500)<br>45,250 | 7,750 | - | (1,500)<br>93,388 | 23.7 | - |
| Textiles | (8,500)<br>60,876 | 600 | - | (3,075)<br>24,487 | (11,575)<br>86,963 | 6.4 | - |
| Agr., Forestry, Marine Products, Food | (51,930)<br>34,900 | (7,850)<br>18,725 | - | - | (59,780)<br>53,625 | 6.4 | 85,65 |
| Miscellaneous | (9,500)<br>22,225 | (15,300)<br>12,275 | 10,350 | - | (24,800)<br>44,850 | 5.3 | - |
| Subtotal | (69,930)<br>158,389 | (24,650)<br>86,850 | 18,100 | (3,075)<br>34,487 | (97,655)<br>297,826 | 7.5 | 85,65 |
| *Others* | | | | | | | |
| Electric Power, Gas | 25,450 | - | 36,250 | 74,436 | 136,136 | 4.3 | 10,25 |
| Land Transportation | (23,599)<br>12,725 | (9,000)<br>20,000 | - | 7,025 | (32,599)<br>39,750 | 2.4 | - |
| Marine Transportation | 10,000 | (10,000)<br>183,875 | - | 13,000 | (10,000)<br>206,875 | 25.7 | 29,95 |
| Real Estate, Construction, Warehousing | 13,800 | (1,000)<br>17,250 | 58,100 | (1,250)<br>32,738 | (2,250)<br>121,888 | 15.5 | 1,00 |
| Commerce and Trade | (4,407)<br>42,175 | 75,000 | - | 6,594 | (4,407)<br>123,789 | 2.7 | (114,65<br>- |
| Subtotal | (28,006)<br>104,190 | (20,000)<br>296,125 | 94,350 | (1,250)<br>133,793 | (49,256)<br>628,438 | 5.7 | (114,65<br>41,20 |
| TOTAL | (145,823)<br>1,217,168 | (83,150)<br>1,190,845 | (36,975)<br>574,400 | (4,325)<br>370,286 | (270,273)<br>3,352,699 | 12.0 | (1,102,72<br>963,60 |
| National Percentage | 4.4 | 4.3 | 2.0 | 1.3 | 12.0 | | 3. |

Source: Holding Company Liquidation Commission, *Japan's Zaibatsu and Their Dissolution*, Data volume, pp. 470-471.

Explanatory notes to this table will be found in Appendix II.

| Asano | Furukawa | Okura | Nomura | "The Five" | Percent-age of National Total | "The Nine" | Percent-age of National Total | National Total |
|---|---|---|---|---|---|---|---|---|
| - | - | - | 15,000 | 15,000 | 1.1 | 314,431 | 23.0 | 1,364,564 |
| - | - | - | 4,750 | 4,750 | 7.5 | 32,250 | 50.8 | 63,561 |
| - | 1,250 | 500 | 400 | 4,900 | 3.2 | 76,975 | 49.7 | 154,993 |
| - | 1,250 | 500 | 20,150 | 24,650 | 1.6 | 423,656 | 26.8 | 1,583,118 |
| | | | | | | | | |
| (22,600)<br>31,188 | 6,000 | (101,700)<br>24,250 | 1,250 | (598,222)<br>312,338 | 11.8 | (659,809)<br>916,647 | 34.8 | 2,635,197 |
| (7,000)<br>179,350 | (5,000)<br>76,200 | (10,000)<br>- | - | (302,000)<br>255,550 | 10.4 | (322,000)<br>557,775 | 22.8 | 2,448,943 |
| 9,000 | (11,375)<br>85,083 | 54,000 | - | (123,875)<br>559,702 | 16.9 | (148,850)<br>1,317,047 | 39.9 | 3,301,745 |
| - | - | - | - | - | - | 10,000 | 1.7 | 592,414 |
| 400 | 17,575 | 3,950 | 3,600 | (21,657)<br>198,260 | 8.7 | (38,457)<br>551,810 | 24.1 | 2,291,810 |
| (29,600)<br>219,938 | (16,375)<br>184,858 | (111,700)<br>82,200 | 4,850 | (1,045,754)<br>1,325,850 | 11.8 | (1,169,116)<br>3,353,279 | 29.8 | 11,270,109 |
| | | | | | | | | |
| - | - | (4,000)<br>2,500 | (7,500)<br>- | (11,500)<br>2,500 | 0.5 | (11,500)<br>21,500 | 3.9 | 545,488 |
| 77,918 | - | (7,800)<br>- | - | (7,800)<br>77,918 | 19.7 | (9,300)<br>171,306 | 43.4 | 394,528 |
| - | 1,400 | 16,136 | 23,965 | 41,501 | 3.1 | (11,575)<br>128,464 | 9.5 | 1,352,469 |
| - | - | 2,000 | 3,000 | 90,650 | 10.8 | (59,780)<br>144,275 | 7.1 | 842,341 |
| 800 | - | (1,600)<br>15,093 | (11,150)<br>11,100 | (12,750)<br>26,993 | 3.2 | (37,550)<br>71,843 | 8.6 | 833,781 |
| 78,718 | 1,400 | (13,400)<br>35,729 | (18,650)<br>38,065 | (32,050)<br>239,562 | 6.0 | (129,705)<br>537,388 | 13.3 | 3,968,607 |
| | | | | | | | | |
| 35,250 | - | - | 51,000 | 96,500 | 3.0 | 232,636 | 7.3 | 3,192,877 |
| 3,100 | - | 22,816 | - | 25,916 | 1.6 | (32,599)<br>65,666 | 4.0 | 1,656,941 |
| 7,200 | - | - | - | 37,150 | 4.6 | (10,000)<br>244,025 | 30.3 | 805,693 |
| 15,285 | - | 9,809 | 3,900 | 29,994 | 3.8 | (2,250)<br>151,882 | 9.2 | 787,827 |
| 17,575 | - | (5,000)<br>10,000 | 7,500 | (119,650)<br>35,075 | 0.8 | (124,057)<br>158,864 | 3.5 | 4,569,809 |
| 78,410 | - | (5,000)<br>42,625 | 62,400 | (119,650)<br>224,635 | 2.0 | (168,906)<br>853,073 | 7.7 | 11,013,147 |
| (29,600)<br>377,066 | (16,375)<br>187,508 | (130,100)<br>161,054 | (18,650)<br>125,465 | (1,197,454)<br>1,814,697 | 6.5 | (1,467,727)<br>5,167,396 | 18.5 | 27,834,981 |
| 1.3 | .7 | .6 | .4 | 6.5 | | 18.5 | | |

Table 3-3: THE ROLE OF THE ZAIBATSU IN JAPAN'S ECONOMY IN 1937 IN TERMS OF PAID-UP CAPITAL

(Unit: 1,000 Yen)

| Industry | Mitsui | Mitsubishi | Sumitomo | Yasuda | "Big Four" | Percentage of National Total | Aikawa |
|---|---|---|---|---|---|---|---|
| *Financial* | | | | | | | |
| Banking | 60,000 | 62,500 | 50,000 | 124,573 | 297,073 | 21.0 | - |
| Trust | 7,500 | 7,500 | 5,000 | 7,500 | 27,500 | 37.2 | - |
| Insurance | 3,000 | 57,000 | 3,250 | 8,825 | 72,075 | 49.0 | 1,250 |
| Subtotal | 70,500 | 127,000 | 58,250 | 140,898 | 396,648 | 22.5 | 1,250 |
| *Heavy Industry* | | | | | | | |
| Mining | (11,350) 162,550 | (7,500) 106,850 | 34,150 | - | (18,850) 303,550 | 20.9 | (30,000) 163,350 |
| Metal Manufacturing | 15,000 | 12,500 | (4,500) 56,000 | - | (4,500) 83,500 | 9.2 | - |
| Machine Tools | 40,625 | 106,625 | (975) 41,900 | 6,250 | (975) 195,400 | 18.6 | 75,927 |
| Shipbuilding | - | - | - | - | - | - | - |
| Chemicals | (500) 80,015 | 36,500 | 38,400 | 2,250 | (500) 157,165 | 11.3 | (9,839) 83,688 |
| Subtotal | (11,850) 298,190 | (7,500) 262,475 | (5,475) 170,450 | 8,500 | (24,825) 739,615 | 14.6 | (39,839) 332,965 |
| *Light Industry* | | | | | | | |
| Paper | - | 8,000 | - | 9,000 | 17,000 | 4.9 | - |
| Ceramics (inc. cement) | 25,680 | 33,000 | 5,500 | - | 64,180 | 21.5 | - |
| Textiles | 40,797 | 5,000 | 30,000 | (3,100) 12,862 | (3,100) 88,659 | 8.2 | - |
| Agr., Forestry, Marine Products, Food | (43,530) 11,184 | (8,600) 15,300 | - | - | (52,130) 26,484 | 3.7 | (1,350) 53,467 |
| Miscellaneous | 7,141 | (300) 4,750 | 1,050 | - | (300) 12,941 | 2.3 | 1,750 |
| Subtotal | (43,530 84,802 | (8,900) 66,050 | 36,550 | (3,100) 21,862 | (55,530) 209,264 | 7.0 | (1,350) 55,217 |
| *Others* | | | | | | | |
| Electric Power, Gas | 11,250 | (5,000) - | 19,125 | 49,887 | (5,000) 80,262 | 3.0 | 6,375 |
| Land Transportation | 7,325 | 8,573 | 45,125 | 7,825 | 68,848 | 5.4 | 138 |
| Marine Transportation | 2,750 | (4,750) 74,250 | - | - | (4,750) 77,000 | 16.2 | 4,000 |
| Real Estate, Construction, Warehousing | 12,500 | (1,000) 12,250 | 57,350 | 20,237 | (1,000) 102,337 | 16.1 | 3,000 |
| Commerce, Trade | (2,184) 125,300 | 23,500 | - | 5,843 | (2,184) 154,643 | 5.3 | 250 |
| Subtotal | (2,184) 159,125 | (10,750) 118,573 | 121,600 | 83,792 | (12,934) 483,090 | 6.1 | 13,763 |
| TOTAL | (57,564) 612,617 | (27,150) 574,098 | (5,475) 386,850 | (3,100) 255,052 | (93,289) 1,828,617 | 10.4 | (41,189) 393,195 |
| National Percentage | 3.5 | 3.3 | 2.2 | 1.4 | 10.4 | | 2.2 |

Source: Holding Company Liquidation Commission, *Japan's Zaibatsu and Their Dissolution*, Data volume, pp. 472-473.

Explanatory notes to this table will be found in Appendix II.

| Asano | Furukawa | Okura | Nomura | "The Five" | Percentage of National Total | "The Nine" | Percentage of National Total | National Total |
|---|---|---|---|---|---|---|---|---|
| - | 1,250 | - | 10,000 | 11,250 | 0.8 | 308,323 | 21.8 | 1,418,994 |
| - | - | - | 4,750 | 4,750 | 6.4 | 32,250 | 43.6 | 73,920 |
| - | - | 500 | 400 | 2,150 | 1.5 | 74,225 | 50.5 | 147,185 |
| - | 1,250 | 500 | 15,150 | 18,150 | 1.1 | 414,798 | 23.6 | 1,640,099 |
| | | | | | | | | |
| (800)<br>18,502 | 14,700 | (11,000)<br>15,650 | - | (41,900)<br>212,202 | 14.6 | (60,750)<br>515,752 | 35.5 | 1,453,489 |
| (7,500)<br>42,675 | 1,200 | 6,000 | - | (7,500)<br>49,875 | 5.5 | (12,000)<br>133,375 | 14.7 | 911,752 |
| - | 42,782 | 17,150 | - | 135,859 | 13.0 | (975)<br>331,259 | 31.6 | 1,047,934 |
| 25,000 | - | - | - | 25,000 | 9.5 | 25,000 | 9.5 | 263,537 |
| 600 | 7,050 | 6,238 | - | (9,839)<br>97,576 | 7.0 | (10,339)<br>254,741 | 18.3 | 1,389,279 |
| (8,300)<br>86,777 | 65,732 | (11,100)<br>45,038 | - | (59,239)<br>520,512 | 10.3 | (84,064)<br>1,260,127 | 24.9 | 5,065,991 |
| | | | | | | | | |
| - | - | (4,000)<br>2,500 | - | (4,000)<br>2,500 | 7.2 | (4,000)<br>19,500 | 12.1 | 346,144 |
| 74,743 | - | (3,300) | - | (3,300)<br>74,743 | 25.1 | (3,300)<br>138,923 | 46.6 | 298,100 |
| - | 1,400 | 10,589 | 10,500 | 22,489 | 2.1 | (3,100)<br>111,148 | 10.3 | 1,074,873 |
| - | 162 | 2,000 | (400)<br>4,500 | (1,750)<br>60,129 | 8.4 | (53,880)<br>86,613 | 12.1 | 717,696 |
| 2,430 | 650 | (500)<br>18,478 | 10,500 | (500)<br>33,808 | 6.1 | (800)<br>46,749 | 8.4 | 553,797 |
| 77,173 | 2,212 | (7,800)<br>33,567 | (400)<br>25,500 | (9,550)<br>193,669 | 6.5 | (65,080)<br>402,933 | 13.5 | 2,990,610 |
| | | | | | | | | |
| - | - | - | 9,400 | 15,775 | 0.6 | (5,000)<br>96,037 | 3.6 | 2,648,980 |
| 3,100 | - | 10,171 | - | 13,409 | 1.0 | 82,257 | 6.4 | 1,278,153 |
| 10,096 | - | - | - | 14,096 | 3.0 | (4,750)<br>91,096 | 19.2 | 475,712 |
| 20,075 | - | 9,144 | 100 | 32,319 | 5.1 | (1,000)<br>134,656 | 21.2 | 634,997 |
| 18,600 | - | 8,050 | 7,500 | 34,400 | 1.1 | (2,184)<br>189,043 | 6.4 | 2,919,974 |
| 51,871 | - | 27,365 | 17,000 | 109,999 | 1.4 | (12,934)<br>593,089 | 7.5 | 7,957,816 |
| (8,300)<br>215,821 | 69,194 | (18,470)<br>106,470 | (400)<br>57,650 | (68,789)<br>842,330 | 5.8[a] | (162,078)<br>2,670,947 | 15.1 | 17,654,516 |
| 1.2 | .4 | .6 | .3 | 4.7* | | 15.1 | | |

[a]An internal inconsistency to the table produces the disparity in these figures.

certain major investors have been omitted—for example, the Japan Nitrogenous Fertilizer Company with its large investments in Korea. With, however, these limitations in mind, it will be noted that the Big Four accounted for 80.1% of foreign investments at war's end. Because the table does not provide individual combine percentage figures, I have added them. Mitsui alone accounted for close to one-third of the total of these investments, and Mitsubishi was close behind with 29%, together they thus accounted for 60% (a rather different picture from the one given by the former prime minister). Further, study of the character of these investments shows that 72.7% occurred in heavy industry, of which Mitsui, Mitsubishi, and Sumitomo accounted for 60%.

It is instructive to note how helpful the war economy was to the position of the major combines. Table 3-2 for 1941 and Table 3-3 for 1937, showing the position of the *zaibatsu* at the beginning of World War II and at the beginning of the China War, include only 9 combines, Nakajima having been omitted. In these two tables, which rest on even less firm data, domestic and overseas investments are jointly presented, the overseas data being given in parentheses.

Study of Table 3-2 reveals the strikingly lower position of the Big Four at the start of the war. It will be observed that in contrast to the 24.5% position of paid-up capital which the Big Four represented at the end of the war their position at the start was 12%. The comparison of the positions of the other leading *zaibatsu* is handicapped by the change in number from 6 to 5. While the Other Six represented a 10.7% position at war's end, the "other five" held a 6.5% position at the start.

The 1941 table, as does the 1946 table, presents overseas investments in absolute amounts only, not providing individual combine figures in percentage terms; these have been added. A comparison of overseas investment positions among the 9 combines indicates the dramatic change in the position of the Aikawa interests (Nissan-Mangyo), going from 75% of the investments of the 9 at the start of the Pacific War to 6% at its close.

If we now turn to the 1937 table, Table 3-3, which again cites 9 combines only, we find several very interesting points. We observe that the Big Four, out of the realignment of the economy in preparation for war on the continent, stood at the start of the "China Inci-

in mining, divided by investments of the 8 in all fields. Therefore there is no relationship between the percentage figures shown in Part A, "Japan Proper," and Part B, "Outside Japan."

dent" ahead of the "other five" in investments in heavy industry, accounting for 14.6% of such investments, in contrast to 10.3% on the part of the "other five." In terms of over-all importance in the economy by the criterion here employed, we note that the Big Four were roughly twice the size of the Other Five, 10.4% compared to 4.7%.

Let us note investments outside Japan. Again individual combine percentage figures have been added. It will be seen that Mitsui leads with better than one-third of the total of the 9, that Aikawa follows at one-fourth, and Mitsubishi stands at one-sixth. The others are small.

With these tables we have been moving back in time. Working in the opposite direction we find that the Big Four not only over-all but specifically in heavy industries as well were in a strong position at the start of the 1937 China War. The recasting of the economy, which took place in the thirties in preparation for this military venture, did not cost the Big Four their dominance. It will be observed that in the next four years, during the war on the continent and during preparations for the Pacific War, the Big Four and the Big Five increased their importance in the economy at roughly the same pace, the Big Four advancing from 10.4% of total paid-up capital in Japan to 12%, and the Big Five from 4.7% to 6.5%. In the field of heavy industries we see that in this 1937-41 period the Big Four grew somewhat more rapidly than the Big Five; it went from 14.6% of the country's investments in heavy industry to 18.0%, the Big Five from 10.3 to 11.8%.

The really significant increase in position in the economy for the Big Four, however, came during the Pacific War. In those four years they made what were, even for them, giant advances. In heavy industry they went from 18% of the country's investment to 32.4%; in finance, from 25.2 to 49.7%. The Other Five and the Other Six, on the other hand, merely advanced from 11.8% of heavy industry to 16.6%; from 1.6% of finance to 3.3. In other words, as far as increasing their position within the economy was concerned, the Pacific War period was a striking success for the largest businesses in Japan. Similarly, by the much more limited evidence which these tables provide on investments outside Japan, the period was also a brilliant success for the Big Four. Comparing the proportion of investment outside Japan by the Big Four among the 9 in 1941 to their position among the 10 in 1946, we find that the Big Four went from 18 percent to 80 percent. In such circumstances it is hard indeed to imagine that there could have been any fundamental antagonism between the big, older combines and the military.

## *The Estate of Wealth*

What were the returns from a system of enterprise made up of "chosen instruments" and "others"? The returns were handsome, even though the statistical documentation leaves much to be desired. Again one turns to the HCLC for information on the size of the family fortunes and again finds discrepancies between the Japanese-language and English-language reports. The Japanese-language report states that the securities holdings of the 56 designated persons of the 10 family groups amounted to Y1.2 billion in paid-up value, a breakdown of which is reproduced here as Table 3-4. The English-language report employs various figures for the wealth of the 56 designated persons. On one page it both speaks of the "total assets" of the 56 persons as "Y700,000,000" and their investments as "Y1,165,000,000." A few pages later it reports that "securities owned" by designated persons amounted to "Y608,957,000."[38] With such confusion it is difficult to know what the commission intended to say in its English report. The Japanese-language report puts holdings of real property at one-fourth total wealth.[39] The English-language report does not mention them at all.

Table 3-4 shows many odd qualities. It will be seen that the Mitsui fortune is shown only moderately larger than the Sumitomo, Y390 million to Y314. But in Table 3-1 we saw that Mitsui companies accounted for 9.4% of total capitalization in the economy, compared to 5.2% for the Sumitomo. Certainly one would expect the much greater size of the Mitsui *zaibatsu* to be reflected in its family wealth. Again one would expect the Iwasaki fortune from the Mitsubishi empire to be larger relative to the others than it is, the Mitsubishi network accounting for 8.3% of total capital. Further, it will be observed that the Yasuda fortune is third from the lowest, being exceeded in smallness only by Asano and Aikawa.

The size of these family fortunes, of course, reflects in part the number of persons "designated." It was puzzling to me how the commission arrived at its designations of persons within each of the several houses, how it was that the 11-house House of Mitsui produced the same number of designated persons as the two Iwasaki Houses. In the opinion of Fujita Fujio, director of research at the Mitsubishi Economic Research Institute, and Suzuki Yasuzo of the staff, designations were made in terms of those holding shares in the top-holding

[38] HCLC, *Final Report*, pp. 67, 75.

[39] HCLC, *Zaibatsu Dissolution*, textual volume, p. 302. The statement is that securities represent three-fourths and real property one-fourth of total holdings.

Table 3-4: THE PAID-UP VALUE OF STOCKS, PARTNERSHIP SHARES AND THE FACE VALUE OF BONDS, CORPORATE AND GOVERNMENT, BELONGING TO THE 10 DESIGNATED FAMILY GROUPS, MARCH 13,1947

(92.6% of the total represents stocks, 4.3% partnership shares, 0.4% corporate bonds, 2.5% government bonds)

| *Family groups* | *Persons* | *Yen* |
|---|---|---|
| Mitsui | 11 | 390,570,000 |
| Iwasaki (Mitsubishi) | 11 | 177,307,000 |
| Sumitomo | 4 | 314,964,000 |
| Yasuda | 10 | 39,591,000 |
| Nakajima (Fuji Industries) | 5 | 71,650,000 |
| Nomura | 4 | 77,895,000 |
| Asano | 4 | 30,080,000 |
| Okura | 4 | 55,746,000 |
| Furukawa | 1 | 43,402,000 |
| Nakagawa | 1 | 308,000 |
| Aikawa (Nissan) | 1 | 484,000 |
| | 56 | 1,201,998,000 |

Source: HCLC, *Zaibatsu Dissolution*, data volume, pp. 290-93. That Nakagawa is included in this listing of 10 family groups, thus seeming to make 11, is to be explained by the fact that he is in fact, if not in name, within the Furukawa circle. Married to the daughter of Furukawa, he was president of Furukawa Electric Industries (Denki Kogyo) and some 30 years senior to the head of the Furukawa House.

companies.[40] Since in the House of Mitsui, only the head of the 11 houses were permitted to hold shares in the top-holding company (in rigidly prescribed proportion according to the family will)[41] only 11

[40] Interview, November 1965.

[41] For actual family holdings in the holding company cf. HCLC, *Zaibatsu Dissolution*, data volume, p. 344. For the rules governing division of House holdings cf. Article 28 of the 1900 will, where it is specified that the proportion would be 23 percent for the senior main family; 11.5 percent for the other five main families; and 3.9 percent for the five associate families. Among possible sources for text of the full will, cf. Hadley, "Concentrated Business Power," in translation, pp. 149-56; in the original, Appendix VI. The original 1722 will had a slightly

Mitsui persons were designated. However, other persons in these families held shares in Mitsui companies even though not in the top-holding company, but from the way Table 3-4 was compiled there is no information on what such holdings may have amounted to.

As stated above, the Japanese-language report puts holdings of real property for the 10 family groups at a quarter of the value of their total assets (securities, three-fourths, real property, one-fourth). Nothing is said, however, how either "end" of this relationship has been taken—whether the securities are paid-in value, net worth, or what, and on the other hand, whether the real property is market value, tax value, or historical cost (though in Japanese practice the latter two are not far apart). If one assumes the commission was speaking of paid-in value of the securities to tax-value of real property, and one wishes to get at net-worth value of the securities and the market value of the real estate, the writer would estimate the fortunes represented in Table 3-4 to have amounted to some Y3 billion, though such adjustments, of course, take no account for the omissions of Table 3-4.[42]

The only *zaibatsu* fortune to have come through the "wringer" of combine-dissolution, capital levy tax,[43] land reform, and severe inflation (a problem when one's fortune has been converted into bonds), is that of Sumitomo Kichizaemon. Sumitomo Kichizaemon is today among the top taxpayers of the nation, an achievement probably explained not only by his "ingenuity" in tax matters, but by his large and long-time holdings of forest land. Forests were not included in the land reform program and so came through intact.

---

different division of House property. For the text cf. *ibid.*, in translation, pp. 109-14; in the Japanese, Appendix VI.

[42] In the textual volume the HCLC tells us that real property is one-fourth of total assets, or in the relationship of 25%:75% of security holdings. Securities are stated to be Y1.2 billion. Real property at tax value is accordingly assumed to be Y400 million. In the judgment of Fujita Fujio, tax value of real property to market value in the 1945 period might be assumed to be 1:3. (Today, on urban land acquired in the past the ratio would be much higher.) Making this assumption would give us a market value for real property of Y1.2 billion.

In the judgment of Director Fujita, the relationship between paid-in capital to net worth among Japanese corporations at war's end might be taken as roughly 1:1.5. If we use this relationship (disregarding the 2.9% of securities which are not shares but rather bonds given the crudity of the whole calculation), this would give us a net worth value of the securities of Y1.8 billion. Adding Y1.2 billion to Y1.8 billion gives us Y3 billion.

[43] The Capital Levy Law, Law No. 52 of November 17, 1946, provided for a levy on personal net assets of Y100,000 and above with rates beginning at 25% and progressing by incremental margins to 90% on assets of Y15 million and above. The tax was not applied to corporations. SCAP, GHQ, *History of the Nonmilitary Activities of the Occupation of Japan*, Vol. XIII, *Finance*, Part A, National Government Finance, p. 134, Office of Military History, Washington, D.C.

# 4.

## Combine Dissolution: Severing Ownership Ties

THE ALLIED policy to dissolve the combines and remove the *zaibatsu* families from their positions of control amounted to a quite different attitude toward history and social change than the one prevailing in Japan, where a strong Marxian tradition tends to see business or industrial organization as beyond human reach. Marxists regard the stages of capitalist development as the product of "natural law," which unfolds in its own ineluctable course. The "stages" progress with a logic unmodifiable by human hands, not something that can be changed by antitrust action, by separating banking from industry, or the like.

This Japanese attitude, incongruously enough, is similar to 19th-century American thinking, where the consequences of the market mechanism were regarded as God-given rather than the product of legislated corporate privileges and the interpretation of property rights by the judiciary. Frederick Lewis Allen in *The Big Change* has described these American attitudes in this way:

> Nobody expounded the folly of tampering with the laws of economics more eloquently than Yale's great teacher of political economy, the dynamic William Graham Sumner. . . . "You need not think it necessary," he would tell his Yale classes, "to have Washington exercise a political providence over the country. God has done that a good deal better by the laws of political economy. . . ."
>
> The irony of the situation lay in the fact that for generations men had been tinkering with economic law to their own advantage, and in the process had produced institutions which were emphatically not God's work,—as most of Sumner's hearers presumably supposed them to be—but man's. The corporation, for instance, was not an invention of God's. It was an invention of man's. It was a creature of the state; its privileges, its limitations, were defined by legislation. As put to work for the furtherance of industry and business in general, the corporation was one of the great inventions of the 19th century: an instrument of incalculable value. Yet, by taking adroit advantage of the legislative acts which defined its privileges,

one could play extraordinary tricks with it. Corporate devices could be used to permit A to rob B—or, let us say, more charitably, to permit A to drain off all the gravy in sight and leave none for B. And it was a little foolish to defend such devices on the ground that one must let economic nature take its course.

It was largely as a result of the discovery of tricks that could be played with corporations, and particularly with their capital stock, that the wealth produced in such a tremendous spate at the turn of the century flowed in large proportion into a few well-placed hands. While the eyes of the boys in Economics A were fastened upon the benignity of the law of supply and demand, the eyes of corporation lawyers and their clients were fastened upon the benignity of the New Jersey Holding-company Act. Most of these gentlemen would have regarded an income tax, let us say, as a flat transgression by man of economic law. But few of them regarded the Holding-company Act in any such light, even though it made the theoretical rewards of capital, as defined by the classical economists, look trifling.[1]

It was because American and Allied policy-makers saw the combines as the product of the "tricks" which could be played with holding companies, as the product of discriminatory government policy, discriminatory credit, discriminatory business practices—and the snowballing effect these can give to concentration after a healthy start has been made—that they did not see them as untouchable.

### *The Structure of Combine Ownership*

It is as true for combines as for watches that to take something apart one must have an idea of how it has been put together. Ownership, it is claimed, was a major building block; what patterns did it take? To show the patterns of combine ownership at war's end, I have prepared tables on the structure of ownership among the core companies of the "big three"—Mitsui, Mitsubishi, and Sumitomo—among those subsidiaries which the respective top-holding companies designated as being peculiarly and vitally important to the operation of their combines.

Tables 4-1, 4-2, and 4-3 which follow show three of the four principal patterns of combine ownership—vertical top-holding company ownership, direct family ownership, and horizontal cross ties. What they do not show is second-level vertical ownership. Virtually all of

[1] Allen, *The Big Change*, Bantam Books, New York, 1961, pp. 59-61.

Table 4-1: OWNERSHIP TIES AMONG THE CORE SUBSIDIARIES IN THE MITSUI COMBINE AS A PERCENTAGE OF ISSUED SHARES, AT WAR'S END

(asterisks indicate companies designated as holding companies by HCLC)

| *First-line designated subsidiaries* | *Top H.C.* | *Families* | *Inter-Sub.* | *Total* |
|---|---|---|---|---|
| Mitsui Trading* | 41.4 | 10.0 | 1.8 | 53.2 |
| Mitsui Mining* | 59.8 | 2.4 | 3.6 | 65.8 |
| Mitsui Trust | 7.7 | 8.3 | 1.8 | 17.8 |
| Mitsui Life Insurance | 25.0 | 50.0 | 0.0 | 75.0 |
| Mitsui Agriculture and Forestry | 60.3 | 30.1 | 9.5 | 99.9 |
| Mitsui Shipbuilding | 49.5 | 33.3 | 10.0 | 92.8 |
| Mitsui Precision Machinery | 89.6 | 10.0 | 0.0 | 99.6 |
| Mitsui Chemicals* | 20.2 | 19.8 | 59.3 | 99.3 |
| Mitsui Real Estate | 0.0 | 100.0 | 0.0 | 100.0 |
| Mitsui Steamship | 72.8 | 0.0 | 15.7 | 88.5 |
| *Second-line designated subsidiaries* | | | | |
| Japan Flour Milling | 49.6 | 0.0 | 3.5 | 53.1 |
| Mitsui Warehouse | 100.0 | 0.0 | 0.0 | 100.0 |
| Taisho Marine Fire Insurance | 48.3 | 0.0 | 2.8 | 51.1 |
| Tropical Produce | 39.2 | 0.0 | 0.0 | 39.2 |
| Toyo Cotton* | 88.3 | 0.0 | 0.0 | 88.3 |
| Sanki Engineering | 97.0 | 0.0 | 0.0 | 97.0 |
| Toyo Rayon | 35.6 | 0.0 | 9.2 | 44.8 |
| Toyo Koatsu[a] | 0.0 | 0.0 | 40.8 | 40.8 |
| Mitsui Petrochemical | 100.0 | 0.0 | 0.0 | 100.0 |
| Mitsui Light Metal[b] | 2.4 | 0.0 | 36.2 | 38.6 |
| *Second-line designated subsidiaries* | | | | |
| Mitsui Wooden Shipbuilding | 30.0 | 0.0 | 67.5 | 97.5 |
| Mitsui Lumber | 100.0 | 0.0 | 0.0 | 100.0 |
| *A noteworthy "ordinary" subsidiary* | | | | |
| Teikoku Bank | 3.7 | 18.2 | 0.8 | 22.7 |

Sources: The names of companies designated as "first-line" ("chokkei") and "second-line" ("junchokkei") subsidiaries are taken from HCLC, *Zaibatsu Dissolution*, textual volume, p. 96. Ownership data are taken from the accompanying data volume, pp. 344-54.

[a]Cited as under top-holding company in textual volume; as under Mitsui Chemical in data volume.

[b]Cited as under the top-holding company in textual volume; as under Mitsui Mining in data volume.

Table 4-2: OWNERSHIP TIES AMONG THE CORE SUBSIDIARIES IN THE MITSUBISHI COMBINE AS A PERCENTAGE OF ISSUED SHARES AT WAR'S END

(asterisks indicate companies designated as holding companies by HCLC)

| *First-line designated subsidiaries* | *Top H.C.* | *Families* | *Inter-Sub.* | *Total* |
|---|---|---|---|---|
| Mitsubishi Heavy Industries* | 22.6 | 0.5 | 17.2 | 40.3 |
| Mitsubishi Trading* | 40.4 | 1.0 | 6.2 | 47.6 |
| Mitsubishi Bank | 30.3 | 2.0 | 6.8 | 39.1 |
| Mitsubishi Mining* | 42.6 | 0.5 | 4.7 | 47.8 |
| Mitsubishi Electric* | 44.3 | 0.3 | 7.0 | 51.6 |
| Mitsubishi Chemical Process* | 12.0 | 14.0 | 28.3 | 54.3 |
| Mitsubishi Oil | 45.0 | 0.0 | 30.0 | 75.0 |
| Mitsubishi Steel Fabricating | 51.0 | 0.0 | 30.2 | 81.2 |
| Mitsubishi Trust | 19.1 | 6.1 | 14.5 | 39.7 |
| Mitsubishi Warehouse | 46.8 | 0.5 | 13.3 | 60.6 |
| Mitsubishi Real Estate | 65.1 | 1.6 | 32.4 | 99.1 |
| *Second-line designated subsidiaries - partial listing* | | | | |
| Tokyo Marine Fire Insurance | 15.3 | 0.8 | 22.6 | 38.7 |
| Meiji Life Insurance | 13.9 | 8.3 | 19.5 | 41.7 |
| Japan Optical | 22.2 | 0.0 | 17.5 | 39.7 |
| Japan Grain Products | 52.2 | 0.0 | 0.0 | 52.2 |
| Japan Aluminum | 13.1 | 0.0 | 23.7 | 36.8 |
| Mitsubishi Steamship | 7.1 | 0.0 | 80.9 | 88.0 |
| Mitsubishi Chemical Machinery | 12.7 | 0.0 | 37.6 | 50.3 |
| Japan Steel Construction | 30.0 | 0.0 | 66.8 | 96.8 |

Sources: The list of first-line companies ("bunkei") is taken from HCLC, *Zaibatsu Dissolution*, textual volume, p. 111. Because no two sources agree on the listing of the second-line companies ("kankei"), eight have been selected on which there is an important measure of agreement. Ownership data are taken from the accompanying data volume, pp. 355-65.

Sources consulted for the names of second-line companies are: HCLC, *Zaibatsu Dissolution*, textual volume, p. 111; a separately published appendix to this two-volume study entitled, "Personnel Interlocks among the Principal Companies of the "Big Four" Zaibatsu ("Shi Dai Zaibatsu Kei Shuyo Kaisha Jinteki Koryuen"); *Capital Accumulation and Control in the Mitsubishi Zaibatsu* (*Mitsubishi Zaibatsu ni okeru* -- ), p. 218; *Mitsui, Mitsubishi, Sumitomo*, pp. 151-52.

the corporations[2] shown in these tables had subsidiary complexes of their own. The companies which are starred had such large subsidiary complexes that the HCLC designated them as holding companies in their own right and called for the dissolution of their holding functions.

Broadly speaking, one can say that the core subsidiaries established the market-breadth of the combine. It was these key subsidiaries which the top-holding company tied, and tied again, to ensure that the whole could move with singleness of purpose. Spokesmen for the Sumitomo combine explained that the distinction between first and second-line core subsidiaries in their organization was a distinction between companies "perfectly" under top-holding company control and companies which were "almost perfectly" so.[3] Those "perfectly" under control, the first-line designated subsidiaries, were in the Sumitomo, as in the other combines as well, the pillars on which the combine structures rested.

Tables 4-1, 4-2, and 4-3 indicate how difficult it is to generalize, to speak of a typical ownership pattern either within a single combine or among the combines. Perhaps the one generalization to be drawn is that the families invested little, if at all, in the second-line core companies. It would be misleading to decide that ownership must be 51 percent in order to speak of a company as an effectively controlled subsidiary. It will be noted in the Mitsui combine that there was even a company listed as a first-line subsidiary, where the top-holding company held no shares in it at all! An instance of

[2] With these tables, which represent the first listing of Japanese company names, comment on translation is in order. There is no clear and unequivocal way of presenting Japanese company names in translation. Problems arise for a number of reasons: (1) the Japanese language abounds in homonyms, a difficulty when one is working from company names phonetically transcribed. For example, "kogyo" —industry, "kogyo"—mining, "kogyo"—development. (2) The Japanese language does not distinguish singular and plural, a difficulty when one is trying to decide whether a corporate name should be translated "industry" or "industries." (3) Frequently Japanese corporations for foreign purposes use a name that is not a translation of their Japanese name. (4) Some words embrace more than one concept, and one cannot be sure which to choose in translation. For example, "kogyo," meaning "development" in the case of the well-known bank with this word in its Japanese name, is translated as the *Industrial* Bank of Japan, whereas in the case of the former Sumitomo company it was translated as the Sumitomo Borneo *Development* Company. (5) Frequently only a part of the Japanese name is to be translated. For example, the bank formed out of the merger of the Mitsui Bank and the Shibusawa's Daiichi Bank is customarily referred to in English as the Teikoku Bank, not the Imperial Bank. Accordingly, there is an inescapably arbitrary quality to the form in which company names are presented.

[3] Memorandum submitted by the Sumitomo Holding Company to GHQ-SCAP, entitled, "The Definitions of the Sumitomo Companies," undated; reproduced in part in Hadley, "Concentrated Business Power," pp. 66-67.

this among the second-line Mitsui subsidiaries is less clear because sources differ as to how in fact the company was classified. Even together, ownership holdings were frequently well under 51 percent. In the Mitsui table the low is 17 percent, in the Mitsubishi table, 36 percent, and in the Sumitomo table, 22 percent. In comparison with American patterns of ownership, these figures would, of course, seem high, not low, but in the case of Japan they are in contrast to the far higher figures found earlier.

If we note the range in the percentage of stock held in the different core subsidiaries it will be seen that in the Mitsui case top-holding company holdings varied from zero to 100 percent, that the House ranged from zero to 100 percent among first-line companies, and that it did not invest at all in the second-line companies. Horizontal cross

Table 4-3: OWNERSHIP TIES AMONG THE CORE SUBSIDIARIES IN THE SUMITOMO COMBINE AS A PERCENTAGE OF ISSUED SHARES AT WAR'S END

(asterisks indicate companies designated as holding companies by HCLC)

(Company names briefly used during the Occupation period will be found in the accompanying notes; name changes which have held are shown in the table.)

| *First-line designated subsidiaries* | *Top H.C.* | *Families* | *Inter-Sub.* | *Total* |
|---|---|---|---|---|
| Sumitomo Mining* | 26.6 | 53.4 | 20.5 | 100.5[a] |
| Sumitomo Electric Industries* | 24.3 | 4.7 | 9.1 | 38.1 |
| Japan Electric* (formerly Sumitomo Communications Ind.) | 11.1 | 2.0 | 6.7 | 19.8 |
| Sumitomo Metal Industries* | 20.9 | 4.3 | 14.5 | 39.7 |
| Manchurian Sumitomo Metal Ind. | 25.2 | 9.1 | 54.0 | 88.3 |
| Shikoku Machinery | 21.0 | 7.2 | 69.0 | 97.2 |
| Sumitomo Chemical Industries* | 17.5 | 7.3 | 6.7 | 31.5 |
| Sumitomo Aluminum Reduction | 24.6 | 10.5 | 46.3 | 81.4 |
| Korean Sumitomo Light Metal | 10.0 | 3.0 | 60.0 | 73.0 |
| Sumitomo Bank | 24.1 | 11.3 | 16.7 | 52.1 |
| Sumitomo Trust | 1.5 | 2.8 | 40.7 | 45.0 |
| Sumitomo Life Insurance | 30.0 | 70.0 | 0.0 | 100.0 |
| Sumitomo Warehouse | 21.7 | 38.2 | 39.9 | 99.8 |
| Nippon Construction Industries (formerly Sumitomo Real Estate & Building) | 26.6 | 34.7 | 22.2 | 83.5 |
| Sumitomo Cooperative Elec. Power | 22.5 | 7.4 | 67.2 | 97.1 |

| *Second-line designated subsidiaries* | *Top H.C.* | *Families* | *Inter-Sub.* | *Total* |
|---|---|---|---|---|
| Japan Plate Glass | 19.2 | 4.6 | 0.4 | 24.2 |
| Antung Light Metal | 10.0 | 0.0 | 15.0 | 25.0 |
| Imperial Compressed Gas | 22.7 | 0.0 | 38.5 | 61.2 |
| Osaka Sumitomo Marine Fire Insur. | 17.0 | 2.6 | 2.7 | 22.3 |
| Sumitomo Borneo Development | 80.0 | 0.0 | 20.0 | 100.0 |

Sources: The list of first-line ("chokkei") and second-line ("junchokkei") companies is taken from HCLC, *Zaibatsu Dissolution*, textual volume, p. 124. Ownership data are taken from the accompanying data volume, pp. 366-74.

Name changes used during the Occupation period are:

Sumitomo Mining - Seika Mining

Sumitomo Metal Industries - Fuso Metal Industries

Sumitomo Machinery - Shikoku Machinery

Sumitomo Chemical - Nisshin Chemical

Sumitomo Chemical Materials - Japan Chemical Industries

Two earlier name changes were:

Japan Electric - Sumitomo Communication Industries.

Nippon Construction Industries - Sumitomo Real Estate and Building.

[a]Exceeds 100% because of rounding of figures.

ties ranged from zero to 67 percent. In the Mitsubishi case, top-holding company ownership varied from 7 to 65 percent, family participation from zero to 14 percent, and cross ties from zero to 80 percent. Cross ties were more significant in the Mitsubishi combine than the Mitsui. In the Sumitomo combine top-holding company ownership varied from 1 to 80 percent, family participation from zero to 70 percent, and cross ties from zero to 69 percent. While the tables indicate that controls other than ownership were important in making these key subsidiaries perfectly responsive to the will of the top-holding company, they also clearly demonstrate the vital role of ownership, and the first step in the *zaibatsu* dissolution program was the dispersal of this ownership base.

### *Holding Company Liquidation Commission*

In the Japan Occupation it was the Japanese government that carried out Occupation reforms, not GHQ-SCAP. Primarily because of the grossly insufficient number of Japanese-language personnel among the Allied powers and because of lack of familiarity with Japanese administrative procedures, Truman, Stalin, and Attlee agreed at Potsdam in July 1945 that in contrast to the situation in

Germany, no military government would be established in Japan. The Japanese government would be used as the instrument of the Allies. As events proved, however, the Japanese government was at times a somewhat balky instrument.

At the outset conversations began between Headquarters and the Japanese government with respect to *zaibatsu* dissolution. On November 4, 1945 the Japanese government submitted for approval by MacArthur a proposal incorporating the "Yasuda Plan," under which, in a consent-decree type of action, the holding companies of the Big Four would enter into dissolution procedures and a Holding Company Liquidation Commission would be created to administer the program.[4]

In the second and third months of the Occupation, MacArthur, lacking a staff adequate to advise him on the suitability of the Japanese proposal, cabled Washington to determine if there were objections to his acceptance of the Japanese government's proposal. Washington cabled back "no objections," but suggested to MacArthur that he might find it advantageous to have a group of technical experts to advise him on the intricacies of combine dissolution. MacArthur agreed, and thus was born the State-War Mission on Japanese Combines, which was in the theatre from January to March 1946. (The policy recommendations of this mission are discussed in detail in Chapter 7, in connection with the "FEC 230" controversy.)

Illustrative of the difficulties MacArthur met in getting the Japanese government to act on measures it was not in the least sympathetic with was the timetable for *zaibatsu* dissolution. MacArthur accepted the Japanese government's proposal on November 6, 1945, two days after it was submitted, but at the same time he made it clear that ". . . full freedom of action is retained by the Supreme Commander for the Allied Powers to elaborate or modify the proposed plan at any time and to supervise and review its execution." It was five months, however, before the Japanese issued a "Potsdam ordinance,"[5] creating the Holding Company Liquidation Commission called for in the plan (Imperial Ordinance 233, April 20, 1946).[6] And it was

[4] Cf. Appendix III for the text of the Yasuda Plan, together with MacArthur's acceptance of it.

[5] Under Imperial Ordinance 542 of 1945, the government was empowered, "in case it is necessary for conducting affairs demanded by the Supreme Commander of the Allied Forces in consequence of the acceptance of the Potsdam Declaration, [to] make the necessary provision . . . [by order]." Thus when the government wanted to act, it was possible to carry out directives with dispatch. Cf. HCLC, *Laws, Rules*, p. 3, for full text of Imperial Ordinance 542, September 20, 1945.

[6] For full text, cf. *ibid.*, pp. 38-46.

August, four months later, before agreement was reached on appointments to the commission. A year from the start of the Occupation, September 1946, the commission held its first meeting and the first "designations" of holding companies were announced. While the commission later acquired other functions, its principal function was putting into new hands the stock through which a small number of family groups and certain holding companies outside the circle of these family groups had exercised control over a large portion of the modern sector of the Japanese economy.

The HCLC had a somewhat peculiar status within the Japanese government—it was of it, yet separate. Although in accordance with the Potsdam agreement it was a part of the Japanese government, nevertheless a SCAP observer attended all meetings of the commission,[7] and the commission took no action without prior SCAP approval. Such close supervision was not exercised over other parts of the Japanese government.

The name of the commission, The Holding Company Liquidation Commission, not Combine Liquidation Commission, is illustrative of the spirit in which the whole program moved. Without exception, successive conservative cabinets[8] attempted to whittle down the program to its barest elements. As was noted at the beginning of Chapter 2, "holding company" refers to the command center of a combine, not the combine as a whole. Top-holding company controls did not exhaust the techniques used to integrate Japan's combines. In the field of ownership alone it is clear from the foregoing tables that under a program restricted to top-holding company dissolution, direct family investments—those made independently of the top-holding companies—would not be touched nor would the intersubsidiary horizontal holdings be included.

The HCLC Ordinance stipulated that securities held by designated holding companies be transferred to the commission, which would dispose of them to new owners and compensate the former owners to the extent of the proceeds of the sales minus the expenses of operating the commission. Current income from the holdings was also due the owners. Because an effective deconcentration program had to prevent the *zaibatsu* families from buying their way back to their former position of preeminence, payment to the *zaibatsu* family

[7] Bisson, *Zaibatsu Dissolution*, p. 100. Various provisions in the Basic Initial Post-Surrender Directive (paragraphs 2, 4c, 12) gave SCAP authority to act directly if in MacArthur's judgement such was necessary to carry out the policies of the United States and its allies.

[8] All cabinets in the postwar period, with the exception of the Katayama cabinet (June 1947 to February 1948) which was coalition, have been conservative.

owners was made in the form of 10-year nonnegotiable government bonds. In this way, it was believed, new owners would have the opportunity to establish themselves before the former *zaibatsu* owners were back in the market. Other owners were reimbursed, as was noted earlier, in liquid form.

Between September 1946 and September 1947 the HCLC designated 83 holding companies (see Appendix IV). The Japanese government had undoubtedly hoped to limit the designations to the five companies named in the original designation, the top-holding companies of the Big Four—Mitsui, Mitsubishi, Sumitomo, and Yasuda, plus Fuji Industries, the renamed Nakajima Aircraft Company. Under SCAP pressure, however, there were additional designations. Two additional designations were made in December 1946, adding 40 and 20 companies, respectively. A fourth, made in March 1947, added two, and the fifth and final one in September 1947 added 18. That 83 holding companies were named does not indicate that there were 83 combines. As has been seen, combines numbered about 15 or 20. Rather, the designation of 83 holding companies came about out of the inclusion of major second-level holding companies within the combines—with the signal exception of financial subsidiaries—as well as certain independent operating companies with complexes of subsidiaries and also some minor *zaibatsu.*

The list of the 83 holding companies was an uneven one, juxtaposing companies of widely different importance to the economy. The first designation appropriately named the Big Four, but also included Nakajima Aircraft, in no sense of the same order of importance. The second designation included a number of other *zaibatsu* of lesser importance, but which still represented important concentrations of economic power. However, this second designation, strangely enough, included eight cotton spinning companies. Inasmuch as the cotton industry had no *zaibatsu* influence, how did it happen that the holding functions of the operating companies in this industry were so much more heavily represented than other industries? The third designation represented major second-level holding companies within the combines, with the exception of the financial subsidiaries. The fourth designation named two companies from the entire utility field, and the fifth was a strange assortment of companies. It included a number of virtually unknown family holding companies, presumably because the commission had come to believe that family holding companies were to be named regardless of their significance or impact on the economy.

In making such criticisms, however, certain considerations need to be kept in mind. While there was a significant lack of familiarity with Japanese industrial organization on the part of SCAP staff, there was also a problem in this regard on the Japanese side. The combines had only themselves to thank for this. Notwithstanding the dominant position of the combines in the economy, the family owners and officials had taken the attitude that these holdings represented private property and were none of the public's business. One of the very striking differences between doing research on Japan's combines today, in contrast to prewar or at the close of the war, is the great difference in the information available. Earlier there was no such information as is available today in the Finance Ministry's quarterly individual corporate reports,[9] or in the Ministry's annual data on the over-all aspects of share capital.[10] Similarly there were no studies of market positions of leading firms such as the Fair Trade Commission now publishes from time to time.[11] One limped along importantly on rumor and gossip. Where there were errors of judgment based on ignorance, the combines were but reaping the consequences of their own minimal disclosure policy. Second, it was at times difficult to escape the conclusion that the combines sought to mislead.[12]

The designation of eight spinning companies raises a different issue. Apparently American pressure was brought to bear which did not reflect the position of the United States government. However, as will be seen in Appendix X, only minimal change occurred among these companies; in fact, five were left untouched.

The list of designated holding companies contained striking omissions—no bank or other financial institution was included. This occurred in spite of the fact that the Basic Directive specifically called for action in this regard and in spite of the fact that MacArthur had specifically informed the Japanese government it would be expected to dissolve the "private, industrial, commercial, *financial*

[9] Okurasho Rizaikyoku Keizaika, *Yuka Shoken Hokokusho Soran.*

[10] Okurasho Rizaikyoku Keizaika, *Kabushiki Bumpu Jokyo Chosa.*

[11] Kosei Torihiki Iinkai: *Nihon ni okeru, Keizai Ryoku Shuchu no Jittai,* 1951; *Shuyo Sangyo ni okeru, Seisan Shuchu,* 1958; *Shuyo Sangyo ni okeru, Seisan Shuchudo,* 1960; *Shuyo Kigyo no Kabushiki Shoyu to Kigyo Godo ni kansuru Shiryo,* 1961; *Nihon no Sangyo Shuchu,* 1964.

[12] How otherwise could one explain that Mitsui listed Toyo Menka Co. in two different submissions to SCAP as having 33 and 9 subsidiaries? Memorandum submitted by the Mitsui Holding Company to GHQ-SCAP entitled, "List of Subsidiary Companies with Percentage of the Investments by Parent Companies as of January 31, 1946," wherein Toyo Cotton is listed with 33, undated, reproduced in part in "Concentrated Business Power," pp. 194-96. Chart prepared by Mitsui Holding Company submitted to GHQ-SCAP entitled, "The Mitsui Interests," wherein Toyo Cotton is shown with 9, February 1946, and reproduced among other places in the pocket of the back cover of Bisson, *Zaibatsu Dissolution.*

and agricultural combines in Japan."[13] Further, this occurred in spite of the key role financial institutions had played in the development of *zaibatsu* power. As has been stated, a real factor in the growth of Japan's pattern of concentrated business power was the partiality with which combine commercial banks extended credit to subsidiaries within their own ranks. The list of designated holding companies not only omitted commercial banks, but all other financial institutions as well—trust banks, property insurance companies, and life insurance companies. In view of the importance of banks and other financial institutions among Japan's combines, the omission of these companies was strange and extremely important.

The explanation probably stems from several factors. Inasmuch as in the United States commercial banks are not permitted to have industrial and trading subsidiaries or affiliates, the American vocabulary and way of thinking is to regard commercial banking as quite separate from industry and commerce. This revealed itself more than once. First, the State-War Mission on Japanese Combines, which outlined a comprehensive program for dissolving Japan's combines (see Chapter 7), did not include representatives from the banking community among its members. The Economic and Scientific Section of Headquarters, the administering unit, was set up with an Antitrust and Cartel Division and a Finance Division, which was a mistake. It was simply an invitation to misunderstanding between the two divisions. The title of the Antitrust and Cartel Division should have clearly reflected the integral nature in Japan of finance with commerce, industry, and mining. The title of the Finance Division should have indicated that the responsibility of this division was limited to finance exclusive of combine ties. The result of the actual arrangement was that the Antitrust and Cartel Division claimed jurisdiction in antitrust matters over the banks, but the staff of the Finance Division insisted that the banks were entirely theirs (and their responsibility included no antitrust assignment!). A further, important, factor in the omission of the banks and other financial institutions was the vigor with which successive Japanese cabinets balked at including these companies. But the omission meant that a major instrument of combine ownership and revival was left outside the program. Such, however, was the framework for dissolving holding company controls.

Because of lack of familiarity with the structure of Japanese combines, the requirements of a combine dissolution program were not initially appreciated by SCAP personnel, and because the Japanese

[13] Scapin 244 (cf. Appendix III).

government was intent on allowing only the minimum of action, the HCLC was established with powers to deal only with holding company ownership. It had no authority to dispose of stock held by *zaibatsu* family members through direct holdings, just the stock held through designated holding companies. However, as was seen in Tables 4-1, 4-2, and 4-3, direct family investments were sizable and would have constituted an invaluable means of sustaining family control. When it became evident to SCAP that a program had to be developed for administering disposal of direct family holdings if *zaibatsu* dissolution were to become a reality, it was necessary for SCAP to instruct the Japanese government to arrange the necessary additional authority.[14] On March 13, 1947 the commission named 56 persons from 10 *zaibatsu* houses as falling within the purview of "designated persons." (A listing of these persons by "house" will be found in Appendix V.) As in the case of designated holding companies, designated persons were to transfer their securities to the HCLC, which would compensate them in the same manner as in the holding company program.

As was seen in Tables 4-1, 4-2, and 4-3, horizontal ownership ties were frequently significant. Although MacArthur's acceptance of the Yasuda Proposal called for eliminating "undesirable intercorporate security ownership," no provision was made in the HCLC Ordinance for dealing with horizontal ties, only the vertical ones. Accordingly, SCAP was obliged specifically to direct the Japanese government to develop, among other additions, a program for severing such ties (Scapin 1079, July 23, 1946), and on November 25, 1946 the Government issued Imperial Ordinance 567 for this and related purposes.[15]

It had been the intent of Headquarters that the ordinance would be focused on the subsidiaries of the 10 designated *zaibatsu*. However, it was written in terms of "restricted concerns" established by an earlier ordinance (the ordinance number of which was confusingly similar, Imperial Ordinance 657 of 1945, to distinguish, hereafter referred to as the 1945 and 1946 ordinances[16]), freezing, except with ministerial permission, the assets of companies with a capitalization

[14] Scapin 1363, November 26, 1946, which resulted in Imperial Ordinance 592 of 1946, which is incorporated in the version of Imperial Ordinance 233 presented in HCLC, *Laws, Rules*.

[15] For the text of Imperial Ordinance 567 of 1946, cf. *ibid.*, pp. 10-22. The obscurity of the text is enough to remind one of a well-known U.S. senator's "confusing amendment" produced at regular intervals to stop passage of a Constitutional amendment he opposed.

[16] For the text of Imperial Ordinance 657 of 1945, see *ibid.*, p. 7.

of Y5 million and above. In other words, this ordinance was intended to supervise the activities of large companies, whether related or unrelated to *zaibatsu* groupings (though the preponderance of large companies were, of course, related).

Companies designated under this earlier ordinance were spoken of as constituting the "Schedule of Restricted Concerns." The 1946 ordinance stated that "restricted concerns" would divest themselves of shares in other companies with the exception of financial companies, where they would be obliged to do so only in the event that their holdings were in "the same chain of capital," i.e., companies within their own combine complex. (Again, it will be noted that while financial institutions were included, they were treated more generously.) "Subsidiaries" and "affiliates" of "restricted concerns" were to divest themselves of stock acquired *after* December 8, 1945. Thus there was an additional stock divestiture program under this ordinance.

As observed in Chapter 2, the HCLC, using 10-percent ownership as its definition of *subsidiary*,[17] found the 10 *zaibatsu* to have some 1,200 subsidiaries. Firms on the Schedule of Restricted Concerns at peak likewise numbered some 1,200.[18] While there was numerical identity between the two lists, there was not full corporate identity. The Schedule of Restricted Concerns gave greater emphasis to textile companies. A comparison of companies listed as subsidiaries of the 10 *zaibatsu* combines, companies designated as "restricted concerns" and companies designated as subsidiaries and affiliates of the 10 *zaibatsu* family groups (see the following chapter) will be found in Appendix VI.

[17] HCLC, *Zaibatsu Dissolution*, data volume, unnumbered page at the beginning of the volume marked "Preface" ("Reigen"), note 4, where it is explained that the 10% is computed by the holding company alone, by the holding company in conjunction with family holdings, or the preceding circumstance plus holdings "in the same chain of capital," i.e., by other members of the combine. The unreliability of any of the specific statistics is demonstrated in the case of Mitsui Trading's subsidiaries. In a memorandum the Mitsui Holding Company submitted to GHQ-SCAP showing Mitsui's Trading's holdings in other companies as of July 31, 1945 (Mitsui Trading alone, without inclusion of top holding company or family holdings) and reproduced in Hadley, "Concentrated Business Power," pp. 220-25, there are 60 companies listed in which Mitsui Trading alone held 10% and more of the shares (exclusive of holdings in various control associations of this amount and more), although as will be noted in Table 4-4 the HCLC listed Trading's subsidiaries on a more generous definitional basis as 49.

[18] The Schedule of Restricted Concerns, which was under the jurisdiction of the Ministry of Finance, was variable by time period; firms were continually added and subtracted. At its peak the schedule numbered 1,200.

Let us note a specific instance of the type of situation to which the 1946 ordinance was intended to apply. As was seen in Table 4-3, Sumitomo Mining (known briefly during the immediate postwar years as Seika Mining) had cross ties amounting to 20.5 percent of issued capital. The breakdown of this 20.5 percent was as follows:[19]

| | |
|---|---|
| Sumitomo Metal Industries (Fuso Metals) | 1.5% |
| Sumitomo Electric Industries | 1.0 |
| Osaka Sumitomo Marine & Fire Insurance | 3.0 |
| Sumitomo Trust | 3.0 |
| Sumitomo Bank | 7.0 |
| Sumitomo Life Insurance | 4.0 |
| Sumitomo Joint Electric Power | 1.0 |

Under the holding-company dissolution program shares held by Sumitomo Metal Industries and Sumitomo Electric Industries, inasmuch as the two companies were designated as holding companies, would have been transferred. The remaining Sumitomo stock, 18 percent of the total, would not have been affected by that program. If Sumitomo ties were to be severed it was clear that action needed to be taken with respect to this block of holdings.

The 1946 ordinance provided that companies submit a plan to the HCLC giving details of proposed transfer of stock to favored categories of buyers, such as (1) the employees of the companies, (2) the residents of the localities in which the stock-issuing companies were domiciled, and (3) any remaining balance to the general public. But the ordinance made no provision regarding the disposition of the balance to the public. Moreover, although all designated companies (that is, companies listed on the Schedule of Restricted Concerns) were required to submit plans, only subsidiary and affiliated companies, with respect to stock acquired after December 8, 1945, were required to get approval! This meant that designated companies, which included major combine firms, could act independently.[20] Considerably later supplementary provisions corrected this.[21] Only a portion of these shares were eventually disposed of (cf. Table 10-1).

While the Japanese government managed to issue the complying

[19] *Ibid.*, p. 366.
[20] SCAP, GHQ, *History of the Non-military Activities of the Occupation of Japan*, Vol. x, Reform of Business Enterprise, Part A, *Elimination of Zaibatsu Control*, p. 147, Office of Military History, Washington, D.C.
[21] *Ibid.*, p. 146.

ordinance within four months of MacArthur's July 1946 directive, the enforcement of the stock disposal program did not take place until May 1948.[22] It was a game which was played again and again. Successive Japanese governments were unsympathetic to the effort to reduce concentration in the capital-intensive sector, and they were splendidly resourceful in devising ways of ostensibly complying with MacArthur while at the same time protecting the interests of those they were supposedly reorganizing. In this case the ruse paid high dividends, for by the spring of 1948 the United States had changed its mind about the desirability of economic deconcentration and was eager to forget the matter. Only a modest amount happened under the program for severing horizontal ties.

Because of the interrelatedness of several of the measures and the multiple programs to which the 83 designated holding companies were subject, the account of the disposal of holding company securities is postponed to Chapter 10 following discussion of these other programs.

[22] *Ibid.*, p. 146, wherein Ordinance No. 24 from the Prime Minister's Office, May 7, 1948, "Amendment to Cabinet Order No. 83 concerning the Enforcement of Imperial Ordinance No. 567 of 1946" is discussed.

# 5.

# Combine Dissolution: Severing Personnel Ties

A STUDY of ownership holdings as presented in Chapter 4 indicates how inadequately ownership alone tells the story of Japanese combine structures. In some of the core subsidiaries the Mitsui, Mitsubishi, and Sumitomo top-holding companies held no more than 7, 13, and 17 percent, and the combine itself held no more than 17, 36, and 22 percent ownership, yet these were described as "almost perfectly" under top-holding company control. To have "perfect" or "almost perfect" control of subsidiaries with low ownership holdings indicates the presence of other controls with unmistakable clearness. Among the most important of these other means of control were the officers.

The controls exercised over the officers were both traditional and modern. The officers were expected to demonstrate a feudal-like loyalty to the controlling families. However, to insure that such loyalty was always in force the families through their top-holding companies: directly or indirectly appointed all officers of the core companies; bound such hand-picked officers through contractual agreements to take virtually no action on their own; and provided numerous interlocks between the top-holding company and the core subsidiaries, and among the core companies. The interlocks with the top-holding company served the dual function of simplifying liaison and providing on the scene watchfulness to ensure that no officer would lose sight of the fact that he was but a servant of the families. Inasmuch as the goal of combine dissolution was to make the member firms of the combine businesses in their own right, businesses that would decide on their own questions of output, product lines, prices, technology, and investment, the need to eliminate the integration by officers who had spent a lifetime in obeisance to the larger whole appeared vitally important. In the Basic Directive the JCS had ordered MacArthur to remove key business figures, because it believed them to be active exponents of "militant nationalism and aggression," which it was the objective of the Occupation to eliminate, not because such persons were a vital part of the combine structures, likewise an objective of the Occupation to eliminate.

The following pages portray how personnel controls operated within the combine structures, the efforts of Headquarters to get at this personnel ingredient, the division of views on the wisdom of such procedures—within Headquarters and from the American public—with a few summary illustrations of the effect of such actions on individual companies. Severing personnel ties was a highly controversial action.

With Japan challenging the United States to war in 1941, it is easy to forget how very recent a phenomenon modern Japan is, but the modern period is just a century old. With the arbitrariness that dating of social trends imposes, it is 1868, the year of the Meiji Restoration which we use to mark the transition into the modern period. From the 13th century to this period Japan existed under feudalism, which, like feudalism everywhere, structured social relations not on equality but on hierarchy and the loyalty of inferiors to superiors. Loyalty, rather than pecuniary gain, was the motivating force of conduct. Classical Japanese literature exudes this spirit. In Tokyo today, the largest city of the world with all the appurtenances of contemporary technology, one can still find striking instances of how vividly the past lives on in human relations. Incense supplied by the person on the street, in reverence to the ideals personified by the 47 *ronin* who gave their lives that the honor of their dead lord might be vindicated, burns continuously at their graves in the Sengakuji Temple, a 10-minute taxi ride from the heart of downtown Tokyo. No performance of Kabuki, the classical theatre, outdraws the attendance of a presentation of this story, a tale every Japanese has heard from the time he was a small child, the classic of all Japanese classics on loyalty. While Japan from Meiji to the Pacific War was avidly developing modern technology it was attempting to perpetuate traditional patterns of human relations. Corporately, the *zaibatsu* represented this fusion.

The *zaibatsu* organizations combined the modern holding company with feudal loyalty. The families at the top were the superiors to whom staff of the entire organization owed fealty. The spirit of subordination of staff to superiors, and ultimately to the families themselves, began on the day the individual joined the combine. The device of company "loyalty oaths" was used to heighten awareness of this quality. Earlier the writer observed,[1]

[1] Hadley, "Concentrated Business Power," pp. 55-57.

. . . each employee upon assignment to his subsidiary in the case of designated companies, or upon directly entering the company in the case of non-designated subsidiaries, swore an oath of loyalty and secrecy to the company, much as in this country one swears an oath of loyalty to the Constitution of the United States on entering Government service. The oaths to the business companies committed the employee to complete obedience to the instructions of all senior officials, devotion to the company, a policy of secrecy concerning business information "large or small, trivial or important," observance of all company rules, and the pledge never to act independently on his own judgment. The oaths were of a standard form. The text of the type of oath in common use prior to the Allied occupation is translated below; it is followed by a translation of the new "democratic" form. In English the two forms reveal less difference than they show in Japanese, because the older oaths were written in extremely formal, literary Japanese, whereas the new ones are written in a style nearer to the colloquial, though employing, of course, honorific and humble forms. Thus, for example, in the new form the word "company" is still prefixed with an honorific (the honorable company), the word "I" . . . [appears in its humble form]. The literary style of the older form made that form a more solemn pledge, but it is evident that this would only be a matter of degree. The text of the older type oath is the form used by a subsidiary of Mitsubishi Mining, Southern Sakhalin Colliery and Railroad Company; the new form, that of Mitsubishi Mining itself.

Oath of the Southern Sakhalin Colliery and Railroad Company:

1. I shall never violate the orders of the president or the instructions of my senior officers.

2. I shall sincerely and assiduously perform my duties, never bringing loss to the company.

3. I shall never divulge to a third party any of the affairs of the company large or small, trivial or important.

4. I shall keenly bear in mind never to violate any of the rules of the company.

5. With respect to any business I transact I shall always follow the instructions of my senior official, never undertaking any transactions on my own judgment.

I accept the foregoing oath.

Year —— Month —— Day ——

Permanent Residence ————

Family Relationship (i.e. relationship to head of the house)
Name ————————
Date of birth ————————
Southern Sakhalin Colliery and Railroad Company.

Employee Oath of Mitsubishi Mining:
Having come into the employ of this company, I pledge this oath.
1. I shall follow the rules of the company and the instructions of the chief under whom I work.
2. I shall at all times strive toward an increase in the business of the company and shall diligently attend to my duties.
3. I shall never divulge secrets of which I am informed in connection with my duties.
Year ——— Month ——— Day ———
[Space for signature and seal]
Mitsubishi Mining Company.

The *zaibatsu* families conceived staff loyalty in personal terms. Loyalty was not to be to the staff person's conception of the business interests of the subsidiary in which he worked, but personally to the families themselves. Not only did such loyalty preclude an officer responding to a more attractive offer from the outside—once a Mitsui man always a Mitsui man—but it required demonstrated personal fealty to the families. It could be said of all the *zaibatsu* organizations that the ultimate test of advance up the ladder to the most coveted positions of all, the presidency of the core subsidiaries and membership on the board of the top-holding company, rested on business ability only where it was conjoined to unquestioning loyalty to the families at the top. A striking illustration of this was seen in the Mitsui *zaibatsu* in the 1930s, in connection with the appointment of the president of Mitsui Trading. For some years Mitsui Trading had had an outstanding managing director who had brought the company from near-bankruptcy to a thoroughly sound position following market collapses both in Japan and the United States in the 1921 recession. Outsiders were confident he would be named to the vacancy that had arisen in the position of president.

On the eve of his election to the presidency of Trading, however, in 1933, a representative of the House called upon Yasukawa to recommend that he resign from Trading. Yasukawa refused to submit, but the following day House pressure compelled him to do so. His error was that he had not liaisoned adequately with the House.

> A similar fate befell Makita Tamaki, son-in-law of Baron Dan. Baron Dan was the chief business advisor to the Mitsuis and senior managing director [banto] of the top-holding company from 1912 to the time of his assassination in 1932. From 1913-32, Makita was managing director and president of Mitsui Mining. An outstanding engineer with foresight and imagination, Makita had developed the chemical undertakings of the combine. . . . Belief was common that he would step into his father-in-law's post. However, because he had acted too independently of the House, he lost prospect of . . . achieving this position even though he was temporarily elevated in 1932 to the board of directors of the holding company.[2]

But loyalty to the *zaibatsu* organizations was not enough alone; the families, acting through their holding companies, determined how the loyalty was to be evaluated and rewarded. Practices with respect to the selection of top officers in the core subsidiaries of the different combines differed in details. In some, the family-appointed top-holding company named all the officers; in others, the top-holding company named the president and one or two other officers and let them nominate, for top-holding company approval, other officers. In all cases the top-holding company effectively controlled personnel among the key subsidiaries.

In the Sumitomo combine, top-holding company control over personnel was very close.

> . . . the holding company in the Sumitomo combine appointed all officers of the first-line subsidiary companies. . . . As to second-line subsidiary companies, the holding company appointed "only the principal officers," that is, the president, chairman, managing directors, and standing auditor. Among the subsidiaries of the designated companies, the holding company appointed the president and standing auditor. In the Sumitomo combine the managing director of the holding company was *ex officio* chairman of the board of all first-line subsidiaries. The staffs of all designated subsidiaries were centrally hired through the top-holding company.[3]

[2] *Ibid.*, pp. 178-79.

[3] Sumitomo Holding Company memorandum submitted to GHQ-SCAP, entitled "Notes and Explanations on Sumitomo Zaibatsu Companies," dated June 17, 1947, reproduced in Hadley, "Concentrated Business Power," p. 71; also interview information from meeting with Sumii Tatsuo, last senior managing director of the Sumitomo Holding Company.

*Interlocking Officerships*

To ensure unity of action among this hand-picked officership group, all of the combines relied on interlocking directorships. The tables in Appendix VII portray for the two years 1937 and 1945 the extent of the interlocking positions among the Big Four. Table 5-1 below summarizes the 1945 interlocks. While the emphasis was less in Mitsui, it will be noted from a study of the Appendix tables how, while the position of key coordinating person or persons differed, each of the combines ensured unity of subsidiary action by having one or two top officers interlock core undertakings. In the 1945 tables it will be seen in the Mitsubishi combine that the president of the top-holding company held 10 positions, that one managing director held 10, that a second held 9, and that a standing director held 9. It will be noted in the Sumitomo combine that the managing director of the top-holding company held 15 officerships, primarily "chairman of the board" positions, and that the auditor of the holding company held 14 auditorships. That interlocks in the Mitsui *zaibatsu* were less extensively resorted to reflects the different historical origins of the Mitsui complex and its greater scale. In the Mitsui combine, key subsidiaries did not grow up as departments of the top-holding company before splitting off into separate corporations; they grew up outside. The enormous size of the Mitsui operations made the Mitsui Holding Company more a coordinating body among its three key subsidiaries, Trading, Mining, and Banking, than the top strategy board, which the holding company was in the case of the other *zaibatsu*.

*Contractual Agreements*

In the Sumitomo combine the family, after appointing through its holding company all officers of the first-line subsidiaries, and providing interlocks on the scale shown below, was still fearful of separatist tendencies. Accordingly, for directors with the power to bind the corporation, the so-called representative directors (*daihyo torishimari yaku*), resort was made to contract. Such officers signed a contractual agreement with the holding company, obligating them to refer virtually every topic that might come up in a board meeting to the top-holding company for guidance before a decision was taken in a board meeting. And among the core subsidiaries of the Sumitomo combine the majority of officers were such "representative" officers. An informative document which the Sumitomo Holding Company submitted to MacArthur's Headquarters, stated that ". . . According to

**Table 5-1:** SUMMARY OF INTERLOCKS BETWEEN OFFICERS OF FIRST-LINE SUBSIDIARIES AND OFFICERS OF THE TOP HOLDING COMPANY IN THE MITSUI, MITSUBISHI AND SUMITOMO COMBINES, 1945

| | Position in Subsidiary | | | | |
|---|---|---|---|---|---|
| | President | Chairman | Director | Auditor | No. Interlocks with holding co. |
| Mitsui | | | | | |
| Mitsui Trading | * | | 1 | | 2 |
| Mitsui Mining | * | | 2 | | 3 |
| Mitsui Trust | * | | 1 | | 2 |
| Mitsui Life Insurance | * | | 1 | | 2 |
| Mitsui Agr. and Forestry | | * | | | 1 |
| Mitsui Shipbuilding | * | | 1 | | 2 |
| Mitsui Precision Machinery | * | | 1 | | 2 |
| Mitsui Chemical Ind. | * | | 1 | | 2 |
| Mitsui Real Estate | * | | 1 | | 2 |
| Mitsui Shipping | | | 1 | | 1 |
| Mitsubishi | | | | | |
| Mitsubishi Heavy Ind. | * | | 3 | 5 | 9 |
| Mitsubishi Trading | * | | 5 | 3 | 9 |
| Mitsubishi Bank | * | | 3 | | 4 |
| Mitsubishi Mining | * | | 4 | 4 | 9 |
| Mitsubishi Electric | * | | 7 | 2 | 10 |
| Mitsubishi Chemical Ind. | * | | 3 | 3 | 7 |
| Mitsubishi Oil | | | 3 | | 3 |
| Mitsubishi Steel Fabricating | * | | 5 | 1 | 7 |
| Mitsubishi Trust | * | | 3 | 2 | 6 |
| Mitsubishi Warehouse | | | 2 | 1 | 3 |
| Mitsubishi Estate | * | | 1 | | 2 |
| Sumitomo | | | | | |
| Sumitomo Mining | * | * | 2 | 2 | 6 |
| Sumitomo Electric Ind. | | * | 2 | 3 | 6 |
| Nippon Electric | * | * | 1 | 2 | 5 |
| Sumitomo Metal Ind. | * | * | 1 | 2 | 5 |
| Manchurian Sumitomo Metal Ind. | | | Not listed on table | | |
| Sumitomo Machinery | | * | 1 | 2 | 4 |
| Sumitomo Chemical Ind. | * | * | 2 | 2 | 6 |
| Sumitomo Aluminum Reduction | | * | 3 | 1 | 5 |
| Korea Sumitomo Light Metal | | | Not listed on table | | |
| Sumitomo Bank | * | | 3 | 1 | 5 |
| Sumitomo Trust | | | 3 | 1 | 4 |
| Sumitomo Life Insurance | | * | 3 | 1 | 5 |
| Sumitomo Warehouse | | * | 2 | 1 | 4 |
| Japan Engineering | * | * | 2 | 2 | 6 |
| Sumitomo Co-op Electric Power | | * | 1 | 2 | 4 |

Source and note: Separately published appendix to HCLC *Zaibatsu Dissolution*, entitled, "A Chart Showing Personnel Ties Among the Principal Companies of the Big Four Zaibatsu" (Shi Dai Zaibatsu Kei Shuyo Kaisha Jinteki Koryuen). For other 1945 interlocks, as well as 1937 interlocks, cf. tables in Appendix VII.

law, an officer of the Board is supposed to possess certain rights within certain limits, but in the case of the Sumitomo zaibatsu structure this is not so [i.e., among designated subsidiaries], because the board is placed under the strict orders of the holding company."[4]

The Sumitomo Holding Company submitted copies of the contract form which "representative" officers of first- and second-line companies signed. Because there is no substantive difference in content between the form used for first-line designated subsidiaries and that for second, excerpts are taken from the form used for first-line companies. (The rules were submitted in English.)

> Private Rules Concerning Officers of First-Line Subsidiaries of the Sumitomo Holding Company.[5]
>
> Art. 1 Officers of the (first-line) subsidiaries of the Sumitomo Holding Company (hereafter referred to as "holding company") who represent the interests of the holding company, shall be nominated by the holding company from among those who have special connection with the holding company or its subsidiaries.
>
> Art. 2 Those who take the post of officer of a (first-line) subsidiary according to the preceding Article are to have the following matters approved by the holding company before decision about them is taken in the companies.
>
> The above does not apply to specially designated cases.
>
> 1. Appointment and discharge, promotion, rewards and discipline of employees above third class,[6] also, transfer of employees down to section chief (*kacho*).
> 2. Decision with respect to retirement allowance of employees. . . .
> 3. Employees' and sub-employees'[7] business trips abroad. . . .
> 4. Bonus . . . to employees and sub-employees. . . . .
>
> 7. Commission of advisors or employees on the non-official staff.
> 8. Making of important rules or codes for employees and laborers, except in specially designated cases.
> 9. Important laws concerning the articles of association or the execution of the business.

[4] *Ibid.*, p. 71.

[5] *Ibid.*, pp. 72-73.

[6] "Third class" employees were defined as those in 1945 receiving Y30 to Y179 per month exclusive of bonus. Information submitted by the Sumitomo Holding Company to Headquarters.

[7] "Sub-employees" were defined as those in 1945 receiving Y20 to Y150 per month exclusive of bonus. Information submitted by the Sumitomo Holding Company to Headquarters.

10. Important contracts and lawsuits.
11. Important donations and receptions.
12. Increases and decreases of capital. . . .
13. Establishment, reorganization, or abandonment of enterprises, planning of enterprises, budget estimates, settlement of accounts each fiscal period.
14. Investment in and dispatch of officers to other companies.
15. Adoption, revision, abandonment of accounting system.
16. Choice of bank.
17. Affairs to be discussed at the general meeting of shareholders.

From the foregoing it would indeed seem that in the Sumitomo combine, policies of the core subsidiaries were under the "perfect" control of the holding company.

A similar document was in use in the Mitsui combine. When, after a four-year gap (1940-44) in which Mitsui Trading Company had acted as top-holding company, the top-holding company was reestablished, it dispatched identical letters to the core subsidiaries. Again because the letters were identical except for the words "first-line" and "second-line," portions of only the first-line document[8] are reproduced here. "Honsha" refers to top-holding company. (The document was submitted in English.)

1. Honsha will assist and encourage the various enterprises of first-line designated-subsidiaries and their expansion.
2. Honsha will act as a liaison organization among the first-line designated-subsidiaries, so that mutual assistance may be given and the power of Mitsui's vast composite organization can be efficiently taken advantage of.
3. The officers of first-line designated subsidiaries shall be recommended by Honsha.
4. The agenda for discussion at the general meeting of shareholders and other important matters must be referred to Honsha before their execution.

From the foregoing it will be seen how officers performed an integrating role in the *zaibatsu* structures. It is evident that if such integration was to be eliminated, several steps must be taken. There would have to be exclusion of those symbols of feudal-like loyalty, the *zaibatsu* family members. There would have to be removal of key officers of the major subsidiaries from positions within the combines,

[8] Reproduced *ibid.*, pp. 200-201.

officers who had spent their entire professional experience being trained to operate as a combine team. There would need to be prohibition of officer-interlocks among such companies. Headquarters spent almost three years taking these steps, by which time the objectives of the Occupation had changed.

In the Yasuda Plan,[9] which was put forward in early November 1945, *zaibatsu* family members offered to resign all positions in business,[10] but the ordinance that made this offer legally binding, Imperial Ordinance 233, took several months to achieve and by April 1946 the Japanese government was no longer feeling so overwhelmed by the catastrophe of August 1945. The ordinance did not include the offer by the family members to "resign all offices." It simply stated that the HCLC would direct the affairs of the holding companies designated for dissolution, thereby superseding the families. Nothing was said about restricting family participation in companies not among the designated holding companies.[11]

To correct the deficiency of the HCLC Ordinance, SCAP in July 1946 instructed the Japanese government to eliminate the influence of *zaibatsu* family members and their appointees from positions of business responsibility and cease appointment of interlocking officers.[12] Five months later, in December 1946, the Japanese government amended Imperial Ordinance 233 to provide for exclusion of *zaibatsu* family members from business positions[13] (it was the same amendment that brought family securities under HCLC jurisdiction). Three

[9] Cf. Appendix III.

[10] "All members of the Mitsui, Yasuda, Sumitomo and Iwasaki families will immediately resign all offices held by them in any financial, commercial, non-commercial, or industrial enterprises and cease forthwith to exercise any influence, either directly or indirectly, in the management or policies of the Holding Companies affected by this dissolution." [Was the offer of ceasing to exert any influence limited to the holding companies?]

[11] If comparison is made of the positions held by the family members in 1945 (Appendix VII, tables) and companies designated as holding companies (Appendix IV), it will be seen that their officerships were more far-ranging than those among the designated holding companies. For example, if restriction on family members had been confined to designated holding companies, it would have been acceptable for Mitsui Takahisa to continue to serve on both the board of the Teikoku Bank and Mitsui Shipbuilding; for Iwasaki Koyata to continue to serve on the board of the Mitsubishi Trust, Tokyo Marine and Fire Insurance, Mitsubishi Steel Fabricating and Mitsubishi Warehouse and Sumitomo Kichizaemon to continue to serve on the Board of the Sumitomo Trust, Sumitomo Bank and Sumitomo Life Insurance Co.

[12] Scapin 1079.

[13] Through amendment, Article 19 now reads, "Designated persons shall not become an officer of a company provided that the foregoing provision shall not apply to a case where the approval of the Commission has been obtained due to an unavoidable cause." [Article 19, 3]

more months were to pass before the "authorizing" authority of the December action was given meaning by naming 56 persons as coming within the meaning of the December amendment (cf. Appendix V). Provision for the elimination of appointees took considerably longer; it was not until January 1948 that specific provision was made for their elimination.

*The Economic Purge*

The JCS had instructed MacArthur:

> You will prohibit the retention in or selection for positions of important responsibility or influence in industry, finance, commerce or agriculture of all persons who have been active exponents of militant nationalism and aggression, of those who have actively participated in the organizations enumerated in paragraph 5 (g) of this directive, and of any who do not direct future Japanese economic effort solely towards peaceful ends. (*In the absence of evidence, satisfactory to you, to the contrary, you will assume that any persons who have held key positions of high responsibility since 1937, in industry, finance, commerce or agriculture have been active exponents of militant nationalism and aggression.*)[14]

This formulation complicated rather than helped MacArthur's task. The weakness of the JCS approach, as T. A. Bisson aptly stated, was, "It was premised not on conditions of . . . [concentration], in Japan's business system but on the system's association with militarists and aggression."[15] Clearly certain Japanese business leaders had worked openly and actively with the militarists in promoting Japan's "New Order in Greater East Asia"—Fujihara Ginjiro, president of the Oji Paper complex, historically within the Mitsui combine, and Sasaki Shiro, previously mentioned, a director of the Mitsui Holding Company and head of its "research department," were among them. But they were, in their outspokenness, more the exception than the rule.

What was more at fault in the business world was the system. More important than the collaboration of various business leaders in the country's military adventures, as has earlier been observed, was the system of enterprise itself, Japan's system of private collectivism. It was the *zaibatsu* which, with the other power blocs within the country, the military (*gumbatsu*), and the bureaucracy (*kambatsu*), supported oligarchy in government and actively opposed individualism and civil liberties. It was this system which resulted in favored treat-

[14] JCS 1,380, paragraph 23, italics mine.
[15] Bisson, *Zaibatsu Dissolution*, pp. 158-59.

ment to a handful of businesses and a lack of concern toward others. And it was this system that produced a stunted domestic market with the resulting additional pressure for overseas markets. The JCS directive called for a change in Japan's system of private collectivism, but failed to tie the action on personnel changes in the business world to the way in which the system had been put together.

*The Mechanics of the Purge*

The economic purge promulgated January 4, 1947 grew out of the political purge a year earlier. That is, public service was expanded to include top positions in major companies in the "private" sector of the economy, if one can call "private" those combines which accounted for up to one-tenth of the paid-up capital of the nation's corporate and partnership businesses. Technically the purge came as a result of the expansion of the final paragraph of the January 4, 1946 directive, calling for the removal of "militarists and ultranationalists." The major part of the economic purge related to persons holding key positions in 245 major companies—160 companies in Japan and 85 companies outside Japan—between the outbreak of the war in China and the end of World War II.[16] The key officers in these 245 companies, which this time included, appropriately enough, financial institutions, were automatically required to give up their positions and were barred from all public service, which in the case of private business organizations was taken to mean *designated positions in designated companies.*

If a purged businessman wished to accept a lower nonspecified position in his same company, or to accept a top position in a company that was not listed, either a nonlisted subsidiary in his own combine or in a company outside, he was free to do so, as well, of course, as to join a new company. While the first circumstance was a possibility, there was little likelihood, with Japan's strong sense of hierarchy, of its being used. Superiors cannot serve under inferiors. In fact, one cannot serve under an equal, as is demonstrated by the custom of resigning in the civil service when one's classmate reaches the position of under-secretary. Therefore, the chief avenue for business "purgees" was either to retire or shift to one of the thousands of companies not among the 245 listed ones. For example, the former chairman of the board of the Mitsui Bank, Mandai Junshiro, who was purged by virtue of holding that position

[16] It will be recalled that the HCLC found there to be some 1,200 companies in the control structure of the 83 designated holding companies. Accordingly, there were numerous combine subsidiaries outside the provisions of this paragraph.

within the specified time period, shifted to the Sony Corporation where he became the chairman of its board, his outstanding business ability thus being contributed to a new and rising company. The object of the economic purge was not to deprive Japan of business talent. It was to sever the personnel ties binding together the constituent parts of the combines.

The 245 companies from which removal of top officers was mandatory were compiled from criteria which repeatedly employed the phrase "conspicuously monopolistic."[17] But inasmuch as concentration in Japan had taken the conglomerate path rather than that of monopoly, there were of course scarcely any instances of "monopolistic" companies in the strict usage of that word (cf. Chapter 14 for market concentration ratios pre- and post-war). Accordingly, for purposes of the purge, the phrase "conspicuously monopolistic companies" was interpreted as companies that had been part of "conspicuous concentrations."

A study of companies named under Paragraph 11 (cf. Appendix VIII for a listing) indicates how difficult administrative decisions can at times be. With the best will in the world, the JCS assignment was extremely difficult to execute. One of the cardinal principles of administration is consistency, treating similar situations similarly. Did the companies listed in Paragraph 11 display this or was the list uneven? Even among those with staff responsibility for the compilation, there would have been few, if any, who would have argued that the list was wholly equitable. There was neither knowledge nor time to make the selection perfectly balanced, and the JCS instruction gave little guidance—"key positions of high responsibility . . . in industry, finance, commerce or agriculture. . . ."

In the original political purge of 1946 "public service" was divided into two categories, "principal public office" and "ordinary public office." Since the economic purge was an extension of the political purge, this distinction continued to exist. Persons holding "principal public office" were automatically removed; those holding "ordinary public office" could, *upon evidence*, be removed, but if unchallenged they were free to continue in their specific positions, though they were not free to shift.[18] "Principal public office" in the case of companies was defined as:

1. President, vice president.
2. Chairman, vice chairman.

[17] Supreme Commander for the Allied Powers, Government Section, *Political Reorientation of Japan*, Sept. 1945 to Sept. 1948, GPO, pp. 48-49.

[18] *Ibid.*, p. 50.

3. Managing director, standing director.
4. Standing auditor.
5. Active advisor or councillor.
6. Principal stockholder who owned 10% or more of capital stocks or who exercised, directly or indirectly, controlling influence in the management of the company.
7. Any other official, regardless of his title, including branch managers in any Japanese-occupied territory, Axis or Axis-occupied country, who in fact exercised authority or influence commensurate with any of the positions listed below.

"Ordinary public office" was defined as director,[19] "auditor, advisor, councillor, head of the business or accounting department and any other official with commensurate authority."

In addition to the 245 "conspicuously monopolistic" companies of Paragraph 11,[20] there were several additional categories under which companies were named where officers might be "evidentially" removed. The groupings are listed according to the paragraph of the purge ordinance:[21]

*Paragraph 6*: special companies, corporation, special banks and companies in which the government was the largest holder. Examples: Bank of Japan, Hypothec Bank of Japan, Industrial Bank of Japan, Japan Coal Co. Number of companies designated: 26

*Paragraph 7*: companies designated under the Temporary Supply Demand Adjustment Law (the legislation under which wartime allocations were handled.) Number of companies designated: (Not indicated in source.)

*Paragraph 8*: organizations established under special legislation; subsidized by the government. Examples: Japan Industrial Club, Japan Iron and Steel Council, Shipbuilders' Federation. Number of companies designated: 87

[19] Through a typographical error, "director" was omitted from the listing.

[20] Prior to the economic purge of 1947 there was a small amount of economic purge activity under "Category E" of the original purge directive, "Officers of Financial and Business Concerns Involved in Japanese Expansion," and earlier interpretations under "Category G." In an ordinance of February 27, 1946 (Imperial Ordinance 109) the Japanese government listed 33 concerns engaged in Japanese expansion. Included in this group were the Banks of Korea, Manchukuo, Taiwan, Mongolia, and Thailand; the Korea, Manchukuo, North China and Central China Development Companies; the Manchurian Investment Securities Company, Southern Manchurian Railway Company, and the Yokohama Specie Bank. SCAP, Government Section, *Political Reorientation of Japan*, p. 21.

[21] *Ibid.*, pp. 555-56.

*Paragraph 12*: influential companies, financial institutions in addition to those listed under Paragraph 11. Examples: Hokkaido Development Company, Maruzen Petroleum, Nissan Steamship Company. Number of companies named: 38

Evidential criteria were based on whether or not there was "conspicuous evidence" of "militarist or ultranationalist" activities.[22] "Conspicuous evidence," under an interpretation worked out by the Japanese government, March 10, 1946, was taken to mean that a person played an important part in (1) the conclusion of the Japanese-Manchurian Protocol, Tripartite Alliance, Sino-Japanese Basic Treaty, Japan-Thai Pact, or in the stationing of Japanese troops in French Indo-China, or in starting the Great East Asia War; (2) the suppression of opponents of militarism; (3) concluding economic agreements with, or in extending economic credits to countries in the sphere occupied by the Japanese armed forces; or (4) the financial or production program for Japan's military activities.[23]

As operations progressed under the economic purge it became evident that the government faced a major loophole in the case of officers who resigned rather than face exclusion under the provisions of the purge, for the "injunctions against continuity of influence [continuing to direct, but from outside the office] . . . applied only to designees of the screening committees."[24] Accordingly, some seven months after the economic purge had begun, legislation was passed which permitted "provisional designation," designating all specified key officers in the designated companies within the specified time periods as falling within the provisions of the purge.[25] If a resigned or "out of office" person wished to appeal his case he could do so within a 30-day period. If appeal was not made within this period the person was purged by "provisional designation."

In Tables 5-2, 5-3, and 5-4 which follow, information is provided on the number of officers affected by the economic purge. The number of executives directly removed from positions came to 639 (639 in Table 5-2, 626 in Table 5-3) and those who had resigned in anticipation of removal or had earlier retired (the time reference for the purge was 1937-1945), came to 896, thus making a total of 1,535 (Table 5-2). If attention is given to "Paragraph 11" data, the heart of the economic purge, it will be seen that 405 officers were removed from the 240 companies, thus indicating that on the average, direct removals, notwithstanding the number of "principal public office" positions specified, were just under two per company. Overall,

[22] *Ibid.*, p. 50. [23] *Ibid.*, p. 22. [24] *Ibid.*, pp. 54-55.
[25] *Ibid.*

Table 5-2: GENERAL SUMMARY OF PURGE STATISTICS

Category G — Additional Militarists and Ultranationalists

| | |
|---|---|
| Number of officers screened | 6,951 |
| Number of officers passed | 6,312 |
| Number of officers coming under the purge | 639 |
| Number barred | 186 |
| Number removed | 453 |
| Number purged by provisional designation | 896 |
| Number originally designated | 914 |
| Number reinstated | 18 |
| Number purged directly or by provisional designation | 1,535 |

Source: SCAP, Government Section, *Political Reorientation of Japan, Sept. 1945 to Sept. 1948*, GPO, p. 553.

inasmuch as some 400 companies were listed (the number of companies listed in Table 5-3 adds to 391, exclusive of "Paragraph 7" companies where the information was not available), and inasmuch as 1,535 officers were affected (including some retirees), it is evident that on the average less than four officers per company were purged. Accordingly it is apparent that the purge was less severe than study of affected positions would suggest.

How much change could be anticipated from removal of four officers from boards consisting of 12, 16, 20, or more officers? Clearly, it was scarcely a "wholesale" amount, particularly when replacements were largely by promotion. Probably the most that can be said is that the removal of a few key officers dramatized the attempt to create more independent boards among companies, most of which had previously been instructed in minute detail on how to act. The hope was that the removal of certain key executives would inspire more independent behavior on the part of other board members.

In a number of circles in Japan and in the United States the economic purge occasioned sharp criticism of the Occupation. It even created dissension within the Headquarters staff. Headquarters by the second year of the Occupation was divided on the advisability of the economic purge. Had it occurred in January 1946, at the time of the political purge, criticism would probably have been

Table 5-3: DETAILED SUMMARY OF ECONOMIC PURGE STATISTICS (According to paragraph groupings in Appendix I to the Cabinet and Home Affairs Ordinance No. 1 of 1947)

| Paragraph | Companies | Number of officers purged |
|---|---|---|
| Paragraph 6<br>special companies, special banks | 26 companies | number of officers purged 99 |
| Paragraph 7<br>Temporary Supply Demand Adjustment Law companies | ? companies | number of officers purged 41 |
| Paragraph 8<br>organizations established by special legislation; subsidized | 87 companies | number of officers purged 60 |
| Paragraph 11<br>(160 companies in Japan, number purged 332;<br>85 companies outside Japan, number purged, 73)<br>(Cf. Appendix VIII for a listing of these companies) | 240 companies | number of officers purged 405 |
| Paragraph 12<br>"other" influential companies | 38 companies | number of officers purged 21 |
| Total number of officers purged (not including provisional designation) | | 626[a] |

Source: SCAP, *Political Reorientation of Japan*, pp. 555-56.

[a]This total, 626, does not agree with that given in Table 5-2, 639, likewise from the same source, but is certainly close enough to give confidence that the "order of magnitude" is correct.

minor, but it did not, largely because of Japanese government obstruction and procrastination. By the second year the cold war was emerging, and there were those who in their new concern with the threat of Communism believed it expedient to forget the reform aspects of the Occupation, even though these were the *raison d'être* of the Occupation and even though in the longer run they provided the best defense against Communist inroads. Most unfortunately of all, there was an ugliness creeping into the differences of view, an ugliness which Senator Joseph McCarthy was later to make synonymous with his name. Critics of the economic purge tended to

Table 5-4: BREAKDOWN OF PARAGRAPH 11 PURGE STATISTICS BY TYPE OF ENTERPRISE

(exclusive of provisional designations)

| | Companies in Japan (a) | Companies Outside Japan (b) |
|---|---|---|
| Financial organizations | 45 | 1 |
| Aircraft companies | 12 | 1 |
| Munitions companies | 72 | 14 |
| Iron and steel companies | 12 | 6 |
| Heavy industries companies | 5 | 9 |
| Chemical companies | 27 | 5 |
| Transportation companies | 22 | 2 |
| Communication companies | 20 | 3 |
| Mining companies | 25 | 13 |
| All others | 92 | 19 |
| | 332 | 73[a] |
| Total | 405 | |

Source: SCAP, *Political Reorientation of Japan*, p. 559.

[a]Corrected for typographical error.

impugn the motives of those who emphasized the integrating role of combine officers. Thus at times it could happen that staff carrying out the orders of the JCS could for this reason find themselves coming to be regarded in the eyes of their own government as doubtful security risks.

Criticism of the purge was heightened by the framework in which it was conceived—"militarists and ultranationalists." It was also heightened by certain inevitable inequities of a largely categorical approach, as well as by the inequities arising from combining categorical removal with evidential. Inequities among business executives arose depending on whether they were "paragraph 11" persons or paragraph something else. As observed, paragraph 11 meant mandatory removal, whereas other paragraphs meant evidential.

Kazuo Kawai sums up the arguments ranging over the entire scope of the purges—political, economic, mass media, teaching—this way:

While the purge was on, it stirred lively discussion among both the Japanese and the Occupation people. Some held that the purging of only 220,000 individuals [of whom about 180,000 were former military officers and 1,500 were business executives] was too mild a measure to have any appreciable effect on the democratization of the country. Others held that this number, including as it did a large proportion of the most capable leaders of the country, was enough to endanger the necessary task of reconstruction. Some argued that in a dictatorial regime like that of pre-surrender Japan, only fifty or a hundred men had any real responsibility for policy and that all the others in even seemingly important posts were not much more than technicians who had no choice but to go along with the established policy. The latter might have been readily won over to support the new regime, whereas instead the purge unnecessarily alienated and embittered these potentially valuable people. Even more argument raged over the inflexible character of the predominantly automatic purge. Many rascals were said to have escaped because they happened not to hold positions that fell within the designated categories, while on the other hand, many fine individuals were caught in the purge on mere technicality. There were not a few individuals fundamentally liberal and unsympathetic toward the wartime policy, who had deliberately stayed at their official posts in the belief that they could more usefully help to moderate the government's action from within than by attacking the government from without. The automatic purge made no distinction between such persons and the others.[26]

[The] rigidly impersonal policy was not, however, always manifest. . . . The case of Finance Minister Tanzan Ishibashi, who eventually became prime minister some time after Japan's recovery of independence, . . . looked suspicious. Ishibashi admittedly had written two or three articles praising some aspects of fascism soon after a visit to Italy, but as editor of a liberal economics journal he had consistently opposed the authoritarian and imperialistic policies of the militarists. No question was raised of his fitness for office when he became finance minister, but later when he began making disdainful remarks about the professional competence of the Occupation's economic planners, SCAP suddenly ordered that he be purged.[27]

[26] Kazuo Kawai, *Japan's American Interlude*, Chicago, 1960, pp. 92-93.
[27] *Ibid.*, pp. 93-94.

> Despite some injustice and irregularities, however, in relation to the tremendous scope and complexity of the operation, the purge was conducted with about as little abuse as could practically be expected. It seems to have worked out better than the "de-Nazification" procedure in Germany, where the semiautomatic purge soon gave way to judicial judgments that carried sentences of stiff fines and other punishments. Whereas the court trials in Germany apparently afforded opportunity for much inconclusive wrangling over questionable testimony inspired by political bias or personal spite, the virtually automatic administrative character of the Japanese purge allowed the intrusion of a minimum of petty politics or subjective influences. Unlike the war crimes trials, it carried practically no punitive connotations; it was primarily a constructive political measure to facilitate the emergence of fresh national leadership.[28]
>
> These results indicate, therefore, that despite its relatively brief duration and other inadequacies, the purge performed its intended purpose. By removing from the scene many of the older undesirable leaders during the first critical formative years of the new regime, it enabled a new generation of leaders at least to gain a foothold. With such a foothold, the new leaders have for the most part been able to resist being displaced by the returning purgees. Although the purge could not of course insure the good quality of the new leaders, it made what must be considered an essential contribution to the process of democratization.[29]

Kawai's sober and careful assessment contrasts sharply with some popular journalism at the time. *Newsweek*, in an extensive article appearing within the month of the beginning of the economic purge, opened a sharp attack on the Headquarters sections involved in the purge. In an article entitled, "Behind the Japanese Purge—American Military Rivalries," of January 27, 1947, the magazine gave support to the suggestion of sending a Congressional committee to Japan "to discover why American capitalist principles are being undermined by American occupation authorities." It reported that "some 25,000 to 30,000" of Japan's "businessmen, financiers, and industrialists faced removal from their jobs." As I have noted, the number was actually 1,500. It claimed that the action had been put over on MacArthur by Government Section, mistakenly referred to throughout as "military government," and that such a Congressional investigation "would help clear General MacArthur of any blame and would repair the

[28] *Ibid.*, p. 95. [29] *Ibid.*, p. 97.

damage already inflicted on his dignity in the eyes of the Japanese." Further, the article asserted: "Even though Whitney's MG [Gen. Courtney Whitney's Government Section] fathered the purge, some MG officers are already claiming that it had to be undertaken because of direct orders from the eleven-nation Far Eastern Commission sitting in Washington where 'the Russians put something over!'" As we have noted, MacArthur undertook it on direct orders of the U.S. Joint Chiefs of Staff.

MacArthur's rebuttal of the *Newsweek* piece, which follows, was timed to coincide with the magazine's publication date:

> The article contained in the January 27th issue of the magazine "Newsweek" in an attack upon the basic concept underlying the purge of active exponents of militant nationalism and aggression from the postwar economy of Japan, reflects a complete lack of knowledge and understanding of the basic facts and issues involved.
>
> The Supreme Commander was directed early in the occupation to "prohibit the retention in or selection for positions of important responsibility or influence in industry, finance, commerce or agriculture of all persons who have been active exponents of militant nationalism or aggression, and of any who do not direct future Japanese economic effort solely towards peaceful ends." In the absence of evidence to the contrary, he was directed to "assume that any persons who have held key positions of high responsibility since 1937 in industry, finance, commerce, and agriculture have been active exponents of militant nationalism and aggression" and to "remove and exclude from positions of important responsibility or influence in all public and private financial institutions, agencies or organizations all persons who have been active exponents of militant nationalism and aggression," it to be "generally assumed, in absence of evidence to the contrary, that any persons who have held key positions in any such institutions, agencies or organizations are active exponents of militant nationalism and aggression." He was also directed to "prevent the retention or in selection for places of importance in the financial field of individuals who do not direct future financial effort solely towards peaceful ends."
>
> In the implementation of the above directive, I used the normal discretion of a field commander. . . .
>
> While there have been natural differences of views on detail, throughout there has been complete unity of purpose by the staff

sections concerned, and every decision has been personally made by me. I have aggressively furthered this objective, not alone because to do so is in compliance with the basic directive by which my course of action as Supreme Commander is bound, but because any other course would be to ignore those very causes which led the world into war, and by so doing to invite the recurrence of future war.

It was these very persons, born and bred as feudalistic overlords, who held the lives and destiny of the majority of Japan's people in virtual slavery, and who, working in closest affiliation with its military, geared the country with both the tools and the will to wage aggressive war. This, to the end that a large part of the earth's surface and inhabitants might be brought under the same economic bondage they had so long maintained over a majority of the Japanese people—and that Japan might weld from conquered nations and peoples of the world a vast totalitarian economic Empire, designed further to enrich them. Those are the persons who, under the purge, are to be removed from influencing the course of Japan's future economy.

Petitions and letters have been received by the thousands from the people of Japan calling for the extension of the purge to which "Newsweek" objects, and since its announcements the press of Japan has been practically unanimous in applauding its purpose. . . .

The details of the purge program have been carefully evolved so as not to disturb the ordinary businessman, nor the technician whose skill and brains did not influence formulation of the policy which directed Japan's course toward aggressive war. It is fantastic that this action should be interpreted or opposed as antagonistic to the American ideal of [a] capitalistic economy. In my opinion, and I believe in the opinion of truly responsible Japanese as well, the action will not unduly disturb the development of a future peaceful industrial economy. But even if this should prove not the case—even if, as "Newsweek" avers, this cleansing of the economy of Japan of undesirable influence is destined seriously to handicap industrial revival for lack of essential leadership—or even if such revival is wholly impossible without the guidance of those several thousand persons involved who directly contributed to leading the world into a war taking a toll of millions of human lives and effecting destruction of hundreds of billions in material resources—then, in that event the interests of those other hundreds of millions of people who want and seek peace leave no alternative than that Japan must bear and sustain the consequences, even at the expense of a new economy geared down to the capabilities remaining.[30]

The economic purge marked the first significant criticism from American quarters of MacArthur's handling of the Occupation. In retrospect it can be seen to have represented the opening assault on the business reform aspects of the Occupation.

### *Law for the Termination of* Zaibatsu *Family Control*

Because the economic purge was conceived in terms of "militarists and ultranationalists" in "conspicuously monopolistic companies," rather than in terms of the appointment pattern of *zaibatsu* personnel, the staff of GHQ-SCAP concerned with deconcentration continued to press for legislation implementing SCAP's directive of July 1946, calling for the elimination of *zaibatsu* appointees. Illustrative of the difference between the two concepts are the following examples: If we compare the lists of companies under "paragraph 11" with the companies listed by the HCLC as subsidiaries of the top-holding companies, we find in the case of the Mitsui combine that 23 subsidiaries of the top-holding company's 75 subsidiaries were included, 52 were not; that in the case of the Yasuda combine, 5 of the top-holding company's 30 subsidiaries were included, 25 not. With SCAP prodding and pushing, the Japanese government finally took action. The result was the "Law for the Termination of *Zaibatsu* Family Control," promulgated January 7, 1948—but it came too late. The reform phase of the Occupation was ending and the law turned out to represent no more than the anomaly of a reform proposal in a nonreform period.

Article I of the "Law Concerning the Elimination of Control by Zaibatsu Families" (Law No. 2, January 7, 1948) reads: "The objective of this Law is to eradicate [the] personal tie which has served influentially for the formation and maintenance of the Zaibatsu enterprises, thereby promoting a sound development of the Japanese economy on the democratic basis."[31]

The law grouped the complexes of *zaibatsu* subsidiaries into seven categories according to their closeness to the top-holding company. Mandatory removal of affected officers was called for in the case of the companies making up the first three categories. The law called for the removal of all officers in category A subsidiaries, officers above standing director in category B subsidiaries, and removal of the

[30] *Political Reorientation*, p. 549.
[31] As cited in *Laws, Rules*, p. 94.

highest representative officers in category C companies.[32] Removals were not from positions in business but from all positions within the particular combine. In the other categories, D, E, F, and G, removals were evidential. The breakdown of companies by combine is shown in Table 5-5. The table indicates that 1,681 companies were deemed to fall within its provisions and that 3,668 officers (both alive and dead!) were affected by its provisions.[33] A study of Table 5-6, showing action taken under the law indicates the scale of achievement—40 removals—beyond those removed by the economic purge.

There is no easy answer as to what the consequences of the purge and related measures were, for history cannot be re-run so that we can know "what would have been if. . . ." Given the GNP record of the economy,[34] it is clear, however, that the economy of Japan was far from being seriously damaged. In fact, some observers of the postwar scene assert that an element in the truly phenomenal growth of the economy has been the new managerial blood which the purges and reorganizations (financial and structural) brought about in the new business environment in which corporate officers have been able to be officers in fact rather than in name only.

The legal prohibitions restricting *zaibatsu* family members from business positions and the removals brought about by the economic purge and the Zaibatsu Appointees Law were in effect somewhat less than four years. While some depurging occurred in 1950, the principal part took place in 1951. In a May 3, 1951 memorandum to the Japanese government on the fourth anniversary of the postwar constitution, General Ridgway authorized the Japanese government "to review existing ordinances issued in implementation of directives from this headquarters, for the purpose of evolving through established procedures such modifications as past experience and the present situation render necessary and desirable."[35] The Japanese government acted with vigor under its new independence. Professor Bisson states that by the end of October 1951, "only 80 . . . economic purgees were still under designation."[36] Yasuba Yasukichi's figures

[32] The writer cannot help but wonder if the intention in the case of category B companies was not to state "standing directors and above." However, both Article 7 of the law as appearing in *Laws, Rules*, and a memorandum from the Secretariat of the Appointees Examination Committee (dated Sept. 2, 1948), as found in the World War II Records Division, use the phrasing of the text.

[33] The law did not specify a beginning date of applicability; by administrative decision the year 1931 was chosen. In this way deceased officers were covered.

[34] For the postwar performance of the Japanese economy, cf. Chapter 17, Table 17-2, and for international comparison, 17-1.

[35] As quoted in Bisson, *Zaibatsu Dissolution*, p. 179.

[36] *Ibid.*

Table 5-5: COMPANIES AND APPOINTEES AFFECTED BY LAW FOR THE TERMINATION OF ZAIBATSU FAMILY CONTROL

| Zaibatsu | Companies by category | | | | | | | Total | Appointees[a] |
|---|---|---|---|---|---|---|---|---|---|
| | A | B | C | D | E | F | G | | |
| Mitsui | 23 | 28 | 15 | 46 | 239 | 61 | 3 | 405 | 1,048 |
| Mitsubishi | 14 | 13 | 8 | 10 | 142 | 61 | 1 | 249 | 548 |
| Sumitomo | 14 | 10 | 13 | 9 | 111 | 74 | 7 | 239 | 564 |
| Yasuda | 5 | 5 | 4 | 16 | 43 | 36 | 1 | 110 | 266 |
| Nissan | 4 | 19 | 26 | 33 | 64 | 63 | 1 | 210 | 601 |
| Okura | 1 | 3 | 4 | 24 | 33 | 12 | 0 | 77 | 129 |
| Furukawa | 1 | 4 | 6 | 9 | 27 | 40 | 1 | 88 | 198 |
| Asano | 1 | 4 | 2 | 2 | 65 | 9 | 0 | 83 | 113 |
| Fuji | 1 | 2 | 2 | 61 | 29 | 78 | 0 | 173 | 65 |
| Nomura | 1 | 3 | 6 | 10 | 18 | 9 | 1 | 48 | 136 |
| Total | 65 | 91[b] | 86 | 220 | 771 | 443 | 15 | 1,682[c] | 3,668 |

A = Direct zaibatsu affiliates

B = Quasi-direct zaibatsu affiliates

C = Zaibatsu associate companies

D = Restricted companies (under Imp. Ord. 657)

E = Subsidiary companies (as defined by Imp. Ord. 567)

F = Connected companies ("affiliate companies," as defined by Imp. Ord. 567)

G = Successor companies (as defined by the Prime Minister)

Source: Document in folder marked "Zaibatsu Appointees Examination Section — Prime Minister's Office," World War II Records Division, National Archives, Suitland, Md.

[a] Figures for "appointees" "based on data available for the period of January 1, 1931 to November 15, 1948."

[b] Correction of arithmetic error. The figure 81 is used in the source.

[c] There is an internal inconsistency to the figures. When added vertically, 1,682 is correct. When added horizontally the total is 1,691.

Note: A list of these companies will be found in HCLC, *Laws, Rules and Regulations Concerning the Reconstruction and Democratization of Japanese Economy*, Tokyo, 1949, pp. 103-16. Names appear in both romanized form and English translation.

Table 5-6: ACTION TAKEN UNDER THE LAW FOR THE TERMINATION OF *ZAIBATSU* APPOINTEES

(The figures are internally inconsistent,[a] but are given as presented by the Appointees Examining Committee in its Memorandum to SCAP, September 2, 1949.)

| | | |
|---|---|---|
| Appointees coming under the law | | 3,668 |
| Exclusions | | 3,054 |
| Latent appointees, resigned or retired 1931 to 1945 | 1,673 | |
| Removed by economic purge (SCAPIN 550) | 758 | |
| Deceased | 623 | |
| Appointees remaining | | 614 |
| Appointees appealing | 715[a] | |
| Appeals approved | 614 | |
| Appeals not approved but temporarily retained | 61 | |
| Removals | 40 | |

Source: Appointees Examining Committee and Appointees Reexaming Committee memorandum transmitted to SCAP, Sept. 2, 1949, in folder marked "Zaibatsu Appointees Examination Section - Prime Minister's Office," in World War II Records Division, National Archives, Suitland, Md.

[a]There could not, of course, be 715 appeals from 614 "remaining appointees."

are slightly different; he reports that by May 1951 "all but convicted war criminals were released."[37] *Zaibatsu* family members' designations were cancelled July 11, 1951, the day the Holding Company Liquidation Commission was dissolved.

It would be helpful if there were good case studies on personnel changes brought about by the foregoing reform measures, but there are few. Part of the difficulty in saying what personnel changes were

[37] Yasuba Yasukichi, "Foreign Economic Policy of the United States Affecting Japan: 1945-1962," mimeographed, p. 69, in a study prepared for the International House of Japan, 1964.

brought about by the purge and the prohibition on *zaibatsu* family members, together with their appointees, is that two further programs which have not yet been discussed had an impact on personnel matters. These were the reorganization of operating companies deemed to be "excessive concentrations of economic power" under the Law for the "Elimination of Excessive Concentrations of Economic Power," Law No. 207 of 1947, and the reorganizations under the twin laws providing special procedures for companies facing bankruptcy out of postwar dislocations, "Financial Enterprise Reconstruction and Reorganization Law," Law No. 39 of 1946, and "Enterprise Reconstruction and Reorganization Law," Law No. 40 of 1946. These measures are taken up in the next chapter.

An example will serve to illustrate how these additional laws brought about personnel changes. Under the "Law for the Elimination of Excessive Concentrations of Economic Power," Mitsubishi Heavy Industry was split into three companies which were at first called East Japan Heavy Industry, Central Japan Heavy Industry, and West Japan Heavy Industry. (They merged in June 1963, once more to constitute a single unit.) This three-way split creating two additional companies, created two additional boards of directors, thereby accelerating personnel promotions. Similarly, for financial reasons, large numbers of companies were corporately split. Financial reorganization created additional companies, and additional companies meant additional boards of directors and accelerated promotions. Thus it would be inappropriate to attribute all personnel changes to the economic purge and to the prohibitions placed on *zaibatsu* family members and their appointees.

Noda Kazuo, in "Postwar Japanese Management" ("Sengo Nihon no Keieisha") presents case evidence on the effect of the purge and related personnel changes, with respect to the presidents or chairmen of the boards of roughly half of the 83 designated holding companies, though unfortunately he does not inform the reader which companies he has used.[38] Presumably Professor Noda used the 30 companies corporately untouched, plus the 11 where there was reorganization but not dissolution.[39] Of the 41 companies studied, 9 continued to have the same president in 1951 or 1952 as at war's end. In the 31 companies where there was change, 19 represented promotion

[38] Noda Kazuo, in Komiya Ryutaro, ed., *Postwar Japanese Economic Growth* (*Sengo Nihon Keizai Seisho*), Iwanami, 1963, pp. 260-61. This has now been brought out in English translation, Komiya Ryutaro, *Postwar Economic Growth in Japan*, Berkeley, 1966.

[39] The final action on the 83 holding companies is summarized in Chapter 18.

(in 4 cases from managing or standing director). In 11 cases the new person was from outside the company. One case was "unclear." Comparing the average age of the top officer in 1951 or 1952 with the situation at war's end, Professor Noda found that the age of the chief officer was lower. In the 1951-52 period the president or chairman of the board was 51.8 years; at war's end, 60.2 years.

In an uneven study on the consequences of the purge which John D. Montgomery undertook for the Department of the Army,[40] data are presented on the impact of the purge measures on boards of directors of a few companies. Three such tables are reproduced compositely here as Table 5-7. In companies undergoing corporate reorganization it is inappropriate, of course, to ascribe all officer changes to the purge. As observed earlier, personnel changes in such cases are a composite of purge and reorganization. Of the four companies shown in Table 5-7, two illustrate corporate reorganization. While study of the table, to the extent that the information is reliable, indicates that "average years of experience as directors" and "average age of directors" was lower in the later period, it will be seen that the later officers all had had long experience with the company.[41] In no case was the experience of officers less than 25 years, and the median figure was 29.

The purge, while far from being an ideal instrument, did weaken combine personnel ties. However, curiously enough, the HCLC, charged with dissolution of Japan's combines, took no cognizance of it. Neither in its two-volume Japanese-language report nor in the English-language report did it so much as mention it. Is it that the commission never understood the meaning of the program awkwardly carried out under the phraseology of exponents of "militant nationalism and aggression," or was the omission the product of not having administrative responsibility? While the HCLC was involved in the program for removing the influence of *zaibatsu* family members and their appointees, it had no connection with the economic purge.

With the benefit of hindsight, it would seem open to question whether personal loyalty, once the *zaibatsu* structures had been brought under dissolution procedures, and the whole "polity" of which they were a part lay in ruins, was as strong as it was imagined

[40] Montgomery, *The Purge in Occupied Japan*, limited edition for the Department of the Army, Baltimore, 1954. The research for the study was done between April and October 1952.

[41] Apparently one of the means used to prevent too much new blood coming into the boards was to reduce their size. In 1943 the size of the boards of the four companies listed in Table 57 was: Heavy Industries, 22; Mining, 20; Bank, 15; Electric, 14. Cf. Securities Exchange Companies Control Association, *Corporation Directory* (Shoken Torihiki Kaisha Tosei Kaihen, *Kabushiki Kaisha Nenkan*), Tokyo, 1943.

Table 5-7: AGE AND EXPERIENCE OF DIRECTORS OF FOUR MITSUBISHI COMPANIES BEFORE AND AFTER THE PURGE

| *Company* | *Date* | *Total no. of dir.* | *Average age* | *Av. yrs. exper. as dir.* | *Av. yrs. seniority in Co.* |
|---|---|---|---|---|---|
| *Mitsubishi Heavy Industries (Split into 3 companies)* | | | | | |
| Mitsubishi Heavy Ind. | 12/46 | 12 | 60+ | 8+ | 38+ |
| East Heavy Ind. | 1/50 | 10 | 54+ | 1 1/2 | 30 1/2 |
| Central Heavy Ind. | 1/50 | 10 | 55 1/2 | 1+ | 30+ |
| West Heavy Ind. | 1/50 | 10 | 53+ | 1/3 | 28- |
| *Mitsubishi Mining (Split into 2 companies* | | | | | |
| Mitsubishi Mining | 10/46 | 10 | 57 | 5+ | 31 |
| Mitsubishi Mining | 4/50 | 11 | 52+ | 1/2 | 27 1/2 |
| Mitsubishi Metal Mining | 4/50 | 12 | 50 1/2 | 0 | 25+ |
| *Mitsubishi Bank (No corporate reorganization. Name change)* | | | | | |
| Mitsubishi Bank | 1/47 | 13 | 59 1/2 | 4 1/2 | 33+ |
| Chiyoda Bank | 2/47 | 12 | 53+ | 1/3 | 29- |
| *Mitsubishi Electric (No corporate reorganization, no name change)* | | | | | |
| Mitsubishi Electric | 12/46 | 8 | 55 | 2 | 29- |
| Mitsubishi Electric | 4/47 | 15 | 53 1/2 | 1 | 29- |

Source: John D. Montgomery, *Purge in Occupied Japan*, limited edition for the Department of the Army. The Johns Hopkins Press, April 1954, Tables 77, 78, 79, pp. 117-18.

to be. This older pattern of human relations would seem close to having been ready to snap of its own accord. After all, the pre-surrender Japanese government devoted great energy to sustaining the pattern—"ethics" courses in the schools, thought control, and the ubiquitous police. All this was shattered in the country's defeat.

The loyalty on which the *zaibatsu* structures rested could only be anachronistic. It was rightfully of the age which "officially" ended with the Meiji Restoration, but which through ardent cultivation had been kept alive. To talk with certain of Japan's business executives today is to be persuaded that they enjoy being officers in their own right, that they like the greater independence the postwar business environment has provided them, and that they find it highly attractive to participate in the gains which their skill and imagination make possible, rather than seeing the fruits of their efforts go largely to *zaibatsu* families. Human relations and technology in Japan are coming to be of the same age.

To say that feudal-like loyalty is a disappearing item is not, however, to say that the "old school tie" is a comparably disappearing item. While feudal loyalty may no longer provide an important tie in business transactions, certainly a common business background does. It is on this more tenuous connection that the present-day groupings are being built (cf. Chapters 11, 12, and 13).

# 6.

# The Deconcentration Law and the Antimonopoly Law

BECAUSE certain of the operating companies of the combines were of such giant size as to deter entry, it was believed important that the HCLC be given the power to reorganize them. But the HCLC, while possessing the power to dissolve companies it designated as holding companies, had no such authority.[1] The Enterprise Reconstruction and Reorganization Law, which provided authority to reorganize corporations in circumstances of insolvency or near-insolvency (a circumstance in which virtually all major corporations found themselves following cancellation of government indemnities in 1946), did not contain standards for reorganization from an antitrust point of view, nor was it administered by the HCLC. The legislation authorizing the HCLC to reorganize operating companies—which resulted from months of SCAP pressure and months of Japanese government resistance—was entitled "Law for the Elimination of Excessive Concentrations of Economic Power." It was also referred to as the Deconcentration Law and as Law No. 207 of 1947.[2] Passage of the legislation was bitterly resisted by the Japanese government, and led to a sharp division of American opinion, which in turn resulted in a reversal of United States policy.

The Deconcentration Law was conceived as a means of promoting more competitive market structures, of promoting the opportunity for entry. Entry, of course, can be of two types—by a new firm or by extension of an existing firm into a new line. The entry being sought was the former.

A few of the operating companies coming under the Deconcentration Law were thought of as deterring entry because of monopolistic or near-monopolistic positions. The Japan Express Company, the Oji Paper Company, and the Toyo Can Company are illustrative of companies in this position. The far bigger part of the problem of

[1] The HCLC did not possess direct authority, but held voting rights on the enormous blocks of stock from the designated holding companies and the *zaibatsu* families which could be used toward reorganizing, from an antitrust point of view, the companies continuing in existence. Cf. HCLC, *Final Report*, p. 22.

[2] For the text see HCLC, *Laws, Rules*; also Bisson, *Zaibatsu Dissolution.* All quotations in this chapter are from the HCLC.

more competitive market structures, however, related to companies occupying oligopolistic positions, frequently in diverse lines—such as Mitsubishi Heavy Industries. With its shipyards and plants extending from the Tokyo area to Nagasaki it was foremost in shipbuilding, ship repair and marine engines, a major producer of diverse types of industrial machinery (for mining, textiles, papermaking, etc.), a leading producer of different types of engines (including diesel engines), the second largest producer of aircraft, a key producer of airplane engines, a major producer of rolling stock (steam, electric, and diesel), and an important producer of automobiles and trucks.[3]

A monopolistic company hinders entry into a market through its potential for price discrimination. A conglomerate company occupying oligopolistic positions in diverse markets has a different effect on entry. It possesses purchasing and selling advantages over the single-market firm; it can buy more cheaply because its size and selling costs are less; it is likely to possess credit advantages over the single-line firm because of its exceptional diversification of risk (when banks are affiliated, the advantages are more so). A conglomerate company permits internal price discrimination, one division making goods and services available to another at below-market prices. As will be seen in Chapter 8 where this practice is illustrated, the logic rests on revenue gains on less than full-cash pricing from additional business. Further, a conglomerate has resources it can fall back on in case of reverses. Where there is a sharp contest for advantageous site, coveted patent arrangement, and so forth, a conglomerate may pool its resources in order to outbid its rivals. Professor Corwin D. Edwards has written:

> A big firm has advantages over a smaller rival just because it is big. Money is power. A big firm can outbid, outspend, and outlose a small firm. It can advertise more intensively, do more intensive and extensive research, buy up inventions of others, defend its legal rights or alleged rights more thoroughly, bid higher for scarce resources, acquire the best locations and the best technicians and executives. If it overdoes its expenditures, it can absorb losses that would bankrupt a small rival.[4]

[3] For a discussion of Mitsubishi Heavy Industries see Mitsubishi Economic Research Institute, *Mitsui, Mitsubishi, Sumitomo*, pp. 176-96. For a brief discussion of the 1964 merger see Chapter 14.

[4] Edwards, in testimony at *Hearings on Economic Concentration* before the Subcommittee on Antitrust and Monopoly, Committee of the Judiciary, U.S. Senate, Part I, *Overall and Conglomerate Aspects*, 88th Cong., 2nd Sess., Washington, D.C., 1964, p. 42.

While in an economic sense, oligopolistic positions in different markets "add" in the foregoing manner, politically they "add" even more easily. A conglomerate has genuine economies of scale resulting from familiarity with government officials, and greater opportunities for favors. The closeness of Japanese government-business ties was an important consideration in the minds of GHQ-SCAP staff in pushing for a business environment cordial to the new entrant.

There were those who argued that, granting the circumstances outlined above, it was quite unnecessary to attempt splits among operating companies because the Antimonopoly Law, the permanent legislation, forbade discriminatory business practices. To those favoring the "direct action" approach taken by the Deconcentration Law, however, it seemed highly improbable that a mere piece of paper would deter behavior unless the business environment was such as to create a vested interest in the provisions being observed. For this reason staff of the Antitrust and Cartels section of Headquarters hoped to see the economy turned over in deconcentrated form to the Fair Trade Commission, the administrative body for the permanent antimonopoly legislation. Otherwise, the Antimonopoly Law was regarded as likely to be either ignored or scuttled as soon as the nation once again became independent.

In seeking reorganization of giant operating companies from the point of view of antitrust, Headquarters staff thought of efficiency in terms of the physical costs of production. Reorganization was to be ruled out if it would increase the costs of materials, labor, and management of companies named under the law. If, on the other hand, reorganization did not affect these items, it would be explored with the presumption in favor of splits. Where major manufacturing sites or mining sites are geographically widely separated, it was believed there would be few economies in physical costs of production. Such an approach definitionally excludes from consideration differences in costs of financing between smaller and larger companies. It likewise excludes differences in selling costs. That research and development was also excluded from such an approach did not represent a difference of view between Japanese and American thinking, for only in the 1960s have Japanese companies begun to operate R and D programs.

The intensity of the Japanese government's resistance to this legislation reflected the different approach taken on such matters. Virtually all Japanese government officials, with the exception of officials in the Fair Trade Commission, appear to believe that economies of scale continue indefinitely, a belief that steps partly from a lack of empirical work on costs-size relationships such as Professor Joe Bain and others have done in industry studies on the American economy.[5] Partly, it stems from a belief that it is unrealistic to exclude costs of financing and selling costs. It also, however, reflects differences brought about by the absence of an antitrust tradition. Where commercial banks and manufacturing companies are tied together, the ability of small independent companies to compete is less than in settings where applicants for loans stand on a more equal footing. Accordingly, out of the Japanese background it seemed more difficult to believe that small business could compete with large. Japanese businessmen having dealings with American business express astonishment and surprise that small manufacturing establishments in the United States can hold their own with large.

That size is required to compete with size is a view by no means confined to Japan. Recently the same opinion has been voiced in Europe; European businessmen are claiming they need greater size in order to compete with American giants.[6]

### *Law No. 207*

The Deconcentration Law of December 1947 was not the product of GHQ-SCAP thinking alone. In view of subsequent charges it is important to keep in mind that the language of the proposed measure had been cleared with Washington through the Department of the Army before a vote was taken in the Japanese Diet,[7] and that, in fact, it paralleled comparable legislation in Germany enacted almost a year earlier (the "Prohibition of Excessive Concentration of German Economic Power," OMGUS 56, approved January 28, 1947).

The Japanese "Law for the Elimination of Excessive Concentrations of Economic Power" was finally passed by the Diet December 8, 1947 and promulgated 10 days later. A SCAP release published in the *Nippon Times* for December 18, 1947 stated of the Law: "Its broad intention is to establish a reasonable basis for competition and freedom of enterprise through the elimination of those concentrations of

[5] Cf. Bain, *Barriers to New Competition*, esp. Chapter 3, "Economics of Large Scale," Cambridge, Mass., 1956, pp. 53-113; also D. L. McLachlan and D. Swann, *Competition Policy in the European Community*, London, 1967, Chapter 8, "Concentration and Market Combination," esp. pp. 227-55.

[6] Cf. *Patronat Français*, "Face à la concurrence américaine les entreprises européennes devront souvent concentrer leurs moyens," Aug.-Sept. 1964, pp. 2-15.

[7] Washington instructions for certain changes in the wording were contained in the Radio DA to CICFE, Dec. 9, 1947, to which reference is made in the document entitled "Deconcentration of Economic Power," by C. M. Hamm, dated August 9, 1950, pp. 15-16, in the files of the World War II Records Division, Suitland, Md.; hereinafter cited as "Hamm."

economic power which stifled efficiency as well as freedom. . . . *It is essential to recognize that this Deconcentration Law is not intended to hamper large-scale production or to prevent efficiently integrated enterprises.* . . . Likewise it should be clear that the Deconcentration Law does not establish any maximum or minimum size for business enterprises and it is to be administered by weighing carefully the actual facts characterizing each company affected by the Law. . . . It should be stressed that the deconcentration program, of which the Deconcentration Law is a major part, is a partner of other programs for the economic recovery of Japan. . . ."[8]

The key provisions of the Law were the two articles, 3 and 6. Article 3 read, in part: ". . . an excessive concentration of economic power shall be defined as any private enterprise conducted for profit, or combination of such enterprises, which by reason of its relative size in any line or the cumulative power of its position in many lines, restricts competition or impairs the opportunity for others to engage in business independently, in any important segment of business." Article 6 specified the criteria to be taken into account by the HCLC in publishing more detailed standards about what constituted an "excessive concentration of economic power." The Article included:

(1) market position including how gained (independent growth or by means of mergers).
(2) number of subsidiaries.
(3) whether parent-company plants stand on their own or are tied together through common raw material purchases, intermediate goods production or joint selling of final goods.
(4) history of monopolistic practices of the company.

The companion German legislation had been phrased similarly; defining "excessive concentration of economic power" as concerted activities "fostering monopolistic control" or "restricting access . . . to markets," the German law stated that "All enterprises having their headquarters in the United States Zone . . . and employing, in Germany . . . more than 10,000 persons shall be examined as prima facie constituting excessive concentrations of economic power. . . ." In addition, however, it sweepingly stated that any enterprise not included in the foregoing definitions, "but whose character or activities are deemed objectionable shall be considered . . . an excessive concentration of economic power." It then specified factors to be taken into account.

Because of the months it had taken to get the Japanese law passed,

[8] *Ibid.*, p. 16, italics mine.

much of the survey work to determine which companies were to be designated had been done by the time of enactment. This was accomplished by SCAP staff and the HCLC initially working independently of one another and then pooling their efforts.[9] Given the uncertainty for businesses as to whether they would be designated, it was decided that designations should be done at the earliest possible date. It was further decided to announce the designations by groupings according to the character of the enterprise. SCAP kept the Department of the Army fully informed of these developments.

In a January 26, 1948 radio message to the Department of the Army, MacArthur said:

> Part 1. Designation for Examination as Excessive Concentrations.
>
> 1. Pursuant to requirements of Article 3 and Article 6 of Japanese Public Law No. 207, passed by the Diet on 9 December 1947 under title: Law for Elimination of Concentrations of Excessive Economic Power, companies will be publicly designated in four categories under classification as (a) industrial, (b) distributive and service, (c) insurance, and (d) banking. Plan is for HCLC to designate companies promptly thereby assuring non-designated institutions that they will not be required to reorganize as excessive concentrations under this Law. . . .
>
> 2. Standards for designation and reorganization will be issued by HCLC for each of the four categories simultaneously with the announcement of designated corporations except that standards for financial institutions will not be made public initially. . . .
>
> 3. Plan is to require HCLC to designate industrial companies first, distributive and service companies second, insurance companies third, and banks under a special procedure. Banking institutions, of which six probably will come under the classification of excessive concentrations, will be designated separately. Banks probably to be affected by deconcentration now are reorganizing pursuant to provisions of the Financial Institutions Reconstruction and Reorganization Law and major changes necessary to eliminate excessive concentration characteristics are being effected insofar as practicable. Objective is to conduct reorganization of banks to maximum degree possible before public announcement is made in order to prevent loss of public confidence in banking structure or in any banking institution.[10]

[9] Hamm, pp. 17-21.

[10] Message from MacArthur to Dept. of the Army, Jan. 26, 1948, cited in Hamm, p. 23.

On February 8, 1948 the HCLC announced the designation of 257 companies from the industrial field and on February 22, 68 companies from the distributive and service fields, making a total of 325 companies.[11] In announcing the first designation of companies from the industrial field under the Deconcentration Law February 8, the HCLC in a Public Notice spelled out in greater detail its criteria for defining a firm as an "excessive" concentration. The following is taken from Section B of the Public Notice.

> Any private enterprise conducted for profit, or combination of such enterprises, will be considered an excessive concentration [among companies designated for review] if it meets any of the following criteria. Each company designated under the Deconcentration Law must furnish a statement explaining carefully the extent to which it meets the following criteria:
>
> 1. Produce or have capacity to produce a sufficient portion of the total supply of a commodity or service that a substantial price increase or hardship to potential buyers or to the general public would result if such a supply were withdrawn from an uncontrolled market;
> 2. Distribute sufficient supply of commodity or commodities that a substantial price increase or hardship to potential buyers or to the general public would result if it withheld such supply from the market;
> 3. Has sufficient influence and power in its field of operations that it could take action which would make it very difficult for another entrepreneur to enter the same field of activity with reasonable opportunity to compete successfully;
> 4. Acquired other organizations, operating units or concerns or any part thereof and enjoyed special monopolistic privileges and dominating controls as a result of war mobilization policy since 1937;
> 5. Has sufficient cumulative influence and power through its activities in unrelated fields of operations to restrict competition or impair opportunity for others to engage in business independently.[12]

Even cursory examination of the 325 firms which were announced in the first two designations indicates the kinds of problems the staff encountered in compiling the list. While a sizable proportion of the firms on the list fell within a plausible "excessive concentration of

[11] A listing of the 325 companies will be found in HCLC, *Japan's Zaibatsu and Their Dissolution* (*Nihon Zaibatsu to Sono Kaitai*), Data volume, pp. 24-88.
[12] HCLC, *Laws, Rules*, pp. 77-78.

economic power" definition, there were large numbers that did not. I have selected the following examples to illustrate the point. Asano Trading Co. was included. Given the scale of operations of Mitsui Trading, Mitsubishi Trading, and the trading activities of the Daiken Industries, it could scarcely be argued that Asano Trading was of such scale as significantly to deter entry. Yet there it was. Probably the reason for its inclusion was its close connection to the Asano Holding Co., but this blurs and distorts the meaning of the Deconcentration Law. There were other instruments for removing family, holding company, and intersubsidiary ties. The problem to which the Deconcentration Law was ostensibly addressed was operating companies of such size as to deter entry when size was not the product of technological economies of scale.

There were other unusual inclusions among the 325 companies. For example, the Daimaru and Matsuzakaya Department Stores were there. Both stores were large, but it would seem difficult, given the number of department stores and the scale of competition not only among themselves but from the competition these stores faced from small shops, to demonstrate that the two large stores deterred entry appreciably. Again in shipbuilding, there were unusual inclusions; the Fujinagata and Japan Shipbuilding Companies were there, yet neither accounted for sizable output at the end of the war.[13]

But while the foregoing examples suggest a too-liberal application of the law, there were certainly large numbers of perfectly appropriate "nominations." Firms such as Tokyo Shibaura Electric, Hitachi Mfg., and Mitsubishi Electric, with their enormously varied product lines and high market-positions were appropriate. So were such companies as the following (for which the position in their dominant market position is included): Japan Light Metals (Furukawa, 52% of aluminum production in 1937; 57% in 1949); Imperial (Teikoku) Petroleum (its predecessor company, Japan Petroleum, with 67% of production in 1937, it, itself, with 94% in 1949); Japan Precision Machinery (a Mitsui subsidiary, with 47% of bearing output in 1937 and 38% in 1949); Mitsui Chemical (with 28% of dyestuff production in 1937 as a department of Mitsui Mining, with 37% of dyestuff output in 1949); Asahi Glass (a Mitsubishi subsidiary, with 73% of plate glass output in 1937 and, as Mitsubishi Kasei Chemical, 65% of output in 1949).[14]

There was alarm and resistance to the Deconcentration Law from

[13] Cf. Fair Trade Commission, *The Realities of Economic Concentration in Japan* (*Nihon ni okeru, Keizai Ryoku Shuchu no Jittai*) for shipbuilding.

[14] *Ibid.*

conservative groups in the United States, which were upset that such a program had been attempted. The Department of the Army reversed its position. Although the Army approved the text of the law before a vote was taken in the Japanese Diet, three months later key officials of the department were able, in effect, to have the law negated. Such an about-face left MacArthur in an embarrassing and awkward position. And timing on the reversal was such that no insurance or banking companies were designated, though the need for a more competitive banking structure was more urgent than change among most of the industrial and commercial companies.

Looking back on the operation, one cannot help regretting that those wrestling with "translating" the phraseology of Article 3 came up with 257 companies from the industrial field and 67 from the distributive and service fields. To many persons, both Japanese and American, this gave the impression that there was such eagerness to achieve competition in the capital-intensive sector that cost considerations were to be disregarded for greater numbers. Undoubtedly both for the program and the critics it would have been wiser to have made total designations including finance of the order of magnitude of 100. Such an observation, however, implies that critics relied on reason instead of emotion in making their charges. Much happened in the months following passage of the Deconcentration Law that would suggest the critics did not confine themselves to reasoned objections.

In judging the Deconcentration Law it is important to bear in mind that at the time of its passage almost all major corporations in Japan—industrial, commercial, and financial—were undergoing corporate reorganization as a result of what in effect was cancellation of war indemnity payments owed them by the Japanese government. This proposed large-scale reorganization was not put forward in a smoothly running, established economy, but in one in which virtually every large corporation was in the throes of reorganization because of insolvency or near-insolvency. By means of the Deconcentration Law it was proposed to add to the other criteria that of determining whether a company would be left as it was, or whether it would be reorganized. Indicative of the scale of corporate reorganization for reasons of near-insolvency is a 1950 report stating that 4,762 companies had submitted reorganization plans under the Enterprise Reconstruction and Reorganization Law.[15] Of the 83 holding companies designated

[15] SCAP, GHQ, "History of the Nonmilitary Activities of the Occupation of Japan," Vol. XIII, Finance, Part D, *Financial Reorganization of Corporate Enterprise 1945 through 31 December 1950*, which reproduces Bank of Japan, Funds

by the HCLC for holding company dissolution, 76 were concurrently engaged in drawing up reorganization plans covering their operating functions. The legislation designed to prevent wholesale bankruptcy was the ERR Law, or in the case of banks and other financial institutions, the Financial Institutions Reconstruction and Reorganization Law.

In an effort (1) to put the Japanese government on a more solid basis, (2) prevent the pumping of large amounts of purchasing power into an economy that was prostrate, which could only be calculated to result in severe inflation, and (3) to prevent the distribution of funds to those who had had a major role in the war, SCAP in the fall of 1946 called for passage of a law which would impose a 100% tax on war indemnity payments, thus in effect cancelling them. The Japanese Diet passed such a law October 19, 1946 under the title, "War Indemnity Special Measures Law" (Law No. 38 of 1946).

The Japanese government's involvement in war financing had been enormous. "The Government had underwritten practically every kind of risk incident to private enterprise associated with the war . . . war damage insurance, contract termination, indemnities for government-ordered plant expansion, and depreciation and obsolescence. . . ."[16] Consequently it had enormous claims against it. (For a somewhat different picture see Chapter 3). Figures for the amount which the government owed business vary widely. Some reports put it in the range of Y100 billion. In noting these figures, it should be remembered that they were borrowings in terms of 1938-45 prices, not the far more severely inflated prices following the war. The Army Historical Service report on financial reorganization puts the figure at Y81 billion.[17] This report describes the circle of indebtedness this way:

> Industry, in turn, owed the banks on unsecured loans some Y85 billion which it had been forced to borrow during the war. Private banks had claims on the Government to the extent of Y25 bil-

---

Bureau "Tables Concerning Special Accounting Companies as of December 31, 1950," p. 26.

[16] *Ibid.*, pp. 4-5.

[17] *Ibid.*, p. 5. Different figures are to be found in the Army Historical Service's monograph, "Money and Banking" (where it is stated that the government owed Y25 billion on guaranteed war production loans and Y80 billion to insurance companies through its reinsurance program, p. 20); and the Army Historical Service monograph, "National Government Finance" (stating that the government's war indemnity debt was estimated at more than Y100 million [*sic*, billion], p. 133).

lion for defaulted industrial loans which the Government had guaranteed. . . . The banks could not meet their deposit liabilities unless they could collect on their unsecured loans and companies could not meet their unsecured loan obligation to the banks or find working capital to continue production unless they could collect from the Government on war damage claims.[18]

Had other measures not been taken, cancellation of the government's obligations in this circle of indebtedness would have thrown nearly all major corporations into bankruptcy. Needless to say, other measures were taken. Emergency legislation was passed to tie the cancellation of war indemnity payments and the consequent financial reorganization to legislation passed a few months earlier, which dealt with bankruptcy situations from the general dislocation of the economy. Here I am referring to the twin laws of August 15, 1946, "Law Concerning Emergency Measures for the Accounts of Financial Institutions," and "Law Concerning Emergency Measures for the Accounts of Companies," Laws No. 6 and No. 7 of 1946 which produced the phenomenon of "special accounting companies." The bridging legislation was provided in Laws 39 and 40 of October 18, 1946, "Financial Institutions Reconstruction and Reorganization Law," and the "Enterprise Reconstruction and Reorganization Law." "Special accounting companies" affected by "special losses" (cancellation of war indemnity payments and others) were to draw up plans to be submitted to the appropriate minister (Commerce and Industry, Transportation, Finance, etc.) for the financial reorganization of their companies. Thus all major corporations in Japan were engaged in drawing up "FIRR" and "ERR" plans.

The financial Institutions Reconstruction and Reorganization Law and the Enterprise Reconstruction and Reorganization Law were designed to provide for an orderly way of handling "special losses" among stockholders and creditors, which occurred from

. . . (1) the loss resulting from the payment of the War Indemnity special Tax, (2) losses of overseas assets, (3) losses resulting from the fact that companies had their bank deposits frozen in restricted accounts (as prescribed by the Emergency Measures for the Accounts of Financial Institutions, Law No. 6, 15 August, 1946) . . . (4) other losses due to the termination of the war, (5) deficits accrued during the preceding business year, and (6) the losses of the old account. . . .[19]

[18] *Financial Reorganization*, p. 5.

[19] *Ibid.*, p. 15.

Where there were large liabilities in the old account, second companies were often established.

> The significance of the separation of accounts lay in the fact that the new account was for the purpose of conducting the business and that all claims on assets transferred to it were frozen for the time being so that the old creditors of special accounting companies were not able to instigate bankruptcy proceedings against them and thus stop production.[20]

A further consideration which must be kept in mind when assessing the Deconcentration Law was that it was intended to permit companies which had been obliged to undergo forced mergers during the war period to resume corporate independence. In an effort to increase national output, the Japanese government had forced smaller corporations (and corporations not so small) to acquiesce in merger with larger corporations, as will be seen in the following figures:

MERGERS AMONG NONFINANCIAL COMPANIES

(capital in millions of yen)

| *Year* | *Cos acquiring other cos* | | *Companies acquired* | | *Total* | |
|---|---|---|---|---|---|---|
| | *no.* | *capital* | *no.* | *capital* | *no.* | *capital* |
| 1940 | 197 | 2,819 | 329 | 1,083 | 526 | 3,902 |
| 1941 | 323 | 6,133 | 698 | 1,464 | 1,021[a] | 7,597 |
| 1942 | 360 | 3,783 | 787 | 1,093 | 1,147[a] | 4,876 |
| 1943 | 492 | 5,686 | 963 | 2,120 | 1,455 | 7,806[a] |

[a]Correction of arithmetic error.

T.F.M. Adams, *A Financial History of Modern Japan*, Tokyo, 1964, p. 145.

REDUCTION IN NUMBER OF BANKS THROUGH CONSOLIDATIONS

| | | | | | |
|---|---|---|---|---|---|
| 1938 | 426 | 1941 | 264 | 1944 | 113 |
| 1939 | 398 | 1942 | 226 | 1945 | 69 |
| 1940 | 366 | 1943 | 150 | | |

Bank of Japan, *Historical Statistics of Japanese Economy*, Tokyo, 1962, Table 31, p. 69.

[20] Bank of Japan, *Historical Statistics of Japanese Economy*, Tokyo, 1962, Table 31, p. 69.

Believing that size made for greater output, the government pushed through hundreds of these consolidations. Only, interestingly enough, GNP did not increase. Japanese national income work is still tentative and subject to frequent revisions, but regardless of present-day sources, there is consensus that Japanese national income was virtually stagnant from 1937 to 1943 when Allied air raids began to show their impact, as will be seen in the following figures:[21]

Japanese National Income in Billions of Yen at Constant Prices (1934-36 Average)

| | | | |
|---|---|---|---|
| 1937 | 21.2 | 1941 | 21.1 |
| 1938 | 21.9 | 1942 | 21.4 |
| 1939 | 22.1 | 1943 | 21.3 |
| 1940 | 20.7 | 1944 | 20.6 |

It was in part as a result of this government policy of forced wartime mergers that Mitsui, Mitsubishi, Sumitomo, and Yasuda made such striking gains in the economy and, lesserly, the Other Six. The figures from the earlier large tables on the proportion of total paid-in capital are,

| | 1937 | 1941 | 1946 |
|---|---|---|---|
| Big Four | 10.4% | 12.0% | 24.5% |
| Other Six | 4.7 | 6.5 | 10.7 |

Social causation is exceptionally difficult, given the multiplicity of factors that typically are present, but at least one can observe that the mergers and consolidations which the government so eagerly pushed did not result in increased output.

A great many companies forced into these wartime mergers desired to undo them[22]—which was not confined to the smaller companies swallowed up in the process. For example, the Shibusawas, who controlled the Daiichi Bank that was obliged to merge with the Mitsui Bank in 1943 to form the Teikoku Bank, wanted very much to reverse this "unnatural merger."[23] The Teikoku Bank was dissolved in October 1948 into its former component parts, Mitsui Bank and

[21] Economic Planning Agency, *1963 National Income White Paper* (Keizai Kikakucho, *Kokumin Shotoku Hakusho*), Tokyo, 1965, pp. 178-79.

[22] For examples of such companies see Chapter 14.

[23] See Dai-ichi Bank, *A Brief History of the Dai-ichi Bank, Limited*, Tokyo, 1955, p. 6, as cited in Ehrlich, *The Role of Banking in Japan's Economic Development*, p. 293.

Daiichi Bank. There were many companies that wanted to undo unnatural mergers; therefore a number of designations under the Deconcentration Law occurred in consequence of "company history."

Such was the background for and the circumstances in which the Deconcentration Law was put forward. Now let us turn to the Antimonopoly Law, which, the critics have asserted, should have been relied on instead of the Deconcentration Law.

Critics of the Deconcentration Law found it difficult to understand how it was that there was both a Deconcentration Law and an Antimonopoly Law on the statute books. Seemingly the two laws were designed for the same purpose. Most critics found the Antimonopoly Law[24] a more acceptable piece of legislation. As observed earlier, the anomaly occurred because the Deconcentration Law was regarded as the surgical procedure necessary for the economy, in order for it to be turned over to the safekeeping of the Antimonopoly Law. The Antimonopoly Law was seen as having a future to the extent to which the Deconcentration Law was effective—means that without the "surgical procedure," observers anticipated that the Antimonopoly Law would either be scuttled or disregarded. For a law to be meaningful there has to be support for it. What made matters more confusing for critics, however, was that the permanent legislation antedated the emergency legislation. The permanent legislation was enacted in April 1947; this temporary emergency measure was enacted in December 1947.

As previously explained, Gen. MacArthur had asked for the permanent legislation in the initial deconcentration directive of November 6, 1945, accepting "in general" the Japanese Government's proposal for holding-company liquidation, the Yasuda Plan. The legislation was not achieved until a year and a half later, which bespeaks the unenthusiasm of the Japanese government for its passage. Perhaps it was premature in the second to third month of the Occupation to have asked for permanent legislation, but MacArthur, who strongly believed in the advantages of a short occupation, was apparently eager to be in a position to present evidence that Occupation objectives had been accomplished. With only a small staff to advise him in those first months, the range of difficulties attaching to the JCS assignment, "dissolve Japanese combines," was apparently not fully evident. With his experience in administration, however, MacArthur made it clear to the Japanese government in accepting "in general" its proposals, "that full freedom of action is retained by the

[24] For text see HCLC, *Laws, Rules*, pp. 195-212.

Supreme Commander for the Allied Powers to elaborate or modify the proposed plan at any time. . . ."

That critics of the program found the Antimonopoly Law more acceptable than the Deconcentration Law is probably to be explained by the more general and more traditionally antitrust wording of the Antimonopoly Law, as well as the fact that no prosecutions were taking place under it. To Americans reared to regard concentrations of economic power as synonymous with monopoly, not with conglomerate enterprise, it was possible to regard the Antimonopoly Law—notwithstanding such concepts as "undue disparities of bargaining power" and "competition" defined to include "potential competition"—as "respectable," whereas the Deconcentration Law had many "unorthodoxies." The Deconcentration Law explicitly recognized conglomerate operations as leading to "excessive concentrations of economic power"; it explicitly spelled out the criteria which were to be taken into account in reaching judgments. To go beyond the traditional limits of antitrust as it had been practiced in the United States seemed to some Americans, notwithstanding the dimensions of the problem at hand, highly questionable, maybe even subversive.

Article 1 of the Antimonopoly Law expressed the objectives of this legislation in this way:

> This Law, by prohibiting private monopolization, unreasonable restraints of trade and unfair methods of competition, by preventing excessive concentration of power over enterprises, and by excluding undue restriction of production, sale, price, technology, etc. through combinations and agreements etc. and all other unreasonable restraints of business activities, aims to promote free and fair competition, to stimulate the initiative of entrepreneurs, to encourage business activities of enterprises, to heighten the levels of employment and national income and, thereby, to promote the democratic and wholesome development of national economy as well as to assure the interest of the general consumer.

Definitions followed in Article 2. "Competition" was defined to include "potential competition." "Monopolization" was defined as those business activities, "by which an entrepreneur, individually, or by combination, conspiracy or any other manner, excludes or controls the business activities of other entrepreneurs, thereby causing, contrary to the public interest, a substantial restraint of competition in any particular field or trade." "Unreasonable restraint of trade" as used in this Law was taken to mean those "business activities by which an entrepreneur, by contract, agreement or any other manner, in conjunction with other entrepreneurs, mutually restricts . . . their . . . activities. . . ." "Undue substantial disparities in bargaining power" meant those disparities between an entrepreneur and his competitors not based on technological considerations which were likely to result in monopolization through domination of output and control of raw materials. "Unfair methods of competition" were taken to include (1) "Unwarranted refusal to receive from or supply to other entrepreneurs, commodities, funds and other economic benefits"; (2) Supplying the foregoing "at unduly discriminative prices"; (3) Supplying the foregoing "at unduly low prices"; (4) "Inducing or coercing, unreasonably, customers of a competitor to deal with oneself by means of offering benefits or that of threatening disadvantages"; (5) Prohibition of exclusive or sole agency contracts.

The next four chapters of the Act contained the substantive provisions of the law. Chapter II, "Private Monopolization and Unreasonable Restraints of Trade," forbade both monopolization and participation in such activities as price-fixing, quantity-fixing, restrictions on either technology or new facilities. Participation in cartels, domestic or international, was outlawed.

Chapter III, in giving the Fair Trade Commission authority to eliminate "undue substantial disparities in bargaining power," broke new ground. Article 8 specified: "When undue substantial disparities in bargaining power exist, the Fair Trade Commission may order the entrepreneur concerned . . . to transfer a part of [his] business facilities, or take any other necessary measures for eliminating said substantial disparities in bargaining power." Among the factors to be taken into consideration by the Fair Trade Commission in issuing an order under this authority were location of factories; terms of possible patents; production capacity; ability to obtain financing as well as materials; investment and other ties with other businesses; "comparison with competitors on all points enumerated. . . ."

Chapter IV spelled out restrictions on stock-holding, multiple directorates, mergers, and acquisition of assets—the major building blocks of combine enterprise. In Article 9 holding companies which represented the key corporate device for creating combines were outlawed outright. A holding company was defined as "a company whose principal business is to control, by holding stocks (including partnership shares; hereinafter the same), the business activities of another company." In a subsequent Cabinet Order (Cabinet Order No. 239 of November 8, 1947), "principal business" was construed to occur "when such stockholdings . . . [exceed] one-fourth . . . of its total assets."

In Article 10 intercorporate stockholding in the case of nonfinancial companies was outlawed except with the permission of the FTC, which might grant approval in situations of single-layer subsidiaries where there was close technological relationship to the parent company. Among financial companies no distinction was made between commercial banks and other financial institutions. In Article 11 banks and insurance companies, while not permitted to own shares in companies with which they were competing, were permitted to own stock when the amount did not exceed five percent of the capital of the company in question.

In view of the *zaibatsu* tradition of enormous family holdings, there were restrictions in Article 14 on stock holdings by natural persons and "noncompany" juridical persons. This restriction was framed in terms of substantially restraining competition.

Although debentures are little used in Japan outside of financial companies, a restriction on debenture-holding with respect to both nonfinancial and financial companies was put in the law. Article 12 specified that neither nonfinancial nor financial companies were to hold debentures of other companies in an amount which was 25% or more of the capital of the issuing company. As this provision related to nonfinancial companies it was largely irrelevant; as it related to financial, it would seem to have been excessively liberal.

There were several restrictions on interlocking directorates. In Article 13 it was stated that no officer or employee could become an officer in a competing company, no person could become an officer in another company if one-fourth or more of the "officers of either of the two companies are holding concurrently positions in a third company" or if concurrent officerships number four or more. The Japanese language does not distinguish singular or plural, which not infrequently clouds matters. If one interprets the former to be "a third company," the provision was without meaning, inasmuch as rarely would such a high proportion of officers be from a single company, even at the height of the *zaibatsu* period. If the provision is interpreted to be "third-companies," then it relates to real-world problems.

In Article 15 mergers and acquisitions of assets were made permissive only. The FTC was empowered to refuse permission if the merger or acquisition of assets did not contribute to the "rationalization of production, supply or management," if "substantial disparities in bargaining power" would arise, if the action caused "a substantial restraint of competition," or if "coerced by unfair methods of trade. Chapter V proscribed "unfair methods of competition."

Because trade associations can very easily be used for cartels as well as legitimate purposes, a special trade association law was believed important to assure that, with Japan's intensive, 15-year plus reliance on control associations (cartels with a bit of government thrown in), trade associations would not become cartels in disguise. Accordingly, the FTC drew up under SCAP pressure the Trade Association Law which became Law No. 191 of 1948, July 29, 1948.[25]

The purpose of the Trade Association Law as stated in Article 1 of the act was, "to define the legitimate scope of activities of trade associations and to provide for a system of their notification to the Fair Trade Commission."

In Article 4 the Law spelled out the legitimate activities of trade associations, 10 in number, which included such items as receiving and publishing voluntarily given statistical data, voluntary interchange of research, fostering development of quality standards. In Article 5 it spelled out 18 illegitimate activities of trade associations. These included such activities as controlling or attempting to control production and/or distribution; controlling or fixing prices; compulsorily requiring constituent entrepreneurs to submit reports on sales, prices, terms, orders, inventories, production, plant capacity, business accounts, activities, or facilities.

Such was the original form of the Antimonopoly Law and the Trade Association Law to be administered by a quasi-judicial commission, the Fair Trade Commission. The Antimonopoly Law was amended in 1949 and again in 1953. In 1953 certain parts of the Trade Association Law were incorporated into the Antimonopoly Law and the remainder of the act was rescinded. Given the ban in the Antimonopoly Law on centralized selling (or allocating) agencies (Article 5); the ban on holding companies (Article 9); the restriction on intercorporate stock holding among nonfinancial companies (Article 10), and among financial companies (Article 11), there was an additional share-disposal program undertaken as a result of the Antimonopoly Law.

[25] For text see *ibid.*, pp. 222-31.

# 7.

# The Public Debate: FEC 230 and All That

THE Deconcentration and Antimonopoly Laws, as well as other aspects of the deconcentration program, were influenced by recommendations by the State-War Mission on Japanese Combines, which was in Japan for about nine weeks in early 1946. Later that spring, the mission report, submitted to the two departments, was placed before the State, War, Navy Coordinating Committee for adoption as United States policy. (On November 4, 1947 the State, War, Navy Coordinating Committee, commonly abbreviated SWINCC, became the State, Army, Navy, Air Coordinating Committee [SANACC]. For convenience, the committee, throughout this book will be referred to as SWINCC.) Finally when the report achieved adoption as U.S. policy in May 1947, it was transmitted through the State Department to the Far Eastern Commission for discussion and adoption as Allied policy. While it was before the Far Eastern Commission it was designated "FEC 230."

The State-War Mission on Japanese Combines was the product of an exchange of cables between MacArthur and Washington. In early 1945, when MacArthur had the "Yasuda Plan" before him for decision, he cabled Washington for approval of his acceptance of it. Washington did approve as a first step in the program, but raised the question with him whether he might find it advantageous to have a technical mission made up of antitrust experts prepare a comprehensive guide for him. MacArthur agreed, and the State-War Mission on Japanese Combines was the result. Headed by Professor Corwin D. Edwards, at that time of the Economics Department of Northwestern University and consultant on cartels to the International Business Practices Branch of the State Department, the mission consisted of seven other members from the following departments and agencies: Antitrust Division of the Department of Justice, three; Federal Trade Commission, one; Securities and Exchange Commission, one; Federal Power Commission, one; and Tariff Commission, one.[1]

[1] The other members were: Chief of Staff, Robert Dawkins, Legal Advisor and Consultant, FTC; William B. Dixon, Special Assistant to the Attorney General,

Notwithstanding the fact that the problem the mission was being sent to advise on was that of an integral fusion of commercial banking with industry and commerce, the mission did not include a financial expert. It submitted its report to the two departments in March 1946; the War Department sought MacArthur's views on it.

SCAP comments on the report, transmitted to the JCS May 17, 1946, revealed a sympathetic appreciation of the general lines of the recommendations, but also contained reservations on particular points.[2] The detailed point-by-point SCAP comment was prefaced with the following:

> The objectives of this report are admirable in purpose but the practical execution of such a program, except in broad outline and along general lines, is quite beyond the size and organization of the Occupation Forces as at present constituted. The report includes in its program the most advanced refinement in the fields of finance, economics, commerce and industry—subjects which are now agitating the governments of the world and ones that are in a constant state of flux and unbalance. . . . .
>
> The basic question is whether the purpose of the Occupation is to establish an ideal economy here or whether it is merely to provide the introduction of such democratic methods and the abolition of such menaces as to insure the disability of Japan to make future war.
>
> If the purpose is the former, a complete reorganization approaching governmental size must be made in the Occupation Forces. This conception conflicts with the budget restrictions of the American Government, which have already been set forth and definitely limit the structure of the SCAP organization to a mere controlling echelon to provide and enforce broad basic principles.
>
> . . . this report must be regarded merely as a . . . study to which

Antitrust Division; James M. Henderson, Special Assistant to the Attorney General, Antitrust Division; Samuel Neel, Special Assistant to the Attorney General, Antitrust Division; Raymond Vernon, Assistant Director, Trading and Exchange Division, Securities and Exchange Commission; R. M. Hunter, Legal Consultant, Federal Power Commission, and professor of law, Ohio State University; and Benjamin Wallace, Special Advisor, Tariff Commission.

[2] For these comments see SCAP, GHQ, "History of Nonmilitary Activities of the Occupation of Japan," Volume x, *Reform of Business Enterprise*, Part A, "Elimination of Zaibatsu Control 1945 through 1950," Appendix 5, pp. 58-66, Office of the Chief of Military History, Washington, D.C. The comments were transmitted by Maj. Gen. W. F. Marquat; SCAP thinking necessarily reflected that of his advisors. Later chiefs of the Antitrust and Cartels Division of ESS were probably more sympathetic to the Edwards Report than the person holding the position at the time these comments were prepared.

every effort will be made in compliance but which contains many details of refinement in practice that may be of great difficulty or even unpracticability of accomplishment. . . .

Detailed SCAP comment not only included many "concurs," but also such observations as "too sweeping," "unworkable," "object," "too liberal," "unwise," "sound in principle."

The problem to which the mission addressed itself was how to eliminate the industrial-commercial-banking combines that dominated the capital-intensive sector of the Japanese economy. As was discussed in Chapter 1, the combines were considered an important pillar of Japan's authoritarian government, and Japan's authoritarian government was considered a major cause of its expansionist foreign policy. Accordingly, in the name of the "security interests" of the U.S., it had been decided in 1945 by the policy-determining interdepartmental committee, SWINCC, to call for the elimination of such concentrated business power and its replacement with competitive free enterprise.

The State-War Mission submitted a comprehensive set of proposals for eliminating Japan's historical pattern of industrial organization in the capital-intensive sector of the economy.[3] It was thought that combine dissolution embraced not only holding company dissolution but prohibition of interlocking directorates, dissolution of contractual and service arrangements, procedures for opening up combine patents, and dissolution of oversized operating companies. Because of the existence of strong business loyalties, the mission recommended that *zaibatsu* members and those close to them be divested of all corporate securities and be removed from participation in business for a 10-year period. Such persons were to be compensated for their property, but the mission cautioned against giving them enough to buy back their former position. It recommended a rapid liquidation of *zaibatsu* properties, preferably over a two-year period, and cautioned that sales should be screened to prevent cloaks for *zaibatsu* interests or formation of new excessive concentrations of economic power. The mission proposals in finance were curiously weak; somehow it never came to grips with a key element of the issue, the integral union of commercial banking with industrial and commercial undertakings.

Under the U.S. Commercial Code, commercial banks are not per-

[3] The account of the Edwards Mission proposals given in this chapter has been written from two documents—a summarized version of the report appearing in *Reform of Business Enterprise*, Part A, Appendix 4, pp. 49-57; and SWINCC 302/4 (FEC 230), which was declassified in 1966. SWINCC 302/4 is reproduced in Appendix IX.

mitted to own on their own account stock in nonbanking companies though they are permitted, of course, to own debt instruments.[4] While calling for a virtual prohibition of intercorporate stock ownership among nonfinancial companies, which is far more stringent than anything in the U.S., the mission did not recommend that banks be prohibited from holding stock in commercial and industrial corporations. Furthermore, it did not call for a separation of investment banking from commercial banking. The mission's proposals[5] in this matter were:

> (a) Banks and trust companies should be prevented from investing as much as 25 percent[6] of their capital and reserves in the securities, loans, bills, advances, and overdrafts of any one company.
> (b) Such concerns should not be permitted to hold in their proper, savings, and trust accounts the stock of any other company to an amount which exceeds 5 percent of the outstanding shares of that company, nor to vote any such stock which they may hold. Exemption should be made to the percentage rule for stock acquired in connection with *bona fide* underwritings or in default of loans, but any such exemption should not run longer than one year.
> (c) Officers and directors of any bank or trust company, and persons holding 5 percent or more of the stock thereof, should be ineligible to hold any office or directorship or a similarly large percentage of stock in any other company. . . .
> (d) No bank or trust company should be allowed to redeposit more than 10 percent of its deposits in any one institution other than the Bank of Japan.

[4] This was provided in the Glass-Steagall Act of 1933, which was enacted as an amendment to the Federal Reserve Act. While the foregoing governs what banks may do, it does not say what a holding company that includes banks among its subsidiaries may do. The Bank-Holding Company Act of 1956 was enacted to prevent holding companies including banks in their networks from breaking down the separation between banking and industry. The Bank-Holding Company Act of 1956 specifies that all holding companies holding 25 percent or more of the stock of a bank must, if there are two or more banks in their networks, divest themselves of control of all nonbanking and nonbank-related businesses. To accommodate what was regarded as a matter of small communities, an exception was provided for one-bank holding companies. Recently under this exception there has been a startling rise in the number of one-bank holding companies, and often the bank is large. Cf. House of Representatives, Committee on Banking and Currency, Staff Report, *The Growth of Unregistered Bank Holding Companies—Problems and Prospects*, 91st Cong., 1st Sess., February 11, 1969.

[5] The quotation is from Appendix 4 of *Reform of Business Enterprise*, Part A.

[6] Both SCAP and SWINCC reviewers found this provision excessively "generous." SCAP comment was "too liberal." While the document was before SWINCC the 25% figure was reduced to 10%.

The Mission proposed deposit insurance as a way of breaking popular discrimination in favor of *zaibatsu* banks; it proposed various measures for breaking government favor to *zaibatsu* banks including bank examinations of all banks (not just non-*zaibatsu* banks) every two years.

In addition, and more generally, the mission called for the termination of "control legislation," including within the term government monopolies, legislation requiring government approval for the formation of new businesses, and repeal of the laws and ordinances establishing "control associations"—the semi-private, semi-government bodies with which Japan had handled wartime allocations. The mission said: "New government monopolies should not be established during the transition period except with the explicit consent of SCAP. The petroleum and alcohol monopolies, which were instituted for war purposes, should be terminated."

The mission urged a systematic review of all forms of subsidy, legal monopoly, trade preference laws, and termination of such as do not have a demonstrable public purpose. It called for enactment of an antitrust law and revision of the patent law, and offered several suggestions for making control of corporations by insiders more difficult, among which was the establishment of independent auditors. As was noted in Chapter 5, auditors are corporation officers and when of the rank of standing auditors are of key importance in integrating combines or groupings of companies.

To prevent the re-formation of combines, the mission called for permanent legislation prohibiting intercorporate stockholdings, "with exceptions for banks, insurance companies, investment trusts, and possibly other types of financial institutions," prohibiting interlocking directorates, prohibition of intercorporate shareholding. It recommended that basic changes be made in Japan's income and inheritance taxes, and concluded with several proposals for creating Japanese support for the program. The policy recommendations of the Edwards Report in its FEC 230 form will be found in Appendix IX.

It was this document which, with relatively minor word changes by SWINCC, became, with State's transmittal of it to the Far Eastern Commission, FEC 230. While it was before SWINCC and the FEC, MacArthur used it as a guide to the broad program for deconcentration, but did not feel bound by specific proposals. In fact, in a number of areas what he called for in the deconcentration program diverged considerably from the document. For example, with respect to divestiture of personally held corporate securities, MacArthur limited this to the 56 *zaibatsu* family members named as "designated persons." No other person's corporate securities were involved in the divestiture program. Furthermore, MacArthur did not follow the mission recommendations about compensation of *zaibatsu* members for such securities. He met the problem of giant fortunes permitting a "buy-back" of former holdings through compensation in the form of 10-year nonnegotiable bonds. In addition he used the capital levy tax[7] as a means of reducing the fortunes of those who had benefited from the war. Also, MacArthur did not employ all of the suggestions the mission made in dispersing holding company and personal securities.

Inasmuch as the State-War Mission proposals were not transmitted to the FEC until May 1947, by which time the deconcentration program was well advanced and when there was no likelihood of redoing portions of the program already executed, it is curious to this writer why SWINCC did not adjust the document to what was actually happening. It is possible that those urging reform were fearful that rewriting would cause a loss of U.S. adherence to a deconcentration policy, but the consequence of not rewriting the document was that it was considerably more extreme than events. Further, it is curious why, since the language changes were but minor ones, it took a year to rework the document. SCAP comments on the report were received in Washington May 17, 1946; it was May 12, 1947 when the document was transmitted to the Far Eastern Commission. Its unauthorized release raised a storm of protest.

Between 1945 and 1948 American "security interests," in the name of which the U.S. undertook the Occupation of Japan, changed, and so did U.S. policy. When the Occupation began, the U.S. and its Allies were concerned with Japan as the former enemy and with the measures needed to guard against future aggression. MacArthur had the Japanese include in their new constitution a "renunciation of war" clause. That it remained, in contrast to the economic deconcentration policy, reflected the fact that constitutional law does not follow shifts of opinion in the manner of other laws.

By 1948 the U.S. was seriously doubting the assumptions on which its postwar policy in Europe and the Far East had been based. U.S. policy in Europe and the Far East had been conceived on the basis of a continuation of the wartime partnership with the Soviet Union. Taking a risk, Roosevelt treated the Soviet Union generously, hoping such a policy would be reciprocated. But this was not the way Stalin operated. The pledge of free elections in the areas of Europe surrendering to the Russian armies meant nothing to him. The pres-

[7] Cf. Chapter 3, note 43.

ence of Russian soldiers in those areas provided an opportunity for the extension of Soviet power, an opportunity Stalin had no intention of letting slip through his fingers.

Prior to the surrender of Germany, the United States at the Yalta Conference, February 4-11, 1945, pressured the Soviet Union into agreeing to enter the Pacific War within 90 days of the cessation of hostilities in Europe. Believing on the basis of faulty intelligence that the crack Kwantung Army was still intact, the U.S. mistakenly foresaw the possibility that the Kwantung Army would not surrender with the defeat of the Japanese home islands. After four years of war in Europe and the Pacific and the fierceness of a number of the island engagements, the U.S. had little enthusiasm for continuing the war against Japan, after the defeat of the home islands, onto the continent of Asia. Accordingly, in a secret agreement Roosevelt offered Stalin various inducements toward the Soviet Union's entering the Pacific War. Russia was promised Southern Sakhalin and the Kurile Islands; it was proposed that Dairen be internationalized, that the lease of Port Arthur as a Russian naval base be restored, and that the Manchurian railroads be under joint Sino-Russian administration.[8] When China learned of the continental features of the agreement, it protested that its sovereignty had been infringed. Stalin accepted the inducements, and true to this pledge, Russia entered the war against Japan on August 8, 1945. With the surrender of Japan a week later, the Soviet Union thus became one of the victors.

The difficulties that had arisen with the U.S.S.R. in the four months between the start of the quadripartite occupation of Germany and the surrender of Japan convinced the U.S. of the folly of repeating a divided Occupation. The solution that was developed, though not until the December 1945 Moscow Foreign Ministers' Conference, was the establishment of an 11-nation Far Eastern Commission which would sit in Washington as the policy-making organ of the Occupation. Its eyes and ears would be a four-nation Allied Council residing in Tokyo. A major part of the weakness of this solution was the lateness of the start. The Far Eastern Commission found itself pronouncing after, rather than before, events. As was noted in Chapter 1, it did not transmit its reworking of the American "Basic Initial Post-Surrender Directive to the Supreme Commander for the Allied Powers" until June 22, 1947, some 21 months after the start of the Occupation. The Soviet Union held a seat on the 11-nation FEC and on the four-nation Allied Council.

[8] Department of State, *United States Relations with China*, Washington, D.C., 1949, pp. 113-16.

Given the stiffening American attitude toward the U.S.S.R. and the very tough attitude MacArthur took toward the Soviet delegate in Tokyo, the seats on the FEC and the Allied council did not net the Soviet Union very tangible returns. Where it did, however, was in taking the surrender of Japanese forces in Manchuria and in Korea south to the 38th parallel. This put Soviet forces in command of these areas and the Soviet Union proceeded to carry out unilateral reparations removals.[9] Booty was good, for Japan had made enormous investments in Manchuria and Korea. Further, with worsening relations between the U.S. and the U.S.S.R. the presence of Soviet forces in Korea south to the 38th parallel resulted in 1948 in the establishment of two regimes in Korea.

Not only by late 1947 had the continuation of the wartime alliance with the Soviet Union gone sour, but events in China were raising questions as to the soundness of the U.S.'s postwar policy of basing its Far Eastern policy on a friendly China. The Communist takeover of China did not occur until 1949 (it is to be noted that unlike the situation in eastern Europe Communist control in China was accomplished by indigenous forces, not with Soviet armies). However, the military performance of the Kuomintang in 1947 and 1948 did not breed a sense of confidence in its ability to overcome the Communist forces. In fact, Mao's success in 1949 betrayed in a sense the whole meaning of the Pacific War. The issue between the U.S. and Japan in 1941 was not with authoritarian Japan's internal policies but with her external policies. The issue of the Pacific War did not concern policy differences over what was happening within Japan but over what Japan was doing outside its national borders, its attempt to gain hegemony over China, "French Indo-China," and to push on to the "Netherlands East Indies," and British Malaya, Burma, and India. China, however, was the bone of contention for the 10-year period, 1931-41. Having fought the Pacific War with its allies and won, the U.S. was beginning to sense it might be without a prize. While Japanese domination of China and areas to the south was distasteful to the U.S., it could not compare in distaste with seeing the area move into the Soviet orbit. (The possibility of antagonism developing between China and the Soviet Union, though only modestly improving things from the American standpoint, was perceived by only a handful of persons.)

The product of these developments was that the Pentagon began to think quite differently about Japan. In fact, by the end of the

[9] *Ibid.*, p. 123 and Annex 60, "Red Army 'War booty' Removals from Manchuria," pp. 596-604.

second year of the Occupation it began to propose that Japan be promoted from "ex-enemy" to partner. Ex-enemy and partner call for quite different policies. With a partner one is concerned only with its foreign policies. With Japan as an ex-enemy the U.S. and its allies were worried about the internal political forces that had produced the foreign expansion. And a number of America's allies were not nearly so ready to forget the Pacific War.

In addition to the Pentagon's desire to effect a fundamental change in the character of the Occupation in Japan, certain conservative spokesmen were urging a reversal—for different reasons. Businessmen, first permitted to enter Japan in August 1947, were dismayed at what they found. Believing, as they did, in the sanctity of private property in all circumstances, they could not bear to see legal and procedural niceties set aside, even temporarily, for the purpose of creating a competitive, free-enterprise environment. To criticize with effectiveness one needs knowledge of what one is criticizing. It was not until businessmen saw the situation with their own eyes that they acquired the knowledge needed for effective criticism. American political mores require everyone to denounce monopoly and cartels, which all conservative critics were careful to observe, but when this had been dispensed with they indicated in unmistakable terms their distaste for both the attempt to break up the giant combines and the measures being used to accomplish the objective.

Frequently the way one casts an issue for public debate has little to do with the realities of the issue, and so it was with respect to reversing American policy in Japan. Much of the public debate on reversing policy in Japan centered on the burden to the American taxpayer of the Occupation of Japan.

The financial burdens to which so many references were made did not have to do with the costs of office space, heat, housing, transportation and recreation of the Occupation forces in Japan. These were being assumed by the Japanese government and in the first years of the Occupation amounted to roughly one-third of total Japanese government expenditures.[10] The burdens had to do with the salaries of the small number of Occupation personnel, their food, and, more importantly, imports for the Japanese people under a "disease-and-unrest" formula of food, fertilizer, and certain other items. Such imports amounted to $194 million from the start of the Occupation to December 1946 and came to $404 million during calendar

[10] Army Historical Branch. In series cited, note 2, Vol. XIII, *National Government Finance*, p. 72.

1947.[11] These figures, while sizable, were not overwhelming, either by comparison with the costs of the war or with the foreign aid program the U.S. was proposing under the Marshall Plan in 1947. World War II cost the U.S. some $330 billion, of which $100 billion is estimated to be attributable to the war with Japan.[12] Since the war lasted four years, expenditures averaged out at $25 billion a year. By comparison with $25 billion, the expenditure of less than 500 million to secure the peace does not seem excessive. Nor by comparison with the U.S. aid extended to Germany, which totaled $1 billion in fiscal 1949 and $3.5 billion in fiscal 1950,[13] does the expenditure of $74 million in fiscal 1949 or $165 million in fiscal 1950[14] in rehabilitation seem unduly burdensome. The Pentagon, in urging rehabilitation funds for Japan, was eager to build a "bulwark against Communism" in the Far East.

The Basic Directive under which the Occupation was initially governed made economic recovery a Japanese responsibility. Given the mood of 1945, this was understandable, but it was a mistake. Politics and economics are much too closely related. Quite apart from "bulwarks," economic recovery in Japan was important to the taking hold of other measures of the Occupation. What enthusiasm can there be for democratic reforms when living conditions are drastically below normal and stagnant?

Whether the poor performance of the Japanese economy during 1946 and 1947—it was only about half the output of the economy during the latter 1930's[15]—was a result of Japanese ineptness or skill is not clear to the writer. Given Japanese ability to manage Japan's own affairs, it could have been the Japanese conservatives' way of arguing their case: let the situation deteriorate to the point where it was

[11] SCAP, GHQ, "History of the Nonmilitary Activities of the Occupation of Japan." *Introduction 1945 through 1951*, Office of the Chief of Military History, Washington, D.C., p. 36. American aid is cited in calendar years, 1945-50. The source for these figures is *Japanese Economic Statistics*, Bulletin 62. In 1948 American aid amounted to $461 million, in 1949, $534 million, and in 1950, $361 million.

[12] The cost of World War II is taken from a document in the Office of the Chief of Military History, based on data appearing in *Treasury Bulletin*, February, 1952, Table 6, p. 19. The estimate of Pacific War costs was made in 1964 for this writer by C. F. Romanus, Chief, General Reference Branch, Historical Services Division, Office of the Chief of Military History, Washington, D.C.

[13] Henry C. Wallich, *Mainsprings of the German Revival*, New Haven, 1955, p. 355.

[14] Department of the Army, *Program for a Self-Supporting Japanese Economy*, January 1949 (popularly referred to as the "Army Blue Book"), Table 2, "Balance of Payments Position of Japan," which shows U.S. Economic rehabilitation appropriations.

[15] See Table 17-2.

hopeless and the U.S. would enter. In its enthusiasm for getting on top of the recovery problem everything would be subordinated to that goal. Whether this gives the conservatives undue credit or no, it was the way things worked out. With increasing indication of an emphasis on economic recovery, the staff at Headquarters working on recovery enjoyed greater and greater prestige, presently the staff found reform measures interfering with the building up of the Japanese economy. There was division within Headquarters on reform.

Passage of the Deconcentration Law in December 1947 brought policy differences to a head and out in the open. Hitherto arguments had been between Army and State as the two key members of the interdepartmental Coordinating Committee determining American policy on Japan, and between different sections at Headquarters. Now, with the admission of private businessmen into Japan and businessmen doing assignments for the Department of the Army, the argument became public. The opening shot was the publication by *Newsweek*, December 1, 1947, of portions of a report which James Lee Kauffman was doing on a supposedly confidential basis for the Army.[16] Captioned "A Lawyer's Report on Japan Attacks Plan to Run Occupation . . . Far to the Left of Anything Now Tolerated in America," the article attacked not only the whole range of economic measures attempting to bring about a fairer, more democratic economy—land reform, the capital levy tax, cancellation of war indemnity payments, the labor laws, and the many measures involved in dissolving the *zaibatsu*—but challenged as well the conception of the Occupation as reform. Reform would make Japan a less attractive place for American investment:

> Heretofore the purpose of an occupation has been to demilitarize the occupied country, restore order, and protect and conserve property until a peace treaty could be concluded. . . . In Japan, however, it was decided that demilitarization included the complete reformation of the nation's ideology. One of the means for bringing this about has been the imposition of an economic theory which . . . [while] not Communistic . . . is far to the left of anything tolerated in this country.
>
> Of course, the family holding companies should have been dissolved and their hold on Japan's economic life broken. But the manner in which this is now being done makes one wonder whether . . . the remedy may not prove worse than the disease.
>
> . . . [The] purge is being used . . . as a lethal weapon in the so-

[16] *Newsweek*, December 1, 1947, pp. 36-38.

cialization of Japan. . . . By use of this purge both the Japanese Government and business have been stripped of older men of ability and experience. The purge is tragic for those who come under it. I talked with two or three of the purgees . . . and found that their funds are blocked and nothing can be done by them without the consent of SCAP. [Mr. Kauffman talked with two or three of the zaibatsu family members.] They are forbidden to work for their old companies and others are afraid to employ them.

There is grave danger that the entire Japanese economy may collapse. . . .

Japan is costing the American taxpayers millions of dollars a year. Theoretically, Japan is paying the costs of occupation. . . . But in fact, the American taxpayer is paying in the form of millions of dollars' worth of food and other necessities to Japan.

Were economic conditions otherwise, I am convinced Japan would be a most attractive prospect for American capital.

Under the heading, "The Troublesome FEC-230," *Newsweek* continued in editorial fashion:

Last spring . . . State Department economists drew up an amazingly detailed document known as FEC-230. It was submitted to the Far Eastern Commission on May 12 [1947] and communicated to General MacArthur's headquarters. . . .

In Sept. the new Under Secretary of the Army William H. Draper Jr. visited Japan. Draper, who gained an outstanding reputation as economic adviser to General Clay in Germany, became aware of FEC-230 during this visit. He and other officials found that FEC-230 not only provided for the abolition of the Zaibatsu but also for a virtual destruction of Japanese business and sale of its assets at nominal prices to selected purchasers, including Japanese labor unions, of which about one-half are Communist-dominated. On his return to Washington Draper warned the State Department that the application of the directive would make Japan a permanent ward of the U.S.

A heated discussion on the future of FEC-230 is now going on between the Army and State Departments.[17]

Passage of the "Law for the Elimination of Excessive Concentrations of Economic Power" was the issue around which the reversal of U.S. policy in Japan revolved. Prior to the *Newsweek* story, differ-

[17] Due to the absence of quotation marks, it is difficult to be sure where Mr. Kauffman leaves off and *Newsweek* begins; the length of the quotation is my surmise.

ences of view had been confined to differences between Army and State in SWINCC and within Headquarters. The differences were sharp; with its excellent intelligence on Allied Headquarters, the Japanese government was encouraged to believe it could get by without passage of the law. But, having explicitly called for the Deconcentration Law, MacArthur could not back down. Furthermore, for other reasons, he construed the American criticism to represent legitimate fears as to the impact of the legislation on recovery rather than using the impact as a smokescreen to cover a reversal of policy.

Senator Knowland of California obtained a copy of FEC 230 from a "nongovernment source," on December 15, 1947[18] and on December 19 opened the Congressional attack with a speech on the floor of the Senate. Mr. Knowland began with the required obeisance: "Although I am in complete accord with the policy of breaking up cartels and trusts in both Germany and Japan, I believe FEC 230 and other policies being followed in Japan go far beyond this. . . . If some of the doctrine set forth in FEC 230 had been proposed by the government of the U.S.S.R. or even by the labor government of Great Britain, I could have understood it. As a statement of policy being urged by the Government of the United States, I find a number of the proposals so shocking that I have today written a letter to the Secretary of State. . . ."[19]

The senator was shocked by the Deconcentration Law of December 1947, the establishment of the Holding Company Liquidation Commission, the procedures for dismantling of holding companies, and the allocation-distribution machinery replacing the wartime, cartel-like bodies (control associations) for handling distribution of materials in very short supply. He was dismayed that the U.S. could be calling for divestiture and removal from positions of responsibility of those who had exercised a "controlling voice" in the large business organizations. He was highly displeased that the amount of compensation to the former *zaibatsu* owners was to be subordinated to the interests of speed in dispersing their properties to new owners. Senator Knowland continued:

> Mr. President, it was unbelievable to me that such a document could be put forward as representing the policy of the Government of which I am a part. . . .
>
> Mr. President, the Congress and the country should be told who the originator of this proposal is. . . . The country and the Con-

[18] *Congressional Record,* January 19, 1948, p. 298.
[19] *Congressional Record,* December 19, 1947, pp. 11,686-88.

gress should be informed as to whether Gen. Douglas MacArthur was consulted in advance regarding these economic policies being followed in the name of the American Government in Japan, or whether he has been given directives from Washington which he has no choice but to carry out.

The next move in effecting the reversal was set forth by Secretary of the Army, Kenneth Royall, in a speech in San Francisco, January 6, 1948.

> It is clearly understandable—and it was fully in accord with the . . . feelings and opinions of our people—that in 1945 the main purpose of occupation should be protection against an enemy which had viciously attacked us and which had committed brutal atrocities against our troops and our private citizens.
>
> Since then new conditions have arisen—in world politics and economics, in problems of national defense, and in humanitarian considerations. These changes must now be fully taken into account in determining our future course, but it should be remembered that these developments arose in large part after the original policies were met. . . . .
>
> In the business field, the Zaibatsu, or "money cliques," dominated completely and ruthlessly the Japanese economy—through holding companies and monopolies. . . . The influence over the Japanese Government of these and other monopolies was almost unbounded, and they were linked inseparably with the militarists. . . . .
>
> The Japanese Government has been directed to prepare legislation prohibiting international cartels. Stringent antitrust and deconcentration legislation has been prepared and passed in part. A Holding Company Liquidation Commission has been established and is functioning in the supervision of the entire program.
>
> While these various steps were being taken, new developments were arising, and old factors were changing in importance. . . .
>
> But the Department of the Army and the Department of State—which shares the policy responsibility of occupation—both Departments realize that for political stability to continue and for free government to succeed in the future, there must be a sound and self-supporting economy. . . .
>
> We also realize that the United States cannot forever continue to pour hundreds of millions of dollars annually into relief funds for occupied areas. . . . Earlier programs are being reexamined—as, for example, the details of the program stated in the paper sub-

mitted some months ago to the Far Eastern Commission, and recently given wide publicity as FEC 230.

We are not averse to modifying programs in the interests of our broad objectives. . . .[20]

On January 19, 1948 Senator Knowland renewed his attack on policy in Japan with a second speech on the floor of the Senate. His target was the Deconcentration Law of December 1947[21]:

> On April 12, 1947, the "law relating to prohibition of private monopoly and methods of preserving fair trade" was promulgated and has been in effect in Japan since then. This law, which is broader and perhaps better than our own antitrust laws, prevents monopolies and combinations in restraint of trade. [Probably, however, had Mr. Knowland studied this law he would have been shocked by several of its features.]
>
> If the Government of Japan in following S.C.A.P. . . . directives was dissolving corporations for the violation of the provisions of this law, there would be a basis for commending S.C.A.P. for some big-scale trust busting. But FEC 230 and certain other policies go far, very far, beyond trust-busting. . . . .
>
> Mr. President, FEC 230 is an 18-page document outlining a "policy" . . . [on] excessive concentrations of economic power in Japan." It was submitted by the United States representatives and was circulated among the other members [of the Far Eastern Commission] on or about May 12, 1947. Section 5 of that document provides:
>
> > All individuals who have exercised controlling power in or over any excessive concentration of economic power, whether as creditors, stockholders, managers, or in any other capacity should be:
> > (a) Divested of all corporate security holdings, liquid assets, and business properties;
> > (b) Ejected from all positions of business or governmental responsibility;
> > (c) Forbidden from purchasing corporate security holdings or from acquiring positions of business or governmental responsibility at any time during the next 10 years.

Which, as we have noted, was in point of fact considerably more extreme than anything which was happening. Mr. Knowland quoted other portions of FEC 230 as well as portions of the Law Concerning

[20] As quoted by Hamm, *Deconcentration of Economic Power*, pp. 33-35.
[21] *Congressional Record*, January 19, 1948, pp. 298-99.

the Elimination of Excessive Concentrations of Economic Power. He then pointed to what to him were "socializing" trends, and concluded:

> I have a very high regard for Gen. Douglas MacArthur. His contribution to the winning of the war is known to every American. The restoration of law and order in Japan, the demilitarization and repatriation of troops were all carried out under the most skillful and intelligent leadership of the supreme commander. But the military phase of the occupation was completed months ago and was succeeded by the necessity of restoring the Japanese economy to the point where it can be self-supporting and not a continual drain upon the United States Treasury. . . . .
>
> Either originating among doctrinaire New Dealers who found their activities limited in Washington and signed up for overseas occupation service, or finding its fountainhead in the Far Eastern Commission, which initiates some policies for transmission to Gen. MacArthur, certain activities are open to serious question by both Congress and the people.

The Senator concluded with another reference to American mores: "It seems to me that in both Germany and Japan our policy should be to eliminate trusts and cartels, but not to promote socialism or a controlled economy. . . ."

It would have been interesting to get the reaction of Senator Knowland, Mr. Kauffman, and others who shared their thinking, had they realized that the Japanese Communist Party was equally unhappy with the Deconcentration Law. While American conservative spokesmen held that the Deconcentration Law would handicap foreign investment, the Japanese Communist Party saw the legislation as a means of inducing foreign capital! In the report on the deconcentration efforts of Headquarters, prepared by C. M. Hamm, it is stated,

> Under date of 22 January 1948, the Central Committee of the Japan Communist Party issued Directive No. 198 in which the Deconcentration Program was described as a plan mapped out by the Government to colonize Japan by inducing foreign capital. This directive called on all labor unions to fight this program "because it is a scheme of the traitorous, monopolistic capitalists." Directive 212 of 20 February 1948 stated that the Deconcentration Program was being run by those opposed to labor and that it actually was being "run by certain outside forces." It went on to state that it was the Communist Party's fighting policy to oppose possible readjustment under the Deconcentration Law and that through enforcement of

such Law "Japan's economy will be destroyed and the Japanese race will be put into a slavery system again." The document stated further that the Communist Party's "fight against the Deconcentration Law must not be ended with mere negotiations . . ., we must organize the public demands with the fight and get them developed into strikes, sabotage, or production management. . . ." A leaflet distributed by the Tokyo District Committee of the Japanese Communist Party on 19 March 1948 included "opposition to the Economic Deconcentration Law" as one of its slogans. Communist members of both houses of the Diet expressed themselves emphatically in opposition to the Deconcentration Law. Communist elements in the labor union of the HCLC organized a "Fight Committee" and put up many placards and issued a number of pamphlets in opposition to the Deconcentration Program.[22]

With Senator Knowland believing Law No. 207 to be near-Communist and the Japanese Communist Party regarding it as an expression of monopoly capital, one has a rather striking example of the limitations of emotion as a tool of social analysis.

MacArthur responded to the growing American criticism of policy in Japan both publicly, by replying to Senator Knowland's speech with a letter read to the Senate, and through channels by proposing the creation of a Deconcentration Review Board to determine whether the plans of reorganization under the Deconcentration Law would, in the opinion of an independent group of observers, have a retarding influence on Japanese economic recovery. Apparently MacArthur assumed the critics were concerned with the impact of the December legislation on economic recovery rather than, as we shall see, using the question of impact merely as a device for scrapping the entire combine-dissolution program.

MacArthur's reply to Senator Knowland's remarks was contained in a letter to Senator Brian McMahon, which McMahon read to the Senate on February 17, 1948. The letter, in part, stated:

> The discussion by Senator Knowland covers the policy paper of the United States (FEC 230) formulated by the State, War and Navy Departments and referred to the Far Eastern Commission. . . .
>
> For your information, however, I did publicly state my view with respect to the underlying purpose of the policy paper known as FEC 230 on New Year's Day last. . . .
>
> In any evaluation of the economic potential here in Japan, it must be understood that tearing down the traditional pyramid of eco-

[22] Hamm, p. 28.

nomic power which has given only a few families direct or indirect control over all commerce and industry, all raw materials, all transportation, internal and external, and all coal and other power sources is the first essential step to the establishment here of an economic system based upon free, private competitive enterprise which Japan has never before known.....

The Japanese people, you may be sure, fully understand the nature of the forces which have so ruthlessly exploited them in the past. They understand this economic concentration not only furnished the sinews for mounting the violence of war but that its leaders in partnership with the military shaped the national will in the direction of war and conquest.....

These things are so well understood by the Japanese people that apart from our desire to reshape Japanese life toward [a] capitalistic economy, if this concentration of economic power is not torn down and redistributed peacefully and in due order under the Occupation, there is not the slightest doubt that its cleansing will eventually occur through a blood bath and revolutionary violence. For the Japanese people have tasted freedom under the American concept and they will not willingly return to the shackles of authoritarian government and economy or resubmit otherwise to their discredited masters.[23]

To meet the criticism that the breakup of companies deemed "excessive concentrations of economic power" would retard economic recovery, MacArthur in a radio message of several parts to the Department of the Army in January 1948, proposed the establishment of a review board. Part III was headed, "Review and advice with reference to the impact of deconcentration proposed upon the operating efficiency of the enterprise as reflected in the domestic economy." Though MacArthur carefully laid out the role and functions which the Deconcentration Review Board was to perform, his stipulations, in the new climate of opinion, came to nothing:

1. It is proposed that analysis of the impact of the deconcentration action proposed by the HCLC upon the operating efficiency of the industrial, distributive, insurance and banking enterprises concerned as reflected in the domestic economy, be made by an advisory group to be designated as the Deconcentration Review Board functioning under SCAP.

2. This Board will receive from SCAP the HCLC Reorganization Order, review it together with statements of the companies

[23] *Congressional Record,* February 17, 1948, p. 136.

concerned and make an independent assessment of the situation. Its investigation will include direct conference contacts as desired.

3. *In general this Board accepts the plan of reorganization for purposes of review as it is presented* and appraises the effects of such plan on the operating efficiency of the enterprise as reflected in the economy. This provision simplifies the Board action and makes possible the most rapid review of any claims presented.

4. The Deconcentration Review Board states its findings to the Supreme Commander for the Allied Powers as follows:

a. The company may be reorganized as per plan without drastically reducing operating efficiency with manifest impairment of the economy, or

b. The company may not be reorganized as per plan without drastically reducing operating efficiency with manifest impairment of the economy, or

c. The plan contains fundamental defects preventing its use in meeting the requirements of deconcentration without drastically reducing operating efficiency with manifest impairment of the economy.

5. Based on its findings, the Board advises the Supreme Commander when, in its opinion, he should exercise his inherent right to intervene for the purpose of staying, modifying, or setting aside any action or order of the HCLC or any other Japanese governmental agency charged with implementing the deconcentration program.

6. The Supreme Commander decides whether to intervene in the HCLC action after consideration of all facts made available to him by the HCLC and the Deconcentration Review Board.[24]

Under Part VI, "Constitution of the Deconcentration Review Board," MacArthur requested that "a group of five specially selected and outstanding individuals on a policy-making level" be named. He requested that the Board should include representation of the following fields: antitrust, securities, and finance; corporate management; and industrial engineering and plant management, and that one member should be selected for his ability as a presiding officer. Further, MacArthur cautioned against any member being selected who had any relationship with firms in Japan or in the United States of a nature which might result in a prejudicial attitude toward the deconcentration program.

The radio message stated: "It is believed that the foregoing procedure will implement the directive contained in proposed revision

[24] From Part III of Message, MacArthur to Dept. of the Army, January 26, 1948, as quoted in Hamm, pp. 47-49.

of SANACC 302/2[25] [FEC 230] in a manner consonant with the intent of the United States Government, while providing proper safeguards for adequate consideration for any possible adverse effects upon industrial production, finance, price levels, or general economic recovery." The Department of the Army set about to find five persons who would be appropriate and able to accept the assignment.

By these actions MacArthur clearly felt he had met the criticism leveled against the program, for he permitted the HCLC to announce a week and a half later the designation of 257 industrial companies as excessive concentrations of economic power and a month later 68 distributive and service companies, as was discussed in the preceding chapter. His report to the Department of the Army as to how the administration of the Deconcentration Law would be handled was in fact in the same radio message in which he outlined his request for establishment of a Deconcentration Review Board. Further, from the concluding paragraph of the message it is clear that MacArthur had no intimation that FEC 230 was about to be scrapped. He interpreted the revision of SANACC 302/2 (FEC 230), which was before him for comment in January 1948,[26] as merely evidencing a shift of emphasis in U.S. policy rather than being a prelude to reversal. If MacArthur had had greater intimation of what was about to happen in Washington he would undoubtedly not have permitted the naming of such a large number of companies, for in reversing policy the cancellation of these designations could not help but be embarrassing. On March 12, 1948, however, he did learn what official Washington was thinking in unmistakable terms when he was informed that the United States had withdrawn support from FEC 230.[27]

The Draper-Johnston Mission, whose role it was to underscore the changed U.S. policy, served the purpose not only of reorienting Headquarters to the new United States policy, but also reorienting public thinking. Inasmuch as the mission, with no background on the Far East, drew up its recommendations, including a new set of reparation proposals, on the basis of two weeks in Japan, it is clear that it did not come in search of information but rather a rostrum from which to enunciate the new policy.

Technically, the visit was one by the Undersecretary of the Depart-

[25] *Ibid.*, p. 30.

[26] Inasmuch as SANACC 302/2 (the superficially rewritten policy recommendations of the State-War Mission on Japanese Combines) had been superseded by 302/3 and 302/4 by April 30, 1947, it is curious why MacArthur had 302/2 for comment in January 1948, as asserted in the series cited in note 2, Part B, "Deconcentration of Economic Power," p. 23. The April 1947 date is taken from the cover page of the document as supplied to me by the Washington National Records Center.

[27] *Ibid.*, p. 24.

ment of the Army, Mr. Draper, who was advised by a group of big business representatives known as the Johnston Committee. The Johnston Committee consisted of Percy H. Johnston, chairman of the Chemical Bank and Trust Co., Paul G. Hoffman, formerly president of Studebaker, who had just been named administrator of the European Recovery Program, Robert F. Loree, chairman of the National Foreign Trade Council and formerly vice president of the Guaranty Trust Company, and Sidney H. Scheuer, senior partner of Scheuer and Co. However, the committee's report was to the Secretary and was officially published as the Johnston Report. Mr. Draper, who in civilian life was an investment banker with Dillon Reed, had been an economic advisor in the Germany Occupation before becoming Undersecretary in 1947. He was influential in effecting a reversal of United States decartelization policy in Germany, and now turned his attention to United States policy in Japan.

The Johnston Committee saw the "problem" of Japan in 1948 as one of economic recovery. The focus on recovery (including Japan as a site for foreign investment) suggests that in the committee's judgment other problems had essentially been met. Its concern with this issue is shown in the following excerpts from its report.

> The first economic need of Japan is increased production. . . . The Committee, therefore, looked into the present obstacles. . . . The three main deficiencies in the physical means available to Japan are: (1) lack of essential raw materials, (2) the bad condition of many existing factories, (3) the poor state of transport. . . . .[28]
>
> Despite all physical limitations, production could even now be at a higher level, were it not for other deterrent influences affecting adversely the desire to produce, work, plan and invest. . . . .
>
> The threat of removal for reparations hangs over much of Japan's industry, especially heavy industry. . . .
>
> Another element of uncertainty derives from the changes being effected in the control of Japanese industry. A very large part of Japanese industry before the war was dominated either by the government or by private monopolistic groups. . . . a small number of family groups, through holding companies and controlled banks, owned and directed a large part of all Japanese industry, shipping and finance. . . .
>
> The period of uncertainty caused by this economic reform should be made short and the area of uncertainty lessened as rapidly as possible. The possible disturbing effect should be allayed by care

[28] Report to the Secretary of the Army, "Report on the Economic Position and Prospects of Japan and Korea and the Measures Required to Improve Them" ["Johnston Committee" report], April 26, 1948, p. 4.

not to hurt production, and by limiting reorganization to the minimum necessary to insure reasonable competition.[29]

Various obstacles to foreign investment remain which must be removed before any substantial flow of such investment can be anticipated. . . . (1) Protection of foreign investments from confiscation and discriminatory taxation, (2) reasonable freedom of export of dividends and profits, (3) a tax structure which would permit earning and payment of reasonable profits, (4) permission to foreign nationals to control enterprises proportionately to their investments.[30]

The shift in the climate of opinion with respect to Japan in the change from ex-enemy to partner is clearly seen in the matter of reparation removals, for reparation policy was of course also integrally involved in the softening attitude. During the ex-enemy period, proposals for reparation removal were high; now that partnership was being considered, proposals were strikingly reduced. Any number of reparation-removal studies were made. The recommendations of three are cited—that of the Pauley Mission in the fall of 1945; the proposals made by Overseas Consultants, Inc. during a five-month study in the fall of 1947 and into 1948 (with which Mr. Kauffman was associated); and Draper-Johnston Mission recommendations, in March 1948. Summarized, these are:[31]

Recommended Removals for Reparations
(in thousands 1939 yen)

| | *Fall 1945* | *March 1948* | *April 1948* |
|---|---|---|---|
| Industry total | 990,033 | 172,269 | 102,247 |
| Primary war facilities | 1,475,887 | 1,475,887 | 560,000 |
| | 2,465,920 | 1,648,146 | 662,247 |

Again the U.S. found its Allies far less enthusiastic about whittling down reparation removals than it was itself. The Far Eastern Commission was unable fully to resolve the issue which had to be settled by Japan, in certain cases, bilaterally in individual peace treaties.

[29] *Ibid.*, pp. 4-6.

[30] *Ibid.*, p. 16. The committee assumed in the circumstance of favorable economic opportunity that the Japanese government would welcome direct foreign investment. With the benefit of hindsight it is evident that the Japanese government, 20 years later, still does not view direct investments enthusiastically. A limited number of direct investments have been approved (for discussion cf. Chapter 16); but in less than a handful of instances has 51% stock control been allowed. Further, the limited opening of the Japanese economy to outside direct investment has occurred only because of strong outside pressure such as that exerted by the OECD.

[31] Jerome B. Cohen, "Reform versus Recovery," in *Far Eastern Survey*, June 23, 1948, p. 140.

# 8.

## The Dissolution of Two Trading Giants; Financial Institutions Untouched

THE effort to get authority for the HCLC to reorganize operating companies created a host of critics of the deconcentration effort in the United States and resulted in a dramatic reversal of U.S. policy, but the dissolution of the two trading giants, clearly the most drastic action taken in the whole deconcentration program, occasioned no criticism at all! By the stroke of his pen, July 3, 1947, MacArthur caused Mitsui Trading and Mitsubishi Trading to be dissolved. Was the absence of criticism to be explained by ignorance of the event; endorsement of dissolution over reorganization; disapproval of trading companies; or the loyalty of Republican critics to a fellow Republican? The decision to call for dissolution was taken within Headquarters itself. It was not the product of the State-War Mission or any other advisory group. It is not clear to the writer how to interpret this seemingly strange behavior. It is difficult to believe that critics were unaware that dissolution had been ordered, and it is difficult to believe that critics favored dissolution over reorganization. It is doubtful that the critics so disapproved of trading companies that they would endorse their dissolution. Seemingly, the only explanation is that supporters of MacArthur did not wish to embarrass him in a situation where responsibility was clearly his alone.

The directive ordering the dissolution, Scapin 1741, contained highly restrictive terms concerning successor companies. The severity of its conditions will be seen in the following excerpts taken from the HCLC *Final Report*:

> 2c. Prohibit any persons who have been officers, directors, advisors, branch managers of foreign or domestic branches, or department or section heads of said companies, during a period of ten years prior to the date of this memorandum, from associating together to form a new company, or more than two being employed by or advising any one existing company or company hereafter formed.
>
> 2d. Prohibit any group of employees in addition to those specified in paragraph c above, being employed by any one existing

company, or any company hereafter formed, without permission of the Holding Company Liquidation Commission or such other agencies as may be designated. The Holding Company Liquidation Commission or such other agencies shall grant such permission if it shall conclusively appear that a possibility of re-creation of the dissolved companies or other monopolistic combinations shall not result.

2e. Prohibit any trading company in which any officers or employees of both said companies shall be employed from occupying any office now used or formerly used by either of said companies as a business office, and further prohibit any company from using the firm name Mitsubishi Trading Company or Mitsui Trading Company or any resemblance thereof.

Fragmentation could only result from such stated conditions. In the weeks and months following this order some 200 successor companies were established out of each of the two companies.[1] SCAP's action against the Mitsui and Mitsubishi Trading companies seems harsh, but let us note their role within the combine structures and how their activities deterred entry.

While earlier in Japan's modernization, cultural and language difficulties no doubt contributed to the establishment of companies specializing in transactions with foreigners, the more important reason for the establishment of trading companies had to do with the logic of combine enterprise. Through the device of the "sole agency contract" the key subsidiaries of the combine bound themselves to buy and sell through their combine's trading company. Thus in the Mitsui combine, Mitsui Mining, Mitsui Shipbuilding, Mitsui Chemical, and the other subsidiaries did not buy and sell on their own but through the Mitsui Trading Company. In this way the bargaining strength of the entire combine could be brought into the terms of each purchase and sale. The trading companies accepted outsiders' accounts but only to the extent that they did not interfere with any of the combine's existing or planned activities. The pattern in the West was that trading companies rose to power via political franchise—such companies as the British East India Co. and the Hudson's Bay Co. comes to mind. In Japan trading companies achieved dominance on the basis of the sole-agency contract.

Let us note a few examples of how such sole-agency contracts operated; the Mitsui combine is illustrative. The quotation is from my earlier study based on copies of the contracts filed with GHQ-SCAP.

[1] *Oriental Economist*, "Zaibatsu Revival?", March 1958, for Mitsui Trading, p. 154; the same article continued, May 1958, p. 241 for Mitsubishi Trading.

*Contracts with Core Companies*

Trading's contract with Mitsui Mining is illustrative of an arrangement with a first-line designated subsidiary. The "gentleman's agreement" first concluded in 1889 between Trading and Mining gave to Trading an exclusive sales agency for the entire output of coal by Mining for all markets, domestic and foreign. The commission averaged 2 1/2% of the selling price. Building upon the sizeable percentage of total production which Mining accounted for, Trading negotiated selling arrangements with Hokkaido Colliery and Steamship Company following the latter's inclusion within the Mitsui orbit. The contract with Hokkaido which went through several changes but remained substantially unaltered from its 1927 form gave sole agency rights on Hokkaido's coal to Trading for all markets with the exception of the island of Hokkaido where the right was not exclusive. . . .

Further strengthening its position in coal, Trading gained exclusive selling rights in coal from Mining's subsidiaries. It had exclusive arrangements with Keeling Coal Mining, Matsushima Coal Mining, Yamato Coal Mining, Pacific Coal Mining, Hainan Coal Mining and Chunghsing Coal Mining. . . . The cumulative effect of these various arrangements was to give Trading some 30% of Japan's total output of coal with which to bargain. Mitsubishi Trading with control over some 15% was Trading's nearest rival. . . .[2]

The contract with Japan Flour Milling will serve to illustrate Trading's arrangements with a second line designated subsidiary. Japan Flour Milling and the somewhat larger Nisshin Flour Milling were Japan's two major flour milling companies. In 1940, Japan Flour Milling accounted for 25% of the wheat flour produced in Japan. Trading had a sole agency agreement with Flour Milling covering its entire output of wheat flour and bran for not only the domestic market, but markets abroad. The agreement provided that Flour Milling would turn over any inquiries concerning its produce to Trading which alone was entitled to handle sales. On the other hand, Trading pledged Flour Milling that it would handle no other domestic flour milling business without Flour Milling's consent. It was agreed that prices would be determined by mutual consent. The fee rate was dependent on whether sales were in the Japanese empire exclusive of Formosa or abroad. In the former, the rate was one percent, in the latter, one and a quarter percent. . . .[3]

[2] Hadley, "Concentrated Business Power," pp. 230-32.
[3] *Ibid.*, p. 232.

*A Contract with a Former Subsidiary*

Examination of contracts with companies over which the Mitsui combine exercised, in its own words, "absolutely no control" is revealing. Oji Paper . . . will serve as illustration. . . .

Oji retained domestic sales, while its sole agency contract with Trading concerning export markets (reserving even certain export areas to Oji), reflected greater independence of action than the previously examined subsidiary contracts. Oji's explanation for handling domestic sales itself was that it found an important part of its domestic market in towns and villages. It alleged that Trading's college graduate men were not able to press sales in these rural communities as effectively as it could do itself. How much weight should be given this explanation is problematical. Oji's grant of sole agency rights abroad to Trading with the exception of three reserved areas—Manchuria, Kwantung Leased Territory and the Netherlands East Indies—should be interpreted as the "quid" of a "pro quo" bargain. In return for giving over the selling rights of its products to Trading, Oji significantly reduced its foreign competition because the sole agency contract bound Trading to handle the products abroad of no other paper producers—domestic or foreign. With its worldwide connections, Trading had it quite within its power to import into Japan and the other Far Eastern Countries the cheaper Scandinavian and Belgium papers. Mitsui holding company (as the result of appropriate Oji pressure) disapproved of Trading's exercising that right within Japan but abroad was not adverse to extracting certain concessions from Oji.

Under Trading's arrangement with Oji, the commission fee was made dependent on Trading's sales efforts. Sales of "standing stock" (stock stored at Tientsin, Shanghai, Hankow, Hongkong, and Canton), the size of which was based on average normal sales, netted two percent. Where "market expansion" was involved Oji granted Trading a three percent sales commission. Oji's independent spirit was nowhere better reflected than in Article 16 of the agreement which stated, "If and when required, a member or members of the staff of 'A' [Oji] shall be dispatched to any branch of 'B' [Trading] to give support to negotiations and other affairs and to inspect the account books and documents concerned."[4]

*Extending Selling Arrangements through Patents*

In addition to its various exclusive sales arrangements attained through acquisition of sole agency rights, Trading had further ex-

[4] *Ibid.*, pp. 235-36.

clusive sales arrangements through its extensive patent holdings, since patents confer a monopoly not only on the manufacturing process but also on use and sale. The agreements between Trading and Aktieselskabet Burmeister and Wain, . . . illustrate this type of arrangement.

The Burmeister-Trading agreement provided exclusive manufacture and sales rights on the Burmeister and Wain type of Diesel engines to Trading for the area of Japan, Korea, Formosa, Sakhalin and Manchukuo, although Burmeister and Wain reserved the right, if they so chose, to sell and deliver in "the territory" all varieties of their Diesel engine manufactured by themselves in Copenhagen. Also they reserved to themselves and their other licensees the right to effect in any part of "the territory" repairs to any vessel using any kind of Diesel engine manufactured by them. Correlatively the right was extended to Trading to effect repairs in any part of the world on any vessel using a Diesel engine manufactured by it.

The purpose of the agreement was stated to be "to promote in the territory the use of the Burmeister and Wain Diesel engines." Trading bound itself "to work energetically" toward this end. Restrictive in character the fee arrangement bound Trading not only to obtain Burmeister and Wain's permission for dealing with other types of Diesel engines but also to pay Burmeister and Wain a royalty "on all Diesel engines, whether they are of Burmeister and Wain's design or not, manufactured or dealt in by the Licensee." The agreement was made irrevocable to August 13, 1951. Although Trading was not free to transfer the license without prior consent nor similarly to sublicense, it was agreed and understood "that the licensee grants and delegates all his rights with obligations under this agreement exclusively to his affiliated company, Kabushiki Kaisha Tama Zosensho. . . ." (Kabushiki Kaisha Tama Zosensho became Mitsui Shipbuilding.) This latter provision should be taken to apply only to manufacturing privileges, since Article 1 of the supplement to the Agency Agreement provided that Mitsui (i.e. Trading) shall as sole agents in Japan of Burmeister's always work to the best of their abilities to sell Diesel engines manufactured in Copenhagen by Burmeister when they cannot sell engines of Burmeister design built by Kabushiki Kaisha Tama Zosensho under the license agreement.[5]

*Nakajima Aircraft.* Mitsui Trading's arrangement with Nakajima Aircraft represented a buying and selling arrangement with an os-

[5] *Ibid.*, pp. 238-40.

tensible outsider which seemingly began out of the credit advantages which Trading represented to Nakajima but which was further strengthened by means of patent technology. Again quotation is from the writer's earlier study.

> Nakajima Aircraft, founded in 1920 by Nakajima Chikuhei, a navy lieutenant of World War I, with stock entirely held by the Nakajima family, grew with exceptional speed from the latter 1920's. During the Pacific War, Nakajima and Mitsubishi were Japan's principal producers of aircraft and aero engines.
>
> Trading's first sole agency agreement with Nakajima was concluded in 1920 giving Trading sole agency for "the 'Nakajima' type airplane and its accessories" for the territory of Japan. Not until 1937 did Trading agree at the insistence of the Army to relinquish its sales agency with respect to sales to the Army and not until 1940, at the insistence of the Navy, did Trading relinquish its privileges covering sales to the Navy. It was noteworthy that in the thirties when Trading was negotiating numerous aircraft manufacturing licensing agreements from different American corporations—Bendix Aviation, Chance Vought, Douglas Aircraft, Hamilton Standard Propeller—that in its license agreement with the Fokker Aircraft Corporation concerning the Fokker super-universal airplane engine the contract read in part, "Mitsui shall not divulge or entrust to any person not directly connected with its own or its subsidiary (Nakajima Aircraft Works and/or other subsidiaries) technical staff and responsible sales or manufacturing personnel, the drawings, specifications or other data provided by Fokker. . . ."
>
> . . . The explanation for Trading's remarkable performance in getting a sole agency for a product needing no agent and with a company in which no part of the combine held any stock apparently lay in the technological and financial advantages Nakajima derived from the arrangement. From the point of view of technology there was . . . distinct advantage in being related to Mitsui Trading, which was Japan's principal acquirer of America's aviation technology if not also of Germany's. From the point of view of finance there was advantage in selling to the Government through Trading. The Japanese Army and Navy, like government agencies elsewhere . . . [did not pay] for their purchases in cash. Settlement of accounts sometimes took up to three months. Financial stringency was [thus] an additional factor leading Nakajima to make its sales through Trading where it could obtain payment on the day of delivery. . . . Under the 1923 agreement the fee was .25%; under the

1932 agreement it was .2%. Under the 1940 agreement which of course, excluded sales to the Army and Navy, it varied depending upon the size of the contract—under 1,000,000 yen, 5%; 1 to 5,000,000, 3%, over 5,000,000, 1%.[6]

From the point of view of Nakajima Aircraft there was advantage to the arrangement. On its sales to the government, Nakajima in this way could get immediate settlement and on more attractive terms from Trading than from the Mitsui Bank or other commercial banks. This is to say, Trading's fee was lower than bank interest. Further, Nakajima put itself in a preferred access position to the aircraft and aero-engine technology that Trading was buying throughout the world. From the Mitsui side, the arrangement gave the combine a further key product line with which to argue its views either in commercial transactions or when pressing the Government with some request. The price that Nakajima paid for the credit terms on Government sales was giving Trading exclusive selling rights throughout the "territory of Japan." There are those who may argue that one cannot have a subsidiary relationship without stock participation in some form, but when a company entirely gives up its right to sell its own product, then, however classifiers wish to classify it, it has in a very real sense put itself in a subsidiary position to the firm marketing its product. So it was in the case of Nakajima Aircraft with Mitsui Trading.

The consequence of bargaining as Mitsui Trading did, with the strength of the whole of the Mitsui combine, was a trading position of preeminence both within Japan and between Japan and foreign countries, as well as a position of a "major" in "entrepot" or third countries' trade. The writer does not have information with respect to the prewar position of Mitsui Trading in buying and selling within Japan, but Table 8-1 indicates the position of the company in Japan's foreign trade. There it will be seen that in 1941 Trading accounted for better than a fifth of the nation's imports and an eighth of total exports.

### *"Entrepot" Trade*

Quotation is once again from the writer's earlier study.

The surprising fact is that prior to 1939 the most important aspect of Mitsui Trading's foreign activities was its trade between foreign countries in which the trade did not relate to Japan at all. In the years shortly preceding 1939, this entrepot trade amounted to Y1.2 billion. The main avenues of this entrepot trade were between

[6] *Ibid.*, pp. 236-38.

Table 8-1: MITSUI TRADING'S POSITION IN THE TOTAL EXPORT AND IMPORT TRADE OF JAPAN PROPER, 1936-45

| *Year* | *Percent of Japan's Exports (value terms)* | *Percent of Japan's Imports (value terms)* |
|---|---|---|
| 1936 | 9.7 | 12.3 |
| 1937 | 10.7 | 16.9 |
| 1938 | 10.3 | 16.7 |
| 1939 | 11.8 | 16.8 |
| 1940 | 10.4 | 22.0 |
| 1941 | 12.8 | 21.8 |
| 1942 | 10.8 | 21.3 |
| 1943 | 9.1 | 15.5 |
| 1944 | 5.8 | 9.2 |
| 1945 | 5.7 | 6.3 |

Source: Data submitted to SCAP, as reproduced in Hadley, *Concentrated Business Power*, p. 216.

China and Manchuria, Australia and China, India and China, Philippines and China, China and the United States, Manchuria and Southwest Asia, and Southwest Asia and the United States. Mitsui Trading's activities in Singapore rubber and tin were an example of this trade. Because rubber and tin were commodities of a speculative nature, uncertainties in the business were high. Mitsui Trading, however, was able to do a successful business in this field, more so frequently than were British merchants. The explanation would appear to involve several factors. Trading with its combine backing enjoyed unlimited credit facilities from the Big Five Banks of the City of London until, . . . 1937, the year of the outbreak of the China War. To Trading's great credit advantage should be added the fact that it could ship on its own fleet of fast running Diesel motorships on which it could get a special price, that it could insure with a Mitsui insurance company from which it could expect special consideration, and that it had its own branches or subsidiaries to handle the cargo on its arrival in the United States or England. It was therefore, not surprising that independent businesses, either Japanese or Western found it a formidable opponent.[7]

[7] *Ibid.*, pp. 212-13.

*Examples of Price Discrimination in Insurance*

Price discrimination, in favor of subsidiaries within the combine and against outsiders, was the rule by which combine enterprise operated. As buyer and seller for the whole of the combine, one saw price discrimination with particular clarity in the operations of the trading companies. Let us note the kind of financial arrangements which could be played between Mitsui Trading and Mitsui's two insurance companies.

> Trading's arrangement with Taisho Fire Marine, a second-line designated subsidiary, is illustrative of the type of preferential understandings possible within a combine organization. A tacit understanding existed between the two companies whereby Trading agreed to do all its insuring with Taisho, that is to say, all insuring both at home and abroad. The significance of this arrangement can be better appreciated if it is remembered that in 1939, Trading's total foreign commercial activities reached close to two billion yen. As would be expected under this arrangement, Taisho reinsured this business with Tokyo Marine Insurance (Tokyo Kaijo Kasai), the great Mitsubishi company . . . [and] with other Japanese or foreign underwriters. Nevertheless, Taisho was able to come off with the greater part of the premium payments even when permitting Trading a reduction of 15% of the "general tariff" and 10% on contracts under any other tariff. Trading also found the arrangement satisfactory not only with respect to the reduced fees but also with respect to the dividends earned on close to one-third of Taisho's stock. Taisho's profit rate for the year ending December 1940 amounted to 135%. Although Tokyo Marine Insurance (Mitsubishi) dominated the non-life field in Japan, Taisho was one of the four non-life companies in 1940 with assets above fifty million yen.
>
> Trading's agreement with Life Insurance, another "directly controlled" subsidiary, provides a further illustration of a preferential intra-combine arrangement. Life Insurance was established in 1926 when Dan arranged for the Mitsuis to acquire the insignificant Takasago Life Insurance Company which was transformed into Mitsui Life Insurance. The first president of the company was Trading's Osaka manager, Noyori, who, within a year or two, worked out an arrangement between Trading and Life which, from the point of view of the House and combine proved very satisfactory. Trading agreed to direct the patronage of its thousands of employees to Life Insurance (in 1945, Trading had eighteen thousand employees, over half of whom were Japanese) by the device of offer-

ing employees monetary inducements to insure with Life Insurance, for which it was, of course, reimbursed by Life Insurance. Depending upon the size of the policy taken out with Life Insurance (with no other life insurance company, of course, did Trading have such an arrangement) Trading would pay a portion of the premium. For example, if the premium in question were one thousand yen, Trading might offer one hundred yen. Life Insurance prospered under these arrangements. With a paid-up capital of Y500,000 in 1941, and authorized capital of 2,000,000, Life Insurance controlled assets of Y193,057,000 and managed to earn profits in that year of 1,349%. Of a total of forty thousand shares the House and Takakimi held 28,400. In 1944, its insurance policies amounted to Y3,275,000,000.[8]

This then was the background against which SCAP made the decision to call for dissolution of the two trading giants, Mitsui Trading and Mitsubishi Trading. Clearly it was basic to the objectives of the deconcentration program that the power of these two companies, which far exceeded other trading companies, be scaled down, for not only were they a key combine-control device but, as buyer and seller for their affiliated companies, arch practitioners of price discrimination. Should Headquarters, however, have not only called for their dissolution, but imposed such harsh terms on successor companies? Opinions will differ, but in my judgment this action was disproportionate to other actions taken. As an administrator one seeks to treat similar cases similarly. In the stipulations governing successor companies the two giant trading companies were dealt with more severely.

While entry was deterred by conglomerate firms occupying major positions in several markets; while entry was deterred by buying and selling through trading companies so that the weight of the entire combine might be brought to bear in each transaction; entry was further fundamentally deterred by industrial companies having affiliated banks and other financial institutions from which it was possible to obtain preferential access to credit.

It might almost be said that the distinguishing feature between the Big Four and Other Six was the presence, and conversely the absence, of a commercial bank. Each of the Big Four had a commercial bank; one of the Other Six had a commercial bank. Each of the Big Four had a trust bank; none of the Other Six had a trust bank. Each of the Big Four had insurance companies; four of the Other Six had insurance companies. *Zaibatsu* subsidiaries relied on the combined fi-

[8] *Ibid.*, pp. 244-45.

nancial resources of their affiliated financial institutions. Needless to say, subsidiaries of the Big Four had considerably more on which to rely than subsidiaries of the Other Six. It would be my strong guess that an important ingredient in the differing growth rates of the Big Four and the Other Six in the war economy was the product of this differential financial base. Using the data from the tables in Chapter 3, we find that between 1937 and 1945 and between 1941 and 1945, the two groups, measured in terms of paid-up capital, expanded as follows: 1937-45; Big Four, 235%, Other Six, 184%; 1941-45: Big Four, 204%, Other Six, 164%.

Internally the combines used credit extension as a means of further "tying" their packages. The conditions under which credit was offered applicant subsidiaries provided an additional opportunity to supervise their operations.

While supervision through credit was the internal consequence of affiliated financial institutions, the public consequence was to make access to credit different depending on whether the applicant was an insider or outsider. While it would not seem likely that combine banks would have frequently offered different rates of interest on borrowings to affiliated and nonaffiliated companies (though this may have occurred on occasion), there are more variables than the rate of interest by which favoritism can be expressed. The most basic of all is access to credit—will the bank make the loan? In addition, terms of repayment can markedly differ, the same with opportunity for renewal. Though interest charges to affiliated companies and interest charges to those outside may, in terms of the books, have been identical, credit was not offered impartially. The continuing duality of the Japanese economy is evidence of this observation. In the case of the Mitsubishi combine, its commercial bank had frankly been described as an "organ" (kikan) bank.[9] During the early development of the combine, its bank was but a department of the top-holding company—until the expansion growing out of the World War I years led to separate incorporation. When a bank is but a department of a top-holding company it is abundantly clear what the uses of its credits are conceived to be.

In 1945 what did the structure of Japan's banking and related financial markets look like? Neither by the measure of deposits nor paid-in capital would it at first appear that there was striking concentration in commercial banking. In September 1945 the Big Four com-

[9] Cf. for example, Economic Planning Agency, *Fund Acquisition and Control in the Mitsubishi Zaibatsu* (Keizai Kikaku Cho, *Mitsubishi Zaibatsu ni okeru, Shikin Chotatsu to Shihai*), Tokyo, 1958, p. 89.

mercial banks accounted for 48.5 percent of total deposits.[10] Individually, the percentages were: Mitsui, 12.9; Mitsubishi, 11.8; Sumitomo, 10.2; Yasuda, 13.5. Coincidentally, by the measure of paid-in capital, as seen in the tables in Chapter 3, their position was virtually identical—48.0 percent. In terms of paid-in capital, the Big Four and the Other Six in banking, trust banking, and insurance in 1945 were as follows:

| | *Big Four* | *Other Six* |
|---|---|---|
| banking | 48.0% | 2.4% |
| trust banking | 85.4 | 0.0 |
| insurance | 51.2 | 9.1 |

The above figures, for the 10, however, give an inadequate description of concentration among financial institutions because of their failure to reflect two factors. First, in Japan, there were and still are two commercial banking markets; second, the figures do not convey the strength that comes from cumulating financial resources out of a commercial bank, a trust bank, a life insurance company and a marine and fire insurance company.

The existence in Japan of two commercial banking markets, one made up of city banks and the other of provincial banks, stems from differences in their relationship with the Bank of Japan and from the scale of their branch banking. Although there is nothing in the legislation governing the Bank of Japan which prevents it from lending to provincial banks, it, in point of practice, lends only to city banks.[11] The ability of the city banks to borrow from the Bank of Japan means that the city banks have far greater resources and strength behind them. The lending authority of provincial banks, by contrast, is limited by their deposit position.

Similarly, city banks and provincial banks are distinguished by the scale of their branch banking. While legally, provincial banks are not restricted in their branches to the province of their head office, provincial banks do not have branches outside the general region. By contrast, city banks have branches throughout the country.

Out of these circumstances two quite distinct banking markets have developed. City banks and long-term credit banks finance the greater part of the needs of the capital-intensive sector of the economy; provincial banks finance medium and small-scale industry and commerce. (For 1964 this point will be seen with particular clarity in Table 12-

[10] Ehrlich, *The Role of Banking in Japan's Economic Development*, p. 268, indicates that the statistics were derived from individual bank balance sheets provided her by the Bank of Japan. The Mitsui figure is that of the Teikoku Bank.

[11] I am indebted to discussion with Royama Shoichi for this point.

11. Accordingly, if one wishes to know the strength of the combine banks at the end of the war, it would be more appropriate to gain percentage figures for deposits and paid-in capital from city banks and long-term credit banks rather than city banks and provincial banks. Unfortunately, so far as I have been able to determine, the statistics do not come in this form. If this were done, however, it is evident that the position of the Big Four in banking would be found to be quite different than the foregoing statistics suggest.

In addition, the foregoing statistics fail to indicate the cumulative financial power resulting from an affiliated trust bank, an affiliated life insurance company, and an affiliated marine and fire insurance company. Data indicating the extent of the financial loans from these institutions to combine companies are not available for the predeconcentration period, when, if anything, one might have expected proportionately even higher amounts than today. To gain some feel for the contribution of the "other financial institutions" to the operations of present-day groups, and by extension to the combines, I have compiled Tables 8-2, 8-3, and 8-4, which show borrowings during the first half of 1961 for present-day "core subsidiaries" of the Mitsubishi, Mitsui and Sumitomo groupings. (In Chapter 11 these present-day groupings are discussed.)

It will be seen from the tables that one cannot speak of the contribution of "other financial institutions" more specifically than that they are "substantial." If comparison is made of the amounts of credit extended by the bank and *other financial institutions*, it will be seen in the Mitsubishi grouping that other financial institutions contributed close to two-thirds as much as the Mitsubishi Bank; that in the Mitsui group, half as much as the Mitsui Bank; in the Sumitomo grouping, that they were even somewhat larger. The tables make clear the resultant scale of financing from the combined resources of the grouping. In the Mitsubishi grouping, 9 of the 20 companies listed obtained 50% and above of their credit needs from Mitsubishi institutions. In the Mitsui grouping, over half of the companies listed gained more than one-third of their credit needs from Mitsui institutions. In the Sumitomo grouping, 7 of the 10 companies listed obtained 45% or more of their credit needs from Sumitomo sources. The tables make clear what it means to have financial institutions within a grouping.

It would be extremely interesting to have reliable figures for both the predeconcentration period and for the post-Occupation period on combine financing the other way around, that is, the proportion of combine bank credit that has been extended to combine firms. But for the pre-1945 period it is difficult to get data on bank loans, and for

**Table 8-2:** BORROWINGS FROM THE MITSUBISHI BANK, MITSUBISHI TRUST BANK, MITSUBISHI INSURANCE COMPANIES BY MITSUBISHI CORE COMPANIES AS A PERCENTAGE OF THEIR TOTAL BORROWINGS, SEPT. 1961; ALSO LARGEST OUTSIDE BORROWING IN PERCENTAGE

Unit: 1,000,000 yen

| *Company* | *Total Borrowings* | *Mitsubishi Bank* | *Other Mitsubishi Financial Institutions* | *Mitsubishi Percentage* | *Largest Outside Borrowing* | *Percentage* |
|---|---|---|---|---|---|---|
| Mitsubishi Mining | 12,459 | 1,484 | 754 | 17.96 | Industrial Bank | 8.80 |
| M. Metal Mining | 5,325 | 1,702 | 926 | 49.35 | Industrial Bank | 18.05 |
| M. Heavy Ind. Reorg. | 44,772 | 7,522 | 5,396 | 28.86 | Sumitomo Bank | 10.16 |
| M. Japan Heavy Ind. | 22,827 | 4,690 | 4,127 | 38.64 | Industrial Bank | 7.74 |
| M. Shipbuilding | 32,246 | 5,661 | 2,164 | 24.27 | Industrial Bank | 6.7 |
| Mitsubishi Electric | 38,867 | 6,188 | 4,915 | 30.11 | Long-Term Credit Bk. | 12.67 |
| Mitsubishi Steel | 3,681 | 1,498 | 1,576 | 83.51 | Toho Bank | 3.26 |
| M. Steel Mfg. | 2,856 | 671 | 545 | 42.57 | Industrial Bank | 7.49 |
| M. Chemical Machinery | 461 | 291 | 122 | 89.56 | Daiwa Bank | 3.26 |
| | | | | | Sanwa Bank | 3.26 |
| M. Chemical Industry | 19,290 | 2,284 | 2,777 | 26.24 | Industrial Bank | 11.10 |
| Asahi Glass | 11,783 | 4,000 | 700 | 39.89 | Hypothec Bank | 14.43 |
| | | | | | Fuji Bank | 14.43 |
| Mitsubishi Rayon | 11,217 | 2,792 | 1,475 | 40.04 | Industrial Bank | 12.83 |
| Edogawa Chemical | 3,190 | 966 | 844 | 56.74 | Industrial Bank | 9.40 |
| Mitsubishi Oil | 11,364 | 2,360 | 3,385 | 55.43 | Industrial Bank | 16.40 |
| Mitsubishi Paper | 4,780 | 1,165 | 1,385 | 53.35 | Toyo Bank | 7.32 |
| Mitsubishi Cement | 6,577 | 1,134 | 2,733* | 75.01 | Long-Term Credit Bk. | 13.65 |
| Mitsubishi Trading | 65,142 | 15,778 | 3,002 | 28.83 | Tokyo Bank | 13.28 |
| Mitsubishi Warehouse | 1,744 | 885 | 509 | 79.93 | Eighty-Second Bank | 5.16 |
| Mitsubishi Shipping | 7,461 | 425 | 495 | 12.33 | Industrial Bank | 5.13 |
| M. Real Estate | 10,788 | 2,727 | 4,026 | 62.60 | Long-Term Credit Bk. | 5.38 |
| Total | 316,830 | 64,223 | 41,856 | 33.48** | | |

*Plus 409 from Mitsubishi Mining.

**Calculated from totals, not an average of individual entries.

Source: Economic Investigation Council, *Research on Business Groupings* (Keizai Chosa Kyokai, *Keiretsu no Kenkyu*), Tokyo, 1962, pp. 44-50.

Note: Two of the core companies, Mitsubishi Monsanto Chemical and Mitsubishi Petrochemical, have not been entered in the table because the source from which this information is taken does not list them.

the present period it is difficult to know the full range of affiliates. Those who know don't talk and those who talk don't have adequate information. Occasionally today one comes upon figures for "affiliates" of Mitsui, Mitsubishi and Sumitomo, but these are very likely to turn out not to be affiliates in general but the companies successor to the former "designated subsidiaries." For example, in the discussion of Mitsubishi Bank in *Mitsui, Mitsubishi, Sumitomo*, the statement occurs: "Loans to those concerns which were the affiliates of former

Table 8-3: BORROWINGS FROM THE MITSUI BANK, MITSUI TRUST BANK, MITSUI INSURANCE COMPANIES BY MITSUI CORE COMPANIES AS A PERCENTAGE OF THEIR TOTAL BORROWINGS, SEPT. 1961; ALSO LARGEST OUTSIDE BORROWING IN PERCENTAGE

Unit: 1,000,000 yen

| *Company* | *Total Borrowings* | *Mitsui Bank* | *Other Mitsui Financial Institutions* | *Mitsui Percentage* | *Largest Outside Borrowing* | *Percentage* |
|---|---|---|---|---|---|---|
| Mitsui Mining | 24,166 | 3,146 | 2,570 | 23.65 | Hokkaido Devel. Bk. | 11.81 |
| Mitsui Metal Mining | 5,833 | 1,070 | 1,200 | 38.92 | Industrial Bank | 29.45 |
| Hokkaido Colliery & SS | 10,004 | 1,326 | 748 | 20.73 | Industrial Bank | 15.29 |
| Japan Steel Works | 8,678 | 1,985 | 1,087 | 35.40 | Hokkaido Devel. Bk. | 16.56 |
| Mitsui Shipbuilding | 6,832 | 1,639 | 500 | 31.31 | Hypothec Bank | 23.86 |
| Sanki Engineering | 586 | 115 | 154 | 45.90 | Tokai Bank | 11.09 |
| Showa Aircraft | 637 | 624 | 0 | 97.96 | Fuji Bank | 1.41 |
| Toyo Koatsu Industries | 15,861 | 1,000 | 2,390 | 21.37 | Industrial Bank | 14.15 |
| Miike Gosei Ind. | 1,157 | 302 | 290 | 51.16 | Industrial Bank | 25.93 |
| Mitsui Chemical | 8,515 | 2,512 | 1,484 | 46.93 | Long-Term Credit Bk. | 13.15 |
| Toyo Rayon | 17,542 | 3,205 | 1,920 | 29.22 | Long-Term Credit Bk. | 22.35 |
| Mitsui & Co. (Trading) | 82,881 | 20,387 | 2,731 | 27.89 | Tokyo Bank | 19.39 |
| General Trading | 7,771 | 1,725 | 941 | 34.31 | Fuji Bank | 6.96 |
| Tokyo Foods | 7,787 | 1,955 | 161 | 27.18 | Hypothec Bank | 14.77[a] |
| Mitsui Warehouse | 1,190 | 426 | 376 | 67.40 | Japan Life Insurance | 9.75 |
| Mitsui Real Estate | 11,675 | 2,517 | 3,104 | 48.15 | Joyo Bank | 8.03 |
| Mitsui Shipping | 23,796 | 742 | 1,563 | 11.09 | Industrial Bank | 7.01 |
| Mitsui Norin (Agr. & Forestry*) | 582 | 169 | | 29.04 | Central Agr. Coop. Bk. | 29.21 |
| Mitsui Construction | 1,446 | 387 | 496 | 61.06 | Hokkaido Devel. Bk. | 7.40 |
| Total | 236,939 | 45,232 | 21,715 | 28.25** | | |

*Mitsui Agriculture and Forestry is an exception. It will be noted that borrowings from the Central Cooperative Bank for Agriculture and Forestry slightly exceeded borrowings from the Mitsui Bank. In all other companies borrowings from the grouping were highest.

**Calculated from totals, not an average of individual entries.

a) Correction of arithmetic error.

Source: Economic Investigation Council, *Research on Business Groupings* (Keizai Chosa Kyokai, *Keiretsu no Kenkyu*), Tokyo, 1962, pp. 38-44.

Note: Three of the core companies, Mitsui Precision Machinery, Mitsui Petrochemical, and Toyo Cotton, have not been entered in the table because the source from which this information is taken does not list them.

Mitsubishi enterprises accounted for only 14% of its total loans, which *is a very low rate as compared with that of pre-war days.*[12]

Because minimum partiality in access to credit is an imperative if entry is to be encouraged, Headquarters staff working on economic deconcentration believed it of crucial importance that sources of

[12] Mitsubishi Economic Research Institute, *Mitsui, Mitsubishi, Sumitomo*, p. 231. Italics added.

**Table 8-4:** BORROWINGS FROM THE SUMITOMO BANK, SUMITOMO TRUST BANK, SUMITOMO INSURANCE COMPANIES BY SUMITOMO CORE COMPANIES AS A PERCENTAGE OF THEIR TOTAL BORROWINGS, SEPTEMBER 1961; ALSO LARGEST OUTSIDE BORROWING IN PERCENTAGE

Unit: 1,000,000 yen

| *Company* | *Total Borrowings* | *Sumitomo Bank* | *Other Sumitomo Financial Institutions* | *Sumitomo Percentage* | *Largest Outside Borrowing* | *Percentage* |
|---|---|---|---|---|---|---|
| Sumitomo Metal Mining | 8,196 | 1,897 | 2,022 | 47.82 | Industrial Bank | 16.37 |
| Sumitomo Coal Mining | 12,238 | 2,282 | 1,574 | 31.51 | Industrial Bank | 13.81 |
| Sumitomo Metal Mfg. | 42,255 | 2,084 | 8,962 | 30.60 | Industrial Bank | 15.31 |
| Sumitomo Elec. Ind. | 10,689 | 3,042 | 3,150 | 57.94 | Industrial Bank | 21.81 |
| Nippon Plate Glass | 8,009 | 2,411 | 2,379 | 59.81 | Industrial Bank | 12.92 |
| Nippon Electric Ind. | 23,585 | 5,241 | 5,621 | 46.05 | Industrial Bank | 12.08 |
| Sumitomo Machinery | 2,673 | 903 | 718 | 60.03 | Mitsubishi Bank<br>Industrial Bank | 8.52<br>8.52 |
| Sumitomo Chemicals | 23,733 | 4,266 | 5,612 | 41.60 | Industrial Bank | 23.76 |
| Sumitomo Trading | 27,084 | 10,906 | 5,458 | 60.42 | Tokyo Bank | 8.63 |
| Sumitomo Warehouse | 979 | 532 | 306 | 55.60 | Industrial Bank | 8.17 |
| Total | 159,441 | 33,564 | 35,802 | 43.50* | | |

*Calculated from totals, not an average of individual entries.

Source: Economic Investigation Council, *Research on Business Groupings* (Keizai Chosa Kyokai, *Keiretsu no Kenkyu*), Tokyo, 1962, pp. 52-59. Sumitomo Real Estate is not listed because of omission in source.

credit be expanded, but banks became excluded from the Deconcentration Law as earlier they had been excluded from other measures. In his January 26, 1948 radio message MacArthur reported to the Department of the Army that financial institutions—first insurance companies and then banks—would be designated under the Deconcentration Law, but they were not. As a SCAP historical report put it,

> Every effort was made at this time to bring about a solution of the program relative to the dissolution of banking combines and various propositions [were] analyzed in order to coordinate the divergent viewpoints on this matter of basic policy. One proposition considered was that of dividing Japan into approximately seven financial market areas with an arrangement whereby no bank would be permitted to have branch banking operations except within one of such areas. This plan would have effectively divided the largest banks in Japan which were virtual networks of branch banks throughout the Japanese islands. This plan was eventually discarded and a second plan given consideration wherein only the five largest banks [would] be designated and that each such bank [would] be divided into no less than two and no more than three separate, independent banks; however, after receiving recommendations from the Deconcentration Review Board and the reports from the Johnston and Draper Missions, a decision was made effecting no change in the basic policy but providing for reorganization of the banking structure by means other than designation under the Deconcentration Law.[13]

In my earlier study, which rests on materials up to 1946, it is observed on the basis of private information, that:

> Although [Mitsui] Banking certainly did not confine extension of credit to the combine alone, combine interests naturally came first. More than this, Banking gave combine firms preferential interest terms[14] and was slow to extend credit to outsiders who challenged or might challenge an important subsidiary in a particular field. . . . .[15]
>
> [Historically] Loans to industrial companies where Banking could

[13] Hamm, *Deconcentration of Economic Power*, p. 24.

[14] This statement contradicts the previous statement with respect to preferential interest rates, which is made on the basis of an interview in 1965 with the Mitsui Bank President, Mr. Sato, wherein Mr. Sato stoutly denied there were ever differences in interest rates. This information, earlier in its time reference, is likewise from an internal Mitsui source. How the two statements are to be reconciled is not clear to me.

[15] Hadley, "Concentrated Business Power," p. 272.

> not have a controlling voice were "adjusted." In the case of companies over which Banking could exert control, further financial assistance was rendered, the outstanding examples being Kanegafuchi Spinning, Oji Paper and Shibaura Engineering.[16]

The characteristic Mitsui pattern of asking control as the price of credit extension is seen very clearly in the establishment of one of the newer combines, Japan Nitrogenous Fertilizer (Nippon Chisso Hiryo, contracted to Nitchitsu, though today through a name change, Chisso), which was named as one of the 83 designated holding companies. Noguchi, the founder, had acquired a Far East license for the manufacture and sale of calcium cyanamide under the Frank Carl cyanamide patent, but a gentleman's agreement provided that he

> . . . would not attempt to work the patent by himself but that he would make an arrangement with an organization like Mitsui for joint exploitation.
>
> As a result of this gentleman's agreement, Noguchi discussed joint working of the cyanamide patent with Mitsui. While interested in the venture, Mitsui proposed that it should hold over fifty per cent of the shares of the new company and that it should have the right to appoint the directors. Noguchi rejected this. He next turned to Kondo, president of NYK, Mitsubishi's great shipping subsidiary, who in turn discussed the matter with Toyokawa, president of Mitsubishi Bank. The Mitsubishi proposal was that Noguchi and his co-operators could subscribe to as many shares as they could handle and that Mitsubishi would subscribe to the remainder. Mitsubishi credit facilities were also pledged. This offer was accepted.[17]

Throughout the combine-dissolution program, financial institutions were consistently treated preferentially. No bank became a designated holding company though banks qualified for such designation a good deal more fully than certain other operating companies named. Under Imperial Ordinance 567 combine subsidiaries, with the exception of financial institutions, were supposed to divest themselves of holdings in other companies; in the case of financial institutions, only when such holdings were in the "same chain of capital." The Antimonopoly Law, the permanent legislation, continued the distinction between nonfinancial and financial enterprises. Nonfinancial companies were not to own stock in other companies (with the exception of approved single-layer subsidiaries); financial institutions could own stock up to 5 percent except in companies with which

[16] *Ibid.*, p. 132.

[17] *Ibid.*, p. 78.

they were competing. When under the Deconcentration Law effort was made to get at operating companies of such size as to deter entry, no bank was named under this.

Even by the back-door route of reorganization for reason of solvency, banks came out preferentially. While under the Enterprise Reconstruction and Reorganization Law many industrial companies found themselves with splits, with "second companies" ostensibly, if not in fact, for reasons of solvency, under the companion legislation, Financial Institutions Reconstruction and Reorganization Law, no bank found itself obliged to split.

The net effect of the foregoing was that the banks came through the wringer of the deconcentration program virtually intact, whereas elsewhere there were numerous changes. Many Japanese have regarded the combine banks as inheriting the mantle of the former top-holding companies. For the reasons set forth in Part II of this study, I do not subscribe to this point of view, but there is no question financial institutions represented the least part of the deconcentration effort.

The contrast in action between trading companies and financial institutions was striking. That the scale of the disparity in treatment was the product of reversing policy makes it no less incongruous though it does become more understandable.

# 9.

# The United States Reorients Its Economic Policy in Japan

Following the withdrawal of U.S. support for FEC 230 on March 12, 1948, together with the Report of the Draper-Johnston Mission later that month, MacArthur realized that the 325 companies designated under the Deconcentration Law were excessive and set about to effect large-scale releases. He now believed that only those concerns which were "interfering seriously with economic recovery" should be reorganized under the Deconcentration Law. A rather balder statement of the change in policy is to be found in a Headquarters memorandum of mid-April 1948 in which the new policy was summarized:

> (1) no banks were to be considered as excessive concentrations or reorganized under the Deconcentration Law; (2) no more than twenty companies were to be subject to reorganization under the Law [the final number was 19] and these were to be chosen on the basis that they were interfering with Japanese economic recovery; (3) all the rest were to be removed from designation with no less than 100 companies taken off in the first such action and, where necessary, be remanded to the Fair Trade Commission for surveillance.[1]

Action followed swiftly. An announcement was made by SCAP on May 1, 1948, stating that the HCLC was releasing 194 industrial and distributive companies from continued designation under Law No. 207.

> . . . 50 would be released as not actually constituting excessive concentrations [that is, outright] and 144 others were regarded as relatively minor concentrations whose operations would continue

[1] ESS/AC, Memorandum to ESS/C, "Change in Deconcentration Policy, April 19, 1948, reproduced in SCAP, GHQ, "History of the Nonmilitary Activities of the Occupation of Japan," Vol. x, *Reform of Business Enterprise*, Part B, "Deconcentration of Economic Power," p. 27, Office of the Chief of Military History, Washington, D.C.

under surveillance or concurrently with the accomplishment of organizational readjustments such as divestment of certain subsidiary relationships and other action to remove monopolistic characteristics. The announcement emphasized that this list of 194 companies was an initial list and other removals would follow subject to the completion of investigation by the Holding Company Liquidation Commission.[2]

On July 1, 1948 an additional 31 firms were removed from designation, making a total of 225 firms that were removed from the original designation of 325. The Army historical report stated: "Further action, by the [Holding Company Liquidation] Commission in respect to the cancelling of company designations were momentarily deferred, however, so as to give the opportunity for the Deconcentration Review Board, which had arrived in Tokyo in May, to make further recommendations concerning the deconcentration program."[3]

*The Deconcentration Review Board*

On April 28, 1948, SCAP announced the names of the members of the Deconcentration Review Board.[4] They were: Roy S. Campbell, chairman, president, and general manager of the New York Shipbuilding Corp.; Joseph B. Robinson, industrial engineer and owner of the Robinson Connector Co.; Edward J. Burger, vice-president of the Public Service Co., Cleveland; Walter R. Hutchinson, former Assistant U.S. District Attorney from north Iowa and formerly special assistant to the U.S. Attorney General; and Byron D. Woodside, assistant director of Corporation Finance, Securities Exchange Commission. Incidentally, with the exception of Mr. Woodside, no member is either listed currently in *Who's Who* or *Who Was Who* for 1943-50.

The members of the Review Board arrived in Tokyo in May 1948 and spent most of the first month familiarizing themselves with their duties.[5] On June 4 the board sent to MacArthur a document entitled "Deconcentration Review Board—Basic Interpretation of Authority," in which the purpose of their review was stated:[6]

The Deconcentration Review Board is to make an independent review of the Reorganization Order issued by the HCLC for the purpose of appraising the impact and effect of the deconcentration

[2] C. M. Hamm, *Deconcentration of Economic Power*, August 9, 1950, p. 45, World War II Records Division, National Archives and Records Services, Suitland, Md.

[3] "Nonmilitary Activities, *Deconcentration*," p. 29.

[4] Hamm, *Deconcentration of Economic Power*, pp. 30-31.

[5] *Ibid.*, p. 46

[6] *Ibid.*, pp. 49-51.

action upon the operating efficiency of the industrial, distributive, insurance or banking enterprise concerned, and its consequent effect upon the general industrial, financial, or commercial economy of the country.

Under "Findings," the board repeated MacArthur's instructions that its sole criterion would be the effect of the reorganization plan on the efficiency of the company and acknowledged the limits on its authority in this way:

> The Deconcentration Review Board is specifically limited in its deliberations to the terms of reference previously set up except as specifically called upon by direction in writing from the Supreme Commander for the Allied Powers for such other appraisals as he requires.

Having explicitly reiterated MacArthur's instructions governing creation of the Deconcentration Review Board (DRB) as the board's understanding of its responsibilities and jurisdiction in its memorandum to MacArthur, it ignored its terms of reference; not one of its judgments was determined on the basis of the effect of the reorganization plan on efficiency. Instead, the DRB in reviewing its first case, that of Nippon Soda, the holding-operating company of one of the lesser *zaibatsu*, enunciated "four points" which were to "guide" the HCLC in determining which companies were and which were not excessive concentrations. Various comments come to mind. The DRB had not been invited to Japan by MacArthur to determine what companies were excessive concentrations; it had been invited to determine the effect of the proposed reorganization plan of companies, deemed excessive by the HCLC working with ESS, on economic recovery. Accordingly, in departing to this field, the DRB was leaving its area of responsibility and moving out into an area in which it had no formal authority. Secondly, as shall become apparent, having enunciated its "four points," the DRB used them only for eliminating companies. In none of the 11 cases in which it recommended structural reorganization did the DRB itself refer to them.

### *The Four Points*

Given the critical role assumed by the DRB's four points, it will be worthwhile to quote the memorandum in which the four points occurred, a memorandum dated August 28, 1948 from the DRB to MacArthur, entitled "Recommendations with Reference to Certain Aspects of the Deconcentration Program."[7]

[7] *Ibid.*, pp. 55-56.

1. Japanese Public Law No. 54 (Law Relating to Prohibition of Private Monopolies and Methods of Preserving Fair Trade) and Japanese Public Law No. 207 (Law for the Elimination of Excessive Concentrations of Economic Power) were enacted pursuant to Allied Policy in Japan.

2. The Board believes that the basic principle of this policy, as it relates to the Deconcentration Program, and as expressed in Article 1 of Law No. 54 and in Article 3 of Law No. 207, is to *eliminate and prohibit monopolies, combinations in restraint of trade and commerce, and excessive concentrations which prevent or restrict competition.* [Emphasis in original.]

3. The Board views with apprehension the present status of the Deconcentration Program and the apparent failure to observe the basic principle stated in paragraph "2" above in administering Law No. 207.

4. The Board believes that the administrative policy and procedure under Law No. 207 should be required to conform to that principle. The Board believes—

a. That no Order should be issued under the Deconcentration Law unless there is a showing of a prima facie case that the company "restricts competition or impairs the opportunity for others to engage in business independently in any important segment of business." In the absence of such showing the company should be removed from designation.

b. That the mere possession of non-related lines of business is not in itself sufficient in any case to establish that a company is an excessive concentration within the law.[8]

c. That the submission of a plan of reorganization as a voluntary plan is not in itself sufficient to confer upon the HCLC authority to issue an Order under Law No. 207.

d. That the action a company is ordered to take by the HCLC under Law No. 207 should be directly related to the facts upon which that company was determined to be an excessive concentration. (We have been advised that ESS/AC and the HCLC do not consider such a relationship necessary. In our opinion Orders issued contrary to this principle involve the arbitrary interference with and invasion of fundamental property rights and freedom of action and exceed the authority granted under the Law.)

5. The Board recommends that the Supreme Commander for the

[8] I.e., the DRB disapproved of Article 3 of Law No. 207.

Allied Powers direct that the principles stated in the preceding paragraphs "2" and "4" be followed in the administration of the Deconcentration Law.

By this memorandum, the DRB introduced an additional law into the operation, a law which was not being used for the problem at hand. Law No. 54 of 1947 was the permanent antitrust legislation which SCAP had earlier directed be enacted for the purpose of keeping the economy deconcentrated; as permanent legislation for a normal situation it contained appropriate safeguards to property rights. Law No. 207 of 1947 was a temporary, emergency measure enacted for the purpose of getting the economy deconcentrated, so that Law No. 54 could take over. As an emergency, temporary measure with the purpose of restructuring the Japanese economy, it did not—it could not—contain the safeguards to property rights that the permanent legislation would be expected to have.

Further, Law No. 54 was administered by the Fair Trade Commission and Law No. 207 by the Holding Company Liquidation Commission. The FTC in late 1947 and early 1948 was new and inexperienced, the HCLC experienced. By proposing the addition and/or substitution of Law No. 54 for Law No. 207, the DRB was proposing inexperienced for experienced administration. It was also proposing two groups of administrators, with all the confusion that implied.

It is most unusual legal procedure to announce that those parts of a law which are favored are applicable, and those that are not, are not. Legally there was nothing giving Articles 1 and 3 of Laws No. 54 and No. 207 any greater standing than other articles contained in the two laws. The Deconcentration Review Board found Article 3 of Law No. 207 less objectionable than Article 6. Not only did Article 6 have quite as much legal standing as Article 3, but in addition, the DRB had no authority to put forward its opinion as prevailing in this matter. It was merely in Japan at the invitation of the Supreme Commander to advise on the effect of reorganization plans on efficiency. If MacArthur had not been caught up in a major reversal of U.S. policy, with all its attendant awkwardness for those with administrative responsibility, it is doubtful he would have acquiesced in such unusual procedures.

In stating that a reorganization order required a prima facie showing that the company "restricts competition or impairs the opportunity for others to engage in business independently," not only was the DRB introducing its own ideas (the legislation said nothing about prima facie evidence[9]), but ideas which the DRB itself later admitted were unworkable. In the circumstance of an economy that had been significantly controlled since 1931 and tightly controlled since 1938, it was virtually impossible for there to be 'prima facie' evidence. Rather, orders necessarily had to be issued largely on analytical grounds. An analytic basis for antitrust action was at this time not an unknown procedure in American antitrust practice. The *Second American Tobacco* case, which the Supreme Court decided in 1946, was a decision based on economic analysis of the market situation. In its final report to MacArthur, July 15, 1949, the DRB said that inasmuch as the Japanese economy had since 1938 been generally characterized by the absence of competition, "there was not available to SCAP Headquarters or to the Board contemporary data which . . . might have been utilized in appraising the possible effects of reorganizing companies from a competitive point of view."[10]

By announcing that the "mere possession of non-related lines of business is not in itself sufficient . . . to establish that a company is . . . excessive," the DRB evidenced its inability to grasp the meaning of conglomerate enterprise. As previously observed, business in the West historically attained to concentrated power by the avenue of monopoly, business in Japan by conglomerate undertakings in which individual market positions were for the most part of the order of magnitude of 10 to 20 percent of the markets in question. Inasmuch as in Japan there were less than a handful of monopolistic positions, the DRB was saying that Mitsui's range of undertakings across the gamut of the Japanese economy and, on a lesser scale, Mitsubishi and Sumitomo, were nothing to alert one to concern.

Items 4c and 4d in the board's report were procedural. What the members of the board never understood—possibly because they did not want to understand, and further perhaps because they were unalterably opposed to the matter—was that Law 207 was an instrument for effecting major social change as part of the revolution being carried out under the Occupation. The DRB did not want a revolution; it wanted a continuance of the industrial structure Japan had had all along. Therefore, obstructing procedural points were added to obstructing *substantive* points. It will be noted that nothing in the foregoing memorandum had anything to do with the effect of reorganization plans on operating efficiency.

The four points were the DRB's public expression of their views.

[9] In fact, Law No. 54 defined "competition" in Article 2 to include "potential competition."

[10] Office of Military History, "Deconcentration of Economic Power," p. 81.

A franker statement of its thinking is to be found in a memorandum circulated among DRB members: "It is becoming quite clear that the implementation of these laws is being carried on on a 'police-state' basis, bordering on (if not actually) the methods used by so-called communist States today."[11]

### *The HCLC and the Four Points*

In the new climate of Washington opinion, MacArthur bowed completely to the wishes of the Deconcentration Review Board, and instructed the chief of the Economic and Scientific Section to hold a meeting of all interested persons for the purpose of explaining the DRB's four points to the HCLC.[12] On September 11, 1948 representatives from the Economic and Scientific Section, Legal Section, and the members of the DRB met with the seven members of the Holding Company Liquidation Commission for the purpose of informing them of the DRB findings in the Nippon Soda case and acquainting them with the DRB's concepts of the deconcentration program. The HCLC was informed that the DRB had determined in the Nippon Soda case that:

> The facts and evidence contained in the basic files submitted do not establish that the Nippon Soda restricts competition or impairs the opportunity for others to engage in business independently in any important segment of the company's field or fields of operation within the meaning of the definition of an excessive concentration of Economic Power set forth in Article 3 of Public Law 207. It is recommended, therefore, that the HCLC be instructed to stay its above Order No. 172, unless evidence is presented that the company is an excessive concentration within the meaning of Article 3 of Public Law 207, [and] that the Company should be removed from designation under the Law.[13]

The chief of the Economic and Scientific Section then read the board's four points, after which Gen. Marquat stated:

> These four points just given to you will influence the decisions of the Board in review of subsequent cases referred to it. These have been presented to you for your information and as a basis for further discussions in order that you may understand thoroughly

[11] Memorandum from Walter Hutchinson in folder marked "Deconcentration Review Board," in World War II Records Division, National Archives and Records Services, Suitland, Md.

[12] Hamm, *Deconcentration of Economic Power*, p. 60.

[13] *Ibid.*

> the basic conception of the Review Board as to the method in which Public Law 207 should be implemented. You have the decision on the Nippon Soda Case and these four points, and we invite [you] to ask any questions you care to submit in further development of consonant operating procedures. At this point I would like to emphasize that nothing [that] has been presented to you indicates any change in the Deconcentration procedures. SCAP contemplates no change in the Law, the Standards, or implementation procedures. This is the concept of the way it was originally intended that the deconcentration procedures be accomplished and it is no change in policy.[14]

In the discussion that arose, Mr. Noda of the commission pointed out:

> . . . the HCLC had established a certain prestige in Japan and that if they were to announce to the Japanese public that a mistake had been made in the administration of the Law and procedure not only in one company but in 175 companies [of the 225 companies removed, 50 were removed outright and the remaining 175 were to continue under surveillance or make minor, non-structural changes], it would greatly injure their prestige. In replying to this question it was suggested that "HCLC permanently discard the attitude that they have made mistakes." Implementation of the Law is primarily a matter of interpretation of the provisions of the legal statute and not a personal position assumed on a basis of advocacy or opposition to the purpose of the legislation. . . . There was no intention to indicate that the HCLC had made an error. A re-examination of the 175 companies in the light of the interpretations submitted by the Board should be taken advantage of and could be referred to without any loss of prestige by the HCLC. . . .[15]

The news of the meeting was released to the press, together with the four points. On Sept. 12, 1948 the *Nippon Times* carried a straight news story on it.[16] However, other portions of the press, less under the influence of SCAP, were not slow to realize the implications of the announcement. The *Asahi Shimbun* on September 14, announced the news under a story captioned "Deconcentration—To be Liberalized on Great Scale. Re-Investigation for Those Already Decided."[17] The Central News Agency of China transmitted the following dispatch from its Tokyo office on September 17: "The economic deconcentration law aimed at breaking the 'Zaibatsu' monopolies in Japan

[14] *Ibid.*, p. 61.
[15] *Ibid.*, pp. 62-63.
[16] *Ibid.*, pp. 63-64.
[17] *Ibid.*, p. 64.

is on its way to the scrap heap. A most reliable source today opined that instead of reaffirmation of the Far Eastern Commission policy the four basic principles recently laid down by the SCAP deconcentration review board actually takes another step towards the law's complete abolition. He quoted a top-ranking holding company liquidation commission official as saying that the 'law will eventually be scrapped in Japan as in Germany due to the fundamental change of the US policy in the Far East.'"[18]

Over the next weeks and months the HCLC had a difficult time grasping what the board meant by "prima facie," and numerous conferences ensued. The ESS, in an effort to give a clear illustration, transmitted to the board on October 15, 1948 its findings in the case of the iron and steel industry:

> pointing out in detail the practices in restraint of trade which had been exercised in the steel industry since 1931 and showing further the extent to which these practices continued at the present time. These restraints included division of territory, division of production, fixing of prices, and domestic cartel agreements. In addition, individual studies were prepared in respect to each of these companies and the Board now gave consideration based on the proposed orders or reorganization of three important steel companies; The Japan Steel Tube Company (Nippon Kokan K.K.), Fuso Metal Industries, Ltd. (Fuso Kinzoku Kokyo K.K.), and Kobe Steel Works, Ltd. (K.K. Kobe Seikosho). . . . Notwithstanding this proof of restriction of competition . . . the Board did not consider it met the prima facie case required by the Board. . . . It shortly became obvious from other actions of the Board in respect to reorganizations which it ordered, that the four points had ceased to be the guide of the Board's actions but served simply as a reference basis in certain cases, to support the Board's actions when it was of the opinion that a company should not be reorganized.[19]

Of the companies it examined over the following months, the board approved structural reorganization of 11 companies, of which seven were illustrative of monopoly, which the board defined to be 70 percent and above of the market, probably the entire number of monopoly cases in the economy. The remaining four structural reorganizations were the Mitsubishi Heavy Industries Co. and the three mining companies of Mitsui, Mitsubishi and Sumitomo. In addition to the 11 structural reorganizations, the board recommended eight cases of adjustments of assets, subsidiaries, or the like.

[18] *Ibid.*, p. 65.

[19] *Ibid.*, pp. 68-69.

A study of the DRB's decisions indicates how difficult it is to describe any guidelines or principles to its actions. With the exception of the monopoly cases, which the DRB, with its American background, understood, the decisions seem capricious. The DRB showed no understanding of conglomerate oligopoly structures. If we look at the nonmonopoly cases where the DRB approved structural reorganization, we find that it did not refer to its four points at all. In fact, the four cases seemed to require a "pep memo" from a member to the other members to get any action. The memorandum, dated March 23, 1949, contained the following remarks:

> . . . Some members of the Board may not now like the Law [No. 207] in the form in which it stands before us, and perhaps never liked it in that form. I can see reasons for that feeling if it exists. But the fact remains that the Law is before us in clear terms and with our own acquiescence as to those terms. I am not prepared to fly in the face of it—and I most earnestly hope the Board will not do so. If there be instances in which, on this presentation of the Law, I have failed to observe the Law in my work on the Board I now apologize to SCAP, to the Board and to the company or companies then involved. If the Law now stands in the way of remedial measures the Board believes should be taken in respect of certain companies, the proper procedure would seem to be for the Board to ask SCAP for *interpretive revisions of the Law* such as would give the Board wider latitude it may need for the purposes in mind. But until the Law is revised it seems to me the duty and obligation of the Board is to enforce it in the form handed to us, and not in the form we may think it would have been best had the law taken or should take now.[20]

With this memorandum before it the DRB two weeks later recommended that the Mitsubishi Heavy Industries be divided into three companies. In its recommendation of April 12, 1949, the Board,

> . . . made reference only to the size of the company and made no finding that the company restricted competition or impaired the opportunity for others to engage in business independently in the same field. In fact, it made no finding that the company was an excessive concentration of economic power nor did it specifically concur in the HCLC finding to this effect. After reviewing the size of

[20] From a memorandum prepared by Joseph Robinson and entitled, "Board Procedure" in Deconcentration Review Board folder in World War II Records Division. (Italics added.)

the company and the questions of reparations, it stated, "we are of the opinion, however, that Mitsubishi should be reorganized."[21]

After two months without any approval of structural reorganization, the DRB recommended the separation of metal mining from coal mining in the case of the Mitsui, Mitsubishi, and Sumitomo (Seika) Mining Companies. On June 14, 1949 it disapproved of structural reorganization of Nippon Mining, out of which the Nissan-Mangyo complex developed. But the next day it approved reorganization of Seika [Sumitomo] Mining, a company with 4.2 percent of the national coal capacity, 10 percent of the copper capacity, and 16 to 21 percent of the national smelting and refining capacity. In this case the DRB concluded that the company should be reorganized into two companies, one coal and one metal.[22] The DRB did not explain why mining in the case of the big three should have been treated differently from other combine mining or excessive concentrations of economic power.

Later in June the DRB ordered Mitsui Mining's coal and metal activities separated. The following is excerpted from the DRB's statement:

> . . . the Board is not convinced . . . that Mitsui by reason of its ownership and operation of the largest and most successful coal mines in Japan is sufficiently dominant to necessitate the division of its coal business under Law No. 207. It is true that as the largest producer of lead and zinc in Japan Mitsui has control of these basic raw materials, but there is no recommendation before the Board for division of the company on that basis. The Proposed Order is directed mainly to the company's position as a producer of coal and secondly to its metal mining capacity. While the Board concurs with that portion of the Proposed Order dividing the metals operation from the coal division, it does not feel that under present conditions years of projected forward development by the company, able management and efficient operation should be sacrificed or disrupted in order to further uproot the former Zaibatsu aspects of the property.
>
> Mitsui is credited with 16.4.% of the national capacity to produce coal. The Board does not believe that this percentage enables the company to restrict competition or that, taken by itself, the percentage is sufficient to bring the company within Law No. 207.

Parenthetically, as was noted in the preceding chapter, with subsidiaries not fully severed, Mitsui Mining accounted for 35% of output of the industry, with the next nearest competitor Mitsubishi at 15%.

[21] Hamm, *Deconcentration of Economic Power*, pp. 73-74.
[22] *Ibid.*, p. 74.

Furthermore, designation under 207 was definitionally designation of the activities of the whole company, coal and metals. A company was not designated for a piece of itself. The statement continued:

> There is no evidence before the Board indicating restrictive practices or direct impairment of opportunities for others. The significant evidence relates to the Zaibatsu roots of the company and the fact that it was the foundation of one of the most powerful industrial and financial combines in Japan. Of major consideration also is the fact that under existing conditions division of the company's coal properties would handicap production and retard industrial recovery in Japan, not only by reason of the separation itself but also because of labor difficulties that would attend it.
>
> Moreover, restraints of trade on the company's part resulting from control association connections and cartel agreements have been or are being removed in compliance with post-war Japanese laws and ordinances or Occupation directives. The company's activities in the future will be subject to the Anti-Monopoly Law and the new Trade Association Law. Its holdings of securities of other companies have been or will be disposed of pursuant to HCLC regulations, and the company's relationships with the Mitsui interests have been or will be dissolved.
>
> The Board recommends that Mitsui Kosan K.K. [Mitsui Mining] be ordered to prepare under the supervision of the HCLC a reorganization plan for division into two independent companies, one company to be engaged principally in the mining of coal and the other company in the mining of metals; that only one of the two independent companies needs necessarily be a new company, and that the Miike Machinery Works shall be allotted to the coal company.[23]

The board made its Mitsubishi Mining decision the following day, June 28, 1949, concluding with: "It would be a mistake against the democratic principles we advocate here and are expected to exemplify here, to base division of this company on the ground alone that it is an alleged coal monopoly [which no one was doing] or an alleged metals monopoly [which no one was asserting]. The company's Zaibatsu history, its reputation for exerting influence in high places, and its control of certain raw materials, taken together, justify division by separation of metal from coal."[24]

A summary of the DRB's actions will be found in Table 9-1.

From the following, it becomes apparent that the "four points" were used by the DRB only for purposes of nonreorganizing com-

[23] *Ibid.*, pp. 77-78.

[24] *Ibid.*, pp. 78-79.

Table 9-1: REORGANIZATIONS UNDER THE LAW FOR THE ELIMINATION OF EXCESSIVE CONCENTRATIONS OF ECONOMIC POWER

Part A: Corporate Reorganizations - 11 Companies

| *Company, number of plants, mines, etc.* | *Products* | *Percent of Nat. Prod.* | *Reorganization Plan together with New Capitalization* | |
|---|---|---|---|---|
| Japan Iron and Steel | pig | 86 | Old company dissolved; 2 new companies | |
| 5 complexes | ingot | 42 | Final plan: old co. dissolved, 4 new cos. | |
| | large shapes | 75 | Yawata Iron & Steel | Y800,000,000 |
| | | | Fuji Iron & Steel | Y400,000,000 |
| | | | Nittetsu Steamship | Y 40,000,000 |
| | | | Harima Fire Brick | Y 20,000,000 |
| Mitsubishi Heavy Industries | shipbuilding | 23 | Old company dissolved; 3 new companies | |
| 31 mfg. establishments | turbines | 46 | East Jap. Heavy Ind. | Y700,000,000 |
| and shipyards | boilers | 68 | Central Jap. Heavy Ind. | Y1,300,000,000 |
| | airbrakes | 50 | West Jap. Heavy Ind. | Y900,000,000 |
| | electric locomotives | 18 | | |
| Mitsui Mining | | | Old company dissolved or old company continued; separate coal from metal | |
| 7 coal mines | coal | 16 | | |
| 14 metal mines | crude lead | 41 | Final Plan: Old company continued, coal; metal separated | |
| | crude zinc | 53 | | |
| | electrolytic zinc | 42 | Mitsui Mining | Y1,200,000,000 |
| | | | Kamioka Mining | 600,000,000 |
| Mitsubishi Mining | coal | 12 | Old company dissolved or old company continued; separate coal from metal | |
| 17 coal mines | tin | 92 | | |
| 20 metal mines | copper | 24 | Mitsubishi Mining | Y900,000,000 |
| 9 "other" | electrolytic tin | 100 | Taihei Mining (metal) | 700,000,000 |
| Seika (Sumitomo) Mining | coal | 04 | Old company dissolved or old company continued; separate coal from metal | |
| 13 coal mines | copper | 09 | | |
| 9 metal mines | electrolytic copper | 21 | Final Plan: Old co. continued, 3 new cos. | |
| 3 "other" | electrolytic silver | 20 | Seika Mining (coal) | Y290,000,000 |
| | | | Besshi Mining (metal) | 310,000,000 |
| | | | Besshi Construction | 5,000,000 |
| | | | Besshi Dept. Store | 6,000,000 |
| Oji Paper | "grand pulp" | 59 | Old company dissolved; 6 new companies | |
| 15 factories | western pulp | 52 | Final Plan: Old company dissolved; 3 new companies | |
| | newsprint | 94 | | |
| | | | Tomakomai Paper Mfg. | Y400,000,000 |
| | | | Jujo Paper Mfg. | 280,000,000 |
| | | | Honshu Paper Mfg. | 250,000,000 |
| Teikoku Fiber | flax fiber | 100 | Old company dissolved or old company continued, but enterprise to be in 3 parts | |
| 33 factories | linen thread | 80 | | |
| | staple fiber | 22 | Imperial Hemp | Y180,000,000 |
| | spun silk thread | 10 | Central Textile | 240,000,000 |
| | | | Toho Rayon | 120,000,000 |

| Daiken Industries | cotton spinning | 11 | Final Plan: Old company dissolved, |
|---|---|---|---|
| 13 factories | trading | (first position) | 4 new companies |
| 13 "branch establishments" | | | Kureha Cotton Spinning ¥700,000,000 |
| | | | Marubeni Trading 150,000,000 |
| | | | C. Itoh Trading 150,000,000 |
| | | | Amagasaki Nail 10,000,000 |
| **Toyo Can** | cans for canning | 85 | Old company continued; 1 second company |
| 11 factories | 5 gal. cans | 33 | out of Otaru plant |
| | miscellaneous cans | 18 | Hokkai Canning ¥ 50,000,000 |
| | crowns | 09 | |
| **Dainippon Beer** | beer | 72 | Old company dissolved; 2 new companies |
| 9 factories | soft drinks | 32 | Japan Beer ¥100,000,000 |
| | | | Asahi Beer 100,000,000 |
| **Hokkaido Dairy Coop.** | butter | 78 | Old company dissolved; 2 new companies |
| 51 establishments | cheese | 85 | Disposal of 2 plants |
| | evaporated, powdered | | Hokkaido Butter ¥120,000,000 |
| | milk | 52 | Snow Brand 360,000,000 |
| | fluid milk | 63 | |

Part B: Disposal of Some Plants, Divestiture of Securities - 7 Companies

| *Company, number of plants, mines, etc.* | *Products* | *Percent of Nat. Prod.* | *Reorganization Plan* |
|---|---|---|---|
| **Hitachi Manufacturing** | generators | 18 | Dispose of 19 factories |
| 35 factories | Electric Machinery | 18 | |
| | steam locomotives | 20 | |
| **Toshiba** | generators | 20 | Dispose of 27 factories and 1 research |
| 43 factories | electric machinery | 13 | laboratory. Toshiba Locomotive to |
| | vacuum tubes | 28 | be merged |
| | light bulbs | 15 | |
| **Teikoku Petroleum** | crude | 96 | a) Divestiture of securities; |
| 3,794 wells | | | b) Disposal of unexploited rights above and below ground |
| | | | New capitalization, ¥1,000,000,000 |
| **Japan Explosives** | explosives | 25 | Divestiture of securities with exception |
| 14 factories | black powder | 85 | of holdings in Japan Chemical Enterprise |
| | fuses | 39 | New capitalization, ¥500,000,000 |
| | percussion cap detonators | 53 | |
| | paint | 33 | |
| **Shochiku Motion Pictures** | movie production | 15 | Divestiture of securities |
| 35 studios | movie distribution | 28 | |
| | movie development | 03 | |
| | theatre development | 01 | |
| **Toho Motion Pictures** | movie production | 15 | Divestiture of securities |
| 17 studios | movie distribution | 26 | |
| | movie development | 03 | |
| | theatre development | 0.5 | |

| | | | |
|---|---|---|---|
| Japan Express<br>9 principal branch off.<br>378 ord. branch off. | express handling | 83 | a) Sale or lease to national or private railroads of its terminal facilities on land of national or private railroads;<br>b) Divestiture of majority of securities<br>c) Disposal of 72 out of 300 tugs and tenders owned |

Part C: Electric Utility, A Special Case - 1 Company

| *Company* | *Products* | *Percent of Nat. Prod.* | *Reorganization Plan* |
|---|---|---|---|
| Japan Electric Generation and Transmission* | generation and transmission of electric power | 100 | HCLC delegated reorganization, Jan. 8, 1951, to the newly created Public Utilities Commission |

*It is not clear to the writer when the Japan Electric Power and Transmission Co. was designated. For some reason it is not among the 325 companies listed in the HCLC data volume nor is it cited in the chart in the textual volume. The *Final Report* speaks only of its transfer from the HCLC, cf. pp. 60-61.

Sources: HCLC, *Zaibatsu Dissolution*, textual volume, pp. 346-49; HCLC, *Final Report*, pp. 62-64. Number of factories, etc., market positions from *Zaibatsu Dissolution*. Terms of reorganization from both reports. Capitalizations from *Final Report*.

panies. In the case of ordered reorganizations, the four points had nothing to do with the matter.

The board ended its activities in August 1949. At a press conference held on August 3rd, the chairman of the DRB stated that the board had recommended a reorganization of 19 major companies, and that, in his opinion, excessive concentration of economic power in Japan was completely broken and a condition for free competition in all fields had been created.[25] By contrast, E. C. Welsh, Chief, Antitrust and Cartels Division of Headquarters, observed in late 1948: ". . . what was initially considered . . . a major objective of the Occupation [had] become . . . a major embarrassment to the Occupation. Without formally questioning the desirability or broad purposes of the policy, it was decided to take measures which would minimize the actions prepared for carrying out the policy. Facts of the last war faded . . . and conjectures [on] the next war took their place."[26]

The Pentagon and conservative opinion had been successful in reversing U.S. antitrust policy in Japan.

25 "Story from Start to End of Deconcentration Told," *Nippon Times*, October 18, 1949.

26 Memorandum dated November 29, 1949, prepared by Welsh for ESS, entitled "Assessment of Deconcentration Situation," World War II Records Division, National Archives, Suitland, Md.

# 10.

# The Sale of Securities and Other Deconcentration Developments

THE various programs for dissolving combine ownership ties and reducing other forms of concentration in the economy added up to a tremendous stock-disposal program. By any count—and there were several—the disposal of securities from holding companies, *zaibatsu* family members, and, far lesserly, of cross ties under the HCLC program, amounted to a huge undertaking. The combined HCLC program was the largest of the securities transfer programs under the Occupation's "surgical procedures," but there were three other programs involving sale of securities. Under the capital levy tax[1] of October 1946, payment of the extraordinary tax was permitted in kind. Accordingly, the Finance Ministry held stock which needed to be disposed of to the public. There was also a disposal program because of stock held in other corporations by "closed institutions." Closed institutions were corporations that had been integrally involved in Japan's program of expansion—for example, the South Manchurian Railroad Company, the Bank of Korea, the Bank of Formosa—or in controlling allocation and distribution in the wartime economy, such as the myriad control companies and control associations. Finally, there was a securities disposal program under the Antimonopoly Law supervised by the FTC. The following figures, as an approximation of the scale of the program, are suggestive:

| | |
|---|---|
| HCLC | Y8.9 billion in proceeds from sale[2] |
| Closed institutions | 3.1 billion in proceeds from sale[3] |
| Capital levy tax | 1.7 billion in proceeds from sale[4] |
| Antimonopoly Law | 1.3 billion in paid-up value[5] |
| | 15.0 |

[1] Cf. Chapter 3, note 43.

[2] Source cited in Table 10-1. Data are as of July 1951.

[3] Source cited in Table 10-2. Data are as of November 1949.

[4] *Ibid.*

[5] Calculation shown in text under "The Antimonopoly Law and Stock Divestiture."

It might be expected that the two bases, proceeds and paid-up value, would produce different figures, but from an HCLC table providing entries both ways,[6] it is clear that it does no violence to add them together. An additional complication is the different dates of the figures. The HCLC figure represents the full program; it is for 1951, while the other three figures are for 1949. Thus there is some understatement to the figure of 15 billion, but it seems improbable that the total would have amounted to more than 16 billion.

The scale of the securities disposal program can better be appreciated in terms of relatives than from the absolute figures themselves. It will be recalled from Chapter 3 that the three figures provided by the Ministry of Commerce, Finance Ministry and Bank of Japan on paid-up capital of all corporations and partnerships in Japan in 1945 were 32, 43, and 48 billion yen, respectively. Thus, depending on which agency's figures are used, the disposal program involved a sale of securities from nearly one-half to almost one-third of the 1945 paid-in value of all corporate securities in Japan. And, as if disposal of securities of such scale were not defeating enough, there was in addition a sale of new issues going on in the market at the same time, a result of recapitalization of reorganized companies and American ideas as to what constituted proper equity levels.

Also there were numerous, complicating background factors. Given *zaibatsu* "exclusiveness" and the skewed nature of income distribution in prewar Japan,[7] there had been no tradition of popular participation

[6] From a table showing the manner of disposal of HCLC securities appearing in HCLC Final "Monthly Report," July 5, 1951, World War II Records Division, National Archives, Suitland, Md. In this table the paid-up value of holding company securities and securities held by the 56 designated persons is shown as Y7.5 billion, whereas proceeds from sale are given as Y8.0. When the securities of restricted concerns are included with holding companies and designated persons, the two totals are Y8.6 billion in paid-up value and Y8.9 billion in proceeds from sale.

[7] Professor Alan H. Gleason in "Economic Growth and Consumption in Japan," in Lockwood, *The State and Economic Enterprise*, argues that statistical evidence does not support the widespread belief that historically Japan's income distribution was skewed. To share Professor Gleason's conclusions would be to deny that ownership patterns affect income distribution—which is highly questionable. It has been seen that at war's end four family groups controlled one-fourth of the corporate and partnership capital of the nation. In agriculture tenancy was widespread and rents were high. ("In 1943 almost 70% of the Japanese farmers rented a part of the land they cultivated; approximately 50% rented more than half of the land they cultivated . . . ," p. 364; for paddy, ". . . the tenant paid somewhat more than 50% of the yield to the landlord"—both quotes from Jerome B. Cohen, *Japan in War and Reconstruction*, Minneapolis, 1949, p. 442.) That even the language has included a word for the "estate of wealth" would suggest the vividness of income disparities to Japanese persons. It would seem doubtful that Marxism would have produced the term (as I suspect) if there had not been keen and

in corporate ownership in the modern sector of the economy. Furthermore, the securities disposal program came at a time when enormous economic adjustments were required to reorient production in a heavily damaged economy away from military to civilian items, and when, in addition to the uncertainties for management resulting from the reform phases of the Occupation, there was no assurance that all would not be lost in reparation removals. And last, inasmuch as MacArthur did not authorize the reopening of the stock exchanges until the spring of 1949, the bulk of the giant sale of stock took place without benefit of the exchanges.[8] The marvel is that transfer *was* effected.

Different methods were used to transfer the stock. The three most important were public tender, underwriting sales, and employee sales.[9] Using public tender, including local tender, securities were auctioned off to the highest bidder, down to a minimum price set by the offering agency. Through "underwriting sales," "large blocks of securities . . . [were] offered to underwriting groups of securities dealers on a competitive bid basis for resale to the public at a fixed price. Public notice . . . [was] made by press and radio announcement "calling for bids" and the usual period of time elapsing between the public announcement and closing of bids . . . [was] ten days to two weeks, depending on the size of the offering."[10] Employee sales provided employees (and local residents of the area of the head office or fac-

---

general feeling. For comment on certain postwar changes in national income distribution, cf. Chapter 17, note 20. What would seem probable is that Professor Gleason has been handicapped by the available statistics, though procedurally it seems questionable to attempt time-series of the length which Gleason has done from a single base.

[8] SCAP gave permission to reopen the Tokyo, Osaka, and Nagoya Stock Exchanges on May 12, 1949. The Tokyo Exchange reopened May 16, Osaka and Nagoya about a month later. Other exchanges reopened in the summer, with the exception of Sapporo, which reopened in April 1950. Cf. T.F.M. Adams, *A Financial History of Modern Japan*, Tokyo, 1964, p. 208.

[9] Other methods were "sales at fixed prices," "consignment sales," and "off-market sales." These three employed the services of dealers. "Sales at fixed prices" and "consignment sales" were very similar. Securities were turned over to dealers for disposal at fixed prices with a commission to them for services rendered. Consignment sales, used in the case of less popular stocks, not only provided a longer time period but required no financial commitment on the part of the dealer. Under the method of "off market sales," which became applicable after the opening of the exchanges in the spring of 1949, shares were offered to dealers from time to time at the closing market price after the close of the exchange, without prior announcement as to quantity or titles. Cf. Economic and Scientific Section, Fair Trade Practices Division, Memorandum, "Policies and Procedures for Securities Program," 25 October 1959 [*sic*, 1949], World War II Records Div., National Archives, Suitland, Md.

[10] *Ibid.*

tories) with the opportunity to purchase securities at a price approved by the Securities Coordinating Liquidation Commission.

### *The Establishment of the Securities Coordinating Liquidation Commission (SCLC)*

Since more than one agency of the Japanese government was involved in the disposal of securities, it quickly became evident that a coordinating group was necessary if the government was to avoid the spectacle of the government competing with itself. Accordingly, the SCLC (it also appears in English as "Committee") was established by Law No. 8 of January 17, 1947.[11] Its objective was "to effect necessary adjustment and coordination with respect to the time, price and quantity of disposal in conformity with the conditions of the securities market and at the same time to attain widest possible distribution of such securities among the nation."

Securities from the HCLC, the Closed Institutions Liquidation Commission, and the Finance Ministry were sold through the SCLC; securities disposed of under the Antimonopoly Law were not. Companies affected by the provisions of this law were not obliged to hand over to the FTC the securities which were to be sold. Rather, the companies submitted disposal plans to the FTC for its approval. In the Cabinet Order dealing with share disposal under the Antimonopoly Law of intercorporate stock-holding by financial and nonfinancial institutions, there was a provision that, "The Fair Trade Commission, if it is deemed necessary . . . [may? shall?] order that the transfer be entrusted to the Securities Coordinating Liquidation Commission."[12] Inasmuch as the records of the SCLC do not show entries from the FTC, and under "Others" shows proceeds from sale of only $16,000, it may be presumed that the FTC did not believe there were cases where companies were not complying with the act.

Tables 10-1, 10-2, and 10-3, which follow, give the story of the disposal program in figures. Because the *zaibatsu* securities were by far the largest part of the disposal program, and combine dissolution the focus of this study, Table 10-1 presents *zaibatsu* securities in some detail. In many cases there were several figures from which to choose. Those in the table represent my best judgment as to which are the most probable. Table 10-1 provides some dramatic relatives. One gains a sharp impression of the enormity of the holdings by the top-holding companies of the Big Four (plus Nakajima Aircraft) in

[11] For the text, cf. HCLC, *Laws, Rules*, pp. 121-26.

[12] Cabinet Order No. 43, February 27, 1948, Article 6. For text, cf. *Laws, Rules*, pp. 216-22.

observing that these companies, which made up the first designation, accounted for 30 percent of the shares which the 83 designated holding companies transferred to the HCLC for disposal. Further, one gains some feel for the magnitude of the personal holdings of the *zaibatsu* families in observing that the holdings of the 56 designated individuals were roughly of the order of magnitude of the shares transferred to the HCLC by the 20 companies making up the third designation, mostly giant second-level holding-operating companies, often key subsidiaries of the Big Four.

Table 10-1 shows a wide discrepancy between combine securities ostensibly coming under the program and securities actually sold. Apparently the disparity largely represented the equity in companies undergoing outright dissolution.[13] In the case of the *zaibatsu* families, the disparity of Y685 million is probably to be explained by the capital levy tax. The families paid Y600 million under the capital levy[14] tax and, as previously noted, the tax could be paid in kind. In the case of securities coming under Imperial Ordinance 567, the discrepancy would appear to be explained simply by nonperformance. Although at peak the number of restricted firms was some 1,200, only 468 concerns participated. Furthermore, of the shares transferred, only approximately 60 percent were disposed of. One gains further insight into performance under Imp. Ord. 567 by studying corporation yearbooks. Under the ordinance, financial institutions were forbidden to hold shares in companies of their "same chain of capital." Yet corporation yearbooks for 1949, 1950, and 1951 reveal case after case where such institutions did so. Clearly the stock divestiture provisions of Imp. Ord. 567 had only a modest impact.

Tables 10-2 and 10-3 present the full range of the securities disposal program, with the exception of shares corporately disposed of under the Antimonopoly Law. Unfortunately the time period of the tables falls short of the conclusion of the program, though the bulk of the disposal is covered. In the case of HCLC shares, the tables provide information on over four-fifths of the securities disposed. With respect to disposal methods, the tables make it clear that disposal by auction (down to a specified minimum price) was the most important route followed by underwriting sales through securities dealers and sales to employees. Further, the tables indicate that 1948 and 1949 were the two key years in the disposal program.

In perpsective it is difficult to understand how such a gigantic share disposal program could have been effected—but it was. The program

[13] Source cited in note 6.
[14] HCLC, *Zaibatsu Dissolution*, textual volume, p. 301.

Table 10-1: SIZE OF THE HCLC SECURITIES DISPOSAL PROGRAM

(Because the figures from the indicated sources are not at all times internally consistent the actual sums of entries shown are presented in parentheses)

| | Shares, paid-up value (1) | Bonds, face value (2) | Total (3) |
|---|---|---|---|
| *Holding Companies (N = 83)* | | | |
| Total securities held in other companies[a] | Y8,326,635,000 | Y790,681,000 | Y9,117,316,000 |
| Total securities transferred to HCLC[b] | 7,026,735,548 | 47,971,451 | 7,074,706,999 |
| 1st designation ( 5 companies) | 2,231,855,423 | 32,721,802 | 2,264,557,226 |
| 2nd designation (40 companies) | 2,914,464,453 | 10,819,356 | 2,925,283,809 |
| 3rd designation (20 companies) | 1,636,991,696 | 3,690,550 | 1,635,682,246 (1,640,682,246) |
| 4th designation ( 2 companies) | 65,696,762 | 256,502 | 65,953,265 |
| 5th designation (16 companies) | 182,727,212 | 483,240 | 183,210,452 |
| (actual sum of entries shown) | (7,031,735,546) | (47,971,450) | (7,074,686,998) |
| Discrepancy between securities held and those transferred[c] | 1,299,899,452 | 742,709,549 | 2,042,609,001 |
| *Designated Persons (56 Zaibatsu persons)* | | | |
| Securities held[d] | Y1,113,951,000 | Y88,048,000 | Y1,201,999,000 |
| Securities transferred to HCLC[b] | 448,393,784 | 8,555,092 | 496,948,877 (456,948,876) |
| Discrepancy between securities held and those transferred[e] | 665,557,216 | 79,493,008 | 745,050,124 |
| *Holding Companies and Designated Persons* | | | |
| Grand tot. securities transferred to HCLC | 7,475,129,332 | 56,526,543 | 7,571,655,876 |

*Restricted Concerns: Imp. Ord. 567*

(Note: Of the 1,203 firms on the Schedule of Restricted Concerns, 468 "participated.")

| | *Shares held in other companies* | *Shares "to be disposed"[f] (as of Nov. 22, 1946) paid-up value* | *Shares disposed paid-up value* |
|---|---|---|---|
| 468 restricted companies | ? | Y1,475,876,000 | |
| 147 "related" companies[g] | ? | 61,021,000 | |
| Total | | 1,536,897,000 | Y982,545,000[h] |

[a]*Zaibatsu Dissolution*, data volume, p. 289. By contrast, the HCLC's English-language report, p. 75, gives the value of shares held as Y7,507,604,000.

[b]HCLC, final "Monthly Report," July 5, 1951. World War II Records Division, National Archives, Suitland, Md.

[c]This line is the subtraction of "securities transferred" from "securities held" using HCLC totals. By contrast, the HCLC "Monthly Report," June 30, 1951, cites as the amount of holding company securities "not yet transferred," Y432,897,720 (paid-in value). World War II Records Division, National Archives, Suitland, Md.

also produced some conservative Japanese, whom one might expect to take a highly critical attitude toward the combine-dissolution program, turned out not infrequently to hold a favorable view, inasmuch as the program provided them, for the first time, with the opportunity to acquire "blue chip" securities.

### *The Antimonopoly Law and Stock Divestiture*

While the intent was that the HCLC, under the Holding Company Liquidation Commission Ordinance, Imp. Ord. 567, and the Deconcentration Law, would hand over the economy in deconcentrated form to the safekeeping of the FTC, which was administering the Antimonopoly Law, there were some divestiture procedures taken under the Antimonopoly Law. The Antimonopoly Law had been drafted to ban intercorporate stock ownership among nonfinancial companies (with the exception of single-layer subsidiaries held close to 100 percent), thus making it much more stringent than pratice in the United States; yet it permitted holdings by financial companies up to 5 percent of the total issued stock, which provided a latitude not allowed in American practice. The toleration of bank holdings in industrial, commercial, and mining companies was unfortunate, and the severity of the ban on intercorporate holdings was both unwise and out of keeping with other parts of the program. The stringency probably came about because of the projection of intercorporate patterns to the extreme of a combine network. But just as some observers deplore mild inflation because severe inflation is ruinous, so the staff wrestling with deconcentration in the Japanese economy came to deplore all intercorpate shareholding because when carried to the scale of combine-building it spelled discriminatory business.

Article 9 of the Antimonopoly Law banned the *establishment* of

---

[d] *Zaibatsu Dissolution*, data volume, p. 293. By contrast, the English-language report gives the strikingly different figures for shares owned of Y608,957,000, a half-billion yen lower. Cf. *Final Report*, p. 75.

[e] This line is the subtraction of "Securities transferred" from "Securities held." In view of the various arithmetic errors in column 3. The figure in parenthesis has been subtracted. The HCLC "Monthly Report," June 30, 1951, cites as the value of securities "not yet transferred," Y112,009,073.

[f] *Zaibatsu Dissolution*, textual volume, p. 466. These amounts do not include a small amount of preemptive share rights and holdings, belonging to Allied nationals. It is curious to have such data put forward three days before the pertinent ordinance was promulgated.

[g] 131 "subsidiary" companies and 16 "affiliated" companies.

[h] *Zaibatsu Dissolution*, textual volume, p. 467. Data are as of March 31, 1950.

Table 10-2: SECURITIES DISTRIBUTED BY THE SECURITIES COORDINATING AND LIQUIDATION COMMISSION, JUNE 1947 TO NOVEMBER 1949

*Classified by Offering Organization*

| *Distributing Agency* | *No of Shares (1,000's)* | *Proceeds (1,000's yen)* |
|---|---|---|
| HCLC | 113,324 | 8,364,403 |
| CILC [Closed Institutions] | 37,867 | 3,121,744 |
| Government [Min. of Finance] | 27,441 | 1,740,447 |
| Bank of Japan | 195 | 80,644 |
| Others | 101 | 5,930 |
| Total | 178,928 | 12,313,168 |
| (sum of figures shown | | 13,313,168) |

*Classified by Means of Disposal*

| *Type of Sale* | *No. of Shares (1,000's)* | *Proceeds (1,000's yen)* |
|---|---|---|
| General, including local, tender | 56,370 | 4,913,486 |
| Underwriting sales | 63,958 | 4,232,124 |
| Employee sales | 44,554 | 2,094,588 |
| General, including local, sales | 12,792 | 952,650 |
| Consignment sales | 701 | 26,716 |
| Off-market sales | 553 | 93,604 |
| Total | 178,928 | 12,313,168 |

Source and notes: SCAP, GHQ, History of Nonmilitary Activities of the Occupation of Japan, Vol. XIII, Finance, Part C, *Money and Banking 1945 through June 1951*, App. 1, F, based on *Japanese Economic Statistics Bulletin No. 39* (November 1949), Section IV, p. 42, Office of Military History, Washington, D.C. For contrasting published figures on the amount of sales, cf. Bisson, p. 114, and *Oriental Economist*, June 28, 1947, p. 510.

Table 10-3: SECURITIES DISTRIBUTED BY THE SECURITIES COORDINATING AND LIQUIDATION COMMISSION, JUNE 1947 TO NOVEMBER 1949

*By Period of Disposition*

| *Period* | *No. of Shares (1,000's)* | *Proceeds (1,000's yen)* |
|---|---|---|
| To December 31, 1947 | 2,844 | 113,126 |
| 1948 | 76,432 | 5,041,212 |
| 1949 | 99,652 | 7,158,830 |
| January | 12,951 | 1,026,148 |
| February | 6,423 | 474,803 |
| March | 8,667 | 720,815 |
| April | 8,385 | 536,388 |
| May | 11,862 | 1,096,930 |
| June | 9,017 | 696,164 |
| July | 5,016 | 252,780 |
| August | 12,023 | 1,005,062 |
| September | 17,553 | 937,316 |
| October | 6,421 | 368,336 |
| November | 1,334 | 44,088 |
| Total | 178,928 | 12,313,168 |

Source: Source cited in Table 10-2, Appendix 1,F, 1949 total has been added.

holding companies (those with 25 percent or more of their assets in securities of other companies), yet Article 105 stated that disposal of securities of *existing* ones would "be provided by separate order." While Article 10 of the Law stated that nonfinancial companies "shall not *acquire*" stocks in other companies, Article 107 stated that stocks *owned* by a nonfinancial company at the time of enforcement of the law would be governed by provisions "to be provided by separate order." Article 11 specified the conditions under which financial companies were *not to own* stocks in other companies—if the companies were competitors, or if the owning company's assets were Y5,000,000 or more, it was not to own more than five percent of the issued shares of another company—but Article 108 stated that *disposal*, where indicated, would "be provided for by separate order." These separate orders, reflecting the procrastinating ways of the Japanese government, occurred months after passage of the law. The Cabinet Order governing disposition of existing holding company securities (Cabinet Order 239) was issued November 8, 1947, some seven months after passage of the act.[15] The Cabinet Order dealing with disposal of securities of nonfinancial and financial companies (Cabinet Order 43) was issued February 27, 1948, 10 months after passage of the law.[16]

Operations under these provisions are presented in Table 10-4, which shows some 4,000 companies affected by the Cabinet Order, notwithstanding that there were at this time about 104,000 joint stock companies in Japan[17] and that intercorporate shareholding was the overwhelmingly dominant form of stockholding. Clearly the law was not applied across-the-board, but, apparently, selectively. In addition to the three categories of stock disposal under the Antimonopoly Law, Table 10-4 shows an additional entry—shares to be disposed of under the Deconcentration Law. It will be recalled that out of the release of 225 of the original companies in the May and June 1948 cutbacks, 175 companies were to continue under "surveillance" and in a number of cases make disposition of certain securities. Several such "cases" were placed under the jurisdiction of the FTC which enjoyed a higher standing among critics of the deconcentration program than did the HCLC. Inasmuch as under the 1949 amendments to the Antimonopoly Law the virtual prohibition of intercorporate stockholding was removed—though financial institutions continued to be restricted to the 5 percent limit until 1953, when through amendment this was raised to 10 percent—the table presents nearly the full story of disposal of intercorporately held shares.

Table 10-4 reveals a strikingly different performance with respect to disposal of shares among the different categories of companies. The securities of financial institutions were much further along toward disposal than were the securities of the other three categories. While the other three programs were one-fourth to one-third complete by June 1949, disposal of shares which financial institutions held in other companies was over 80 percent complete. To me this suggests the hand of SCAP. Although MacArthur was obliged to give up plans to

[15] For text, cf. *Laws, Rules*, pp. 213-15.

[16] For text, *ibid.*, pp. 216-22.

[17] This statistic which is for September 30, 1948 is taken from Hamm, *Deconcentration of Economic Power*, p. 17. It is difficult to find out what the figure actually was. In FTC, *The Realities of Economic Concentration in Japan* (*Nihon ni okeru, Keizai Ryoku Shuchu no Jittai*), Tokyo, 1951, the Appendix Table 5, shows there to have been 207,898 companies in 1949.

Table 10-4: PROGRESS OF STOCK DISPOSAL UNDER THE ANTI-MONOPOLY LAW, JUNE 15, 1949

| | *Cos. Aug. 1948* | *Cos. June 1949* | *Difference* | *Shares Held* (A) | *Shares Disposed* (B) | *Ratio* B/A |
|---|---|---|---|---|---|---|
| Cabinet Order 43 - Divestiture of stocks intercorporately owned | | | | | | |
| Non-financial companies | 3,523 | 3,564 | +41 | 31,822,450 | 8,343,714 | 26% |
| Financial companies | 78 | 83 | + 5 | 10,620,395 | 8,849,907 | 83% |
| Cabinet Order 239 - Dissolution of existing holding companies | 298 | 294 | - 4 | 14,946,718 | 3,653,849 | 24%[a] |
| Companies, designated under the Deconcentration Law, ordered to sell certain securities | 80 | 97 | +17 | 12,494,141 | 3,495,294 | 28% |
| Total | 3,979[b] | 4,038 | +59 | 69,883,704 | 24,342,764[c] | 35%[d] |

[a]Arithmetic error corrected. Document lists ratio at 37%.

[b]Arithmetic error corrected. Document lists total at 3,977.

[c]Arithmetic error corrected. Document lists total at 26,342,764.

[d]Arithmetic error corrected. Document lists ratio at 37.6.

Sources: August 1948 data from FTC report, "Brief Outline and Record of the Fair Trade Commission Covering the Period of Time from 23 July 1948 to 31 August 1948," World War II Records Division, National Archives, Suitland, Md. June 1949 data from FTC 1949 *Annual Report* (April 1, 1949 to March 31, 1950), pp. 98-99, World War II Records Division.

reorganize the banking system, pressure was exerted toward disposal under the Antimonopoly Law. But pressure under the law was not tantamount to disposal under Imp. Ord. 567, for the Antimonopoly Law contained no restriction on holdings "in the same chain of capital." Thus, even with the disposal record that Table 10-4 shows, Mitsui Bank could continue to hold share in Mitsui Trust Banking, Mitsui Shipbuilding, Mitsui Chemical, and similarly the other city banks in their former affiliates up to 5 percent.

The information in Table 10-4 is presented in terms of shares held rather than by value, but what was the yen scale of the disposal program? The FTC stated that all shares under this program were 50-yen shares.[18] While 50-yen shares are by far the most common denomination of shares, 500-yen shares are also used; it would seem highly improbable to me that all shares were 50 yen. (For a contemporary breakdown of shares by denomination, cf. note—23 below.) If the FTC statement is accepted, however, and if it is assumed that all shares were fully paid up, the total of the program by June 1949 was Y1.3 billion in paid-up value, which among the four programs breaks down in round numbers as follows: Nonfinancial companies, Y415 million; Financial companies, Y440 million; Holding companies, Y280 million; Deconcentration companies, Y174 million. Elsewhere, figures of Y3.3 billion[19] and Y12 billion[20] have been cited for the value of all securities affected by the Antimonopoly Law. The first figure would seem high, the latter quite implausible.

### *The Effect of Securities Transfer on Ownership Patterns*

In a sense, one might say that the Occupation's measures for diversifying the pattern of corporate ownership in Japan accelerated the historical trend. It is the genius of the corporate form to pool bits and pieces of capital into giant aggregates. Enormous fortunes are not required to produce the capital necessary for modern production. Far greater amounts than any fortune could produce are obtained through aggregating pieces.

The *zaibatsu* families were largely successful in restricting ownership in their key operating companies to insiders (personal and corporate) until the expansion after the Manchurian War, in preparation for the China and Pacific Wars. This expansion saw old industries greatly

[18] Fair Trade Commission, "Brief Outline and Record of the Fair Trade Commission Covering the Period of Time from 23 July 1948 to 31 August 1948," World War II Records Division, Suitland, Md.

[19] Bisson, *Zaibatsu Dissolution*, p. 114.

[20] *Oriental Economist*, June 28, 1947, p. 510.

enlarged, along with the start of entirely new ones. Because of the scale of their capital needs in these years, the *zaibatsu* began to open securities to public subscription, as was illustrated in Chapter 2. The securities disposal program under the extraordinary measures of the Occupation gave this process a major boost.

The transfer of the billions of yen in securities did effect some changes in the overall pattern of corporate ownership in Japan. If a comparison is made of the pattern prior to the start of the deconcentration effort in 1945 with that 15 years later, when the economy had once again come into its own, certain significant differences will be seen. The Occupation effort resulted in a decline in the role of government; it unintentionally produced a great increase in the role of financial institutions, and it left individual holdings at much the same percentage level as they had been. These patterns will be seen in Table 10-5.

From a study of Table 10-5 it might appear at first that personal holdings had declined from 53% in 1945 to 46% in 1960. This would not be a correct conclusion, however, for inasmuch as "investment trusts" importantly represent personal holdings, it is appropriate to add these (6%) to "individuals," thus making individual holdings essentially the same. Although individual holdings as a percentage of total holdings may have remained the same, the number of individuals participating has dramatically risen. In 1960 there were 13.3 million persons holding shares, compared to 1.6 million in 1945.[21] Making allowance for differences in size of the population for the years in question,[22] one finds there has been a roughly sixfold increase in the number of individual shareholders. No longer does one find entries for major corporations, such as one used to do in corporation yearbooks in prewar years, with a total of 11 shareholders. While the eventual effect of the program was to leave individual holdings at the percentage figure where they had been, the table indicates that the initial effect was to greatly expand the percentage figures for individual holdings. It will be seen that during the peak period of the securities disposal program individual holdings rose to 69%.

However, a caveat is in order, with respect to the basis for the percentage figures of Table 10-5. To obtain the figures presented in the table, the Ministry of Finance simply counted shares—in effect treat-

[21] Finance Ministry, *Investigations of the Distribution of Shareholding* (Okurasho, *Rizaikyoku Keizaika, Kabushiki Bumpu Jokyo Chosa.* In the 1953 issue, pp. 8-9; in the 1960 issue, pp. 22-23.

[22] Population was 72 million in 1945; 93 million in 1960.

Table 10-5: DISTRIBUTION OF SHARES BY TYPE OF SHAREHOLDER IN PERCENTAGE TERMS

| | *(1945-53 listed shares only)* | | | | | | *(1954-60 listed and unlisted shares)* | | | | | | |
|---|---|---|---|---|---|---|---|---|---|---|---|---|---|
| | 1945 | 1949 | 1950 | 1951 | 1952 | 1953 | 1954 | 1955 | 1956 | 1957 | 1958 | 1959 | 1960 |
| Gov't and public bodies | 8.29 | 2.8 | 3.14 | 1.76 | 1.0 | 0.7 | 0.85 | 0.57 | 0.57 | 0.56 | 0.65 | 0.53 | 0.46 |
| Financial institutions | 11.17 | 9.91 | 12.63 | 18.24 | 21.82 | 22.94 | 20.31 | 2 .48 | 22.46 | 22.93 | 25.42 | 25.88 | 26.69 |
| Investment trusts | - | - | - | 5.22 | 6.03 | 6.67 | 5.67 | 3.39 | 3.20 | 2.44 | 5.52 | 6.35 | 6.25 |
| Security dealers | 2.82 | 12.56 | 11.90 | 9.22 | 8.44 | 7.34 | 6.50 | 7.17 | 6.49 | 5.22 | 4.11 | 3.52 | 3.51 |
| Other corporate persons | 24.65 | 5.59 | 11.03 | 13.80 | 11.75 | 13.54 | 16.19 | 16.69 | 18.72 | 19.53 | 19.17 | 20.79 | 21.34 |
| Individuals | 53.07 | 69.14 | 61.30 | 56.98 | 55.79 | 53.79 | 54.39 | 53.35 | 50.26 | 50.30 | 48.63 | 47.24 | 46.18 |
| Foreigners | - | - | 3.14 | 1.76 | 1.2 | 1.7 | 1.57 | 1.48 | 1.32 | 1.20 | 1.17 | 1.21 | 1.07 |
| Actual Total | 100.00 | 100.00 | 103.14 | 106.98 | 106.03 | 106.68 | 105.48 | 103.13 | 103.02 | 102.18 | 104.67 | 105.52 | 105.50 |

Source and notes: Finance Ministry, *Investigation of the Distribution of Share Holding* (Okurasho Rizaikyoku Keizaika, *Kabushiki Bumpu Jokyo Chosa*). The data for this table have been compiled from Table I in the reports for the two years 1953 and 1960. The reports are not altogether consonant. The 1953 report is for listed shares only; the 1960 report covers both listed and unlisted stock (of companies with a capitalization of Y50 million and above). "Listed" refers to stocks listed on the first section of the Tokyo Stock Exchange; "listed and unlisted" refers to all stocks of the indicated capitalization. It will be observed that with the exception of the first two columns, the percentage figures have the unusual quality of adding to more than 100.

ing all shares as if they were of equal value.[23] Not only are differences in par value ignored, a 50-yen share being added to a 500-yen share to equal two shares, but market worth is entirely disregarded. If, however, it is assumed that the different varieties of shares and share worth were roughly equally distributed among different types of shareholders, then the table does provide approximate information.

Although it was in Chapter 4 that the designation of the 83 holding companies was discussed, it has been necessary to postpone discussion of what became of these companies to this point, inasmuch as a large proportion of them were operating companies, as well, and were subject for this reason to other Occupation actions. Of the 83 holding companies 76 were designated "special accounting" companies under the Enterprise Reconstruction and Reorganization Law to handle reorganization of operating functions;[24] 51 were initially designated under the Deconcentration Law, of which 10 remained designated after DRB review.[25] The summarized results of the holding-company dissolution program, reorganization under the ERR Law, and reorganization under the Deconcentration Law will be found in Appendix X.

Because of the several laws to which the 83 holding companies were subject, it is possible, apart from the divestiture of their securities, to summarize the actions taken with respect to these companies in successor form under four headings—(1) dissolution, (2) dissolution with "second companies," (3) no dissolution and "second companies," and (4) "untouched." The two extremes are clear—outright dissolution and company untouched. The distinction between the two middle categories—dissolution with successor companies, and no dissolution

[23] Finance Ministry, *Investigation of the Distribution of Shareholding*, 1960 issue, pp. 22-23. In 1960 the distribution of shares by share-worth among issuing companies and shareholders was as follows: Out of a total of 3,919 companies, 2,518 issued 50-yen shares, and 1,126 issued 500-yen shares. Out of a total number of shareholders of 13,806,921, 12,336,148 held 50-yen shares, and 1,162,801 held 500-yen shares. Out of a total of 41,440,556,000 shares outstanding, 39,242,221,000 were in 50-yen shares and 1,021,049,000 were in 500-yen shares.

[24] The designations are shown in HCLC, *Zaibatsu Dissolution*, Data volume, in the listing of the holding companies, pp. 6-20. While certain companies which were designated "special accounting companies" under the Enterprise Reconstruction and Reorganization Law were dissolved (thus indicating that such designation was not sufficient to prevent dissolution, for example, Asano Holding Co.), curiously enough, certain companies which are shown with "second companies" are not listed as "special accounting companies," for example, the Mitsubishi Holding Co. Inasmuch as Mitsubishi Holding Co. is discussed as reorganized under the Enterprise Reconstruction and Reorganization Law in the HCLC, textual volume, p. 198, such may perhaps merely represent typographical oversights.

[25] Initial designations are listed in *ibid.*, Data volume, pp. 24-88; final designations are listed, *ibid.*, textual volume, pp. 346-49, and in the English-language *Final Report*, pp. 62-64.

and successor companies—was largely dictated by accounting necessities under the ERR Law. The antitrust dimension of these middle categories is to be seen in the number of companies which resulted from these operations. It would be inappropriate to imply that all expansion of corporate units stemmed from antitrust considerations. Some stemmed from financial solvency alone, but the antitrust dimension of the ERR Law should be recognized. For example, it was under the ERR Law that Mitsubishi Chemical Industries (Mitsubishi Kasei) became three companies: Nippon Chemical Industries (later Mitsubishi Chemical Industries), Mitsubishi Rayon, and Asahi Glass. It was under the ERR Law that Mitsubishi Steel became Mitsubishi Steel and Mitsubishi Steel Mfg. (Consolidation took place in 1964, so that today, there is only Mitsubishi Steel.)

Using the numbers of the four categories of actions, it is possible to summarize the results of the actions taken with respect to the operating functions of the 83 holding companies under the several laws as follows: (1) 16 companies—dissolved (no operating functions); (2) 26 companies—dissolution with successor companies; (3) 11 companies—no dissolution and successor companies; (4) 30 companies—continued.

Only a few of the companies in the first category, "outright dissolution," were *zaibatsu* companies, according to the customary usage of that confusing term. *Zaibatsu* companies were represented by the top-holding companies of the Mitsui combine, Asano combine, Nomura combine, and Shibusawa combine. A number of the other companies were small family operations, the product of the fifth and final designation of holding companies. None of the companies in Category 1 were designated under the Deconcentration Law.

Most of the holding companies falling in Category 2 were large operating companies. The top-holding companies of the Mitsubishi, Sumitomo, and Yasuda combines were here, but this was because of operating activities. The two giant trading companies, Mitsui Trading and Mitsubishi Trading, were here, but their presence obscures what really took place. The two trading companies are shown with one successor company. Normally dissolution with one successor company would mean no corporate reorganization at all—merely an accounting reorganization. That these two companies were thus shown is somewhat puzzling, for it is misleading in view of the nature of the action taken. Other companies in this grouping were key subsidiaries of the Big Four—Nakajima Aircraft (renamed Fuji Industries), holding companies outside the network of the 10 designated *zaibatsu* families (Nitchitsu, Riken, Okura), certain key national policy companies (Japan Iron and Steel, International Telecommunications), as well as a few small companies from the final designation of holding companies. Twelve of the companies in Category 2 were designated under the Deconcentration Law.

As stated, there was no substantive difference between categories 2 and 3. It was the exigencies of accounting that created the two categories. Accordingly, it is not surprising that the companies in Category 3 were of the same type as found in Category 2. All 11 companies in Category 3 were designated under the Deconcentration Law.

Category 4, the untouched companies, represented a highly uneven collection of companies—some major subsidiaries of the Big Four, certain major subsidiaries of the Other Six, and cotton spinning companies. Twenty-eight of the 30 companies in this grouping were designated under the Deconcentration Law.

Most of the textile companies were to be found in Category 4, the "untouched" category. Two companies, however, were in Category 2, "dissolution with successor companies," and three in Category 3, "no dissolution with successor companies." Thus, in what earlier had seemed a somewhat curious action, little change occurred.

### *Revision of the Antimonopoly Law*

Given the views of the Japanese government toward the original version of the Antimonopoly Law, it was predictable that it quickly responded to the change in American policy signaled by enunciation of the Deconcentration Review Board's four points of September 11, 1948. While it had taken MacArthur a year to get the Japanese Cabinet to submit an antitrust bill to the Diet and a year and a half to get the law on the statute books—not to mention the additional months required for issue of the implementing Cabinet Orders—it took less than three weeks from the September 1948 publication of the four points for the Japanese government to announce its proposals for revision. The chairman of the Fair Trade Commission informed the Deconcentration Review Board that the Japanese government intended to amend the provisions of the law governing "corporate securities holdings, international contracts, multiple directorates, individual stockholdings, mergers and transfers of business." He said:

> As it was pointed out in your press release of 11 September 1948, I believe the time is now appropriate that the Anti-monopoly Law be restudied and reconsidered in light of the basic principles of anti-trust legislation as they are internationally recognized. While it is felt that there is no need for the Japanese Anti-monopoly Law to

> be a translation of the American or Canadian antitrust legislation and that all reasonable improvements provided in experience to be practical and effective from an antitrust viewpoint should be incorporated, it is going a little too far when all provisions of the law are written for the sole purpose of enabling the strictest possible enforcement of the law. In light of the foregoing thought, reconsideration and amendment of our present law should be made as suggested above.
>
> . . . it is the intention of our government to introduce into the coming extraordinary session of the Diet a bill covering the amendments to the Anti-monopoly Law. . . . . While certain proposals have been submitted [to the Headquarters], our government as well as this Commission are of the opinion that the whole question of amending the present Anti-monopoly Law must again be reconsidered in light of the newly indicated four basic principles for carrying out the deconcentration program under the Deconcentration Law. This Commission, in coordination with other Ministries of our Government, has drawn up a preliminary draft of our proposed amendments along the lines indicated above, which are attached herewith for your study and reference.[26]

This revision resulted in the 1949 amendments.

The Anti-monopoly Law was amended by Law No. 214, June 18, 1949:

> By this revision, the overall prohibition of intercorporate stockholding and mergers was abandoned. The restriction on multiple directorates was lifted. The revision authorized intercorporate stockholding and multiple directorates on the condition that the positions were not obtained by unfair methods of competition and did not tend to lessen competition in any particular field of trade or between the companies concerned.
>
> Mergers or acquisitions by a company of the assets of another company became permissible so long as they were not forced by unfair methods of competition or . . . [did not result in] disparities in bargaining power. Any proposed merger or acquisition by a company of the assets of another company must be reported [i.e., not permission, but reporting] to the FTC 30 days in advance. The FTC

[26] Fair Trade Commission document, entitled "Statement to be read by Mr. K. Nakayama, Chairman of the Fair Trade Commission, at a meeting with the Deconcentration Board to be Held on Tuesday, 28 September 1948," World War II Records Division, National Archives, Suitland, Md., paragraph 4d, 5.

must act within the 30-day period if it decides that the action violates the above restriction and should be stopped.

With regard to international agreements, it was no longer necessary to obtain the permission of the FTC as previously required, but a report must be filed with the FTC within 30 days after the conclusion of an agreement. The ban on international agreements to restrict the exchange of scientific knowledge or information necessary for business activities was also lifted.[27]

With the imminent occurrence of the Peace Treaty, September 1951, the Japanese government in June 1951 established an inquiry commission to comprehensively study the Anti-monopoly Law and make recommendations for its improvement. The commission reported in July 1951: ". . . while upholding the basic principle of the law [the commission] expressed the opinion that the law was too strict and should be made more moderate in order to accelerate the nation's economic recovery."[28] These recommendations did not occur as amendments until 1953.[29]

Amendment was achieved through Law No. 259 of September 1, 1953.[30] The provision proscribing disparities in bargaining power was deleted. Resale maintenance was limitedly authorized (copyrighted books, records and commodities "which are in daily use by the general consumer and easily identifiable by trademarks and other labels, in free competition with other similar commodities"). The flat prohibition on cartels was removed; instead, with the approval of the FTC, two types of cartels were authorized, depression and rationalization. Restrictions on intercorporate stockholding and interlocking multiple directorates were further modified. The stipulation that these not be attained by unfair methods of business was deleted, and the only restriction remaining was that the result would not be a substantial restraint of competition in any particular field of trade. Reporting of intercorporate stock ownership and interlocking directorates was required for companies whose assets were valued at 100 million yen

[27] *Foreign Trade and Antitrust Laws*, Hearings before the Subcommittee on Antitrust and Monopoly of the Committee of the Judiciary, U.S. Senate, 89th Cong., 1st Sess., Part 2 (Appendix), "Antitrust Development and Regulations of Foreign Countries," p. 982. Cf. Iyori Hiroshi, *Antimonopoly Legislation in Japan*, pp. 18-19.

[28] *Ibid.*

[29] Professor Yasuba asserts the delay in enactment was caused by SCAP displeasure. Given the great latitude extended to the Japanese government by General Ridgway's May 1951 order, this does not seem altogether plausible. Cf. Yasuba Yasukichi, "Foreign Economic Policy of the United States Affecting Japan: 1945-1962" mimeo., a study prepared for the International House of Japan, 1964, p. 103.

[30] *Foreign Trade and Antitrust Laws*, pp. 982-83.

(about $278,000). The Trade Association Law was repealed and some of the prohibited acts were incorporated in a new Article 8 in the Antimonopoly Law.

As we shall see in Part II, the Japanese government has attempted further revision, but not successfully. At the present time, the chief avenue for change in the provisions of the Antimonopoly Law is not amendment but legislation exempting businesses from its provisions. In addition, businesses can escape the ban on cartels through cartels described as "administrative guidance," primarily under the direction of the Ministry of International Trade and Industry (commonly abbreviated MITI).

Interestingly enough, however, the prohibition in the Antimonopoly Law with respect to holding companies (Article 9) still stands. Writing some 10 years after the height of the deconcentration effort, a Restrictive Practices Study Team of the Japan Productivity Center commented: "Against the outlawing of the holding company there has been no open criticism. . . . The evil[s] of the holding company have been so deeply impressed upon the popular mind that, in spite of significant contributions by some of them toward the advancement of the Japanese economy at large, no voice is raised favouring openly its revival, whatever different people may feel inwardly."[31]

As will be evident in Part II, the proscription of holding companies in the Antimonopoly Law has in no way inhibited the development of subsidiary complexes around today's majors. They are large and growing. But a company whose "principal business is to control . . . the business activities of another company" has not yet reappeared, though officials of MITI and elsewhere in the Japanese government are asserting that this prohibition is handicapping to Japan's full economic performance.

In the foregoing chapters I have outlined the measures adopted in the attempt to create a more competitive structure of industrial organization in Japan and to widen the distribution of income and ownership of the means of production, together with the problems encountered and the setbacks faced. As these chapters make abundantly clear, there was frequent uncertainty and a lack of knowledge with which to proceed. The implementation of the program was not well conceived, but improvised and guessed at. And MacArthur's problems were certainly not lessened when in midstream, the United States changed the objectives of the Occupation.

[31] Japan Productivity Center, *Control of Restrictive Trade Practices in Japan*, Tokyo, 1958, p. 7.

Measured against the original instructions, MacArthur had both successes and lack of accomplishment. Holding companies were dissolved, an achievement which, as will be seen in Part II, has made for quite a different pattern of industrial organization in the modern sector of the economy. Ownership in the modern sector has been distinctly broadened. Where accomplishment was least was in the matter of banking-industrial ties. These were not severed, so that impartial access to credit remains a problem to those who subscribe to the goal of equality of business opportunity. The brilliant growth of Japan's economy which followed the Occupation years demonstrates with a clarity, which no amount of argumentation could achieve, how badly mistaken not only in description but in analysis the Mitsuis were when in 1955 they wrote:

> With the ruinous diminution of the Mitsui families' wealth, the dissolution of [the top-holding company] Mitsui Honsha, Ltd., the complete democratization of the shareholding system of Mitsui companies and the retirement of the Mitsui family members and former executives, the powerful organization of Mitsui enterprise has been thoroughly dissolved as a business concern from the point of view of both capital and personnel. In this respect the dissolution of the big business concerns with the object of democratizing Japanese economy, as aimed at by G.H.Q., has been more than realized. On the other hand, this is one of the main reasons rendering Japan's post-war economy very weak and making its reconstruction exceedingly difficult. In particular, it cannot be denied that the dissolution of big companies such as Mitsui [Trading] Bussan Kaisha, Ltd., has made it exceedingly difficult for Japan to recover its former markets.[32]

In Part II we turn to the state of the economy 15 to 20 years after this bold experiment in antitrust.

[32] Mitsubishi Economic Research Institute, *Mitsui, Mitsubishi, Sumitomo*, Tokyo, 1955, p. 30.

# Part II 系列

# 11.

## *Zaibatsu* Yesterday, Business "Groupings" Today—Is There a Difference?

In the preceding chapters the logic of the Allied experiment in antitrust and the steps taken (some reversed) have been outlined. Now let us look at the situation today, nearly 20 years after the peace treaty with Japan, to determine the extent to which "the most ambitious antitrust action in history" has taken hold or been rejected, the extent to which the *zaibatsu* have returned, or if they have not returned, how much they have been replaced by similar concentrations of business power.

In both Japan and the U.S. the press has been reporting a steady series of recombinations. The *Oriental Economist* in its English edition in 1955 published a series entitled "Zaibatsu Renaissance,"[1] and in 1958-59, "Zaibatsu Revival?"[2]—the gist of which was that the question mark in the title was unnecessary. In 1963 the *Japan Economic Journal* (*Nihon Keizai*), Japan's *Wall Street Journal*, published a series of articles under the general heading, "Industrial World Washed by Waves of Regroupings."[3] In the same year the monthly publication of the large investment house, Nikko Securities, made an extensive examination of present patterns, called "The Direction of Industrial Regroupings."[4] *Time* magazine, in its summer 1963 account of the Mitsubishi Heavy Industries merger, began its story with "Just Like Old Times."

> The postwar U.S. breakup of Japan's *zaibatsu*, the huge and powerful prewar cartels [*sic*, combines] that controlled practically all of Japanese industry, was the most ambitious antitrust action in history. The re-emergence of the *zaibatsu* has been hardly less ambi-

[1] *Oriental Economist*, February-July 1955.

[2] *Oriental Economist*, December 1958, August 1959.

[3] "Sangyo Kai o Arau, Saihensei no Nami," January 1, 4-6, 8-15, 17, 19-23, 1963. These articles were later expanded and printed in book form under the title, *The Direction of Industrial Regroupings* (*Sangyo Saihensei no Doko*), Tokyo: Nihon Keizai Shimbun Sha Hen, 1963.

[4] "Kigyo Keiretsu Saihensei no Doko," Nikko Shoken, *Toshi Geppo*, April 1963, pp. 111-39.

> tious. With scarcely a murmur to mark it, the steady reconcentration of the three biggest *zaibatsu*—Mitsui, Mitsubishi and Sumitomo—has been going on quietly but steadily since 1952. The three now account for more than one-third of Japan's total industrial and commercial business—and they are not finished yet. Last week executives from three big prewar Mitsubishi heavy industry groups were at work on what promises to be the biggest postwar reunion of them all: the merger of the three into the old Mitsubishi Heavy Industry Co., which would rank as Japan's second biggest firm and trail only [one other] *zaibatsu* firm, Hitachi Ltd.[5]

And in 1965 the *Mainichi Newspaper* ran a series of articles on "New Waves of Industrial Re-Groupings."[6]

Let us examine the nature of industrial organization in Japan today by dividing the problem into three parts. In this chapter today's Mitsubishi, Mitsui, and Sumitomo groupings will be examined to see how they compare to their predeconcentration forms. Then, in the following chapters attention will be given to other groupings in the economy, to the resulting concentration ratios, and to cartelization. Further, I shall note the postwar performance of the economy.

### *Defining Core Companies*

Before examination of the Big Three can be undertaken it will be necessary to decide the corporate membership of the three groupings. Because virtually every writer and research group uses different lists of companies making up the present Mitsubishi, Mitsui, and Sumitomo, let us again employ the device of studying the patterns among the core companies, which not only represent consensus as to membership but show the group's organizational form most vividly.

In Chapter 4 the term "core" was used, as defined by the former top-holding companies. Today there are no holding companies, but there *are* "presidents' clubs": in the Mitsubishi grouping the presidents of 25 key companies constitute the Friday Club (Kinyo Kai); in the Sumitomo grouping the heads of 17 companies are in the White Waters Club (Hakusui Kai).[7] The Mitsui grouping has two such clubs, the 27-member Monday Club (Getsuyo Kai), and the more exclusive

[5] *Time* magazine, Atlantic International edition, August 30, 1963, p. 52.

[6] "Atarashii Nami, Sangyo Saihensei," *Mainichi Shimbun*, Nov. 25-27, 1965.

[7] "White Waters" has a historical Sumitomo ring. The original Sumitomo enterprise dating back to the latter 16th century was called "Izumi," meaning "spring" (of water). "Izumi" is written with a Chinese character which is made up of two components, "white" above, and "water" below. These components have been split apart to provide the name for the present club. I am indebted to Uramatsu Samitaro for calling this to my attention.

17-member Second Thursday Club (Nimoku Kai). For our purposes, the companies from which membership is obtained in these clubs come under today's definition of the core companies of the Big Three.

In the Mitsubishi group the 1966 Friday Club membership is drawn from companies listed in Table 11-1. If this listing is compared with that of the former core companies cited in Table 4-2, several points emerge. Of the former 11 first-line companies all 11 are still present, though now numbering 14 because of splits and reorganizations in the Occupation period. Mitsubishi Trading, which along with Mitsui Trading suffered the most drastic Occupation action, is present. It was reconstituted in 1954 from a merger of the small second company, Kowa Jitsugyo, with other splinter parts of the old "Shoji" (Trading).[8] Mitsubishi Heavy Industries, split into three companies under the De-

Table 11-1: FRIDAY CLUB COMPANIES OF THE MITSUBISHI GROUPING (1966)

| | |
|---|---|
| *Finance* | |
| Mitsubishi Bank | Meiji Life Insurance |
| Mitsubishi Trust & Banking | Tokyo Marine Insurance |
| *Mining and industry* | |
| Mitsubishi Mining | Mitsubishi Rayon |
| Mitsubishi Metal Mining | Mitsubishi Monsanto Chemical |
| Mitsubishi Heavy Industries | Mitsubishi Edogawa Chemical |
| Mitsubishi Electric | Mitsubishi Oil |
| Mitsubishi Steel | Mitsubishi Petrochemicals |
| Mitsubishi Chemical Machinery | Mitsubishi Paper |
| Mitsubishi Chemical Industries | Mitsubishi Cement |
| Mitsubishi Plastic Industries | Kirin Beer |
| Asahi Glass | |
| *Commerce and "other"* | |
| Mitsubishi Shoji (Trading) | Nippon Yusen Kaisha (NYK) |
| Mitsubishi Warehouse | Mitsubishi Estate |

Source: Economic Investigative Council, *Research on Business Groupings* (Keizai Chosa Kyokai, *Keiretsu no Kenkyu*), Tokyo, 1967, p. 11.

[8] Cf., for example, *Oriental Economist*, May 1959, p. 241.

concentration Law, received Fair Trade Commission approval to integrate in 1963. The ERR reorganization of Mitsubishi Steel into Steel and Steel Mfg. lasted until 1964, when the two companies merged. The Deconcentration Law split of Mining into Mining and Metal Mining remains. The ERR reorganization of Chemical Industries into Mitsubishi Chemical Industries, Asahi Glass, and Mitsubishi Rayon remains, though mergers are rumored. Of the remaining 11 companies, four second-line companies have been "promoted"—Meiji Life Insurance, Tokyo Marine Insurance, Mitsubishi Chemical Machinery, and Mitsubishi Shipping—though in 1964 the last-named was replaced by "NYK" with which it was merged. Two "ordinary" subsidiaries have been promoted,—Mitsubishi Edogawa Chemical and Mitsubishi Paper. Kirin Beer is in a separate category, although with long Mitsubishi ties, it was not a subsidiary. Today, due to some shareholding, but overwhelmingly to credit, it is not only in the grouping but has been promoted to a core company. The remaining four companies are new: Mitsubishi Petrochemicals, Mitsubishi Monsanto Chemicals, Mitsubishi Plastics, and Mitsubishi Cement. It would, therefore, at first glance seem like "old times."

Let us turn next to the Mitsui grouping to see how today's core companies compare with yesterday's. Because the Monday Club membership is that of the Second Thursday Club, plus 10 companies, only a single listing is presented in Table 11-2, with those companies starred whose presidents constitute the Second Thursday Club. Again there should be a comparison of this grouping with the former first- and second-line, directly-controlled companies as listed in Table 4-1. The two tables are strikingly similar. Changes in the composition of the two tables can be noted by observing dropouts and additions. Formerly, there were 22 core companies; now there are 27; the change is a product of five dropouts and 10 additions. Dropouts are: Tropical Produce; Mitsui Light Metal Fabrication; Mitsui Oil and Fat; Mitsui Wooden Shipbuilding; and Mitsui Lumber. Additions are: Mitsui Bank; Mitsui Metal Mining; Hokkaido Colliery; Japan Steel Works; Showa Aircraft; Mitsui Miike Mfg.; Mitsui Petrochemicals; General Petroleum; Toshoku (Tokyo Foods); and Mitsui Construction.

A word on certain of the inclusions and additions: Table 11-2 indicates that Mitsui & Co. (i.e., Mitsui Trading), notwithstanding its breakup during the Occupation, is present once more. The climaxing merger of its fragments occurred in February 1959.[9] However, certain parts of the old Mitsui Trading have not been reintegrated. General Petroleum and Toshoku (Tokyo Foods) continue their independence

[9] Cf., for example, *ibid.*, March 1959, p. 154.

Table 11-2: MONDAY CLUB AND SECOND THURSDAY CLUB COMPANIES OF THE MITSUI GROUPING (1966)

(Asterisk indicates Second Thursday Club companies)

| | |
|---|---|
| *Finance* | |
| Mitsui Bank* | Taisho Marine Insur.* |
| Mitsui Trust & Banking* | Mitsui Mutual Life Insur.* |
| *Mining and industry* | |
| Mitsui Mining* | Toyo Koatsu Industries* |
| Mitsui Metal Mining* | Mitsui Miike Mfg. |
| Hokkaido Colliery and Steamship* | Mitsui Chemical* |
| Japan Steel Works* | Mitsui Petrochemical* |
| Mitsui Shipbuilding & Engineering* | Toyo Rayon* |
| Mitsui Precision Machinery | Japan Flour Milling |
| Showa Aircraft | |
| *Commerce and "other"* | |
| Mitsui & Co. (Mitsui Trading)* | Mitsui Real Estate* |
| General Petroleum | Osaka Shosen-Mitsui Shipping |
| Toshoku (Tokyo Foods) | Mitsui Norin (Agr. & Forestry) |
| Toyo Menka (Toyo Cotton) | Sanki Engineering* |
| Mitsui Warehouse* | Mitsui Construction |

Source: Economic Investigative Council, *Research on Business Groupings*, 1967, p. 11.

and are now part of the new core group. It may at first seem surprising that Mitsui Bank is an addition. This is because of the five-year Teikoku-Bank period in which Mitsui Bank and Daiichi Bank were merged. In this period, because of the participation of Shibusawa capital, the Teikoku Bank was not a "core" company of the Mitsui *zaibatsu*, merely an "ordinary" subsidiary. Mitsui Metal Mining is the product of the Deconcentration Law split of Mining. Hokkaido Colliery, Japan Steel Works, and Showa Aircraft represent advances of "ordinary" subsidiaries. Mitsui Miike Mfg., Mitsui Petrochemicals, and Mitsui Construction represent the inclusion of new operations. Thus again, it might seem appropriate to conclude that things were much as before except for a few additions.

Now to the Sumitomo grouping. Table 11-3 is a listing of the members of the Hakusui Kai. If we compare this listing with Table 4-3, we again find ourselves in familiar territory. Eleven of the former 15 first-line subsidiaries are represented in the Hakusui Kai, though they now number 12 because of the split in Mining. The four omissions are two domestic companies (Sumitomo Aluminum Reduction and Sumitomo Cooperative Electric Power), and two empire companies (Korea Sumitomo Light Metal and Manchurian Sumitomo Metal Industries). Promotions are two former second-line subsidiaries, Nippon Sheet Glass and Sumitomo Marine Insurance. Sumitomo Shoji (Trading) is in something of a special category. Formerly it was part of the top-holding company; now it is separately incorporated. Sumitomo Cement[10] and Sumitomo Light Metals are additions.

Table 11-3: WHITE WATERS CLUB OF THE SUMITOMO GROUPING (1966)

| | |
|---|---|
| *Finance* | |
| Sumitomo Bank | Sumitomo Marine Insur. |
| Sumitomo Trust & Banking | Sumitomo Mutual Life Insur. |
| *Mining and industry* | |
| Sumitomo Coal Mining | Nippon Electric |
| Sumitomo Metal Mining | Sumitomo Machinery |
| Sumitomo Metal Industries | Sumitomo Chemicals |
| Sumitomo Electric Industries | Sumitomo Cement |
| Nippon Sheet Glass | Sumitomo Light Metals |
| *Commerce and "other"* | |
| Sumitomo Shoji (Trading) | Sumitomo Real Estate |
| Sumitomo Warehouse | |

Source: Economic Investigative Council, *Research on Business Groupings*, 1967, p. 11.

[10] Sumitomo Cement is a name change of the former Iwaki Cement Company following purchase of a sizeable block of its shares by several companies of the Sumitomo grouping. There has been confusion over the meaning of the development out of mistaking the Iwasakis of Iwaki Cement for the Iwasakis of the Mitsubishi grouping. Cf. for example, the treatment of Iwaki Cement in the Fair Trade Commission, *The Realities of Economic Concentration in Japan* (*Nihon ni okeru, Keizai Ryoku Shuchu no Jittai*), 1951, p. 158. I am indebted to Professor Togai (Togai Yoshio) for pointing out that the two Iwasaki families are unrelated.

Under the combine system, "core company" meant, as was seen earlier, that the company had no freedom of action, that it was obliged to seek "guidance" on virtually every aspect of its business operations. It was not free to buy and sell on its own. It was not free to determine new undertakings or the abandonment of old ones. It could not negotiate patent licensing arrangements, nor make political contributions. It did not determine salaries, the accounting system, or the choice of a bank. In brief, it meant a denial of the company's corporate character and an arrangement whereby these companies were in effect but departments of the top-holding company. Expressed differently, it meant an arrangement whereby decision-making for the combine network was overwhelmingly concentrated in the top-holding company, which in turn meant an arrangement whereby officers of the core companies renounced their true executive roles and accepted subordinate ones.

Holding-company direction of these corporations was exercised in various ways—ownership, personnel, credit, centralized buying and selling. Ownership was in big chunks principally by the top-holding company. Officers of the core companies were not only directly or indirectly appointed by the top-holding company, but many, in addition, were bound through contractual arrangements to refer virtually every policy matter to the top-holding company before decision was taken at their own board meetings. To enhance unified action, interlocks were established between the top-holding company and the core subsidiaries. Credit needs, with the exception of the trading companies, with their enormous requirements for short-term financing, were met through the combine's financial institutions. Thus the combine bank could serve as a further check on subsidiary activity. In addition, the top-holding company not infrequently itself borrowed from the bank and lent to the core subsidiaries. As we have seen, the trading companies were used to achieve the daily, immediate sort of coordination that would be difficult without centralized buying and selling.

In today's groupings, are controls as tight? To understand what it means to be a core company today, the control patterns will be compared with those of yesterday, for it is out of controls that it is possible to determine the extent to which policy is unified. In assessing these groupings, it must always be remembered that we are examining structures in which integration, because of the highly conglomerate nature of member companies, must come out of controls. Market forces, by definition, are not capable of material assistance.

Granted, there is a certain basis for common action among member companies simply out of common trade names and trademarks, as for example, in joint advertising.[11] Further, "old school ties" can lead to joint undertakings, such as the creation of a new company in petrochemicals, atomic energy, or the like. But as was seen in Part I, combine strength did not rest on such intangibles; it rested on solid, compelling controls.

*Group Ties Through Ownership*

Ownership, which formerly was basic, was presented in Chapter 4 in terms of family, top-holding company, and horizontal cross-ties. Today, among the successor groupings there are with minor exception no *zaibatsu*-family holdings, and holding companies do not exist. Accordingly, what remains are "cross-subsidiary" ties, as it were.

A research group, the Economic Investigative Council (Keizai Chosa Kyokai), supported by business contributions, has since 1960 made annual studies of cross-subsidiary ties. The studies present intragroup share-ownership among what the Council understands to be the corporations making up the different business groupings—Mitsubishi, Mitsui, Sumitomo, and the others. The scale of intragroup shareownership is, of course, influenced by the way corporate membership in the different groupings is defined. The Council states that its criteria for corporate membership in the grouping are:

(1) That the financial institutions of the grouping have, over each of the last three years, been the top supplier of credit, or, that the financial institutions have accounted for at least 20 percent of the intragroup shareholding.
(2) That the Bank of the grouping, over each of the last three years, has supplied at least 40% of the credit, or, that there is a sizeable difference between the Bank in first position and the next largest credit source.
(3) That the company has traditionally been included within the grouping.[12]

Examination of credit sources and shareholding among the Council-defined members of the groupings indicates many exceptions to its first two criteria, even among the core companies.[13] The latter, how-

[11] See note 23 for a brief discussion of the Occupation attempt to change these.

[12] Economic Investigative Council, *Research on Business Groupings* (Keizai Chosa Kyokai, *Keiretsu no Kenkyu*), Tokyo, 1967, "Introductory Remarks" (Hanrei), unnumbered page before the table of contents.

[13] Under the Council's methodology, there is something of a turnover in companies in its year-to-year definition of the different groupings. If, for example, one

ever, handsomely qualify for membership on the more subjective grounds of "traditional inclusion."

Table 11-4 presents cross-ownership ties among Mitsubishi core companies for 1961, 1964, and 1966. If the 1966 data are arranged by size of holdings from Kirin Beer at 6% to Mitsubishi Cement at 89%, it will be found that the median cross-ownership for these companies is 20%. If, on the other hand, the former first- and second-line companies of the combine are arranged by scale of ownership (top-holding company, *zaibatsu*-family, and cross ties), as seen in Table 4-2, from Japan Aluminum at 30% to Mitsubishi Real Estate at 99%, the median position is between 47% and 50%, over twice as high. The combine data are for war's end, following the wartime expansion. If combine data for the years before the war buildup were used, combine ownership would be even higher. Ownership ties are thus far lower among Mitsubishi core companies today.

However, there is a further highly significant difference in the character of the ownership pattern then and now. Group holdings are far more fractured than previously, which is but to say that the need for coordination is greater if there is to be any meaning to such a thing as "Mitsubishi" ownership. The percentages cited in Table 11-4 were obtained by summing the total of investments by the 48 companies

---

compares its 1964 definition of the Mitsubishi, Mitsui, and Sumitomo groups with its 1961 definition, the following differences result:

Mitsubishi

somewhat under 30% of the 1964 companies are not in the 1961 listing
somewhat under 25% of the 1961 companies are not in the 1964 listing

Mitsui

roughly 15% of the 1964 companies are not in the 1961 listing
somewhat under 25% of the 1961 companies are not in the 1964 listing

Sumitomo

somewhat under 25% of the 1964 companies are not in the 1961 listing
slightly more than 30% of the 1961 companies are not in the 1964 listing

(Tables 206, 207 and 208 in the 1965 edition; Tables 27, 28 and 29 in the 1962 edition.)

In view of the foregoing observations, it may be wondered whether the Council's data make a reliable base for drawing conclusions with respect to intragroup ownership. The turnover companies, however, are for the most part the more "marginal" companies. Typically these companies do not have large intragroup stock holdings. Therefore, the weakness does not affect the findings as much as might at first be thought, though it certainly has some effect. The alternative to using the Council's data is going to the reports filed by the individual companies with the Ministry of Finance. The time element precludes a single writer from doing this when a large number of companies are at issue. Accordingly, the Council's data have been used.

Table 11-4: OWNERSHIP TIES AMONG MITSUBISHI CORE COMPANIES AS OF SEPT 1961, 1964, 1966, EXPRESSED AS A PERCENTAGE OF ISSUED CAPITAL (n.l. = not listed)

| | 1961 | 1964 | 1966 | | 1961 | 1964 | 1966 |
|---|---|---|---|---|---|---|---|
| *Finance* | | | | | | | |
| Mitsubishi Bank | 27.30 | 27.85 | 28.64 | Mitsubishi Trust & Banking | 35.40 | 33.17 | 35.35 |
| Meiji Life Insur. | | (mutual) | | Tokyo Marine Insur. | 12.13 | 14.43 | 12.41 |
| *Mining and Industry* | | | | | | | |
| Mitsubishi Mining | 23.96 | 21.94 | 19.02 | Asahi Glass | 22.02 | 22.97 | 20.63 |
| M. Metal Mining | 18.25 | 15.33 | 13.90 | Mitsubishi Rayon | 29.90 | 25.94 | 20.27 |
| M. Heavy Ind. | * | 14.57 | 11.77 | M. Monsanto Chem. | n.l. | n.l. | n.l. |
| M. Electric | 07.69 | 6.26 | 6.39 | M. Edogawa Chem.*** | 18.69 | 19.28 | 18.22 |
| M. Steel | * | 19.02 | 17.93 | M. Oil | 16.51 | 13.53 | 10.08 |
| M. Chemical Mach. | 32.13 | 30.71 | 25.86 | M. Petrochemicals | 73.17 | 69.90 | 69.90 |
| M. Chemical Ind. | 25.61 | 23.23 | 20.50 | M. Paper | 21.23 | 26.28 | 32.64 |
| M. Plastic Ind.** | n.l. | 60.22 | 56.71 | M. Cement | 90.13 | 93.03 | 89.55 |
| Kirin Beer | n.l. | 7.25 | 6.24 | | | | |
| *Commerce and "other"* | | | | | | | |
| Mitsubishi Shoji (Trading) | 34.15 | 34.78 | 33.53 | Nippon Yusen Kaisha (NYK) | * | 10.56 | 9.40 |
| M. Warehouse | 31.96 | 31.90 | 26.57**** | Mitsubishi Estate | 38.16 | 26.32 | 21.94 |

*Because of mergers, 1961 figure not comparable.

**The omission of Mitsubishi Monsanto from the source table produces this figure. With inclusion, the 1966 figure is 65.59%.

***In 1961, Edogawa Chemical.

****An apparent error in the source table omits the holdings of Heavy Industry. With inclusion the 1966 figure is 30.02%.

Source: Economic Investigative Council, *Research on Business Groupings* (Keizai Chosa Kyokai, *Keiretsu no Kenkyu*), 1962, 1965, 1967 editions. In the 1962 edition, Table 28, pp. 146-55; in the 1965 and 1967 editions, Table 207, pp. 80-87 and pp. 92-99, respectively.

which the Council is using for its 1966 definition of the Mitsubishi grouping.[14] The fact that two companies happen to be included in the Council's definition of the grouping for a particular year does not, in the absence of controls, indicate that they will automatically pull together, nor is the fact that they may both have investments in a third company, say Mitsubishi Bank. Therefore, before more information is available, we cannot conclude that because the Mitsubishi Bank is listed at 28.6% "Mitsubishi" ownership this means that this 28.6%

[14] With respect to Mitsubishi, the Council's figure for 1964 was 51 companies, for 1961, 54 companies; Mitsui for 1964, 51 companies, for 1961, 55 companies; Sumitomo for 1964, 50 companies, for 1961, 55 companies.

represents a single voice. In fact, the 28.6% represents the combined holdings of 46 companies out of the 47 companies (48 companies minus the Bank) which the Council lists in its 1966 tables. In this regard it is noteworthy that of the 46 companies with holdings in the Mitsubishi Bank, the issued capital of which is $61,111,111, 19 have holdings of under $139,000. While there is wider group participation in the bank than in any of the other companies, the pattern here is not unrepresentative; in fact, fragmented holdings are typical of most of the companies. In the case of Heavy Industries, 23 companies make up the 11.7% "Mitsubishi" ownership; for Metal Mining, 12 companies make up the 13.9%; Chemicals, 13 make up 20.5%; Electric, 15 make up 6.3%. In less than a handful of cases are intra-group holdings suggestive of yesterday. Illustrative of this latter category are two new companies—Petrochemicals, where 4 companies make up the 69.9%, and Cement with 14 companies making up the 89.5%. In contrast to today's typical fragmentation, holdings at the end of the war were in significant blocks. In 1945 the top-holding company alone held 22% of Heavy Industries, 33% of Banking, 42% of Mining, 44% of Electric, and so on.

In today's form, the heaviest Mitsubishi holders of stock in the Mitsubishi grouping are the four financial institutions, Mitsubishi Bank, Mitsubishi Trust and Banking, Tokyo Marine Insurance, and Meiji Life Insurance. In 1966 these four institutions accounted for more than half of the Mitsubishi holdings in the grouping, 10.9% out of 16.8%, divided among the four as follows: the Bank, 2.8%; Trust and Banking, 2.3%; Marine Insurance, 2.2%; and Life Insurance, 3.4.%

While intragroup shareholding in the core companies is fragmented, it is to be compared, of course, with fragmented holdings by outsiders. Among Japan's largest corporations, shareholding today is typically in "bits and pieces." The position of the top 10 shareholders among the core companies of the Mitsubishi group, which range from large to very large, is shown in Table 11-5. It will be seen that outsiders' holdings are frequently on the scale of individual Mitsubishi holdings, if not greater, so that the preeminence of the Mitsubishi position is dependent on the Mitsubishi companies acting in concert. Let us reserve judgment on the extent to which the companies achieve coordination until studying the nature of the other group ties.

In the Mitsui grouping an even more dramatic contrast in ownership patterns can be seen. Present-day intragroup holdings among the core companies of the grouping are given in Table 11-6. There is a considerable difference between these figures and those in Table 4-1.

Table 11-5: TOP 10 SHAREHOLDERS AMONG MITSUBISHI CORE COMPANIES, 1966

(Holdings by those outside the *keiretsu* are underlined.)

| Company | Paid-up capital, millions yen | Top 10 shareholders, percentage of issued shares | | | | | | | | | | Total Top 10 | Mitsubishi Total Among Top 10 |
|---|---|---|---|---|---|---|---|---|---|---|---|---|---|
| | | 1 | 2 | 3 | 4 | 5 | 6 | 7 | 8 | 9 | 10 | | |
| Mitsubishi Mining | 7,473 | 4.83 | 3.38 | 2.81 | 2.69 | 2.03 | 1.81 | 1.56 | 1.43 | 1.39 | 1.33 | 23.26 | 15.75 |
| M. Metal Mining | 10,000 | 9.18 | 6.20 | 2.72 | 2.60 | 2.60 | 1.85 | 1.60 | 1.59 | 1.39 | 1.18 | 30.91 | 10.77 |
| M. Heavy Ind. | 79,555 | 4.04 | 3.70 | 2.93 | 2.87 | 2.46 | 2.23 | 1.38 | 1.37 | 1.23 | 1.09 | 23.30 | 10.40 |
| M. Electric | 43,200 | 3.96 | 2.68 | 1.74 | 1.74 | 1.32 | 1.23 | 1.23 | 1.16 | 1.10 | 0.75 | 16.91 | 4.71 |
| M. Steel | 4,767 | 5.07 | 4.47 | 2.95 | 2.09 | 1.81 | 1.47 | 1.44 | 1.36 | 1.25 | 1.05 | 22.96 | 17.83 |
| M. Chem. Mach. | 1,200 | 5.00 | 4.17 | 4.17 | 3.75 | 3.33 | 2.90 | 2.77 | 2.50 | 2.17 | 1.33 | 32.09 | 25.86 |
| M. Chemicals | 22,722 | 6.40 | 6.16 | 5.85 | 3.54 | 3.28 | 3.04 | 2.75 | 2.16 | 2.09 | 1.76 | 37.03 | 17.23 |
| M. Edogawa Chem. | 2,400 | 6.15 | 5.00 | 5.00 | 3.17 | 3.11 | 2.08 | 2.04 | 1.73 | 1.67 | 1.67 | 31.62 | 15.93 |
| M. Plastics | 3,150 | 41.41 | 9.14 | 8.38 | 3.54 | 1.67 | 1.57 | 1.52 | 0.95 | 0.95 | 0.87 | 70.00 | 65.59 |
| Asahi Glass | 21,600 | 6.46 | 5.64 | 4.91 | 4.51 | 4.12 | 4.06 | 3.99 | 2.78 | 2.25 | 2.11 | 40.83 | 23.11 |
| Mitsubishi Oil | 10,000 | 48.70 | 3.38 | 3.00 | 2.08 | 1.64 | 1.35 | 1.29 | 1.00 | 1.00 | 1.00 | 64.44 | 9.02 |
| Mitsubishi Rayon | 7,780 | 8.68 | 6.59 | 4.68 | 4.44 | 3.86 | 2.45 | 2.25 | 2.13 | 1.74 | 1.71 | 38.53 | 15.41 |
| Mitsubishi Paper | 5,600 | 9.65 | 6.18 | 5.20 | 5.11 | 4.58 | 4.41 | 4.08 | 3.32 | 2.68 | 2.36 | 47.57 | 32.37 |
| Kirin Beer | 23,014 | 4.95 | 3.03 | 2.90 | 2.74 | 2.31 | 1.77 | 1.44 | 1.42 | 1.32 | 0.98 | 22.86 | 5.93 |
| Mitsubishi Trading | 22,500 | 6.95 | 6.03 | 5.20 | 4.13 | 4.00 | 3.42 | 2.72 | 1.63 | 1.60 | 1.60 | 37.28 | 25.30 |
| M. Real Estate | 24,750 | 4.55 | 4.04 | 3.87 | 3.84 | 2.66 | 2.35 | 2.21 | 1.93 | 1.69 | 1.69 | 28.83 | 17.30 |
| NYK | 14,600 | 6.60 | 3.66 | 3.32 | 2.44 | 2.06 | 1.56 | 1.48 | 1.17 | 0.91 | 0.90 | 24.10 | 8.67 |
| Mitsubishi Warehouse | 2,000 | 8.24 | 7.23 | 5.11 | 4.64 | 3.84 | 3.71 | 3.46 | 2.76 | 2.51 | 2.03 | 43.53 | 30.02 |

Source: Economic Investigative Council, *Research on Business Groupings*, 1967, Table 221, pp. 138-191

Table 11-6: OWNERSHIP TIES AMONG MITSUI CORE COMPANIES, SEPT 1961, 1964, 1966, EXPRESSED AS A PERCENTAGE OF ISSUED CAPITAL (n.l. = not listed)

| | 1961 | 1964 | 1966 | | 1961 | 1964 | 1966 |
|---|---|---|---|---|---|---|---|
| | | | *Finance* | | | | |
| Mitsui Bank | 31.60 | 31.16 | 31.77 | Taisho Marine Insur. | 30.20 | 23.23 | 24.82 |
| Mitsui Trust & Banking | 18.00 | 19.88 | 22.52 | Mitsui Mutual Life Insur. | | (mutual) | |
| | | | *Mining and industry* | | | | |
| Mitsui Mining | 4.88 | 4.65 | 5.87 | Showa Aircraft | 36.49 | n.l. | n.l. |
| Mitsui Metal Mining | 9.37 | 11.18 | 11.64 | Toyo Koatsu Industries | 11.15 | 11.58 | 10.59 |
| Hokkaido Colliery & SS | 3.77 | 4.24 | 3.21 | Mitsui Miike (Ind.)[a] | 36.53 | n.l. | n.l. |
| Japan Steel Works | 15.73 | 14.45 | 13.06 | Mitsui Chemical | 8.33 | 11.24 | 9.34 |
| Mitsui Shipbldg. & Eng. | 2.87 | 8.67 | 8.48 | Mitsui Petrochemical | 83.50 | 74.44 | 66.87 |
| Mitsui Precision Machinery | n.l. | 56.04 | 56.04 | Toyo Rayon | 4.32 | 3.99 | 2.53 |
| Japan Flour Milling | 16.20 | 19.59 | 19.56 | | | | |
| | | | *Commerce and "other"* | | | | |
| Mitsui & Co. (Trading) | 15.79 | 15.88 | 14.30 | Mitsui Real Estate | 30.51 | 27.45 | 27.05 |
| General Petroleum[b] | 9.06 | 9.44 | 10.11 | Osaka Shosen-Mitsui Shipping | * | n.l. | n.l. |
| Toshoku (Tokyo Foods) | 15.74 | 15.36 | 15.36 | Mitsui Norin (Agr. & Forestry) | 63.33 | 51.02 | 51.02 |
| Toyo Menka (Toyo Cotton) | 18.63 | 9.97 | 9.97 | Sanki Engineering | 12.80 | 12.93 | 18.23 |
| Mitsui Warehouse | 13.34 | 19.24 | 22.56 | Mitsui Construction | 91.75 | 57.16 | 57.09 |

*Because of mergers, 1961 figure not comparable.

a) In 1961 Miike Gosei Industries.

b) In 1961 and 1964 General Bussan.

Source: Economic Investigative Council, *Research on Business Groupings*, 1962, 1965, 1967 editions. In the 1962 edition, Table 27, pp. 136-45; in the 1965 and 1967 editions, Table 206, pp. 72-79 and 84-91 respectively.

Today there are three companies in which combined holdings are under 6%; 20 years ago there were four companies with holdings of 100%. If today's companies are arranged by size of 1966 "Mitsui" ownership, from Toyo Rayon at 2.5% to Mitsui Petrochemical at 66.8%, the median position is 15%. If, on the other hand, the companies in Table 4-1 are arranged by size of combine-holding, from Mitsui Trust at 17% to the four companies at 100%—Real Estate, Warehouse, Oil & Fat, and Lumber—the median size of combine investment is 88%.

But for the same reasons as in the Mitsubishi case, this understates the distinction, great as it already is. The present-day percentages are the sum of the large numbers of small investments. The 31% Mitsui holding in the Mitsui Bank is the sum of the holdings of 44 of the 49 companies (50 minus the bank), which the Council has used in its 1966 Mitsui table. Nine companies make up the 5.8% Mitsui block in

Mining, 16 companies the 14.3% in Trading, 5 companies the 8.48% in Shipbuilding, and so forth. Clearly holdings are in small pieces. Again, as with the Mitsubishi grouping, the four financial institutions account for nearly half the holdings, constituting 5.5% of the 1966 Mitsui total of 10.5%. As is evident from a study of the tables, Mitsui group ties are a mere shadow of their former strength and distinctly weaker than those found in the Mitsubishi group.

Table 11-7 gives information on the top 10 shareholders in the core companies of the Mitsui grouping. Not only are Mitsui ties weaker than the Mitsubishi from the point of view of the grouping, but weakness also shows up among the top 10 shareholders. As the table makes abundantly clear, there is far more outside capital in top position among the core Mitsui companies than in Mitsubishi.

Does the Sumitomo grouping present a similar dramatic contrast between yesterday and today? Table 11-8 provides a summary of present holdings among the core companies by the 50 companies, which

Table 11-7: TOP 10 SHAREHOLDERS AMONG MITSUI CORE COMPANIES, 1966

(Holdings by those outside the *keiretsu* are underlined.)

| Company | Paid-up capital, millions yen | Top 10 shareholders, percentage of issued shares | | | | | | | | | | Total Top 10 | Mitsui Total Among Top 10 |
|---|---|---|---|---|---|---|---|---|---|---|---|---|---|
| | | 1 | 2 | 3 | 4 | 5 | 6 | 7 | 8 | 9 | 10 | | |
| Mitsui Mining | 3,000 | 16.24 | 7.34 | 1.80 | 1.67 | 1.67 | 1.56 | 1.25 | 1.25 | 0.83 | 0.82 | 34.43 | 2.92 |
| Mitsui Metal Mining | 10,800 | 6.22 | 4.17 | 2.43 | 1.99 | 1.98 | 1.87 | 1.83 | 1.33 | 1.06 | 0.99 | 23.87 | 9.04 |
| Hokkaido Colliery & SS | 7,002 | 7.36 | 5.00 | 3.33 | 2.25 | 1.70 | 1.17 | 0.99 | 0.96 | 0.93 | 0.91 | 24.60 | 3.21 |
| Japan Steel Works | 8,788 | 6.40 | 6.14 | 4.00 | 3.66 | 1.76 | 1.42 | 1.29 | 1.24 | 1.08 | 1.06 | 28.05 | 13.06 |
| Mitsui Shipbuilding | 11,900 | 6.56 | 5.36 | 2.90 | 2.52 | 2.12 | 2.12 | 1.93 | 1.71 | 1.47 | 1.43 | 28.12 | 8.23 |
| Toyo Koatsu | 13,143 | 8.60 | 3.98 | 2.87 | 2.83 | 2.56 | 2.43 | 2.40 | 2.11 | 1.63 | 1.54 | 30.95 | 8.44 |
| Mitsui Chemical | 8,809 | 7.36 | 2.56 | 1.89 | 1.72 | 1.39 | 1.15 | 1.01 | 0.91 | 0.86 | 0.84 | 19.66 | 8.76 |
| Mitsui Petrochemical | 5,000 | 22.98 | 8.80 | 8.79 | 8.78 | 7.50 | 4.67 | 3.40 | - | - | - | 64.93 | 56.14 |
| Sanki Industries | 2,500 | 10.00 | 9.90 | 7.40 | 5.03 | 3.40 | 3.32 | 3.30 | 2.25 | 2.00 | 1.80 | 48.40 | 17.10 |
| Mitsui Construction | 2,040 | 26.66 | 20.22 | 5.32 | 2.45 | 2.45 | 1.42 | 1.31 | 1.25 | 0.77 | 0.74 | 62.59 | 55.96 |
| Japan Flour Milling | 3,450 | 9.56 | 5.08 | 4.49 | 4.45 | 4.34 | 3.94 | 3.61 | 3.26 | 3.19 | - | 41.92 | 16.33 |
| Toyo Rayon | 42,060 | 4.13 | 3.94 | 3.78 | 3.69 | 3.44 | 2.11 | 2.02 | 1.93 | 1.76 | 1.72 | 28.52 | 1.93 |
| Mitsui & Co. | 13,308 | 7.97 | 7.14 | 4.88 | 3.61 | 3.37 | 2.78 | 2.68 | 2.14 | 2.08 | 1.67 | 38.32 | 12.06 |
| Toyo Menka | 7,425 | 8.61 | 8.28 | 6.06 | 4.04 | 3.37 | 3.37 | 3.21 | 3.03 | 2.88 | 2.80 | 45.65 | 7.41 |
| Toshoku | 2,800 | 7.1 | 5.0 | 4.3 | 4.3 | 3.6 | 2.9 | 2.7 | 2.7 | 2.5 | 2.1 | 37.2 | 14.80 |
| General Petroleum | 1,714 | 4.17 | 3.33 | 3.27 | 2.33 | 2.22 | 1.67 | 1.59 | 1.39 | 1.35 | 1.34 | 22.66 | 8.89 |
| Mitsui Real Estate | 4,197 | 9.75 | 7.11 | 5.55 | 4.95 | 3.33 | 3.13 | 2.43 | 2.09 | 2.08 | 1.95 | 42.37 | 19.21 |
| Osaka Shosen-Mitsui Shipping | 13,100 | 6.43 | 4.93 | 3.60 | 3.04 | 2.36 | 2.14 | 2.12 | 2.00 | 1.92 | 1.72 | 30.26 | 2.14 |
| Mitsui Warehouse | 2,027 | 5.58 | 5.42 | 5.21 | 5.20 | 5.07 | 5.00 | 4.30 | 3.32 | 3.00 | 2.36 | 44.46 | 18.30 |

Source: Economic Investigative Council, *Research on Business Groupings*, 1967, Table 221, pp. 138-191 passim. Totals columns have been added.

the Council is using as its 1966 definition of the Sumitomo group. If these holdings are arranged by size, from Sumitomo Chemicals at 14.73% to Sumitomo Light Metals at 53.76%, the median position lies between 33 and 34%. This turns out to be roughly half the median range of combine investments, which by reference to Table 4-3, is between 61 and 73%.

However, today's Sumitomo ownership, like that of Mitsubishi and Mitsui, is the sum of numbers of companies. The investments of 43 companies make up the 35.9% Sumitomo holding in the Sumitomo Bank, 13 companies the 26.2% in Metal Mining, 25 companies the 18.5% of Metal Industries. Again, it is the financial four which are the largest holders; they account for 10.1% of the 18.4% Sumitomo holdings in 1966.

Table 11-9 concerns information on the top 10 shareholders in the core companies of the Sumitomo grouping. Not only does the Sumitomo grouping show the highest intra-group ownership, but it shows the strongest group positions among the top 10 shareholders.

From the foregoing examination of ownership patterns in the Mitsubishi, Mitsui, and Sumitomo groupings today, it should be evident that ownership ties are far weaker than they were in the combine period. The extent to which there is meaning behind the sum of the individual Mitsubishi, Mitsui, and Sumitomo positions awaits examination of the character of the other ties.

## *Control Through Lending*

We have been looking at the cross-ties arising from ownership. Corporate capital in Japan today, following close to 15 years of extraordinary growth is, however, far more importantly bank capital than equity capital. In most corporations borrowings from banks amount to two, three, or even four times the scale of equity ownership. Accordingly, many observers see today's control pattern within the groupings stemming more from bank lending than from ownership. For industry as a whole, the figures on the net supply of industrial funds, exclusive of retained earnings and depreciation, in millions of yen for 1964, are cited below.[15] The portion of the several amounts used for equipment funds is shown in parentheses.

| | | |
|---|---|---|
| Total | Y5,094,050 million | (2,108,862) |
| Stock | 791,382 | (605,561) |
| Industrial bonds | 154,017 | (153,794) |
| Loans and discounts | 4,148,651 | (1,349,507) |

[15] Bank of Japan, *Economic Statistics of Japan, 1964*, Tokyo, March 1965, Table 14, pp. 33-34.

Table 11-8: OWNERSHIP TIES AMONG SUMITOMO CORE COMPANIES AS OF SEPT 1961, 1964, 1966, EXPRESSED AS A PERCENTAGE OF ISSUED CAPITAL (n.l. = not listed)

| | 1961 | 1964 | 1966 | | 1961 | 1964 | 1966 |
|---|---|---|---|---|---|---|---|
| | | | *Finance* | | | | |
| Sumitomo Bank | 31.07 | 34.64 | 35.90 | Sumitomo Marine Insur. | 21.07 | 18.80 | 23.24 |
| Sumitomo Trust & Banking | 36.13 | 37.43 | 38.74 | Sumitomo Mutual Life Insur. | | (mutual) | |
| | | | *Mining and industry* | | | | |
| Sumitomo Coal Mining | 34.63 | 34.62 | 33.67 | Nippon Sheet Glass | 17.26 | 15.61 | 14.78 |
| Sumitomo Metal Mining | 28.10 | 27.41 | 26.22 | Nippon Electric Mfg. | 40.96 | 38.55 | 36.50 |
| Sumitomo Metal Ind. | 19.86 | 25.46 | 18.54 | Sumitomo Machinery | 52.91 | 40.82 | 40.70 |
| Sumitomo Electric Ind. | 27.51 | 24.36 | 23.68 | Sumitomo Chemicals | 16.86 | 17.14 | 14.73 |
| Sumitomo Light Metals | n.l. | 57.75 | 53.76 | Sumitomo Cement | n.l. | 38.65 | 34.75 |
| | | | *Commerce and "other"* | | | | |
| Sumitomo Shoji (Trading) | 59.51 | 49.60 | 46.61 | Sumitomo Real Estate | n.l. | 16.75 | 35.93 |
| Sumitomo Warehouse | 35.13 | 30.60 | 31.84 | | | | |

Source: Economic Investigative Council, *Research on Business Groups*, 1962, 1965 and 1967 editions. In the 1962 edition, Table 29, pp. 56-65; in the 1965 and 1967 editions, Table 208, pp. 88-95 and pp. 100-107 respectively.

Table 11-9: TOP 10 SHAREHOLDERS AMONG SUMITOMO CORE COMPANIES (1966)

(Holdings by those outside the *keiretsu* are underlined.)

| Company | Paid-up capital, millions yen | Top 10 shareholders, percentage of issued shares | | | | | | | | | | Total Top 10 | Sumitomo Total Among Top 10 |
|---|---|---|---|---|---|---|---|---|---|---|---|---|---|
| | | 1 | 2 | 3 | 4 | 5 | 6 | 7 | 8 | 9 | 10 | | |
| Sumitomo Coal Mining | 3,308 | 5.95 | 5.78 | 4.23 | 3.17 | 2.68 | 2.56 | 2.50 | 2.49 | 2.30 | 2.06 | 33.72 | 31.23 |
| Sumitomo Metal Mining | 5,572 | 4.73 | 3.29 | 3.24 | 3.16 | 2.45 | 1.97 | 1.89 | 1.79 | 1.75 | 1.52 | 25.79 | 22.48 |
| Sumitomo Metal Ind. | 61,785 | 5.72 | 4.72 | 3.91 | 2.88 | 2.36 | 1.64 | 1.56 | 1.43 | 1.26 | 1.02 | 26.50 | 14.34 |
| Sumitomo Elec. Ind. | 13,500 | 10.11 | 6.11 | 5.38 | 4.41 | 4.28 | 3.75 | 2.96 | 2.63 | 1.74 | 1.70 | 43.07 | 19.52 |
| Sumitomo Light Metals | 5,600 | 36.89 | 5.85 | 4.58 | 3.43 | 2.49 | 1.79 | 1.73 | 1.14 | 1.00 | 0.99 | 59.89 | 50.80 |
| Sumitomo Machinery | 5,400 | 9.01 | 6.48 | 5.08 | 4.24 | 3.44 | 3.37 | 3.10 | 2.81 | 2.78 | 2.78 | 43.09 | 27.26 |
| Nippon Electric | 20,000 | 11.85 | 8.66 | 8.13 | 7.86 | 5.23 | 3.96 | 3.01 | 2.55 | 2.49 | 2.48 | 56.22 | 28.47 |
| Sumitomo Chemical | 25,200 | 5.25 | 4.76 | 3.97 | 3.69 | 3.67 | 3.66 | 2.00 | 1.88 | 1.49 | 1.19 | 31.56 | 11.32 |
| Sumitomo Cement | 5,500 | 9.95 | 7.02 | 6.02 | 5.30 | 4.48 | 3.91 | 3.46 | 3.01 | 2.95 | 1.86 | 47.96 | 29.85 |
| Nippon Sheet Glass | 8,000 | 15.00 | 6.43 | 6.14 | 4.18 | 4.04 | 2.20 | 1.94 | 1.67 | 1.60 | 1.44 | 44.64 | 14.27 |
| Sumitomo Trading | 7,000 | 8.06 | 7.15 | 5.46 | 3.44 | 3.38 | 3.33 | 3.16 | 2.75 | 2.75 | 2.69 | 42.17 | 42.67 |
| Sumitomo Warehouse | 1,800 | 10.00 | 5.67 | 5.04 | 5.00 | 2.95 | 2.67 | 2.54 | 2.09 | 1.72 | 1.67 | 39.35 | 27.38 |

Source: Economic Investigative Council, *Research on Business Groupings*, 1967, Table 221, pp. 138-191 passim.

Table 11-10 presents 1966 data on the relationship between ownership and borrowings for the core companies of the three groupings. No attempt has been made to separate short and long-term borrowing, for the data are too intermixed. In theory, commercial banks are restricted to short-term loans, and insurance companies to long, but there is only casual observance of this. Further, many short-term loans are in fact, through repeated and anticipated renewals, long-term. Therefore, loan data have been presented merely as given in the source from which this table has been constructed.

It will be seen that among the Mitsubishi core-companies, indebtedness to banks is 3.09 times the scale of equity capital; in the Mitsui grouping 4.47 times, and in the Sumitomo grouping 2.58 times. It is this enormous indebtedness to banks that gives rise to the view that banks are the focal point of the groupings in the manner of the former top-holding companies. The very size of the borrowings, however, leads certain other observers to the exactly opposite interpretation. They see banks controlled rather than controlling because the banks are so committed to particular companies they have no choice but to cooperate with the borrower.

Because the role of the banks in today's groupings is crucial to an assessment of the groups, it is worthwhile to examine the position of the banks with care. Whether one sees today's groupings as a revival of the *zaibatsu, sans families,* or as quite different in character, is highly dependent on one's interpretation of the role of the respective banks. Let us look at their position in detail.

Inasmuch as it is frequently difficult to see individual relationships within aggregate figures, the writer has selected four major borrowers from each of the three groups for purposes of examining the sources of their bank funds. Table 11-11 cites sources and amounts of borrowing for companies among those with highest borrowings in the Mitsubishi, Mitsui, and Sumitomo groupings. The selected companies are: Mitsubishi—Mitsubishi Heavy Industries, Mitsubishi Electric, Mitsubishi Shoji (Trading), and Mitsubishi Chemical; Mitsui—Mitsui & Co. (Trading), Mitsui Mining, Toyo Rayon, and Petrochemicals; Sumitomo—Sumitomo Metal Industries, Sumitomo Chemicals, Nippon Electric, and Sumitomo Shoji (Trading).[16]

[16] Selection among the Mitsui grouping was not self-evident. As will be seen from Table 11-10, both Osaka Shosen-Mitsui Shipping and Toyo Menka have higher borrowings, but these two companies were passed over. Osaka Shosen-Mitsui Shipping is an odd, hybrid merger in which "Sumitomo" holding of shares is considerably stronger than the "Mitsui." Further, the company receives essentially two-thirds of its financing from the Government's Development Bank. Only .5% comes from the Mitsui Bank. Toyo Menka was not selected for it would have meant the inclusion of a second trading company.

Table 11-10: A COMPARISON BETWEEN CAPITAL AND LOANS AMONG THE CORE COMPANIES[a] OF THE MITSUBISHI, MITSUI, AND SUMITOMO GROUPINGS, TOGETHER WITH PERCENTAGE OF BORROWINGS OBTAINED FROM THE FINANCIAL INSTITUTIONS OF THE GROUPINGS (1966) (Loans include both long and short) in millions yen

Part A: Mitsubishi

| | Capital | Borrowings | Percentage borrowings from grouping | | Capital | Borrowings | Percentage borrowings from grouping |
|---|---|---|---|---|---|---|---|
| Mitsubishi Mining | 7,473 | 26,935 | 20.33 | Mitsubishi Rayon | 7,780 | 33,924 | 27.77 |
| M. Metal Mining | 10,000 | 21,158 | 40.90 | M. Edogawa Chemical | 2,400 | 8,556 | 57.56 |
| M. Heavy Ind. | 79,555 | 296,219 | 22.65 | M. Oil | 10,000 | 26,854 | 31.44 |
| M. Electric | 43,200 | 81,797 | 30.48 | M. Paper | 5,600 | 14,417 | 35.61 |
| M. Steel | 4,767 | 13,406 | 61.05 | M. Shoji | 22,500 | 131,448 | 32.75 |
| M. Chemical Machinery | 1,200 | 1,873 | 69.46 | M. Warehouse | 2,000 | 3,706 | 73.88 |
| M. Chemical Ind. | 22,722 | 61,721 | 20.02 | Nippon Yusen Kaisha | 14,600 | 75,987 | 4.73 |
| M. Plastic Ind. | 3,150 | 8,244 | 45.84 | M. Estate | 24,750 | 52,413 | 54.09 |
| Asahi Glass | 21,600 | 17,293 | 26.32 | grand total | 283,297 | 875,951 | • |

Table 11-10: (continued)

Part B: Mitsui

| | Capital | Borrowings | Percentage borrowings from grouping |
|---|---|---|---|
| Mitsui Mining | 3,000 | 52,407 | 16.17 |
| M. Metal Mining | 10,800 | 15,358 | 25.90 |
| Hokkaido Colliery | 7,002 | 21,863 | 10.99 |
| Japan Steel | 8,788 | 20,014 | 40.57 |
| M. Shipbuilding | 11,900 | 40,457 | 20.41 |
| Toyo Koatsu Ind. | 13,143 | 38,492 | 21.29 |
| Mitsui Chemical | 8,809 | 31,925 | 38.42 |
| M. Petrochemicals | 5,000 | 46,546 | 34.14 |
| Toyo Rayon | 42,060 | 46,266 | 22.70 |
| Mitsui & Co. (Trading) | 13,308 | 182,431 | 24.53 |
| Toyo Menka | 7,425 | 74,332 | 13.95[b] |
| Toshoku (Tokyo Foods) | 2,800 | 20,820 | 21.71 |
| General Petroleum | 1,714 | 17,157 | 34.58 |
| Sanki Engineering | 2,500 | 2,433 | 51.99 |
| M. Construction | 2,040 | 7,987 | 59.93 |
| Osaka Shōsen-Mitsui | 13,100 | 59,672 | 2.54[b] |
| M. Warehouse | 2,027 | 2,676 | 64.35 |
| M. Real Estate | 4,197 | 32,975 | 42.98 |
| Grand total | 159,613 | 713,811 | |

Table 11-10: (continued)

Part C: Sumitomo

| | Capital | Borrowings | Percentage borrowings from grouping | | Capital | Borrowings | Percentage borrowings from grouping |
|---|---|---|---|---|---|---|---|
| Sumitomo Coal Lining | 3,308 | 28,183 | 40.70 | Sumitomo Light Metal | 5,600 | 15,036 | 56.76 |
| S. Metal Mining | 5,572 | 12,296 | 58.19 | S. Machinery | 5,400 | 9,855 | 56.60 |
| S. Metal Ind. | 61,785 | 94,346 | 38.31 | S. Chemicals | 25,200 | 65,698 | 36.45 |
| S. Electric Ind. | 13,500 | 27,863 | 50.63 | S. Cement | 5,500 | 20,500 | 40.57 |
| Nippon Sheet Glass | 8,000 | 15,927 | 60.42 | S. Shoji (Trading) | 7,000 | 70,859 | 47.19 |
| Nippon Electric | 20,000 | 56,487 | 44.25 | S. Warehouse | 1,800 | 2,853 | 60.39 |
| | | | | grand total | 162,665 | 419,903 | |

[a]Several of the core companies are missing from this table. They were not included in the tables from which this table was constructed. No financial institutions are included. In addition, in Part A of the table, Monsanto Chemicals, Petrochemicals, and Cement are omitted; in Part B, Precision Machinery, Showa Aircraft, Mitsui Miike Gosei Industries, and Mitsui (or M.) Norin (Agriculture and Forestry); in Part C of the table, Real Estate.

[b]Calculated by the writer from Table 222 series, see below.

Source: Economic Investigative Council, *Research on Business Groupings*, 1967. Capital is taken from the Table 221 series, pp. 138-91; borrowings from the Table 222 series, pp. 192-268; percentages, except were otherwise noted, from Table 204, pp. 53-58.

A study of Table 11-11 will indicate the diversity of sources for the enormous borrowings characterizing the present-day scene. Among the 12 companies under study, the Mitsui company, Toyo Rayon, has the greatest number of different sources; it has borrowings from 32 different banks. If, however, for purposes of going forward with an analysis of bank control, loans under one billion yen ($2,777,777) are disregarded, and we omit borrowings of this magnitude from financial institutions of the grouping, it will be found that the four Mitsubishi companies, respectively, had borrowings of $2.7 million and above—from 20, 9, 12, and 6 outside banks; that the four Mitsui companies, respectively, had borrowings of this scale from 12, 5 (plus an additional gigantic government loan), 11, and 6 outside banks; and that the four Sumitomo companies, respectively, had borrowings of this scale from 7, 7, 6, and 6 different outside banks.

The view that corporations are controlled by banks is easier to accept when considered in the aggregate than when looked at in detail. It is not easy to see bank control when 5, 10, 15, or 20 different outside banks are supplying major loans in addition to the financial institutions of the grouping. Japanese analysts characteristically ascribe great significance to the bank from which the largest loan comes; it is the "primary" bank. But again, this analysis is less convincing when examined closely. There is not always a sizable difference between the loan from the primary bank and the next largest loan. The primary bank of one year is not necessarily the primary bank of the next. And loans from nonprimary banks are too large to imagine that these institutions act very differently than the primary bank. Among the core companies of the three groupings being examined here there is greater constancy to the primary bank than is true among less "connected" corporations, as will be seen in the following chapters; but even among core companies there can be changes.

Among the 12 companies under study, the pertinent qualifications for the concept of the primary bank should be noted. Among the four Mitsubishi companies, each of which is regarded as a Mitsubishi Bank company, it will be observed that Heavy Industries has a loan from the Japanese Export-Import Bank of just under Y72 billion, or $200 million, which exceeds its combined borrowing from Mitsubishi institutions. Although Chemicals' largest loan (Y5,958 million) is from the Mitsubishi Bank, it has a loan of Y5,453 million from the Industrial Bank. Among the Mitsui companies it will be seen that while Mitsui and Co. (Trading) has a loan of Y31 billion from the Mitsui Bank it has a loan of Y30 billion from the Fuji Bank. Mining's borrowings from the government (Y15.9 billion from the Development Bank and Y15.6 billion from the Rationalization Fund) exceed by several times its

Table 11-11: SOURCES OF BORROWING FOR HIGHEST BORROWERS AMONG CORE COMPANIES (1,000,000 yen = $2,777) in millions of yen

Part A: Four Major Mitsubishi Borrowers, 1966

| | Heavy Industries | Electric | Trading | Chemical |
|---|---|---|---|---|
| Government | | | | |
| Development Bank | 1,417 | | | 971 |
| Export-Import Bank | 71,165 | 157 | 10,757 | |
| Others | 1 | 149 | | 232 |
| Mitsubishi | | | | |
| Mitsubishi Bank | 33,475 | 12,880 | 32,652 | 5,958 |
| Mitsubishi Trust Bank | 29,222 | 9,335 | 10,391 | 4,648 |
| Meiji Life | 4,400 | 2,716 | | 1,700 |
| Tokyo Marine Insur. | | | | 50 |
| Sumitomo | | | | |
| Sumitomo Bank | 8,945 | 270 | 2,736 | |
| Sumitomo Trust Bank | 12,108 | 3,460 | | 2,721 |
| Sumitomo Life | 1,200 | | | |
| Sumitomo Marine Insur. | | | | |
| Mitsui | | | | |
| Mitsui Bank | 1,080 | 2,330 | 669 | |
| Mitsui Trust Bank | 3,015 | 7,023 | | 794 |
| Mitsui Life | 200 | | | |
| Taisho Marine | | | | |
| Fuji | | | | |
| Fuji Bank | 2,656 | | 3,833 | |
| Yasuda Trust Bank | 3,491 | 2,335 | 365 | 720 |
| Yasuda Life | | | | |
| Yasuda Fire Ins. | | | | |
| Daiichi Bank | | | | |
| Daiichi Bank | 1,580 | | 3,490 | |
| Asahi Life Insur. | 200 | | | |

| | | | | |
|---|---|---|---|---|
| Sanwa | | | | |
| Sanwa Bank | 1,246 | 1,540 | 11,800 | 99 |
| Toyo Trust Bank | 3,077 | 805 | 516 | 160 |
| Daido Life Insur. | | | | |
| Industrial Bank | 17,072 | 395 | 2,530 | 5,453 |
| Long-Term Credit Bank | 11,785 | 7,645 | 947 | 4,116 |
| Hypothec Bank | 2,435 | 834 | | 2,052 |
| Tokyo Bank | 4,397 | | 17,036 | 500 |
| Kangyo Bank | 5,741 | 8,510 | 10,091 | 3,704 |
| Tokai Bank | 10,379 | 1,300 | 10,097 | 620 |
| Daiwa Bank | 295 | | 610 | |
| Kobe Bank | 10,026 | 2,250 | 1,004 | |
| Kyowa Bank | 3,718 | 720 | 1,333 | |
| Hokkaido Develop. Bank | 110 | | 1,114 | |
| Others | (6) | (7) | (7) | (6) |
| Total | 296,219 | 81,797 | 131,448 | 61,721 |

Part B: Four Major Mitsui Borrowers, 1966

| | Trading | Mining | Toyo Rayon | Petro-chemicals |
|---|---|---|---|---|
| Government | | | | |
| Development Bank | | 15,920 | | 420 |
| Export-Import Bank | 23,757 | | 773 | |
| Others | 385 | 528 | 7 | 214 |
| Mitsubishi | | | | |
| Mitsubishi Bank | 9,975 | | 1,440 | |
| Mitsubishi Trust Bank | | | 685 | |
| Meiji Life | | | 495 | |
| Tokyo Marine Insur. | | | | |
| Sumitomo | | | | |
| Sumitomo Bank | 8,642 | | 1,440 | |
| Sumitomo Trust Bank | 872 | | 1,073 | |
| Sumitomo Life | 500 | | 400 | |
| Sumitomo Marine Insur. | | | | |

| | Trading | Mining | Toyo Rayon | Petro-chemicals |
|---|---|---|---|---|
| Mitsui | | | | |
| Mitsui Bank | 31,747 | 4,498 | 4,283 | 7,152 |
| Mitsui Trust Bank | 10,326 | 3,625 | 5,716 | 7,622 |
| Mitsui Life | 1,819 | 300 | 495 | 530 |
| Taisho Marine Insur. | 874 | 50 | | |
| Fuji | | | | |
| Fuji Bank | 30,711 | | 1,440 | |
| Yasuda Trust Bank | 468 | | 830 | |
| Yasuda Life | | | | |
| Yasuda Fire Ins. | | | | |
| Daiichi Bank | | | | |
| Daiichi Bank | 2,219 | | 360 | |
| Asahi Life Insur. | | | 495 | 110 |
| Sanwa Bank | | | | |
| Sanwa Bank | 5,374 | | 1,440 | |
| Toyo Trust Bank | | | 1,986 | 1,137 |
| Daido Life Insur. | | | | |
| Industrial Bank | 2,042 | 1,968 | 1,000 | 8,342 |
| Long-term Credit Bank | 411 | 2,701 | 10,184 | 8,342 |
| Hypothec Bank | 961 | | 840 | 25 |
| Tokyo Bank | 19,886 | | | |
| Kangyo Bank | 4,554 | 2,717 | 2,165 | 4,732 |
| Tokai Bank | 3,787 | | 1,440 | |
| Daiwa Bank | 3,285 | | 1,080 | 2,958 |
| Kobe Bank | 680 | | 880 | |
| Kyowa Bank | 493 | 777 | 360 | 2,858 |
| Hokkaido Develop. Bank | 2,150 | 2,627 | | |
| Others | (6) | (5) | (7) | (5) |
| Total | 182,431 | 52,407 | 46,266 | 46,546 |

Part C: Four Major Sumitomo Borrowers, 1966

| | Metal Ind. | Chemicals | Nippon Electric | Trading |
|---|---|---|---|---|
| Government | | | | |
| Development Bank | 212 | 2,409 | | |
| Export-Import Bank | 174 | | 1,117 | 3,286 |
| Others | 32 | 50 | 139 | 183 |
| Mitsubishi | | | | |
| Mitsubishi Bank | 710 | 470 | 1,834 | 2,459 |
| Mitsubishi Trust Bank | 3,070 | 2,310 | 30 | 100 |
| Meiji Life | 481 | | | |
| Tokyo Marine Insur. | | | | |
| Sumitomo | | | | |
| Sumitomo Bank | 15,802 | 9,609 | 10,775 | 17,961 |
| Sumitomo Trust Bank | 12,536 | 10,619 | 10,511 | 12,172 |
| Sumitomo Life | 7,806 | 3,720 | 3,710 | 3,303 |
| Sumitomo Marine Insur. | | | | |
| Mitsui | | | | |
| Mitsui Bank | | | 290 | |
| Mitsui Trust Bank | 1,420 | 1,342 | | 8 |
| Mitsui Life | | | | |
| Taisho Marine Insur. | | | | |
| Fuji | | | | |
| Fuji Bank | 850 | 350 | 194 | |
| Yasuda Trust Bank | 2,120 | 1,524 | | |
| Yasuda Life | 171 | | | |
| Yasuda Fire Ins. | | | | |
| Daiichi Bank | | | | |
| Daiichi Bank | | | 524 | |
| Asahi Life Insur. | 662 | | | |
| Sanwa | | | | |
| Sanwa Bank | | | | 11 |
| Toyo Trust Bank | | 700 | | |
| Daido Life Insur. | 126 | | | |

| | Metal Ind. | Chemicals | Nippon Electric | Trading |
|---|---|---|---|---|
| Industrial Bank | 9,896 | 9,795 | 5,030 | 3,116 |
| Long-Term Credit Bank | 7,545 | 7,730 | 4,990 | 3,419 |
| Hypothec Bank | 2,321 | 2,522 | 1,413 | 1,258 |
| Tokyo Bank | 194 | 80 | 489 | 8,284 |
| Kangyo Bank | | 100 | | |
| Tokai Bank | | | | |
| Daiwa Bank | 330 | | | |
| Kobe Bank | | | | 5,008 |
| Kyowa Bank | 1,130 | 100 | 2,120 | |
| Hokkaido Develop. Bank | | | | |
| Others | (6) | (7) | (7) | (5) |
| Total | 94,346 | 65,698 | 56,487 | 70,859 |

Source: Economic Investigative Council, *Research on Business Groupings*, 1967, Table 222 series, pp. 192-268 passim.

combined borrowings from Mitsui institutions. Toyo Rayon has as large a loan from the Long-Term Credit Bank as from the Mitsui Bank, Mitsui Trust and Banking, and Mitsui Life combined. Petrochemical has its largest loans from the Industrial and Long-Term Credit Bank—each Y8,342 million. Its loan from the Mitsui Bank is Y7.1 billion, and from Mitsui Trust and Banking Y7.6 billion. Among the four Sumitomo companies one sees a stronger position to the bank of the grouping. In three of the four cases the bank of the grouping is the primary source; in the fourth case it is the trust bank. In all four Sumitomo companies borrowings from Sumitomo sources, when combined, put the financial institutions of the grouping in a preeminent position.

For these 12 companies the percentage figures on the proportion of total borrowings from the bank and the financial institutions of the grouping are as follows:

| | *Bank* | *Grouping* | | *Bank* | *Grouping* |
|---|---|---|---|---|---|
| *Mitsubishi* | | | | | |
| Mitsubishi Heavy Ind. | 11.30 | 22.65 | Mitsubishi Trading | 24.84 | 32.74 |
| Mitsubishi Electric | 15.74 | 30.04 | Mitsubishi Chemical | 9.65 | 19.93 |
| *Mitsui* | | | | | |
| Mitsui & Co. (Trading) | 17.02 | 24.53 | Toyo Rayon | 9.25 | 22.68 |
| Mitsui Mining | 8.58 | 16.16 | Petrochemicals | 15.38 | 30.75 |
| *Sumitomo* | | | | | |
| Sumitomo Metal Ind. | 16.74 | 38.31 | Nippon Electric | 19.07 | 44.25 |
| Sumitomo Chemicals | 14.62 | 36.45 | Sumitomo Trading | 25.34 | 47.18 |

As the above percentage figures show, there is both very substantial reliance on the bank of the grouping, together with the affiliated trust bank and life insurance company, and at the same time major reliance on outside institutions—both banks and other financial institutions of rival groupings, as well as independent institutions and government sources. Among all 12 companies more than 50% of their borrowing is from outside sources; in five cases more than 75% of their borrowing is from outside sources.

Given the widespread Japanese view that banks of the grouping are the directing centers, let us pursue the interpretation further. The foregoing figures indicate that how one treats the relations among the bank and the other financial institutions of the grouping can greatly influence one's judgment as to the position of the bank vis-à-vis the industrial and commercial companies of the grouping. If one views the four financial institutions of the grouping as speaking with one voice—that of the bank—the role of the bank is obviously stronger than if one regards the four institutions as related yet with different voices.

Although the Economic Investigative Council subscribes to the prevailing Japanese view of the pivotal position of the bank in the grouping, the Council supplies markedly less information on the financial institutions than it does on the other members of the grouping. No information on lending among the institutions is given, nor are details on personnel ties provided. Ownership data are supplied, however, which are presented in Chart 11-1. The chart indicates that there is no clear answer from ownership as to the relationship of the four institutions. That there is no shareholding between the bank and the trust bank in the Mitsui and Sumitomo groupings is probably to be explained by the provision of the Antimonopoly Law forbidding shareholding by a financial institution "in a company with which it is competing and which operates in the same field of financial business." It is not clear how the Mitsubishi shareholding falls within the law. On management ties, however, it may be that the presidents of the four financial institutions who are members of the presidents' clubs have their own financial-institutions-presidents' group, which would be small enough to provide effective liaison.

What do the lending patterns of the four institutions indicate? The small sample of lending patterns given in Table 11-11 is enough to indicate that the trust bank is a substantial source of funds for member companies. Table 11-11 suggests, but not as clearly as a larger sample would, that trust banks tend toward a somewhat more catholic lending pattern than does the bank. That is, trust banks lend across group lines more frequently than does the bank of the group-

Chart 11-1: OWNERSHIP TIES AMONG THE FOUR FINANCIAL INSTITUTIONS, EXPRESSED AS A PERCENTAGE OF ISSUED SHARES, 1966.

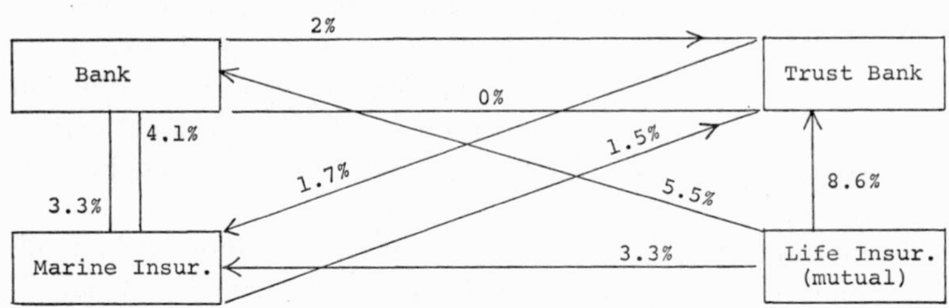


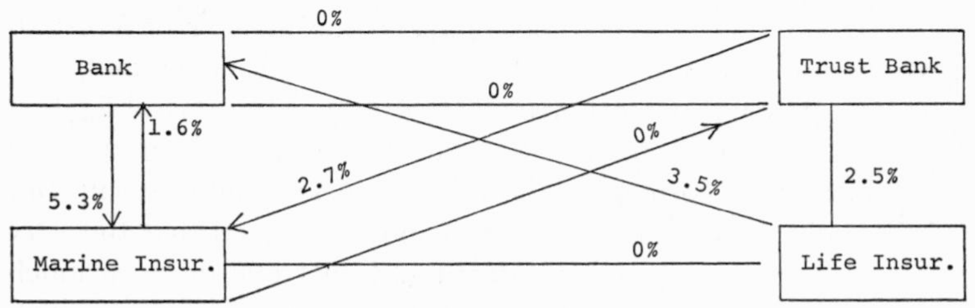


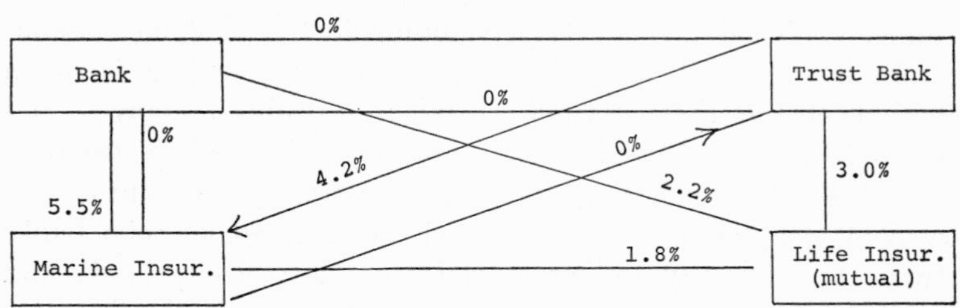


Source: Economic Investigative Council, *Research on Business Groupings*, 1967, Calculated from Tables 206, 207, and 208.

ing. The table also makes evident that life insurance companies, while not rivaling the bank and the trust bank in size of loans, are major lenders. By contrast, the casualty insurance companies only occasionally provide funds. That there is a discernible distinction in lending patterns between the bank and the trust bank of the grouping suggests that the trust bank is not a mere extension of the bank.

The foregoing limited evidence indicates that the ties between the four financial institutions are insufficient for the type of coordination seen in the combine period, yet much too real for independent action. Relations suggest joint action at times, while at other times, indicating separate paths.

In this interpretation, if one regards the lending position of the bank as the product of its own lending position, supplemented, but not always, by the action of the other financial institutions of the grouping, does the bank's position seem strong enough to make it a successor to the former top-holding companies? The point is repeatedly made by persons knowledgeable about the ways of business in Japan that under Japanese mores, bankers do not regard policy guidance to borrowers as part of the province of a bank in the manner of Western bankers. Naturally, if the terms of a loan are not being met, this alters matters, but when the borrower is fully meeting his obligation it is held that it is not customary under Japanese banking practice to tell the borrowing corporation how its business should be run. But even if this point were granted, might it not be argued that the very grant of a loan is in itself policy-directing? Is not one quite as much in a position to shape policy by saying "yes" or "no" to a loan request, especially when three-quarters of financing is done by borrowing, as by putting a director on the board? We will look at bank representatives on boards of the core companies shortly, but what of policy determination from granting or refusing the loan?

Commercial banks achieve their standing in the banking community from the scale of their lending. Because its lending is much below that of the Fuji (former Yasuda), Mitsubishi, Sanwa, and Sumitomo Banks, the Mitsui Bank is no longer in the top group of commercial banks. It is now in the middle group of "city banks." (As observed in Chapter 8, the Japanese divide their commercial banks into two categories, city and provincial; there are 12 city banks and 64 provincial banks.[17]) The 1967 loans of the 12 city banks, plus those of the Bank of Tokyo, may be seen in Table 11-12.

There is a compulsion on the part of the city banks to grant loans

[17] For a brief discussion of the Japanese banking structure see T.F.M. Adams, *A Financial History of Modern Japan*, Tokyo, 1964, pp. 248-62.

in order to maintain their position in the banking community. City banks are not obliged to live with the illiquidity resulting from excessive loans because, unlike the provincial banks, as observed earlier, they are able to meet such crises by borrowing from the Bank of Japan. This is the "overloan" situation about which there has been so much comment. Legally both city and provincial banks are entitled to borrow from the Bank of Japan, but actually the Bank of Japan lends only to the city banks. If a provincial bank were to get itself overloaned it would face bankruptcy. Therefore, with the restraint of bankruptcy removed for the city banks, and with their standing dependent on their scale of lending, there is considerable pressure to grant all plausible loans.

In addition to the pressure to grant loans, the large number of sources to which companies not only can, but do turn, suggests that policy determination from extension of loans is at a minimum. With the number of alternative opportunities open to the companies, and the banks' eagerness to extend loans, the banks are not in a strong position to impose banking conditions for the extension of loans. Further, there is the asserted difference in banker mores. Accordingly, from the point of view of lending alone it would seem difficult to conclude that the banks are in a position to control.

In deference to those observers who see banks controlled rather than controlling because of the scale of their lending to individual corporations, the borrowing relationship is viewed the other way around: the amount of bank loans committed to particular corporations in relation to total lending. This information is presented in Table 11-13. The data in this table are not wholly consonant with Table 11-12, for Table 11-13 presents 1961 information. A study of the relationship between loans and total lending in Table 11-13 indicates that in no instance were loans to the individual core companies by the bank of the grouping up to 5% of the total lending of the bank. In one case they amounted to 4.6%, in one to 2.4%, in two cases to one and a fraction percent, and in the remainder to a fraction of one percent. I, accordingly, would conclude that detailed information on the relationship between total lending and loans to particular companies does not support the view that banks are controlled by their major borrowers.

The bank's position in the grouping is more than the product of lending alone, however the lending is regarded—loans from the bank by itself or in combination with the other financial institutions. The bank's position is the product of its shareholding, lending, and, as we shall shortly see, at times, of personnel ties as well. At the beginning

Table 11-12: Lending by "City Banks," 1967
(in billions yen)

| | March | September | December |
|---|---|---|---|
| Fuji | 1,482 | 1,570 | 1,625 |
| Mitsubishi | 1,422 | 1,514 | 1,564 |
| Sanwa | 1,414 | 1,499 | 1,549 |
| Sumitomo | 1,402 | 1,489 | 1,542 |
| | | | |
| Daiichi | 1,095 | 1,149 | 1,184 |
| Tokai | 1,087 | 1,143 | 1,179 |
| Mitsui | 1,017 | 1,082 | 1,115 |
| Kangyo | 973 | 1,019 | 1,052 |
| | | | |
| Kyowa | 639 | 678 | 703 |
| Daiwa | 639 | 670 | 692 |
| Kobe | 522 | 552 | 569 |
| Hokkaido Devel. | 392 | 410 | 425 |
| | | | |
| Tokyo | 454 | 482 | 506 |
| Total | 12,545 | 13,265 | 13,710 |

Source and Notes: Banking Federation of Japan (Zenkoku Ginko Rengokai), through the courtesy of Miyoshi Masaya of the Japan Economic Federation. The above figures include call loans. The Daiichi Bank has trust bank operations, but the figures cited for Daiichi are exclusive of this.

of this chapter group ownership ties were noted. Now let us look at the bank's shareholding in these companies and combine the results with its own lending and personnel ties where applicable. Table 11-14 provides the information on shareholding by the bank. (It likewise includes information on the company's shareholding in the bank.[18])

[18] Although it is true that bank ownership in the core companies is considerably more significant than core company ownership in the bank, nevertheless it is noteworthy that almost all core companies, as will be seen in Table 11-14, hold (*Cont. p. 241*)

Table 11-13: MITSUBISHI, MITSUI, AND SUMITOMO BANKS' TOTAL LENDING, AND LOANS BY THESE BANKS TO THE CORE COMPANIES OF THEIR GROUPING, SEPT 1961 (in millions yen)

Mitsubishi Bank: total lending, 639,971

| Company | Loans from bank | Percentage of bank's total lending | Company | Loans from bank | Percentage of bank's total lending |
|---|---|---|---|---|---|
| tsubishi Mining | 1,484 | 0.23 | Asahi Glass | 4,000 | 0.63 |
| Metal Mining | 1,702 | 0.27 | Mitsubishi Rayon | 2,792 | 0.44 |
| Heavy Ind. Reorg. | 7,522 | 1.18 | Edogawa Chemical | 966 | 0.15 |
| Japan Heavy Ind. | 4,690 | 0.73 | Mitsubishi Oil | 2,360 | 0.37 |
| Shipbuilding | 5,661 | 0.88 | M. Paper Mills | 1,165 | 0.18 |
| Electric | 6,188 | 0.97 | M. Cement | 1,134 | 0.18 |
| Steel | 1,498 | 0.23 | M. Shoji (Trading) | 15,788 | 2.47 |
| Steel Mfg. | 671 | 0.10 | M. Warehouse | 855 | 0.13 |
| Chem. Mach. | 291 | 0.05 | M. Shipping | 425 | 0.07 |
| Chemicals | 2,284 | 0.36 | M. Real Estate | 2,727 | 0.43 |

Mitsui Bank: total lending, 437,385

| Company | Loans from bank | Percentage of bank's total lending | Company | Loans from bank | Percentage of bank's total lending |
|---|---|---|---|---|---|
| :sui Mining | 3,146 | 0.72 | Mitsui & Co. (Trading) | 20,387 | 4.66 |
| Metal Mining | 1,070 | 0.24 | Gen. Bussan (Trading) | 1,725 | 0.39 |
| kaido Colliery & SS | 1,326 | 0.30 | Toshoku (Tokyo Foods) | 1,955 | 0.46 |
| an Steel Works | 1,985 | 0.45 | Mitsui Warehouse | 426 | 0.10 |
| sui Shipbuilding | 1,639 | 0.37 | Mitsui Real Estate | 2,517 | 0.58 |
| wa Aircraft | 624 | 0.14 | Mitsui Shipping | 742 | 0.17 |
| o Koatsu Industries | 1,000 | 0.23 | Mitsui Agr. & Forestry | 169 | 0.04 |
| ke Gosei Chemical | 302 | 0.07 | Sanki Engineering | 115 | 0.03 |
| sui Chemical | 2,512 | 0.57 | Mitsui Construction | 387 | 0.09 |
| o Rayon | 3,205 | 0.73 | | | |

Sumitomo Bank: total lending, 610,553

| Company | Loans from bank | Percentage of bank's total lending | Company | Loans from bank | Percentage of bank's total lending |
|---|---|---|---|---|---|
| itomo Coal Mining | 2,282 | 0.37 | Nippon Electric | 5,241 | 0.86 |
| Mining | 1,897 | 0.31 | Sumitomo Machinery | 903 | 0.15 |
| Metal Ind. | 2,084 | 0.34 | S. Chemical | 4,266 | 0.70 |
| Electric Ind. | 3,042 | 0.50 | S. Shoji (Trading) | 10,906 | 1.79 |
| pon Sheet Glass | 2,411 | 0.39 | S. Warehouse | 532 | 0.09 |

rces: Total lending by the three banks, Economic Planning Agency, *An Analysis of our Country's k Behavior* (Keizai Kikachucho, *Waga Kuni Ginko no Kodo Bunseki*), Tokyo, 1964, Table 11, pp. 96-97; rowing by companies, Economic Investigative Council, *Research on Business Groupings* 1962, Tables 6, 8, pp. 38-59. Percentages have been calculated.

Table 11-14: SHAREHOLDING BETWEEN BANK AND CORE COMPANIES IN THE MITSUBISHI, MITSUI, AND SUMITOMO GROUPINGS, SEPT 1966 (in thousands of shares)

(All shares have been computed in the form of 50 yen shares)

(n.l. - not listed)

Mitsubishi

| Company | Total issued shares | Bank ownership in Company | | Company's ownership in bank | Percent |
|---|---|---|---|---|---|
| | | shares | percentage | | |
| Mitsubishi Bank | 440,000 | | | | |
| M. Trust & Banking | 200,000 | 4,000 | 2.00 | 0 | 0 |
| Tokyo Marine Insur. | 180,000 | 6,000 | 3.33 | 18,040 | 4.10 |
| Mitsubishi Mining | 149,466 | 3,031 | 2.02 | 800 | 0.18 |
| M. Metal Mining | 200,000 | 3,700 | 1.85 | 2,100 | 0.48 |
| M. Heavy Ind. | 1,591,114 | 48,864 | 3.07 | 15,000 | 3.41 |
| M. Electric | 864,000 | 15,000 | 1.73 | 6,000 | 1.36 |
| M. Steel | 95,342 | 4,264 | 4.47 | 862 | 0.20 |
| M. Chemical Mach. | 24,000 | 1,000 | 4.16 | 300 | 0.07 |
| M. Chemical | 454,447 | 16,080 | 3.53 | 6,000 | 1.36 |
| Asahi Glass | 432,000 | 21,195 | 6.15 | 4,000 | 0.91 |
| Mitsubishi Petrochem. | 202,500 | 16,403 | 8.10 | n.l. | - |
| M. Rayon | 155,603 | 6,916 | 4.44 | 3,200 | 0.73 |
| M. Edogawa Chemical | 48,000 | 2,953 | 5.00 | 1,200 | 0.27 |
| M. Plastics | 63,000 | 1,050 | 1.67 | 500 | 0.11 |
| M. Oil | 200,000 | 2,589 | 1.29 | 400 | 0.09 |
| M. Paper | 112,000 | 6,920 | 6.16 | 2,500 | 0.57 |
| M. Cement | 70,000 | 1,162 | 1.66 | n.l. | - |
| Kirin Beer | 460,000 | 0 | 0 | 2,500 | 0.57 |
| M. Shoji (Trading) | 450,000 | 23,400 | 5.20 | 4,554 | 1.03 |
| M. Warehouse | 37,600 | 1,445 | 3.84 | 1,400 | 0.32 |
| Nippon Yusen Kaisha (NYK) | 292,000 | 4,320 | 1.48 | 2,960 | 0.67 |
| Mitsubishi Estate | 495,000 | 20,000 | 4.04 | 2,000 | 0.45 |

Table 11-14: (continued)

Mitsui

| Company | Total issued shares | Bank ownership in Company shares | Bank ownership in Company percentage | Company's ownership in bank | Percent |
|---|---|---|---|---|---|
| Mitsui Bank | 360,000 | | | | |
| M. Trust & Banking | 200,000 | 0 | 0 | 0 | 0 |
| Taisho Marine Insur. | 128,000 | 6,900 | 5.39 | 6,040 | 1.68 |
| Mitsui Mining | 60,000 | 1,000 | 1.67 | 0 | 0 |
| M. Metal Mining | 216,000 | 4,275 | 1.98 | 2,532 | 0.70 |
| Hokkaido Colliery & SS | 140,441 | 1,343 | 0.96 | 4,000 | 1.11 |
| Japan Steel Works | 175,767 | 11,257 | 6.40 | 3,630 | 1.01 |
| Mitsui Shipbuilding | 238,000 | 0 | 0.00 | 3,760 | 1.04 |
| M. Precision Machinery | 12,240 | 1,224 | 10.00 | n.l. | - |
| Toyo Koatsu Industries | 262,860 | 7,450 | 2.83 | 5,230 | 1.45 |
| Mitsui Petrochemical | 100,000 | 8,800 | 8.80 | 0 | 0 |
| M. Chemical | 176,180 | 3,335 | 1.89 | 3,332 | 0.93 |
| Toyo Rayon | 841,213 | 0 | 0.00 | 2,840 | 0.79 |
| Mitsui & Co. (Trading) | 266,177 | 19,000 | 7.14 | 7,430 | 2.06 |
| Gen. Petroleum (Sekiyu) | 34,285 | 1,143 | 3.33 | 840 | 0.23 |
| Toshoku (Tokyo Foods) | 56,000 | 2,800 | 5.00 | 1,340 | 0.37 |
| Toyo Menka | 148,500 | 5,000 | 3.37 | 3,512 | 0.98 |
| Mitsui Warehouse | 40,540 | 1,216 | 3.00 | 1,240 | 0.34 |
| M. Real Estate | 83,952 | 8,185 | 9.75 | 4,750 | 1.32 |
| Osaka Shosen-Mitsui Ship. | | | | | |
| Mitsui Norin (Agr. & Forestry) | 6,600 | 198 | 3.00 | n.l. | - |
| Sanki Engineering | 50,000 | 1,650 | 3.30 | 1,040 | 0.29 |
| Mitsui Construction | 40,800 | 313 | 0.77 | 217 | 0.06 |

Table 11-14: (continued)

Sumitomo

| Company | Total issued shares | Bank ownership in Company | | Company's ownership in bank | Percent |
|---|---|---|---|---|---|
| | | shares | percentage | | |
| Sumitomo Bank | 440,000 | | | | |
| S. Trust & Banking | 200,000 | 0 | 0 | 0 | 0 |
| S. Marine Insur. | 108,000 | 6,000 | 5.55 | 0 | 0 |
| S. Coal Mining | 66,172 | 3,826 | 5.78 | 5,280 | 1.20 |
| S. Metal Mining | 111,458 | 3,608 | 3.23 | 2,870 | 0.65 |
| S. Metal Ind. | 1,271,467 | 72,709 | 5.71 | 10,000 | 2.27 |
| S. Electric Ind. | 270,000 | 10,125 | 3.75 | 6,600 | 1.50 |
| Nippon Sheet Glass | 160,000 | 6,464 | 4.04 | 9,000 | 2.05 |
| Nippon Electric | 400,000 | 34,646 | 8.66 | 10,000 | 2.27 |
| Sumitomo Machinery | 108,000 | 4,575 | 4.24 | 1,760 | 0.40 |
| S. Chemical | 504,000 | 18,450 | 3.66 | 13,000 | 2.95 |
| S. Trading | 140,000 | 11,277 | 8.05 | 8,000 | 1.82 |
| S. Warehouse | 36,000 | 1,800 | 5.00 | 880 | 0.20 |
| S. Cement | 110,000 | 7,718 | 7.16 | 2,000 | 0.45 |
| S. Real Estate | 24,030 | 1,913 | 7.96 | n.l. | - |
| S. Light Metal | 112,000 | 5,126 | 4.57 | 1,500 | 0.34 |

Source: Economic Investigative Council, *Research on Business Groupings*, 1967, Tables 206, 207, 208, pp. 84-107. Percentage column figures have been computed.

A look at bank holdings in the core companies reveals a number of cases where bank ownership is 5% and above. There is, of course, no magic in this percentage, but in today's fractured holdings (which characterize the large corporation), 5% typically represents a situation where the company is a major shareholder.[19] It will be seen that the bank's position is at this substantial level among 5 of the 21 Mitsubishi companies, 7 of the 21 Mitsui companies, and 9 of the 15 Sumitomo companies for which information is presented. Thus, while the bank does not characteristically have substantial holdings, it does on several occasions. A summary of the information from Table 11-14 shows that the core companies in which the bank does have such holdings in the three groupings are as follows:

| | | | |
|---|---|---|---|
| **Mitsubishi** | | | |
| Petrochemicals | 8.1% | Shoji (Trading) | 5.2% |
| Asahi Glass | 6.1 | Edogawa Chemical | 5.0 |
| Paper | 6.1 | | |
| **Mitsui** | | | |
| Precision Machinery | 10.0 | Japan Steel Works | 6.4% |
| Real Estate | 9.7 | Taisho Marine Insur. | 5.3 |
| Petrochemical | 8.8 | Toshoku (Tokyo Foods) | 5.0 |
| Mitsui & Co. (Trading) | 7.1 | | |
| **Sumitomo** | | | |
| Nippon Electric | 8.6% | Coal Mining | 5.7 |
| Shoji (Trading) | 8.0 | Metal Industries | 5.7 |
| Real Estate | 7.9 | Marine Insur. | 5.5 |
| Cement | 7.1 | Warehouse | 5.0 |
| Light Metal | 5.8 | | |

(*Cont. from p. 236*)
shares in the bank. One gains the impression of shareholding in banks as a "facilitant" to loans most clearly from companies which are not part of any grouping. For example, if one looks at the "portfolio" of some of the cotton companies in the Economic Investigative Council's study, one notes the striking number of banks in which they hold shares. For example, the Nitto Spinning has investments in 21 different banks, and the Kurashiki Spinning Co. in 18. Thus, while we have been looking at bank influence in the core companies from shareholding in them, one must not overlook the reciprocal influence of core company influence in the bank, modest though the shareholdings may be.

[19] In the original form of the Antimonopoly Law, 5% share ownership was the maximum level permitted financial institutions.

The position of the bank as a supplier of funds to these companies will be provided shortly, but now let us observe personnel ties.

In view of the widespread currency of the opinion that banks have inherited the mantle of the former top-holding companies, various studies have been made of officers with a bank background who are on the boards of various companies of the grouping.[20] Such lists tend to be more impressive when viewed without critical examination than when studied in detail. The lists turn out to have only modest consistency one with another or when comparison is made of the findings in different years published by the same source. Furthermore, when some of the persons' dates of transfer are studied, it turns out that transfers back to the immediate postwar years are included. The Japanese phrasing for most such lists is "persons 'dispatched' from the bank." The bank quality of a person in 1966 who transferred from the bank to the core company in 1947 would seem tenuous indeed. Not only is there a question of the time dimension in such lists, there is likewise a question about the appropriateness of certain of the officer inclusions when consideration is focused to policy-affecting officers. As noted earlier, auditors, under Japanese commercial law, are officers. Persons knowledgeable about Japanese business procedures insist that plain auditorships (in contrast to standing ones) are not policy positions, that plain auditorships tend either to be sinecures or springboards for those rising to the officer level.

In compiling Table 11-15 I have deliberately omitted certain officers, so as to present "significant" personnel ties between the bank and the core companies of the grouping. With respect to the time factor, *significant* includes transfers since 1960. *Positions* includes those auditorships where the person has held (or is holding) an important position in the bank; the term excludes auditorships where the bank position was below the officer level. There are striking discrepancies between different lists, and I have arbitrarily chosen to use the material prepared by the Economic Investigative Council.

Detailed examination of bank personnel ties among core companies, as shown in Table 11-15, reveals several surprising features. Such ties do not show a high correlation with the most important companies of the grouping (as indicated by capitalization), with bank ownership in the companies, or with the scale of borrowing from the bank. These observations are shown in Table 11-16, where the material from earlier tables is pulled together. For example, in Table 11-15, in the Mitsubishi grouping it will be seen that Rayon has the strongest personnel

[20] Cf., for example, Diamond, *Management Yearbook* (Diamondo, *Keiei Nempo*), 1965, pp. 333ff. See also *Oriental Economist* article discussed in note 25 below.

Table 11-15: PERSONNEL TIES BETWEEN THE BANK AND THE CORE COMPANIES, 1966 ACCORDING TO THE PRESENTATION OF ECONOMIC INVESTIGATIVE COUNCIL IN THE MITSUBISHI, MITSUI AND SUMITOMO GROUPINGS

Note: Transfers which date from the 1940s and the 1950s (with exception) have been omitted. Auditors are included only when the person was (is) of officer position in the bank.

tsubishi - 9 companies

| npany | *Position in company* | *Date of "dispatch"* | *Position in Bank when transferred, or concurrent position* | *Other financial institutions with which company has personnel ties. (affiliated institutions in parenthesis)* |
|---|---|---|---|---|
| avy Industries | auditor | 1961 | standing director | |
| | auditor | 1962 | councilor | |
| ectric | standing director | 1964 | standing director | Kangyo Bank |
| eel | president | 1963 | standing director | |
| emicals | auditor | 1963 | director | |
| 'on | president | 1959 | director | (Mitsubishi Trust Bank) |
| | standing director | 1960 | branch chief | |
| | auditor | 1966 | director | |
| per | mgr. director | 1959 | councilor | |
| ading | auditor | 1959 | president | (Tokyo Marine Insur.) |
| al Estate | director | 1966 | councilor | (Mitsubishi Trust Bank) |
| | standing auditor | 1959 | standing auditor | |
| rehouse | auditor | 1960 | councilor | |

sui - 7 companies

| pany | *Position in company* | *Date of "dispatch"* | *Position in Bank when transferred, or concurrent position* | *Other financial institutions with which company has personnel ties. (affiliated institutions in parenthesis)* |
|---|---|---|---|---|
| l mining | director | 1964 | director | |
| micals | vice pres. | 1966 | standing director | Kangyo Bank |
| rochemicals | standing director | 1963 | director | (Mitsui Life), (Taisho Marine Insur.) |
| | director | 1955 | chairman | |
| o Rayon | vice pres. | 1963 | vice pres. | |
| | director | 1960 | division head (*bucho*) | |
| ding | director | 1965 | board chairman | |
| l Estate | chairman | 1955 | vice pres. | |
| ka Shosen-sui Shipping | director | 1964 | chairman | Sumitomo Bank |

itomo - 5 companies

| | | | | |
|---|---|---|---|---|
| al mining | director | 1963 | chief of head office | |
| pon electric | vice pres. | 1962 | standing director | |
| ht metals | mgr. director | 1965 | standing director | |
| hinery | director | 1960 | director | (Sumitomo Trust Bank) |
| ent | standing director | 1964 | standing director | (Sumitomo Life) |

e: This listing excludes transfers which occurred in the 1940's and (with exceptions) the 0's and includes auditorships only when the person was (or is) of officer rank in the bank.

rce: Economic Investigative Council, *Research on Business Groupings*, 1967, Table 205, pp. 69-74.

ties with the bank—a president, director, and auditor with bank connections. However, as will be seen in Table 11-16, Rayon is not among the top 10 core companies by capitalization, it is not one of the companies in which the bank has most substantial shareholding (shareholding was 4.44% in 1966), it is not one of the companies with largest absolute borrowings from the bank (its borrowing in 1966 was Y4,380 million), nor relatively was the bank an exceptionally important supplier of funds (10.2% in 1966). Furthermore, in the case of Mitsubishi Electric, bank personnel are not confined to the Mitsubishi Bank; it has an officer from the Kangyo Bank.

This does not suggest to me in the *usual* situation that banks are the inheritors of the former top-holding company role. Certain observers, however, look to the exceptional activities of banks—their role in

Table 11-16: BANK TIES SUMMARIZED AMONG THE CORE COMPANIES OF THE MITSUBISHI, MITSUI AND SUMITOMO GROUPINGS, 1966

Note: Capital and borrowings in millions of yen; companies with asterisk, those in which the Bank holds 5% or above of issued shares; figures in parenthesis, Ranking of top 10 firms within the column.

Mitsubishi

| *Company* | *Capitalization* | *Total borrowing* | *Borrowing from bank* | *Borrowing from affil. fin. inst.* | *Bank personnel ties* |
|---|---|---|---|---|---|
| Mining | 7,473 ( ) | 26,935 ( ) | 2,003 ( ) | 3,472 | |
| Metal Mining | 10,000 (10) | 21,158 (10) | 2,666 (10) | 5,231 | |
| Heavy Industries | 79,555 ( 1) | 296,219 ( 1) | 33,475 ( 1) | 33,622 | 2 aud. |
| Electric | 43,200 ( 2) | 81,797 ( 3) | 12,880 ( 3) | 12,051 | st. dir. |
| Steel | 4,767 ( ) | 13,406 ( ) | 3,857 ( 7) | 4,177 | pres. |
| Chemical Machine | 1,200 ( ) | 1,873 ( ) | 673 ( ) | 628 | |
| Chemicals | 22,722 ( 5) | 61,721 ( 5) | 5,958 ( 5) | 6,398 | aud. |
| Edogawa Chemicals* | 2,400 ( ) | 8,556 ( ) | 2,038 ( ) | 2,887 | |
| Plastics Industries | 3,150 ( ) | 8,244 ( ) | 1,206 ( ) | 2,573 | |
| Asahi Glass* | 21,600 ( 7) | 17,293 ( ) | 2,818 ( ) | 1,516 | |
| Rayon | 7,780 ( ) | 33,924 ( 7) | 4,380 ( 6) | 4,822 | pres., st. dir |
| Oil | 10,000 ( 9) | 26,854 ( 9) | 3,230 ( 8) | 5,214 | |
| Paper* | 5,600 ( ) | 14,417 ( ) | 1,435 ( ) | 3,699 | mgr. dir. |
| Kirin Beer | 23,014 ( 4) | 14,030 ( ) | 3,200 ( 9) | 5,010 | |
| Shoji (Trading)* | 22,500 ( 6) | 131,448 ( 2) | 32,652 ( 2) | 10,391 | aud. |
| Warehouse | 2,000 ( ) | 3,706 ( ) | 1,265 ( ) | 1,473 | |
| Nippon Yusen Kaisha | 14,600 ( 8) | 75,987 ( 4) | 2,506 ( ) | 1,085 | |
| Real Estate | 27,750 ( 3) | 52,413 ( 6) | 6,563 ( 4) | 21,787 | dir., st. aud. |

*Specific Bank holdings are: Petrochemicals (not shown because of lack of data) 8.1%; Paper, 6.1%, Asahi Glass, 6.1%; Shoji (Trading) 5.2%, and Edogawa Chemicals, 5.0%.

Mitsui

(Among Companies of the Second Thursday Club)

| *Company* | *Capitalization* | *Total borrowing* | *Borrowing from bank* | *Borrowing from affil. fin. inst.* | *Bank personnel ties* |
|---|---|---|---|---|---|
| ning | 3,000 ( ) | 50,407 ( 3) | 4,498 ( 6) | 3,975 | dir. |
| tal Mining | 10,800 ( 6) | 15,358 (10) | 1,088 ( ) | 2,890 | |
| kkaido Colliery | 7,002 ( 9) | 21,863 ( 9) | 1,324 (10) | 1,079 | |
| pan Steel* | 8,788 ( 8) | 20,014 ( ) | 4,576 ( 5) | 3,545 | |
| ipbuilding | 11,900 ( 5) | 40,457 ( 6) | 4,301 ( 7) | 3,716 | |
| yo Koatsu | 13,143 ( 3) | 38,492 ( 7) | 3,196 ( 9) | 4,998 | |
| emicals | 8,809 ( 7) | 31,925 ( 8) | 5,130 ( 4) | 7,136 | |
| trochemical* | 5,000 (10) | 46,546 ( 4) | 7,152 ( 2) | 8,152 | st. dir., dir. |
| yo Rayon | 42,060 ( 1) | 46,266 ( 5) | 4,283 ( 8) | 6,211 | vice pres., dir. |
| nki Engineering | 2,500 ( ) | 2,433 ( ) | 378 ( ) | 887 | |
| aka Shosen-Mitsui | 13,100 ( 4) | 59,672 ( 2) | 615 ( ) | 901 | dir. |
| ading* | 13,308 ( 2) | 182,431 ( 1) | 31,747 ( 1) | 13,019 | dir. |
| rehouse | 2,027 ( ) | 2,676 ( ) | 963 ( ) | 700 | |
| al Estate* | 4,197 ( ) | 32,975 ( ) | 5,684 ( 3) | 8,488 | |

pecific Bank holdings are: Precision Machinery 10.0%; Real Estate 9.7%; Petrochemicals, 8.8%; ading, 7.1%; Japan Steel, 6.4%; Taisho Marine Insurance (not listed above because of lack of ta), 5.3%.

Sumitomo

| *Company* | *Capitalization* | *Total borrowing* | *Borrowing from bank* | *Borrowing from affil. fin. inst.* | *Bank personnel ties* |
|---|---|---|---|---|---|
| ning | 3,308 ( ) | 28,183 ( 5) | 6,191 ( 6) | 5,279 | |
| tal Mining | 5,572 ( 8) | 12,296 (10) | 2,710 ( 9) | 4,445 | dir. |
| tal Industries* | 61,785 ( 1) | 94,346 ( 1) | 15,802 ( 2) | 20,342 | |
| ectric Industries | 13,500 ( 4) | 27,863 ( 6) | 6,815 ( 5) | 7,291 | |
| ppon Sheet Glass | 8,000 ( 5) | 15,927 ( 8) | 5,155 ( 7) | 4,468 | |
| ppon Electric* | 20,000 ( 3) | 56,487 ( 4) | 10,775 ( 3) | 14,221 | vice pres. |
| ght Metal* | 5,600 ( 7) | 15,036 ( 9) | 1,790 ( ) | 3,844 | mgr. dir. |
| chinery | 5,400 (10) | 9,855 ( ) | 2,630 (10) | 2,948 | |
| emicals | 25,200 ( 2) | 65,698 ( 3) | 9,609 ( 4) | 14,339 | |
| ment* | 5,500 ( 9) | 20,500 ( 7) | 3,590 ( 8) | 4,727 | st. dir. |
| ading* | 7,000 ( 6) | 70,859 ( 2) | 17,961 ( 1) | 15,475 | |
| rehouse | 1,800 ( ) | 2,853 ( ) | 985 ( ) | 738 | |

pecific Bank holdings are: Nippon Electric 8.6%; Shoji (Trading), 8.0%; Real Estate, 7.9%; ment, 7.1%; Light Metal, 5.8%; Mining, 5.7%; Metal Industries, 5.7%; Marine Insurance (not sted bacause of lack of data), 5.5%, and Warehouse, 5.0%.

mergers—and conclude that they have inherited the top-holding company course.

In the last few years corporations have been merging at an ever-increasing rate. Prior to the Securities Exchange Law of March 1947 commercial banking and investment banking in Japan were one.[21] It was customary for commercial banks to arrange the means of financing corporate reorganization. There is, accordingly, a tradition in Japan for commercial banks to assume such a role. Small items reported in newspapers and periodicals suggest that commercial banks often take important roles in today's mergers. In 1963-64, at the time of the wholesale mergers in shipping, when shipping companies in Japan were grouped into six great complexes, one heard a lot about the role of the respective banks in effecting these mergers. The shipping merger initiative, however, did not come from the banks, but rather from the government. In the case of the merger of the three Mitsubishi Heavy Industries companies, one frequently heard about the role of the Mitsubishi Bank. I am more inclined to view the banks as agents and promoters of amalgamation, however, than as imposers of amalgamation. (As will be seen more fully below, the Japanese government is using the full range of its resources to promote mergers. In discussions with Japanese commercial reporters and young businessmen, no point is more astonishing to them than to learn that the U.S. government tends to take a critical view of mergers—from their own experience they had supposed that all governments promoted them.) Mergers always involve the awkward problem of who among the existing presidents will be the new president, who the board chairman, et cetera. An outsider is helpful here, and no outsider is more logical than the president or board chairman of the bank from which the merging companies have large, if not their largest, borrowings. Thus, even in the exceptional role in mergers, it does not seem to me that banks are playing the role of the former top-holding companies.

### *Control through Trading Companies*

In downturns of Japan's high growth rate (growth at 4 or 5%), a different interpretation of coordination within the groupings has been put forward, namely, that it is the trading companies that provide

[21] For a very brief discussion see Yazawa Makoto, "The Legal Structure for Corporate Enterprise: Shareholder-Management Relations under Japanese Law," in Arthur Taylor von Mehren, ed., *Law in Japan*, Cambridge, Mass., 1963, p. 562; also see Adams, *A Financial History*, pp. 201-202.

overall direction.[22] Again, however, we are dealing with a service organ. Like the banks of the groups, trading companies have a pervasive influence via their buying and selling activities with all the companies of the grouping. During high growth, when sources of funds are the overriding question, it is the banks which are said to be the key; in downturns, such as 1962 and 1965 when the economy was at a slower rate (GNP growing at 5.7 and 3.7%) and selling was consequently more in the forefront, it was said that it was the trading companies which were integrating. From the earlier examination of trading companies in the context of combine enterprise, it is clear that they can be used as a highly effective coordinating mechanism. Then, however, there was the holding company to insist that all buying and selling be done through these companies. Furthermore, there was use of the sole-agency contract, doubly to ensure no slip-ups. Now, however, under Japan's Antimonopoly Law, exclusive dealing is illegal. Article 5 states: "No entrepreneur shall establish, organize or become a party to or a member of a juridical person or any other organization which controls distribution of all or a part of materials or products by methods of exclusive purchase or sale or which undertakes the allocation of all or a part of materials or products."

There is nothing in today's structure of the groupings to compel reliance on the trading companies. Boards of the core companies can buy and sell on their own or they can use the services of the trading company. Certain factors conduce to joint activity; others to individual. That the core companies are typically operating with common trade names and trademarks contributes to the joint activity.[23] In

[22] Cf., for example, *Mainichi Shimbun*, "Atarashii Nami, Sangyo Saihensei," cited in note 6 above.

[23] There was an attempt in the deconcentration program to prohibit the use of *zaibatsu* trade names and trademarks among the 10 combines (the Big Four and the Other Six), but it largely came to naught. In response to a SCAP directive prohibiting the use of trade names and trademarks by the 10 combines, Imp. Ord. 567 was amended to so prohibit (Art. 14). However, enforcement was by Cabinet Order, and the Cabinet Order was drawn to apply to only the Big Three (Mitsubishi, Mitsui, and Sumitomo). They were given until June 20, 1950 to make the necessary changes, but before the deadline was reached it was decided to allow another year for the changes, making new trade names and trademarks mandatory by June 30, 1951. In May 1951, however, it was decided to allow the Big Three another year in which to make the necessary changes, thus extending the deadline to June 30, 1952, safely into the post-Peace Treaty period (cf. HCLC, *Final Report*, pp. 79-80). Some evidence of the attempt to change trade names and trademarks is scattered about. That the Sumitomo company, Nippon Electric, is so named is a product of this period; formerly it was Sumitomo Communications. That the Yasuda Bank is the Fuji Bank is a product of this effort, even though the Cabinet Order was not drawn to include the Yasuda *zaibatsu*.

advertising one Mitsubishi product, one is advertising another; not surprisingly, there is considerable joint advertising. But it costs to sell through the trading companies—in the combine period it was noted that charges were between 1% and 3% of sales—and the issue before individual core companies today is whether the gains from their own point of view match the costs. The question is how much it would cost to handle marketing on their own as compared to using the services of the trading company, and whether their corporate image comes through sufficiently clearly in joint selling.

The trading companies are eager to have the core companies use their services. Core companies are typically leaders in their fields, and it gives the trading companies not only the commissions but prestige to have them included in their product line. Today, however, that with which the trading companies have to argue their case is simply persuasion in the context of common trade names and trademarks and the old school tie. In the Mitsubishi grouping one sees evidence of this persuasion at work in the scale of Trading's interlocks with core companies. Because of possible limitations of the following listing of interlocks, two different years are cited, 1959 and 1964:[24]

In 1959
- Trading's president was
  - a director of the Bank; of Japan Heavy Industries; of Oil; of Cement; of Warehouse; of Rayon; and an auditor of Petrochemicals
- Trading's vice president was
  - a director of Heavy Ind. Reorganized; of Chemical Machinery
- Trading's managing director was
  - a director of Steel Mfg

In 1964
- Trading's president was
  - a director of Heavy Industries; of Chemical Industries
- Trading's chairman of the board was
  - a director of Rayon; of Warehouse; of Cement; and an auditor of Petrochemicals
- One of Trading's vice presidents was
  - a director of Steel
- One of Trading's auditors was
  - a director of Nippon Yusen Kaisha
- Another auditor was
  - an auditor of Oil

[24] *Oriental Economist,* June 1959, p. 349. The 1964 data were supplied me through the courtesy of Iyori Hiroshi; they are taken from the Ministry of Finance, *Corporate Securities Reports* (*Yuka Shoken Hokokusho*).

So far as I know, such extensive interlocks do not occur in the case of Mitsui Trading or Sumitomo Trading.

In the annual corporation reports required by the Ministry of Finance, information is asked on principal buyers and sellers. It is this information that is reproduced in corporation directories under the heading "principal transactions." To study the entries of core companies of the three groupings is to be persuaded that core companies are using both the services of their respective trading companies and buying and selling on their own. The trading companies are in a position to provide integrating leadership to their respective groupings, but the extent to which they do this is dependent on the extent to which they can persuade the individual companies to purchase their services. Today this is elective. Accordingly, I have concluded that while opportunities for leadership exist in the trading companies, the companies are not in a position today to act in a successor role to the former top-holding companies.

### *Control Through Presidents' Clubs and Management Interlocks*

Today it is frequently asserted that one of the by-products of the combine dissolution program in Japan is the separation of ownership from control, that Japan has experienced a managerial revolution, and that it is management which now determines corporate policy. We have seen that today's ownership, in the case of large companies such as the core companies of the three groupings, is in bits and pieces. To what extent, then, is unified direction of the groupings being achieved through presidents' clubs and management interlocks?

The highest management coordinating group in the three groupings is the one from which has been taken the definition of today's core companies, that is, the presidents' clubs. The presidents of the core companies meet regularly to discuss common problems and maintain social ties. No doubt a valuable amount of coordination is achieved, but the clubs in no way represent successor organizations to the boards of the former top-holding companies. For one thing, they are too big. Second, they are made up of persons ostensibly equal, a point not to be treated lightly. Third, they have no way of compelling adoption of their thinking even when they are able to agree on common positions. It will be recalled that in the combine period the top-holding company directly or indirectly appointed all officers of the first- and second-line companies. No one has suggested that today's presidents' clubs are attempting to manage officer appointments in the core companies. But it would be my guess that the clubs find it much easier to agree on such items as share subscriptions in new companies or taking over an outside company, than on telling a member corporation how its business should be run. There have been a number of instances in which the companies of a grouping joined either in establishing a new company or in taking over an existing one. In the Mitsubishi group the high group ownership in Petrochemicals, Plastics, and Cement is a result of joint effort in establishing new companies. Similarly, the high "Sumitomo" ownership in Sumitomo Cement is a result of several of the Sumitomo core companies joining to buy out the Iwaki Cement Company.

The presidents' clubs have not exhausted the efforts at joint management within the groupings. In addition, there are from among the core companies committees of managers, committees of department heads and committees of engineers. One of the most powerful committees within the groups is the committee on trade names and trademarks. It is this committee which decides on applications for the use of the trade name as well as handling problems arising out of use. An examination of today's management situation among the three groupings suggests a situation midway between that found in the former combine period and independence. There is collaboration, but it is of a far weaker variety than formerly.

Common management can be achieved not only out of joint collaboration through committees, but out of interlocks. As we saw in the combine period (Table 4-1 and Appendix VII), interlocks were extraordinarily comprehensive. What do we find now? Because it has not been possible to locate current data on interlocks[25] as adequate as the data appearing in the 1959 English-language edition of the *Oriental Economist*, it is these data which are reproduced as Table 11-17. It is not clear to me whether the much stronger pattern of interlocks in the Mitsubishi grouping is the product of fact or the data. A study of Table 11-17 will show in the Mitsubishi grouping that 11 of the 22 core companies had interlocks, some considerably more

[25] The Japanese-language edition of the *Oriental Economist, Toyo Keizai,* published a major study of current business groupings in 1963 under the title, "An Analysis of the Groupings of Principal Businesses" (Shuryoku Kigyo no Keiretsu Shindan), July 18, 1963, pp. 165-90. It includes material on management ties. Ostensibly it includes the ties reported in the 1959 English-language edition of the magazine, for the table purported to present personnel connections over the preceding 10 years. (How it is possible to present changing ties over a 10-year period without showing dates was not discussed.) In the English-language table, officers who were "dispatched" or were interlocks are named; in the Japanese-language table officers are frequently not named. Ties are indicated by company of origin or very frequently merely by "kei," i.e., "of the grouping." Because this table fails to include officers named in the 1959 table, I have relied on the latter.

extensive than others. The two companies with the highest interlocks, Petrochemicals and Cement, are also two among a small number showing high ownership (Petrochemicals 69.90% and Cement 89.55% in 1966). They are new and represent joint undertakings.

In the Mitsui portion of Table 11-17, interlocks are sparse indeed—three out of 26 companies. It is difficult for me to imagine that they are as weak as the data indicate, but on the other hand, if they had

Table 11-17: INTERLOCKING DIRECTORATES AMONG THE CORE COMPANIES OF THE MITSUBISHI, MITSUI, AND SUMITOMO GROUPINGS (1959 DATA)

Part A: Mitsubishi

| | |
|---|---|
| Mitsubishi Bank | Trading's president, director; Tokyo Fire, Marine Insurance's chairman, director; Meiji Life Insurance's president, director |
| Tokyo Marine, Fire Insur. | Meiji Life Insurance's president, auditor |
| M. Heavy Ind. Reorg. | Trading's vice-president, director |
| M. Japan Heavy Industries | Trading's president, director; Steel Mfg.'s chairman, director |
| M. Steel | Japan Heavy Industries' president, director; Electric's vice-president, director |
| M. Steel Mfg. | Trading's managing director, director |
| M. Chemical Machinery | Trading's vice-president, director; Heavy Ind. Reorg.'s managing director, director |
| M. Rayon | Trading's president, director; Real Estate's chairman, director |
| M. Petrochemicals | Trading's president, auditor; Bank's president, auditor; Metal Mining's president, director; Real Estate's chairman, director; Asahi Glass's president, director; Rayon's president director |
| M. Cement | Trading's president, director; Real Estate's president, director; Mining's president, director; Mining's managing director, director; Asahi Glass's president, director |
| M. Warehouse | Trading's president, director |

Part B: Mitsui

| | |
|---|---|
| Showa Aircraft | Japan Steel's president, director; Mitsui Shipbuilding's president, director; Mitsui Shipbuilding's director, director |
| Tokyo Food Products | Taisho Marine, Fire Insurance's auditor, auditor |
| Mitsui Real Estate | Mitsui Bank's director, chairman |

Part C: Sumitomo

| | |
|---|---|
| Sumitomo Electric Ind. | Nippon Electric's president, director; Warehouse's auditor, auditor |
| Japan Electric | Sumitomo Electric's chairman, director |
| Sumitomo Machinery | Sumitomo Trading's vice-president, director |
| S. Real Estate | Sumitomo Chemical's president, director; Sumitomo Metal Ind.'s president, director; Sumitomo Bank's president, director; Sumitomo Trading's president, auditor |

Source: *Oriental Economist*, June 1959, p. 349 (Mitsubishi); March 1959, p. 122 (Mitsui); July 1959, p. 413 (Sumitomo).

been strong, one would have expected the *Oriental Economist* to be able to see them. Thus they may well be stronger than shown here, but yet are not extensive. The point that stands out from an examination of the Sumitomo section of the table is the extent of interlocks with Sumitomo Real Estate, in which Sumitomo Kichizaemon has holdings. Forest land was not included in the land reform program and so the large forest holdings of Sumitomo Kichizaemon on the island of Shikoku where the Sumitomo enterprise originated were not disturbed. Supposedly, the capital levy tax of 1946 applied to all wealth, including forest-land holdings, but as I have previously noted, Japanese tax valuation is based on historical cost. Where holdings are quite old, it would mean a very low tax valuation. However Sumitomo Kichizaemon managed the matter, he alone among the former *zaibatsu* family members is today a man of wealth. Thus, as was observed, what is noteworthy in the Sumitomo management interlocks is the extent of the ties with the real estate company. While these interlocks are noteworthy, they are, when compared to the scale of interlocks seen in the tables in Appendix VII, not extensive.

In the foregoing pages we have looked at the Mitsubishi, Mitsui and Sumitomo groupings in terms of ownership, borrowings, centralized buying and selling, and joint management. While there is much to suggest the past, there is also much to suggest the new. Perhaps the best way to phrase the difference is to say that formerly the core companies were, in effect, only departments of the top-holding companies; today they are corporations in their own right. The boards of the companies are capable of discussing whatever they wish to discuss and no prior clearances are required. The individual boards determine officer appointments and personnel policies; they determine how financing will be handled; they determine how marketing will be done; they determine new product lines, they determine political contributions. This is strikingly different from the combine period and fundamental to an understanding of the character of the present groupings.

In the combine period the monolithic unity of the groupings was achieved through controls which enforced, reenforced and reenforced again the centralized direction of the top-holding company. Today, as we have seen, these group ties are but a shadow of their former strength; furthermore, they are ties between firms ostensibly equal, not between a holding company that is above the others. Today's unity of action rests on cooperation which stems from common trade names and trademarks and a long tradition of collective action. The top officers of the core companies spent years under the *zaibatsu* form of organization and have lived and breathed the Mitsubishi, Mitsui, and Sumitomo spirit from the time they began their professional careers. The old school tie of the grouping is very real to them; it provides a genuine basis for cooperation. But there are also centrifugal forces which have reality. If there had been nothing to worry about in companies going off on separate paths during the *zaibatsu* period, the former top-holding companies would not have tied their packages so firmly. Today's groupings, while exhibiting much of their past, are significantly different from their combine form.

In terms of most of the published comment, this interpretation of Mitsubishi, Mitsui, and Sumitomo is unusual.[26] A typical comment is

[26] An exception is the article by Kozo Yamamura, "Zaibatsu Prewar and Zaibatsu Postwar," *Journal of Asian Studies*, August 1964, pp. 539-54, reprinted practically verbatim, including a number of factual inaccuracies as well as certain questionable judgments, as Chapter 7, "The Zaibatsu Question," in Yamamura, *Economic Policy in Postwar Japan*, Berkeley, 1967, pp. 110-28.

that which was quoted at the beginning of the chapter, "*zaibatsu* renaissance," "*zaibatsu* revival," "just like old times." How is it that so many observers have come out with such a different interpretation? A large part of the answer may lie in not looking at what is beneath today's label of Mitsubishi, Mitsui, and Sumitomo and assuming because the trade names are the same that the reality beneath them is the same.

There is a second factor which no doubt contributes to the difference of interpretation, and that is regarding corporate mergers as representing comparable consolidation of the grouping. Observers looked at the merger of the three Mitsubishi Heavy Industry companies and concluded that the Mitsubishi grouping was being comparably strengthened. While one can argue that mergers of member companies represent a strengthening of the group, there is not the one-to-one relationship here that is assumed in so many comments. There is a strengthening of the group because there are not so many members to coordinate, not because group ties have become any stronger in the process. The merger of the three Mitsubishi Heavy Industry companies did nothing in itself to group ownership ties, to borrowing ties, to centralized buying and selling, or to joint management. What it did was to eliminate competition among three companies of the grouping that were operating in common and overlapping markets. The reduction of competition is what has prompted most mergers.

With all the comment on the Mitsubishi, Mitsui, and Sumitomo revival, how do the groupings compare in position in the economy today with their "predeconcentration" form? Formerly, Mitsui was preeminent. It is not so today. As was seen in the earlier chapters, its strength rested on its three key subsidiaries, Trading, Mining and Banking. Mitsui & Co. (Trading) formerly was preeminent, today it has close rivals and is not consistently in first place. Mitsui Mining is still the nation's leading coal producer, but in an industry which is declining and with the aid of Y31 billion of government funds ($85 million). (Comparable government aid to Mitsubishi and Sumitomo in coal is 15 and 12 billion, respectively.)[27] Mitsui Bank is, as we have noted, in but a middle position among the city banks. This is a major change indeed. Mitsubishi has pushed ahead in overall position. Sumitomo is probably as strong if not stronger today than yesterday.

One can quantify this impression of the relative position of the

[27] These figures represent the sum of Development Bank loans and loans from the Rationalization Fund (Gorika Jigyodan): Mitsui, Y15.9 plus 15.6, respectively; Mitsubishi, Y8.7 plus 6.6; Sumitomo, Y9.3 plus 3.0.

three groupings by noting total equity and total borrowing of the core companies of the three groupings as seen in Table 11-10. The Y283 billion capital of the Mitsubishi companies contrasts to the Y159 billion of the Mitsui and Y162 of the Sumitomo. The Y875 billion of Mitsubishi borrowings contrasts to Y711 billion on the part of the Mitsui grouping and Y419 billion on the part of the Sumitomo grouping. If equity and borrowings are combined, this puts the Mitsubishi grouping at Y1,158 billion; the Mitsui grouping at Y870 billion, and the Sumitomo at Y581 billion.

The typical Japanese explanation for the change of position of the groupings is that the Mitsui *zaibatsu* rested on strong personalities, whereas both the Mitsubishi and Sumitomo *zaibatsu* gave greater emphasis to organization. It is said that it is this organization and discipline which has stood the latter two in such good stead in the task of revival. I would look elsewhere for an explanation. There would not seem to have been any lesser controls in the Mitsui *zaibatsu* than in the other two. The Mitsui was as tightly organized as the other two. What may be of particular significance in explaining the greater problems of the Mitsui grouping is that its bank underwent the wartime merger with the Daiichi Bank and the subsequent separation; the other two banks did not. There may be, as well, a more subjective factor. The sheer size of the Mitsui organization and the magnitude of Mitsui family wealth may have resulted in more suppressed animosities than in the other groupings. The larger an organization becomes, the more restricting it is to move it with singleness of purpose.

There is a further point that is noteworthy when comparing the Big Three business groupings today with yesterday, and this is the frequency with which transactions cross the lines of the grouping, that is, their external relations. There were occasions when the *zaibatsu* joined together for joint undertakings, and when products could not be supplied from within the grouping they were purchased from other *zaibatsu* or other outsiders. But overwhelmingly where purchases could be made from members of the combine, buying and selling took place within the group. Today there is frequent crossing of boundaries both in buying and selling and in borrowing.[28]

[28] One sees this crossing of lines in the case of the core companies of the three groupings in noting in corporation directories the firms listed as "principal firms from which purchases are made" and "principal firms to which sales are made." The following examples are taken from the 1963 Yamaichi Securities Corporation Directory:

Mitsubishi Heavy Ind. Reorg.—among principal firms from which it buys, Sumitomo Metal Industries; among principal firms to which it sells, Osaka Shosen Kaisha, now Osaka Shosen-Mitsui Shipping.

The answer to the question in the title of this chapter is emphatically yes. Internally the three groupings are very different structures; externally they are different, too. Preference for the grouping is still there, but the old exclusiveness is gone. Further, I would guess, while there has been strong growth, particularly in the case of Mitsubishi and Sumitomo groupings, there has been such dramatic expansion to the economy that, relatively speaking, the three do not occupy the position in the economy today that they did formerly. Markets have been easier to enter and other talent has been able to rise.

---

Mitsui Chemical Industries—among principal firms from which it buys, Mitsubishi Trading; among principal firms to which it sells, Sumitomo Metal Industries.

Sumitomo Metal Industries—among principal firms from which it buys, Mitsubishi Shoji (Trading) and Mitsui & Co. (Trading); among principal firms to which it sells, Mitsui & Co. (Trading).

# 12.

## Other "Headless" Combines and Financial Groupings

JAPANESE newspapers, magazines, and journals abound with references to business groupings, groupings resting on multiple ties such as was characteristic of the former *zaibatsu* (*keiretsu*), those resting on credit sources (*kinyu keiretsu*), on raw material supplier and/or product finisher (*kigyo keiretsu*), and groupings resting on technologically related products where the output of one company's plant is the raw material for another, and where transportation costs range from high to prohibitive (*kombinato*). Typically the Japanese see considerable significance to these groupings. We have explored in detail the present-day form of the Mitsubishi, Mitsui, and Sumitomo groupings which, as successor to the *zaibatsu* of those names, are regarded as the most important groupings in the economy. But given the significance Japanese accord groupings similar to these and other types of groupings, it will be helpful to see what meaning, if any, attaches to them. In this chapter additional *zaibatsu* and *zaibatsu*-like successor groupings will be explored, as well as the groups that rest on bank borrowing. In the following chapter subsidiary grouping and *kombinato* will be examined.[1]

The current general term for business groupings in Japanese is *keiretsu*, which, broken into its component parts, is "kei" meaning "lineage, faction, group" and "retsu" meaning "arranged in order." Used without various modifying adjectives, the term usually refers to the successor groupings of *zaibatsu* companies, or "headless" combines. Although I did not use the expression in the preceding chapter, I was in fact exploring the condition of the Mitsubishi, Mitsui, and Sumitomo *keiretsu*. In other words, *keiretsu* refers to a conglomerate grouping of "majors" with ties to one another of ownership, credit, management, and marketing. The base is thus one of multiple ties, in contrast to other types of groupings which rest primarily on one type of linkage.

[1] Because *kigyo keiretsu* are an entire additional field and because, involving the relations of small and medium business with large, the data are more difficult to acquire, these groupings have not been included in this study. For one of many Japanese studies on *kigyo keiretsu* the reader is referred to Kobayashi Yoshio, *The Realities of Kigyo Keiretsu* (*Kigyo Keiretsu no Jittai*), Tokyo, 1958.

After Mitsubishi, Mitsui, and Sumitomo, the most prominent groupings of majors are two *zaibatsu* successor groupings and a grouping dating from the 1930s: the Fuji Bank *keiretsu*, the Daiichi Bank *keiretsu*, and the Sanwa Bank *keiretsu*. The Fuji Bank is the renamed Yasuda Bank; thus its grouping refers to the former Yasuda *zaibatsu* companies, including additions. The Daiichi Bank historically belonged to the Shibusawa *zaibatsu*, one of the lesser *zaibatsu* families; thus this grouping is a successor to the Shibusawa *zaibatsu*. The Sanwa Bank is the product of a three-way merger in 1933 of the Thirty-Fourth Bank, the Yamaguchi Bank, and the Koike Bank. Its grouping is the complex that developed around this financial institution, but a grouping which, like the other two, rests on more than credit. Let us explore the character of the controls governing these three groupings—the Fuji, the Sanwa, and the Daiichi—to see the degree of meaning attaching to these groupings, to see whether corporate decisions of members are likely to be individual decisions or group decisions. Again we find presidents' clubs, only this time, guidance from membership in the clubs is not comparably helpful.

## *Fuji Bank* Keiretsu

As was noted in the preceding discussion of Mitsubishi, Mitsui, and Sumitomo, it has been widely asserted that the banks of the former *zaibatsu* groupings have taken over the function of the former top-holding companies. Inasmuch as the Yasuda *zaibatsu* concentrated overwhelmingly in finance, and inasmuch as under the Occupation reforms no bank became either a designated holding company or an "excessive concentration of economic power," it might be supposed that the Fuji Bank, the leading city bank, is performing the functions of the former Yasuda top-holding company. Is it? To attempt an answer, ownership, credit, management, and marketing ties among the key companies of the *keiretsu* will be examined.

It is not easy to determine which are the key companies of the Fuji Bank *keiretsu* because of the lack of consensus between the firms ostensibly members of the presidents' club,[2] those the Economic In-

[2] The 25 members of the Fuji Bank line's presidents' club—Fuyo Kai—as of April 1967 are reported to be as follows:

Financial institutions
- Fuji Bank
- Yasuda Fire Insur.
- Yasuda Trust Bank
- Yasuda Life Insur.

Industrials
- Toa Nenryo
- Nippon Kokan
- Showa Kenko
- Hitachi Ltd.
- Oki Electric
- Toho Rayon
- Nisshin Spinning
- Kokusaku Pulp

vestigative Council regards as members of the *keiretsu* and those the Council views as members of the Fuji Bank financial grouping, for which it presents two listings, but without full identity. Where firms ostensibly members of the presidents' club seem to lack a convincing basis for inclusion in the grouping, they have not been listed.[3] Selection of firms, together with ownership, borrowing, and personnel ties, is given in Table 12-1. The table presents 20 of the 48 companies which the Economic Investigative Council has used in its 1966 definition of the Fuji Bank *keiretsu.*

Although ownership percentages are for the most part not high, especially when compared to *zaibatsu* days, ownership in the Fuji Bank *keiretsu* is exceptionally tightly held. Among the 48 companies defined by the Economic Investigative Council as Fuji Bank *keiretsu,* the four financial institutions account for two-thirds (65%) of the cross-ownership ties of the grouping. (The obverse of this statement is, of course, that there is comparatively little cross-ownership among the other companies.) In fact, the Fuji Bank alone accounts for better than one-third of the *keiretsu* holdings. One can gain a sense of per-

---

| | |
|---|---|
| Nissan Motors | Sapporo Beer |
| Nippon Cement | Nisshin Flour |
| Nippon Seiko | Nippon Oil and Fat |
| Commerce and "other" | |
| Marubeni Iida | Tobu Tetsudo |
| Showa Shipping | Taisei Construction |
| Keihin Express | Tokyo Kenbutsu |

as reproduced in the Economic Investigative Council, *Business Groupings,* 1967, p. 11 from the *Japan Economic Journal* (*Nihon Keizai*), April 25, 1967.

[3] The omitted—ostensible—members of the Fuji Bank line presidents' club point up the limitations of accepting such groupings at face value. The following details will serve to illustrate the point. The petroleum company, Toa Nenryo, has far stronger ownership ties abroad than with the Fuji line companies. Esso Standard and Mobile Oil each hold 25% of the shares, while Fuji Bank *keiretsu* ownership is 4.8%, which does not even qualify for position among the top 10 shareholders. Although the company borrows heavily from the financial institutions of the grouping (37% of its borrowings is from this source) the 50% Esso and Mobile ownership would seem far more policy-determining than the 37% borrowings. The electrical equipment firm, Hitachi, is listed as a member of both the Fuji Bank line presidents' club and as a member of the Sanwa Bank line presidents' club which, if presidents' clubs are to have any meaning as coordinating centers, would seem an impossibility. Neither in ownership nor in borrowings is the Fuji Bank grouping impressively connected with the Hitachi Company. Fuji Bank line companies are not listed among the top 10 shareholders; Hitachi's largest borrowing is from the Industrial Bank. The automobile company, Nissan Motors, is likewise listed as a member of the presidents' club, yet it has only weak ties with Fuji Bank line companies. The Fuji Bank line ownership position, while ranking among the top 10, is weaker than a good number of other groupings; Nissan has far larger borrowings from the Industrial Bank than from the Fuji line institutions. Thus, it seems quite unwise to take the reputed membership of these groupings at face value.

spective with respect to the ownership controls of Table 12-1—and the other controls—by comparing the controls shown for other companies with those shown for a company in which the controls are clear, the Tokyo Real Estate Company. Whether one notes the ownership position, the lending position, or personnel "dispatched" from the Bank, the Tokyo Real Estate Company unmistakably indicates control. It provides something of a benchmark for assessing the controls of the other companies.

When we turn to the credit ties of the Fuji Bank *keiretsu*, shown in column two of the table, we find the members of the grouping putting extensive reliance on the bank and its financial affiliates. All of the companies except one are at the level of 20% and above (as a proportion of their total borrowings) in their reliance on the grouping for credit. Over half of the companies are above 30%. Such sizable credit dependency might imply controls were it not for the factors discussed in the previous chapter—the number of credit sources, the frequent lack of distinctive difference between borrowings from the primary bank and next largest borrowings, and the asserted difference in banker mores.

What do we find when we turn to bank participation in the management of the companies, a point to which Japanese observers are likely to attach considerable significance? Table 12-1 does indicate bank participation, but with the conspicuous exception of the Tokyo Real Estate Company, one has much more a feeling of bank participation, bank influence, than direction. Given the way the Economic Investigative Council has constructed the table, from which this information has been taken, it is not possible to determine among persons "dispatched" those who represent interlocks. A person with a bank background who is not concurrently a bank officer represents but a tepid sort of bank influence in management. Presumably, the majority of the persons shown in the table are not interlocks but merely persons who earlier in their career served on the staff or officer level of the bank. When it is not a matter of interlocks, the time dimension has very real bearing. The bank quality of a person who has been away eight or 10 years becomes attenuated indeed.

A further highly relevant point to note in Table 12-1 is that three of the eight companies, which on a relative basis show fairly strong personnel ties, have dual bank representation on their boards. Thus the steel company, Nippon Kokan, has an officer with a Kangyo Bank background; Toho Rayon and Teikoku Seni both have officers with a Mitsubishi Bank background. From a historical point of view the latter two are particularly noteworthy because Toho Rayon was formerly part of Teikoku Seni and Teikoku Seni and Oki Electric his-

Table 12-1: FUJI BANK *KEIRETSU*, 1966

*Financial institutions* - ownership ties, percent issued shares

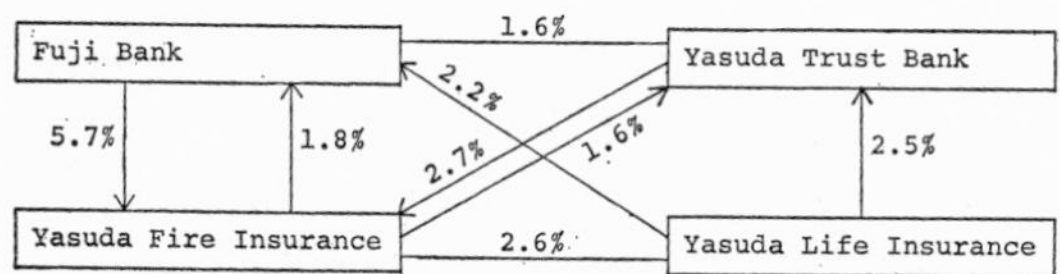


| *Industrials* - 11 | Cross ownership, percent issued shares | Proportion of total borrowing from bank & affil. financial institutions | Personnel ties with Fuji Bank & affil. financial institutions: Position of bank person in co.; date of "dispatch" | Other financial institutions represented on Board |
|---|---|---|---|---|
| Nippon Kokan (steel) | 6.73% | 22.07% | st. dir. '62 | Kangyo Bank 1 |
| Nippon Seiko (bearings) | 23.96 | 27.73 | st. dir. '61 | |
| Oki Electric Ind. | 27.01 | 40.67 | mgr. dir. '59; aud. '61 | |
| Showa Denko (chemicals) | 11.95 | 22.02 | aud. '66; Yasuda Fire Insur. 1 | |
| Canon Camera[a] | 5.00 | 31.22 | | |
| Nippon Oils & Fats | 15.30 | 58.75 | pres. '57; st. dir. '65 | |
| Nippon Cement | 5.40 | 45.94 | aud. '66 | |
| Toho Rayon | 8.07 | 35.91 | mgr. dir. '57 | Mitsubishi Bank 1 |
| Teikoku Seni[a] (textiles) | 16.64 | 28.08 | pres. '57 | Mitsubishi Bank 1 |
| Nippon Reizo | 3.13 | 36.38 | aud. '64 | |
| Sapporo Beer | 1.49 | 29.57 | | |
| *Commercial and "others"* - 5 | | | | |
| Marubeni Iida | 12.55 | 25.09 | | |
| Okura Trading[a] | 15.36 | 57.62 | mgr. dir. '66 | |
| Taisei Construction | 4.76 | 41.11 | | |
| Tokyo Real Estate | 44.56 | 76.83 | chr. '57; pres. '63; st. dir. '59; dir. '58, Yasuda Trust Bank 1 | |
| Showa Shipping[a] | 19.36 | 8.88 | | |

[a]Companies not listed as members of the presidents' club.

Source and notes: All information taken from Economic Investigative Council, *Research on Business Groupings*, 1967.

*Selection of companies.* The financial institutions are clear. The selection of companies for "industrials" and "commercial and 'other'" is based on a comparison of companies listed as members of the Fuji Bank line presidents' club, p. 11; of companies listed as members of the Fuji Bank *keiretsu*, Table 209, pp. 108-15; and two tables, not wholly consonant, listing members of the Fuji Bank *financial keiretsu*, Table 204, pp. 58-59 and Table 203, pp. 49-52, where companies are listed by product line.

*Ownership data.* In the case of the financial institutions, data are calculated from Table 209. For the other companies data are taken from Table 209.

*Borrowing data.* With the exception of companies marked with the supercript "a", borrowing data are taken from Table 204. For companies marked with the superscript, borrowing data are calculated from the Table 222 series, except for Canon Camera which is taken from Table 204.

*Personnel ties.* Data on personnel ties are taken from Table 205, pp. 74-76. For, at times, conflicting data, see Diamond, *Management Yearbook, 1965* (Diamondo, *Keiei Nempo, 1965*), pp. 331-32. Officer transfers during the 1940s and 1950s (with exceptions) have been excluded from this table. Auditorships are included only when the person was of officer rank in the bank. (For a discussion of the position of auditor, cf. Chapter 11.)

torically represented the principal industrial ventures of the Yasuda *zaibatsu.*

In the earlier chapters, in an analysis of *zaibatsu* controls, we found centralized buying and selling to be a key instrument of *zaibatsu* power. The Fuji Bank *keiretsu* has two trading companies—Marubeni Iida and Okura Trading—both postwar acquisitions, but they do not play a significant role in the grouping. Checking principal sources of purchases and sales for the seven largest firms of the Fuji Bank *keiretsu* in the Yamaichi *Corporation Yearbook* for 1962, I found no instance of either trading company figuring distinctively. In two cases, Marubeni Iida was listed among principal sources of purchases and sales, but that was all. Okura Trading was not mentioned. It would accordingly seem appropriate to conclude that marketing was not an important tie in the case of the Fuji Bank *keiretsu.*

From the foregoing analysis of the ties that bind this grouping together, there is evidence of connectivity, but nothing to suggest the controls of the bygone *zaibatsu* era. In analyzing these conglomerate structures, it must always be kept in mind that when one is working among companies lacking market-relatedness, all cohesion, all unifying pressures have to come from the control structure. The market, by definition, is not in a position to assist. The Fuji Bank *keiretsu* is a conglomerate grouping of companies ranging from the base, which is finance, to steel, electrical equipment, chemicals, photographic equipment, textiles, beer, trading, construction, real estate, and shipping. Conglomerate groupings can only have meaning where controls are tight and cohesive. The evidence of connectivity in Table 12-1 does not suggest that there is such a thing as Fuji Bank *keiretsu* policy determination. Rather, it would seem that to a very large extent members of this grouping were operating on corporate policies individually worked out, though putting significant reliance on the Fuji Bank as a source for their borrowings.

### *Daiichi Bank* Keiretsu

The Economic Investigative Council lists the Daiichi Bank *keiretsu* as a grouping of 29 members (two years earlier the Council described it as having 35 members), but with the unusual feature of two subgroups, the Furukawa and the Kawasaki.[4] Table 12-2 presents

[4] The 16 members of the Daiichi-Bank line presidents' club—Godo Shacho Kai—are as follows:

Furukawa group—Sansui Kai—10 members

| | |
|---|---|
| Daiichi Bank | Yokohama Rubber |
| Asahi Life Insurance | Fuji Denki |

Table 12-2: DAIICHI BANK *KEIRETSU*, 1966

*Financial institutions* - ownership ties, percent issued shares

Daiichi Bank ← 2.9% — Asahi Life Insurance

| *Industrials* - 11 | Cross ownership, percent issued shares *keiretsu* | subgroup | Proportion of total borrowing from Bank & Life Insurance | Personnel ties with Bank and Life Insurance: position of bank person in company; date of "dispatch" | Other financial institutions represented on Board |
|---|---|---|---|---|---|
| *Furukawa group* - 6 | | | | | |
| Furukawa Mining | 36.85 | 16.73 | 45.13 | | |
| Furukawa Electric | 21.43 | 11.04 | 33.24 | aud. '65; Asahi Life, 1 | |
| Fuji Denki | 22.49 | 15.89 | 15.09 | st. dir. '63; Asahi Life, 1 | |
| Fujitsu | 52.23 | 42.93 | 19.60 | dir. '61; Asahi Life, 1; aud. '63 | |
| Nippon Zeon | 41.61 | 30.63 | 24.71 | | |
| Yokohama Rubber | 19.98 | 13.90 | 37.27 | st. dir. '63; Asahi Life, 1 | Ind. Bank 1 |
| *Kawasaki group* - 5 | | | | | |
| Kawasaki Dockyard | 10.54 | 3.62 | 16.51 | st. dir. '60; aud. '65 | |
| Kawasaki Steel | 4.91 | 1.13 | 7.51* | | |
| Kawasaki Rolling Stock | 1.17 | 1.17 | 18.57* | | |
| Kawasaki Aircraft | 7.59 | 6.58 | 17.33 | dir. '62 | |
| Kawasaki Shipping | 19.58 | 13.67 | 1.85* | | |
| Ishikawajima-Harima Heavy Industries | 4.19 | | 10.36 | aud. '60 | |
| Isuzu Motors | 6.61 | | 0.49* | mgr. dir. '63; aud. '64 | Sanwa Bank 1 |
| Shimizu Construction | 4.28 | | 36.12 | | |
| Nissho | 4.51 | | 26.53 | | |

Source and notes: All information taken from Economic Investigative Council, *Research on Business Groupings*, 1967.

*Selection of companies for table.* The two financial institutions are clear. Selection of the other companies rests on a comparison of companies listed as members of the Daiichi Bank line presidents' club, p. 11; companies listed as members of the Daiichi Bank *keiretsu*, Table 210, pp. 116-121; and two tables, not wholly consonant, listing members of the Daiichi Bank *financial keiretsu*, Table 204, p. 60 and Table 203, pp. 49-52, where the companies are listed by product line.

*Ownership data.* Ownership ties between the Bank and Life Insurance are calculated from Table 210. *Keiretsu* cross ownership among the other companies is taken from Table 210; subgroup cross ownership is taken from Table 212 for the Furukawa grouping and Table 213 for the Kawasaki grouping, both of which will be found on pp. 130-31.

*Borrowing data.* Except for figures shown with asterisks, percentages are taken from Table 204. For entries with asterisk, percentages are calculated from the Table 222 series, pp. 192-268.

*Personnel ties.* Data on personnel ties comes from Table 205, pp. 76-77. For, at times, conflicting data, cf. Diamond, *Management Yearbook, 1965*, (Diamondo, *Keiei Nempo, 1965*), p. 342. Criteria for listing are those specified in Table 12-1.

ownership, credit, and management ties among 15 key industrial companies of this grouping, including the ownership ties within the subgroups. That the Economic Investigative Council does not regard the two subgroups as *keiretsu* in their own right (the council lists 10 companies in the Furukawa complex and 5 in the Kawasaki) suggests that to be a *keiretsu* grouping member firms must not only be large but numerous.

Table 12-2 indicates that the closest ties in the Daiichi *keiretsu* are with and among the Furukawa subgroup. In the tables from which this table has been constructed, it will be found that Furukawa Mining and Furukawa Electric Industries have holdings in each of the other nine companies making up the subgroup. Another firm of the subgroup has holdings in five members, three in four members. The subgroup holds 18.3 of the shares of its members. Not only are intragroup ownership ties strong among the Furukawa subgroup, but the bank and life insurance company have sizable investments in these companies. In addition, the two key firms, Furukawa Mining and Furukawa Electric both rely heavily on the loan facilities of the bank and the life insurance company. Further, it will be seen that with four of the six listed companies, there are bank-connected officers on the boards of directors. (Under the previously enunciated criterion, auditors are listed only when they come from officer positions in the bank, excluding the position of "plain" auditor.)

The Kawasaki subgroup strongly contrasts with the Furukawa. Both intragroup ties and ties with the Daiichi Bank and Asahi Life Insurance Co. are weaker. The Kawasaki subgroup accounts for 3.0% of the shares of the subgroup companies. The pivotal firm in the Kawasaki group is Dockyard ("Heavy Industries" would be a literal translation), where the Daiichi Bank, at 4.8% of the issued shares, is the largest shareholder (Asahi Life holds 1.3%). The one subgroup member that shows significant cross-ownership ties is Kawasaki Shipping, where combined holdings are roughly 20%. Among the Kawasaki companies lending reliance on the Daiichi Bank and Asahi Life is distinctly weaker than among the Furukawa subgroup. Further-

---

| | |
|---|---|
| Furukawa Mining | Fujitsu |
| Furukawa Electric | Nippon Keikinya |
| Asahi Denka | Nippon Zeon |

Kawasaki Group—Mutsu Kai—6 members

| | |
|---|---|
| Kawasaki Dockyard | Kawasaki Denki Seizo |
| Kawasaki Steel | Kawasaki Shipping |
| Kawasaki Rolling Stock | Kawasaki Aircraft |

as reported in the source cited in note 2 above.

more, there are fewer bank-connected officers. In fact, one might even say that it is stretching things to see the Kawasaki subgroup as part of the Daiichi Bank *keiretsu.*

Ownership among the companies outside the two subgroups is weak, and lending varies from negligible to considerable. It is the company with negligible borrowing which has the most important personnel ties. As has been seen, and will be seen again and again, bank appointments seem to correlate neither with the scale of borrowing, absolutely or relatively, nor with the importance of the company. At times, one is almost tempted to say that appointments correlate inversely with these points. Isuzu Motors with under one-half of one percent of its funds from the Daiichi Bank, is shown with a managing director and an auditor with Daiichi Bank connections. The Shimizu Construction Co., with over a third of its funds from the bank, is without personnel connections.

If we turn to buying and selling arrangements, we do not find other deficiencies being compensated by this channel. Nissho and Company, the trading firm of the Daiichi grouping, in 1966 was the eighth largest trading company on the basis of sales, but an examination of the sources for principal purchases and sales of companies of the grouping in the Yamaichi *Corporation Yearbook* for 1962 does not reveal extensive *keiretsu* reliance on Nissho.

### *The Sanwa Bank* Keiretsu

Let us turn next to the Sanwa Bank *keiretsu,* which the Economic Investigative Council shows to have 38 members and which likewise has a presidents' club.[5] Table 12-3 summarizes cross-ties among the

[5] The 23 members of the Sanwa Bank line presidents' club—Sansuikai—are:

Financial
- Sanwa Bank
- Nippon Life Insurance
- Tokyo Trust Bank

Industrials
- Maruzen Oil
- Kobe Steel Works
- Nakayama Steel Works
- Hitachi Shipbuilding
- Daihatsu Kogyo
- Osaka Cement
- Ube Industries
- Tokuyama Soda
- Kansai Paint
- Tokyo Rubber
- Nippon Rayon
- Nichbo
- Teijin

Commerce and "others"
- Nissho
- Japan Express
- Ohbayashi Gumi
- Takashimaya
- Kei-Han-Shin Kyuko Railroad
- Yamashita Shin Nippon Steamship

as reported in source cited in note 2 above.

Table 12-3: SANWA BANK *KEIRETSU*, 1966

*Financial institutions* - ownership ties, percent issued shares

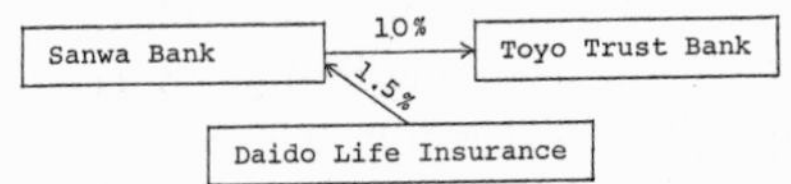


| *Industrials* - 13 | Cross ownership, percent issued shares | Proportion of total borrowing from Bank & affiliated finan. institutions | Personnel ties with Bank & affil. fin. institutions: Position of bank person in co.; date of "dispatch" | Other fin. institutions represented on Board |
|---|---|---|---|---|
| Maruzen Oil | 6.48 | 22.04 | pres. '64; st. dir. '63; dir., '63 | Ind. Bank 1 |
| Nisshin Steel[a] | 7.91 | 26.91 | st. aud. '56 | |
| Nakayama Steel Works | 3.54 | 49.42 | | |
| Daihatsu Kogyo (auto.) | 6.25 | 31.36 | st. dir. '64 | |
| Hitachi Shipbuilding | 3.40 | 14.38 | aud. '62 | |
| Chisso[a] | 2.29 | 19.91 | | |
| Tokuyama Soda | 8.11 | 23.56 | | |
| Ube Industries (chem.) | 5.75 | 20.03 | mgr. dir. '62 | |
| Osaka Cement | 7.64 | 39.75 | | |
| Tanabe Seiyaku (pharmaceut.) | 5.31 | 17.45 | | |
| Nichibo | 4.12 | 15.36 | | |
| Teijin | 5.83 | 25.90 | | |
| Nippon Rayon | 14.59 | 23.69 | aud. '66 | |
| *Commerce and "others"* - 2 | | | | |
| Yamashita Shin Nippon SS | 6.57 | 13.14 | | |
| Ohbayashi Gumi | 8.34 | 24.4 | | |

[a]Companies not listed as members of the presidents' club.

Source and notes: All information taken from Economic Investigative Council, *Research on Business Groupings*, 1967.

*Selection of companies.* The three financial institutions are clear. Selection of companies for "industrials" and "commercial and "others"" rests on a comparison of companies listed as members of the Sanwa Bank line presidents' club, p. 11; of companies listed as members of the Sanwa Bank *keiretsu*, Table 211, pp. 122-29; and two tables, not wholly consonant, listing members of the Sanwa Bank *financial keiretsu*, Table 204, pp. 60-62 and Table 203, pp. 49-52 where the companies are listed by product line.

*Ownership and borrowing data.* Ownership data are taken from Table 211 and with the exception of Chisso, borrowing data from Table 204. For Chisso, borrowing is calculated from Table 222.

*Personnel ties.* Data on personnel ties comes from Table 205, pp. 77-78. For occasional conflicting data, cf. Diamond, *Management Yearbook, 1965* (Diamondo, *Keiei Nempo, 1965*) pp. 338-40. Criteria for listing are those specified in Table 12-1.

principal firms of this group. It should be noted that the Sanwa Bank has 10% of the shares of the trust bank, which would appear to be a direct violation of the Antimonopoly Law's forbidding of financial institutions holding shares in firms with which they compete. Column one of the table indicates that shareholding is for the most part very low in this grouping, though reference to the source for the table indicates considerable cohesion to it. The Sanwa Bank and its affiliated Toyo Trust Bank account for three quarters of the cross-ownership.

The limitation of the type of information given in Tables 12-1, 12-2, and 12-3 is that the impression is conveyed that it is the principal shareholders of the companies in question which are being shown; but this is not necessarily so. The tables present *keiretsu* shareholding in these companies. The distinction between top shareholders and *keiretsu* shareholders is obvious in the case of two companies of the Sanwa Bank *keiretsu*, Maruzen Oil and Nisshin Steel. When attention is directed to "major shareholders" rather than "keiretsu shareholders" in Maruzen Oil, it turns out that Sanwa Bank is not the largest shareholder, but rather Union Oil. Union Oil holds 32% of the shares, its 108 million shares contrasting to the Sanwa Bank's 14 million and its affiliated Toyo Trust Bank's 3 million. Similarly, in the case of Nisshin Steel one would not realize from Table 12-3 that it is Yawata Steel which is the largest shareholder in this company (Yawata holds 56 million shares, compared to 29 million held by the Sanwa *keiretsu*, principally by the bank, Toyo Trust Bank, and the trading company, Iwai & Co.).

When we note credit dependency among the Sanwa *keiretsu* firms shown in Table 12-3, it will be seen that most of the firms are under 30%. With two exceptions—Chisso and Nichibo—all firms listed in the table borrow the heaviest from the Sanwa Bank and its affiliates when the "universe" is *Japanese private* credit sources. An evaluation of the full range of Maruzen Oil's borrowings indicates, however, that while the Sanwa Bank is the largest Japanese private credit source, providing Y12.2 billion ($33.8 million) of its total borrowings of Y55.5 billion, the Bank of America provides Y12.5 billion ($34.7 million).

In Table 12-3 bank personnel ties are noteworthy among three of the 15 industrials shown—Maruzen Oil, Daihatsu Kogyo, and Ube Industries. But inasmuch as Union Oil holds 32% of the shares in Maruzen Oil, where the Bank of America is the largest lender, and where there is representation from a second bank, the Industrial Bank, it is clear that the significance of such personnel is limited. In other words, such appointments have to be interpreted instead of being taken at face value. The Sanwa *keiretsu* also includes two trading companies, Iwai and Nichimen, which do not seem to be significant.

From the foregoing information it will be seen that while there are ownership, credit, and management ties to the *keiretsu*, there are also very real ownership and credit ties extending outside its bounds. *Keiretsu* controls do not seem sufficient to provide unity to the grouping.

### *Are the Newer Groupings Being Ignored?*

Some Japanese scholars in related fields criticize the work being done on business groupings by Japanese economists on the ground that insufficient attention is paid to the newer, postwar groupings. For example, one such grouping is Tokyo Electric Express Railroad (Tokyo Kyuko Dentetsu, commonly referred to by its abbreviated form, Tokyu), a company providing express commuter services in the Tokyo area. There is definitely a network of companies around Tokyu. The Economic Investigative Council put "related" companies in 1964 at 76 (88 in 1966), the Fair Trade Commission in 1964 at 78.[6] The FTC treats these companies as the capital *keiretsu* (*shihon keiretsu*) of Tokyu. The Council treats the Tokyu complex in two ways. The core companies of the complex are listed as a "group," not as a "*keiretsu*." The full range of Tokyu investments is shown in a table combining subsidiaries and investments. That the Council does not treat the Tokyu complex as a *keiretsu* points up two aspects of this term. Most of the members of a *keiretsu* are majors, and a *keiretsu* has many members, not four, six, or eight. Although the degree of conglomeration might be thought of as an element in the distinction between capital groupings and *keiretsu* groupings, in Japanese practice it does not appear to be definitive. Apparently scale is the critical distinction. But, correlatively, because scale is larger among *keiretsu* members, controls are more difficult. Given these qualities of the term "*keiretsu*," it would appear that economists have been correct in not including the newer groups in studies of *keiretsu* groupings. Such groups are being studied as subsidiary complexes.

This brief examination of the other three leading *keiretsu* in the economy leads to the same conclusion as did the study of Mitsubishi, Mitsui, and Sumitomo, namely, that controls are not sufficient to compel unity of behavior, particularly given the conglomerate quality of

[6] FTC, *Capital Keiretsu Among the Principal Companies* (Kosei Torihiki Iinkai, *Shuyo Kaisha ni okeru Shihon Keiretsu no Jokyo*), mimeog., November 1965, pp. 182-83.

the groupings. While among the Fuji Bank, the Daiichi Bank, and the Sanwa Bank *keiretsu*, controls are strongest in the Fuji Bank *keiretsu*—which is what one would expect as successor to the Yasuda complex—they are but a shadow of former years. Corporate decisions may be influenced by member companies, but hardly compelled. In only a small number of instances are controls of sufficient scale to compel behavior.

### *Financial Groupings—Kinyu Keiretsu*

Among Japanese writers about the business scene, much attention is given groupings made up of firms which borrow mostly from a particular bank. In fact, Professor Miyazaki of Yokohama National University has gone so far as to develop a theory of investment out of these groupings.[7] He sees such internal group cohesion to them, and such a strong sense of rivalry among them, that he believes them the key to understanding the pace of recent investment. He describes his theory as "one set-ism," by which he means that each of the groupings seeks as large a complement of industries as the next group. If, for example, one grouping goes into color TV, then all the other groupings are likely to go into it.

The Bank of Japan describes these financial groupings and their significance in this way.

> Under the indirect financing system banks in Japan are very closely connected with their customer enterprises. Large enterprises usually hold accounts with a number of banks, but there is always a bank for every enterprise, which has special relations as the enterprise's principal bank. Following the postwar disorganization of the *zaibatsu* holding companies, each of the leading banks, many of them former *zaibatsu* banks, has become the center of its group of big business customers, promoting the expansion of the group. Under the Anti-Monopoly Law, no bank may hold more than 10 per cent of the total stocks issued of a corporation, but a large enterprise's borrowings from its principal bank usually represent about 30 per cent of its total external debt.
>
> When the relation between banks and enterprises becomes too close, the former become involved in the competition against other groups of enterprises, and find themselves obliged to adopt

[7] Professor Miyazaki (Miyazaki Giichi) published a number of similar articles in 1964 on "excessive competition" and "one set-ism." The central thesis of these articles will be found in his book, *Postwar Japan's Economic Structure* (*Sengo Nippon no Keizai Kiko*), Tokyo, 1966.

an easy lending attitude. This is one of the factors contributing to the tendency to excessive economic expansion in Japan.[8]

The backdrop to the attention given financial groupings in today's economy is the scale of dependency on banks as sources of funds for industrial investment. In the *zaibatsu* period ownership provided the critical cohesive element for business groupings; today it is said to be credit. Banks are currently providing 40 to 50% of total corporate funds, or 70 to 80% if the comparison is to external sources only (cf. Table 12-8 at the end of this chapter). While such dependency on banks for industrial financing is not new in Japan's history, present levels are heavy (cf. Table 12-9).

Much of the time between 1913 and 1930, corporate dependency on banks amounted to 40 and 50% of externally supplied funds. During World War I it rose to 75%. In the early thirties there was greater reliance on equity financing, but with the outbreak of the China War bank borrowings began to increase, and by the end of World War II had risen to the incredible level of 93% of externally supplied funds. In 1966 banks supplied 81%. It is not possible to make direct American comparison because in the United States commercial banks don't finance plant and equipment (but for U.S. sources of corporate funds cf. Table 12-10). The Bank of Japan expresses Japanese procedures this way: ". . . Japanese commercial banks have traditionally engaged in long-term financing, in addition to their orthodox banking functions."[9]

Bank financing is being done primarily through the city and long-term credit banks (cf. Table 12-11). Japan's banking system consists of 12 city banks, 7 trust banks, 65 provincial banks, 3 long-term credit banks, and 1 specialized foreign exchange bank,[10] but broadly speaking, the system, as observed in Chapter 8, divides between city and long-term credit banks on one hand, and the provincial banks on the other. As we observed earlier, that it is the city banks and long-term credit banks which head the financial groupings, and not the provincial banks as well, has nothing to do with legal provisions governing the banking system, but much to do with administrative procedures. Legally, all commercial banks may borrow from the Bank of Japan, but in point of fact the Bank of Japan lends only to the city banks. Thus it is that the city banks can engage in long-term

[8] Bank of Japan, *Money and Banking in Japan, 1964*, pp. 103-104.

[9] *Ibid.*, p. 102.

[10] *Ibid.* Commercial banks, p. 102; long-term credit banks, p. 128; trust banks, p. 136.

loans and very high lending in relation to deposits because they know that if they run into difficulty the Bank of Japan will rescue them. But there is no such prospect of rescue for the provincial banks; they are obliged to live with the consequences of their lending policy.

### *Leading Financial Groupings—Kinyu Keiretsu*

While every compiler provides a different number of these financial groupings, attention centers on 11, 9 of them belonging to the major city banks and 2 belonging to 2 of the long-term credit banks. The size of the membership of these groupings, on which there is also little consensus, is given in Table 12-4 for three periods—1961, 1964, and 1966—as developed by the Economic Investigative Council and contained in its annual publication, *Research on Business Groupings.* For many of the entries there are three numbers. The first figure represents companies that have their largest borrowing from the bank in question and the second, those companies that usually do, but do not as of the period in question. The figure in parenthesis is the sum of these two.

Comparing the size of the groupings in the three different periods, one is tempted to conclude that the Economic Investigative Council changed the criteria on which it based its selection. Certainly for the size disparity between 1961 and 1964 there would seem no other way to explain the difference. The number of companies in the financial groupings clearly did not halve within this three-year period. If the groupings in 1964 and 1966 are compared, there is no apparent change in the scale of the groupings, but there is in the relationship of one grouping to another. In the 1964 listing the Mitsubishi grouping appears as almost one and a half times the size of the Fuji; in the 1966 listing the two groupings are almost the same, which, in turn, raises a puzzling question.

Although the members of a financial *keiretsu* are defined as those companies having their largest borrowing from a particular bank, it is to be expected there would be some correlation between the size of the bank and the number of companies having their largest borrowing from it. However, according to the Economic Investigative Council's compilation, there isn't. The Fuji Bank, the largest city bank, is in fourth position in all three years in size of its financial *keiretsu,* whereas the Mitsui Bank, which is a middle-sized city bank, is shown as consistently larger. The seeming lack of correlation between size of the bank and size of its financial *keiretsu* suggests that traditional ties may be the major influence as to which bank a company turns for

Table 12-4: NUMBER OF COMPANIES IN LEADING FINANCIAL *KEIRETSU*, 1961, 1964 AND 1966

(First figure is the number of "primary" borrowers; the figure following the slash, the number, usually "primary", but not at this time; the figure in parenthesis is the sum of these two.)

| *City banks* | 1961 | 1964 | 1966 |
|---|---|---|---|
| Mitsubishi Bank | 126/20 (146) | 78/9 (87) | 65/16 (71) |
| Mitsui | 117/18 (135) | 55/22 (77) | 65/14 (79) |
| Sumitomo | 128/17 (135) | 62/14 (76) | 62/7 (69) |
| Fuji | 116/23 (139) | 54/18 (72) | 61/11 (72) |
| Sanwa | 86/9 (95) | 45/12 (57) | 46/6 (52) |
| Daiichi | 70/18 (88) | 34/4 (38) | 30/5 (35) |
| Kangyo[a] | 41/5 (46) | 24 | 21 |
| Tokai | 36/13 (49) | 14 | 14 |
| Daiwa[b] | 23/8 (31) | 16 | 14 |
| Kyowa[c] | 11/3 (14) | 6 | 7 |
| Kobe | 11/3 (14) | 6 | 6 |
| Hokkaido Development | 5/4 (9) | 2 | 2 |
| *Long-term credit banks* | | | |
| Industrial Bank | 119 | 66 | 64 |
| Long Term Cridit Bank | 24 | 12 | 17 |
| Hypothec Bank[a] | n.l. | 3 | 3 |

Source: Economic Investigative Council, *Research on Business Groupings*, 1962, 1965 and 1967 editions, pp. 38-95, 45-60, and 53-68, respectively.

Note: That the smaller city-bank *keiretsu* in the 1964 data and the long-term bank *keiretsu* in the 1961, 1964, and 1966 data are not presented with slashed marks probably reflects a change in methodology on the part of the Council rather than the fact that these institutions had no instances of "primary" borrowers using another bank as their "primary" source.

[a]The Kangyo Bank, which formerly under this name, was a special long-term credit bank and formerly was called in English the Hypothec Bank, is not to be confused with the present long-term credit bank, Nippon Fudosan Ginko, now called in English, Hypothec Bank.

[b]Formerly the Nomura Bank.

[c]Formerly Japan Savings Bank, the principal savings bank to emerge from the war period.

primary reliance. But no two compilers of financial *keiretsu* put their information together in the same way.

If, however, one ignores refinements and puts attention on major differences in size some correlation can be seen between the size of the financial grouping and the size of the bank. The smaller banks do have smaller groupings. The city banks of the former Big Four *zaibatsu* have the largest membership; the Sanwa and Daiichi are distinctly lower, but noteworthy. The Kangyo, Tokai, and Daiwa are small, and the next three are so minimal as to be ignored. This is true also of the three long-term credit banks.

### *An Inductive Approach to the Significance of Financial Groupings*

To understand the character of these financial groupings, it will be helpful to start by noting some actual examples of borrowing patterns among Japan's majors, then determine the function of the primary bank. For this purpose I have compiled Table 12-5 from material in the Economic Investigative Council's 1967 *Research on Business Groupings*. The selection of companies was made on the basis of highest 1966 sales among firms in the major industry groupings employed by the Council. For example, Taiyo Fisheries had the highest sales among companies in the grouping, "agriculture, forestry, and marine products"; Mitsui Mining among "coal companies"; Nippon Mining among "nonferrous metal mining companies"; Mitsubishi Heavy Industries among "shipbuilding companies"; Nippon Express among "land transportation companies." With one exception, Osaka Shosen-Mitsui Shipping, the Council regards all of these firms as having membership in a financial grouping. The Council's classification is indicated in Table 12-5 with underlining of the loan from the city or long-term credit bank from which the largest borrowing comes.

Table 12-5 reveals several things, but first and foremost it shows the number of credit sources on which Japan's majors rely. (The borrowings listed in the table are from the main body of the tables in the source. In addition, there is the category, "other borrowings"; in other words, Table 12-5 data are not exhaustive.) If we take some of the more outstanding examples it will be noted that Yawata Steel is listed with 28 credit sources, Mitsubishi Heavy Industries with 27, Hitachi with 26, and Toyo Rayon with 24. The size distribution of these borrowings in several instances does not vary markedly. If the primary bank stood out clearly as the most important supplier, and consistently so, either in its own right or by the inclusion of affiliated

Table 12-5: BANK BORROWINGS OF 20 SELECTED MAJORS, 1966

Companies with Highest Sales in their Product Lines

Underlined borrowing indicates financial grouping to which firm is regarded as being affiliated

(in millions yen)

| *City banks and affiliates* | *Taiyo Fisheries* | *Mitsui Mining* | *Nippon Oil* | *Nippon Mining* | *Furukawa Electric* | *Yawata Steel* | *Mitsubishi Heavy Ind.* |
|---|---|---|---|---|---|---|---|
| Mitsubishi Bank | 1,438 | | | 90 | 1,320 | 11,930 | 33,475 |
| Mitsubishi Trust Bank | 2,990 | | | 824 | 457 | 6,780 | 29,222 |
| Meiji Life Insurance | 555 | | | | | 1,428 | 4,400 |
| Tokyo Marine Ins. | 270 | | | | | | |
| Total for grouping | (5,253) | | | (914) | (1,777) | (20,138) | (67,097) |
| Mitsui Bank | 699 | 4,498 | 5,171 | 3,855 | | 2,180 | 1,180 |
| Mitsui Trust Bank | 1,761 | 3,625 | 1,524 | 2,559 | | 8,620 | 3,015 |
| Mitsui Life Insurance | 422 | 300 | | | | 763 | 200 |
| Taisho Marine Ins. | 93 | 50 | | | | | |
| Total for grouping | (2,975) | (8,473) | (6,695) | (6,414) | | (11,563) | (4,395) |
| Sumitomo Bank | 403 | | | | | 8,485 | 8,945 |
| Sumitomo Trust Bank | 840 | | | 1,916 | | 13,660 | 12,108 |
| Sumitomo Life Insurance | | | | | | 1,660 | 1,200 |
| Sumitomo Marine Ins. | 40 | | | | | | |
| Total for grouping | (1,283) | | | (1,916) | | (23,805) | (22,253) |
| Fuji Bank | 1,335 | | 5,336 | 1,285 | 1,475 | 12,700 | 2,656 |
| Yasuda Trust Bank | 772 | | 1,524 | 2,160 | 1,090 | 14,372 | 3,491 |
| Yasuda Life Insurance | 555 | | | | | 1,080 | |
| Yasuda Fire Ins. | 270 | | | | | | |
| Total for grouping | (2,932) | | (6,860) | (3,445) | (2,565) | (28,152) | (6,147) |
| Sanwa Bank | 1,103 | | | 1,822 | | 8,445 | 1,246 |
| Toyo Trust Bank | 668 | | | 1,469 | 546 | 4,835 | 3,077 |
| Daido Life Insurance | | | | | | 521 | |
| Total for grouping | (1,771) | | | (3,291) | (546) | (13,801) | (4,323) |
| Daiichi Bank | 405 | | 4,939 | | 6,599 | 1,780 | 1,580 |
| Asahi Life Insurance | 624 | | | | 2,558 | 1,271 | 200 |
| Total for grouping | (1,029) | | (4,939) | | (9,157) | (3,051) | (1,780) |

ty banks and affiliates

| *ty banks* | *Taiyo Fisheries* | *Mitsui Mining* | *Nippon Oil* | *Nippon Mining* | *Furukawa Electric* | *Yawata Steel* | *Mitsubishi Heavy Ind.* |
|---|---|---|---|---|---|---|---|
| ngyo Bank | 4,538 | 2,717 | 200 | 1,644 | | 5,005 | 5,741 |
| iwa Bank | 23 | | | 1,129 | | 1,855 | 295 |
| kai Bank | 97 | | 200 | 80 | 270 | 1,060 | 10,379 |
| owa Bank | 907 | 777 | | 1,443 | 2,425 | 2,430 | 3,718 |
| be Bank | 30 | | | | | 1,040 | 10,026 |
| kkaido Development | 651 | 2,627 | | 77 | | | 110 |
| nk of Tokyo | 1,549 | | | 654 | 100 | 1,140 | 4,397 |
| *ng-term credit banks* | | | | | | | |
| dustrial Bank | 7,449 | 1,968 | | 6,749 | | 30,676 | 17,072 |
| ng-Term Credit Bank | 2,092 | 2,701 | | 2,482 | 8,105 | 15,345 | 11,785 |
| pothec | 1,029 | | | 1,314 | 185 | 2,000 | 2,435 |
| *ernment institutions* | | | | | | | |
| velopment Bank | | 15,920 | | 1,064 | | 349 | 1,417 |
| port-Import Bank | 131 | | | 331 | | 428 | 71,165 |
| otal borrowings ncluding "others" | 58,190 | 52,407 | 21,159 | 57,234 | 27,548 | 203,507 | 296,219 |
| inancial *Keiretsu* dependency | | | | | | | |
| Bank alone | 21% | 8.5% | 25.2% | 11.7% | 23.9% | 15% | 11.2% |
| Bank and affiliates | 21% | 16.1% | 32.4% | 11.7% | 33.2% | 15% | 36% |

| *ty banks and affiliates* | *Toyota Motors* | *Hitachi Mfg.* | *Mitsubishi Chemical* | *Bridgestone Tires* | *Asahi Glass* | *Taisei Const.* | *Kirin Beer* |
|---|---|---|---|---|---|---|---|
| subishi Bank | | 4,341 | 5,958 | 300 | 2,818 | 410 | 3,200 |
| itsubishi Trust Bank | 828 | 5,656 | 4,648 | 1,070 | 1,516 | 2,830 | 4,010 |
| eiji Life Insurance | | 1,750 | 1,700 | | | 100 | 1,000 |
| okyo Marine Ins. | | | 50 | | | | |
| Total for grouping | (828) | (11,747) | (12,356) | (1,370) | (4,334) | (3,340) | (8,210) |
| sui Bank | | 2,185 | | | | 10 | |
| itsui Trust Bank | 1,328 | 4,689 | 794 | 1,075 | | | |
| itsui Life Insurance | | 100 | | | | | |
| aisho Marine Ins. | | | | | | | |
| Total for grouping | (1,328) | (6,974) | (794) | (1,075) | | (10) | |
| itomo Bank | | 4,328 | | 1,653 | | | |
| umitomo Trust Bank | 945 | 7,636 | 2,721 | 1,135 | | 1,134 | |
| umitomo Life Insurance | | 500 | | 75 | | 200 | |
| umitomo Marine Ins. | | | | | | | |
| Total for grouping | (945) | (12,464) | (2,721) | (2,863) | | (1,334) | |

| *City banks and affiliates* | *Toyota Motors* | *Hitachi Mfg.* | *Mitsubishi Chemical* | *Bridgestone Tires* | *Asahi Glass* | *Taisei Const,* | *Kir Bee* |
|---|---|---|---|---|---|---|---|
| Fuji | | 12,153 | | 826 | 1,430 | 8,702 | |
| Yasuda Trust Bank | 424 | 8,306 | 720 | 1,056 | | 4,495 | |
| Yasuda Life Insurance | | 200 | | | | 150 | |
| Yasuda Fire Ins. | | | | | | | |
| Total for grouping | (424) | (20,659) | (720) | (1,882) | (1,430) | (13,347) | |
| Sanwa Bank | | 13,085 | 99 | | 400 | 131 | |
| Toyo Trust Bank | 893 | 6,336 | 160 | | | | |
| Daido Life Insurance | | | | | | | |
| Total for grouping | 893 | 19,421 | 259 | | 400 | 131 | |
| Daiichi Bank | | 13,085 | | 514 | 150 | | |
| Asahi Life Insurance | | | | | | | |
| Total for grouping | | 13,085 | | 514 | 150 | | |
| *Other City banks* | | | | | | | |
| Kangyo Bank | | 4,079 | 3,704 | 826 | 1,550 | | 1,3 |
| Daiwa Bank | 693 | 2,560 | | | | 2,118 | |
| Tokai Bank | | 3,962 | 620 | 100 | 1,000 | 180 | 6 |
| Kyowa Bank | | 2,353 | | 514 | | 195 | |
| Kobe Bank | | 2,007 | | | 500 | 794 | 1,4 |
| Hokkaido Development | | | | 50 | | 331 | |
| Bank of Tokyo | | 1,305 | 500 | 226 | 846 | | |
| *Long-term credit banks* | | | | | | | |
| Industrial Bank | | 25,184 | 5,453 | | 816 | 1,710 | |
| Long-term credit bank | 6,760 | 1,095 | 4,116 | 3,424 | 798 | 2,150 | 1,1 |
| Hypothec Bank | | | 2,052 | | | 2,643 | |
| *Government banks* | | | | | | | |
| Development Bank | | | 971 | | | | |
| Export-Import Bank | 182 | 2,890 | | 257 | 1,578 | | |
| Total borrowings including "others" | 21,429 | 151,849 | 61,721 | 15,352 | 17,293 | 32,465 | 14,0 |
| *Keiretsu* dependency: | | | | | | | |
| Bank alone | 31.5% | 16.5% | 9.6% | 22.3% | 16.2% | 26.3% | 22.8 |
| Bank and affiliates | 31.5% | 16.5% | 20.02% | 22.3% | 25% | 44.5% | 58.5 |

| *City banks and affiliates* | *Toyo Rayon* | *Mitsui & Co.* | *Daimaru Dept. Store* | *Nippon Express* | *Osaka S. Mitsui Shipping* | *Tokyo Elec.* |
|---|---|---|---|---|---|---|
| Mitsubishi Bank | 1,440 | 9,975 | 1,039 | 3,450 | 306 | 1,7 |
| Mitsubishi Trust Bank | 685 | | 140 | 900 | 45 | 15,7 |
| Meiji Life Insurance | 495 | | | | | 1,9 |
| Tokyo Marine Ins. | | | | | 13 | |
| Total for grouping | (2,620) | (9,975) | (1,179) | (4,350) | (364) | (19,5 |

| *banks and affiliates* | *Toyo Rayon* | *Mitsui & Co.* | *Daimaru Dept. Store* | *Nippon Express* | *Osaka S. Mitsui Shipping* | *Tokyo Elec. Power* |
|---|---|---|---|---|---|---|
| Bank | 4,283 | 31,747 | 40 | | 615 | 3,510 |
| sui Trust Bank | 5,716 | 10,326 | 90 | 2,800 | 666 | 17,782 |
| sui Life Insurance | 495 | 1,819 | | | 195 | 2,036 |
| sho Marine Ins. | | 874 | | | 40 | |
| Total for grouping | (10,494) | (44,766) | (130) | (2,800) | (1,516) | (23,328) |
| omo Bank | 1,440 | 8,642 | 580 | | 591 | 858 |
| itomo Trust Bank | 1,073 | 872 | 215 | 1,200 | 677 | 8,049 |
| itomo Life Insurance | 400 | 500 | | | | 2,403 |
| itomo Marine Ins. | | | | | 42 | |
| Total for grouping | (2,913) | (10,014) | (795) | (1,200) | (1,310) | (11,310) |
| Bank | 1,440 | 30,711 | 60 | 3,350 | 359 | 1,753 |
| uda Trust Bank | 830 | 468 | 100 | 300 | 204 | 11,718 |
| uda Life Insurance | | | | | | 1,612 |
| uda Fire Ins. | | | | | 47 | |
| Total for grouping | (2,270) | (31,179) | (160) | (3,650) | (610) | (15,083) |
| Bank | 1,440 | 5,374 | 70 | 4,300 | 54 | 858 |
| o Trust Bank | 1,986 | | | 2,480 | | 4,509 |
| do Life Insurance | | | | | | 325 |
| Total for grouping | (3,426) | (5,374) | (70) | (6,780) | (54) | (5,692) |
| hi Bank | 360 | 2,219 | 21 | 1,650 | 73 | 1,753 |
| hi Life Insurance | 495 | | | | | 2,640 |
| Total for grouping | (855) | (2,219) | (21) | (1,650) | (73) | (4,393) |
| *City banks* | | | | | | |
| o Bank | 2,165 | 4,554 | 60 | 5,800 | 333 | 858 |
| a Bank | 1,080 | 3,285 | 80 | 50 | 25 | 288 |
| Bank | 1,440 | 3,787 | | 600 | 159 | 288 |
| a Bank | 360 | 493 | 90 | | 183 | 858 |
| Bank | 880 | 680 | 80 | | 20 | 108 |
| aido Development | | 2,150 | 20 | 500 | 34 | |
| of Tokyo | | 19,886 | 156 | | | |
| *-term credit banks* | | | | | | |
| strial Bank | 1,000 | 2,042 | | | 2,004* | 32,035 |
| -Term Credit Bank | 10,184 | 411 | | 7,125 | 1,884 | 27,479 |
| thec Bank | 840 | 961 | | | | |
| *rnment banks* | | | | | | |
| lopment Bank | | | | | 41,088 | 67,045 |
| rt-Import Bank | 773 | 23,757 | 143 | | | |
| tal borrowings cluding "others" | 46,266 | 182,431 | 3,287 | 34,577 | 59,672 | 260,801 |

| City banks and affiliates | Toyo Rayon | Mitsui & Co. | Daimaru Dept. Store | Nippon Express | Osaka S. Mitsui Shipping | Tokyo Elec. |
|---|---|---|---|---|---|---|
| *Keiretsu* dependency: | | | | | | |
| Bank alone | 22% | 17.4% | 31.6% | 20.6% | 3.3% | 12.2 |
| Bank and affiliates | 22.68% | 24.5% | 35.8% | 20.6% | 3.3% | 12.2 |

Source: Economic Investigative Council, *Research on Business Groupings, 1967*, Table 221 series, pp. 192-268. Selection of companies is from Table 202, pp. 41-48; borrowing data are from the Table 221 series; City banks are arranged according to the 1966 ranking of their financial *keiret.* Table 12-4.

*Inasmuch as borrowings of the OSAKA SHOSEN-Mitsui Shipping are highest from the Industrial Bank, I have placed it in the financial *keiretsu* of the Industrial Bank. The Economic Investigative Council appears to place it in no grouping in its 1967 edition.

financial institutions it would be easier to see real significance in the position of the primary bank in Table 12-5 material.

It is notable that in establishing *kinyu keiretsu* affiliation, borrowings from government sources are ignored (by the Council, but not by all Japanese compilers), as well as borrowings from foreign sources. Thus, although Tokyo Electric Power has borrowings twice the size of its Industrial Bank loans from the Development Bank, a government institution, it is classified as belonging to the Industrial Bank's grouping. Similarly, although Mitsui Mining's borrowings from the Development Bank and from the Rationalization Fund are 7 times the scale of its borrowings from the Mitsui Bank and over 3½ times the scale of its borrowings from all Mitsui institutions combined, this is disregarded by the council in developing its financial groupings.

Table 12-5 amply illustrates what it means to a city bank to have affiliated financial institutions (the long-term credit banks do not have them), for it will be observed that in many cases the primary position of the city bank comes not from borrowings from it alone, but in combination from the city bank, trust bank, and the marine and fire insurance and life insurance companies. Borrowing from the bank of the primary-bank line is shown for each company after total borrowings, along with the percentage figures when affiliated financial institutions are included.

### *Scale of Borrowing from Primary Bank—with Time Dimension*

In the Bank of Japan quotation given earlier, 30% was cited as typical of the scale of reliance on primary banks. It will be recalled from Chapter 11 that the Economic Investigative Council stated that it used—ostensibly—40% as a criterion in determining membership in a *keiretsu* grouping. My sample of the borrowing patterns of 20 majors indicates that for 1966 30% is high; 14 of the 20 companies were below 30%. (Only two companies met the 40% figure). To give the reader a better feel for the scale of reliance on the primary bank and its affiliated institutions, I have given in Table 12-6 such information for the years 1964, 1961, and 1959. The 1966 figures are repeated for ease of comparison. If one notes the degree of reliance in the earlier years, it will again be seen that the majority of companies are below the 30% level. For 1964, 13 of the 20 companies are below 30%; for 1961, 15 of the 20; and for 1959, 13 of the 20.

Table 12-6, with its "over time" dimension (over a period of time), shows another important point about the financial groupings. Between 1959 and 1964 five of the 20 companies changed their bank line: Nippon Oil, Nippon Mining, Bridgestone Tires, Nippon Express, and Tokyo Electric Power. Between 1964 and 1966 two of the above, plus a third, changed affiliations: Bridgestone Tires, Nippon Express, and Osaka Shosen-Mitsui Shipping.

### *Influence of Bank Shareholding and Management Participation on Financial Groupings*

While it is customary to see financial groupings resting on the power of credit, observers not infrequently point in addition to ownership and management as strengthening elements. Table 12-7 presents information on this point. For convenience it repeats the lending reliance on the primary bank and then shows the primary bank's holdings in the major, as well as the major's holdings in the primary bank. In addition, the table indicates the number of other banks in which the major has investments and the scale of management ties with the primary bank.

Overall, ownership ties are not substantial. However, by inference, Table 12-7 clearly reveals the significance of affiliated financial institutions in equity control. While the Antimonopoly Law restricts bank holdings to a maximum of 10%, there is nothing in it that says the Mitsubishi Bank and the Mitsubishi Trust Bank may not each have 10%. Shareholding by financial institutions, then, will be seen in three instances to be above 10%. It is noteworthy that these three cases are among companies formerly key members of the Mitsui and Mitsubishi *zaibatsu*. Apart from these cases, bank ownership was not large among the companies in question. In three instances, no bank ownership at all is indicated. Conversely, in column four it will be

Table 12-6: THE BORROWING PATTERNS OF 20 SELECTED MAJORS WITH A TIME DIMENSION

Highest and second highest *private Japanese* borrowing sources when affiliated financial institutions are included with the city bank as a percentage of the firm's total borrowing

(Underlined companies = where affiliation changed during period)

Abbrev:

| | | | |
|---|---|---|---|
| AgrC | Central Agr. & Forestry Coop | Ko | Kobe |
| D | Daiichi | LTC | Long-Term Credit |
| Dw | Daiwa | M | Mitsui |
| F | Fuji | Mb | Mitsubishi |
| HD | Hokkaido Development | S | Sumitomo |
| Ind | Industrial | Sa | Sanwa |
| Kan | Kangyo | T | Tokyo |

| *Company* | 1966 Highest | 1966 2nd Highest | 1964 Highest | 1964 2nd Highest | 1961 Highest | 1961 2nd Highest | 1959 Highest | 1959 2nd Highest |
|---|---|---|---|---|---|---|---|---|
| Taiyo Fisheries | Ind 12.8 | AgrC 9.0 | Ind 16.5 | Mb 9.5 | Ind 14.7 | AgrC 11.0 | Ind 15.7 | Mb 11.5 |
| Mitsui Mining | M 16.1 | Kan 5.1 | M 16.8 | HD 5.1<br>Kan 5.1 | M 23.6 | HD 11.8 | M 21.9 | Kan 10.5 |
| Nippon Oil | F 32.4 | M 31.6 | F 32.4 | M 31.8 | M 33.6 | D 33.3 | M 35.4 | F 32.8 |
| Nippon Mining | Ind 11.7 | M 11.2 | M 12.1 | Ind 12.0 | Ind 16.8 | M 14.2 | Ind 23.1 | M 14.9 |
| Furukawa Electric | D 33.24 | LTC 21.4 | D 32.3 | LTC 30.1 | D 36.9 | LTC 28.8 | D 44.3 | LTC 23.4 |
| Yawata Steel | Ind 15.0 | F 14.0 | Ind 16.1 | F 13.9 | Ind 17.6 | LTC 10.8 | Ind 19.9 | LTC 12.3 |
| Mitsubishi H. Ind. | Mb 22.6 | S 7.5 | Mb 24.4 | S 6.4 | (three companies before 1963 merger) | | | |

| Company | 1966 Highest | 1966 2nd Highest | 1964 Highest | 1964 2nd Highest | 1961 Highest | 1961 2nd Highest | 1959 Highest | 1959 2nd Highest |
|---|---|---|---|---|---|---|---|---|
| Toyota Motors | LTC 31.5 | M 6.2 | LTC 33.6 | M 9.0 | LTC 55.8 | | LTC 82.9 | |
| Hitachi Mfg. | Ind 16.5 | F 13.6 | Ind 14.4 | F 12.6 | Ind 15.1 | F 11.8 | Ind 18.3 | F 10.5 |
| Mitsubishi Chem. | Mb 20.0 | AgrC 17.4 | Mb 23.5 | Ind 8.3 | Mb 26.2 | Ind 11.1 | Mb 38.4 | Ind 11.8 |
| Bridgestone Tires | LTC 22.31 | S 18.6 | S 25.7 | LTC 21.1 | LTC 24.7 | S 24.2 | n.l. | |
| Asahi Glass | Mb 26.3 | K 8.9 | Mb 28.4 | F 10.0 | Mb 39.8 | F 14.4<br>Kan 14.4 | Mb 35.1 | F 16.7 |
| Taisei Construction | F 41.1 | Mb 10.2 | F 38.6 | Dw 13.9 | F 52.1 | Dw 19.4 | F 34.6 | Dw 27.2 |
| Kirin Beer | Mb 58.5 | Ko 9.9 | Mb 46.2 | LTC 16.6 | n.l. | | n.l. | |
| Toyo Rayon | M 22.7 | LTC 22.0 | M 25.5 | LTC 19.0 | M 29.2 | LTC 22.3 | M 29.0 | LTC 18.3 |
| Mitsui & Co. | M 24.5 | F 17.0 | M 28.4 | T 14.8 | M 27.8 | T 19.3 | M 22.9 | T 19.2 |
| Daimaru Dept. Store | Mb 35.8 | S 24.1 | Mb 33.8 | S 29.6 | Mb 29.5 | S 20.1 | Mb 28.8 | S 21.1 |
| Nippon Express | LTC 20.6 | Sa 19.6 | Kan 22.8 | Sa 20.1 | Kan 26.3 | LTC 17.4 | Ind 29.6 | Kan 25.3 |
| Osaka S.-M. Shipping | Ind 3.3 | LTC 3.1 | M 4.5 | Ind 3.6 | (OSK)S 8.5<br>(M)M 11.0 | Ind 5.4<br>Ind 7.0 | (OSK)S 6.2<br>(M)M 8.1 | Mb 2.8<br>Ind 5.0 |
| Tokyo Elec. Power | Ind 12.2 | LTC 10.5<br>M 8.9 | Ind 12.0 | LTC 10.6<br>M 9.7 | M 10.9 | Ind 10.5 | Ind 9.8 | LTC 9.0 |

Source and notes: Economic Investigative Council, *Research on Business Groupings*, 1967, 1965, 1962 editions. 1966 data are from the 1967 edition, Table 204, pp. 53-68; 1964 data, the 1965 edition, Table 204, pp. 45-59; 1961 and 1959 data from the 1962 edition, Tables 6-20, pp. 38-95. By definition of the way the table has been constructed, borrowings from the Development Bank and from the Export-Import Bank are excluded from consideration.

Table 12-7: TIES BETWEEN 20 SELECTED MAJORS AND THEIR "PRIMARY" FINANCIAL INSTITUTIONS

With specified exceptions, information is as of 1966

| *Company* | Primary bank (1) | Percent borrowings from primary bank and affiliates (2) | Percent ownership by primary bank & financial affiliates in major (3) | 1963-64 data, percent ownership by major in primary bank (4) | No. of banks in which major has holdings exclusive of primary bank (5) | No. prim bank sent to m ( |
|---|---|---|---|---|---|---|
| Taiyo Fisheries | Ind | 12.8 | 2.0 | .8 | 4 | |
| Mitsui Mining | M | 16.1 | 1.6 | 0.0 | 0 | |
| Nippon Oil | F | 32.4 | 2.1 | 1.8 | 2 | |
| Nippon Mining | Ind | 11.7 | 3.5 | 2.2 | 8 | |
| Furukawa Electric | D | 33.2 | 9.9 | 3.8 | 7 | |
| Yawata Steel | Ind | 15.0 | 2.6 | 4.5 | 4 | |
| Mitsubishi Heavy Ind. | Mb | 22.6 | 9.5 | 8.8 | 4 | |
| Toyota Motors | LTC | 31.5 | 0 | .1 | 3 | |
| Hitachi Mfg. | Ind. | 16.5 | 1.4 | 3.0 | 3 | |
| Mitsubishi Chemical | Mb | 20.0 | 15.1 | 2.7 | 3 | |
| Bridgestone Tires | LTC | 22.3 | 0 | 1.1 | 5 | |
| Asahi Glass | Mb | 26.3 | 19.0 | 1.8 | 3 | |
| Taisei Construction | F | 41.1 | 3.6 | 0.0 | 4 | |
| Kirin Beer | Mb | 58.5 | 5.9 | 0 4 | 1 | |
| Toyo Rayon | M | 22.7 | 1.9 | 1.6 | 1 | |
| Mitsui & Co. | M | 24.5 | 12.0 | 4.1 | 8 | |
| Daimaru Dept. Store | Mb | 35.8 | 5.5 | 0.5 | 3 | |
| Nippon Express | LTC | 20.6 | 1.6 | 4.4 | 5 | |
| Osaka S.-M. Shipping | Ind | 3.3 | 2.0 | 0.1 | 0 | |
| Tokyo Electric Power | Ind | 12.2 | 1.9 | 0.0 | 0 | |

Sources and notes: Economic Investigative Council, *Research on Business Groupings*, 1965; Tokyo Stoc Exchange, *First Section Corporation Directory* (Tokyo Shoken Torihiki Shohen, *Daiichibu Jojo Kaisha S* 1963. Abbreviations employed in column 1 are those given in Table 12-6; columns 1 and 2 from Counci Table 204, pp. 45-59. Column 3 calculated from Table 221 series, pp. 138-91, where top 10 sharehold are shown. If holdings are not among the top 10, they are accordingly not included in this column. Column 4 calculated by the writer: 1964 information on *shares held* in primary bank and affiliates t from Council (1965 edition) Table 300 series, pp. 260-607; 1963 information on total bank *shares iss* taken from 1963 Tokyo Stock Exchange Directory with the exception of the Long-Term Credit Bank, wher information was supplied me through the courtesy of the Bank of Tokyo, Seattle Branch. There may be inaccuracies in column 4 data, inasmuch as "shares held" represent 1964 information and "issued shar 1963. Column 5, taken from Council (1967 edition) Table 302 series, pp. 331-601, refers to the numb of banks exclusive of the primary bank and trust banks in which the firm has holdings. Column 6 is from Council (1967 edition), Table 205, pp. 69-83. Where a "representative" from an affiliated fina institution holds a position in the major, the entry occurs in two parts, first the number from the and in parentheses the number from affiliated institutions. For purposes of column 6, all officers been counted regardless of date of transfer, including "plain" auditors.

seen that with three exceptions—Mitsui Mining, Taisei Construction, and Tokyo Electric Power—the majors hold ownership in the primary bank. However, column five indicates clearly that bank holdings by the major are not confined to the bank of primary reliance and its affiliated institutions. In fact, Nippon Mining had holdings in 11 other banks, Mitsui & Co. in 9. Only Mitsui Mining, Osaka Shosen-Mitsui Shipping, and Tokyo Electric were without bank investments. From a study of the investment portfolios of these and other majors, I have gained the impression that generally there is some correlation between the number of banks in which the major holds investments and the degree of closeness to the primary bank. It would appear that the looser the ties are to a primary bank, the greater the number of bank investments—no doubt as "facilitants" to loans.

Let us note bank participation in the management of the 20 companies. The word "participation" does not here, for the most part, refer to that clear and tangible form—interlocks. Instead, in the majority of cases I am talking about officers who earlier in their careers held a position in the bank in question, not infrequently in a non-officer capacity. In the last column of Table 12-7, 10 of the 20 companies have bank participation, while 10 have none, thus dividing half-and-half. Typically, one gains an impression of stronger bank representation in businesses when starting with lists of companies to which a particular bank is said to have "dispatched" officers (which on detailed examination range from large to small), than when the process is reversed, as has been done in Table 12-5 and 12-7. One works backward from a given criterion for selection of companies toward bank ties.

A study of bank-industrial personnel ties invariably leaves one with many questions, for there does not appear to be any discernible pattern to those "dispatched" (terminology which, as earlier observed, is something of an overstatement). For example, in Table 12-7 there are two Mitsui Bank-connected officers on the board of Toyo Rayon, while there is only one on the board of Mitsui and Co. Toyo Rayon is a leading company, but it is not of equal importance to Mitsui and Co. to the Mitsui grouping. Mitsui and Co. was one of the historic triumvirate of operating companies heading the Mitsui *zaibatsu* (see Chapter 5), which acted, during a four-year period, concurrently as holding company for the *zaibatsu*. Not only do the historical factors make Mitsui and Co. of more importance, so do functions. A strong trading company is in a position to knit the complex together more effectively than a strong industrial company. Further, Mitsui and Co.'s borrowings from the bank are far greater than those of Toyo Rayon.

From Table 12-5 it will be seen that Mitsui and Co. has borrowings from the bank of Y31 billion, while Toyo Rayon has borrowings of Y4 billion.

In the case of the Industrial Bank, it is similarly difficult to discern the criteria that determine personnel ties. Five of the 20 companies in Table 12-7 have the Industrial Bank as their primary bank—Taiyo Fisheries, Nippon Mining, Yawata Steel, Hitachi, and Tokyo Electric Power. Two of the companies are shown as having bank "representation," Taiyo with two officers and Hitachi with one. Yet in Table 12-6 the amounts borrowed by these five in billions of yen are: Taiyo, 7; Nippon Mining, 6; Yawata, 30; Hitachi, 25; Tokyo Electric Power, 32. Taiyo, a company with a relatively low borrowing has two officers (plus an officer from the Kangyo Bank, as is seen in the table); Hitachi, with a large borrowing, has one officer. The two companies with borrowings larger than Hitachi, plus the one with borrowings of the approximate size of Taiyo, do not have representation. Clearly, Yawata Steel is far more important on the industrial scene than Taiyo, yet it is without "representation."

Toyota Motors, as seen in Table 12-6, has had a strong record of reliance on its primary bank, the Long-Term Credit Bank. In 1966, 31% of its borrowings were from this source; in 1964, 33%; in 1961, 55%; and in 1959, 82%. Seemingly, there is no representation from the Long-Term Credit Bank on its board, but the president is shown, in the source table, as connected with the Mitsui Bank, from which institution borrowing has been relatively small. The date of transfer, however, may provide an explanation—1950! This example serves to point up the limitations of lists of bank personnel "dispatched" when dates are not included. Clearly, when reference is to transfers and not interlocks, ties with the bank are highly attenuated 18 years after service on the staff of the bank. From the above discussion, the question becomes, "What is it that prompts decisions to put persons of bank background on the boards of companies?"

In only one case among our 10 companies showing primary bank representation is there plural bank representation—Taiyo Fisheries. But judging from the material presented by the Economic Investigative Council on officers of other companies (additional to the 20 shown here) having a bank background, it turns out there are quite a few instances of plural bank representation. Mitsui Chemical, in addition to having two directors with a Mitsui Bank-background, has an officer with a Kangyo Bank background. Teikoku Seni, a part of the Fuji Bank *kinyu keiretsu* and *keiretsu,* has, in addition to an officer from the Fuji Bank, a standing auditor from the Mitsubishi Bank.

Onoda Cement, regarded by the council as part of the Mitsui *keiretsu*, has in addition to an officer from the Mitsui Bank on its board, an officer from the Industrial Bank and an officer from the Kyowa Bank. Maruzen Oil, regarded as part of the Sanwa Bank *keiretsu*, has in addition to three officers from the Sanwa Bank, an officer from the Industrial Bank. What does this plural bank representation do to the notion of special relations with the primary bank? Does not this multiple bank influence weaken the notion of the special position of the primary bank?

### *The Source of Direction of the Groupings*

We have been examining the nature of the ties that bind the *kinyu keiretsu* into single wholes, but we have not taken up the pertinent question of the source of direction of the groupings. From the discussion in Chapter 11 of the core companies of the Mitsubishi, Mitsui, and Sumitomo, where "*keiretsu-ness*" and "*kinyu keiretsu-ness*" coexist, we found differences of view as to where leadership lies, though certainly the overwhelmingly dominant view is that it lies with the respective banks. In the quotation from the Bank of Japan cited earlier in this chapter, the primary banks are described both as promoters and followers,

Yet it seems doubtful to me that the primary bank is in a position to conceive and to carry out an overall strategy. In the sample of 20 companies, credit reliance is frequently not as high as that customarily ascribed; in a five-year period five companies changed affiliation, and in a seven-year period, six. These six companies, plus an additional five, show only a small difference in the scale of reliance on the primary bank line and their second highest source. In addition, while there is appointment to officer positions of persons formerly with the primary bank, and at times interlocks, such appointments do not appear to be related either to the scale of the borrowing or to the importance of the company. Yet Japanese observers believe the banks are in a crucial position. May the answer not lie in the phrasing of the second portion of the Bank of Japan quotation—"When the relation between banks and enterprises becomes too close, the former . . . find themselves obliged to adopt an easy lending attitude"?

The special ties between industrials and their primary bank, rather than implying bank conception and promotion of projects, may well be a matter of what happens to objective judgment in loan requests. When ties are of such a character that a bank finds it difficult to say no to a loan request, where the bank feels itself "obliged to adopt an easy lending attitude," then a special relation clearly exists. It seems to me that it is this situation that is likely to be the nature of the particular ties with the primary bank, on which the *kinyu-keiretsu* analysis rests. And the longer the association between the industrial and the bank the more likely is this to be true.

### *"One Set-ism"—A Characteristic of Financial Groupings?*

Let us return to Professor Miyazaki's theory of one set-ism. As is apparent, the analysis rests on the assumption of a strong sense of group, and a commitment of funds (as we have seen, *borrowed* bank funds), to projects not undertaken on the basis of anticipated returns, but rather for reasons of group rivalry and prestige. One of Japan's leading businessmen once remarked to me that while Western businessmen always made decisions rationally, he would not so characterize Japanese businessmen. Joseph Schumpeter was wont to observe, however, that economic activity is inherently a rationalizing process, that double-entry bookkeeping is a clarifying calculus between outgo and income, between expenses and returns. In an economy as demonstrably successful as Japan's, it is hard to believe that the underlying rationale behind investment is not a balancing of costs and returns. It is possible to imagine that around the "edges," as it were, Japanese decision-makers might allow themselves to decide projects on the basis of prestige, but such should not describe the bulk of the commitment of new funds.

In the analysis of Mitsubishi, Mitsui, and Sumitomo above, a question was raised with respect to the extent of the sense of group, with the implication that by comparison with *zaibatsu* days, it was weak. One set-ism suggests the opposite. While in the discussion of the Big Three various instances were noted of group collaboration in new undertakings, comparable group direction of ongoing operations was not found. But to collaborate in new undertakings requires much less sense of group than to collaborate in existing undertakings. That is, the core companies of the Big Three may not object to putting up a few tens of millions of yen as their pro rata share of a new undertaking, but they would find it difficult to allow the group to tell them how they should be handling sales or purchases or what they should or should not be doing in expansion of their own enterprises.

While one set-ism is applied to the relations between Mitsubishi, Mitsui, and Sumitomo, it is also used to describe the relations between financial groupings in general. But the seeming imitative behavior which Professor Miyazaki ascribes to internal group cohesion and external group rivalry could be explained in other terms, in individual terms. Might not the rush to enter a new market be explained in terms of the difficulty of later entry? That color TV producers would rush into production ahead of the market may in fact be perfectly rational behavior. Entry in any economy is seldom easy, but in an economy which does not strive toward an impartial banking system, which fosters concentration and blesses groupings, it could well be that entry at any other time than the beginning is extremely difficult.

The Confucian heritage of each man in his proper place, knowing his proper place and not aspiring to leave it, has overtones in business. Recognizing one's position and not aspiring to leave it is just the opposite of the way Schumpeter used to liken the business community to passengers on a bus with those crowding to get on pushing out some of those already in. Within the Japanese pattern, if a producer does not get started directly on a new technology he is likely to be regarded, if he later seeks entry, as working to the "detriment of the old established concerns."

Japan's entire modern period (1868 to the present) has been built on discriminatory bank credit. On the plus side are the majors of today's economy; on the minus side is the ongoing duality of the economy, the continuance of its medium and small enterprise which is not competitive with large. It will be recalled from Chapter 1 that as recently as a decade ago two-thirds of Japan's labor force in manufacturing was in plants with less than 200 workers. This is the price paid for a banking system committed to "related" companies, rather than one committed (however short it may fall of its goal) to serving all who ask on the merits of their loan requests, a view admirably stated by Dr. Edna Ehrlich in *The Role of Banking in Japan's Economic Development.*

It was because ties between banks and industrials inevitably make for favoritism in the extension of credit that those who were engaged in the program of economic deconcentration in Japan sought to include the banking system within the deconcentration effort as originally prescribed in the Basic Directive. But this policy was reversed. Certain historical trends, however, may be working toward a weakening of financial and industrial ties—the fact that the credit needs of today's majors are quite beyond the capability of any financial line, and the general, pervasive trend in Japanese society, as in all modern societies, toward more impersonal human relations. The personal loyalty that underlay the *zaibatsu* system is a vanishing phenomenon.

Table 12-8: NET SUPPLY OF INDUSTRIAL FUNDS — INCREASE AND DECREASE, 1931-64

Calendar years except where entry is marked with asterisk when fiscal. Two asterisks indicate that calendar year data and fiscal data have been added together.

(in millions yen)

| Year | Grand total | Internal capital | | | External capital | | | |
|---|---|---|---|---|---|---|---|---|
| | | subtotal | depreciation | retained earn. | subtotal | shares | bonds | loans & discounts |
| 1931 | 638 | 277 | 450 | -173 | 361 | 204 | 108 | 49 |
| 1933 | 1,013 | 1,066 | 885 | 181 | -53 | 315 | -40 | -328 |
| 1935 | 2,479 | 1,280 | 930 | 350 | 1,199 | 816 | 26 | 357 |
| 1937 | 5,597 | 1,864 | 1,238 | 626 | 3,733 | 1,986 | -7 | 1,754 |
| 1940 | 10,996 | 3,343 | 2,122 | 1,221 | 7,653 | 2,940 | 609 | 4,104 |
| 1942 | 15,280 | 4,762 | 2,586 | 2,176 | 10,518 | 3,930 | 1,362 | 5,226 |
| 1945 | 56,527 | 6,122 | 3,136 | 2,986 | 50,405 | *3,082 | 325 | 46,998 |
| 1947 | **152,280 | *18,877 | *19,932 | *-1,055 | 133,403 | *9,030 | 10 | 124,363 |
| 1950 | **856,541 | *341,643 | *149,733 | *191,910 | 512,898 | 31,919 | 43,476 | 437,503 |
| 1952 | 1,468,439 | 447,144 | 291,007 | 156,137 | 1,021,295 | 122,359 | 37,047 | 861,889 |
| 1955 | 1,389,358 | 712,887 | 460,909 | 251,987 | 676,471 | 95,547 | 26,548 | 554,376 |
| 1957 | 2,974,996 | 1,176,743 | 670,867 | 505,876 | 1,798,253 | 285,652 | 52,399 | 1,460,202 |
| 1960 | 5,037,737 | 2,108,491 | 1,130,014 | 978,477 | 2,927,246 | 471,918 | 152,814 | 2,302,861 |
| 1962 | 6,926,675 | 2,722,787 | 1,753,414 | 969,373 | 4,203,888 | 797,820 | 133,199 | 3,272,869 |
| 1963 | 9,028,363 | 3,301,032 | 2,090,939 | 1,210,093 | 5,727,331 | 589,404 | 163,672 | 4,974,255 |
| 1964 | - | - | - | - | 5,094,050 | 791,382 | 154,017 | 4,148,651 |

Sources and notes: Bank of Japan, *Economic Statistics of Japan, 1961, and, 1964* (1962 and 1965 editions). The pertinent tables are Table 12 of the 1962 edition, pp. 29-32 and Table 14 of the 1965 edition, pp. 31-34. While published by the Bank of Japan, the data for these tables in fact come from two sources – that on internal capital from the Economic Planning Agency, that on external capital from the Bank of Japan. I have added these two totals to obtain the first column, "Grand Total." It is disturbing that the data on depreciation, a major source of internal financing, are markedly different in two tables in the 1965 edition, Table 14 and Table 179 (p. 325), both prepared by the same source. The scale of disparity is to be seen in the following illustrations, which are given in billions of yen:

| | Table 14 depreciation | Table 179 depreciation |
|---|---|---|
| 1935 | 0.9 | 1.2 |
| 1940 | 2.1 | 2.8 |
| 1950 (fiscal) | 149.0 | 207.0 |
| 1955 | 460.0 | 633.6 |
| 1960 | 1,130.0 | 1,453.8 |
| 1963 | 2,090.0 | 2,583.2 |

Table 12-9: SHARE OF BANK ADVANCES IN EXTERNALLY SUPPLIED INDUSTRIAL FUNDS

| | in millions yen | | | | in percent | | |
|---|---|---|---|---|---|---|---|
| Year | Total external supply | Bank advances | Shares of stock | Corporate debentures | Bank advances | Shares of stock | Corporate debentures |
| 1913 | 480 | 224 | 227 | 29 | 46.7 | 47.3 | 6.0 |
| 1915 | 305 | 170 | 99 | 36 | 55.7 | 32.5 | 11.8 |
| 1916 | 1,126 | 844 | 267 | 15 | 75.0 | 23.7 | 1.3 |
| 1918 | 3,930 | 2,331 | 1,536 | 63 | 59.3 | 39.1 | 1.6 |
| 1920 | 2,131 | -127 | 2,263 | -5 | -6.0 | 106.2 | -0.2 |
| 1921 | 2,093 | 843 | 1,074 | 176 | 40.3 | 51.3 | 8.4 |
| 1923 | 2,448 | 1,088 | 1,205 | 155 | 44.4 | 49.2 | 6.3 |
| 1925 | 1,177 | 496 | 307 | 374 | 42.1 | 26.1 | 31.8 |
| 1926 | 1,043 | 368 | 488 | 187 | 35.3 | 46.8 | 17.9 |
| 1928 | 137 | -712 | 334 | 515 | -519.7 | 243.8 | 375.9 |
| 1930 | -69 | -179 | 13 | 97 | - | - | - |

Source: Edna E. Ehrlich, *The Role of Banking in Japan's Economic Development*, p. 378, based on data supplied Dr. Ehrlich by the Bank of Japan.

Table 12-10: SOURCES OF U.S. CORPORATE FUNDS
(in billions dollars)

| | Internal Sources | | | | External Long-term Sources | | | | Short-term Sources | | | | |
|---|---|---|---|---|---|---|---|---|---|---|---|---|---|
| | Total | Subtotal | Profits | Deprec. | Subtotal | Stocks | Bonds | Other debts | Subtotal | Bank loans | Trade pay. | Inc. Tax Liabil. | Other |
| 1950 | 44.2 | 20.8 | 13.0 | 7.8 | 4.2 | 1.7 | 2.0 | 0.5 | 19.2 | 2.1 | 8.8 | 7.3 | 1.0 |
| 1955 | 50.3 | 26.6 | 10.9 | 15.7 | 8.6 | 2.7 | 4.2 | 1.7 | 15.1 | 3.7 | 5.5 | 3.8 | 2.1 |
| 1958 | 39.4 | 26.0 | 5.7 | 20.3 | 10.9 | 3.6 | 5.9 | 1.4 | 2.6 | -.4 | 3.8 | -2.5 | 1.7 |
| 1960 | 46.2 | 29.1 | 6.2 | 22.9 | 9.8 | 3.0 | 5.0 | 1.7 | 7.4 | 1.3 | 4.5 | -1.6 | 3.2 |
| 1961 | 52.3 | 29.7 | 5.6 | 24.1 | 11.8 | 4.5 | 5.1 | 2.2 | 10.8 | 0.4 | 7.4 | 0.7 | 2.3 |
| 1962 | 59.2 | 35.2 | 7.7 | 27.5 | 11.3 | 2.1 | 5.0 | 4.2 | 12.8 | 3.0 | 5.6 | 0.9 | 3.2 |
| 1963 | 62.5 | 36.8 | 8.0 | 28.8 | 10.9 | 0.6 | 5.2 | 5.0 | 14.8 | 4.3 | 6.8 | 1.2 | 2.5 |
| 1964 | 66.6 | 42.1 | 11.6 | 30.5 | 13.4 | 2.9 | 6.1 | 4.4 | 11.1 | 2.6 | 5.8 | 0.7 | 2.0 |

Source: U.S. Dept. of Commerce, *Statistical Abstract of the United States*, 1965, p. 502.

Table 12-11: THE SOURCES OF BANK BORROWINGS BY JAPAN'S PRINCIPAL ENTERPRISES[a]

(in percent, September 1964)

| | *Short-term borrowings* | *Long-term borrowings* | *Long & short combined* | *Receivables, discounted paper* | *Total borrowin* |
|---|---|---|---|---|---|
| *Proportion of total borrowings* | (41.5%) | (40.6%) | (82.1%) | (17.9%) | (100%) |
| City banks[b] | 76.1 | 50.7 | 63.5 | 77.6 | 66.1 |
| Provincial banks | 10.4 | 1.4 | 6.0 | 18.1 | 8.1 |
| Mutual and credit banks | 0.7 | 0.3 | 0.5 | 2.3 | 0.8 |
| Government financial institutions | 3.5 | 23.1 | 13.2 | 0.2 | 10.9 |
| Other | 9.3 | 24.5 | 16.8 | 1.8 | 14.1 |

[a]"Principal enterprises" refers to 500 firms selected by the Bank of Japan as the majors of the economy.

[b]In this table "city banks" include "long-term credit banks" and "trust banks."

Source: Bank of Japan, *An Analysis of the Management of Principal Enterprises, 1964* (Nippon Ginko Tokei Kyoku, *Shuyo Kigyo Keiei Bunseki, Showa 39 Nendo Geki*), p. 95.

Table 12-12: CITY BANKS AND THEIR AFFILIATED FINANCIAL INSTITUTIONS

| *City bank* | *Trust bank* | *Marine and fire insurance* | *Life insurance* |
|---|---|---|---|
| Fuji Bank | Yasuda Trust and Banking | Yasuda Fire Insur. | Yasuda Life Insur. |
| Mitsubishi Bank | Mitsubishi Trust & Banking | Tokyo Marine Insur. | Meiji Life Insur. |
| Sanwa Bank | Toyo Trust & Banking | | Daido Life Insur. |
| Sumitomo Bank | Sumitomo Trust and Banking | Sumitomo Marine Insur. | Sumitomo Life Insu |
| Tokai Bank | Chuo Trust Bank | | |
| Daiichi Bank | (within city bank not separately incorporated) | | Asahi Life Insur. |
| Mitsui Bank | Mitsui Trust & Banking | Taisho Marine Insur. | Mitsui Life Insur. |
| Kangyo Bank | | | |
| Daiwa Bank | | | |
| Kyowa Bank | | | |
| Kobe Bank | | | |
| Hokkaido Development | | | |

# 13.

## Still More Groupings: Subsidiaries and *Kombinato*

An examination of "plain" *keiretsu* groupings and financial *keiretsu* groupings reveals a situation in which ties are tenuous and unclear, yet a study of subsidiary groupings indicates a quite different picture. The Fair Trade Commission calls subsidiary groupings "capital [*shihon*] *keiretsu*." In the case of capital *keiretsu*, parent-company ownership is high, management interlocks are numerous, and credit extension is frequent. Although Article 9 of the Antimonopoly Law forbids holding companies, and Articles 10 and 13 forbid intercorporate stockholding and interlocking directorates where the effect is "substantially to restrain competition," these provisions have not impeded the buildup of subsidiary complexes of market-related, as well as non-market-related, firms.

In a 1965 study[1] the FTC took for examination the subsidiaries of the top 100 nonfinancial firms of the first section of the Tokyo Stock Exchange on the basis of paid-in capital. In this study, subsidiaries are defined as firms with parent-company stockholdings amounting to 30% and above, or holdings in the range of 10 to 29%, when accompanied by management interlocks or loans or both. Under this definition, it was found that the top 100 firms had 4,270 dependent firms. It was learned that better than half of the subsidiaries (58.8%) were controlled at 50% stock ownership and above; slightly over four-fifths (82.4%) were controlled at 30% and above. In addition, three-quarters of the subsidiaries (75%) had interlocking officerships, a far stronger management device than persons "dispatched," and further, that 36% were the recipients of loans from the parent company.[2]

[1] Fair Trade Commission, *Capital Keiretsu Among the Principal Companies* (Kosei Torihiki Iinkai, *Shuyo Kaisha ni okeru Shihon Keiretsu no Jokyo*), mimeog., November 1965. The selection of companies was made as of March 1963, but the data presented on the 100 are, for the most part, as of 1964.

[2] FTC, press release, "An Investigation into Corporate Capital Concentration and Capital Keiretsu" ("*Kaisha no Shihon Shuchu oyobi Shihon Keiretsu ni tsuite no Chosa*"), January 14, 1966; pages are not numbered.

In absolute rather than percentage figures the FTC's findings were:[3]

| | Parent Company Shareholding | | |
|---|---|---|---|
| | 10-29% | 30-49% | 50% & above |
| 4,207 companies | 740 companies | 991 companies | 2,476 companies |
| Of which 3,196 companies have parent company management interlocks | 649 | 659 | 1,888 |
| Of which 1,548 companies have parent company loans | 192 | 304 | 1,052 |

To have parent-company ownership among four-fifths of the subsidiaries at the 30% level and above is not only evidence of effective controls and therefore groupings which can be knit together, but it is also evidence that the scale of enterprise has changed. This is clear from the proportion of total corporate capital which the "controllers" and the "controlled" account for. The FTC found that the top 100 firms themselves accounted for 39.4% of total paid-in capital; that the 4,270 satellite firms accounted for 13.8%.[4] Thus indirectly the top 100 firms accounted for 53.2% of corporate capital.

One sees this change of scale spelled out in Table 13-1, which is reproduced from the FTC's study giving the size distribution of the 4,000-odd subsidiaries. Stock control of 30% and above characteristically refers to the medium and smaller enterprises in the subsidiary networks. It is not typical of the large-scale companies of the groupings.

Notwithstanding the clarity and tangibility of subsidiary controls, different sources give different accounts of the number of companies in the subsidiary complexes of the majors of the economy.[5] Even the same source, the Economic Investigative Council, gives different data in different annual editions of its *Research on Business Groupings.* While one would expect some change of numbers over time, subsidiaries will obviously not double or halve within a short period. When

[3] FTC, *Capital Keiretsu*, p. 19. All tables in this study occur in the form, for example. "10% ijo—30 miman." I have accordingly listed entries in the form "10—29%".

[4] *Ibid.*, p. 13.

[5] This discussion compares the findings of the above cited FTC study, in which corporations are arranged by industry groupings, with the Investigative Council in its 1965 and 1962 editions of *Research on Business Groupings.* (The 1965 edition presents 1964 information; the 1962 gives 1961 information.) In both editions information is taken from the Table 300 series, in which firms are listed according to industry groupings.

Table 13-1: SUBSIDIARIES OF TOP 100 FIRMS, RANKED BY SIZE OF CAPITALIZATION

| | No. companies | Percent |
|---|---|---|
| Under $13,888 (Y5 million) | 604 | 14.2 |
| $13,888 to $27,777 (Y5 million to Y10 million) | 581 | 13.6 |
| $27,777 to $138,888 (Y10 million to Y50 million) | 1,351 | 31.6 |
| $138,888 to $277,777 (Y50 million to Y100 million) | 577 | 13.5 |
| $277,777 to $2,777,777 (Y100 million to Y1 billion) | 971 | 22.7 |
| $2,777,777 and over (Y1 billion and above) | 186 | 4.4 |
| | 4,270 | 100.0 |

Source: FTC, *The Condition of Capital Keiretsu Among the Principal Companies* (Kosei Torihiki Iinkai, *Shuyo Kaisha ni Okeru Shihon Keiretsu no Jokyo*), October 1965, mimeog. Table III, p. 20.

there is this degree of difference, it is evident definitions have been changed. A few examples will illustrate the problem. The Economic Investigative Council shows the Fuji Iron and Steel Corporation in 1964 with 22 "related companies," in 1961 with 42; the FTC shows it in 1964 with 43. The Council shows the Sumitomo Chemical Company for 1964 with 24 subsidiaries, in 1961 with 13; the FTC shows it in 1964 with 38. The Council shows the Isuzu Motor Company with 21 subsidiaries in 1964 and 66 in 1961; the FTC shows it in 1964 with 74. The FTC spells out its criteria for speaking of a firm as a subsidiary, as part of the capital *keiretsu* of a major. It would have been most helpful if the Economic Investigative Council had spelled out its definition of "related companies" and done this from edition to edition.

In the FTC study the number of companies within the subsidiary groupings of the 100 top-ranking firms ranges from a high of 285 (Matsushita) to a low of 3 (Hokkaido Electric), with an arithmetic average of 42. The combined capitalizations of the subsidiary companies of the different groupings range from a high of Y39 billion ($110.7 million, Yawata Steel) to a low of Y27 million ($75,000, Mitsukoshi Department Store). Among the 20 majors used for study in the preceding chapter, there is likewise a wide range in size of subsidiary groupings. As seen in Table 13-2 (where, except for reasons of lowness of capital, merger, etc., they were not included in the FTC

Table 13-2: ILLUSTRATIONS OF INDUSTRIAL *KEIRETSU* IN JAPAN'S ECONOMY TODAY

(Companies with an asterisk not with top 1966 sales in their lines; see note to table.)

| Major | Number subsid. in grouping | Subsid. Capitalized at $2.7 million above | Combined capitalization of subsidiaries billions yen | Parent company stock control | | |
|---|---|---|---|---|---|---|
| | | | | 10-29% | 30-49% | over 50% |
| Taiyo Fisheries | 68 cos. | 22 cos. | Y14.2 | 10 cos. | 15 cos. | 43 cos. |
| Hokkaido Colliery & SS* | 54 | 13 | 5.4 | 5 | 7 | 42 |
| Nippon Oil | 22 | 10 | 16.2 | 6 | 3 | 13 |
| Nippon Mining | 41 | 11 | 17.4 | 5 | 10 | 26 |
| Furukawa Electric | 39 | 14 | 16.0 | 11 | 6 | 22 |
| Yawata Steel | 55 | 37 | 39.8 | 19 | 18 | 18 |
| Ishikawajima-Harima H.I.* | 27 | 14 | 6.7 | 7 | 6 | 14 |
| Toyota Motors | 28 | 21 | 31.9 | 11 | 11 | 6 |
| Hitachi Mfg. | 76 | 39 | 27.6 | 10 | 7 | 59 |
| Mitsubishi Chemical | 27 | 18 | 16.0 | 7 | 8 | 12 |
| Bridgestone Tires | 129 | 1 | 3.1 | 2 | 12 | 115 |
| Asahi Glass | 21 | 10 | 3.7 | 3 | 2 | 16 |
| Kajima Construction* | 19 | 6 | 1.3 | 5 | 3 | 11 |
| Kirin Beer | 15 | 3 | 0.7 | 0 | 0 | 15 |
| Toyo Rayon | 21 | 10 | 2.3 | 5 | 2 | 14 |

| Major | Number subsid. in grouping | Subsid. capitalized at $2.7 million above | Combined capitalization of subsidiaries billions yen | Parent company stock control | | |
|---|---|---|---|---|---|---|
| | | | | 10-29% | 30-49% | over 50% |
| Mitsui & Co. | 134 | 29 | 11.0 | 48 | 38 | 48 |
| Mitsukoshi Dept. Store* | 13 | 0 | 0.02 | 0 | 0 | 13 |
| Nippon Express | 143 | 23 | 11.0 | 27 | 24 | 92 |
| Osaka S-Mitsui Shipping | 45 | 11 | 4.1 | 15 | 12 | 18 |
| Tokyo Electric Power | 11 | 5 | 3.5 | 0 | 1 | 10 |

Sources and notes: Companies with top 1966 sales taken from Economic Investigative Council, *Research on Business Groupings*, 1967 edition, Table 202, pp. 41-48; company data are taken from FTC, *Capital Keiretsu of Major Companies* (Kosei Torihiki Iinkai, *Shuyo Kaisha ni okeru, Shihon Keiretsu no Jokyo*), mimeog. 1965, *passim*. Starred companies represent substitutions for the majors previously used. The FTC study, based on the top 100 firms judged on the basis of *capital*, does not include certain of the companies now in top position. While March 30, 1963 represents the FTC's date of selection of the top 100, the statistical material on these companies is, for the most part, as of March 1964. The date of the material for each company is indicated in the tables from which this table has been constructed.

study), the range in number of subsidiaries is 143 (Nippon Express) to 11 (Tokyo Electric Power); the range in combined capitalization of subsidiaries is from Yawata Steel to the Mitsukoshi Department Store, the high and low of the full study. Table 13-2 presents further information on the capital *keiretsu* of the previously noted 20 majors.

*Some Examples of Subsidiary Complexes*

To get something of a feel for these groupings, let us briefly examine a few of them, using the FTC information.

MATSUSHITA: The (nonfinancial) firm with the largest number of subsidiaries in the economy, Matsushita is an electrical goods manufacturer which in 1964 and 1966 ranked sixth highest among industrials, in sales.[6] The bulk of Matsushita's subsidiaries, when judged by number, are distributors, but the core of the complex, judged by capitalization, is in manufacturing. In manufacturing, Matsushita has seven subsidiaries at or above Y1 billion ($2.7 million) in capitalization.

In absolute figures the Matsushita subsidiary complex appears as follows:

| | Parent Company Shareholding | | |
|---|---|---|---|
| | 10-29% | 30-49% | 50% above |
| 285 companies | 11 companies | 37 companies | 237 companies |
| Of which 281 have parent company management interlocks | 11 | 35 | 235 |
| Of which 11 have parent company loans | 1 | 2 | 8 |

Matsushita's shareholding—it will be seen that 83% of the complex is at or above 50% control—leaves no doubt that we are viewing subsidiaries in the real meaning of the term. While the FTC study does not break down management interlocks by the number of officers involved, it is noteworthy that only four companies of the entire complex of 285 do not have officer interlocks. Parent-company lending in the Matsushita complex is infrequent. It will be observed that only 11 of the subsidiaries are the recipients of loans from the parent company. While the FTC presents its management interlocks and lending

[6] Economic Investigative Council, *Research on Business Groupings*, 1965 and 1967 editions, Table 202.

in summarized form only, the Economic Investigative Council provides specific company information. The Council for 1964 shows a Y932 million loan ($2.5 million) from the parent company to the Matsushita Electric Association (*Kyozaikai*); it shows loans in the range of 500 thousand dollars from the parent company to Kyushu Matsushita Real Estate, to Kyushu Matsushita Electrical Industries (*Dengu*), and to the Tokyo Research Works (*Tokyo Kenkyujo*).

*Itoh and Company*: Among the leading firms of that peculiar Japanese institution, the trading company, Mitsui and Company, has the largest subsidiary complex on the basis of numbers. But it is C. Itoh and Company that has the largest, if the measure is combined capitalization. Itoh and Marubeni Iida, another trading company, are two of four successor companies carved out of the former giant, Daiken Industries, which was dissolved under the Excessive Concentration of Economic Power Law. In terms of 1964 sales among trading companies, Mitsubishi Shoji was first, Mitsui second. Marubeni Iida third, and C. Itoh fourth.[7] (In 1966 Mitsui was first and Mitsubishi second; Marubeni Iida and C. Itoh were third and fourth.)

In Itoh's complex of 119 subsidiaries, somewhat less than a third of the companies are in wholesale and retail trade, but their industrial activities range from construction to cotton spinning, chemicals, metal and machinery, electricity and gas. The FTC gives the control pattern among these 119 firms as follows:

| | Parent Company Shareholding | | |
|---|---|---|---|
| | 10-29% | 30-49% | 50% above |
| 119 companies | 37 companies | 33 companies | 49 companies |
| Of which 110 have parent company management interlocks | 36 | 28 | 46 |
| Of which 53 have parent company loans | 11 | 13 | 29 |

*Yawata Steel and Nisshin Steel*: According to the 1965 FTC study, the major with the largest subsidiary complex in terms of the combined capitalization is Yawata Steel, a company likewise the product of action under the Excessive Concentration of Economic Power Law. Under this law the steel activities of Nippon Seitetsu (frequently translated as Japan Iron Manufacturing) were split into two parts,

[7] *Ibid.*

Yawata Steel and Fuji Steel. The 1968 "intention to merge" announcement of these two companies would thus bring the two parts together again. (In the 1965 FTC study, Fuji Steel is shown with 43 subsidiaries having a combined capitalization second only to Yawata.)

The Yawata subsidiary complex does not display as high parent-company ownership as do most of the subsidiary complexes, but this is undoubtedly a function of the greater size of the capitalizations involved. The control pattern of the Yawata complex is as follows:

| | Parent Company Shareholding | | |
|---|---|---|---|
| | 10-29% | 30-49% | 50% above |
| 55 companies | 19 companies | 18 companies | 18 companies |
| Of which 48 have parent company management interlocks | 18 | 14 | 16 |
| Of which 9 have parent company loans | 2 | 3 | 4 |

According to the FTC, the largest subsidiary in the Yawata complex is Nisshin Steel, capitalized at $45 million (Y16.2 billion). Yawata's holdings of Nisshin stock amounted in 1964 to 12.4%.[8] Equity was reinforced at this time by one management interlock. The standing auditor of Yawata was a director of Nisshin.[9]

In Nisshin Steel we have a company which, between the Economic Investigative Council and the FTC, is classified as a member of a "plain" *keiretsu*, of a financial *keiretsu*, and of a capital *keiretsu*. The council treats Nisshin as part of the Sanwa Bank's plain *keiretsu*, as well as financial *keiretsu*; the FTC treats it as a member of Yawata's subsidiary complex.

The three types of groupings might be summarized as follows: the plain *keiretsu* grouping rests on the advantages stemming from being part of a conglomerate complex of majors; the financial *keiretsu* on the advantages arising from being part of a grouping, all members of which place their largest borrowing reliance on the same city bank; the capital grouping on the advantages to a parent company of having a complex of affiliated firms.

Nisshin, as a member of the plain *keiretsu* of the Sanwa Bank, is

[8] *Ibid.*, Table 202.

[9] Cf. Tokyo Stock Exchange, *Corporation Yearbook, 1963* (Tokyo Shoken Torihiki Sho, *Daiichibu Jojo Kaisha Soran, 38*).

one of some 30 majors in diverse lines of activity. Operations of member firms include oil, coal, chemicals, metals, automobiles, shipbuilding, pharmaceuticals, textiles, and construction (see Table 12-3 for the 1966 form). While there is some market-relatedness for Nisshin among this grouping, neither of the two most obviously market-related firms—Daihatsu Kogyo, the auto manufacturer and Hitachi Shipbuilding—list Nisshin among its principal suppliers.[10]

The Economic Investigative Council, in its 1965 and 1967 editions, treats Nisshin Steel not only as a member of the *keiretsu* of the Sanwa Bank[11] but as a member of the *financial keiretsu* of the Sanwa Bank. Usually financial *keiretsu* are somewhat larger in membership than plain *keiretsu.* While the financial *keiretsu* have the bank as the head, the highly conglomerate character of the groupings makes it difficult to develop a guide to member behavior. Controls are those of the dependency generated in consequence of the bank being the largest credit resource. In the case of Nisshin, the Sanwa Bank, together with its affiliated trust bank, is supplying a quarter of Nisshin's total borrowing.

While financial *keiretsu* have directing centers—the banks—the fact that the majors choose the bank and not the other way around, restricts the bank's capacity for direction. Firms do from time to time change their primary banks. Membership in a financial *keiretsu* would seem to reduce to a sort of mutual accommodation between the primary bank and major borrower. That the Bank of Japan describes the primary bank both as a promoter and follower bespeaks the ambiguity of many Japanese observers about what really is the role of the primary bank. With city banks competing to grant loans, and with the number of possibilities that exist for borrowing, a commanding role would not seem appropriate for the primary bank. Were we not talking about the majors of the economy, it would be easy to view the banks in a strong position, but the *financial keiretsu* analysis refers to the relationship between the primary bank and large borrowers.

Turning to subsidiary relations we find that the FTC in its 1965 study treats Nisshin as one of 55 firms comprising the subsidiary network of Yawata Steel, the great majority of which are market-related. Nisshin is by far the largest firm in the network. Yawata's formal con-

[10] Yamaichi Securities Co., *Corporation Yearbook, 1962* (Yamaichi Shoken, *Kabushiki Kaisha Nenkan, 37*).

[11] *Keiretsu* ownership, 10%; *keiretsu* borrowing, 25%; *keiretsu* marketing, through reliance on *keiretsu* trading company, Iwai and Company, in both purchases and sales. As noted in the preceding chapter, Nisshin, according to one of the sources cited there, has two officers, a managing director and a standing auditor, who have a Sanwa Bank background.

trols over Nisshin are not strong—in 1964 it held 12.4% of its capital with one officer interlock—yet because the subsidiary firm and parent firm are in the same market, its actual controls are undoubtedly stronger. In 1964, in the iron and steel industry, Yawata was in the top position in sales, Nisshin in seventh.[12] Statistics of production further delineate the disparity in market power. The FTC, in a study relying on 1962 data, reports that Yawata accounted for 26.6% of Japanese production of pig iron and Nisshin 1.0%, that Yawata accounted for 20.8% of ingot and Nisshin 2.3%.[13] In these circumstances it is not difficult to see that market forces would materially assist Yawata in bringing Nisshin into line. Yawata does not need an absolute majority of shareholding in Nisshin in order to have Nisshin toe its mark; the market materially assists in the task.

In the above pages we have seen how the lines of the different groupings cross and recross. Depending on the source consulted, Nisshin Steel is found to be a member of the Sanwa Bank's plain *keiretsu*, its financial *keiretsu*, and a member of Yawata Steel's capital *keiretsu*; Yawata, in turn, is regarded as a member of the Industrial Bank's financial *keiretsu*. If the controls of these groupings were effective, wouldn't it be reasonable to expect conflicts of loyalty out of such crossing? Japanese discussants of these groupings do not raise this point, which would suggest that conflicts are not a problem, and this in turn would suggest the controls are not very meaningful.

The plurality of membership for a single firm in different groupings indicates weaknesses in the controls. Nisshin is not an isolated case. Matsushita, for example, is regarded by the Economic Investigative Council (in its 1965 and 1967 editions) as both a member of the Sumitomo *keiretsu* and a member of the Industrial Bank's financial *keiretsu*. Similarly, in both editions, Kawasaki Steel is regarded as a part of the Daiichi Bank's *keiretsu* and a member of the Long-Term Credit Bank's financial *keiretsu*.

Not only is there the problem of plurality of membership, but one of changes in membership affiliation. In the preceding chapter we saw how five of the 20 majors noted changed their financial *keiretsu* classification over a five-year period, and six over a seven-year period. In Chapter 11 we noted that in a four-year period there was a 25 to 30%

[12] Economic Investigative Council, *Research on Business Groupings*, 1965 edition, Table 202. In 1964 Yawata's sales were Y272 billion, Nisshin's Y60.

[13] FTC, *Industrial Concentration in the Principal Industries* (Kosei Torihiki Iinkai Shuyo Sangyo ni okeru, *Sangyo Shuchudo*), 1964, mimeog.; "Pig," p. 83; "ingot," p. 85.

turnover in companies which the council regarded as part of the Mitsubishi, Mitsui, and Sumitomo *keiretsu*. The frequency of change reinforces my impression that the groupings are not strong. But most basic of all, controls don't match the size of the coordinating task.

However, when we turn to subsidiaries we do for the most part come upon strong clear corporate controls, but this is because the size of our units has changed. In noting firms which are a part of a company's capital *keiretsu*, we are looking for the most part at smaller-scale enterprise. And in the case of subsidiaries held with majority control or at the 30% level and above, it would be my guess there was not much turnover.

Because of the scale of the controls needed to control the majors of today's economy, particularly when groupings are conglomerate, and because of the difficulty in forging effective control centers among members ostensibly equal, it would seem doubtful that it would be possible to build conglomerate structures in the manner of the former *zaibatsu* groupings. Rather, it would appear likely that concentration in the Japanese economy will take the path of increasing the size of the majors themselves—in part, through internal growth but more significantly through merger—with controls over other businesses exercised primarily through subsidiary complexes. As has been noted, controls are less difficult in the case of subsidiaries because typically the firms are smaller; neither is there ambiguity about where policy determination lies, nor for what ends it is sought. Before taking up recent merger trends, let us note one additional type of grouping—*kombinato*—regarded by many Japanese as the wave of the future.

### *Kombinato*

The thrust of the *kombinato* concept is technological connexity. *Kombinato* refer to plants physically clustered together which are key suppliers of basic raw materials for one another. The companies to which the plants belong may or may not be related through capital, credit, management, and/or selling. These clusters are to be found primarily in the field of chemicals—petrochemicals and iron and steel chemicals.[14]

In referring to their own *kombinato*, the Japanese always speak of plural corporate undertakings. In speaking of what they call *kombinato* in the United States and in Europe, they frequently cite single

[14] These and other fields are listed in *Keiretsuka, Kombinato*, Vol. 3 of *Monopoly Capital in Present-Day Japan* (*Gendai Nippon no Dokusen Shihon*), ed. Imai Noriyoshi, Minosou Hitoshi, Miyazaki Giichi, and Nakamura Norihide, Tokyo, 1964, p. 216. In this section of the volume, Shibamura Yogo is the author.

corporate operations, the plants in a particular location of, for example, Gulf Oil, Esso, ICI, ENI (Enta Nazionale Idrocarboni), I. G. Farben.[15] Attention centers on the actual physical production, the flow of inputs resulting in many end products.

Typical of the way many Japanese observers regard these complexes is the following quotation found in the showroom of the Nippon Petrochemical Company's Center in Tokyo.

> Following the first industrial revolution in the 18th century, industry developed dramatically and living was greatly enriched. But until recently, each industry and each enterprise has gone its own way with duplication in equipment, in labor and consequent waste. In the *kombinato*-type of enterprise-organization, however, one has related enterprises using common raw materials located together so that successive stages of manufacture and by-product materials can mutually be taken advantage of. Clustered together, with factories organically related, large and small enterprise is tied into a pipeline with attendant economies. . . .[16]

To believe that *kombinato* represent an entirely new level of industrial efficiency, that outside the *kombinato* groupings there is inherently duplication and waste is to misunderstand the nature of the market mechanism. The market mechanism, while permitting entrepreneurial independence, compels—compels, that is, if the market is competitive—efficient use of resources and efficient production. A basic reason, among several, for the emphasis in classical economic theory and in the public policy of many countries concerning competitive markets, is this very matter of efficiency. Certainly there may well be efficiency in other types of market structures—oligopolistic and monopolistic—but it is the competitive market which compels efficiency, which makes efficiency "nonelective." A major reason for the emphasis in the public policy of such countries on free entry (free entry being one of the defining characteristics of a competitive market) is just this. Efficiency among existing producers is underscored when there is the opportunity for someone who sees a better way of organizing production, a better source of raw materials, a better way of handling distribution, to enter and demonstrate. To assert that industrial organization up until the emergence of *kombinato* has represented waste and inefficiency is to miss the meaning of the way in which the market mechanism functions.

[15] *Ibid.*, especially pp. 185-203.

[16] Quoted in the study published by the Japan Economic Journal, *The Direction of Industrial Regroupings* (Nihon Keizai, *Sangyo Saihensei no Doko*), Tokyo, 1963, p. 47.

The circumstance giving rise to *kombinato* complexes is not a new level of industrial efficiency, but rather the use of raw materials that cannot be transported economically and that have interrelated end uses. *Kombinato* represent a special instance of location theory. Most commodities can be economically transported; Japan's iron and steel industry is an obvious case in point. With virtually no iron ore of its own, with insufficient scrap resources, and lacking coal suitable for coking, Japan in 1965 became the world's third largest producer of steel, outdistancing even Germany, surpassed only by the United States and Russia. Japan has achieved this feat by bringing iron ore from Malaysia, Chile, Australia, Peru, India, Goa, the United States, and Canada (scrap primarily from the U.S., Australia, and India), and by bringing coal suitable for coking from the U.S., Australia, India, the U.S.S.R., and Canada.[17] If iron ore, scrap, and coal were not economic to transport, Japan would have no iron and steel industry. Earlier, Japan rose to major power industrial status on textiles. While historically Japan did grow cotton, its late 19th and 20th-century cotton textile industry did not depend on domestic cotton production but on imports from the United States, India, and Egypt.

The gaseous chemicals are an exception. It is because they are for the most part not economically transportable and because they result in interrelated end products that plants using common raw materials are grouped together. *Kombinato* do not represent efficient utilization of resources in an otherwise sea of entrepreneurial waste, nor do they represent the coming pattern of industry organization. Instead, they are the exceptional circumstance of raw materials whose costs greatly increase when transported.[18]

Table 13-3 presents Japan's petrochemical *kombinato*—in operation and under construction as of the spring of 1968.[19] Table 13-3 indicates

[17] For iron ore and scrap steel, the specific country proportions of supply will be found in Foreign Capital Research Society, *Japanese Industry*, Tokyo, 1965, p. 49.

[18] As will be seen in Table 13-3 in instances where companies are parenthesized, there is occasional transportation, but this is clearly the exception. Transportation is by pipeline and special ships.

[19] In a 1964 study, Professor Shibamura reported the following *kombinato* resting on coal tar chemicals—in operation "O", under construction "C", and planned "P":

| *Location* | *Status* | *Participating Companies* |
|---|---|---|
| *Fuji Seitetsu Group* | | |
| Muroran | O | Fuji Steel, Muroran Steel Chemical, Toyo Koatsu Industries |

both *keiretsu* influence on the composition of the participating firms (whether the name of the *kombinato* reflects *keiretsu* affiliation or not), as well as a disregard for *keiretsu* lines. The two Mitsui Petrochemical complexes are heavily Mitsui. The Osaka Petrochemical complex, on the other hand, divides largely between Mitsui interests and Sanwa Bank *keiretsu* companies. In the Tonen Petrochemical *kombinato* one sees extensive crossing of lines. Tonen Petrochemical, a 100% subsidiary of Toa Nenryo (but a company in which, as observed in the preceding chapter, Esso and Mobil Oil each hold 25% of the shares) and Showa Denko are both members of the Fuji Bank *keiretsu*. Nitto Unicar represents a joint venture between Union Carbide and Nitto Chemical, a subsidiary of Mitsubishi Rayon. Asahi Chemical Industries is a member of the Sumitomo *keiretsu* (not to be confused with Asahi Electro Chemical of the Daiichi line). Thus, without noting all of the members of this *kombinato*, one has companies belonging to the Fuji Bank *keiretsu*, the Mitsubishi *keiretsu*, and the Sumitomo *keiretsu*, not to mention the foreign interests represented.

In Table 13-3 it will be observed that one and the same company may be a member of more than one *kombinato*. Thus it will be seen that the Nippon Petrochemical *kombinato* and the Tonen Petrochemical *kombinato*, both located at Kawasaki, share the following firms in common—Nippon Olefin, Showa Denko, Asahi Chemical Industries, Japanese Geon, and Asahi Dow (a joint venture between Asahi Chemical Industries and Dow Chemical). In the table from which Table 13-3 is taken, companies common to the two complexes are listed as producing the same products in the two complexes. Thus, for example, Nippon Olefin is producing "medium, low-pressure polyethylene"

| | | |
|---|---|---|
| Hirohata | O | Fuji Steel, Steel Chemicals |
| *Nippon Kokan Group* | | |
| Kawasaki | O | Nippon Kokan, Kokan Chemicals (now Olefin) |
| *Kawasaski Steel Group* | | |
| Chiba | P | Kawasaki Steel, Steel Chemical |
| *Yawata Steel Group* | | |
| Tobata | C | Yawata Steel, Yawata Chemicals, Kyushu Chemical, Shin Nippon Chisso (now Chisso) |
| *Mitsubishi Group* | | |
| Onahama, Fukushima | O | Nippon Suiso, Mitsubishi Metal Mining, Sakai Chemical |

Source: *Keiretsuka, Kombinato*, Vol. 3 in *Monopoly Capital in Present-Day Japan* (*Gendai Nippon no Dokusen Shihon*), ed. Imai Noriyoshi, Misonou Hitoshi, Miyazaki Giichi, and Nakamura Norihide, Tokyo, 1964, p. 217.

Table 13-3: JAPAN'S PETROCHEMICAL *KOMBINATO* — IN OPERATION AND PLANNED, 1968

(Within each complex, the first company listed, the oil company, is the producer or importer of the naphtha; companies not physically a part of the *kombinato* are listed in parenthesis.)

*Mitsui Petrochemical*

| | |
|---|---|
| Iwakuni | Koa Oil, Mitsui Petrochemical,[1] Mitsui Polychemical,[2] Mitsui Chemical |
| Chiba | Kyokuto Oil;[3] Mitsui Petrochemical, Mitsui Polychemical, Mitsui Conoco, Japan Synthetic Rubber |

*Mitsubishi Petrochemical*

| | |
|---|---|
| Yokkaichi | Showa Yokkaichi Oil;[4] Mitsubishi Petrochemical,[5] Mitsubishi Monsanto, Mitsubishi Chemical Ind., Japan Synthetic Rubber, Kurare Oil |
| Kashima | Kashima Oil; Mitsubishi Petrochemical, Kanegafuchi Chemical, Kashima Vinyl Chloride |

*Sumitomo Chemical — Oe, near Niihama*

(Idemitsu Kosan), (Nippon Mining); Sumitomo Chemical, Atlantic Oil

*Sumitomo Chiba Chemical*[6] *— Chiba*

Idemitsu Kosan, Fuji Oil; Sumitomo Chiba Chemical,[7] Nippon Polyvinyl Chloride Center, Japan Synthetic Rubber

*Nippon Petrochemicals — Kawasaki*

Nippon Petroleum Refining;[8] Nippon Petrochemicals,[8] Furukawa Chemical, Nippon Olefin, Japan Catalytic Chemical, Nippon Polystyrene, Asahi Dow, Showa Denko (Asahi Electro Chemical), (Nippon Soda), Asahi Chemical Ind., Japanese Geon,[9] Nisseki Detergent, Toyo Rayon

*Tonen Petrochemical* — Kawasaki

Toa Nenryo Kogyo; Tonen Petrochemical,[10] Nitto Unicar,[11] Asahi Dow, Nippon Olefin, Central Chemical, (Toagosei Chemical), Showa Denko, (Mitsui Chemical), Nitto Chemical Ind., Asahi Chemical Ind., Japanese Geon, Nippon Butyl[12]

*Maruzen Petrochemical* — Chiba

Maruzen Oil; Maruzen Petrochemical,[13] Ube Ind., Nissan Petrochemical, Nisso Yuka, Denki Kagaku, Denko Petrochemical, Chisso Petrochemical, Japan Synthetic Rubber, Nissan Conoco

*Daikyowa Petrochemical* — Yokkaichi

Daikyowa Petrochemical;[14] Kyowa Petrochemical, Japan Synthetic Rubber

*Osaka Petrochemical*[15] — Sakai

General Oil Refining, Kansai Oil; Kansai Petrochemical, Toyo Koatsu, Ube Ind., (Kanegafuchi Chemical), Shin-etsu Chemical, Nichibo

*Kasei Mizushima* — Mizushima

Mitsubishi Oil; Kasei Mizushima,[16]. Mizushima Yuki, Mizushima Gosei, Asahi Dow, Mitsubishi Oil

*Asahi Chemical Ind.*[17] — Mizushima

Nippon Mining; Asahi Chemical Ind., Asahi Dow, Nissan Chemical Chisso

*Idemitsu Petrochemical* — Tokuyama

Idemitsu Kosan; Idemitsu Petrochemical, Nippon Petrochemical, Tokuyama Petrochemical, Shunan Petrochemical, Toyo Soda, Sun Arrow, Japanese Geon, Teikoku Yuka

*Tsurusaki Petrochemical*[18] — Oita

Kyushu Sekiyu; Tsurusaki Petrochemical, Nippon Polychemical, Nippon Olefin, Showa Denko, Ajinomoto

[1] A company recently established through the joint efforts of several of the companies of the Mitsui *keiretsu*, illustrates high cross-ownership. In 1966, 66.8% of its shares were held by members of the *keiretsu*. Toyo Rayon is by far the largest shareholder, with the Mitsui Bank, Toyo Koatsu, and Mitsui and Company other large shareholders. (EIC)

[2] A joint venture between Mitsui Petrochemical and DuPont.

[3] A joint venture between a number of Mitsui companies headed by Mitsui and Company and Mobil Oil.

[4]Cf. Figure 13-1 below for the corporate ties of Showa Yokkaichi Oil.

[5]A company recently established through the joint efforts of several of the companies of the Mitsubishi *keiretsu* illustrates high cross-ownership. In 1966, 69.9% of its shares were held by members of the *keiretsu*. The three highest shareholders are Mitsubishi Chemical, Asahi Glass, Mitsubishi Rayon, with the Bank, the Tokyo Marine Insurance, and Meiji Life Insurance Company likewise with sizeable shares. (EIC)

[6]As presented by the *Oriental Economist* there are two additional members of the *Kombinato* — Aldehyde, and Kao Ethyle. Because these do not appear to be identifying company names, they have not been included in the table.

[7]A subsidiary of Sumitomo Chemical.

[8]Subsidiaries of Nippon Petroleum.

[9]B. F. Goodrich holds 32.6% of the shares of Japanese Geon and Furukawa Denko, Yokohama Rubber and the Daiichi Bank, all of the Daiichi Bank *keiretsu*, hold 25%.

[10]A 100% subsidiary of Toa Nenryo, of which Esso Standard and Mobile Oil each hold 25%. Toa Nenryo is a member of the Fuji Bank *keiretsu*.

[11]A joint venture of Nitto Chemical Ind. and Union Carbide. Nitto Chemical Ind. is a subsidiary of Mitsubishi Rayon.

[12]Jointly established by Esso Standard and Japan Synthetic Rubber.

[13]An affiliate of Maruzen Oil. (EIC)

[14]A subsidiary of Kyowa Chemical Ind. (EIC)

[15]The *Oriental Economist* does not show the Osaka Petrochemical Company as a participant in its own *kombinato*, which would seem an omission. It has accordingly been added. The *Oriental Economist* reports that the *kombinato* was established in February 1965 as a joint undertaking

by Mitsui Chemical, 25%, Toyo Koatsu, 25%, and Kansai Petrochemical 50%. Kansai Petrochemical is the product of equal capital subscriptions by Maruzen Oil, Hitachi Shipbuilding, Ube Ind., Osaka Soda, Chisso, Sekisui Chemicals, Toyo Rubber, Teijin, Nichimen, and Nippon Express.

[16]It is not clear from the *Oriental Economist* presentation, but Kasei Mizushima appears to be Mitsubishi Kasei at Mizushima.

[17]It is presumed that the proper company entry is Asahi Chemical Ind. Textually, the *Oriental Economist* makes many references to Asahi Chemical Ind. and employs it in the table from which this table has been constructed. In another table, however (p. 36), it lists a quite different company but with the confusingly similar name, Asahi Electro-Chemical. Two entries with respect to member companies are not clear: "Acetaldehyde" and a "new firm jointly financed by Japanese Geon and others."

[18]The *Oriental Economist* does not list Tsurusaki Petrochemical as a participant in its own *kombinato*, which would seem an omission. It has been accordingly added. It lists a new firm for the production of acetaldehyde, and confusingly lists for the producer of vinyl acetate, "Showa Denko-Ajinomoto."

Sources: "Changing Pattern of Petrochemical Ind.," *Oriental Economist*, April 1968, pp. 35-41. The source does not clearly distinguish between *kombinato* already in operation and those under construction. Where information on group affiliation has been taken from the Economic Investigative Council, *Research on Business Groupings*, 1967, in these notes it is indicated by "EIC" in parentheses. Otherwise it is taken from the *Oriental Economist* article.

at the Nippon Petrochemical and Tonen Petrochemical complexes. In Table 13-3 it will be noted that Japanese Synthetic Rubber is a participant in the Mitsui Chiba complex, in the Sumitomo Chiba Chemical complex, in the Mitsubishi Yokkaichi complex, in the Daikyowa Petrochemical complex, and in the Maruzen Petrochemical complex.

The location of these petrochemical complexes (and the other

JAPAN
Kashima
Kombinato Cities
Sapporo
Reference Cities
Sapporo
Sea of Japan
Sendai
Kashima
Tokyo
Kawasaki
Chiba
Yokohama
Nagoya
Yokkaichi
Kobe
Osaka
Sakai
Mizushima
Tokuyama
Iwakuni
Kitakyushu
Niihama
Oita
Tsurusaki
gasaki
Pacific Ocean
0
100
200
Miles

*kombinato* referred to in footnote 19) are shown on the accompanying map. As is evident from Table 13-3, the petrochemical *kombinato* are both clustered together and widely spread. There are three complexes at Chiba—a Mitsui complex, the Sumitomo Chiba Chemical complex, and the Maruzen complex. Both Nippon Petrochemical and Tonen Petrochemical are located at Kawasaki. There are two complexes at Yokkaichi—a Mitsubishi Petrochemical complex and the Daikyowa Petrochemical complex. There are two at Mizushima—Kasei Mizushima and Asahi Chemical Industries, a member of the Sumitomo *keiretsu*. The remainder of these *kombinato* are elsewhere along the shores of the Inland Sea. Inasmuch as Japan lacks petroleum resources to match the needs of today's economy, the raw material resources for these *kombinato*—petroleum or the naphtha derivative—depend on imports. Accordingly, the *kombinato* are located with a view to easy access to such imports.

Let us look in some detail at two of the *kombinato* in order to get a better understanding of this type of enterprise organization. For this purpose the Nippon Petrochemical complex at Kawasaki and the Mitsubishi complex at Yokkaichi have been selected.

NIPPON PETROCHEMICAL *kombinato*: The Nippon Petrochemical Co. (Nippon Sekiyukagaku), the pivotal firm in the complex which bears its name, was established in 1955 as a 100% subsidiary of Nippon Petroleum, a very old firm dating from the middle Meiji years.[20] Nippon Petroleum, a major in the oil industry, has a highly fractured ownership pattern, with Sumitomo, Mitsubishi, Fuji Bank, and Mitsui affiliates among its top shareholders. The Economic Investigative Council regards it as part of the Fuji Bank financial *keiretsu*, but in fact borrowings from the Fuji line and the Mitsui line are almost identical, and borrowings from the Daiichi Bank are not far behind.[21]

Membership in the Nippon Petrochemical *kombinato* illustrates much crossing of *keiretsu* lines. Different sources are not wholly consonant as to the membership,[22] but using the one given in Table

[20] *Ibid.*, pp. 232-33.

[21] For ownership see *Research on Business Groupings*, (1967), Table 221 series, pp. 140-41; for credit dependency, *ibid.*, Table 204 series and Table 222 series, p. 58 and p. 194, respectively.

[22] For example, in the earlier material on this complex there is not full identity of member firms in Professor Shibamura's listings in *Keiretsuka, Kombinato*, pp. 217, 236. There are sizable differences between his listings and the listing prepared by Professors Sugioka and Nagae in *Forms of Monopoly* (*Dokusen Keitai*), Vol. 1 of the same series (1964), p. 78. The volumes are only a month apart in publication date, so that publication data cannot serve as explanation. There are differences, understandably, because of time between these and the listings employed by the *Oriental Economist*.

13-3 we will find—in addition to subsidiaries of Nippon Petroleum (Fuji Bank financial *keiretsu*) and Nippon Olefin also of the same financial line (Nippon Olefin represents a merger of Kokan Chemical, a subsidiary of Nippon Kokan, and Showa Petrochemical, a subsidiary of Showa Denko)—firms belonging to other groups: Asahi Chemical Industries of the Sumitomo *keiretsu* and it subsidiaries, and Japanese Geon of the Daiichi *keiretsu*, together with Furukawa Chemical, a subsidiary of Furukawa Electric Industries, also of the Daiichi line.

Apparently the composition of the complex stems in part from a Ministry of International Trade and Industry decision. Even earlier than Nippon Petrochemical's planned complex at Kawasaki, it would seem that Furukawa Electric Industries, Asahi Electro-Chemical (Denka), Japanese Geon, Nippon Soda, and Tokyo Gas planned a complex there. However, MITI did not give approval to their scheme, so the group decided to get the desired ethylene from the Nippon Petrochemical complex.[23]

Illustrative of the way in which a *kombinato* operates was the initial agreement which, according to Prof. Shibamura, provided that Nippon Petrochemical would supply ethylene to Showa Petrochemical (now in merged form, Nippon Olefin) and to Nippon Soda; propylene to Asahi Electro-Chemical; and butadiene to Japanese Geon. Further, in the plan it was agreed that Showa Petrochemical (now Olefin) would provide polyethylene to Asahi Chemical Industry. It was understood that during changes in its factory, Showa Denko would acquire naphtha from the Toa Nenryo group, also located in Kawasaki. In this way, these several companies began their *kombinato* operation.[24] Table 13-4 lists products and makers in the Nippon Petrochemical complex at Kawasaki.

THE MITSUBISHI *kombinato*: Although again, different sources do not fully agree on member companies,[25] the pivotal firms in this complex are Showa Yokkaichi Oil, a subsidiary of Showa Oil, and Mitsubishi Petrochemical, a subsidiary of Mitsubishi Chemical Industries, with numerous other Mitsubishi companies holders of its stock and the Shell Oil Company not very far in the background. In the

[23] According to Shibamura's account, cf. *Keiretsuka, Kombinato*, p. 233. One finds the same strong hand of MITI reported in current developments; cf. "Changing Pattern of Petrochemical Industry," *Oriental Economist*, April 1968, pp. 35-41.

[24] *Keiretsuka*, p. 233.

[25] As in the case of the Nippon Petrochemical *kombinato*, one finds discrepancies in member companies between the listing presented by Prof. Shibamura, *Keiretsuka, Kombinato*, p. 217, and the listing presented by Professors Sugioka and Nagae in *Forms of Monopoly*, p. 78, as well as between these sources and the later *Oriental Economist* source.

Table 13-4: PRODUCTS AND MAKERS IN THE NIPPON PETROCHEMICAL *KOMBINATO*

(Two sources have been combined to produce this table. Asterisk indicates source "one." Companies from source "two" cited within parentheses are not physically a part of the *kombinato*. Source "one" does not so distinguish.)

| Product | Maker |
|---|---|
| I *Ethylene and derivatives* | |
| ethylene* | Nippon Petrochemicals |
| high-pressure polyethylene | Nippon Petrochemicals |
| medium low-pressure polyethylene | Furukawa Chemical |
| | Nippon Olefin |
| ethylene oxide | Japan Catalytic Chemical |
| styrene monomer | Nippon Polystyrene |
| | Asahi Dow |
| II *Propylene and derivatives* | |
| propylene* | Nippon Petrochemical |
| isopropyl alcohol* | Nippon Petrochemical |
| acetone | Nippon Petrochemical |
| propylene oxide | Showa Denko |
| | (Asahi Electro-Chemical) |
| | (Nippon Soda) |
| acrylonitrile | Asahi Chemical Industries |
| | Showa Denko |
| III *Butylenes and derivatives* | |
| butadiene* | Nippon Petrochemical |
| polybutadiene | Asahi Chemical Industries |
| polybutene* | Furakawa Chemical |
| styrene butadiene rubber | Japanese Geon |
| | Asahi Dow |
| butylene rubber | Nippon Petrochemical |
| IV *Aromatics and derivatives* | |
| benezene* | Nippon Petrochemical |
| toluene* | Nippon Petrochemical |
| xylene* | Nippon Petrochemical |
| paraxylene | Toyo Rayon |
| alkylbenzen | Nisseki Detergent |
| cyclohexane | Toyo Rayon |

Sources and notes: Entries indicated with an asterisk have been taken from *Keiretsuka, Kombinato* (which is volume 3 of *Monopoly Capital in Present-Day Japan* (*Gendai Nippon no Dokusen Shihon*), edited by Imai Noriyoshi, Misonou Hitoshi, Miyazaki Giichi, and Nakamura Norihide, Tokyo, 1964, p. 236. Shibamura Yogo is the author of the section from which these entries have been taken. Entries without an asterisk have been taken from "Changing Pattern of Petrochemical Industry," *Oriental Economist*, April 1968, pp. 38-39. I am indebted to Mr. Daniel F. McCarthy of Washington, D.C., for grouping the product entries according to their product-relatedness.

1965 edition the Economic Investigative Council regards Showa Oil, the parent company, as a part of the Daiichi Bank's financial *keiretsu* on the basis of 11% of its borrowings from this source (and 1.6% stockholding), but what would seem considerably more significant is that the Anglo-Saxon Petroleum Co. of London holds 50% of its stock and provides some 30% of its loans.[26] (In the 1967 edition of the Economic Investigative Council's report, Showa Oil is shown as part of the Long-Term Credit Bank's financial *keiretsu* on the basis of 10.8% of its borrowings from this source and 0.5% stockholding. Anglo-Saxon Petroleum's shareholdings remain at 50%, though borrowing from this source has been reduced to about 20%.)

Apparently Mitsubishi's interest in the Yokkaichi site began in 1950 when, in collaboration with Monsanto Chemical, Mitsubishi Chemical Industries (then called Nippon Chemical Industries, one of three companies into which Mitsubishi Chemical Industries was split under the Enterprise Reorganization Law—the other two being Asahi Glass and Mitsubishi Rayon) established a vinyl factory there.[27] Mitsubishi Chemical Industries attempted to move into the petrochemical field by relying on Shell for certain critical imports, but was blocked in this by the government's policy on imports of raw material. Following this, Shell and Mitsubishi jointly attempted to acquire title to the former Navy fuel works at Yokkaichi, but again were not successful. The government decided to dispose of the plant to Showa Oil.[28] As in an earlier era, the disposal of government property has had ramifying repercussions. Seemingly, under the heading of "if you can't beat them, join them," Mitsubishi, Shell and Showa Oil are today intricately tied together, as will be seen in Figure 13-1.

Whether or not acquisition of the Navy installation made the critical difference, Showa Yokkaichi Oil in 1962 was the nation's leading producer of naphtha with 21.5% of total output.[29] It was not the leading seller, however; in fact it was not a seller at all, for reputedly Showa Yokkaichi Oil is not permitted to make sales. Sales are to be handled by the parent company.[30] That all Showa Yokkaichi's sales are made through the parent company is the sort of corporate arrangement which one would expect where controls are real.

[26] For ownership information see Economic Investigative Council, *Research on Business Groupings* (1967), Table 221 series, pp. 140-41; for information on loans, *ibid.*, Table 222 series, p. 194.

[27] According to information presented by Professor Shibamura, *Keiretsuka, Kombinato*, pp. 227-28. This whole discussion rests on Professor Shibamura's presentation.

[25] *Ibid.*, p. 228.

[29] FTC, *Industrial Concentration*, pp. 77-78.

[30] Shibamura, *Keiretsuka, Kombinato*, p. 229.

Figure 13-1: CORPORATE TIES IN THE MITUSBISHI *KOMBINATO* AT YOKKAICHI approximately 1963
(solid connecting line: shareholding; dashed connecting line: lending)

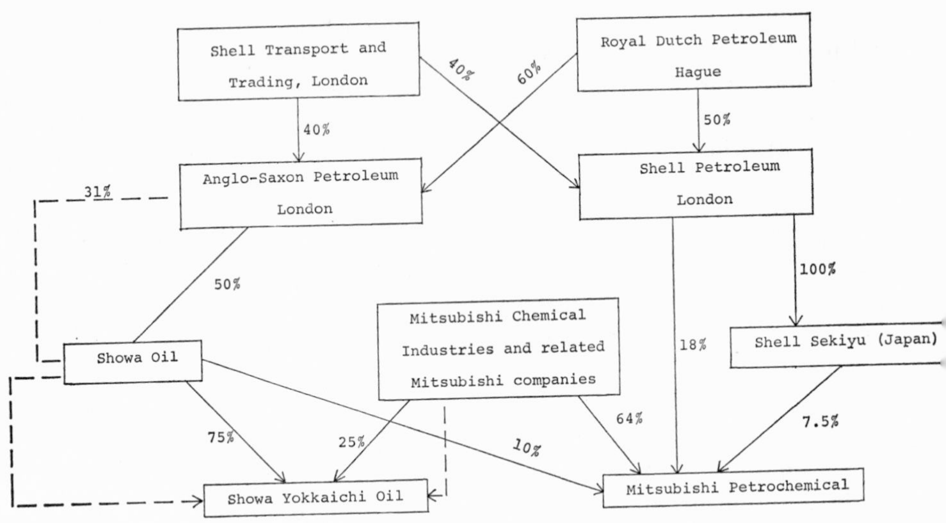


Source and notes: *Keiretsuka, Kombinato*, Vol. 3 of *Monopoly Capital in Present-Day Japan*, ed. Ima Noriyoshi et al., p. 229. I have changed the order of the lower part of the layout — "Mitsubishi group" to "Mitsubishi Chemical Industries and related Mitsubishi companies" — inasmuch as Mitsubis Petrochemicals is a subsidiary of Mitsubishi Chemical Industries. I have corrected an apparent er in double-listing Mitsubishi share ownership in Showa Yokkaichi Oil. The source from which this figure is taken shows both Mitsubishi Petrochemical and the "Mitsubishi group," with 25% ownership in Shows Yokkaichi Oil. Inasmuch as the accompanying text (p. 229) reports Showa Oil holding 75% of Showa Yokkaichi's stock (which has been added to Figure 13-1), it is clearly impossible for bot Mitsubishi Petrochemical and the Mitsubishi grouping each to have 25%. I am *guessing* that it is "Mitsubishi Chemical Industries and related Mitsubishi companies," which have the 25% and have so listed this in Figure 13-1. The source shows Showa Yokkaichi Oil lending to Showa Oil. Not only does this seem improbable, but the Economic Investigative Council *Research on Business Groupings*, 1965, (p. 279) shows Showa Oil with a $24 million (Y8,655.5) loan to Showa Yokkaichi Oil. I have accordingly changed the direction of the arrow. The source does not show the scale of lending from Anglo-Saxon Petroleum to Showa Oil. I have added this on the basis of information in the Economic Investigative Council (p. 184).

It might be said that *kombinato* are at once a respecter and not a respecter of the lines of "plain" *keiretsu* and financial *keiretsu*, and that they do include capital *keiretsu*, parent-subsidiary, relationships. Membership in particular *kombinato* both reflects affiliation based on plain *keiretsu* and financial *keiretsu*, and shows a fine disregard for their boundaries. A study of the *keiretsu* influence on these groupings once again suggests that *keiretsu* influence is more perceptible when members are joining together to finance the new than in direction of ongoing operations of member companies.

I would expect to see *kombinato* develop wherever mutually needed raw materials were uneconomic to transport. But it would seem unlikely that such groupings would spread to other situations.

# 14.

## Concentration Without Monopoly

NEITHER before nor after World War II were observers able to agree on the nature of concentration in the Japanese economy. Economists such as G. C. Allen argue that Japan's economy was and is highly competitive. Professor Allen said of the prewar economy: "At first sight it seems perhaps surprising that competitive conditions should flourish in a country where the large scale trades are dominated by a few groups and where the State has had historically a large role; yet if the true nature of Japan's political and economic system is appreciated the apparent inconsistency disappears."[1] In 1965 he observed, ". . . Japan today possesses one of the most highly competitive economies in the world. This characteristic is revealed most obviously in the conduct of small and medium-sized firms in manufacturing industry and distribution, but it is also present among large-scale enterprises. Indeed, the fierce rivalry among oligopolists has undoubtedly been responsible for much of the breathless innovation and lavish investment in new equipment during the last few years."[2]

During the years 1945-48, when the U.S. government's position was under the influence of the International Business Practices Branch, Commodities Division, of the Department of State and the State-War Mission on Japanese Combines, it was the view of the United States that Japan's prewar economy had been very highly concentrated. The State-War Mission began Part I of its report: "Something has been seriously wrong with the social system of Japan. . . . Doubtless no single condition is responsible for these peculiarities. The excessive concentration of economic power in Japan is, however, one of the more important factors."[3]

General MacArthur expressed this viewpoint when he stated:

> In any evaluation of the economic potential here in Japan it must be understood that tearing down the traditional pyramid of eco-

[1] G. C. Allen, in E. B. Schumpeter, ed., *The Industrialization of Japan and Manchukuo*, New York, 1940, p. 682.

[2] G. C. Allen, *Japan's Economic Expansion*, London, 1965, p. 250.

[3] State-War Mission on Japanese Combines, *Report*, Part I, March 1946, p. vii.

nomic power which has given only a few families direct or indirect control over all commerce and industry, all raw materials, all transportation, internal and external, and all coal and other power sources, is the first essential step to the establishment here of an economic system based upon free, competitive enterprise which Japan has never before known.[4]

On the other hand, beginning in the spring of 1948, it was much as if the U.S. government had decided that Japan's economy did not show excessive concentration after all. Naturally the reversal was phrased in terms of having already accomplished deconcentration, but those who reversed official thinking, in off-the-record remarks indicated their belief in the lack of wisdom of the whole of what had been American and Allied policy. While, as we saw in earlier chapters, the reversal was emotional, probably the root of the difference in economic terms came down to whether conglomerate activities pose a threat to competitive enterprise, whether concentration can exist in other than monopoly terms. Members of the Deconcentration Review Board could see no threat from conglomerate activities of single firms, for as they wrote MacArthur in their "four points"—". . . the mere possession of non-related lines of business is not in itself sufficient . . . to establish that a company is an excessive concentration. . . ." and one can imagine that the members may well have felt the same way about the holding companies that directed conglomerate combine operations. It would be fair to say of the board that monopoly and monopoly alone, in their view, posed a threat to competitive enterprise. For the board, monopoly consisted of market positions of more than 70% of output.[5]

In a sense, Eugene Rotwein agrees with the point of view that there cannot be concentration without market concentration, for he has based his findings of present-day concentration in the economy on concentration ratios. Moving from concentration ratios to concentration in the economy, he writes,

The evidence, as seen, does not support the view that Japanese markets are generally highly concentrated. These findings cannot be compared directly with those of studies for the United States, owing to various differences. But even with the incomparabilities removed it is unlikely, conservatively speaking, that the results would

[4] General MacArthur's letter to Senator MacMahon of January 1948, as quoted in C. M. Hamm monograph, "Deconcentration of Economic Power," dated August 9, 1950, World War II Records Division, Suitland, Md., p. 36.
[5] *Ibid.*, p. 69.

> reveal a substantially higher level of concentration in Japan than in the United States. In Japan the overall degree of concentration may indeed be lower.[6]

I would argue, however, that while market concentration ratios in the capital-intensive sector of Japan's economy and the U.S. may not look much different, they do not tell the whole story of concentration in an economy. If one turns to prewar concentration ratios, the patterns would not be substantially different between the two countries, and yet concentration *was* vastly different. This is because, unlike the pattern known in Europe and the United States, Japanese big business did not seek a limited number of high-occupancy positions, but rather a wide range of oligopolistic ones. The greatest of the combines held oligopoly positions in mining, manufacturing, finance, and commerce. It is an intriguing question why Japanese business groups did not seek to move from their oligopoly positions to monopoly. As suggested in Chapter 1, it may be that the returns from "cordial oligopoly" were as handsome as monopoly profits would have been. In any event, there appeared to be little incentive to try to get out of a circumstance, which made the oligopolists the same oligopolists in markets running the gamut of the capital-intensive sector of the economy. With positions varying among themselves in the different markets from strength to weakness, Oligopolist A did not challenge Oligopolist B in markets of A's strength because it faced B in markets where B was stronger.

G. C. Allen does interpret Japan's conglomerate operating companies (and presumably formerly its conglomerate combines) as the result of lack of specialization which is likely to disappear as Japan becomes more heavily engaged in world trade:

> [that] the degree of concentration is usually lower in Japan than in the United States or the United Kingdom . . . may be explained . . . by the highly diversified character of Japan's great industrial groups, in other words, by a lack of specialization among enterprises. It may be expected that as Japan strives to raise her scales of production to match those of her competitors, her concentration ratios will increase.[7]

Apart from whether market concentration in the Japanese economy, as contrasted to market concentration in the United States or the United Kingdom, is lower, Allen may be taking a very Western point of view.

[6] Eugene Rotwein, "Economic Concentration and Monopoly in Japan," *Journal of Political Economy*, Vol. LXXII, No. 3, June 1964, pp. 275-76.

[7] Allen, *Japan's Economic Expansion*, pp. 193-94.

If one is engaging in speculation, it might with equal plausibility be imagined that business in the United States and Great Britain is becoming more like Japan's, that is, increasingly conglomerate. Certainly there are considerable indications of this in the American economy.[8]

The widespread confusion over the circumstance of modest concentration positions within markets and exceptional concentration in the Japanese economy has been augmented by the Japanese practice of referring to the *zaibatsu* as representing "monopoly capital." While the *zaibatsu* may have represented "monopoly capital" in Japanese Marxist usage which has long since become general Japanese usage, the *zaibatsu* clearly did not represent monopoly in a market sense. Accordingly, to use concentration ratios for the measure of concentration in an economy where the *zaibatsu* achieved concentration through a series of oligopoly positions and where today's majors continue in conglomerate form, is to use as indicator that which is not indicative.

To understand concentration in the capital-intensive sector of the Japanese economy one needs far more than market concentration data. One needs to know the number of markets in which the same major appears, the extent to which subsidiaries enhance market positions, the relations between the majors in the same market, and the relationship between the majors in the different markets. Further, one should know the rigidity/fluidity of positions within the markets and the extent of cartelization. Also, in an economy in which, while it is private enterprise, the government plays an extraordinary role, one needs a knowledge of how pressure is effectively exerted on the government.

Because Japan's economy was and is a dualistic one, findings are easily misleading when the "divisor for concentration ratios" is all enterprise rather than that of the capital-intensive sector. In speaking of concentration in the Japanese economy, Allen points out that competition is the hallmark of medium and small-scale enterprise. Of course it is, but when one is talking about concentration one is talking about the capital-intensive sector. Japan's national income is generated in high-concentration markets (which he defines as the top four producers accounting for 50% of domestic output).[9] But is it meaningful to include agriculture and the small-scale trades when describing Japanese concentration? It may be that spokesmen on both sides of

[8] Cf. the testimony at the Hearings of the U.S. Senate Antitrust and Monopoly Subcommittee, 88th Cong., 2nd Sess., *Economic Concentration*, esp. testimony of Corwin D. Edwards, pp. 36-56; Walter Adams, pp. 248-62; John M. Blair, p. 85.

[9] Rotwein, "Economic Concentration," p. 264.

the discussion of concentration in Japan have erred: that those who have emphasized concentration have failed each time to use the phrase, "in the capital-intensive sector of the economy"; that those who talk about the medium and small-scale trades fail to point out the gulf that typically separates these entrepreneurs from—in the words of former Prime Minister Yoshida—"those who built Japan."

*Market Structure*

But let us begin a study of concentration by noting market patterns both before and after World War II. While they are by no means the single indicator of concentration which many writers would make of them, they obviously are an element. Table 14-1 presents for selected markets the proportion of domestic output accounted for by the top firm, top-three firms, and top-five firms for three periods: 1937, the year of the outbreak of the "China Incident" (with indicated exceptions); 1949, which represented the virtual completion of the reform phase of the Occupation; and 1962, for the most recent data. The next three tables give for these three periods essentially the same information as Table 14-1, but the markets are rearranged by descending orders of concentration for the top firm, top-three firms, and top five. However, before we can meaningfully discuss these ratios, a few observations are in order, for, by definition, concentration ratios are no better than the markets from which they come.

Japanese concentration ratios are not presented in terms of uniform definitions of markets such as results from using (with adjustments) the Standard Industrial Classification, with its two, three, four, five, and seven-digit definitions.[10] Accordingly, out of the hundreds of markets that go to make up the Japanese economy, it has not been easy to decide which to include in a selective study, and Japan's dualistic economy has increased the difficulty. Basic markets such as principal foodstuffs and principal textiles, major energy sources, the principal metal, principal chemicals, the leading manufactured items of the economy, transportation, communication, finance, and foreign trade have seemed indicated, but how to select

[10] The digit definitions are illustrated as follows:

| | |
|---|---|
| two digit—major industrial group | (e.g., food and kindred products) |
| three digit—industry group | (meat products) |
| four digit—industry | (meat packing) |
| five digit—product class | (fresh beef) |
| seven digit—product | (whole carcass beef) |

Cf. Bureau of the Census, *Concentration Ratios in Manufacturing Industries, 1958*, a report prepared for the United States Senate Subcommittee on Antitrust and Monopoly, 87th Cong., 2nd Sess., Washington, D.C., 1962, p. 2.

among them, how to define, and what of additional markets? From the essentially 50 markets presented in Tables 14-1 through 14-4, it will be seen that we have a moderately representative sample of the capital-intensive sector of the economy, but clearly there could be many changes and the samples would still be representative.

Part of the problem of representative selection that Table 14-1 reveals is the time period it spans—25 years. Given the dramatic changes the Japanese economy has undergone in this period, it is especially difficult to arrive at a representative sample of manufactured items. If one were to compile a sample for 1937, the sample would need to be weighted by defense items. If for the two postwar periods defense items were virtually zero in 1949 and still exceptionally low in 1962, there would need to be a different range of manufactured items. For in this period the Japanese economy has gone from specializing in light industry to heavy industry and chemicals. Also, consumer products have changed radically.

I am calling attention to this matter of the selection of markets because it is easy to disregard their representativeness and to argue as if one really had a good picture of the economy from whatever concentration ratios he might be working. But just because the figures happen to be the only statistics available does not make them representative.

In its successive reports on concentration, the Fair Trade Commission, on which one relies in this area, has expanded its market coverage. In its first report in 1951 it presented 50 markets; in its last report, released in 1964 (data for 1962), there were 170 markets. This increase, however, cannot be attributed entirely to the inclusion of hitherto uncovered material. In part, it is a matter of redefinition. Although the 1964 study is more comprehensive than the original 1951 report, the trend has been to define markets in narrower terms.

How a market is defined bears greatly on what one finds in the way of concentration ratios. If the market is "automobiles," the findings will be different than if, as it was in the FTC's recent (1964) study, the market is broken into three markets—"ordinary cars" (which includes trucks), "small, four-wheeled cars," and "light, four-wheeled cars"—with buses, three-wheeled cars, and motorcycles seemingly omitted. In general, the broader the market the lower the concentration figures. But it is not easy to decide what constitutes the best definition. And, of course, it is important to keep a common standard of inclusiveness; otherwise, one is attempting to gain an impression from items not fully comparable. The original FTC study in 1951 demonstrated comparability of market definition, which is not uniformly true of more recent

Table 14-1: POSITION OF THE TOP FIRM, TOP THREE FIRMS AND TOP FIVE FIRMS IN SELECTED MARKETS, 1937, 1949, 1962

market position in percent

(where 100% of production has been attained before size grouping in question, 100% appears in parentheses)

| | | 1937 | | | 1949 | | | 1962 | | |
|---|---|---|---|---|---|---|---|---|---|---|
| | | Top 1 | Top 3 | Top 5 | Top 1 | Top 3 | Top 5 | Top 1 | Top 3 | Top 5 |
| coal | | 15 | 35 | 44 | 16 | 35 | 43 | 15 | 31 | 40 |
| crude oil | | 67 | 91 | 95 | 94 | 97 | 99 | n.l. | n.l. | n.l. |
| petroleum products | | n.l. | n.l. | n.l. | n.l. | n.l. | n.l. | 14 | 36 | 55 |
| electric power | (1936) | 10 | 21 | 27 | 78 | 84 | 89 | 23 | 55 | 73 |
| pig iron | | 83 | 97 | n.l. | 65 | 89 | 91 | 26 | 65 | 83 |
| steel[1] | | 41 | 56 | 66 | 32 | 58 | 68 | 20 | 48 | 64 |
| aluminum | | 52 | 91 | (100) | 57 | 100 | (100) | 49 | 100 | (100) |
| electrolytic copper | | 37 | 74 | 98 | 34 | 70 | 92 | 28 | 65 | 88 |
| elec. wire & cables | | n.l. | n.l. | n.l. | 21 | 51 | 66 | 16 | 40 | 56 |
| elec. engines | (1943) | 36 | 72 | 91 | 23 | 52 | 67 | 22 | 53 | 74 |
| shipbldg. | | 35 | 67 | 86 | 14 | 38 | 56 | 15 | 37 | 51 |
| locomotives[2] | | 28 | 71 | 95 | 21 | 54 | 78 | 28 | 74 | 95 |
| RR passenger cars | | 40 | 77 | 94 | 31 | 56 | 74 | n.l. | n.l. | n.l. |
| RR freight cars | | 38 | 71 | 91 | 22 | 56 | 76 | 29 | 68 | 91 |
| automobiles[3] | (1938) | 59 | 100 | (100) | 45 | 98 | (100) | 26 | 66 | 90 |
| bearings | | 47 | 100 | (100) | 38 | 66 | 79 | 26 | 68 | 85 |
| elec. light bulbs[4] | | n.l. | n.l. | n.l. | 27 | 47 | 54 | 41 | 83 | 96 |
| sewing machines | (1939) | 25 | 52 | n.l. | 11 | 32 | 50 | 10 | 30 | 40 |
| caustic soda | (1940) | 22 | 55 | 72 | 16 | 38 | 56 | 8 | 23 | 35 |
| ammonium sulphate | | 22 | 60 | 78 | 15 | 39 | 57 | 13 | 32 | 48 |
| calcium superphosphate | | 24 | 46 | 59 | 30 | 47 | 61 | 16 | 32 | 45 |
| lime nitrate | | 40 | 86 | 94 | 31 | 75 | 91 | 40 | 83 | 94 |
| synthetic dyestuffs | (1939) | 28 | 56 | 61 | 37 | 74 | 88 | 24 | 62 | 79 |
| celluloid | | 59 | 77 | 85 | 43 | 68 | 78 | 63 | 80 | 87 |
| photographic film | (1940) | 72 | 100 | (100) | 72 | 100 | (100) | 76 | 100 | (100) |
| auto tires/tubes | (1939) | 41 | 100 | (100) | 33 | 89 | 100 | 41 | 76 | 91 |
| plate glass | | 73 | 100 | (100) | 65 | (100) | (100) | 55 | 100 | (100) |
| cement | | 23 | 40 | 54 | 22 | 52 | 70 | 18 | 47 | 62 |
| pulp[5] | (1941) | 49 | 65 | 76 | 21 | 43 | 57 | 13 | 33 | 47 |
| western paper | | 71 | 83 | 90 | 27 | 62 | 74 | 15 | 39 | 49 |

| | | 1937 | | | 1949 | | | 1962 | | |
|---|---|---|---|---|---|---|---|---|---|---|
| | | Top 1 | Top 3 | Top 5 | Top 1 | Top 3 | Top 5 | Top 1 | Top 3 | Top 5 |
| tton spinning | | 15 | 33 | 42 | 14 | 38 | 57 | 5 | 16 | 26 |
| yon yarn[6] | | 13 | 36 | 53 | 25 | 66 | 94 | 23 | 60 | 82 |
| tton goods | | 7 | 16 | 22 | 7 | 20 | 31 | 2 | 6 | 10 |
| nthetic fibers | | n.l. | n.l. | n.l. | n.l. | n.l. | n.l. | 37 | 67 | 80 |
| our milling | | 34 | 71 | n.l. | 20 | 40 | 44 | 30 | 60 | 66 |
| er | | 63 | 99 | (100) | 38 | 100 | (100) | 45 | 97 | (100) |
| tter | (1943) | 80 | 90 | 92 | 67 | 85 | 89 | 48 | 74 | 88 |
| oking oil | | n.l. | n.l. | n.l. | 10 | 22 | 30 | 17 | 42 | 62 |
| y oil | | 12 | 20 | 24 | 10 | 18 | 21 | 16 | 25 | 30 |
| ndensed milk[7] | (1943) | 42 | 80 | 86 | 35 | 79 | 86 | 31 | 82 | 91 |
| tches | (1940) | 28 | 38 | 48 | 22 | 33 | 42 | 9 | 18 | 27 |
| ipping | | 14 | 29 | 37 | 9 | 20 | 26 | 6 | 18 | 28 |
| press service | (1941) | 51 | n.l. | n.l. | 78 | n.l. | n.l. | n.l. | n.l. | n.l. |
| rehousing | | 16 | 37 | 46 | 13 | 30 | 39 | 10 | 20 | 25 |
| nking | | 11 | 25 | 39 | 8 | 22 | 35 | 6 | 19 | 32 |
| sualty insur. | | 16 | 31 | 42 | 15 | 35 | 52 | 16 | 33 | 48 |
| fe insur. | | 16 | 41 | 63 | 25 | 46 | 59 | 19 | 43 | 61 |

937 and 1949, "steel fabricating"; 1962, "crude steel."

937 and 1949, "locomotives"; 1962, "electric locomotives."

937 and 1949, "automobile chassis (including trucks & buses)"; the 1962 data are divided into three markets, "ordinary automobiles" (including trucks); "small, four-wheeled cars" and "light, four-wheeled cars." "Ordinary cars" is what is reproduced here.

937 and 1949, "electric light bulbs"; 1962, "fluorescent light tubes."

In the 1962 statistics, the market is divided into two kinds of pulp. "Paper pulp" is reproduced here.

1937 and 1949, "rayon yarn"; 1962, "rayon filament."

1943 and 1949, "condensed milk"; 1962, "powdered milk."

ources and notes: The data for 1937 (with indicated exceptions) and for 1949 are taken from FTC, *he Realities of Economic Concentration in Japan* (Kosei Torihiki Iinkai, *Nihon ni okeru, Keizairyoku huchu no Jittai*), 1951, passim; the 1962 information from FTC, *Production Concentration in the rincipal Industries* (*Shuyo Sangyo ni okeru, Seisan Shuchudo*), 1964, mimeog. passim.

FTC studies. In the 1964 report one finds "coal" and "ham sausages" (a particularly unimportant item in the Japanese diet) side by side.

The duality of Japan's economy presents some unusual problems in definition. Even if market definition is kept consistent, some markets cross the duality of the economy, and if treated as one, result in unrepresentative concentration ratios. For example, it will be noted in Table 14-1 that "banking" (which is compiled on the basis of loans extended) is shown with an exceptionally low concentration.[11] This is largely because the divisor is the total number of banks, 471 in 1937, 74 in 1949 (resulting from wartime amalgamations), and 88 in 1962.[12] But as we saw in the preceding chapter, Japanese banking practice is not to consider banks a single market, but instead two, wherein city, trust, and long-term credit banks are in one market and provincial banks in the other. Broadly speaking, city, trust, and long-term banks serve the credit requirements of large-scale enterprise, and provincial banks those of medium and small. (In Table 12-11 we observed for 1964 that the city, trust, and long-term credit banks supplied two-thirds of the borrowing needs of the country's leading enterprises.) Therefore, it distorts practice to treat them as if they were

[11] From reading Professor Yamamura's article, "Zaibatsu, Prewar and Zaibatsu, Postwar," *Journal of Asian Studies*, August 1964, pp. 539-54, one gains a different idea of the role of the Big Four banks. In his Table I (p. 540), entitled "Loans Made by Four Zaibatsu Banks, 1944," Professor Yamamura shows the Mitsui Bank (which did not exist as such in 1944) with 29% of total bank loans, Mitsubishi with 19%, Sumitomo with 14%, and Yasuda with 11%, thus amounting to a total for the Big Four of 74%. These figures bear no relationship to anything I have ever seen, and furthermore, they have the extraordinary quality of making Yasuda the smallest. Yamamura cites as his source the HCLC, *The Japanese Zaibatsu and Their Dissolution* (*Nihon Zaibatsu to Sono Kaitai*), but he fails to indicate to which volume of the two-volume study (which he also misdates) his page reference applies; it in fact applies to neither. Further, inasmuch as virtually all HCLC data of this period are for war's end, the time reference would seem in all probability in error.

In my earlier study, *Concentrated Business Power in Japan*, I gave data on the position of the Big Four banks in terms of their deposits as a proportion of total deposits for 1944, on the basis of information submitted to GHQ-SCAP. The Teikoku Bank (Mitsui and Shibusawa) is shown at 13.8%; Yasuda, 12.4%; Mitsubishi, 12.0%; and Sumitomo, 10.6% (cf. p. 379).

The data volume of the HCLC study in question shows the position of the Big Four banks at the end of the war in terms of capital. Computing the percentage figures from the absolute figures shown, the banks are as follows: Teikoku, 14.7%; Mitsubishi, 8.7%; Sumitomo, 5.3%, and Yasuda, 19.2% (cf. data volume, p. 468).

[12] The 1937 and 1949 figures for numbers of banks are taken from FTC, *The Realities of Economic Concentration in Japan* (Kosei Torihiki Iinkai, *Nihon ni okeru, Keizai Ryoku Shuchu no Jittai*), 1951 (hereafter referred to as 1951 Concentration Ratio Study), pp. 237 and 239, respectively. The figure for 1962 is taken from FTC, *Production Concentration in the Principal Industries* (*Shuyo Sangyo ni okeru, Seisan Shuchudo, Sokatsu Hen*) (hereafter referred to as the 1964 Concentration Ratio Study), mimeog., 1964, p. 32.

one. Further, in the *zaibatsu* period the market had more unusual qualities. Given the practice of internally supplying their own credit needs, it was much as if each of the big three *zaibatsu* constituted a financial market of its own.

Further, it is important to keep in mind that Japanese concentration ratios, like their American counterparts, do not take imports or exports into account. A domestic monopoly can be significant or insignificant according to the proportion of the whole market—domestic output plus imports—that it supplies. In the Japanese context, with its important reliance on foreign raw materials as well as in many cases manufactured products, this has genuine bearing.[13]

And last, it should be observed that the assumption underlying all concentration ratios is that in counting firms one is counting separate entities, a pitfall in working with Japanese figures.

### *The 1937 Concentration Ratios*

With these observations in mind, let us note the 1937 patterns of market concentration as shown in Tables 14-1 and 14-2. Their material clearly indicates that high, single-firm occupancy of market positions was not characteristic. By mere count (with all the limitations that this implies) it will be seen that in only 12 of the 45 markets presented does the top firm occupy a position above 50% of output. For an economy described by a number of observers as most extraordinarily concentrated, this at first glance does not seem like much. If we note the information on position of the top three firms in these markets, we see that in about 28 markets is the position above 50%; in the case of the top five, some 33 markets. Oligopoly is the prevailing pattern.

In the markets we are working with here, a competitive structure is unusual; in only a few cases does it exist—cotton textiles,[14] electric

[13] Professor Rotwein, who has studied this point, asserts, however, that the impact is not large.

> A study of manufacturing . . . indicates that the effects [of international trade] would be relatively small. In over half of ninety Census manufacturing industries (covering all manufacturing) imports would reduce the concentration ratios by 2 per cent or less, in over two-thirds they would reduce the ratios by 5 per cent or less, and in only seven cases would they reduce the ratios by more than 25 per cent. In only two cases where concentration ratios are available would the adjustment remove an industry from the high-concentration class. The removal of exports would increase the high-concentration component in manufacturing from 34.6 to 36 per cent (assuming that the removal of exports would not alter the domestic concentration ratios in each industry).

Rotwein, "Economic Concentration," pp. 264n-65n.

[14] Nakagawa Eiichiro, professor of economic history at Tokyo University, has suggested that market concentration patterns may reflect the pattern of demand in the overseas market to which the goods are being exported. Because cotton

Table 14-2: MAJOR PREWAR (1937) MARKETS ARRANGED IN DESCENDING ORDER OF CONCENTRATION BY TOP FIRM, TOP THREE FIRMS AND TOP FIVE FIRMS

market position in percent

(where 100% of production has been attained before size grouping in question, 100% appears in parenthesis)

| *Top Firm* | | *Top 3 Firms* | | *Top 5 Firms* | |
|---|---|---|---|---|---|
| iron | 83 | plate glass | 100 | plate glass | (100) |
| butter | 80 | photog. film | 100 | photog. film | (100) |
| plate glass | 73 | automobiles | 100 | automobiles | (100) |
| photog. film | 72 | bearings | 100 | bearings | (100) |
| western paper | 71 | auto tires/tubes | 100 | auto tires/tubes | (100) |
| crude oil | 67 | beer | 99 | beer | (100) |
| beer | 63 | iron | 97 | aluminum | (100) |
| celluloid | 59 | cast iron pipe | n.l. | iron | n.l. |
| automobiles | 59 | aluminum | 91 | electrolytic copper | 98 |
| cast iron pipe | 55 | crude oil | 91 | cast iron pipe | n.l. |
| aluminum | 52 | butter | 90 | crude oil | 95 |
| express service | 51 | lime nitrate | 86 | locomotives | 95 |
| pulp | 49 | western paper | 83 | lime nitrate | 94 |
| bearings | 47 | condensed milk | 80 | RR passenger cars | 94 |
| condensed milk | 42 | celluloid | 77 | butter | 92 |
| auto tires/tubes | 41 | RR passenger cars | 77 | RR freight cars | 91 |
| steel | 41 | electrolytic copper | 74 | electric engines | 91 |
| RR passenger cars | 40 | electric engines | 72 | western paper | 90 |
| lime nitrate | 40 | flour milling | 71 | shipbldg. | 86 |
| RR freight cars | 38 | locomotives | 71 | condensed milk | 86 |
| electrolytic copper | 37 | RR freight cars | 71 | celluloid | 85 |

textiles historically went in large measure to south and southeast Asia, to economies of low concentration, Professor Nakagawa hypothesizes that a competitive structure for the industry was possible in Japan, whereas in the case of goods exported to Europe and the U.S. it was not.

One does not usually think of the consumer-demand side of the market shaping the structure of supply, though in J. K. Galbraith's concept of "countervailing power" this notion is put forward with respect to the factor markets: concentration in the demand for labor (concentration in production units) is held likely to induce concentration in the supply arrangements of labor (Galbraith, *The American Economy*, Cambridge, Mass., 1952, esp. Chap. 9). Applying Nakagawa's hypothesis to the structure of consumer demand at home, as well as abroad, there is the question of whether historically the concentrated nature of much of the demand for the output of the capital-intensive sector of Japan's economy (i.e., the army and navy, the national railroads, and communications) may have been a factor conducive to concentration on the supply side, and conversely, whether the diversified nature of demand for textiles has been a factor conducive to its low concentration.

It will be helpful to distinguish the various forms of concentration: fewness

| | | | | | |
|---|---|---|---|---|---|
| electric engines | 36 | shipbldg. | 67 | flour milling | n.l. |
| shipbldg. | 35 | pulp | 65 | ammonium sulphate | 78 |
| flour milling | 34 | ammonium sulphate | 60 | pulp | 76 |
| locomotives | 28 | synthetic dyestuffs | 56 | caustic soda | 72 |
| synthetic dyestuffs | 28 | steel | 56 | sewing machines | n.l. |
| matches | 28 | caustic soda | 55 | steel | 66 |
| sewing machines | 25 | sewing machines | 52 | life insurance | 63 |
| superphosphate of lime | 24 | express service | n.l. | galvan. iron sheets | 63 |
| cement | 23 | galvan. iron sheets | 48 | synthetic dyestuffs | 61 |
| ammonium sulphate | 22 | superphosphate of lime | 46 | superphosphate of lime | 59 |
| caustic soda | 22 | life insurance | 41 | cement | 54 |
| galvan. iron sheets | 19 | cement | 40 | artificial fibers | 53 |
| casualty insurance | 16 | matches | 38 | express service | n.l. |
| warehousing | 16 | warehousing | 37 | matches | 48 |
| life insurance | 16 | artificial fibers | 36 | warehousing | 46 |
| cotton spinning | 15 | coal | 35 | coal | 44 |
| coal | 15 | cotton spinning | 33 | cotton spinning | 42 |
| shipping | 14 | casualty insurance | 31 | casualty insurance | 42 |
| artificial fibers | 13 | shipping | 29 | banking | 39 |
| soy oil | 12 | banking | 25 | shipping | 37 |
| banking | 11 | electric power | 21 | electric power | 29 |
| thread | 10 | soy oil | 20 | soy oil | 24 |
| electric power | 10 | thread | n.l. | thread | n.l. |
| cotton goods | 7 | cotton goods | 16 | cotton goods | 22 |

Source: FTC, *The Realities of Economic Concentration in Japan* (Kosei Torihiki Iinkai, *Nihon ni okeru, Keizairyoku Shuchu no Jittai*), 1951 Appendix 2.

---

of numbers within a market (in the concentration-ratio sense of the word); conglomerate enterprise; and cartelization. Given the pattern of Japan's textile industry, Professor Nakagawa is clearly referring to the first two circumstances—to the industry's relatively low concentration ratio (lower in cotton goods than in spinning), to the absence of conglomerate enterprise—but not to the cartel which characterized the industry's development from the early Meiji period through the Second World War.

The capital-intensiveness of technology is undoubtedly the single most important factor affecting the structure of supply. That in any modern economy steel mills are scarce and dry cleaning establishments numerous reflects the scale of the barriers imposed by the capital requirements of the two industries. A product of this scale—yet a separate facet—is the consequent differences in the shape of the cost curves among different-sized enterprises. The cost curves of large enterprise, though showing individual differences from industry to industry, are downward sloping to large amounts of output, thus making entry more difficult. A refreshingly realistic discussion of cost curves, in the petrochemical industry, is to be found in the *Oriental Economist* for April 1968, pp. 35-41, but esp. p. 35.

power, banking. As already observed, the material on banking is misleading and so is the presentation of electric power, though for different reasons. In 1937 electric power occurred in the form of regional markets; there was no national market for it; accordingly, it is meaningless to present it on a national basis.

It was suggested earlier that among the relevant considerations which concentration ratios do not measure are the relations between the majors in the same market; the amount which subsidiaries add to market position; the number of markets in which the same major appears; the group ties between majors in different markets; the rigidity/fluidity of market positions; and the prevalence of cartels. Let us use coal as an illustration. In 1937, the market positions of the big three in coal were:[15] (1) Mitsui Mining, 15.1%; (2) Mitsubishi Mining, 12.1; (3) Hokkaido Colliery and Steamship, 8.2—for a total 35.4%. Since both Mitsui Mining and Hokkaido Colliery and Steamship were subsidiaries of the Mitsui top-holding company, it is meaningless to speak of the concentration ratio for the top three firms in coal as being 35.4% for the top three did not speak with three voices; they spoke with two. Thus what we have is Mitsui at 23.3% and Mitsubishi at 12.1%. But all three companies had subsidiaries of their own. According to FTC material (which seems questionable to the writer), other Mitsui subsidiaries in 1937 added only 1.6% to the Mitsui position, but 5.7% to the Mitsubishi position.[16] In other words, Mitsui stands at 24.8% and Mitsubishi at 16.3%.

Mitsui Mining and Mitsubishi Mining strengthened these positions through the coal cartel they were instrumental in establishing in the

---

In a developing economy the strongest way in which demand affects the structure of supply may well be, as Ragnar Nurkse emphasized, in terms of the size of the market. Nurkse, *Problems of Capital Formation in Underdeveloped Countries*, New York, 1955, esp. Chapter 1. The fact that textiles, with the large overseas market, in addition to the domestic market, had a larger number of majors in the market than most of the other capital-intensive industries may have been partly a reflection of the greater size of the market.

It is a highly interesting question why the combines did not participate in textiles as they did in all other sectors of the capital-intensive portion of the economy. To suggest that the answer may be primarily a matter of numbers among final consumers would seem too strong. I would guess that some of the answer is historical in part, an intuition as to where the greatest profit opportunities were. When considering the combines it must be borne in mind that they operated in a world of abundant investment opportunities under generous government favor. The lesser appeal of textiles than metallurgy, ships, machinery, and finance may reflect a thinking which finds it more worthy to engage in products that build a nation rather than clothe ordinary folk.

[15] FTC, 1951. Concentration Ratio Study, p. 48.

[16] *Ibid.*, p. 49.

early 1920s. One of a small number of cartels set up following World War I (cf. Table 15-1), the Coal Mining Federation (Sekitan Kogyo Rengokai), attempted to meet the problems arising from the 1921 recession through the establishment of production quotas. For a time the arrangement was threatened by increased imports from Manchuria, but in 1926 the cartel concluded an agreement with the South Manchurian Railroad Company which established import quotas for Manchurian coal. To further strengthen its position, the cartel in 1932 established a centralized selling agency, the Showa Coal Company (Showa Sekitan). By 1933 the cartel controlled 65 to 70% of output. Its restrictive arrangements were effective, as is suggested by the fact that between 1932 and 1934 the price of coal increased 30%. In 1936 the government, using the Major Industries Law, compelled the cartel to increase its production quota by one million tons; but at the same time, under authority to oblige outsiders to join a private arrangement representing two-thirds of the industry, the government forced those coal producers outside the cartel to join it. The cartel continued in virtually this form until 1941, when it was transformed into the Coal Control Association.[17]

Of course, the activities of Mitsui Mining and Mitsubishi Mining were not confined to the coal market. Mitsui Mining was the largest producer of lead and zinc in Japan and active in numerous other fields of metal mining, as well as in metallurgy and coal derivatives. Mitsubishi Mining was also metallurgy—lead, zinc, copper, gold, and silver.

However, to fully appreciate the position of these two companies, one has to take into consideration the combines of which they were a part. In the prewar days of party government, the coveted coal contract for the national railroads alternated between Mitsui, when the Seiyukai was in power, and Mitsubishi, when the Minseito was in power. This situation reflected more than a bargaining position of the two top-holding companies arising out of mining activity.[18] It reflected their position in ordnance, aircraft, shipbuilding, machinery, heavy and light electrical equipment, chemicals, imports and exports, banking, insurance, shipping, and other important markets. A series of oligopolistic positions were intended to—and did—add to power. It will be recalled that in the 1944 circular letter from the Mitsui top-holding company it was stated that the top-holding company "will act as a liaison organization among the . . . designated subsidiaries, so that mutual assistance may be given and the power of Mit-

[17] Hadley, "Concentrated Business Power in Japan," pp. 263-64.
[18] *Ibid.*, p. 262.

sui's vast composite organization can be efficiently taken advantage of."

In coal, the situation was one of Mitsui strength and Mitsubishi weakness. In other markets, positions were reversed. In shipbuilding, for example, Mitsubishi Heavy Industry accounted for 35% of output, and Mitsui Shipbuilding 15%. The highly unusual circumstance of the oligopolists being the same (i.e., belonging to a few top-holding companies which covered the capital-intensive sector of the economy and which possessed sufficient powers to compel the behavior they sought of their subsidiaries) is what led me earlier to describe "cordial oligopoly" as the hallmark of inter-*zaibatsu* relations. (In the discussion of 1962 concentration ratios below, it will be suggested that the inability of today's groupings to compel behavior is what accounts for the more cutthroat oligopoly, the "excessive competition," of markets in recent years.)

To convey an idea of the spread of prewar combine activities, I have gone through the top 10 firms listed in the 50 markets for which individual market positions are shown by the FTC for 1937. By rough count, it would appear that Mitsui subsidiaries held positions in 24 of the markets. Since we are talking here about the top 10 firms of these markets, we are talking about only those subsidiaries that were majors. Summarized, the market position of these 24 Mitsui majors was: 70% and over, 2; 60-69%, 0; 50-59%, 1; 40-49%, 3; 30-39%, 1; 20-29%, 5; 10-19%, 4; a fraction of 1% to 9%, 8. It is clear that the Mitsui network was not after monopoly positions. In fact, in 8 markets the position was under 10%.[19] (For mention of a similar situation, see Table 1-1.) That market positions were of this character indicates how misleading it is to attempt to measure concentration under the *zaibatsu* system by concentration ratios.

While the Mitsui combine appeared in 24 of the 50 markets shown by the FTC for 1937, there are, from a Mitsui *zaibatsu* point of view, significant omissions. The most striking is the omission of foreign trade, where, as we saw in Table 8-1, Mitsui Trading in 1937 accounted for 16.9% of imports and 10.7% of exports—this was exclusive of the trade accounted for by that other major Mitsui trading company, Toyo Menka, which specialized in the textile trade, and was exclusive of Trading's roughly 125 subsidiaries, though the bulk of activity of these subsidiaries was probably in the domestic market. Other significant Mitsui omissions are petroleum refining, machine tools, rubber, batteries, lumber products, aircraft, ordnance, and the trust business.

[19] Professor Rotwein comes up with essentially the same findings; see his article, "Economic Concentration," Table 4, p. 270.

Does a series of oligopoly positions, many of them in the 10% range of domestic output, stretching the breadth of the capital-intensive sector of the economy, add to business power? It is futile to debate. The relevant question is not whether it did, but how it did, which is a study in conglomerate enterprise.

Imbued with the notion that concentration engenders monopoly we find divestment difficult. Professor Kozo Yamamura unwittingly reflects such thinking when he writes: "The so-called revival of the Zaibatsu connotes a highly concentrated market structure and a tendency for the larger firms to become larger and perhaps monopolistic."[20] But the *zaibatsu* connoted no such thing. They connoted business structures frequently resting on oligopoly positions in the 10-20% range of domestic output, which joined market after market after market.[21]

That Professor Allen and I can have such marked differences of opinion, with respect to whether the capital-intensive sector of Japan's prewar economy was concentrated or not, probably has to do with two factors, the absence of monopolistic markets and the internal structure of the *zaibatsu* organizations. It would be my guess that Allen does not see concentrated business power as arising from conglomerate activities. Further, with respect to internal structure, Allen does not believe that the *zaibatsu* top-holding companies possessed controls sufficient to compel desired behavior from the key subsidiaries. This may be because the supporting "chapter and verse" did not become available until the Occupation (before the war, all aspects of these structures were regarded as strictly private matters to which the public was not privy) and has not been extensively publicized since.

But under the *zaibatsu* system, concentration (most unusual concentration) occurred, wherein, as we saw earlier (by the Ministry of Commerce and Industry divisor), four family groups at war's end con-

[20] Yamamura, "Zaibatsu, Prewar and Zaibatsu, Postwar," *Journal of Asian Studies*, August 1964, p. 549.

[21] Rotwein repeats this thinking when he remarks, "markets in the prewar Japanese economy were not as highly concentrated as several observers have supposed." But a check of such reserves quotations indicates that no source has suggested high market concentration in talking about concentration in the Japanese economy. It was Professor Rotwein who imagined this. With market concentration the only form of concentration that we Westerners have known, it is difficult to read the word "concentration" without having it register in our minds as "market concentration." Cf. Rotwein, "Rejoinder to Yamamura," *Journal of Political Economy*, October 1965, p. 527, which in turn compares with his article, "Economic Concentration and Monopoly in Japan," p. 263 of the June issue of the same journal.

trolled one quarter of the corporate and partnership capital of the nation. The pertinent percentages for the Big Four, as a proportion of total corporate and partnership capital, from the tables of Chapter 3 for 1937, 1941, and 1945 are:

| | 1937 | 1941 | 1945 |
|---|---|---|---|
| Mitsui | 3.4% | 4.6% | 9.4% |
| Mitsubishi | 3.1 | 4.2 | 8.3 |
| Sumitomo | 2.1 | 2.0 | 5.2 |
| Yasuda | 1.4 | 1.3 | 1.6 |
| | 10.0% | 12.1% | 24.5% |

In addition to the concentration represented in these individual structures, concentration was increased through the cordiality of inter-*zaibatsu* relations producing a united front against outsiders. Not the least of the obstacles to entry was the fact that the *zaibatsu* dominated the city, trust, and long-term credit banks, and thus had it within their power to deny outsiders access to credit.

*The 1949 Market Concentration Ratios*

Let us turn to the 1949 portion of the material presented in Table 14-1, which again is arranged by descending order of concentration in Table 14-3. One cannot regard 1949 merely as reflecting wartime developments minus Occupation reforms, for 1949 represented the fourth postwar year with all of its staggering readjustments—loss of overseas assets, reorientation of output, uncertain reparation removals, and severe inflation. The data are valuable, however, for what they reveal (with indicated exceptions) concerning the effect of the Occupation reforms on market structure. Study of the position of the top firm, top three, and top five indicates that the Occupation changes that did occur (*proposed* changes would have brought a somewhat different result) scarcely resulted in the fracturing of Japanese business.

If the position of the top firm in the listed markets in 1937 is compared with the top firm in 1949, and the position of the top three firms is compared in the two years, it will be seen that with a few exceptions there are no sharp breaks. True, the majority of top positions in 1949 are below those of 1937, but the decreases in the case of the top firms are in the range from 41 to 33%, from 49 to 43%, and from 47 to 38%. The results of the actions taken under the Excessive Concentration of Economic Power Law are to be seen in shipbuilding (35 to

14%); in pulp and western paper (pulp, 49 to 21%; paper, 71 to 27%); in beer (63 to 38%). Other Excessive Concentration Law changes which occurred among the markets presented, but which are not reflected in the 1949 figures, are electric power and iron and steel. The latter should have been represented in the figures; electric power could not have been because a decision on how to deal with the Japan Electric Generation and Transmission Co. was not reached until after the HCLC handed the problem over to the FTC in 1951, when it was decided to establish nine regional public utility companies on the American pattern. Markets where changes occurred under the Excessive Concentration Law, but which are not included in these tables, are tin cans, flax spinning, and milk.[22]

The 1949 material indicates that certain high occupancy positions went untouched by Occupation changes—crude oil, photographic film, plate glass, and the express business. The first was not changed, which probably reflects the fact that Japanese domestic output is insignificant when imports are included. A monopoly of domestic oil is not meaningful when the nation relies overwhelmingly on foreign sources. Photographic film and plate glass were not included probably because of the new climate of official thinking, while the omission of the express business was the product of skillful lobbying.

At first glance it might seem highly surprising, in view of the Occupation's "trust busting" activities, that the 1949 market positions are for the most part so little changed from those in 1937. But inasmuch as the focus of the Occupation effort was combine-dissolution and the combines in question were overwhelmingly conglomerate, it is evident that market positions would be little affected by such dissolutions. One dissolves a combine by cutting the ties that hold together in one package a commercial bank, an electric equipment manufacturing firm, a mining company, a firm in the import-export trade, and so forth. In fact, even the reorganization of the conglomerate operating companies when reorganization was along product, rather than geographic, lines, would not show up in concentration ratios. Thus, for example, the separation of coal and metal mining in the case of the mining companies belonging to the Big Three is not reflected in the concentration ratios, for these ratios take no account of the number of different markets in which the same firm appears. Nor would the three-way split of Daiken Industries into a flax company, a rayon company, and into trading be evident, though the division of its trading activities into two companies would. The reorganization of Mitsubishi

[22] Cf. Table 9-1.

Table 14-3: MAJOR POSTWAR (1949) MARKETS ARRANGED IN DESCENDING ORDER OF CONCENTRATION BY TOP FIRM, TOP THREE FIRMS AND TOP FIVE FIRMS

market position in percent

(where 100% of production has been attained before size grouping in question, 100% appears in parenthesis)

| *Top Firm* | | *Top 3 Firms* | | *Top 5 Firms* | |
|---|---|---|---|---|---|
| crude oil | 94 | plate glass | (100) | plate glass | (10[illegible] |
| electric power | 78 | photog. film | 100 | photog. film | (10[illegible] |
| express service | 78 | aluminum | 100 | aluminum | (10[illegible] |
| photog. film | 72 | beer | 100 | beer | (10[illegible] |
| butter | 67 | automobiles | 98 | automobiles | (10[illegible] |
| iron | 65 | crude oil | 97 | auto tires | 10[illegible] |
| plate glass | 65 | galvan. iron pipe | 93 | crude oil | 9[illegible] |
| galvan. iron pipe | 63 | auto tires | 89 | galvan. iron pipe | 9[illegible] |
| aluminum | 57 | iron | 89 | hemp spinning | 9[illegible] |
| automobiles | 45 | butter | 85 | fiber thread | 9[illegible] |
| hemp spinning | 45 | electric power | 84 | electrolytic copper | 9[illegible] |
| celluloid | 43 | hemp thread | 82 | iron | 9[illegible] |
| beer | 38 | condensed milk | 79 | lime nitrate | 9[illegible] |
| bearings | 38 | express service | n.l. | electric power | 8[illegible] |
| synthetic dyestuffs | 37 | lime nitrate | 75 | butter | 8[illegible] |
| condensed milk | 35 | synthetic dyestuff | 74 | synthetic dyestuff | 8[illegible] |
| electrolytic copper | 34 | sulphur ore | 72 | condensed milk | [illegible] |
| auto tires | 33 | electrolytic copper | 70 | sulphur ore | [illegible] |
| steel | 32 | celluloid | 68 | express service | [illegible] |
| RR passenger cars | 31 | artificial fibers | 66 | wool combing spinning | [illegible] |
| lime nitrate | 31 | bearings | 66 | bearings | [illegible] |
| superphosphate of lime | 30 | western paper | 62 | celluloid | [illegible] |
| sulphur ore | 30 | steel | 58 | locomotives | [illegible] |
| electric light bulbs | 27 | wool combing spinning | 57 | RR freight cars | [illegible] |
| western paper | 27 | RR passenger cars | 56 | RR passenger cars | [illegible] |

| | | | | | |
|---|---|---|---|---|---|
| ife insurance | 25 | RR freight cars | 56 | western paper | 74 |
| rtificial fibers | 25 | locomotives | 54 | cement | 70 |
| lectric engines | 23 | electric engines | 52 | steel | 68 |
| alvan. iron sheets | 22 | cement | 52 | electric engines | 67 |
| R freight cars | 22 | electric wire & cables | 51 | elec. wire & cables | 66 |
| ool combing spinning | 22 | superphosphate of lime | 47 | superphosphate of lime | 61 |
| ement | 22 | electric light bulbs | 47 | galvan. iron sheets | 61 |
| atches | 22 | life insurance | 46 | life insurance | 59 |
| ulp | 21 | galvan. iron sheets | 45 | staple fiber | 59 |
| ocomotives | 21 | pulp | 43 | ammonium sulphate | 57 |
| lec. wire & cables | 21 | flour milling | 40 | pulp | 57 |
| lour milling | 20 | staple fiber | 40 | cotton spinning | 57 |
| hread | 17 | ammonium sulphate | 39 | shipbldg. | 56 |
| austic soda | 16 | caustic soda | 38 | caustic soda | 56 |
| taple fiber | 16 | shipbldg. | 38 | light bulbs | 54 |
| oal | 16 | cotton spinning | 38 | casualty insurance | 52 |
| asualty insurance | 15 | coal | 35 | sewing machines | 50 |
| mmonium sulphate | 15 | casualty insurance | 35 | flour milling | 44 |
| hipbldg. | 14 | matches | 33 | coal | 43 |
| otton spinning | 14 | sewing machines | 32 | matches | 42 |
| arehousing | 13 | warehousing | 30 | warehousing | 39 |
| ewing machines | 11 | thread | 30 | banking | 35 |
| oy oil | 10 | bicycles | 26 | thread | 35 |
| ooking oil | 10 | carded wool spinning | 24 | bicycles | 34 |
| icycles | 9 | banking | 22 | carded wool spinning | 33 |
| hipping | 9 | cooking oil | 22 | cotton goods | 31 |
| arded wool spinning | 9 | shipping | 20 | cooking oil | 30 |
| anking | 8 | cotton goods | 20 | shipping | 26 |
| otton goods | 7 | soy oil | 18 | soy oil | 21 |

ource: FTC, *The Realities of Economic Concentration in Japan*, 1951, Appendix 3.

Heavy Industries, which was along geographic lines rather than product, would be reflected in the figures.

Even today there is considerable confusion among knowledgeable Japanese about the purpose of the Occupation deconcentration effort. A number of them apparently believe that the emphasis was not on combine dissolution, but rather change in market concentration patterns. In a chapter which grew out of a 1961 legal conference at Harvard University, Professor Kanazawa of Hokkaido University, one of the leading antitrust scholars in Japan, observed that "the occupation authorities sought to prevent any reversion to the prewar oligopolistic structure of Japanese industry. . . ."[23] One finds the same thought repeated in a 1964 article coauthored by Mrs. Ariga, now a commissioner of the Fair Trade Commission, and Professor Rieke: "The legislation and dissolutions compelled during the immediate postwar days by the Occupation forces were primarily designed to eliminate the oligopolistic structure which had dominated Japan's industry."[24] But this was not the case; the focus of the deconcentration effort was combine dissolution. Where combines are conglomerate—which all Japan's combines were—there can be combine dissolution with virtually no effect on market position. Even under the Excessive Concentration of Economic Power Law, which did attempt to alter the market structure, there was no attempt to eliminate oligopoly; the intent was to eliminate "excessive concentrations," and the two are not synonymous. It will be observed that *after* the three-way split of Mitsubishi Heavy Industries, the top four companies in shipbuilding accounted for 48.8% of output. Conventionally, output by the top four firms at 50% of the market is taken to represent high concentration. It is accordingly misleading to describe the Occupation effort as one of attempting to eliminate oligopoly; the attempt was to eliminate combines and excessive concentrations.

Even though 1949 market positions, while lower, were not greatly different from the 1937 statistics, concentration in the Japanese economy was distinctly changed. This was because the top-holding companies, formerly the command centers, were undergoing dissolution; because the holdings of the *zaibatsu* families were undergoing sale to the public; because there was some reshuffling of top management out of the economic purge; and because there was some weakening of

[23] Kanazawa Yoshio, "The Regulation of Corporate Enterprise: The Law of Unfair Competition and the Control of Monopoly Power," in Arthur Taylor von Mehren, ed., *Law in Japan*, Cambridge, Mass., 1963, p. 485.

[24] Ariga Michiko and Luvern V. Rieke, "The Antimonopoly Law of Japan and Its Enforcement," *Washington Law Review*, Vol. 39, Number 3, August 1964, p. 461.

horizontal ties through actions under Imp. Ord. 567 and the Anti-Monopoly Law. The most important action in this regard was the restriction under the original provisions of the Anti-Monopoly Law of limiting banks to the level of 5% holdings in companies in industry, mining, and commerce. Further, concentration was different because of the proscription of cartels. These elements, which do not appear in concentration ratios, probably had far more to do with lessened concentration than the split of Mitsubishi Heavy Industries and a handful of other companies, the results of which in part do appear in concentration ratios.

### *1962 Concentration Ratios*

Let us note the 1962 market positions shown in Tables 14-1 and 14-4, but first a few additional general observations. With the dramatic growth of the Japanese economy involving many new industries, the sample of 50 markets is increasingly less representative. Furthermore, although 1962 was the latest year for which data were available, at the time of writing (the FTC has now released a concentration study covering 1963-66), a number of important mergers have since occurred. For the markets with which we are working, a comparison of 1962 with 1949 will not show a striking change in concentration ratios. When comparison is made at the top-firm level increases have occurred in 13 of the markets, but the increases for the most part are not large; 26 markets show decreases. If a comparison is made at the three-firm level, there are 10 cases of increase and 26 of decrease.

Professors Eugene Rotwein and Kozo Yamamura have done considerable research on postwar trends in concentration ratios in Japan.[25] Both found a slight decline in concentration during the greater part of the 1950s.[26] This was noted regardless of whether it was the position of the top firm, the top three firms, or the top five. At the top-10 level the situation was not as clear. Carrying the research forward to the latest year for which statistics were available at the time he wrote, Professor Yamamura called attention to a reverse movement beginning essentially in 1958 and 1959, when concentration ratios show a slight tendency to increase, up to 1962 when data cease.[27]

Professor Rotwein reached his deconcentrating conclusion on the

[25] Rotwein, "Economic Concentration"; Yamamura, "Zaibatsu," (referred to as "article one"), as well as "Market Concentration and Growth in Postwar Japan" (referred to as "article two"), *Southern Economic Journal*, April 1966, pp. 451-64.

[26] Rotwein, "Economic Concentration," esp. pp. 264-65; Yamamura, "Zaibatsu," pp. 549-50.

[27] Yamamura, "Market Concentration," esp. pp. 457-60.

**Table 14-4:** MAJOR POSTWAR (1962) MARKETS ARRANGED IN DESCENDING ORDER OF CONCENTRATION BY TOP FIRM, TOP THREE FIRMS AND TOP FIVE FIRMS

market position in percent

(where 100% of production has been attained before size grouping in question, 100% appears in parenthesis)

| *Top Firm* | | *Top 3 Firms* | | *Top 5 Firms* | |
|---|---|---|---|---|---|
| photog. film | 76 | aluminum | 100 | aluminum | (1 |
| celluloid | 63 | photog. film | (100) | photog. film | (1 |
| plate glass | 55 | plate glass | 100 | plate glass | (1 |
| aluminum | 49 | beer | 97 | beer | (1 |
| butter | 48 | elec. light bulbs | 83 | elec. light bulbs | |
| beer | 45 | lime nitrate | 83 | locomotives | |
| auto tires/tubes | 41 | condensed milk | 82 | lime nitrate | |
| elec. light bulbs | 41 | celluloid | 80 | RR freight cars | |
| lime nitrate | 40 | auto tires/tubes | 76 | auto tires/tubes | |
| synthetic fibers | 37 | locomotives | 74 | condensed milk | |
| condensed milk | 31 | butter | 74 | automobiles | |
| flour milling | 30 | RR freight cars | 68 | electrolytic copper | |
| RR freight cars | 29 | bearings | 68 | butter | |
| locomotives | 28 | synthetic fibers | 67 | celluloid | |
| electrolytic copper | 28 | automobiles | 66 | bearings | |
| pig iron | 26 | pig iron | 65 | pig iron | |
| automobiles | 26 | electrolytic copper | 65 | rayon yarn | |
| bearings | 26 | synthetic dyestuffs | 64 | synthetic fibers | |
| synthetic dyestuffs | 25 | rayon yarn | 60 | synthetic dyestuffs | |
| electric power | 23 | flour milling | 60 | electric engines | |
| rayon yarn | 23 | electric power | 55 | electric power | |
| electric engines | 22 | electric engines | 53 | flour milling | |
| steel | 20 | steel | 48 | steel | |

| | | | | | |
|---|---|---|---|---|---|
| king oil | 19 | cement | 47 | cooking oil | 62 |
| e insurance | 19 | life insurance | 43 | cement | 62 |
| ent | 18 | cooking oil | 42 | life insurance | 61 |
| oil | 17 | elec. wire & cables | 40 | elec. wire & cables | 56 |
| cium superphosphate | 16 | western paper | 39 | petroleum products | 55 |
| ualty insurance | 16 | shipbldg. | 37 | shipbldg. | 51 |
| c. wire & cables | 16 | petroleum products | 36 | western paper | 49 |
| l | 15 | pulp | 33 | ammonium sulphate | 48 |
| pbldg. | 15 | casualty insurance | 33 | casualty insurance | 48 |
| tern paper | 15 | ammonium sulphate | 32 | pulp | 47 |
| roleum products | 14 | calcium superphosphate | 32 | calcium superphosphate | 45 |
| p | 13 | coal | 31 | coal | 40 |
| onium sulphate | 13 | sewing machines | 30 | sewing machines | 40 |
| ing machines | 10 | soy oil | 25 | caustic soda | 35 |
| ehousing | 10 | caustic soda | 23 | banking | 32 |
| ches | 9 | warehousing | 20 | soy oil | 30 |
| stic soda | 8 | banking | 19 | shipping | 28 |
| pping | 6 | matches | 18 | matches | 27 |
| king | 6 | shipping | 18 | cotton spinning | 26 |
| ton spinning | 5 | cotton spinning | 16 | warehousing | 25 |
| ton goods | 2 | cotton goods | 6 | cotton goods | 10 |
| de oil | n.l. | crude oil | n.l. | crude oil | n.l. |
| passenger cars | n.l. | RR passenger cars | n.l. | RR passenger cars | n.l. |
| press service | n.l. | express service | n.l. | express service | n.l. |

urce: FTC, *Production Concentration in the Principal Industries* (Kosei Torihiki nkai, *Shuyo Sangyo ni okeru, Seisan Shuchudo*), 1964, mimeog. passim. The markets lected have been chosen to match the earlier FTC study. For certain differences in tries, cf. footnotes to Table 14-1.

basis of concentration ratios for "64 major industries in manufacturing." Professor Yamamura, using different sources in his two articles and "Comment," reached this conclusion in "article one" on the basis of 40 markets for the period 1952-57, and 81 markets for the period 1955-58.[28] In his criticism of Rotwein's findings and in "article two" he used 53 markets for study of trends during the 1950-62 period and 156 markets for the period 1959-62.[29]

What stands out from the work of these two economists is that the downward trend during the first five to eight years is indeed slight. Similarly, the rising trend in concentration ratios which Yamamura notes for the period 1959-62 is not strong. However, if data were available for the post-1962 period, it is evident that there would be a gain in the momentum of this movement. Rotwein found that the unweighted average concentration ratios for his 64 manufacturing markets, presumably at the three-firm level, were "64 per cent in 1950 and 61 per cent in 1955."[30] Yamamura in "article one" states: ". . . we showed that the postwar concentration ratios are falling rather than rising. . . . The largest [firm], three largest, and five largest show a slight downward trend of concentration, while we detect an uneven movement for the largest firms."[31] In his "Comment" and in "article two" he maintains different positions.

Where I would principally differ with these two economists is in the conclusion to be drawn about concentration in the Japanese economy in consequence of these findings. Professor Rotwein's conclusion is that "a study of this pattern does not bear out the contention that the Japanese economy is highly concentrated or oligopolistic."[32] But one cannot suppose that there is a one-to-one relationship between concentration ratios and concentration in an economy—certainly not Japan's. Rotwein has merely shown that for six years, 1950-55, there was a slight downward trend. It is bold, indeed, to make a pronouncement in 1964, using 1950-55 data, on concentration patterns, especially in an economy as dynamic as Japan's. It is equally bold to assume—in an economy characterized by conglomerate firms, increasing subsidiary networks, and increasing cartelization—that these findings represent concentration in the economy. It is puzzling how Rot-

[28] Rotwein, "Economic Concentration," p. 265; Yamamura, "Zaibatsu," pp. 549-50.

[29] Yamamura, "Comment," *Journal of Political Economy*, October 1965, p. 524; "Market Concentration," p. 451. The information on the number of markets for 1959 to 1962 is taken from the manuscript version of the "Comment."

[30] Rotwein, "Economic Concentration," p. 265.

[31] Yamamura, "Zaibatsu," first portion of quote p. 553, second p. 550.

[32] Rotwein, "Economic Concentration," p. 264.

wein would conclude that oligopoly was absent from Japan's economy. By his own admission, 44 of his 64 markets in 1950 were "high-concentration," with the top four firms accounting for 50% and above of total output.[33] According to most experts, a situation in which two-thirds of the markets under study was at this level, would spell oligopoly in capital letters.

That Yamamura focused his entire criticism of Rotwein's article on his handling of concentration ratios, when there was much else to comment on, and that he has written on postwar industrial organization solely from the point of view of concentration ratios, leads me to the conclusion that he sees a great deal of significance in them. In his 1966 concentration ratio study Yamamura commented: "Whatever view one takes of the postwar Japanese economy, the conclusion to be drawn is that the postwar Japanese economy has followed, and steadily continues to follow, the path of increased market concentration."[34]

Professor Allen, like me, views concentration ratios as much less revealing: "These statistical inquiries [about concentration ratios] are of limited value in solving the problems of major economic interest. They afford little help in estimating the power of the great concerns to influence economic policy, for the statistics apply to individual companies rather than to groups and they cover shares in the output of particular products rather than shares in the aggregate industrial production."[35]

Although Rotwein believed that in 1964 concentration was decreasing in Japan, he nevertheless attributed considerable revival to the "*zaibatsu*." Having done little independent work on business groupings, he adopts the prevailing Japanese attitude that the combines have been revived, though admittedly in looser form. Certainly the attitude one adopts on this point has much to do with the way one interprets concentration ratios. Seeing the origin of the *zaibatsu* in the shortage of capital and resources with which Japan began the task of industrialization, Rotwein writes: "Postwar Japan did not see the disappearance of the conditions which originally spawned the *zaibatsu*, and under the circumstances a reversion to older and traditional forms of doing business—with the careful guarding of scarce economic opportunity for the members of the group—was to be expected."[36] On the other hand, Yamamura, who has done his own research on the

[33] *Ibid.*, p. 265.

[34] Yamamura, "Market Concentration," p. 463. These articles of Yamamura's have now been published as a book, Yamamura, *Economic Policy in Postwar Japan*, Berkeley, 1967.

[35] Allen, *Japan's Economic Expansion*, p. 194.

[36] Rotwein, "Economic Concentration," p. 266.

subject, comes to the conclusion that, "the term Zaibatsu as used in postwar years must be understood as different from the prewar Zaibatsu. We could perhaps go as far as to say that in prewar terms, Zaibatsu no longer exist in Japan."[37]

Judging from the material presented in the preceding chapters, it does not seem possible to see the strong ties so commonly attributed by Japanese writers to today's groupings. It is much as if "all the king's horses and all the king's men" couldn't put them together again. Neither the successor *keiretsu* groupings nor the financial groupings, *kinyu keiretsu*, would appear to provide effective controls. But while I do not see concentration increasing through conglomerate groupings of majors or through bank domination of majors, there is no question that by other routes it has been increasing these last years. These are primarily mergers, expanding subsidiary networks, and cartelization.

### *Capital, an Aggregate Measure of Concentration*

Although such aggregate measures of concentration as capital, assets, employment, sales, value-added, and profits are in use, the aggregate measure overwhelmingly used in Japan is capital. Frequently it is stated in terms of the proportion of corporate and partnership capital represented by the top 100 firms. For such purposes, it is not customary in Japanese practice to group firms by broad sector (industrials, utilities, etc.), nor to exclude government corporations. Thus the top 100 firms cut across all parts of the capital-intensive sector of the economy and include government corporations. Because utilities tend to be capitalized at higher figures than other firms, all such lists include a disproportionate number of them.

Statistics on the position of the top 100 firms as a proportion of total corporate and partnership capital, for a few selected years, are listed here:[38] 1937, 37.4%; 1949, 30.4%; 1953, 32.1%; 1958, 35.4%; 1963, 39.4%. From these figures we have another insight into the effects of the Occupation deconcentration effort, though one which, like the concentration ratio, has distinct limitations. The position of the top 100 tells us only the proportion represented by 100 firms; it tells nothing about the scale or character of relations among the top 100. By rough count

[37] Yamamura, "Zaibatsu," p. 552.

[38] The figures for 1937 and 1949 are taken from FTC, 1951 Concentration Ratio Study, Appendix Table 4. The figures for the three latter years are from an FTC press release entitled "An Investigation Regarding the Concentration of Capital and Capital Keiretsu" (Kaisha no Shihon Shuchu oyobi Shihon Keiretsu ni tsuite no Chosa), January 14, 1966.

it would appear that firms belonging to the Big Three groupings in 1937 and 1949 among the top 100 are as follows:

| | 1937 | 1949 |
|---|---|---|
| Mitsui | 6 | 8 |
| Mitsubishi | 6 | 6 |
| Sumitomo | 5 | 3 |
| | 17 | 17 |

But, as I interpret the situation, there is no comparison at all with what it means to "belong." In the *zaibatsu* period there were compelling powers and a singleness of purpose; in today's groupings there are diverse aspirations at a time when ties are insufficient to enforce uniform behavior.

But in spite of the limitations of this measurement, what do the statistics for the top 100 firms reveal about the effect of the Occupation on concentration? It is evident that it is *decrease*. But the real decrease is probably greater than the 37.4% to 30.4% shown above for 1937 and 1949—because the end of the war percentage for the top 100 firms would surely have been considerably above that for 1937. As noted, the years between the "China Incident" and the end of World War II were years of unusual merger and consolidation. Then, as now, the Japanese government believed that GNP is benefited by corporate consolidation. The continuous mergers of this period represented not only the strength of big capital but the persuasion of the government. Under its quasi-, then full, war powers, the Japanese government compelled consolidation after consolidation (see Chapter 6). Thus, in many instances proposed splits under the Excessive Concentration of Economic Power Law met enthusiastic response from former officers eager to have previously merged corporations resume their independent life. Not having the necessary data, I could not hazard a guess as to the position of the top 100 firms at war's end. Regardless of what the figure is, part of the subsequent decrease represented the exclusion of businesses closed under the Closed Institutions Law, as, for example, the South Manchurian Railroad, the largest corporation in Japan in 1937, and the Bank of Korea. No doubt, however, the greater part of the decrease reflected reorganizations "induced" under the Enterprise Reconstruction and Reorganization Law (such as the three-way split of Mitsubishi Chemical) and required under the Excessive Concentration of Economic Power Law (the three-way split of Mitsubishi Heavy Industries). When the top 100 firms account for

30.4% of the corporate and partnership capital of the nation, one cannot, however, assert that enterprise has been atomized.

It will be observed that the figure for 1963—39.4%—exceeds that for 1937—37.4%. But it would not be appropriate to conclude that concentration in 1963 was higher than in 1937, for there is so much left out of the figures. The position of the top 100 firms, as a proportion of total paid-in capital, tells nothing about the scale of their subsidiary networks, nothing of interrelations among the 100 or with firms outside such ranks, and nothing of the extent of cartelization.

Information on the subsidiary networks of the top 100, over time, is sketchy; it meshes for only one year with that of the previous data for the top 100. We do know, however, that in 1963 the top 100 had 4,270 subsidiaries, which represented 13.8% of the total capitalization of the nation.[39] Thus, in 1963 the true position of the top 100 was not 39.4%, but 53.2. For only two earlier years do we have data—1956 and 1960—but here the information is in absolute numbers only. In 1956 the top 100 had 1,860 subsidiaries, in 1960, 3,020.[40] To guess on the basis of 1963 data (i.e., assuming subsidiaries were of the same size distribution) might be to suppose that in 1956 they added about 6% to the position of the top majors, and in 1960, about 9%.

In using overall measures of concentration, it is noteworthy that among the several aggregate measures capital tends to give a higher index of concentration than the others. For example, if we compare the position of firms capitalized at Y10 billion ($27 million) and above in 1963, the 78 corporations in this category accounted for 31.9% of total capitalization, but only 12.8% of sales.[41] Of course, the more vertically integrated a firm is, the lower proportionally are its sales. If we take firms capitalized at the Y1 billion and above level in 1963, the positions[42] are: capital, 75%; assets, 66%; sales, 41%. Thus, in having the FTC statistics for the top 100 in the form of the proportion of total capitalization, I am using a measure that gives a stronger indication of concentration than other measures.

While both concentration ratios, with their market measures and the overall index of concentration as measured by capital, show recently increasing concentration, obviously the trend, it is significant

[39] *Ibid.*

[40] *Ibid.*

[41] Tax Bureau, Ministry of Finance, *The Realities of Corporate Enterprise 1963* (Kokusetsucho, *Hojin Kigyo no Jittai, Showa 38 Nenbun*), April 1965, calculated from Table 1-1.

[42] Ministry of Finance, *Statistical Yearbook of Corporate Enterprise, 1963* (Okurasho, *Hojin Kigyo Tokei Nempo, Showa 38 Nendo*), December 1964, calculated from Table 1-2.

that these developments are taking place amidst fierce struggles for position.

### *Fluidity in Market Positions*

A most interesting feature of Japan's leading markets in recent years has been the dramatic shifts in position among the majors. The ranking of the top firms in coal may have been the same in 1937, 1949, and 1962, but this is not the situation in a number of the industrial markets. There the amount of rivalry has been exceptional. The major in first place one year may be in fourth place two years hence, a circumstance the Japanese are prone to describe as "excessive competition." The tendency to see something wrong with struggles for position now, as in the early 1930s, is probably in part a consequence of the Confucian heritage with its emphasis on status. To many Japanese there is something improper about a struggle for position, though the strength of this viewpoint would seem to be related to one's "location." While former Prime Minister Yoshida disparaged new businesses which participated in undertakings "to the detriment of the old established concerns," one finds a lively sense of competition among new firms. Now that the old established concerns are no longer so "established," there is vigorous competition among them. Examples of what has been happening to individual firms will be seen in Table 14-5.

The fluidity in market rankings that has characterized a large num-

Table 14-5: EXAMPLES OF MARKET FLUIDITY BETWEEN 1959 AND 1962 AMONG TOP 10 FIRMS

| *Product* | *1962 compared to* | *Rankings* | *Percent mkt represented 1959* | *Percent mkt represented 1962* |
|---|---|---|---|---|
| urea | 1959 | 1, 4, 5, 2, 3, 6, 7, 10, 8, n.l. | 97 | 91 |
| ethylene | 1960 | 2, 4, 3, 1, n.l. | 100 | 100 |
| syn. fibers | 1959 | 1, 3, 2, 4, 6, 7, 8, 5, 9, 10 | 100 | 96 |
| petroleum products | 1959 | 2, 3, 4, 1, 5, 6, 8, 7, n.l. 9 | 86 | 86 |
| turbines | 1960 | 1, 3, 2, 5, 4, 7, 6, 8 | 100 | 100 |
| bearings | 1959 | 3, 2, 1, 4, 5, 6, 8, 7, n.l. 10 | 95 | 92 |
| generators | 1960 | 2, 3, 1, 5, 4, 7, 8, 6, 9, 10 | 93 | 95 |
| elec. locomotives | 1960 | 3, 1, 4, 2, 5, n.l. | 100 | 100 |
| steel shipbldg. | 1959 | 5,* 1, 2, 3, 4, 6, n.l. 8, 9, n.l. | 67 | 75 |

Source: FTC.

*The comparison is not valid because of mergers. The firm in 5th position in 1959 was Harima Shipbuilding; the firm in first position in 1962 was Ishikawajima-Harima Heavy Industries.

ber of markets in recent years ties directly into the interpretation of the successor *keiretsu* and *kinyu keiretsu* which I put forward earlier in this book. That is, the fluidity is a product of their weakness. It seems that what has happened during these last few years is that, though the corporate names have remained the same, the meaning behind them has changed. Because of the ineffectiveness of *keiretsu* and *kinyu keiretsu* controls, there is no longer unified group behavior. Oligopolist A does not hesitate to challenge B because he is in fact only facing B in markets of A's strength. While there is a common interest among members of the *keiretsu* and *kinyu keiretsu* groupings, the common interest is not enough to cause a corporation to disadvantage itself for the good of the whole.

It has been suggested that the principal avenues to concentration in these years have been mergers, expanded subsidiary networks, and cartelization. Inasmuch as all three were highly restricted or prohibited outright by the Antimonopoly Law, the "permanent" legislation which was to ensure the continuance of a deconcentrated economy, let us briefly recall developments to see how these avenues have been opened up.

Because expansion via merger had greatly enhanced the position of the *zaibatsu*, the provisions of the Antimonopoly Law were stringent, both with respect to straight mergers and to acquisition of assets (Japan, it is to be noted, had a "Celler amendment" three years before its enactment in the U.S.). Originally, mergers and the transfer of assets required FTC approval. Grounds for disapproval were: (a) when the merger was not considered to contribute to the rationalization of the enterprise; (b) when it resulted in disparities in bargaining power; (c) when it resulted in a substantial restraint of competition; and (d) when induced by unfair means.[43] The 1949 amendments dropped the rationalization proviso for mergers and transfer of assets.[44] Furthermore, prior FTC approval for mergers and transfer of assets was likewise deleted and a reporting system substituted. Intent to merge or transfer assets had to be reported to the FTC 30 days in advance; if the FTC disapproved, the disapproval was to be indicated

[43] Discussions in English of the law and its amendments are to be found in various sources; see esp. Kanazawa Yoshio, "Regulation of Corporate Enterprise," Sung Yoon Cho, "Japan," in *Antitrust Development and Regulations of Foreign Countries*, which is part 2 of *Hearings on Foreign Trade and Antitrust Laws* before the United States Senate Subcommittee on Antitrust and Monopoly, 89th Cong., 1st Sess., pp. 977-1,011; Ariga Michiko and Luvern V. Rieke, "The Antimonopoly Law of Japan and Its Enforcement"; Corwin D. Edwards, *Trade Regulations Overseas*, Dobbs Ferry, N.Y., 1966, the chapter entitled, "Japan," pp. 647-726; and Iyori Hiroshi, *Antimonopoly Legislation in Japan*, New York, 1969.

[44] Kanazawa, "Regulation of Corporate Enterprise," p. 488.

within the 30-day period.[45] The 1953 amendments removed the "disparities in bargaining power" proviso, thus causing the FTC decision to object to rest on "substantial lessening of competition" and "unfair business practices."[46] Intent to merge or transfer assets must still, however, be reported to the FTC 30 days in advance.

Originally the Antimonopoly Law made intercorporate shareholding and interlocking directorates—the stuff of which subsidiaries are made—highly restrictive. Among non-financial companies, intercorporate shareholding had to be approved by the FTC.[47] Approval was likely in the case of single-layer subsidiaries having some technological connexity with the parent firm, where the parent firm would hold close to 100% of the stock. Otherwise, no nonfinancial company was to hold stocks of another. As we have seen, both Japanese business and American business criticized such strait-jacketing, and in 1949 the law was amended to provide that intercorporate shareholding was legal provided that it was not obtained by unfair means and did not constitute a substantial lessening of competition.[48] The 1953 amendments reaffirmed this. Financial institutions were prohibited from holding shares in institutions with which they were competing, but were treated more liberally regarding stockholding elsewhere. Originally they were limited to 5% stockholding, which under the 1953 amendments was raised to 10%.[49]

The provisions governing restrictions on personnel interlocks underwent comparable transformation. Originally the law said no officer could become an officer in a competing company; that an officer could not become an officer in a company where more than one-fourth or more of the officers of such company were already officers of a third company; and that no person could be an officer of four or more companies.[50] The 1949 amendments on personnel interlocks were modified along the same lines as intercorporate stockholding, that is, that they were legal if not obtained by unfair means and if they did not tend substantially to lessen competition,[51] which is the form in which the provision stands today.

[45] *Ibid.*

[46] Cf. Japan Productivity Center, *Control of Restrictive Trade Practices in Japan*, p. 9.

[47] Intercorporate shareholding among nonfinancial companies is governed by Article 10.

[48] Kanazawa, "Regulation of Corporate Enterprise," in von Mehren, *Law in Japan*, p. 488.

[49] Intercorporate shareholding among financial institutions is governed by Article 11.

[50] Personnel interlocks are governed by Article 13.

[51] Kanazawa, "Regulation of Corporate Enterprise," p. 488.

In the original Antimonopoly Law, cartels were banned outright;[52] in the 1953 amendments the *per se* tests of illegality were removed and two categories of cartels were authorized, antidepression and rationalization.[53] However, because of the cumbersomeness of this route, compared to the ease of other paths, the Antimonopoly Law has been little used for cartelization.

*Mergers*

Mergers are an increasingly important avenue to the growth of concentration in the Japanese economy. The most dramatic merging for an entire industry occurred in shipping on April 1, 1964, when 97 companies were consolidated into six groupings. To effect this consolidation 12 key companies merged to become six, while the remaining companies were grouped around these six either in the form of *keiretsu* firms or firms "especially attached." A summary of this grand consolidation which the Japanese government took the lead in effecting, will be seen in Table 14-6. Under the Law for the Adjustment and Reconstruction of Shipping, passed by the Diet on June 5, 1963, only companies operating fleets of one million deadweight tons or more (500,000 of their own tonnage, 500,000 chartered) are eligible for a five-year moratorium on interest payments to the Japan Development Bank and to receive a subsidy from the Japanese government.[54] The industry initially balked at accepting such a proposal, the loss of corporate identity not being a cheering prospect, but under skillful government lobbying and the bait of special consideration on interest payments to the debt-ridden firms, companies were brought into line. A similar bill had failed to pass the previous Diet. The industry had been dealt a severe blow in the cancellation of government indemnity payments (October 19, 1946; cf. Chapter 5), for virtually the entire Japanese commercial fleet had been wiped out during World War II. Accordingly, borrowings which are large in all major Japanese industries are huge in the case of shipping companies. Therefore, proffered assistance on interest payments was heady inducement.

Not only shipping but shipbuilding has undergone dramatic mergers. There was a major merger in 1960 when Harima Shipbuilding and Ishikawajima Heavy Industries formed the Ishikawajima-Harima Heavy Industries Co. The merger brought the company to

52 The prohibition of cartels was stated in general language in Article 3, in precise terms in Articles 4 and 5, and the proscription from membership in international cartels by Article 6.

53 Articles 3 and 4 were rescinded. Permission to form antidepression and rationalization cartels was given in additional provisions to Article 24.

54 English edition of *Mainichi Shimbun*, October 29, 1963.

Table 14-6: CONSOLIDATION OF JAPAN'S SHIPPING INDUSTRY

APRIL 1, 1964

| | Deadweight tons |
|---|---|
| *Nippon Yusen Kaisha (NYK)* | 2,278,739 |
| Nippon Yusen Kaisha, Mitsubishi Kaiun merged | 1,046,942 |
| 7 *keiretsu* companies | 1,008,434 |
| 7 affiliated companies | 223,363 |
| *Yamashita-Shin Nippon Kisen* | 1,113,615 |
| Yamashita Kisen, Shin Nippon Kisen merged | 570,031 |
| 4 *keiretsu* companies | 421,112 |
| 9 affiliated companies | 122,472 |
| *Japan Lines* | 1,016,948 |
| Nissan Kisen, Nippon Yusosen (oil tanker) merged | 608,977 |
| 2 *keiretsu* firms | 355,320 |
| 4 affiliated companies | 52,651 |
| *Showa Kaiun* | 1,078,112 |
| Nitto Shosen, Daido Kaiun merged | 897,348 |
| 1 *keiretsu* company | 116,074 |
| 2 affiliated companies | 64,690 |
| *Kawasaki Shipping* | 1,531,382 |
| Kawasaki Kisen, Iino Kaiun merged | 932,715 |
| 8 *keiretsu* companies | 378,211 |
| 8 affiliated companies | 220,456 |
| *Osaka Shosen-Mitsui Steamship* | 2,317,911 |
| Osaka Shosen, Mitsui Steamship merged | 1,228,253 |
| 5 *keiretsu* companies | 312,157 |
| 27 affiliated companies | 777,501 |

| | | |
|---|---|---|
| merged tonnage | (12 cos.) | 5,284,266 |
| *keiretsu* tonnage | (28 cos.) | 2,591,308 |
| affiliated tonnage | (57 cos.) | 1,461,133 |

Source: Ministry of Transportation, Shipping Bureau, "The Quantity of Shipping According to the Groupings" (Unyusho, Kaiun Kyoku, "Gurupu betsu Sempaku Ryo"), mimeog., Dec. 21, 1963.

second place in the industry in 1961 and first place the following year.[55] But undoubtedly, until very recently, the merger with the greatest repercussions both at home and abroad was the 1964 merger of the three Mitsubishi Heavy Industries companies.

Although the 1949 three-way split of Mitsubishi Heavy Industries took place under the Excessive Concentration of Economic Power Law, it will be recalled that the Deconcentration Review Board, while reluctantly approving the split, never declared Mitsubishi Heavy Industries an excessive concentration; nor did it make any finding that the company restricted competition or impaired the opportunity for others to engage in business independently in the same field. The three-way split was not according to product lines, but rather to geography: the Nagasaki and Hiroshima works became, under slightly later nomenclature, Mitsubishi Shipbuilding; the Kobe and Nagoya works, Mitsubishi Heavy Industries Reorganized; and the Tokyo and Yokohama works, Mitsubishi Japan Heavy Industries.[56] The consequence of dividing the corporation along geographic lines was that competition kept breaking out. There was no agreeable division of the markets in which they were operating: shipbuilding, ship repair; diesel engines, turbines; automobiles, trucks and buses; railroad cars; paper-making machinery, agricultural machinery, mining machinery, salvage machinery; bridge materials; aircraft; ordnance; and warships.[57] It would be my guess that had the three successor companies been operating under *zaibatsu* controls, competition could have been contained. Although the three companies had shared a common corporate existence as recently as 1949; although the officers had had "Mitsubishi" rearing; although the three presidents were members of the Friday Club; and although the three companies were members of the *kinyu keiretsu* of the Mitsubishi Bank—these factors, in combination, were not sufficient to inhibit competition. Is the "failure" not something of a commentary on today's groupings?

In accordance with the Antimonopoly Law, the three Mitsubishi companies filed an intent to merge with the FTC 30 days in advance. Inasmuch as the presently remaining grounds for disapproval of mergers are "substantial lessening of competition" and "unfair busi-

[55] FTC, 1964, Concentration Ratio Study.

[56] The original names under a short-lived program to eliminate *zaibatsu* trade names did not contain "Mitsubishi," but were, in the order cited, West Japan Heavy Industries, Central Japan Heavy Industries, and East Japan Heavy Industries.

[57] Yamaichi Securities Co., *Corporation Yearbook* (Yamaichi Shoken, *Kabushiki Kaisha Nenkan*), under the entries for the three companies.

ness practices," and the question to which members of the FTC addressed themselves was—would competition be substantially reduced if the three companies came together? The FTC held mid-winter hearings on the matter. Like Western economists, who seek concentration answers from concentration ratios, the members proceeded to seek an answer to this question by asking what would be the combined position of the three companies in the markets in which they were operating. In a press release following the hearings, the commission stated that, on the basis of production positions for the latest years, the merged company would likely account for the following positions:[58]

| | |
|---|---|
| shipbuilding | 28% |
| ship repair | 27 |
| marine diesels | 27 |
| marine turbines | 27 |
| turbines for electric power companies | 24 |
| boilers for electric power companies | 46 |
| turbines and boilers for factory use | 35-42 |
| paper-making machinery | 63 |
| trucks (including "ordinary" automobiles) | 25 |
| buses | 26 |

While the commission may have considered the several other markets in which the three companies were engaged—agricultural machinery, steel-fabricating machinery, chemical-machinery, mining machinery, salvage machinery, bridge materials, railroad cars, aircraft, ordnance, warships—for some odd reason its press release contained only the markets listed above. That the discussion of this merger by Commissioner Ariga and Professor Rieke makes no reference to the other markets in which the companies were engaged, leads me to conclude that the commission gave no attention to these other markets.[59] The eventual result of the commission's approach was approval of the merger, provided there would be divestiture of some of the company's capacity in paper-making machinery!

But one cannot gain an appropriate sense of restraint or absence of restraint from individual consideration of these markets. In addition,

[58] FTC press release, "Concerning the Merger of the Three Mitsubishi Heavy Industries Companies" ("Mitsubishi Sanjuko no Gappei ni tsuite"), January 21, 1964.

[59] Ariga and Rieke, p. 466.

the firm needs to be viewed whole. What effect would the firm considered whole have on an entrant to the markets in which it was engaged? Would it not seem altogether reasonable to suppose that it would be considerably more inhibiting than the percentage figures would indicate? In 1964 Mitsubishi Heavy Industries had the third highest sales among industrials in Japan—Hitachi, Y301 billion ($836 million); Yawata Steel, Y272 billion ($755 million); and Mitsubishi Heavy Industries, Y263 billion ($730 million). In 1966 it was in first place.[60]

While the mergers in shipping and shipbuilding have been dramatic, mergers in recent years have been increasing across the board in size and numbers. A study of Table 14-7 will make this abundantly clear, and if data for the most recent years were available it would but further underscore it. Not all mergers are cause for concern to those dedicated to the maintenance of an unconcentrated economy in Japan. Table 14-7 will indicate the small size of many of the mergers, and

Table 14-7: MERGERS BY SIZE OF ENTERPRISE, 1948-63 FISCAL YEAR

(size is post-merger)

| *Capital* (in dollars) | 1950 | 1952 | 1954 | 1956 | 1958 | 1960 | 1961 | 1962 | 1963 | 1964 | 1965 |
|---|---|---|---|---|---|---|---|---|---|---|---|
| Under 1,388 | 27 | 15 | 6 | 10 | 4 | 2 | 2 | 6 | 0 | 3 | 1 |
| 1,388-2,777 | 34 | 24 | 15 | 18 | 10 | 8 | 6 | 9 | 11 | 5 | 6 |
| 2,777-13,888 | 215 | 162 | 151 | 150 | 152 | 144 | 147 | 146 | 188 | 182 | 220 |
| 13,888-27,777 | 62 | 71 | 33 | 75 | 85 | 100 | 125 | 131 | 187 | 160 | 169 |
| 27,777-138,888 | 68 | 70 | 73 | 89 | 81 | 94 | 176 | 221 | 320 | 313 | 318 |
| 138,888-277,777 | 7 | 17 | 15 | 17 | 16 | 33 | 63 | 72 | 115 | 67 | 57 |
| 277,777-1,388,888 | 7 | 19 | 23 | 13 | 23 | 41 | 45 | 91 | 116 | 90 | 93 |
| 1,388,888-2,777,777 | 0 | 4 | 5 | 2 | 2 | 8 | 9 | 10 | 15 | 14 | 16 |
| 2,777,777-13,888,888 | 0 | 3 | 4 | 6 | 7 | 9 | 13 | 23 | 28 | 17 | 8 |
| 13,888,888-27,777,777 | 0 | 0 | 0 | 1 | 1 | 0 | 3 | 3 | 5 | 4 | 3 |
| 27,777,777 and above | 0 | 0 | 0 | 0 | 0 | 1 | 2 | 3 | 12 | 9 | 3 |
| | 420 | 385 | 325 | 381 | 381 | 440 | 591 | 715 | 997 | 864 | 894 |

Source: Economic Investigative Council, *Research on Business Groupings*, 1967 edition, p. 17, where it is stated that the information is taken from the FTC's *Annual Report* for 1965. It is not clear to me whether the information is from the 1965 *Report* or the annual *Reports* up to and including the 1965 *Report*.

[60] 1964 figures from Economic Investigative Council, *Research on Business Groupings*, 1965, pp. 33-40. In 1965, according to *Fortune* magazine's 1966 listing, it ranked second within Japan and 19th in the world, exclusive of American corporations. *Fortune*, August 1966, pp. 148-51. 1966 figures from Economic Investigative Council, *Research on Business Groupings*, 1967, pp. 41-48.

will show that genuine economics of production might be expected to follow. The mergers that are cause for concern, however, are those occurring at the largest and next to largest level. On the basis of American experience, with respect to economies of scale, it would seem most improbable that economies could be expected to follow in the case of the last two size categories.[61] However, Mrs. Ariga and Professor Rieke observe in their 1964 article: "The astonishing thing is that, except for . . . [one case] the Commission has issued no complaints."[62] The commission has, however, bolstered its courage sufficiently to argue that tax concessions should not be used as bait to induce mergers![63]

An analysis of Table 14-7 will indicate that between 1952 and 1960 the total number of mergers held fairly steady. 1961 was roughly one-third higher than 1960; 1962 was somewhat over one-fifth higher; and 1963 was two-fifths higher than 1962. Both 1964 and 1965 were below 1963. In Japan mergers through the "acquisition of assets" route are reported separately from regular mergers, and are shown in Table 14-8. In this table 1963, likewise, represents the high for the years shown. Combining the two types of consolidation, we find the following totals:

| | | | | | | | |
|---|---|---|---|---|---|---|---|
| | | 1954 | 492 | 1960 | 584 | 1963 | 1,220 |
| 1950 | 629 | 1956 | 590 | 1961 | 753 | 1964 | 1,059 |
| 1952 | 509 | 1958 | 484 | 1962 | 908 | 1965 | 1,096 |

Again it will be seen from the combined figures that it is 1961 that represents the beginning of the sharp upturn.

Studies of the effect of subsidiaries on the market position of majors are only beginning to be made, but recently the FTC released a report on the effect of subsidiaries in the iron and steel industry. Its story is dramatic and underscores the hazards of disregarding subsidiaries when talking about market concentration figures. The findings are reproduced here as Table 14-9. It will indicate that, depending on the iron and steel submarket in question, concentration when subsidiaries are included in the calculation increases from a few percentage points to many. As will be seen, in pig iron and steel pipe the change is minimal. In such lines as cold-rolled steel plates, on the other hand, the increase is 12 percentage points for the top firm; 22 percentage points

[61] J. S. Bain, *Barriers to New Competition*, Cambridge, 1956, esp. Chap. III.
[62] Ariga and Rieke, "The Antimonopoly Law of Japan," *Washington Law Review*, August 1964, p. 465.
[63] *Ibid.*, p. 468.

Table 14-8: MERGERS THROUGH ACQUISITION OF ASSETS

(capital is that of the company acquiring the assets at the time of the acquisition)

| *Capital* (in dollars) | 1950 | 1951 | 1952 | 1953 | 1954 | 1955 | 1956 | 1957 | 1958 | 1959 | 1960 | 1961 | 1962 | 1963 | 1964 | 1965 |
|---|---|---|---|---|---|---|---|---|---|---|---|---|---|---|---|---|
| Under 1,388 | 13 | 9 | 1 | 4 | 4 | 1 | 6 | 0 | 0 | 2 | 0 | 1 | 0 | 0 | 1 | 1 |
| 1,388-2,777 | 15 | 23 | 5 | 3 | 6 | 4 | 2 | 2 | 4 | 2 | 2 | 2 | 3 | 3 | 1 | 2 |
| 2,777-13,888 | 78 | 64 | 44 | 34 | 44 | 31 | 55 | 18 | 20 | 31 | 29 | 36 | 48 | 59 | 31 | 39 |
| 13,888-27,777 | 30 | 26 | 22 | 15 | 27 | 16 | 32 | 26 | 20 | 22 | 19 | 36 | 30 | 27 | 30 | 31 |
| 27,777-,38,888 | 36 | 39 | 30 | 31 | 35 | 40 | 52 | 35 | 34 | 21 | 35 | 34 | 49 | 58 | 63 | 53 |
| 138,888-277,777 | 12 | 3 | 4 | 16 | 15 | 12 | 17 | 17 | 15 | 11 | 15 | 13 | 16 | 22 | 21 | 22 |
| 277,777-1,388,888 | 15 | 9 | 12 | 15 | 21 | 17 | 26 | 26 | 5 | 24 | 21 | 29 | 29 | 32 | 25 | 30 |
| 1,388,888-2,777,777 | 8 | 1 | 6 | 3 | 3 | 7 | 8 | 5 | 5 | 11 | 7 | 2 | 5 | 5 | 9 | 8 |
| 2,777,777-13,888,888 | 2 | 5 | 0 | 5 | 11 | 13 | 11 | 11 | 0 | 15 | 16 | 8 | 11 | 14 | 14 | 10 |
| 13,888,888-27,777,777 | 0 | 3 | 0 | 0 | 1 | 2 | 0 | 0 | 0 | 0 | 0 | 1 | 1 | 1 | 0 | 2 |
| 27,777,777 and above | 0 | 0 | 0 | 0 | 0 | 0 | 0 | 0 | 0 | 0 | 0 | 0 | 1 | 2 | 0 | 4 |
| | 209 | 182 | 124 | 126 | 167 | 143 | 209 | 140 | 103 | 139 | 144 | 162 | 193 | 223 | 195 | 202 |

*Correction of apparent arithmetic error. The source shows 1950 total as 207; the 1958 total as 118.

Source: EIC, *Research on Business Groupings*, 1967 edition, p. 18.

**Table 14-9: EFFECT OF SUBSIDIARIES ON MARKET CONCENTRATION RATIOS IN THE STEEL INDUSTRY (1963)**

(market position in percent)

| | *Top firm* | | *Top 3 firms* | | *Top 5 firms* | |
|---|---|---|---|---|---|---|
| | major | with subs | majors | with subs | majors | with subs |
| pig iron | 25 | 28 | 63 | 65 | 83 | 86 |
| crude steel | 19 | 23 | 45 | 51 | 63 | 69 |
| ordinary, hot-rolled steel prod. | 20 | 24 | 47 | 54 | 66 | 73 |
| special, hot-rolled steel prod. | 13 | 18 | 35 | 46 | 50 | 62 |
| wide, cold-rolled steel sheets | 38 | 51 | 61 | 89 | 79 | 98 |
| cold-rolled steel plates | 17 | 29 | 45 | 67 | 61 | 85 |
| galvanized iron sheets | 15 | 25 | 35 | 59 | 50 | 78 |
| tin-plate sheets | 42 | 66 | 81 | 88 | 89 | 91 |
| steel pipe | 25 | 25 | 57 | 60 | 72 | 75 |
| light steel shapes | 18 | 20 | 38 | 44 | 48 | 56 |

Source: FTC, *The Effect of Keiretsu-ization on Industrial Concentration — The Steel Industry* (Kosei Torihiki Iinkai, *Keiretsuka ni yoru Seisan Shuchu no Jittai-Tekkogyo*), Press release dated Dec. 1965, without indication of day.

for the position of the top three firms and 24 percentage points for the top five. From our examination of subsidiaries in the preceding chapter it should be evident that while there is much that is conglomerate about these groupings there is also much that is market-related. If one is attempting to get at concentration from concentration ratios it is risky indeed to disregard the effect of these companies on the market positions of the majors.

From the foregoing it is evident that concentration in an economy and concentration within markets, as measured by concentration ratios, do not necessarily reveal a one-to-one relationship. Where subsidiary networks are strong, where the majors are conglomerate, where ties among majors cut across market boundaries, where cartelization is significant, concentration ratios do not reveal the extent of concentration in an economy. Similarly, one cannot use the position of the top 100 firms as a proportion of total paid-in capital as a single indicator of concentration in an economy.

# 15.

## Cartels

In English, "cartel" refers to a treaty-like arrangement among firms within a market, with the typical objective of enhancing profits.[1] The restrictive devices for accomplishing this objective, or attempting to accomplish it, may differ. They may take the form of an agreed upon price; centralized selling to assure that no slip-ups occur with respect to the pricing; restriction of production and division of markets; limitation on new investment, control over new technology; or other arrangements. In English usage, *cartel* refers only to form. Nothing is implied about the degree of resulting market power. Cartel strength depends on a variety of factors—the proportion of the market represented by the cartel; the ability of the cartel to keep members sufficiently satisfied that they will agree to remain members and accordingly abide by its decisions; the elasticity of demand for the commodity in question; the ease of entry into the market, and so forth.

Judged by its usage among leading Japanese writers, "karuteru" refers only in part to what is covered by the English usage of the word. Japanese writers regard a cartel as synonymous with oligopoly. For example, Misonou Hitoshi, a prominent Japanese economist, uses cartel to describe different levels of market concentration. He speaks of markets in which the top 10 firms account for 80% of output as representing the "cartel form"; those in which the top 10 account for 50% of output are "quasi-cartel" in form.[2]

In English, however, *cartel* and *oligopoly* are two separate concepts. *Oligopoly* refers to a situation in which numbers in a market are sufficiently few that the interdependence of firms is sensed and accordingly taken into account in deciding on behavior. It contrasts with competition where numbers are so great that an individual firm (because of its small size in relation to the whole) acts as if its behavior would have no effect on others. One could therefore say that oligopoly

[1] One cannot explore the subject of cartelization in Japan without first defining the key word. Japanese-English dictionaries may render "karuteru" as "cartel," but it is evident the meanings in Japanese and in English are not the same. Japanese writers use the term to cover various situations, and only in part the circumstance indicated by the English use of the term.

[2] Misonou Hitoshi, *Monopoly in Japan* (*Nihon no Dokusen*), Tokyo, p. 84.

represents understood interdependence, cartel, an explicit agreement.

But in addition to using "cartel" in the sense of *oligopoly*, Japanese writers use the term in other ways. One finds "cartel laws" covering holding companies, combine control devices, and all other kinds of restrictive business practices or arrangements, either on a market basis or in a conglomerate setting. In a 1964 publication, *Cartels in Japan* (*Nihon no Karuteru*) edited by Yoshida Jimbu, chief of the Economic Division of the Fair Trade Commission, there is a table entitled, "Japan's Cartel Laws," which begins with the ordinance calling for the dissolution of the Mitsui, Mitsubishi, Sumitomo, and Yasuda top-holding companies, and includes the entire range of Occupation measures dealing with economic deconcentration, as well as subsequent legislation selected on an equally broad basis.[3]

It is difficult to discuss a problem when usage of a key term varies so widely. This diversity in usage may account for the wide differences of view which are likely to emerge when English-language economists, using "cartel" in the English sense of the word, begin to discuss Japan's cartel history with Japanese lawyers and economists. It may further account for widespread foreign misapprehension, perhaps stemming originally from Japanese sources, as to what cartelization in Japan's past has been. Japanese usage, while considerably broader than the English, does include horizontal associations. Unless otherwise specified, for purposes of discussion in this chapter, "cartels" will only be used in the sense of horizontal associations.

## *The Paucity of Cartels Before the 1920s*

Japan does not have a long tradition of cartels. As will be seen from Table 15-1, there were but three cartels in Japan before the 1920s. Given the tradition toward economic concentration, this may seem extremely surprising. I would hypothesize here that the historical paucity of cartels in Japan was the product of the "cordial oligopoly"

[3] Yoshida Jimbu, ed., *Cartels in Japan* (*Nihon no Karuteru*), Tokyo, 1964, pp. 104-14. In this sense, Japanese usage appears to follow German practice. As pointed out in the OECD publication, *Glossary of Terms Relating to Restrictive Business Practices*, Paris, 1965, pp. 29-31:

> "Kartell" in German law denotes an agreement made by enterprises or by an association of enterprises for a common purpose, or a decision of an association of enterprises which is apt to influence by restraint of competition, the production or market conditions with respect to goods or services. Generally, under the prevailing situation in Germany, only horizontal restraints of competition by agreement are termed "Kartell." However, the term "Kartellrecht" (cartel law) is used in a broad sense to denote the entire law of restrictive business practices. The terms "kartellbehorde" (cartel authority) and "Bundeskartellamt" (Federal Cartel Office) are to be understood in this sense.

Table 15-1: JAPANESE DOMESTIC CARTELS, 1868-1931,
(Listed by date of establishment)

Note: This table has been compiled from two sources. Cartels which are found in both sources are without superscript. Those found in source one alone are marked with "a"; those in source two alone, with "b". Primary reliance has been placed on source two for indication of control objectives. The letter designations come from source two.

Abbreviations employed in describing control objectives

| | | | |
|---|---|---|---|
| A | Price agreement | G | Money pool |
| B | Quality standards agreement | H | Profit pool |
| C | Agreement on fields of production | I | Allocation of orders |
| D | Supply agreement | J | Division of sales |
| E | Production agreement | K | Joint selling |
| F | Geographic division of the market | L | Joint raw-material purchases |
| | | M | Agreement on shipping charges |

| | | |
|---|---|---|
| Japan Paper Manufacturers Federation (Nippon Seishi Rengokai) | 1880 | A, D, E |
| Japan (Cotton) Spinning Federation (Dai Dippon Boseki Rengokai) | 1882 | E, M |
| Japan Fertilizer Manufacturers Federation[1] (Dai Nippon Hiryo Rengokai) | 1907 | production control |
| Bleaching Powder[a] (Sarashiko Rengokai) | 1920 | production control |
| Japan Wool Industry Association[a] (Nippon Yomo Kogyo Kai) | 1920 | production control |
| Canned Crab Sales Association[a] (Kani Kanzume Kyodo Hambai KK) | 1920 | marketing controls |
| Copper - called the Wednesday Association (Suiyokai) | 1920[2] | A, D, K |
| Coal Mining Federation (Sekitan Kogyo Rengokai) | 1921 | D |
| Cement Federation[b] (Cemento Rengokai) | 1924 | E |

| | | |
|---|---|---|
| Pig Iron Association<br>(Sentetsu Kyodo Kumiai) | 1926 | A, K |
| Bar Steel Association<br>(Joko Bunya Kyoteikai) | 1926 | C, E |
| Western Paper Corp.[b]<br>(Kyodo Yoshi KK) | 1926 | K |
| Kanto Steel Sales Association<br>(Kanto Kozai Hambai Kumiai) | 1927 | A, C, E, K |
| Association of the Spun Silk Industry<br>(Kembo Kogyo Kai) | 1927 | B, E |
| Sugar Association[a]<br>(Sato Kyokyu Kumiai) | 1927 | marketing |
| Japan Rayon Federation<br>(Nippon Jinken Rengokai) | 1927[3] | A, D, E, F |
| Gasoline Agreement[b]<br>(Kihatsuyu Kyotei) | 1928 | A |
| Steel Federation<br>(Kozai Rengo Kai)<br>bars and flat steel | 1929 | production |
| All-Japan Lime Nitrate Joint Sales Association<br>(Zenkoku Sekkai Chisso Kyohan Kumiai) | 1929 | A, D, E, H, J, K |
| Sheet Iron and Steel Sales Association<br>(Chuban Kyohan Kumiai)<br>sheet iron & medium thick steel | 1930 | marketing |
| Japan Wire Sales Association<br>(Nippon Senzai Kyohan Kumiai)<br>steel wire | 1930 | marketing |
| All Japan Flour Milling Sales Association<br>(Zenkoku Seifun Hambai Kumiai) | 1930 | marketing |
| Tokyo Petroleum Association[a]<br>(Tokyo Sekiyu Kyokai) | 1930 | marketing |
| Ammonium sulphate agreement[a] | 1930 | marketing |
| Hemp agreement[a] | 1931 | production |
| Steel Bar Sales Association<br>(Chugata Yamagatako Kyohan Kumiai)<br>medium-sized chevron bars | 1931 | marketing |

| | | |
|---|---|---|
| Steel Bars Sales Association (Kogata Yamagatako Kyohan Kumiai) small-sized chevron bars | 1931 | marketing |
| Japan Sheet Iron and Steel Sales Assoc. (Nihon Atsuban Kyohan Kumiai) Thick sheet iron and steel | 1931 | marketing |
| Japan Sales Association (Nippon Kurohan Kyohan Kumiai) black sheet | 1931[4] | marketing |
| Japan Canned Salmon Association[a] (Nihon Sakemasu Kanzumegyo Suisan Kumiai) | 1931 | marketing |

Sources: Source one, Hadley, *Concentrated Business Power in Japan*, pp. 27-29 where acknowledgment is made to Kugai Saburo who prepared the table for me. Source two, Shibagaki Kazuo, *Mitsui and Mitsubishi, One Hundred Years* (Mitsui, Mitsubishi no Hyaku Nen), Tokyo, 1968, p. 99. Professor Shibagaki lists among his sources, Minobe Ryokichi, *Cartels, Trusts, Konzern* and Oshima Shotaro, *Cartel-like Controls Among the Major Industries in our Country*, (Waga Kuni Shuyo Sangyo ni okeru, Karuteru-teki Tosei).

Notes:

1. It is not clear but it would appear that this cartel taken from source one and a Calcium Superphosphate Manufacturers Association (Karinsan Dogyosha Kai) listed as established in 1920 in source two are one and the same cartel, for it is explained in source one that the fertilizer cartel dealt in calcium superphosphate. Source two lists the control objectives as covering A, D, F, L. I have not been able to resolve the discrepancy in dates.
2. Listed in source two as established in 1921.
3. Listed in source one as established in 1929.
4. Source two lists this as being established in two parts, "black sheet" - thin in 1930 and "black sheet" - thick in 1931.

that characterized the handful of combines dominating the economy. Where the oligopolists were the same from market to market, joint behavior could be handled on an intuitive basis; explicit agreements were unnecessary. It is significant that in textiles—a key market in Japan's developing economy, a market characterized, with one exception, by the absence of the combines—there was a sustained and powerful cartel, which we will look at briefly.

In a 1939 article, the *Oriental Economist* described the Japan Cotton Spinners' Association as "the oldest autonomous cartel in Japan, having been organized in October 1882. . . . Today 80 companies with an aggregate spindlage of 12,550,000 are affiliated with the association, and in Japan proper, there are only two independent companies, both with a very limited capacity. . . ."

"The first of these contracts, which was entered into between the Spinners' Association and the Nippon Yusen Kaisha in 1893, stipulates that the Nippon Yusen Kaisha in principle shall not transport Indian cotton bought for the account of persons other than the regular or associate members of the Association; that the N.Y.K. is to quote two different freight rates on Indian cotton, namely the net rate and a slightly higher formal rate, and that the N.Y.K. shall rebate to the Spinners' Association the difference between the two rates. Later, the Spinners' Association entered into the same arrangements with the Osaka Shosen Kaisha and two foreign shipping companies. By this monopoly of shipping space the association has been able to protect the member companies from the adverse pressure of foreign capital, and also virtually to prevent the existence of outsiders."[4] (According to Professor Lockwood 60% of Japan's raw cotton in the years just before World War I came from India.[5]) The article continued: "The association spends a small part of the rebated freight charges to maintain its Bombay branch office, and the remainder is rebated to the member companies according to the volume of their purchases of Indian cotton. Actually, however, the membership fees which the affiliated companies pay to the association, and which are fixed according to their spindlage, are paid from the rebates. . . . The contracts also have constituted an important financial source of the association, the amount of the freight difference rebated by the N.Y.K. to the Spinners' Association for the 1937 cotton year having amounted to about Y3,700,000. . . ." Likewise referring to this shipping arrangement, Professor Lockwood summarizes the role of the association in this way: "Its functions included (1) the encouragement of technical

[4] *Oriental Economist*, January 1939, pp. 29-30.
[5] Lockwood, *The Economic Development of Japan*, Princeton, 1954, p. 32.

improvements; (2) regulation of competition for workers; (3) representation of the spinners in negotiations at home and abroad over markets, credit facilities, freight rates, taxes, etc., and (4) production control exercised on eleven different occasions between 1890 and 1936."[6]

It seems plausible to me that there is a connection between the majors which operated in this industry alone and the industry's cartelization. The relations between the oligopolists of the textile industry appear to be different in kind from those among the oligopolists in other industries, where, because of top-holding company affiliation, they turn out to be related in market after market after market. However, Professor Kanazawa, who employs my "cordial oligopoly" thesis, uses it exactly opposite from the way I do. He asserts that this "situation [cordial oligopoly] placed a premium upon the achievement of stability through cartel understandings and organizations."[7] But inasmuch as there were only three cartels before the 1920s, it may be terminology that is at the basis of the difference.

The cartels that developed during the twenties and which spread rapidly in the thirties are probably explained by a combination of the sharp price adjustments—occasioned by the postwar recession, the financial crisis of 1927, and the Great Depression—in conjunction with the start of a long period of military engagements and preparations for larger ones. In this latter regard, there was the Manchurian War of 1931, the "Shanghai Incident" of 1932, the start of the China War in 1937, the takeover of Hainan and Indochina in 1940, and the outbreak of World War II the following year. Thus Japan's economy was on a partial or complete war footing for 14 years.

Japanese government officials have always felt that the Japanese economy required guidance, which preparations for military engagements and their prosecution made even more urgent. Not even the most ardent advocate of laissez-faire would propose to run a war economy on the market mechanism alone.

Earlier in Japan's modernization, "guidance" was handled through conversations between the pertinent ministers and the favored business houses. By the 1930s, however, with the expansion of the economy and an increase in the number of majors, more formal machinery was required. The recently developed cartels were the economic instruments relied on. In their article, Mrs. Ariga and Professor Rieke put forward a similar hypothesis about the origin of cartelization

[6] *Ibid.*, p. 231n.

[7] Kanazawa Yoshio, "The Regulation of Corporate Enterprise," in Arthur T. van Mehren, ed., *Law in Japan*, Cambridge, Mass., 1963, p. 482.

in Japan: "Need for development of industrial controls generated by the depression of the 1930's, the Manchurian Incident, and by an increased dependence on foreign trade brought about general and ultimately compulsory cartelization of Japan's economy."[8]

Future research may show that a combination of sharp price adjustments and orientation of the economy to a war footing may not be the whole explanation of the genesis of widespread cartelization in Japan in the 1920s and 1930s. But at the present time there do not seem to be stronger explanations, though there are certainly other explanations. The most common explanation among Japanese expositors follow along two lines frequently associated in presentation. The key concepts of these two lines are "big capital" and "confrontations."[9] According to the first, cartels cannot develop until capital is "big," and it is claimed that Japanese capital was not big until the 1920s. "Big" appears here to be used in two different senses—in that of oligopoly levels such as those suggested by Professor Misonou in stating that the cartel form is represented when the top 10 firms account for 80% of output; and in the sense of *konzern*, or combines. In this latter connection, it will be recalled that Japanese typically see the combines developing out of the World War I years. Why they should associate big capital with cartels is not clear. However, while concentration ratios are a recent phenomenon in Japan, I would think there was little doubt of substantial oligopolistic concentration throughout Japan's modern period.

The other commonly proffered explanation of cartels has to do with confrontations. The claim is that there were no serious confrontations until the 1920s. Granted that the twenties and thirties represented exceptionally sharp price adjustments, severe price adjustments were certainly not something unknown in the Japanese economy before this time. Any economic account of the Meiji period will not only include reference to the "Matsukata deflation," but to numerous other sharp price adjustments. Professor Tsuru of Hitotsubashi University, a leading economist in Japan, has authored an article dealing specifically with these early price adjustments.[10]

Whatever explanation one chooses to adopt, it is evident that it was in the twenties that widespread cartelization got started. While at no point during Japan's modern period had cartels been viewed un-

[8] Ariga and Rieke, "The Antimonopoly Law of Japan and its Enforcement," *Washington Law Review*, August 1964, p. 437.

[9] From discussion in a seminar of Japanese scholars who criticized the first draft of this book.

[10] Tsuru Shigeto, "Economic Fluctuations in Japan, 1868-1893," *Review of Economics and Statistics*, Vol. xxiii, No. 4, November 1941, pp. 176-89.

favorably, the government in 1925 gave positive encouragement to their formation through passage of two laws, the Export Society Law and the Major Export Commodities Industrial Association Law, both of which provided specific legal sanction for them. Professor Kanazawa comments:

> The first law authorized the establishment of cartels of traders; the second permitted cartels of producers. These cartels could fix prices, establish quotas, curtail production, and allocate markets. Furthermore, the minister having jurisdiction over the particular trade in question was authorized to order firms not party to the cartel agreement or association to observe the terms of the agreement. These laws are considered the first in modern times to provide for compulsory adherence to cartels. In them the Japanese government moved affirmatively to support and strengthen the cartels which had independently arisen throughout Japanese economic society without formal government sanction. [Though, as will be noted from Table 15-1, these were few.] . . .[11] The success of the cartels under the early laws led the government to extend the policy of statutory governmental support of cartels to almost all major industries in the economic depression of the 1930s. . . . [The Major Export Commodities Industrial Association Law, broadened through amendments in 1931 and renamed the Industrial Society Law, included] production of important industrial goods, whether for the domestic or export markets. In 1932 the Mercantile Society Law authorized cartels among wholesalers and retailers. The most extensive of these laws, however, was the Law Concerning the Control of Important Industries of 1931, which authorized support of cartel agreements (called "control agreements") among producers generally.[12]

The key provisions of the Major Industries Control Law were:

> Wherever a scheme for controlling output and prices or for the allocation of market and sales quotas has been agreed to by half of the producers in an industry designated as a "major industry" by the appropriate Government authority, then the provisions of that scheme together with information about the capacity, annual output and sales of the constituent firms must be reported to the Ministry of Commerce and Industry (Article I). If more than two-thirds of the members of an association recognized under this Law make ap-

[11] Kanazawa Yoshio, "Regulation of Corporate Enterprise," p. 482.
[12] *Ibid.*, p. 483.

> plication, then the Minister may, if he thinks fit, require all the producers in the trade to abide by the regulations imposed under the scheme (Article II). On the other hand, the Minister can require that agreements be modified or abrogated if they are found to be detrimental to the interests of the industry in question or to those of other industries and of the public.[13]

The Law was twice modified, in March 1933 and in July 1936.

> A new clause was added in March, 1933, to compel manufacturers to send in further reports on the quantity and value of monthly output and sales and on stocks at the end of each month; but it was not until July, 1936, that the Law was revised so as to meet some of the objections raised to it. The position of the larger firms was strengthened by the provision that participants in the recognized cartel agreements must represent not merely more than one-half of the producers but also more than one-half of the aggregate output (or sales) of the industry. The Minister of Commerce and Industry was also empowered to adopt a license system for the purpose of preventing the increase of capacity in a "major industry" in which agreements for restricting production existed; while the Law was applied to the whole of the Japanese Empire [thus including the colonies and Manchukuo].[14]

This law was the product of the recommendations of the Temporary Industrial Inquiry Commission appointed by the Hamaguchi Cabinet in January 1930, the membership of which comprised the "most prominent captains of industrial and financial experts."[15] In wording highly reminiscent of what one would expect to hear from spokesmen

[13] G. C. Allen, in E. B. Schumpeter, ed., *The Industrialization of Japan and Manchukuo*, p. 687. Cf. Appendix II for cartels formed under this law.

[14] *Ibid.*, p. 688.

[15] Fujita Keizo, "Cartels and Their Conflicts in Japan," Osaka University of Commerce *Journal*, December 1935, p. 73. The membership of the commission as given in the *Official Gazette* (*Kampo*), January 22, 1930, p. 455, was:

Machida Chuji
Tawara Magoichi
Inouye Junnosuke
Koizumi Matajiro
Matsuda Genji
Shiba Chuzaburo
Okochi Masatoshi
Dan Takuma
Hijikata Hasaakira
Go Seinosuke
Shimura Gentaro
Nezu Kaichiro
Inahata Katsutaro
Yukawa Hirokichi
Kimura Kusuyata
Matsuoka Kimpei
Ikeda Seihin
Isaka Takashi
Kushida Manzo
Kagami Kenkichi
Abe Fusajiro
Matsunaga Yasuzaemon

for MITI today, the commission recommended mergers and cartelization as a way of meeting "excessive competition." The Temporary Inquiry Commission recommended:

> *Encouragement of the amalgamation of enterprises*—competition among an excessive number of enterprises in a branch of industry means (1) excessive investment of capital in that particular industry and (2) difficulty in lowering the cost of production and stabilizing enterprises. Particularly in the field of industries relating to export commodities, it may lead to unnecessary competition among enterprises, which will considerably handicap our participation in international trade rivalry. In view of the foregoing, it is most essential in our present industrial situation to effect the amalgamation of enterprises on a large scale, with due consideration of the problems of production, distribution and consumption in each branch of the industry. While success in this undertaking depends much on the cooperation and awakening of those engaged in that industry, it is still more important that the government provide active leadership for the end in view.
>
> *Encouragement of Combination and Agreement*—In order to obtain the largest possible return from the capital investment, it is necessary, besides amalgamating enterprises in various industries, to encourage the adoption of business agreements among the enterprises in one branch or connected branches of industry, such as agreements concerning the amount of production, division of markets, sales prices, and other measures for the prevention of unnecessary competition.[16]

### *The War Control Framework*

By 1938 the Japanese government held the view that the prosecution of the war in China and its other military plans required a stronger control mechanism than was provided by the Major Industries Control Law. The military's wishes resulted in the National General Mobilization Law of 1938, of which Professor Kanazawa writes:

> The . . . law provided for government enforcement of cartel-agreements among both members and nonmembers of the cartel and the establishment of industry-wide associations, in which membership was compulsory, controlling activities in almost every field of commerce and industry. The Commerce and Industry Society Law, enacted in 1943, provided for the establishment of smaller cartels controlling a particular subdivision of industry. These wartime

[16] *Ibid.*, p. 72.

"control" associations were patterned after similar organizations, the *Wirtschaftsgruppen*, found in Nazi Germany. Their distinguishing features were compulsory establishment, enforced membership, and the development and regulation of association policy by a single director appointed by the government (*Fuhrerprinzip*) instead of the decision of a majority of the members of the association.[17]

By the war's end this network of control organs had grown to a vast size. In a GHQ-SCAP memorandum for the file, it is reported that at the national level there were 1,538 control organizations "coming to the attention of SCAP," and at the local level, 6,588.[18]

Let us note a few illustrations taken from the textile industry of the type of events which occurred under the National Mobilization Law and the Commerce and Industry Society Law. Mergers are prominent. A 1940 *Oriental Economist* article reported: "The spinning industry of Japan has finally entered upon a new era of great mergers. At the spinners' joint conference held on November 8, an outline of the plan concerning adjustments and consolidation of the spinning mills was unanimously adopted. According to the approved proposal, 77 existing spinning companies will be merged into a dozen or so firms within the short period of less than three months hence."[19]

Two years later the *Oriental Economist* reported that agreement had finally been reached on the control organs in textiles:

> . . . four different textile control associations will be organized. They are the Cotton-Staple Fiber Control Association, Rayon-Silk Control Association, Woolen Control Association and Hemp Control Association. . . . For the rationalization of distribution, adjustment of demand and supply of different textiles and control over processed textile goods, the authorities have decided to bolster the structure of the existing Textile Goods Distributing Council. The proposed control council will act as an organ to maintain close liaison among the different textile control associations. It has further been decided to have the Manchou Textile Federation and Association of Japanese Spinners in China participate in the projected Textile

17 Kanazawa Yoshio, "Regulation," p. 484.

18 Supreme Commander for the Allied Powers, General Headquarters, History of Nonmilitary Activities of the Occupation of Japan, Vol. X, *Reform of Business Enterprise*, Part C, Elimination of Private Control Organizations, p. 71, Office of Military History, Washington, D.C. (Part C was never completed. It exists in draft form only. It has the further handicap of being misentered on the Department of the Army's Historical Manuscript Accession Sheet.) The quotation in question is from an ESS/AC memorandum for the file dated April 15, 1948.

19 *Oriental Economist*, December 1940, p. 707.

Control Council so that the latter may be able efficiently to formulate measures to control on an uniform basis the textile industries in Japan, Manchukuo and China.[20]

In an ESS staff memorandum commenting on these developments it is observed: "Division of the control power formerly lodged in the cartel organization (Japan Cotton Spinners' Association) among the new control associations did not lessen the influence and domination of the large companies or decrease their participation in restrictive trade practices since such companies had expanded into the various branches of the industry and thus became members of each of the new control organs. They thereby continued to receive benefits from preferential treatment in the allocation of raw materials, acquisition of fixed assets through forced sales of securities of merger, etc."[21]

The same ESS memorandum further observed that the benefits of this system for the large firm were statistically evident in the fact that in 1937 the Big Ten in spinning accounted for 60% of spindlage capacity, whereas by 1945 they accounted for 98%.

At the time of enactment of the Law for the Elimination of Excessive Concentrations of Economic Power, various petitions were filed for relief from forced wartime mergers. The following is taken from the ESS memorandum in question:

(1) Yamamoto Kenjiro on behalf of the former Yamamoto Wool Spinning Company which was absorbed into the Dai Nippon Cotton Spinning Co. The petitioner states in part,

Our factory was equipped with 18 cards which was less than half of the minimum units required by the law. The Japan Wool Spinning Industry Union, which exerted a great influence over individual companies, [was] entrusted with the right to determine the quantity of production by, and allotment to each company, and controlled prices, threatened that, if we should not amalgamate ourselves with another bigger concern, it would suspend further allotments of materials for us. Thus, under pressure of the military and financial cliques, our whole stock was taken over by the Dai Nippon Spinning Co. in August, 1941 for the sum of Y4,300,000. Consequently, our company's officers were made to resign en bloc to be succeeded by the staff of Dai Nippon Spinning, and our factory was wholly turned over to the concern. . . .

[20] *Ibid.*, September 1942, p. 434.

[21] Attachment to a memorandum entitled, " 'Big Ten' Spinning Companies and Deconcentration Policy," to Maj. Gen. Marquat from E. C. Welsh, dated August 27, 1948, in file entitled, "Deconcentration: Textile Companies," World War II Records Division, National Archives, Suitland, Md.

(2) Matsuo Shojiro on behalf of the former Matsuo Wool Spinning Company which was absorbed into the Dai Nippon Cotton Spinning Co. The petitioner states in part,

> At the same time, the Wool Spinning Industry Union, a control organization, announced that the supply of raw materials would be suspended to those mills failing to abide by the Government's enterprise adjustment policy.

(3) Yamagata Dyeing Works in a petition for relief from its absorption into the Daiwa Cotton Spinning Co., in part stated,

> The military authorities strongly demanded that we let the Daiwa Spinning join this company through the financial channel. They hinted that if we refused, no order will be forthcoming from the army, which virtually meant closing down of the plant. Therefore, we were compelled, much against our will, to hand over to Daiwa Spinning, 75% of our shares.

While the foregoing concerns only the textile industry, where the *zaibatsu* were not present, it explains how the combines grew at such an extraordinary pace during the war years, how it was while the Big Four in 1937 accounted for 12% of total corporate and partnership capital, that by war's end they accounted for 24%.

### *The Occupation Bans Cartels*

The preceding discussion suggests the nature of cartel development in Japan. The Occupation proscription of cartels occurred against this background. While MacArthur called for the abrogation of domestic and international cartels in his qualified acceptance of the Yasuda Plan, November 1945, it was not until April 1947 that his instructions were put into law. The prohibition on cartels was included in the Antimonopoly Law. Anticartel provisions were found in Articles 3, 4, 5, and 6. Article 3 generally prohibited "unreasonable restraint of trade." The other three articles were specific. Article 4 stated,[22]

> No entrepreneur shall participate in any one of the following types of concerted activities:
>
> 1. Establishment, stabilization or enhancement of prices;
> 2. Restriction of volume of production or that of sales;
> 3. Restrictions on technology, products, markets or customers;
> 4. Restrictions on construction or expansion of facilities or on adoption of new technology or methods of production.

[22] Quotation is from HCLC, *Laws, Rules and Regulations.*

> The provisions of the preceding paragraph shall not apply in case the effects of such concerted activities on competition within a particular field of trade is negligible.

Article 5 stated:

> No entrepreneur shall establish, organize or become a party to or a member of a juridical person or any other organization which controls distribution of all or a part of materials or products by methods of exclusive purchase or sale or which undertakes the allocation of all or a part of materials or products.

Paragraph 6 of the same law dealt with international cartels. It read:

> No entrepreneur shall participate in an international agreement or an international contract with a foreign entrepreneur or participate in an agreement or contract on foreign trade with a domestic entrepreneur with regard to any one of the following Items:
>
> 1. Any matter which comes under any one of the Items of Paragraph 1 of Article 4.
> 2. An agreement or a contract relating to restrictions on exchange of scientific or technological knowledge or information necessary for business activities.
>
> The provisions of the preceding paragraph shall not apply in case the effects of such agreement or contract on competition in any particular field of international or domestic trade is negligible.

Because of the total disruption of the Japanese economy in the immediate postwar years, with demand far in excess of supply, it was not possible to eliminate the wartime control organs without making alternative arrangements for allocation of scarce raw materials. Just as no modern nation can operate a war economy without resorting to controls, so no badly damaged economy can effect recovery without them. Left to itself, the market mechanism is likely to allocate scarce timber to teahouses rather than to shoring up mine shafts. Because it was thoroughly unpalatable to continue the wartime control associations with their domination by the combines, and yet control organs were necessary, MacArthur resorted to the creation, in a limited number of cases, of agencies completely under government control, of "*kodan.*" It was this development which led Senator Knowland to conclude that the U.S. government was socializing the Japanese economy.

## *The Japanese Reaction to Proscription*

In the 20-odd years of living under a cartelized economy, 1925-45, Japan's business leaders had come to like the cartel way of doing business; certainly it was enthusiastically subscribed to by a number of the ministries, in particular the Ministry of Commerce. Japanese commentators on the proscription of cartels in the original Antimonopoly Law are likely to emphasize Japan's long tradition of cartels, while in fact the tradition was only two decades old. The Restrictive Practices Study Team of the Japan Productivity Center commented in 1958: ". . . faith in the benefit of this [the cartel] way of regulating competition is so deep-rooted that the general run of businessmen appear simply unable to comprehend why its legality should be called into question."[23] Mrs. Ariga and Professor Rieke commented: "Businessmen with a long tradition of cartels and trade associations can understand regulations arrived at after discussion among the competitors, much more readily than they can the bizarre notion that concerted actions constitute an unreasonable restraint of trade."[24] That a coauthor such as Mrs. Ariga, with her deep commitment to competitive free enterprise, would describe the condemnation of concerted business actions as "bizarre" probably reflects the wide difference in the Western and Japanese heritage. The Japanese tradition puts emphasis on the group, and further lacks the notion that power is likely to be abused. In our Western individualistic tradition we worry about power and suspect the motives of businessmen gathering together to discuss output, prices, etc. Just as we have all been reared on Lord Acton, so likewise have we all been reared on the words of Adam Smith: "People of the same trade seldom meet together, even for merriment and diversion, but the conversation ends in a conspiracy against the public or in some contrivance to raise prices."[25]

In the Japanese literature comments on Occupation changes in the business world one even—astonishingly enough—comes upon the phrase "nostalgic longing" of businessmen for "the prewar days of laissez-faire."[26] But as Mrs. Ariga and Professor Rieke explain, "The term "laissez-faire" . . . [in such references] means the freedom of gov-

[23] Japan Productivity Center, *Restrictive Practices*, p. 17.

[24] Ariga and Rieke, "Antimonopoly Law," p. 459.

[25] Smith, *An Inquiry into the Nature and Causes of the Wealth of Nations*, Book I, Chapter X, Part II.

[26] This phrase was used in the Japan Productivity Center, *Restrictive Practices*, p. 7. It is used by Ashino Hiroshi, a Commissioner of the FTC from July 1947 to November 1958, as are many other portions of the source in question, without benefit of quotation marks in his article, "Experimenting with Anti-Trust Law in Japan," *Japanese Annual of International Law*, 1959, pp. 34-35.

ernment to favor some businesses and the freedom of businessmen to contract for a wide variety of restrictive practices"[27]—which should surely stand as the all-time classic in definitions of "laissez-faire."

But cartels in the Western sense do not have a long tradition in Japan. That some Western writers join the Japanese in speaking of their long standing may in part stem from confusion in usage of the word. It will be recalled that Robert Fearey, who was quoted in Chapter 1, asserted, "Japan's experience throughout the formative period of its industrialization was with cartels on the German model." Further, it will be recalled from Chapter 14 that *Time* magazine, in reporting on the merger of the three Mitsubishi Heavy Industries, described the *zaibatsu* as "the huge and powerful prewar cartels that controlled practically all of Japanese industry. . . ." If oligopolistic markets are to be called cartels, and if combines are to be called cartels, then Japan does indeed have a long tradition of them. But if the term is restricted to overt, explicit agreement among businesses independent of one another, then the tradition is essentially of the 20 years preceding the end of the Pacific War.

Although, under the reversal of U.S. policy toward business organization in Japan, SCAP was agreeable to changing certain provisions of the Antimonopoly Law, MacArthur did not favor any changing of the proscription of cartels. So far as I know, not even the Deconcentration Review Board urged elimination of these provisions. Accordingly, modification of the outright ban on cartels had to wait until the Japanese government once again possessed autonomy. Amendment came in 1953, when the *per se* conditions of illegality were removed through deletion of Articles 4 and 5 and when two categories of cartels, anti-depression and rationalization, were specifically authorized through additions to Article 24. The Antimonopoly Law's proscription of cartels, domestic and international, is now governed by Article 3, which deals with "unreasonable restraints of trade," by Article 6, which governs international cartels, and by additions to Article 8 dealing with restriction of competition. The Trade Association Law was abolished at this time, but certain prohibited restrictive trade acts were lifted out of this law and inserted in Article 8 of the Antimonopoly Law.[28]

### *Antidepression and Rationalization Cartels*

Article 24 has been little used. Table 15-2 lists the cartels formed under the antidepression and rationalization exemptions permitted by

[27] Ariga and Rieke, "Antimonopoly Law," p. 439n.

[28] Iyori Hiroshi, "Cartels in Japan," *Oriental Economist,* January 1964, p. 25.

Table 15-2: CARTELS ORGANIZED UNDER THE ANTI-MONOPOLY LAW (presumably as of 1964)

| *Product* | *Nature of restrictions* | *Companies participating* | *Time Period* |
|---|---|---|---|
| | *Anti-Depression Cartels* | | |
| linen thread | sales restrictions | 5-12 | 4/56-9/61 |
| pressed yeast | production controls | 8 | 6/58-12/60 |
| chlorinated vinyl | production, sales restrictions, price | 13 | 11/58-3/59 |
| celluloid | production controls, price | 7 | 12/58-11/59 |
| chlorinated vinyl pipe | production controls, sales restriction, price | 10 | 3/59-5/60 |
| synthetic dyes | sales restriction | 6 | 7/60-6/61 |
| medium steel shapes | production controls, sales restrictions | 21 | 1/63-9/63 |
| carbon electrodes | production | 7 | 10/63-3/64 |
| | *Rationalization Cartels* | | |
| scrap copper purchases | price, quantity | 108 | 4/55-3/57 |
| scrap steel purchases | price, quantity (five different agreements depending on type of furnace equipment and area) | 13-42 | 4/55-9/64 |
| mixed cotton staple thread | quality controls (obliged to label thread as to proportion of cotton and staple) | 150 | 5/55-5/64 |
| pure staple thread | quality controls | 53 | 9/55-10/65 |
| bearings | allocation of production fields | 5 | 11/55-9/64 |
| margerine, shortening | quality controls | about 20 | 5/59-5/65 |
| synthetic dyes | allocation of production fields | 6 | 8/61-1/64 |
| linen thread | quality controls | 10 | 3/62-3/64 |
| automobile tires | quality controls (standardized sizes) | 6 | 7/63-6/65 |
| polynogic thread | quality controls | 8 | 10/63-10/65 |
| worsted thread | quality controls | 71 | 12/63-11/65 |

Notes and sources: Yoshida Jimbu, ed., *Japan's Cartels* (*Nihon no Karuteru*), Tokyo, 1964, antidepression cartels, pp. 40 and 117; rationalization cartels, pp. 42 and 117. Material on number of companies participating was supplied me on FTC worksheets.

Certain of the time periods of the rationalization cartels exceed the publication date of the volume because the reference is to authorized duration.

the amended Antimonopoly Law. The table reveals not only that the exemptions granted in Article 24 of the amended act have not been a particularly fruitful avenue for cartelization, but that it was some two years after passage of the amendment before it was first used. In a 10-year period only 19 cartels have been formed in this way. The paucity of cartels by this route, contrasted to the abundance under legislation exempting industries from the provisions of the Antimonopoly Law, undoubtedly reflects the difference in administration. Cartels formed under the Antimonopoly Law require FTC approval; those formed under other special authorizing legislation do not. Such cartels merely require that the pertinent minister consult with the FTC, which, since FTC assent is not necessary, would not seem a very meaningful provision. In fact, under the Export-Import Transactions Law, not even MITI approval is necessary. As Professor Kanazawa points out: "Originally, MITI had to approve agreements with the concurrence of the FTC before they became effective, but at present [1961] export agreements become effective ten days after they are filed with MITI."[29]

The history of the exempting legislation has been an expanding one. The Antimonopoly Law originally exempted public utilities (Article 21) and mutual aid groups of small-scale entrepreneurs and consumers (Article 24). Subsequently, titles of laws were added to Article 24, providing further exemptions. In addition, there has developed a whole body of legislation written or amended to provide exemption from application of the Antimonopoly Law. Speaking of natural monopolies such as public utilities, Professor Kanazawa said:

> These exempted industries are, for various reasons, inherent in their nature and structure, exempted in every country to a greater or less degree from legislation designed to promote free competition. As early as the spring of 1952, however, industries with a less clear case for special treatment began to receive exemptions. The cotton and synthetic-textile industries, at the urging of officials of the Ministry of International Trade and Industry (MITI), took measures to restrict their operations, with a resultant reduction of production, in order to meet an overproduction crisis resulting from the conclusion of the Korean War. In August 1952, the Medium and Small Enterprise Stabilization Law was enacted to legalize this action. Furthermore, at the same time, the Export-Import Transaction Law was adopted for the asserted purpose of enabling exporters to stabilize the prices and volume of exports and forestall complaints

[29] Kanazawa Yoshio, "Regulation," p. 497.

of dumping activities, the complaints coming mainly from the United States.[30]

Professor Kanazawa continues:

> In 1957, the Medium and Small Enterprise Stabilization Law was replaced by the Law Concerning the Organization of Medium and Small Enterprise Organizations, which broadened the coverage of the earlier law to include dealers and service enterprises as well as producers. Pursuant to its provisions, large enterprises are permitted to combine with small and medium enterprises to restrict production, fix prices, and allocate markets. By June 1961, 634 commerce and industry societies existed. Furthermore, MITI can order both members and nonmembers of the society to observe restrictions on competition imposed by MITI to accomplish the purposes of the society and order medium and small enterprises which are nonmembers to enter it. The parallel with the prewar statutory-supported cartels is obvious: once again the government is lending a hand to support and direct privately regulated competition, particularly in the export industries.[31]

Professor Kanazawa observes that because the MITI "has the power to exempt groups from the antimonopoly laws, its suggestions respecting the formation of cartels have great force."[32] He continues,

> This legislation does not go to the extremes of compulsory establishment and the *Fuhrerprinzip* (abolition of majority rule) embodied in Japanese wartime legislation for associations in the field of economic activities. But the "organizations" for which the Law Concerning the Organization of Medium and Small Enterprise Organizations provides are not entirely free from the danger of totalitarian tendencies, although they purport to be autonomous and democratic.
>
> Article 55 of this law provides for compulsory cartel membership for the first time since World War II; it must, therefore, be examined in the light of Article 21 of the Japanese Constitution which guarantees freedom of association. . . . The national legislature, with the constitutional problem in view, inserted a rather clumsy "attestation" clause which provides that those who do not want to join a cartel may remain outside, even if an administrative order for compulsory membership is in force, by seeking "attestation" from the competent administrative authorities. But attested outsiders are

[30] *Ibid.*, pp. 496-97. [31] *Ibid.*, pp. 498-99. [32] *Ibid.*, p. 498n.

subject to the restrictions that are established for the commerce and industry society. If they violate these measures, they are liable to monetary penalties imposed by the society. Such penalties seem improper because the monetary penalty is imposed directly by the society, a private body. Moreover, members have no freedom of secession so long as the administrative order for compulsory membership remains in force. Therefore the attestation clause does not change the character of the law in regard to the freedom of the association.

Table 15-3 contains a summary of the laws exempting industries from the Antimonopoly Law.

Writing of the scale of cartelization in Japan, on the basis of the 1964 FTC study, Iyori Hiroshi stated in the *Oriental Economist* for January 1964: "Of the 1,002 cartels in existence at March 31, 1963, 90% were in connection with medium and small operations, and with foreign trade. Of the medium and small enterprise cartels, 591 have been formed under the Medium and Small Enterprise Organization Law, and 95 are those formed under the Environment Sanitation Proper Management Law. Of the foreign trade cartels, 194 have been formed under the Export and Import Trade Law, and 11 were established under the Export Marine Product Industry Promotion Law. Fifty-five agreements are shipping conferences in the ocean freight area under the Marine Transportation Law."[33]

But besides the number of cartels one must also have some way of judging their relative importance. This information is available from the research done by the FTC, and is reproduced as Table 15-4. There is one qualification to this data, however—it is based only on the cartels that are called cartels. It does not include cartels that operate under the nomenclature "administrative guidance" (which will be discussed below). It is for this reason that "oil and coal" is listed in Table 15-4 at zero cartelization.

Table 15-4 indicates that the importance of cartelization varies greatly among the 20 "two digit" industries in the table. In textiles, better than three-quarters of shipments come under cartel regulation. In steel, on the other hand, the fraction is one-third, in nonferrous metals, one-half, in food and kindred products, one-third. However, if "administrative guidance" cartels were included in the above calculations we would have different figures in a number of cases. Some industries have both regular cartels and "administrative guidance" cartels.

[33] Iyori Hiroshi, "Cartels in Japan," p. 27.

Table 15-3: LAWS CONTAINING EXEMPTIVE PROVISIONS FROM APPLICATION OF THE ANTIMONOPOLY LAW

(Note: year of enactment refers to the date of the exemption.)

| *Industry* | *Name of Law* | *Year enacted* | *Type of cartel* | *Outsider restriction* |
|---|---|---|---|---|
| **medium and small enterprise in general** | Medium & Small Enterprise Law, Law 185 of 1957. | | | |
| | Art. 17-1-4; Art. 31 | 1957 | for prevention of "excessive competition" | yes |
| | Art. 17-1-5; Art. 31 | 1962 | rationalization cartel | yes |
| | Art. 17-2 | 1957 | joint operation | no |
| | Medium & Small Enterprise Coop. Association Law, Law 181 of 1949 | 1949 | joint operation | no |
| | Law Concerning Exemption from the Antimonopoly Law, Law 138 of 1947 | | | |
| | Art. 2-4 | 1947 | activities of small-scale entrepreneurs | no |
| **foreign trade** | Export & Import Law, Law 299 of 1947 | | | |
| | Art. 5; Art. 11-2 | 1952 | export cartels (price, quantity, product standards) | yes |
| | Art. 5-2; Art. 11-4 | 1955 | domestic cartels of exporters | yes |
| | Art. 5-3 | 1955 | domestic cartels of producers who are exporting | no |
| | Art. 7-2; Art. 19-4 | 1953 | import cartels (price, quantity for import and also in domestic transactions) | yes |
| | Art 7-3; Art. 23 | 1955 | export and import cartels | yes |
| | Art. 5-2 | 1961 | joint operation | no |
| **manufacturing industry** | Machinery Industry Promotion Temporary (10-years) Law, Law 154 of 1961 | 1961 | rationalization cartel | yes |
| | Electronics Industry Promotion Temporary (7-years) Law, Law 171 of 1957 | 1957 | rationalization cartel | no |
| | Textile Industry Promotion Temporary (10-years) Law, Law 130 of 1956. | 1956 | equipment restriction cartel | yes |
| | Ammonium Sulphate Industry Rationalization & Ammonium Sulphate Export Adjustment Temporary (10 year) Law, Law 173 of 1954 | 1954 | domestic cartel of exporters | no |
| | Art. 17-1-4<br>Art. 17-2-2 | 1957 | raw material purchasing cartel | no |
| | Art. 18 | 1954 | cartel for prevention of excessive competition | yes |

| | | | | |
|---|---|---|---|---|
| | Liquor Tax & Liquor Enterprise Association Law, Law 7 of 1953 | | | |
| | Art. 42-5; Art. 82-1-3 | 1953 | excessive competition prevention cartel | yes |
| | Art. 42-6; Art. 82-1-3 | 1959 | rationalization cartel | yes |
| | Art. 42-5 (excl. 6) | 1953 | joint operation | no |
| | Cocoon Industry Law, Law 57 of 1945 | 1953 | price-fixing on raw materials | no |
| | Salt Industry Law, Law 107 of 1953 | 1953 | joint operations | no |
| mining industry | Loal Mining Industry Rationalization Temporary (22-years) Law, Law 15 of 1955 | 1955 | depression cartel | no |
| | Metal Mining Stabilization Temporary (5-year) Law, Law 116 of 1963 | 1963 | depression cartel | no |
| agriculture, forestry and fishery industry | Agricultural Cooperative Law, Law 132 of 1947 | 1947 | joint operation | no |
| | Tobacco Cultivation Law, Law 135 of 1958 | 1958 | joint operation | no |
| | Forest Law, Law 249 of 1951 | 1951 | joint operation | no |
| | Marine Products Cooperative Law, Law 248 of 1948 | 1948 | joint operation | no |
| | Fishery Production Adjustment Law, Law 128 of 1961 | 1961 | fishing restriction cartel | yes |
| commerce and service | Environmental Sanitation Management Law, Law 164 of 1957 | 1957 | for prevention of excessive competition | yes |
| | Shopping Area Promotion Law, Law 141 of 1962 | 1962 | joint operation | no |
| | Wholesale Market Law, Law 32 of 1923 | 1956 | for prevention of excessive competition | no |
| financing business | Credit Law, Law 238 of 1951 | 1951 | joint financing of business | no |
| | Labor Food Law, Law 227 of 1953 | 1953 | joint financing of business | no |
| insurance business | Casualty Insurance Law, Law 41 of 1939 | 1947 | terms & conditions for insurance & re-insurance. | no |
| | Casualty Insurance Rates Law, Law 193 of 1948 | 1948 | rate cartel | no |
| | Law Concerning Foreign Insurance Cos. Law 184 of 1949 | 1949 | insurance cartel | no |
| | Fishing Boat Damage Insurance Law, Law 28 of 1952 | 1952 | insurance cartel | no |
| transportation industry | Local Railway Law, Law 52 of 1919 | 1947 | transportation cartel | no |
| | Tramways Law, Law 76 of 1921 | 1947 | transportation cartel | no |
| | Land Transportation Adjustment Law, Law 71 of 1938 | 1947 | transportation cartel | no |
| | Road Transportation Law, Law 183 of 1951 | 1951 | transportation cartel | no |
| | Express Business Law, Law 241 of 1949 | 1951 | transportation cartel | no |
| | Harbor Transportation Law, Law 161 of 1951 | 1951 | agreement among harbor transport operators | no |

| | | | | |
|---|---|---|---|---|
| | Marine Transportation Law, Law 187 of 1949 | | | |
| | Art. 28 | 1949 | shipping cartel, price, quantity | no |
| | Art. 30-2 | 1951 | agreement among harbor transport operators | no |
| | Small Vessels Transportation Law, Law 162 of 1957 | | | |
| | Art. 8-1-1 through 6 | 1957 | shipping cartel | yes |
| | Art. 8-1-7 through 13 | 1957 | joint operation | no |
| | Aviation Law, Law 231 of 1952 | 1952 | aviation cartel | no |
| warehousing | Warehousing Law, Law 121 of 1956 | 1956 | warehousing cartel | no |
| electric power industry | Temporary Measures for Electricity Law, Law 31 of 1952 | 1950 | adjustment cartel | no |

[a]The Antimonopoly Law itself contains three exemptive provisions: the original provision in Article 24 concerning mutual assistance; and through amendment in 1953, provision for depression cartels and rationalization cartels.

Source: Iyori Hitoshi, "Cartels in Japan," *Oriental Economist*, January 1964, p. 27, which in turn is taken from Yoshida Jimbu, ed., *Japan's Cartels* (*Nihon no Karuteru*), Tokyo, 1964, Table 2.3, "A Summary of Legislation Permitting the Formation of Cartels" (Karuteru Kyoyo Horei Gaikatsu Hyo), following p. 116. This list is less inclusive than that found in the Restrictive Trade Practices Specialists Study Team of the Japan Productivity Center, *Control of Restrictive Trade Practices in Japan*, mimeog., Tokyo, 1958, in part IV entitled, "Exemptions from the Applications of the Antimonopoly Law," pp. 63-111. Since the Productivity report is a 1958 publication, however, and the FTC report, 1964, the FTC has the advantage of bringing the material up to a more recent date.

A number of nations will be interested in the proportion of Japan's export trade that is cartelized. In 1962 the proportion was somewhat above 40% on a value basis. Mr. Iyori, in his *Oriental Economist* article states: "The value of items affected by export cartels (including domestic agreements for export goods by manufacturers), computed on the basis of the 1962 edition of "Trade of Japan," a publication of the Ministry of Finance, stood at $2,072 million or 42.4% [a typographical error resulted in these being printed as $1,193 and 24.4%] of the total exports which were valued at $4,890 million."[34]

## *"Administrative Guidance" Cartels*

Administrative guidance cartels are those handled under the aegis of a ministry, typically the MITI. Professor Kanazawa comments,

> . . . another device which has been widely employed to effect cartelization in the purely domestic market . . . is the "recommended restriction of production" whereby an official of one of the

[34] *Ibid.*, p. 29.

Table 15-4: STATUS OF CARTELIZATION IN JAPAN, 1963

(exclusive of "administrative guidance" cartels)

| *Major industry groups* | *Number commodity items* | *Cartelized items* | *Percent* | *Total delivery amt. millions dollars* | *Cartelized item delivery amt. millions dollars* | *Percent* |
|---|---|---|---|---|---|---|
| food and related products | 81 | 22 | 27.2 | 5,027.6 | 1,710.0 | 34.21 |
| textile mill products | 201 | 127 | 63.2 | 4,068.7 | 3,175.9 | 78.05 |
| apparel & other finished products | 59 | 32 | 54.2 | 422.6 | 273.8 | 64.78 |
| lumber and wood products | 49 | 3 | 6.1 | 1,406.1 | 137.4 | 9.77 |
| furniture and fixtures | 19 | 2 | 10.5 | 393.1 | 22.5 | 5.72 |
| paper, pulp, and products | 59 | 7 | 11.9 | 1,616.2 | 442.9 | 27.40 |
| publishing printing, etc. | 12 | 3 | 25.0 | 812.2 | 370.7 | 47.01 |
| chemical and allied products | 291 | 50 | 17.2 | 3,969.4 | 896.3 | 22.58 |
| oil and coal products | 23 | 0 | 0 | 1,008.3 | 0 | 0 |
| rubber products | 40 | 6 | 15.0 | 629.2 | 83.2 | 13.22 |
| leather and products | 42 | 2 | 4.8 | 185.8 | 13.8 | 7.41 |
| ceramics, stone, and clay | 97 | 16 | 16.5 | 1,516.9 | 624.7 | 41.19 |
| iron and steel | 64 | 9 | 12.5 | 4,320.6 | 1,489.2 | 34.47 |
| nonferrous metals | 79 | 19 | 22.8 | 1,717.4 | 872.6 | 50.81 |
| fabricated metal products | 70 | 5 | 7.1 | 1,618.1 | 113.4 | 7.01 |
| machinery | 192 | 17 | 8.9 | 3,289.7 | 508.4 | 15.45 |
| electrical machinery and equipment | 100 | 3 | 3.0 | 3,318.6 | 273.8 | 8.25 |
| transportation equipment | 101 | 1 | 1.0 | 3,382.1 | 64.7* | 1.92 |
| precision machinery | 54 | 7 | 13.0 | 451.8 | 116.5 | 25.79 |
| ordnance and accessories | 6 | 0 | 0 | 9.9 | 0 | 0 |
| miscellaneous | 109 | 5 | 4.6 | 1,034.0 | 69.5 | 6.73 |
| Total | 1,748 | 336 | 19.2 | 40,197.8 | 11,269.5 | 28.4 |

*Correction of entry. Yoshida figure used.

Source and note: Iyori Hiroshi, "Cartels in Japan," p. 26, from Yoshida Jimbu, ed., *Japan's Cartels*, Table 4.1.2, "A Summary [of the Existing Condition of Cartels] ("Gaikatsu Hyo [Karuteru Genjo]"), pp. 172-73. Mr. Iyori somewhat confusingly states that the "figures [are] as of March, 1963," that the "value of delivery is based on the Census of Manufactures - Report by Commodities (1960)." It is difficult to be sure where this brings one out. "Commodity items" are based on the Standard Commodity Classification for Japan.

ministries, usually MITI, recommends to each of the firms in an industry that it observe certain restrictions on its production or pricing practices. The official has no authority in law to enforce his recommendations, and the effectiveness of his suggestions probably depends on two factors. In the first place, the proposals may be followed because of the time and expense necessary to resist whatever official pressure might be brought, and because, other things being equal, a producer may feel that his long-run interests are served by cooperating with the government agency that regulates him. More important, however, may be the underlying desire of

> the industry group in question to reach some form of agreement. If such is the case, the governmental suggestion offers a convenient focus for compromise of the individual claims of each producer. Furthermore, an industry which suffers from overproduction or excessive competition and desires to create a cartel may find it difficult to obtain the cooperation of a sufficient proportion of producers; in these circumstances the industry may turn to the ministry concerned for assistance in the form of a "recommendation." Such a recommendation is particularly effective when the ministry is in a position to exercise a persuasive influence through its control over the import of necessary raw materials.[35]

Table 15-5 lists the industries that have been cartelized under the umbrella of administrative guidance up to mid-1963. The practice continues to flourish, so the time limitation needs to be borne in mind in analyzing the table.

Let us note a few examples of how administrative guidance has worked out in practice. The following items are taken from the *Japan Times*:

> *November 30, 1963*: "Dissatisfied Idemitsu Quits Petroleum Group." Idemitsu . . . second largest producer of petroleum products in Japan . . . seceded from the Petroleum Association of Japan after expressing dissatisfaction with the PAJ production adjustment scheme for the latter half of fiscal 1963.
>
> The association, composed of 21 leading petroleum refining firms in Japan, is a major organ within the industry. Recently, under the administrative guidance of the International Trade and Industry Ministry, the industry had voluntarily decided the production quota by each firm to ensure stabilized prices in the nation's petroleum market. . . .
>
> MITI officials said . . . they would try to persuade Idemitsu to remain in line, adding that certain steps based on the Petroleum Industry Law may be taken to advise restrictive production if necessary.
>
> *December 6, 1963*: "Federation Urges MITI Refuse Aid to Idemitsu." The Japan Petroleum Federation . . . voted that the current production adjustment under MITI's administrative guidance should be carried on regardless of Idemitsu's secession.
>
> The meeting also voted that Idemitsu be placed under direct Government supervision.

[35] Kanazawa Yoshio, "Regulation," p. 501.

Table 15-5: "ADMINISTRATIVE GUIDANCE" CARTELS

(presumably as of mid-1963)

| *Commodity* | *Type of restriction* | *Effective dates (for latest time periods, authorized dates)* | *Notes* |
|---|---|---|---|
| coal | production restriction | 6/58-3/59<br>7/62-3/63 | 15% for large cos; 10 for medium-small |
| petroleum | production restriction | 6/58-3/59, 10-12/61 | penalty, denial of foreign exchange |
| electrolytic copper | production restriction | 10/57-11/58 | |
| | "pegged" price with short range flexibility | 4/59-3/62 | price reporting |
| lead | production restriction | 3-12/58, 7/62- | cutbacks decided in accordance with decisions at International Lead and Zinc conference |
| zinc | production restriction | 7/62- | |
| ingot | production restriction | 1-3/58, 7/62-10/63 | |
| steel materials | production restriction | 3/58-6/59 | for some items, the period is slightly different |
| | "open market selling system" | 7/58- | |
| | inventory freeze | 4/62- | |
| scrap steel shapes | production restriction | 4-6/58 | |
| special steel | production restriction | 12/58-5/59 | |
| ferro-alloy | production restriction | 12/58-3/59 | |
| fireproof brick | production restriction | 3-12/58 | |
| phosphate fertilizer | production restriction | 8/57- | |

| | | | |
|---|---|---|---|
| sulphate fertilizer | production restriction | 8/59-7/60 | |
| | market stability pricing | 12/59-7/60 | "open market selling system" |
| | inventory freeze | 1-3/62 | |
| lime nitrate | production restriction | 8/58-7/60 | during 1958 MITI advised expansion of production |
| carbide | restriction on shipments | 4/58-3/59 | "adjustment" of carbide used in vinyl in order to keep fertilizer use constant |
| chlorinated vinyl plastic | production restriction | 10/57-11/58 | 11/58 - 3/59 production regulated by a depression cartel |
| chlorinated vinyl pipe | production restriction | 11/57-3/59 | 3/59 - 5/60 production regulated by depression cartel |
| celluloid | production restriction | 4-11/59 | 12/58-11/59 production regulated by depression cartel |
| methanol | production restriction | 9-12/58 | oral "advice" |
| formalin | production restriction | 9-12/58 | oral "advice" |
| pulp | restriction of sales | 1-9/58 | paper-use only |
| | restriction of investment | 2/58- | pine pulp only |
| paper | production restriction | 1-10/58 | (the details of the applicable paper types will be found in the source from which this table is taken). |
| | operations suspended | 2/62- | |
| | investment controls | 12/62-1966 | |
| rayon thread | production restriction | 8/57-10/62 | time period varies according to products |
| staple cotton | production restriction | 4/57-5/63 | "advice" given monthly on |

| | | | |
|---|---|---|---|
| staple thread | mothballing equipment | 9/57-7/60 | |
| | maintaining market "order | 9/57- | max. 16 hrs. per day, 25 days per month |
| | inventory freeze | 6/58-6/59 | |
| cotton thread | production restriction | 10/57-3/58 | |
| | mothballing equipment | 4/58-7/60 | penalty, foreign exchange quota |
| | maintaining market "order" | 6/57- | max. 16 hrs. per day, 308 days per year |
| cotton cloth | inventory freeze | 8/58-11/59 | applicable only to cos. which both spin and weave |
| woolen thread | production restriction | 12/57-3/58; 10/62- | |
| | mothballing equipment | 4/58-7/60 | penalty, foreign exchange quota |
| | maintaining market "order" | 3/58- | max. 16 hrs. per day |
| sugar | "standard pricing" system | 10/31-6/58 | penalty, foreign exchange quota |
| | inventory freeze | 6/58- | |

Source: Yoshida Jimbu, ed., *Japan's Cartels*, Table 6, "Restricting Competition by Means of Administrative guidance" (Kosei Shido to ni yoru, Kyoso Seigenteki Koi"), pp. 54-55. Because of what seems to me the confusing way in which the data for rayon, staple cotton, staple, and cotton thread are presented in the printed version, I have relied on FTC worksheets made available earlier. In the printed table there is a typographical error in the data for production restriction of cotton thread, the beginning date of 1958 having been printed instead of 1957. I have also relied on the worksheets for additional material on woolen thread.

*January 10, 1964*: "Oil Refiners Said Working as Cartel." Kikuzo Watanabe, chairman of the Fair Trade Commission, told the press . . . that the current "reduction adjustment" of petroleum products . . . was suspected of constituting a cartel activity banned by the Antimonopoly Law.

*January 15, 1964*: "Idemitsu Defying Oil Law: Fukuda." International Trade and Industry Minister Hajime Fukuda declared . . . Idemitsu . . . apparently is defying the nation's Oil Business Law. . . . Challenging the firm to return to the fold, Fukuda indicated he might have to invoke a special order if it kept turning down mediations.

"If this failed to prove persuasive enough, we would even study modifications to the present Oil Business Law" the minister said.

*January 27, 1964*: "Idemitsu, MITI Agree on Oil Production Plan." The president of . . . Idemitsu . . . repeated his earlier promise to the International Trade and Industry Ministry that he will accept the new oil production readjustment plan offered by the ministry . . . provided that the readjustment measures be discontinued in the future. . . . The new MITI steps reportedly are more favorable to the oil company than the previous ones. . . . Idemitsu said he did not intend to rejoin the Petroleum Federation at the present moment. The oil firms affiliated with the federation expressed dissatisfaction over the new MITI oil plan which was favorable to Idemitsu. . . .

*April 4, 1964*: "Nippon Oil Announces It Will Raise Gas Prices." Eisuke Kamimura, president of the Nippon Oil Co. announced . . . he is raising the wholesale prices of gasoline "by a considerably wide margin." He then hinted at the possibility of all refiners and gasoline suppliers eventually raising prices. . . . The decision . . . was prompted by International Trade and Industry Minister Hajime Fukuda's bid to normalize the highly competitive price situation in the industry. Idemitsu . . . the second largest supplier with a sales share of . . . 15.2% [Nippon Oil, 18%], is reported . . . willing to follow in its step.

Two years later an essentially similar series of items was running in the press with respect to Sumitomo Metal Industries' rejection of the crude-steel quota assigned it by MITI.

And so cartelization mounts in Japan's postwar economy. Only the strongest business leaders dare to take issue with the government. Professor Rotwein may have supposed, on a sample of 17 cartels out of the thousand plus which exist in Japan today, that "the growth of cartels in Japan should not be equated with a widespread growth of highly restrictive practices."[36] But it would seem doubtful that many would agree with him.

A discussion of cartels in Japan cannot be closed without mentioning the anomalous situation in which the United States in certain instances promotes Japanese cartelization—the United States that so firmly believes in the inadvisability of cartels, which in 1961 put some of its leading businessmen in jail for forming a cartel in heavy electrical equipment; which during the Occupation outlawed all cartels in Japan. The inconsistency comes about as a result of informal and formal arrangements for quotas on certain goods exported to the United States. But the inevitable effect of a quota, whether voluntary or governmental, is the formation of a cartel among exporters of the commodity in order to have some way of dividing the market.

There are varying opinions as to the scale of "voluntary" quantitative restrictions on Japanese exports to the United States, depending on whether one is relying on Japanese or American sources. The Japanese government contends that the voluntary quantitative controls Japan has been obliged to adopt on exports to the United States amounted in 1961 to some 30% by value of its total exports to this country. The United States government, on the other hand, argues that the appropriate category when considering voluntary controls is *unilateral* controls, and argues that unilateral controls in 1963 applied to only 18% of Japanese exports to the United States.[37]

By defining "voluntary" as "unilateral," the U.S. excludes: (1) exports governed by bilateral or multilateral governmental agreements; (2) exports under tariff quotas;[38] (3) exports for which there is reason to think that controls exist for reasons other than "orderly marketing" abroad; and (4) exports on which "controls are not effective or have recently been abandoned."[39] If, however, one is observing the cartel-inducing effects of quantitative restrictions, it does not matter whether the quantitative restrictions were imposed because of formal or in-

[36] Rotwein, "Economic Concentration," p. 275.

[37] Airgram #149 from the American Embassy in Tokyo to the Department of State, dated August 11, 1964, which includes as enclosures, "Japanese Quantitative Voluntary Export Quotas Affecting the U.S." and "Japanese Data Presented at U.S.–Japan Businessmen's Conference, Tokyo, May 18-23, 1964," as reproduced in *Hearings on Foreign Trade and Antitrust Laws* before the United States Subcommittee on Antitrust and Monopoly, 89th Cong., First Sess., Part 1, pp. 582-98.

[38] Under a tariff quota a stipulated quantity of the goods is permitted to enter at a lower rate than entries over this amount. For a discussion of tariff quotas see Heinrich Heuser, *Control of International Trade*, London, 1939, pp. 77-79.

[39] Airgram #149 (see note 37 above), p. 583.

formal governmental procedures or as a result of direct industry pressures.

The scale of the disparity in the quantity of trade in the early 1960s affected by this induced cartelization—30% compared to 18%—stems from the difference in treatment, in view of the above considerations, of two key items, cotton goods and secondary cotton goods on the one hand, and transistor radios on the other. The U.S. calculation excludes the former altogether, on the grounds that the quotas are bilateral and multilateral and places the latter at a much lower figure than the Japanese. In this latter connection, one is handicapped in using the document on which this discussion rests by the fact that the Japanese data are for 1961 and 1962, while the U.S. are for 1963. However, as the American Embassy discussion indicates, the disparity in the value of the trade in transistor radios is due to the fact that "the value of total exports was listed [in the Japanese figures], while only so-called Class C radios (simple single-band sets of six transistors or less) are actually under quantitative controls (we have estimated that these constitute something less than one-half by value of Japanese transistor radios exports to the United States)."[40] While it is appropriate that only the portion of the trade that is under quota restriction be included in such calculation, and while it is appropriate to exclude commodities where there is reason to believe that quantitative controls exist for reasons of "orderly marketing" in the domestic market, rather than foreign markets, it does not make sense to exclude governmentally negotiated agreements if one is looking at the cartel-inducing effects of such quantitative restrictions. And for the government of the United States, with its strong opposition to cartels, it would seem doubly important for it to be conscious of the fact that import quotas imply export cartels.

Given the strong argument it makes for the Japanese side, there is pressure to overstate the scale of the trade affected by quotas, to include, for example, an entire industry when only a portion is under restriction. The foregoing discussion shows abundantly that many leading Japanese businessmen strongly support the cartel approach, and it is equally evident that the Japanese government, with the exception of the FTC—enthusiastically subscribes to this way of doing business. Accordingly, for Japan to be indignant about suffering cartelization at the hands of the United States is almost as incongruous as it is for the United States to be promoting cartelization.

Professor Kanazawa comments on the "voluntary" export-quota system:

[40] *Hearings* (note 37 above), p. 582.

> Voluntary export-quota systems have been established to restrict the export of such commodities as textiles [which the U.S. Government argues are not "voluntary" because official], stainless-steel flatware [which is, in fact, a tariff quota], and plywood [controls on a major item in this trade, Lauan plywood, were abolished April 1, 1964]. Their purpose is to forestall the erection of mandatory barriers to such imports by the United States government at the behest of domestic producers of these commodities. While the United States government has participated in discussions of, and has strongly supported, these various voluntary export quotas, only the quota for the cotton-textile industry has been formalized by the exchange of diplomatic notes. Quotas and standards of price and quality can be established by exporters on their own initiative under articles 5 and 11 of the Export-Import Transactions Law; or by MITI under article 28 of the same law if, as often happens, the exporters are unable to reach an agreement on these points. In either case, MITI can assist in the implementation of the established quotas through its licensing of exports pursuant to the Foreign Exchange and Foreign Trade Control Law.[41]

It is anomalous, however, for the United States to pursue trade policies which inevitably result in cartelization.

In the next and final chapters of this study we will examine the role of the Government in the economy; note the performance of the economy during the postwar period; and attempt to answer the question: Viewed in the perspective of hindsight should the United States and its Allies have attempted to dissolve the leading combines and to have implanted an antitrust policy?

[41] Kanazawa Yoshio, "Regulation," pp. 502-503.

# 16.

## Government in the Economy

INVARIABLY outsiders are astonished at the omnipresence of the Japanese government in the economy. In addition to such "macro" responsibilities as the governments of all free-enterprise economies have come to assume—growth, full employment, stable prices, and a viable balance-of-payments position—and as part of and in addition to its own particular form of "*planification indicativ*," the Japanese government directly supports particular industries, enters into the terms of technological agreements, advises on desirable prices, promotes changes in firm size and encourages cartelization. Few Japanese businessmen regard this as an infringement of their rights.

Japanese government officials believe business to be incapable of making satisfactory decisions by itself, that it is essential for government to provide guidance on virtually every aspect of operations. In a briefing paper prepared for the 1965 Tokyo meeting of Business International, an organization made up of corporations operating on a worldwide basis, the observation is made: "Japan is a country of paradox. A vigorous private enterprise system in which the state has only marginal economic activity coexists with heavy official supervision of business activity. No other private enterprise economy approaches the same degree of government control of business. But most of this control is expressed not in legal enactments, but in administrative action, or in even less definable 'guidance' and persuasion."[1]

This very different relationship between government and business in an ostensibly free enterprise economy reflects the historical absence of events in any way resembling the political revolution that accompanied the industrial revolution in the West, plus the fact that up to the present, Japan has been engaged in forced economic development rather than normal growth. Earlier in Chapter 3 we observed the different role played by business leaders in Japan in the overthrow of the feudal government from that by business leaders in the West. In Japan there was no assertion of business leadership; there was no

[1] Business International, *Japan*, Briefing Paper, Japanese Roundtable, New York, 1965, p. 5.

awareness of the extent to which market forces are capable of directing production and distribution.

In Japan government enterprise is limited essentially to activities in transportation, communication, and banking. The government operates the trunk system of railroads (the Japan National Railroad), and, together with private interests, the two airlines—overseas, Japan Airlines, and domestically, All Nippon Airways. In communication it is the sole operator within Japan of telephone and telegraph service through the Japan Telegraph and Telephone Company. It participates with private interests in the International Telegraph and Telephone Company (Kokusai Denshin Denwa). The government participates also in radio and TV, and operates the Japan Broadcasting Company. Without doubt, the strongest impact on the economy from government enterprise, however, comes from its activities in the field of banking. There it has a number of institutions—the Japan Development Bank (Nippon Kaihatsu Ginko); the Japan Export-Import Bank (Nippon Yushutsu Ginko); and People's Finance Corporation (Kokumin Yukoko); Agriculture, Forestry and Fisheries Finance Corporation (Noringyogyo Kinyu Koko); Small Business Finance Corporation (Chusho Kigyo Kinyu Koko); and the Hokkaido and Tohoku Development Corporation (Hokkaido Tohoku Kaihatsu Koko).

The low esteem in which the market mechanism is held, and the absence of fear of the abuse of power are but facets of the different orientation to political economy that one finds in Japan. Inasmuch as in Japanese conservative opinion the market mechanism is regarded as incapable of providing direction to the economy, no importance is attached, from this point of view, to market form. And inasmuch as efficiency is uncritically associated with larger and larger firm size, there tends to be the view that the higher the market concentration the greater the effective use of resources. In Japanese conservative opinion it is the government which steers, with producers the vital agents. Accordingly, the orientation of thinking is toward "producer satisfaction," not "consumer satisfaction." And inasmuch as those outside the conservative ranks of the Liberal-Democratic Party, predominantly Marxian Socialists, take an equally low view of the market mechanism, but for quite different reasons, there is little support in the political spectrum for a public policy of competitive enterprise.

In the liberal tradition of the West a nation's growth can be left largely to market forces. The government's role, apart from agriculture, is seen as primarily that of promoting through the use of monetary and fiscal policy an environment in which business can operate and prosper. Because different market structures are regarded as producing different results, market form is important. In the liberal view, competitive markets are to be preferred to concentrated markets on a number of counts: (1) allocation of resources and efficiency of production; (2) consumer responsiveness; (3) diffusion of power; (4) accommodation of the "right to entry."

Liberals almost uniformly believe competition makes for the most effective use of resources. In a competitive economy, not only will resources be successfully "bid" to the areas of greatest public desire, but production and distribution will be most efficient. In competitive markets, price, for the firm, is "given," so that cost reduction is the avenue to profits. In other markets where price may be manipulated, corporate gain and public benefit may not coincide. Because liberals take as an axiomatic truth that the object of production is consumption, they support competitive markets as being most responsive to consumer wishes.

Inasmuch as the competitive market both diffuses private power and, giving strong performance, makes it unnecessary for government to intervene, it is desirable on these grounds. Since in the Anglo-American tradition (now more American than Anglo) there is distrust of governmental as well as private power, minimizing the need for government is regarded as advantageous in itself.

There is an additional political dimension to the thinking of liberals about market form. In the liberal tradition there is what amounts to a "right to enterprise." It is believed that persons have a right to try their hand at enterprises, with the market acting as arbiter of those who remain and those who leave. Because the competitive market is both believed to constitute the best arbiter and because it permits the freest entry, competition is desirable on these grounds.

But again, this is in contrast to conservative opinion in Japan. Lacking a tradition of democracy, though democratic values have clearly been gaining ground in the postwar years, there is no feeling there is such a thing as a right to enterprise. "Chosen instruments"—that which 18th-century Britains and Americans protested so vigorously—seem perfectly natural. Therefore, if concentrated markets make entry difficult or impossible, no injustice is done because no right to enterprise is seen to exist in the first place.

The difference in the position of consumers in Japanese conservative and liberal opinion contrasts the two approaches. By definition, the market mechanism puts consumers in a strategic position; even though in real life the position may be appreciably less exalted than the kingly role of textbook presentation, the object of market-directed production remains consumer satisfaction. But in Japan's modernization the object of production has not been personal consumption, but national strength and power. Because producers have been the vital agents toward this goal, conservatives use producer satisfaction as the criterion of policy determination in the same way liberals use consumer satisfaction.[2]

Various aspects of today's Japan suggest the difference in the consumer's position between the two approaches. With its superb public buildings, outstanding rail, steamship, and air transportation; with its top factories the match of any anywhere, housing lags far behind. From an outsider's point of view, not only is housing severely cramped, but much of it is substandard. Only in the late 1960s is the city of Tokyo becoming adequately connected with sewers. Household heating is done entirely with portable units using kerosene, electricity, and gas. But housing, as a consumer item, has not seemed important to the Japanese government.

That Japanese are now permitted for the first time in some 30 years to go abroad as tourists does not reflect Japanese government initiative, but rather international opinion. It is the OECD, in the context of trade liberalization, which has promoted tourism. That the Japanese government did not believe it worthwhile to permit the use of foreign exchange for mere tourism again reflects the unimportance of the buying public.

It is difficult to escape the feeling that the disregard of the consumer is reflected in the Japanese government's emphasis on the role of exports. Obviously, in a nation with few natural resources, exports will necessarily play a crucial role, but one's impression of a disproportionate emphasis on exports is substantiated by the fact that exports have played a lesser role in Japan's postwar economy than in its prewar economy. Japan's economy in the early sixties was roughly three times the size of the 1934-36 economy. Exports as a proportion of GNP were roughly only two-thirds what they were in the mid-1930s.[3]

An additional view of the position of the consumer in Japan's economy is to be seen in life-expectancy figures. It is in the postwar period that life expectancy has dramatically risen—increasing in the 15-year period 1947 to 1962, 17 years for women and 16 years for

[2] This may, however, also tie in with the role of government. In American agriculture, where the government plays a major role, one sees this same focus on producer interests and lack of attention to consumer interests.

[3] Economic Planning Agency, *1963 National Income White Paper*, p. 180. For the average of the period 1934-36, exports and imports were each 24.3% of GNP; for 1956-58, exports were 14.4% and imports 16.1%; for 1961-63, exports were 15.3% and imports 20.5%.

men. In the roughly 50 years of Japan's development before the war life expectancy for women increased five years and for men, four. Demographers caution that Japan's early figures should be regarded as tentative, but even if one employs the statistics for the period just prior to World War I and compares them to figures for the mid-thirties, change is small. Life expectancy, prior to World War I, was 44.2 for men and 44.7 for women by contrast to the situation in the mid-thirties when it was 46.9 for men and 49.6 for women. By contrast, the figures in 1962 were 66.2 for men and 71.2 for women.[4] No one would assert that there was a one-to-one relationship between economic conditions and life expectancy, but on the other hand, the two are not wholly unrelated.

There is more to the explanation of the different relationships between government and business in Japan than the absence of an industrial-political revolution. There is the fact that in Japan economic development has been forced, whereas in nations with a liberal tradition it has been "natural." In forced development the market is not capable of steering. In forced development consumers cannot occupy the critical guiding role, for the criterion is necessarily new product lines, new technologies, with the basis of decision frequently national rather than individual; with the time reference tomorrow rather than today. In forced development change is necessarily programmed. In forced development the criterion of economic performance is not as of a given point in time, which is the primary basis for judging competitive markets, but over time.

Americans seeking to understand the realities of forced development may find it useful to think of our atomic energy and space programs. In these programs, notwithstanding the strong, free enterprise, laissez-faire tradition of the U.S., one sees the government occupying the directing role. In each case the government conceived the program (i.e., not the technology but the program), provided the direction, the stimulus, and the money. What the U.S. has achieved in atomic energy, and what it may achieve in its space program, has less to do with market forces (though private enterprise is integrally involved) than with the AEC and NASA.

One might think of Meiji Japan's task of modernizing the economy

[4] Welfare Ministry's Secretariat, Division of Health and Welfare Statistics [Annual Reports] (Koseisho Daijin Kambo Chosabu). Figures for the years prior to 1948 are taken from the 1951 report, p. 122; for 1962, from the 1962 report, p. 11.

as constituting a series of space and atomic energy programs—a space program in metallurgy, in shipbuilding, in textiles, etc. In one sense, the Japan case represented a less difficult problem, for technology could be purchased, it did not have to be developed; but on the other hand, there was a much more difficult problem: the whole economy had to be geared to new methods of production, whereas in the American case it has been but a few fields. Probably Meiji Japan viewed the consequences of a modern iron and steel industry, shipbuilding industry, textile industry, banking industry, much as the U.S. today views the space and atomic energy programs. In each case a crucial determinant of national welfare appeared to have been involved.

Does the foregoing suggest that in situations of forced development market forces have little place? The answer is no. On the other hand, it suggests market forces will have a different role in such circumstances than in an economy which has developed naturally. For allocating existing resources and technologies (and the "marginally" new), the market has no peer. Even Soviet leaders appear to be realizing that there is much to be said for it. But market forces are not necessarily the fastest route either to the development of altogether new technologies or to their dissemination. Market forces are predicated on *discernible* profit opportunities, and the altogether new—even when perceived—is almost by definition high risk. Further, the scale of resources commitment in the case of certain new technologies is a further deterrent to private development.

Some observers may hold that the above offers an explanation of the role of government in Japan's earlier development, but little with respect to the present scene. Though differently motivated, the Japanese government today, however, acts as if time were as precious a factor as earlier. Yesterday it was national power and prestige that drove the nation to concentrate on economic development; today it appears to be prestige alone. The Japanese government wants to bring the Japanese economy abreast of the level of European economies measured in per capita income terms—and it is doing so. In the postwar period there has been the penetration of the mass market in durable consumer goods, a truly exciting thing to watch. It is difficult to believe that the government's motivation has had much to do with consumer welfare, but inasmuch as one cannot have growth—and in the present case, high growth—without at the same time benefiting consumers, the consumer position has clearly improved. One prominent observer of the Japan scene, Martin Bronfenbrenner, has used the phrase, "The figures prosper; the people suffer," to describe the contemporary scene.[5] But as one watches the penetration of the first mass market in durable consumer goods in all of Asia, it seems exaggerated to contend that the people suffer. True, domestic consumption as a proportion of national income has decreased during the high growth,[6] but even though a lower proportion, the increase of GNP has been so dramatic as to result in real advances in living standards. Personal gains have not been proportionate to the gains in GNP, but they have been genuine.

It does not seem likely to me that when the Japanese economy reaches the level of the European economies the government will relinquish its strong role and let market forces have their head. The position of the government in the economy will decline only to the extent that Japanese business leaders contest direction. With increasing involvement with business leaders in other free enterprise economies, it is possible that Japanese businessmen will feel they have outgrown the period of government tutelage and direction and insist on taking greater leadership—but this is mere speculation. Speaking to the present, it is observed in the briefing paper of Business International, that: "Japan is avid to import the world's most advanced technology, and to contribute a share to it, but loath to adopt the international outlook and spirit of private competition that is the more intangible, but no less essential ingredient of modern business practice."[7]

### *A Japanese View of Political Economy*

A 1962 article by Morozumi Yoshihiko, a MITI bureaucrat, is typical of the type of thinking prevailing in government circles concerning government participation in private enterprise.[8] Mr. Morozumi focuses his attention on certain aspects of market structure, disregarding equally pertinent facets and argues for government guidance. Throughout the article he speaks of the need for "moderate concentration" (literally his phrasing is "'low-level' concentration"), but when I asked him in a 1964 interview which Japanese industry did not

[5] Bronfenbrenner, "Economic Miracles and Japan's Income-Doubling Plan," in Lockwood, p. 523.

[6] Economic Planning Agency, *1963 National Income*, pp. 166-67. In 1955 consumption as a proportion of GNE was 62.1%, in 1963, 52.8%.

[7] Business International, *Japan*, p. 4.

[8] As an idea man Mr. Morozumi has enjoyed a prominence beyond his position in MITI. He was widely regarded as father of the 1963 Specified Industries bill. Because of the unusual reading of the characters of his surname, one not infrequently encounters him in foreign publications under other names—as "Ryokado" in Yamamura's "Market Concentration and Growth in Postwar Japan," *Southern Economic Journal*, April 1966, p. 458.

show "excessive competition," he thought for a moment and then replied—"Plate glass." Plate glass is essentially a duopoly with a small postwar newcomer. In most vocabularies Mr. Morozumi's moderate concentration would be *high* concentration. Mr. Morozumi observes:

> The classic belief that the public welfare will be promoted by the invisible hand of free competition is held even today, but actuality is something else. Free competition neither provides the most suitable scale nor a guarantee of proper prices. Free competition means excessive equipment and low profits. In our country, the problem of excessive competition is being discussed.
>
> [As instances of excessive competition, Mr. Morozumi cites the fact that there are 64 Japanese trading companies in New York and 38 in Hongkong. He continued: "53 Japanese companies have entered into technical arrangements with RCA. Peabody and Co. receives royalties from 17 Japanese companies on the Sanforizing process. Thus can one conclude there is an 'invisible hand'?"]
>
> Eliminating excessive competition and pursuing economies of scale, we must conclude that a policy of moderate concentration is a desirable thing. Advancing concentration results in greater specialization from the technical point of view and from the management aspect, the elimination of inefficient enterprises. In other words we have the conditions for workable competition. The rise in GNP of Japan's economy which has as its central axis, exports, will then be stabilized. The method of distributing the benefits of high growth—prices, wages, profits—must not be awarded to the law of free competition which stifles the conditions of growth. If we have a problem in the suitable distribution of the economies of scale, it is an ex post facto inspecting function, for the Fair Trade Commission or the results should be corrected through public finance measures. The pressing, urgent business is the formation of a business system which will promote economic growth. [This statement was made in 1962 when growth of the GNP had averaged 15.6 per year for the last three years.]
>
> When the role of moderate concentration in the Japanese economy is being discussed, it is necessary to give consideration to the developments for the division of labor, production specialization, equipment modernization, and operations on an efficient scale. . . . There is a headlong trend here. We cannot wait to theorize about the sort of influence which a policy of concentration will have. To the extent that our export strength is assured, the growth of our economy is assured.

With respect to our recent splendid technical advances, we must note the requirements thereby implied for an increase in enterprise scale. . . . This is proved by the fact that postwar foreign technical agreements have been nearly all with large enterprises. In meeting the present technically revolutionary age, we must recognize that our enterprise scale is too small.

Further, we should see the need for moderate concentration which is indicated in trade liberalization. . . . It is unnecessary to illustrate with the automobile industry. The freeing of exports and imports means that we should work to advance the strength of our industry's scale in comparison with the international level.

In addition, a policy of moderate concentration strengthens the ability of business to resist business conditions. . . .

In this way, the application of the policy of moderate concentration is supported by various internal and external factors. It is regarded as a necessary trend in the Japanese economy. Not only is it asked that there be a single industry way of doing things, but such concentration will lay the foundation for a cooperative management of the future national economy.

*A "Concerted" Economy*

A "concerted" economy represents the middle way between 19th century laissez-faire [in the West] and the controls of the war period of the 1930s in Japan. . . . In place of the strife under freedom and the compulsion under controls, it is possible to have a "consent economy." . . . Out of discussions between the government and private enterprise, mutually determined national targets are worked out. Private enterprise pledges to carry these out. Government, on its side, pledges special favors . . . such as subsidies and taxation measures. . . . Mutual consent and bilateral methods obviate the need for legal compulsion. . . .

There are two restricting conditions for such a system to be successful. There must be confidence between the parties. In this way, mutually consented objectives become the objective which actually is possible. The second condition is the existence of market order among the bilateral parties. The contracting parties, with the Government and among themselves, have many private industry groupings, which assure that moderate concentration will be realized. . . .[9]

[9] MITI, Industrial Research Paper #100, "A Discussion of Cooperative Industrial Organization" (Tsusansho, Sangyo Kenkyu, #100, "Sangyo Kyochotai Seiron," reproduced in FTC, *A Collection of Views with Respect to Industrial*

### *Japanese "Planification Indicativ"*

The Japanese government sets goals for the economy and actively promotes their attainment. The last decade has witnessed a series of economic plans, almost all of which have experienced performance outstripping objectives. In the 1955 "Five-Year Plan for Economic Self-Support," developed under Mr. Hatoyama, a target growth rate of 5.5% was set.[10] However, with the increase of national income in 1955 over twice this rate and 1956 somewhat larger (cf. Table 16-1),

Table 16-1: GNP GROWTH RATES CALCULATED IN 1960 PRICES

(Percent increase over preceding year)

| | | | |
|---|---|---|---|
| 1955 | 10.9 | 1962 | 5.1 |
| 1956 | 8.7 | 1963 | 12.1 |
| 1957 | 7.0 | 1964 | 14.4 |
| 1958 | 3.4 | 1965 | 3.7 |
| 1959 | 17.5 | 1966 | 10.7 |
| 1960 | 14.0 | 1967 | 13.7 |
| 1961 | 15.4 | | |

Source: For 1955-63, Economic Planning Agency, *National Income White Paper, 1963* (Keizai Kikakucho, *Kokumin Shotoku Hakusho, 38*), Tokyo, p. 176. For 1964-67, Economic Planning Agency, *National Income Statistics, 1968* (Keizai Kikakucho, *Kokumin Shotoku Tokei, 43*), Tokyo, pp. 78-79.

a "New Long-Range Economic Plan" was drawn up under Mr. Kishi in 1957. This plan called for a target growth rate of 6.5%. With "most of the aims laid down for 1962 . . . already . . . achieved by 1960,"[11] work was begun in 1960 on another plan, Mr. Ikeda's famous 10-year "Income-Doubling" plan.[12] Calling for an average growth rate

---

*Structure and the Antimonopoly Law* (Kosei Torihiki Iinkai, *Sangyo Taisei to Dokusen Kinshiho o meguru Iken Shu*), mimeog., Tokyo, 1962, pp. 8-22. This translation was done from the reproduction. Because the styles of writing in the two languages are so very different, I have done a "free" translation.

[10] Organization for Economic Co-operation and Development, *Japan* in series, Economic Surveys by the OECD, Paris, 1964, p. 21.

[11] *Ibid.*

[12] For the English text, see Economic Planning Agency, *New Economic Plan of Japan* (1961-1970), published by the Japan *Times*, Tokyo, 1961.

of 7.2%, the plan envisaged a "1970 per capita national income that will approach the 1960 level of West Germany and France and will exceed that of Italy."[13] The "five pillars" of this plan[14] were officially expressed as:

1. strengthening social overhead capital
2. shifting the industrial structure toward heavy industries
3. encouraging foreign trade and international economic cooperation
4. raising the quality of human resources and promoting science and technology
5. eliminating the "dual structure" and improving social stability.

With growth again much beyond expectation, a new "medium term plan" for 1964-68 has been put forward as a replacement.[15] Basic to all of the government's programs is the belief that industrial concentration and cartelization encourage growth. Regardless of the plan in operation, concentration and industry agreements are encouraged.

The Japanese government does not stop at indicating the areas in which it believes investment may be most prospective or overseas trade most advantageous. Primarily through reliance on the carrot, though occasionally with the threat of the stick, the government experiences, for the most part, little difficulty in getting business to carry out its wishes. The principal means for effecting its views are lending from Japanese government sources; tax favors; until 1964, exchange controls; approval of capital imports; validation of technological agreements; and "administrative guidance." Since private borrowings from the IBRD carry the requirement of a government guarantee, the Japanese government, through the Japan Development Bank, is assured of a voice in borrowings from this source.

The Japanese government no longer doubly controls imports through tariff measures and foreign exchange. This does not reflect the view of the government, but again outside voices. In 1959 the International Monetary Fund accelerated other international efforts to liberalize trade by announcing that governments with current receipts in convertible foreign currencies would no longer be in a position to justify exchange controls.[16] Reluctantly Japan agreed to move by 1964

[13] Japan Development Bank, *Postwar Growth in the Japanese Economy*, Tokyo, 1964, p. 64.

[14] *Ibid.*, p. 65; Japan Development Bank, *Facts and Figures on the Japanese Economy*, Tokyo, 1964, p. 167.

[15] *Ibid.* P. 167.

[16] General Agreement on Tariffs and Trade, *Activities of GATT 1959/60*, Geneva, 1960, p. 24.

to "Article 8" status at the Fund. "Amid torrents of self-pity and forebodings of doom,"[17] the Japanese government during the four-year period 1960 to 1964 largely relinquished exchange control, a power it had held for about 30 years. Although imports now are for the most part subject only to tariffs, the government maintains a strong voice concerning invisibles and what might at best be described as an embracive voice on capital imports.[18]

Capital imports fall under the Foreign Investment Law which, to read it, does not seem unusual. The criteria for foreign investment are, according to Article 8 of the Law, positively, that the investment contribute to Japan's balance of payments and to the development of key industries; negatively, that contracts must be fair, not contravene existing laws or regulations, and that payments arising from acquisition of stocks, debentures, and the like, or claims in the forms of loans, must be made in appropriate currencies.[19] But as Business International comments out of the experience of foreign firms operating under this law:

> Under this umbrella, the Government operates a framework of regulations that delegates almost complete discretion to officials in judging whether to grant approvals for investments. They in turn operate a system of their own internal rules, known as "naiki" (private laws), which are neither publicly available, nor in any sense formal elements of the law. All direct investments, whether in joint ventures or branches, and licensing agreements must move through these procedures, except a few small ventures approvable by the Bank of Japan.
>
> The pattern of these "naiki" can be fairly accurately surmised from a study of the experience of foreign firms seeking to set up or expand businesses in Japan. Only in rare cases can a foreign company obtain even 50% equity in a manufacturing venture, and 49% is usually the limit. At least half of the directors and auditors must be from the Japanese side, and the president must be a Japanese citizen....
>
> These are inviolable rules, but other conditions may also be imposed on particular ventures—limitations on product line, scale of

[17] Business International, *Japan*, p. 28.

[18] In general, OEEC (predecessor to OECD) members used 1948 as the reference year in working out commitments for trade "liberalization" percentages; Japan's trade "liberalization" percentages are based on 1959. In 1964, on this criteria, Japanese trade was "93% liberalized." Cf. OECD, *The OECD at Work*, Paris, 1964, p. 40, 44. For a discussion of invisibles and capital imports, cf. Business International, *Japan*, pp. 9-14.

[19] Business International, *Japan*, pp. 9-10.

production, access to markets, advertising and promotion campaigns, payments for technology, royalty rates, and exchanges of know-how for equity. Interest rates on loans by foreign partners may be laid down as a condition for approval of the investment. It does not matter that the foreign and Japanese parties have reached amicable agreement on the details of their joint venture. The agreement may be, and frequently is, rewritten by MITI officials. The enforced changes invariably favor the Japanese party. In the course of these validation procedures, as they are called, MITI will frequently consult competitive firms, although often these do not wait to be consulted before making known their objections to a new venture backed with foreign technology and capital. Time taken to obtain validation is often in direct ratio to the clamor made by these groups.[20]

In the case of a proposed joint venture, as reported by Business International, between Hohnen Oil, Japan's largest producer of edible oils, and Unilever for the manufacture of margarine, shortening, and similar products, validation took close to three years. When approved in 1963, it imposed, in addition to limitations on the equity ratio, restrictions on output. Output was limited to 26,000 tons, or 10% of the market up to 1969. It was specified that the new company would join the edible oil industry association, cooperate with its members and give them technical aid.[21]

Similarly, Business International reports that in the case of the joint venture between Showa Denko, Yawata Steel, and Kaiser Aluminum and Chemical for establishment of an aluminum rolling mill, there was much delay in getting government approval of the equity proportions. Permissible output was another snag. The original plan called for output of 71,000 tons by 1971, but MITI reduced this to 58,000 by 1970 and the new company was directed not to make certain items in which small producers specialized.[22]

Abandonment of exchange control was carried out in a manner calculated to strengthen the power of the government elsewhere in the economy, in compensation for the loss of this powerful tool. "On the hour every hour" Japanese were told of the measures which must be taken to prevent the economy from being swamped by cheap foreign goods. The increase in large mergers which was noted in Chapter 14 for the years 1960-63 ties directly into these other avenues of government pressure.

MITI bureaucrats are troubled that Japan's automobile companies

[20] *Ibid.*, p. 10. [21] *Ibid.*, p. 11. [22] *Ibid.*

are but a fraction the size of General Motors. Although it was the government's decision to help the automobile industry by advantageous loans through the Japan Development Bank, loans were not extended until the mergers, which the government sought, had occurred. Thus Nissan, the largest automobile company, was given no JDB loans until after absorbing through merger, Prince, as the government wished it to do.[23]

The government has three times unsuccessfully sought Diet authorization for a stronger voice in "specified industries" (those considered in need of a boost in the face of trade liberalization)—automobiles, tires, special steels, ferro alloys, and petrochemicals. It sought authorization in specified industries for preferential treatment in taxes and loans for firms "desiring" to merge or cartelize.[24] Among other factors in the failure the memory of the thirties was too vivid. However, the fact that the Specified Industries bill did not pass has made little difference in the government's actions. What it failed to obtain by the front door, it has accomplished by the back door.

Early in the postwar period the government decided help should be focused on four basic industries—electric power, coal, iron and steel, and shipping—in order to provide for the growth of other industry. Electric power and coal would supply the energy sources for the economy, iron and steel the basic building material, and shipping, transportation for the vital foreign trade. Substantial government help was extended in the form of advantageous credit, primarily through the Japan Development Bank. As will be seen in Table 16-2 these four industries have claimed a wholly disproportionate amount of loans from the JDB, although since 1956 a lesser proportion than initially.

Up to 1964 just under 2,000 firms had received loans from the JDB in local and foreign currency, loans which totaled the enormous sum of $2.6 billion.[25] It would not seem accidental that "77 of the 100 largest Japanese enterprises in terms of sales (excluding financial and trading companies) [have] either received financial assistance from the JDB in the past or are currently [1964] receiving it."[26]

But to more fully see the role of the government in the basic industries, let us turn the picture around and look at the proportion of total borrowing supplied by the JDB and other government sources to the chosen industries. In 1964 the government was supplying to the

[23] Interview with Japan Development Bank officials, December 1965.

[24] *Japan Times*, March 23, 1963, February 9, 1964.

[25] Japan Development Bank, *Postwar Growth of the Japanese Economy*, Tokyo, 1964, p. 77.

[26] *Ibid.*

Table 16-2: JDB LOANS TO SELECTED INDUSTRIES

(in millions yen, fiscal years)

| *Loans in domestic currency* | *1951-55* | | *1956-63* | | *Total* | |
|---|---|---|---|---|---|---|
| | *amount* | *proportion* | *amount* | *proportion* | *amount* | *proportion* |
| electric power | 117,376 | 46.3% | 194,972 | 30.9% | 312,348 | 35.3% |
| marine transport. | 64,121 | 25.3 | 149,602 | 23.7 | 213,723 | 24.2 |
| iron and steel | 14,223 | 5.6 | 12,885 | 2.0 | 27,108 | 3.1 |
| coal mining | 16,591 | 6.6 | 57,683 | 9.2 | 74,274 | 8.4 |
| Subtotal | 212,311 | 83.8 | 415,142 | 65.8 | 627,453 | 71.0 |
| others | 41,025 | 16.2 | 215,375 | 34.2 | 256,400 | 29.0 |
| Total | 253,336 | 100.0 | 630,517 | 100.0 | 883,853 | 100.0 |
| *Loans in foreign currency* | | | | | | |
| electric power | 12,868 | 96.0 | 41,442 | 41.6 | 54,310 | 48.0 |
| iron and steel | 534 | 4.0 | 56,379 | 56.5 | 56,913 | 50.3 |
| others | 0 | 0 | 1,849 | 1.9 | 1,849 | 1.7 |
| Total | 13,402 | 100.0 | 99,670 | 100.0 | 113,072 | 100.0 |

Source: Japan Development Bank, *Postwar Growth of the Japanese Economy*, Tokyo, 1964, p. 70.

nine leading companies in electric power more than one-third of their total borrowed funds. In hundreds of billions of yen, the JDB supplied 320 out of the total of 922.[27]

The coal industry has continued to be sick, in spite of large loans from the JDB and the "Rationalization Fund." In 1964 loans from the JDB and the Fund to the 13 leading coal companies were just under half of the coal companies' borrowings. In hundreds of billions of yen, borrowings from the JDB were 41.5 and 35.7 from the Rationalization Fund (altogether, 77.2), out of a total of 155.[28] But still coal does not prosper. Oil is its powerful competitor. As the JDB commented in 1964:

> Although the government policies for the coal mining industry were especially strengthened since 1955, the quickening tempo of the energy revolution since 1960 with the rapid spread of the use of heavy oil has brought a crisis to the industry anew. Thus the Government organized the Coal Mining Research Group in 1962; and on the basis of the latter's findings and recommendations, it has decided to take more effective measures for the industry including the following: (1) in order to secure stable demand for coal, to urge large coal consumers such as steel and electric power companies to cooperate (2) in order to insure stable production of coal, to concentrate its production to [*sic*] the efficient mines and close the less efficient ones; and (3) in order to cope with the related social problems, to relieve unemployed miners and to promote industrial development in the coal mining regions. In obtaining funds for fixed investment, only the efficient mines will be able to expect government assistance in the future. . . .
>
> Through the program of rationalization and consolidation, the number of mines has been reduced from 795 in 1959 to 420 in 1962, and the number of regularly employed miners declined from 309,000 at the end of fiscal 1952 to 165,000 at the end of fiscal 1962.[29]

In steel today, the government does much less lending.[30] In the case of the largest companies, its principal lending function would appear to be that of guarantor through the JDB of IBRD loans. "Ad-

[27] Calculated by the author from firm data appearing in Economic Investigative Council, *Research on Business Groupings* (Keizai Chosa Kyokai, *Keiretsu no Kenkyu*), 1965, pp. 258-59.

[28] *Ibid.*, pp. 183-84.

[29] Japan Development Bank, *Postwar Growth*, p. 95.

[30] Calculated by the author from *Research on Business Groupings*, 1965, pp. 187-88.

ministrative guidance," however, provides the government with another means for effecting its views.

In shipping, the government continues to play a dominant lending role. Of the total loans outstanding among the 17 largest shipping companies in 1964, the JDB supplied more than half—in hundreds of billions of yen, 165 out of 286, or 57%.[31] It is accordingly not surprising that the government was able to overcome industry opposition and force it to consolidate into six groupings, which occurred in 1964.

Another major avenue of Japanese government lending is the Japanese Export-Import Bank. In industries with important export trade, loans have been very large. For example, in shipbuilding, loans from the bank in 1964 to the 10 major builders amounted to almost one-third of their total borrowings (in hundreds of billion of yen, the bank supplied 160 out of a total of 492, or 32%.[32]

In addition to gaining a voice through lending and tax favors, primarily in the form of accelerated amortization, the government assures itself a key position through the device of administrative guidance, which amounts to government-sponsored cartelization. In this way, the government has gained participation—temporary and at times sustained—in industry decisions. As was observed in Chapter 15, the government has participated in such industries as coal, petroleum, iron and steel, the nonferrous metals, chemicals, pulp and paper, textiles, and sugar. It exerts a strong voice on price, output, and rationalization schemes. Since the government is oriented toward the producer, not the consumer, its power frequently contributes to price increases and cutbacks in output.

Whether it be lending, accelerated amortization, cartelization, or permissible arrangements for foreign capital, government banks and the ministries act as spokesmen for a basic policy determined at the cabinet level. Key voices are the Economic Planning Agency, MITI, and the Ministry of Finance. With respect to overall objectives for the economy, the Economic Planning Agency is the strongest. MITI is the strongest agency for achieving the goals because its jurisdiction covers the largest portion of the economy. The Ministry of Finance is powerful as the dispenser of tax advantages.

While government favors—credit, tax, or otherwise—may greatly facilitate the performance of the economy, to which the postwar Japanese economy is clearly brilliant testimony, there is a price to be paid for this manner of operation even under Japanese criteria. Dispensation of government favors is highly susceptible to "inducements," and government-business relations in Japan today, as in the

[31] Calculated from *ibid.*, pp. 254-56. [32] *Ibid.*, pp. 196-97.

past, have been clouded by such practices. That the ordinary Japanese takes such an exceptionally low view of government officials is no doubt the result of the magnitude of past scandals. As was noted when discussing the "research department" of the Mitsui top-holding company, all transactions were on a cash basis for which no records were kept. Further, a practice not uncommon in the past continues to be used: establishing dummy corporations to take the rap in the event of leaks.

Although government-business relations are inherently subject to partiality and favoritism, it is noteworthy that the hallmark of market forces when markets are competitive is their impartiality. Merit is the basis of success. On the other hand, in concentrated markets with entry blocked, private power substitutes for government in favoritism and partiality. In Japan's past, the partiality of government favors was a major contributory factor to the development of the *zaibatsu.*

Although there is lacking in Japan a tradition of the abuse of power, it is difficult to be sanguine about events in the last quarter century without concluding that there is much here that is typical of human behavior. Japanese, no less than Westerners, may abuse power. Westerners believe the most effective way to prevent the abuse of power is to keep it diffused. It may well be that increasing numbers of Japanese will come to hold that diffusion of power in Japan is a comparably beneficial arrangement.

# 17.

## The Postwar Performance of the Economy

In contrast to the dour predictions Mitsui and other former *zaibatsu* spokesmen made for Japan's future following the Occupation reforms, and in contrast to the dim view taken by many American government spokesmen, as well as international agency officials, Japan's economy has prospered as never before. As Orville J. McDiarmid has commented: "As late as 1952, Secretary of State Dulles observed, perhaps in a rare humorous vein, that suicide was not an illogical step for anyone concerned about Japan's economic future. To spread the laurels of prescience further, the World Bank, in 1955 and even later, was appraising Japan's total future creditworthiness at a figure much below what it now lends to that country in a single year."[1]

In 1954 the Japanese economy regained its previously achieved peak performance, the level of the 1939 GNP. With the economy sustaining an average growth rate just under 10% during the seven-year period 1955-62, and just over 10% during the four-year period 1963-67, it is difficult indeed to argue that the Occupation reforms, among which the deconcentration program played a prominent role, damaged the Japanese economy. Did the reforms contribute to the high growth? Here examination will be made only of the deconcentration program. Attention will be focused on what role, if any, the breakup of the *zaibatsu* played in the nation's high growth rate.

Table 17-1 presents growth rates among leading free enterprise nations for the period 1955-62, as well as for the Soviet Union for the period 1952-61. Whether comparison is with free enterprise economies or the Soviet Union, Japan comes out ahead. For the most recent years the Japanese GNP has increased unevenly but sharply. Increases in these years in terms of 1960 prices were: 1963, 12.1%; 1964, 14.3; 1965, 3.7; 1966, 10.7; 1967, 13.7.[2]

In a world varying from a keen to a desperate interest in national

[1] McDiarmid, "Japan and Israel," *Finance and Development*, June 1966, p. 36.

[2] The 1963 percentage is from Economic Planning Agency, *1963 National Income White Paper* (Keizai Kikakucho, *38 Nendo Kokumin Shotoku Hakusho*), p. 176. The 1964-67 are from Economic Planning Agency, *1968 National Income Statistics* (Keizai Kikakucho, *43 Nendo Kokumin Shotoku Tokei*), pp. 78-79.

Table 17-1: PART A: AVERAGE ANNUAL INCREASE IN REAL GNP, 1955-62, AMONG MAJOR FREE ENTERPRISE COUNTRIES

| | | | |
|---|---|---|---|
| Japan | 9.9% | West Germany | 5.7 |
| U.S.A. | 2.8 | Italy | 6.2 |
| Canada | 3.6 | Holland | 3.7 |
| England | 2.3 | Sweden | 4.0 |
| France | 4.9 | | |

Source: Economic Planning Agency, *1963 National Income White Paper* (Keizai Kikakucho, *Kokumin Shotoku Hakusho*), Tokyo, p. 2, where it is indicated that the material has been taken from the United Nations, *Yearbook of National Income Statistics*, for 1962 and 1963.

income growth, the question everywhere has been, how has Japan achieved this? Possibly the foregoing should be rephrased—*the question almost everywhere has been*—for some do not join in the acclaim of Japan's accomplishment.[3] Such observers hold that in a basic sense the accomplishment has been a matter of "building back" rather than new growth, which is a simpler process. They point out that if Japan's long-term growth trend—4.37%[4]—is projected from the performance of the economy in the thirties, the nation up to the mid-sixties had been merely building back. Had other events not impinged, Japan's economy would be where it was in 1963 simply on a continuation of the long-term growth trend. Increase at the rate of 4.37% yearly means a doubling in 17 years and a tripling in 26 years.

## *National-income Study in Japan*

In this, the first extended reference to historical GNP calculations, it will be well to pause and observe that study of national income in Japan was only beginning in the decade before World War II. The preliminary quality of the initial research is indicated by the scale of disparities among the different estimates of income at that time.

[3] Martin Bronfenbrenner is prominent among these observers. See his "Economic Miracles and Japan's Income Doubling Plan" in Lockwood, *The State and Economic Enterprise in Japan*, pp. 523-54.

[4] An average of the overlapping growth rates per decade, calculated from figures cited by Ohkawa and associates in *The Growth Rate of the Japanese Economy*, Tokyo, 1957, p. 21, where averages have been used in the form: 1878-87—1883-92; 1883-92—1888-97; etc.

**Table 17-1:** PART B: A COMPARISON OF GROWTH RATES BETWEEN JAPAN AND THE U.S.S.R., WITH "NATIONAL INCOME" CALCULATED FOR BOTH JAPAN AND THE U.S.S.R., ON THE SOVIET METHOD IN 1960 PRICES, WITH 1952 AS 100

| | *Japan* | *U.S.S.R.* |
|---|---|---|
| 1952 | 100 | 100 |
| 1953 | 111 | 109 |
| 1954 | 118 | 123 |
| 1955 | 130 | 137 |
| 1956 | 141 | 152 |
| 1957 | 153 | 163 |
| 1958 | 164 | 184 |
| 1959 | 188 | 199 |
| 1960 | 222 | 214 |
| 1960* | 226 | 214 |
| 1961* | 268 | 230 |

**Source:** Japanese Ministry of Foreign Affairs, European Affairs Bureau, *The Growth of the National Economies of Japan and the Soviet Union*, Tokyo, 1963, p. 10, where it is indicated that sources are as follows: Japan, 1952-1960, Economic Planning Agency, *1960 White Paper on National Income; for 1960,* 1961,** Economic Planning Agency, Research Bureau, Economic Outline, 1963. U.S.S.R, 1952-1960, *Statistical Yearbook, 1960; 1960,* 1961,* Statistical Yearbook, 1961.*

For example, for the year 1937 estimates in current yen ranged from Y15 billion by the *Oriental Economist* to Y20 billion by both the Mitsubishi Economic Research Bureau and the Japan Economic Federation.[5] The calculations of Professors Takahashi, Hijikata, and Shibata for 1937 were 18, 19, and 17 billion respectively.[6] All of these calculators used Y10 billion for their 1930 estimate, the GNP figure de-

[5] Japanese statistics are typically presented as gross national expenditures rather than gross national product. GNE equals GNP.

[6] Reproduced in Jerome B. Cohen, *Japan's Economy in War and Reconstruction*, Minneapolis, 1949, p. 6, where sources are cited.

veloped by the Cabinet Bureau of Statistics.[7] The Cabinet Bureau developed GNP figures for three year-periods—1925, 1930, and 1934.[8] However, no one at this time was adequately deflating estimates to get rid of increases out of price rises alone, which became sharper, and sharper as the thirties went on.[9] One can accordingly only conclude that Japan's leaders began World War II unaware that the economy, notwithstanding seemingly higher and higher national income figures, had not grown since 1939 and was but little changed from its 1937 performance.

Not surprisingly, in view of the recentness of work in the national income field, revisionism continues to characterize not only the historical projections but to some extent recent estimates as well. In the historical field Professor Ohkawa and associates and Professor Rosovsky have been doing the leading work, though they have been recently challenged in their estimates of agricultural income by Professor James Nakamura.[10]

Illustrative of the scale of the revisionism in progress is the difference in the data presented by Professor Ohkawa and associates of Hitotsubashi University's Economic Research Institute in the Japanese-language edition of their *Growth Rate of the Japanese Economy* (*Nihon Keizai no Seicho-Ritsu*), which appeared in 1956, and the English-language edition of the study which came out the following year. The income statistics for the years 1937 to 1941 from the two editions follow.[11] Although the two editions employ different deflators for the years in question, this should not affect the pattern of the growth.

Similarly one sees revisionism in the national-income work of the government. Postwar national income calculation is now the responsibility of the Economic Planning Agency, which succeeded the Economic Stabilization Board. While initially the ESB was responsible for national-income work (publication on an annual basis began in 1953),

[7] That is, all used the Y10 billion figure, though not all the 10.635 billion yen calculated by the Cabinet Bureau.

[8] United Nations, Department of Economic and Social Affairs, *National Accounting Practices in Sixty Countries* (Provisional Issue), Studies in Methods, Series F, No. 11, New York, 1964, p. 123.

[9] I am indebted to a discussion with Royama Shoichi for this point.

[10] Cf. Ohkawa-Rosovsky, "A Century of Japanese Economic Growth," in Lockwood, *The State and Economic Enterprise*, and Nakamura, "Growth of Japanese Agriculture, 1875-1920," in Lockwood, *State and Economic Enterprise.*

[11] The Japanese-language edition figures are taken from their reproduction in *Japanese Economic Statistics* (Nippon Hyoron Shin Sha, *Nippon Keizai Tokei Shu*), Tokyo, 1958, pp. 340-41, the English-language edition figures from *Growth Rate*, p. 234.

| | 1956 Jap.-lang. edn., income in 1928-32 prices | 1957 Eng.-lang. edn., income in 1934-36 prices |
|---|---|---|
| 1937 | Y15.1 billion | Y16.2 billion |
| 1938 | 16.5 | 15.9 |
| 1939 | 18.9 | 16.8 |
| 1940 | 17.6 | 16.1 |
| 1941 | 18.2 | 16.7 |

since 1958 it has been the National Income Division of the Economic Research Institute of the Economic Planning Agency.[12] The EPA has carried its projections back to 1930. But likewise with it, findings have been substantially altered. In the White Papers for 1955 and 1956, GNP for the immediate prewar years, in 1934-36 prices, was shown as follows.[13] For comparison the more recent estimates presented in Table 17-2 from the 1963 report are shown.

| | 1955 & 1956 reports | 1963 report |
|---|---|---|
| 1937 | 16.1 | 21.2 |
| 1938 | 15.8 | 21.9 |
| 1939 | 16.7 | 22.1 |
| 1940 | 16.0 | 20.7 |
| 1941 | 16.7 | 21.1 |

As can be seen from Table 17-2 (bearing in mind the still tentative quality of the material), Japan would be where it is merely on a continuation of its long-term growth trend; it would nevertheless seem appropriate to distinguish between the attainment of previously achieved levels and the attainment of "what might have been if. . . ." Building back to demonstrated performance is clearly different from building back to what might have been but was not. The "building back to where the nation might have been" explanation of Japan's high growth rate would appear to be pertinent primarily in the psychological sense of an impatience to be where Japan might have been, of, as the Japanese-English phrase goes, "catch up." And it should indeed be remembered that Japan was not the only nation to have had its long-term growth trend interrupted.

Japan's accomplishment of sustaining a GNP growth rate just under

[12] United Nations, *National Accounting Practices*, p. 123.

[13] Figures from the 1955 and 1956 yearbooks are taken from their reproduction in *Japanese Economic Statistics* (*Nihon Keizai Tokei Shu*), Tokyo, p. 341.

Table 17-2: JAPANESE GNE, 1930-63

(in billions 1934 yen)

| | | *Increase over preceding year* | | | *Increase over preceding year* |
|---|---|---|---|---|---|
| 1934-36 | 16.7 | | 1946 | 11.5 | |
| 1930 | 13.4 | | 1947 | 12.5 | 8.4% |
| 1931 | 13.9 | 3.4% | 1948 | 14.2 | 13.0 |
| 1932 | 14.0 | 1.0 | 1949 | 14.5 | 2.2 |
| 1933 | 14.6 | 4.2 | 1950 | 16.1 | 10.9 |
| 1934 | 16.2 | 10.8 | 1951 | 18.2 | 13.0 |
| 1935 | 16.6 | 2.4 | 1952 | 20.2 | 11.1 |
| 1936 | 17.1 | 3.1 | 1953 | 21.6 | 7.0 |
| 1937 | 21.2 | 23.7 | 1954 | 22.4 | 3.7 |
| 1938 | 21.9 | 3.4 | 1955 | 24.9 | 11.2 |
| 1939 | 22.1 | 0.8 | 1956 | 26.5 | 6.4 |
| 1940 | 20.7 | -6.0 | 1957 | 28.3 | 6.8 |
| 1941 | 21.1 | 1.6 | 1958 | 29.5 | 4.0 |
| 1942 | 21.4 | 1.3 | 1959 | 34.3 | 16.4 |
| 1943 | 21.3 | -0.2 | 1960 | 38.8 | 13.0 |
| 1944 | 20.6 | -3.4 | 1961 | 44.3 | 14.2 |
| | | | 1962 | 46.8 | 5.7 |
| | | | 1963 | 52.2 | 11.5 |

Notes and Source: Economic Planning Agency, *1963 National Income White Paper* (Keizai Kikakucho, *38 Nendo Kokumin Shotoku Hakusho*). Absolute figures, pp. 178-79; 1934-63 percentage figures, pp. 180-81. The years 1930-44 are calendar years, 1946-63, fiscal.

10% over the seven-year period 1955-62 and just above 10% in the four-year period 1963-67 is the product of several elements—a high growth tradition, some good fortune, and deliberate policy-planning. The postwar pattern builds on the noteworthy long-term growth trend of 4.3% which rested on high investment, high savings, good entrepreneurship teamed with government foresight, and a labor force which was literate, disciplined, and industrious. The recent growth pattern, roughly double the long-term trend, is the product initially of some good fortune but overwhelmingly of national skill. American aid, which totaled some $2 billion,[14] was helpful in getting the economy moving again after its near-paralysis of August 1945; the Korean war was also a stimulant. Furthermore, the terms of international trade have been advantageous to Japan, though as much as good fortune this has been the product of good management, of the government's steering the economy into fields where it would reap such international advantage.

Other elements entering into Japan's high postwar growth have been: investment (as a proportion of GNP) roughly double the level of the thirties and savings markedly higher; exceptionally large increases to the labor force out of the high birthrate in the immediate postwar years; skillful government direction of the economy, shifting resources out of areas of low-growth potential and into high-growth areas; and factors stemming from the deconcentration program and other postwar changes.

Dissolution of the top-holding companies created far more independent "members," with the result that in market after market there has been a tough battle for position. Such struggles, occurring as they have, in the context of impressive technological change, have pushed private investment to exceptional levels. Government investment likewise is far greater, a consequence among other things of the greatly reduced armaments burden; large amounts of government expenditure now go into capital items rather than military goods.

The scale of technological change in the Japanese economy, with much of the change representing foreign technology, not only reflects hunger for outside developments after the isolation of the war period and the fact that Japan today is such a much more widely known area for investment by foreign corporations, but the freer trading patterns stemming from the dissolution of the top-holding companies and the temporary dissolution of the two giant trading companies. The two giant trading companies were formerly the chief avenue for en-

[14] In a manuscript study, "Banking in Japan," prepared for a client and dated October 1965, T.F.M. Adams states on p. 65 that total help came to about $2 billion. "Besides some doubts concerning the character of the debt (there was never any formal agreement regarding the aid), the amount was disputed. MITI said that it possessed no accurate figures for the help received." Mr. Adams states that ESS records for the period September 1945 to March 1951 showed a total of $1,197 million of aid (of which $1,131 was in civilian goods and $66 million in released military supplies). From April 1951 to March 1956, when MITI kept its own records, it reported that aid amounted to $853 million (of which $847 million was in civilian goods and $6 million in goods released by the United States Army). This figure, added to the earlier ESS amount, would make a total of $2,151 million. However, Mr. Adams states that according to figures released by MITI in June 1961, American aid under GARIOA, EROA, and other civilian programs totalled $1,795 million.

trance of foreign technology into the country. Their imports were not for corporations in general, but for members of their combine groupings. Their temporary dismemberment in the context of the generally freer trading patterns established by Occupation measures has meant a far wider diffusion of foreign technology than would have occurred if the *zaibatsu* structures had been intact. These factors will be examined in turn.

### *Investment Levels—An International Comparison*

Let us begin the analysis of Japan's extraordinary post-1954 national income growth by noting investment levels, and let us begin this by making comparison of investment in Japan with investment in other economies. As will be seen in Table 17-3, capital-formation has been higher in Japan than elsewhere. On the other hand, it has not been so much higher than the levels in West Germany, Holland, and Canada as to explain the difference in performance of the economies. Putting GNP growth rates from Table 17-1 with "fixed domestic capital formation" as a percentage of GNP from Table 17-3, we find, for the period 1955-62:

| | Table 17-3 data<br>*Fixed investment as percent of GNP* | Table 17-1 data<br>*Aver. per annum increase in GNP* |
|---|---|---|
| Japan | 27.6 | 9.9 |
| West Germany | 23.2 | 5.7 |
| Holland | 23.9 | 3.7 |
| Canada | 23.7 | 3.6 |

Thus, fixed investment in Japan has been only some 15% greater than in the other three countries, yet the growth rate of GNP has been 1¾ to 2¾ times greater.

### *Exceptionally High Inventories*

The Table 17-3 figures on Japanese investment may seem surprisingly low in view of other published material on investment levels (such as the final column in Table 17-4). The explanation is that in Table 17-3 capital formation is broken down between "fixed capital formation" and "inventories." If the two are treated together, one gains the impression that capital-formation in Japan has been markedly above the levels occurring in other countries, but this stems from the unusually high levels of inventory in Japan.

Table 17-3: AN INTERNATIONAL COMPARISON OF GNP COMPONENTS, 1955-62 (in percent)

| | *Japan* | *U.S.* | *Canada* | *U.K.* | *France* | *W.Germany* | *Italy* | *Holland* | *Sweden* |
|---|---|---|---|---|---|---|---|---|---|
| 1. Personal consumption | 56.6 | 63.6 | 64.0 | 65.9 | 65.6 | 58.3 | 63.3 | 58.1 | 60.5 |
| 2. General govt. consumption | 9.8 | 18.3 | 14.5 | 16.9 | 13.5 | 13.5 | 14.6 | 14.3 | 17.4 |
| 3. Domestic capital formation | 27.6 | 16.6 | 23.7 | 15.5 | 18.9 | 23.2 | 21.5 | 23.9 | 21.1 |
| private | 19.2 | 13.8 | 17.0 | 9.0 | 16.6 | 20.1 | 18.9 | 16.0 | 12.8 |
| govt. enterprise | 3.1 | 0.4 | 2.8 | 5.1 | | | | 3.8 | 4.9 |
| govt. - general | 5.3 | 2.4 | 3.9 | 1.4 | 2.3 | 3.1 | 2.6 | 4.1 | 3.4 |
| 4. Inventories | 5.7 | 0.8 | 0.9 | 1.1 | 1.6 | 2.2 | 0.9 | 1.9 | 1.3 |
| 5. Net export, goods, services | 0.6 | 0.2 | -1.6 | -0.5 | 0.4 | 2.9 | -0.6 | 0.6 | -0.5 |
| export, goods, services | 12.5 | 4.7 | 19.5 | 20.8 | 13.9 | 21.4 | 14.4 | 48.2 | 26.8 |
| import, goods, services | 11.9 | 4.5 | 21.1 | 21.3 | 13.5 | 18.5 | 15.0 | 47.6 | 27.3 |
| *Gross Domestic Product* | 100.3 | 99.5 | - | 98.9 | 100 | 100 | 99.7 | 98.8 | 99.8 |
| 6. Net income from abroad | -0.3 | 0.5 | -1.6 | 1.1 | 0.0 | -0.1 | 0.3 | 1.2 | 0.2 |
| *Gross National Product* | 100 | 100 | 100 | 100 | 100 | 100 | 100 | 100 | 100 |

**Source: Economic Planning Agency, *1963 National Income White Paper*, p. 15.**

A comparison of the inventory data in Table 17-3 will indicate that inventories in Japan have in recent years run seven times the level found in the United States and over twice the level of West Germany, the nation with inventories next highest to Japan. One might be tempted to explain Japan's high inventories by its high growth, but study of material showing historical patterns indicates that inventories as a percentage of private capital formation were at the same level in the thirties as more recently.[15] Further, some observers have professed to see a relationship between inventories and market organization, suggesting that the higher the concentration the lower the inventories. In a very broad sense this is true, but in the breakdown of the data both small and large business show high inventory.[16] But inasmuch as it is fixed capital formation, not inventories, which basically affects output levels, let us concentrate attention on fixed investment.

To understand the present very high investment levels in Japan it will be helpful to compare them with the scale of investment in the thirties when the nation was preparing for the China and Pacific wars. Investment broken down as between private and government and as between fixed and inventory as a proportion of GNE for the period 1930-63 is presented in Table 17-4.

Comparing the information on investment levels in Table 17-4 with GNP growth rates from Table 17-2, we will find that from 1931 to 1939, inclusive, fixed capital formation averaged 14.8% of GNE while GNP increased, on the average, 5.8% over the preceding year. During the next four years, 1940-43, inclusive, fixed capital formation averaged 22.2%, but GNP *decreased* at 0.57% per annum, thus underscoring that growth is dependent on more than the scale of the investment and the need for information on the scale of disinvestment. By contrast, during the 1955 to 1962 period fixed investment averaged 27.9% while GNP increased at 9.7%, both close to double the period of the thirties.

In seeking to understand the national-income consequences from the levels of fixed investment in Japan, we should take note of the exceptionally small proportion of total investment which housing occupies. In its first survey of Japan the OECD observed that while housing in 1962 constituted only 8% of fixed capital and 2.5% of GNP in Japan, in other OECD countries in that year it constituted 25% of fixed capi-

[15] Cf. *1963 National Income White Paper,* p. 167, where data on inventory as a proportion of private capital formation will be found, 1930 to 1963. For the decade of the thirties, inventories averaged 21.9% of private investment; for the period, 1955 to 1962, inventories averaged 21.3%.

[16] Cf. Ohkawa, *Growth Rate,* p. 224; 1963 *White Paper,* p. 167.

Table 17-4: CAPITAL FORMATION IN JAPAN, 1930-63 AS A PERCENTAGE OF GNE (in 1934-36 prices)

| *Calendar* | *Private* | *(Fixed+Inventory)* | *Govt.* | *Total* | *Fiscal* | *Private* | *(Fixed+Inventory)* | *Govt.* | *Total* |
|---|---|---|---|---|---|---|---|---|---|
| 1930 | 7.5 | ( 5.3 + 2.2) | + 3.8 | =11.3 | 1946 | 26.3 | (14.2 + 12.1) | + 8.8 | =35.1 |
| 1931 | 8.6 | ( 4.5 + 4.1) | + 3.1 | =11.7 | 1947 | 22.8 | (12.5 + 10.3) | + 15.7 | =38.5 |
| 1932 | 7.4 | ( 7.6 -0.2) | + 3.8 | =11.2 | 1948 | 22.9 | (12.2 + 10.7) | + 12.2 | =35.1 |
| 1933 | 9.5 | ( 9.8 -0.3) | + 2.9 | =12.4 | 1949 | 17.7 | (11.1 + 6.6) | + 10.2 | =27.9 |
| 1934 | 14.7 | (11.2 + 3.5) | + 3.5 | =18.2 | 1950 | 19.5 | (11.0 + 8.5) | + 4.6 | =24.1 |
| 1935 | 15.8 | (11.3 + 4.5) | + 3.1 | =18.9 | 1951 | 19.5 | (10.6 + 8.9) | + 6.4 | =25.9 |
| 1936 | 16.8 | (11.3 + 5.5) | + 3.0 | =19.8 | 1952 | 17.1 | (11.5 + 5.6) | + 6.7 | =23.8 |
| 1937 | 18.7 | (12.2 + 6.5) | + 2.8 | =21.5 | 1953 | 17.3 | (12.0 + 5.3) | + 8.3 | =25.6 |
| 1938 | 18.6 | (15.6 + 3.0) | + 3.1 | =21.7 | 1954 | 14.7 | (11.3 + 3.4) | + 7.5 | =22.2 |
| 1939 | 23.7 | (19.8 + 3.9) | + 3.5 | =27.2 | 1955 | 16.0 | (10.8 + 5.2) | + 8.4 | =24.4 |
| 1940 | 24.7 | (18.9 + 5.8) | + 3.9 | =28.6 | 1956 | 22.5 | (15.4 + 7.1) | + 6.6 | =29.1 |
| 1941 | 25.2 | (18.7 + 6.5) | + 3.9 | =29.1 | 1957 | 21.4 | (16.7 + 4.7) | + 7.1 | =28.5 |
| 1942 | 26.6 | (15.8 + 10.8) | + 4.1 | =30.7 | 1958 | 16.8 | (16.6 + 0.2) | + 8.2 | =25.0 |
| 1943 | 23.0 | (19.1 + 3.9) | + 4.4 | =27.4 | 1959 | 25.0 | (18.0 + 7.0) | + 8.3 | =33.3 |
| 1944 | 26.2 | (19.4 + 6.8) | + 5.1 | =31.3 | 1960 | 28.2 | (21.9 + 6.3) | + 8.8 | =37.0 |
| | | | | | 1961 | 32.7 | (24.3 + 8.4) | + 9.6 | =42.3 |
| | | | | | 1962 | 25.8 | (22.3 + 3.5) | + 11.9 | =37.7 |
| | | | | | 1963 | 29.3 | (22.1 + 7.2) | + 12.3 | =41.6 |

Source and notes: Data for the category "private," and the breakdown between "fixed" and "inventory" are taken from the *1963 National Income White Paper*, p. 179; data for "government" from, p. 180. A different set of figures for private fixed investment as a percentage of GNP will be found in Japan Development Bank, *Postwar Economic Growth*, p. 51, where the source is EPA "national income statistics," without indication of the year. Illustrative of the scale of the differences are the following examples: 1948, 7.9%; 1950, 9.9%; 1955, 9.0%; 1960, 20.1%; 1962, 20.8%; 1963, 18.3%.

Data cited in the chapter, "Century of Growth," by Professors Ohkawa and Rosovsky, in Lockwood, *The State and Economic Enterprise*, p. 85 and p. 90, although based on EPA material (the *1960 White Paper*), is slightly different than the data reproduced here from the 1963 edition.

Professor Alan Gleason of Tokyo Christian University has likewise been engaged in work in this field, primarily directing his attention to deflators. Using Ohkawa, Rosovsky, and Emi data, he has developed somewhat different figures by using different deflating methods. Although Gleason cautions that the material for the decade of the thirties from the Hitotsubashi University 1887-1940 series is not to be used in comparisons of magnitude with the EPA series, 1930 to the present, the scale of the disparity in relative terms nevertheless reveals the continuing "tentative" quality of the findings. For example, the Gleason data for selected years in the 1930 decade indicate: 1930, private 9.5%, government 6.5%; 1932, private 9.6%, government 7.0%; 1935, private 12.3%, government 5.4%; 1938, private 10.1%, government 3.5%; 1940, private 13.9%, government 3.5%. The foregoing is taken from mimeographed tables dated May 1965, and marked "A.H. Gleason."

tal and 4.5% of GNP.[17] The OECD's finding for Japan in 1962 is typical of housing over the years in that nation's fixed-investment "mix." During the 1930s housing constituted 7% of fixed-capital formation and 1.2% of GNP; for the period 1955-62 it constituted 8.1% of capital formation and 2.3% of GNP. In the immediate postwar years, when housing was desperately tight, even by Japanese standards—because of the loss of hundreds of thousands of homes from the incendiary raids—it still constituted an insignificant proportion of fixed investment. In the 1946 to 1954 period, when need was enormous, housing amounted to only 7.9% of fixed investment and 1.5% of GNP.[18] Given the consistency of the small allocation of resources to housing, it will be seen there is no difference in patterns between the thirties and the recent period. However, when making international comparisons of the scale of national income gains from given levels of investment, the high growth rate in Japan is undoubtedly in part explained by the low proportion of funds into "unproductive" housing.

Both by comparison with fixed investment levels in most other leading free enterprise nations, and by comparison with the country's own past, Japan's recent investment levels will be seen to be high. In seeking to understand the factors responsible for the recent exceptional investment, let us begin by distinguishing between government and private investment. Although capital formation in Japan is predominantly private, a study of Table 17-4 will show that in the recent period government capital-formation has constituted some 30% of fixed investment. One can gain a feel for the striking increase in the role of government in capital-formation by taking averages of the percentage figures presented in Table 17-4. If private fixed capital-formation and government capital-formation is averaged for the decade of the thirties and for the eight years 1955-62, inclusive, it will be found that in the decade of the thirties: private capital-formation amounted to 10.5% of GNE, government capital-formation amounted to 3.26% of GNE; for the period 1955-62, inclusive: private capital-formation amounted to 18.25% of GNE, government capital-formation amounted to 8.90% of GNE. Thus the increase in percentage of private fixed investment is 1.7 times while the increase in the percentage of government investment is 2.7 times.

In these bare figures one finds a major corroborating element of the often repeated Japanese observation that freedom from the burden of armaments has been a significant factor in the higher postwar growth rate. That the role of military expenditures in the health of

[17] OECD, *Economic Surveys by the OECD, Japan* and Paris, July 1964, p. 12.

[18] Calculated from data given in absolute figures in *1963 National Income White Paper*, pp. 164-65.

the economy has been viewed so oppositely in recent years in Japan and in the U.S. reflects in part the difference between an economy long on investment opportunities in contrast to one in which its affluence results in problems of finding investment outlets—problems, that is, when public needs are neglected and attention concentrated on private "wants."

While private fixed-investment in Japan constituted on the average 10% of GNE during the decade of the thirties, it was 18% for the period 1955-62. Although a number of factors enter into the historical trend of high investment in Japan, two appear to have particular pertinence in explaining the much higher recent investment levels—higher profits and the sharp rivalry resulting from oligopolists finding themselves essentially independent agents. This rivalry has been fought out in a period of major technological change, which has further enhanced the scale of investment.

In its analysis of Japan's exceptional capital-formation the OECD attributes a major role to high profits.[19] While profits are unrelated to the much higher level of government investment in recent years, they are certainly pertinent to private investment. And in Table 17-5, in which national income is broken down into distributive shares, profits will be seen to be a higher proportion of national income in recent years than in the thirties. (The factor obscuring ready interpretation of the wage data is the striking recomposition of the economy. Wages appear to be a higher proportion of national income today by comparison with yesterday. This is to be explained partly as a taxonomic phenomenon—a shift in classification of remuneration stemming from the movement out of agriculture, classed as entrepreneurial income, into factory work, which is wage income.[20]) It has been stated that profits

[19] OECD, *Japan*, 1964, p. 14.

[20] To try to separate the real from the taxonomic let us compare the relationship between the proportion of employment in the secondary and tertiary sectors and wages as a proportion of national income between three periods, 1938, 1955, and 1962. The statistics on sectoral employment as a percentage of total employment are taken from the Japan Development Bank, *Facts and Figures*, p. 2. As in other cases, differences in the statistics, depending on the source employed, hold true here. Because the time spread is helpful, the JDB material is used. The statistics of wages as a proportion of national income are taken from Table 17-5 data.

| | *Employment in secondary and tertiary sectors* | *Wages, as a proportion of national income* |
|---|---|---|
| 1938 | 56.3 | 39.2 |
| 1955 | 57.1 | 48.5 |
| 1962 | 70.0 | 53.2 |

Employing the familiar "product of the means equals the product of the extremes"

Table 17-5: DISTRIBUTIVE SHARES OF JAPANESE NATIONAL INCOME (IN CURRENT PRICES)

(the first four entries are calendar years; the remaining, fiscal)

| | Wages | Entrepre. income | Rent | Interest | Profits | Proportionate Uses of Profits | | |
|---|---|---|---|---|---|---|---|---|
| | | | | | | Taxes | Distributed | Retained |
| 1934-36 av. | 38.9 | 31.3 | 9.1 | 9.1 | 8.7 | (27.4) | (45.2) | (27.4) |
| 1938 | 39.2 | 30.4 | 7.8 | 8.7 | 11.5 | (35.6) | (39.5) | (24.9) |
| 1940 | 36.6 | 33.7 | 6.5 | 8.8 | 12.7 | (37.8) | (31.2) | (31.0) |
| 1942 | 38.4 | 31.7 | 5.1 | 9.7 | 13.7 | (40.8) | (21.4) | (37.8) |
| 1948 | 42.2 | 55.6 | 0.8 | 0.9 | 2.6 | (78.6) | (16.8) | (4.6) |
| 1950 | 41.8 | 45.6 | 0.9 | 1.2 | 9.9 | (32.6) | (9.6) | (57.8) |
| 1952 | 45.7 | 42.9 | 1.0 | 1.6 | 9 3 | (47.2) | (11.3) | (41.5) |
| 1955 | 48.5 | 38.7 | 1.7 | 2.8 | 8.9 | (39.2) | (15.0) | (45.8) |
| 1956 | 48.8 | 34.8 | 1.9 | 2.9 | 12.3 | (32.3) | (11.1) | (56.6) |
| 1957 | 49.8 | 33.0 | 2.0 | 3.2 | 11.9 | (43.1) | (13.1) | (43.8) |
| 1958 | 52.7 | 31.4 | 2.2 | 3.7 | 9.9 | (44.6) | (16.1) | (39.3) |
| 1959 | 50.7 | 29.0 | 2.3 | 4.0 | 14.0 | (34.9) | (11.4) | (53.7) |
| 1960 | 49.8 | 27.4 | 2.2 | 4.1 | 16.4 | (34.6) | (11.2) | (54.2) |
| 1961 | 50.9 | 26.3 | 2.2 | 4.0 | 16.3 | (36.5) | (11.9) | (51.6) |
| 1962 | 53.2 | 25.7 | 2.2 | 4.3 | 14.5 | (41.0) | (15.5) | (43.5) |
| 1963 | 53.8 | 24.8 | 2.2 | 4.2 | 15.0 | (38.0) | (14.6) | (47.4) |

Source: Economic Planning Agency, *1963 National Income White Paper*, pp. 162-63.

in recent years in Japan as a proportion of national income were considerably higher than they were in the thirties. If one were speaking of the American economy this would not be saying very much. But the thirties in Japan were, in terms of what is known from present national income work, a period of growth. The beginning years reflected the impact of the world depression, but by 1934 the economy was in an upward momentum, as is seen in Table 17-2. If we consider the period 1934-40, profits as a percentage of national income averaged 9.8%; for the last three years of the period, 1938, 1939, and 1940, they averaged 11.6%. For the period 1955-62, however, profits averaged 13.0% of national income; and for the three years, 1960, 1961, and 1962, they average 15.7%. Such profit levels are indeed investment-inducing.

How have such generous profits come about? Basically because un-

formula to employment and wages, one has, when comparing 1938 with 1955: 56.3 : 39.2 = 57.1 : x, where x turns out to be 39.5%. Wages in 1955 instead of being 39.5%, however, were 48.5% so that one can see very real gains for labor from various of the Occupation measures. However, if we repeat the exercise, applying the 1955 relationship to 1962 (57.1 : 48.5 = 70 : x), wages would be expected to be 57.7% whereas they are only 53.8%. In other words, there were striking gains in the initial period, but since the mid-fifties labor, while gaining from national income growth, proportionately has not held its own.

til the last years wages have not risen as fast as productivity: "Between 1953 and 1962 the value-added in mining and manufacturing rose, in current prices, by 222% . . . the total wage bill [rose] by only 175%."[21] With respect to the 1960-64 period, the same pattern is to be seen in the data presented in Table 17-6, though there are discon-

Table 17-6: RECENT PRODUCTIVITY AND WAGE INCREASES IN JAPAN
Percent Increase Over Preceding Year

| | Productivity | | | |
|---|---|---|---|---|
| | *Japan Productivity Center* | *Ministry of Labor* | *Nominal wages* | *Real wages* |
| 1960 | 13.0 | 8.7 | 8.0 | 4.2 |
| 1961 | 10.2 | 8.3 | 11.8 | 6.2 |
| 1962 | 2.8 | 2.9 | 10.0 | 2.9 |
| 1963 | 9.4 | 7.6 | 10.8 | 3.0 |
| 1964 | - | 14.0 | 11.0 | n.a. |

Sources and notes: Business International, *Japan*, p. 57, which reproduced the material from a report of the Fuji Bank, Research Division. Not only are there large productivity differences between the Japan Productivity Center statistics and Ministry of Labor findings as shown in Table 18-1, but the Japan Productivity Center figures do not agree with Japan Productivity Center figures reproduced in the *1964 Economic White Paper*, p. 333. The *White Paper* shows in chart form Japan Productivity Center findings on changes in productivity in manufacturing, 1955 to 1963. It likewise gives changes in wage rates (which also do not agree). Productivity figures shown in the *White Paper* are below those shown here. While the figures reproduced here as Table 18-1 are not labeled "in manufacturing," which is the caption to the *White Paper* chart, manufacturing changes would be leading other sectors of the economy.

certingly large differences in the productivity increases, depending on whether the figures are those of the Japan Productivity Center or the Ministry of Labor, as well as which publication one finds them reproduced in.

That wages have not risen as fast as productivity is largely ex-

[21] OECD, *Japan*, 1964, p. 14.

plained by the scale of increases in the labor supply and the degree of slack which existed in the economy—and here we come to that other major determinant of national-income growth: increases in the labor supply. While the population between 1954 and 1964 increased 10%, the labor supply increased 15% (those of working age increased 23% but more remained in school).[22] Thus the age composition of the population arising out of the high birthrate in the immediate postwar years has put a large number of young workers into the market. Given Japanese wage practice, wherein wages are a function of age rather than job skill or responsibility, the large number of young workers has been advantageous for employers.

In addition to the absolute additions to the labor supply there have been additions to manufacturing employment from a recomposition of the economy. Employers in the manufacturing sector, the sector of high growth, have been able to bid workers ranks from agriculture, the scale of which is seen in the following figures on the proportion of employment by sector:[23]

| | *primary* | *secondary* | *tertiary* |
|---|---|---|---|
| 1955 | 41.0% | 23.5% | 35.5% |
| 1963 | 28.5% | 32.5% | 39.0% |

In 1955 the primary sector, while accounting for 41% of employment, represented but 23% of national income; in 1962, while accounting for 30% of employment, it represented only 14% of national income.[24]

Not only have wage contracts been advantageous to Japanese employers, but so likewise the nation's international terms-of-trade. Prices of imports have fallen faster than exports. Comparing the import-export price index for "all commodities," 1955 to 1964, wherein 1960-62 prices equal 100, one finds that import prices have gone from 119 in 1955 to 102 in 1964, whereas export prices have gone from 108 to 100.[25] In other words, 1964 import prices are 84% of the 1955 level, whereas export prices are 94.6% of their 1955 level.

One associates profits not only with those cost-price items which are "givens" for the firms, that is, bought or sold in competitive markets, but also with elements within the maneuverability of the firm such as sales prices in oligopolistic markets. Such advantageous prices may be

[22] Calculated from absolute figures in Bank of Japan, *1964 Economic Statistics*, p. 341 and 311.

[23] Economic Planning Agency, *1963 National Income*, p. 7.

[24] Japan Development Bank, *Fact and Figures*, p. 2.

[25] Bank of Japan, *1964 Economic Statistics*, pp. 299-300.

the product of market structure, market agreements, or both. Given the limitations of data, as we saw in Chapters 14 and 15, it is difficult to make other than rough judgments about market structure and agreements, but there do not appear to be substantial changes in market structures, today compared to yesterday. With respect to recent cartelization it may well be somewhat under the scale of the thirties. These elements apparently do not contribute to an explanation of the higher profit levels and far higher investment levels; wages would appear the major part of the explanation.

While market structure may not be appreciably different today, what *is* different is that in market after market the oligopolists are essentially on their own. Instead of being restrained from challenging competitors because their top-holding company faced competition from these same competitors in markets where their combine was weak, it has been each member for himself. Nothing reveals the vigor of the resultant rivalry better than Table 14-5, which shows examples of market fluidity between 1959 and 1962 among the top 10 firms of eight different markets.

If this rivalry were not occurring in the context of important technological change, it is doubtful the stakes would have been as high as they obviously have been regarded. But in the circumstance of a fundamental retooling of much of the economy, the competition has been extraordinary. In emphasizing product competition, in contrast to price competition, Joseph Schumpeter used to liken the difference to a bombardment in comparison to forcing a door.[26] In Japan these last years, competition has been of bombardment proportions. During the *zaibatsu* period, the key subsidiaries were but extensions of their top-holding companies, which necessarily operated in terms of the combine's total position in the economy, not in terms of individual markets. For these subsidiaries to find themselves free to act in terms of their individual market positions would be expected to produce some vigorous competition. To have had this circumstance coincide with major retooling of the economy has resulted in extraordinary rivalry and levels of investment. At issue is much more than position this year or next. In a basic sense the new technology establishes position for years to come.

The retooling is the product of a complex of factors—the isolation of the war years; Japan's better visibility as a market today; the government's direction of the economy into new fields; the wider access to technology in consequence of the deconcentration program. Japan's

[26] Schumpeter, *Capitalism, Socialism and Democracy*, 2nd edn., New York, 1947, p. 84.

war years were appreciably longer than they were for most other countries—1937 to 1945. While foreign technology did not begin to be cut off until Japan was well into the China War, Japanese foreign exchange restrictions growing out of the Manchurian War and disorganization of the world economy put effective barriers for many industries on the acquisition of foreign technology much earlier in the decade. If Japan had had a longer innovative history in modern technology than it had at the time of these conflicts, the isolation from the outside world would undoubtedly not have been so keenly felt. As it was, however, many industries were isolated for some 15 years, when to the isolation of the prewar and war years is added the dislocation of the immediate postwar period. For Europe and the United States the war years were years of technological advance; for Japan, depending so heavily on outside technology and being so geographically separated from its Axis partners, the years represented very modest gains indeed, and such limited advances as occurred were restricted to industries of key strategic significance. Thus catching up has become vital.

One of the unexpected consequences of the Occupation was that it introduced Japan to thousands of foreigners. While the immediate postwar years with all their agonizing readjustments did not present a market of interest to foreign investors, the situation was radically altered in the early fifties. Foreign investors began to appreciate the exceptional opportunities presented by initial penetrations in diverse lines. No growth rates can compare to the rates resulting from initial penetration of a market. The Japanese economy was full of initial-penetration opportunities. Accordingly, a factor in the scale of the retooling has been that foreign investors were eager to participate.

The government has shown great skill in perceiving foreign markets of high potential growth for the economy and pushing Japanese investors into such lines. The loss of the Chinese market and the heavy dependence on American products was compensated for by skilled government analysis of products which could successfully be sold in the new markets. Broadly expressed, the government has attempted to shift exports from goods for markets with low purchasing power into goods for markets of high purchasing power, from cheap manufactures into quality ones. The change in the character of exports has required significant retooling.

The scale of the penetration of the new technologies is also related to the deconcentration program. Under the *zaibatsu* system the trading companies were the principal avenue for entrance of outside technology into Japan. The Mitsui Trading Company and the Mitsubishi

TABLE 17-7: MAJOR TECHNICAL ASSISTANCE CONTRACTS, FISCAL 1950-63

(in numbers of contracts)

| *Industrial Group* | *1950-59* | *1960* | *1961* | *1962* | *1963* | *Total* |
|---|---|---|---|---|---|---|
| spinning and weaving | 54 | 8 | 23 | 3 | 16 | 104 |
| paper and pulp | 10 | 4 | 5 | 6 | 7 | 32 |
| chemicals | 220 | 77 | 59 | 83 | 93 | 532 |
| petroleum | 34 | 7 | 5 | 5 | 17 | 68 |
| glass, ceramics, cement | 16 | 7 | 7 | 12 | 4 | 46 |
| rubber and leather | 30 | 12 | 8 | 2 | 1 | 53 |
| metals and fabrication | 111 | 19 | 27 | 22 | 16 | 195 |
| electrical machinery | 236 | 99 | 59 | 82 | 122 | 598 |
| transport machinery | 62 | 17 | 24 | 17 | 4 | 124 |
| other machinery | 228 | 71 | 101 | 94 | 272 | 766 |
| construction | 14 | | 1 | 1 | 9 | 25 |
| foodstuffs | 1 | 4 | | | 2 | 7 |
| others | 7 | 2 | 1 | 1 | 2 | 13 |
| Total | 1,023 | 327 | 320 | 328 | 565 | 2,563 |

Source: Business International, Japan, p. 19, where the Ministry of Finance is cited as the source.

Trading Company did not serve the economy as a whole; they served the member companies of their two combines. Thus the advanced technology of the outside world tended to be highly concentrated among combine firms. The temporary dismemberment of the two giant trading companies in the context of the other measures resulted in a freer business system. Firms unrelated to the combines were in a position to enter into negotiations with foreign firms—that is, to the extent that MITI would permit. MITI officials have had a propensity to believe that only large, established firms are worthy of foreign exchange for technological agreements. Although, as we have seen, trade has been largely liberalized, all technological agreements continue to require MITI validation.

The foregoing factors in the context of a business climate of rising profit produced a veritable river of technological agreements, as will be seen in Table 17-7 and as extraordinary an investment level as is likely ever to occur. When inventories are included in investment figures, it will be noted in Table 17-4 that in 1961 and again in 1963 investment pushed over the 40% level. To sustain investment as a rising proportion of national income would require that the economy grow at an increasing rate, an obviously impossible long-run condition. But as we have seen, a number of factors producing the extraordinary investments are inherently short-run in character. The major retooling of existing industries and the technology required for new industries are not factors which can continue in the scale of these past years. Initial penetrations are by definition one-time affairs.

### *The Managers*

Attention has been given to the massive investment and increases in the labor supply as factors in Japan's high national-income growth, but the managerial aspect, or entrepreneurial aspect, as Schumpeter was wont to emphasize, also deserves note. When we speak of "managerial" in the Japanese economy we are speaking, as we have seen, of both government and private enterprise. Each is stronger today than yesterday.

Although some students of Japan's national-income growth see the thirties as a period of high growth,[27] the period 1930 to 1943 has odd qualities if one observes yearly changes rather than averaging the changes for the period as a whole. Two exceptional years greatly affect the average of the 1930-40 period: 1934 at a 10.8% increase over 1933 and 1937 at a 23.7% increase over 1936 (which seems impossible to believe). During the decade, apart from these two years, only 1933 was up to the long-run norm of 4% increase. Moving into the forties, one finds 1940 at a 6% *decrease* from the preceding year, with 1941 and 1942 showing increases of only 1.6% and 1.3%. Broadly speaking, it could be said that the economy was stagnant from 1937 to the middle of World War II. (Thereafter the decline represented only the mounting destruction of the war.) As we saw from Table 17-2, GNP, expressed in billions of 1934-36 yen, was 21.2 in 1937 and 21.3 in 1943, with the range 22.1 to 20.7. This strikingly poor performance of the economy occurred during a period of seemingly substantial fixed-investment. For the years 1930-43, inclusive, the EPA figures cited in Table 17-4 result in fixed investment averaging 16.1% of GNP, with the range (if 1930 and 1931 are disregarded) from 11.4 to 23.5%. My guess as to the extraordinarily poor performance of GNP on such substantial levels of investment, would be that it has much to do with the quality of management during that period, as

[27] Professors Ohkawa and Rosovsky hold this view. In their chapter, "A Century of Japanese Economic Growth," in Lockwood, *State and Economic Enterprise*, one finds several references to the thirties as a period of strong growth. "A renewed spurt [of growth] . . . begins in 1931 . . ." (p. 81); "Once Japan had decided to follow a policy of military expansion, it was a relatively simple matter to step up the growth of the economy" (p. 82).

well as the fact that the data do not provide us with material on disinvestment. It may well have been that a substantial part of the capital-formation at this time came at the price of net disinvestment elsewhere.

During this period the Japanese government geographically spread itself over wider and wider areas, and further, attempted much more direct control of the domestic economy than was true of the traditional pattern of shared leadership with the combines. In 1931-32 it moved to control Manchuria, in 1937 North China and then all of China, in 1940 Hainan and then French Indochina, and finally all of Southeast Asia.

The legislation signaling the change in government orientation to the domestic economy was the National General Mobilization Law of 1938. The administrative development was the increased power of the Cabinet Planning Bureau. In contrast to the bureaucrats of the Ministry of Commerce and Industry (predecessor of MITI), the Ministry of Finance, and other departments, those holding key positions in the CPB were not aligned with the combines. They viewed them critically. One can gain some understanding of what officials of the bureau wanted to see take place in Japan from what they were able to shape in Manchukuo. There direction of the economy was essentially in government hands; it was not shared with the older combines. That the legend grew up that the army kept the older combines out of Manchukuo, may have arisen from the fact that the older combines were excluded from participation in leadership.

But the CPB was not able to bring off in Japan what it achieved in Manchukuo. The combines had no intention of relinquishing the role held since the Meiji years. Judging by the results, one may believe that the outcome represented the worst of both worlds. It was neither what the Bureau wanted nor was it the traditional pattern under which government and business had operated for so many decades. The combines were able to transform the Bureau's scheme into one for their own aggrandizement. As noted in Chapter 3, the Big Four were able to advance in the years between 1937 and 1945 from 10% of the paid-up capital of the nation to 24% of the capital.

During this period the Japanese government attempted to substitute its judgment for market forces rather than using market forces as partial guides, but with little knowledge of the likely consequences. As has been demonstrated in many settings, governments can substitute their decisions for market forces, but to do this with any success there has to be some foresight. I have noted that national income work in Japan was only in the most rudimentary form prior to the war and, further, that it was not understood how to get at real national income as distinguished from apparent national income. Looking back on those years, one is somewhat reminded of China's recent "Great Leap Forward." In both instances, will, drive, determination were to substitute for economic knowledge. Such qualities are invaluable "additives" but scarcely substitutes.

The quality of government direction of the economy today in Japan is vastly superior. The government has the benefit of economists trained in national-income work, so that it now has information to work from. Because of these and other economists, it has analytical understanding of national-income determination. Also, the government has the advantage, like others, of the statistical materials prepared by the United Nations and its agencies. As a member of OECD, Japan benefits from the dialogue between it and other governments on its domestic policies. Accordingly, one finds the Japanese government providing sophisticated direction, pushing and nudging private enterprise into areas of growth potential.

Not only is the quality of government leadership vastly better in postwar Japan, but so, it would be my guess, is business leadership because of the demise of the top-holding companies and from the changed status of the defense forces. In pre-1945 Japan there was great prestige in belonging to the army and navy; there is next to none in today's Self-Defense Force.

Under the combine format, officers of the key subsidiaries were officers in name only. All key decisions lay with the top-holding company. These officers were all salaried men. The rewards of ownership were kept for the families alone—until, that is, expansion in the thirties obliged some sharing with officers and outsiders. Out of the demise of the holding companies, today's officers are officers in fact as well as name. While the boards of the former subsidiaries may be influenced in their thinking by the bank of their grouping, by the trading company or some other "member," the decision is theirs. In terms of the national economy, there would seem to be only advantage from letting creative people be creative. Under the combine system creativeness was restricted to the holding companies, where only those who combined sycophancy and subserviency with talent stood a chance of appointment.

Further, in today's pattern, incentives are far stronger for executives. In the past, incentive consisted of advancement in position but very little in material rewards. Today's executives are able to share in what they create rather than see the fruits of their labor go to favored business families.

We have been speaking of Japan's high growth in terms of the scale of investment stemming from high profits and keen market rivalry, from additions to the labor supply, and from the stronger quality of the leadership shown by both government and business. But one can only carry forward dreams if there is capital. How have the recent high levels of investment been financed?—by high savings, taxes, undistributed profits and depreciation, foreign borrowing, and by credit. Table 17-8 provides the pertinent statistics on the sources of financing for fixed investment.

TABLE 17-8: FIXED INVESTMENT IN JAPAN AND SOURCES OF ITS FINANCING

(all columns expressed as a percentage of GNP)

| | 1 | 2 | 3 | 4 | 5 | 6 |
|---|---|---|---|---|---|---|
| | *Fixed investment* | *Personal savings* | *Government current surplus* | *Corporate reserve* | *Total of 2, 3, & 4* | *Other including foreign borrowing* |
| 1934-36 | 14.4 | 12.2 | -0.7 | 2.1 | 13.6 | 0.8 |
| 1950-62 | 24.1 | 11.6 | 6.9 | 4.7 | 22.2 | 1.9 |
| 1955-62 | 27.9 | 12.2 | 6.7 | 5.1 | 24.0 | 3.9 |
| 1960-62 | 33.1 | 14.3 | 8.4 | 6.3 | 29.0 | 4.1 |

Sources and notes: column 1 is taken from Table 17-4 data. In so doing the year-periods have been construed on an inclusive basis. Columns 2-5 are taken from Japan Development Bank, *Facts and Figures on the Japanese Economy*, Tokyo, 1964, p. 3. Column 6 represents the difference between column 5 and column 1.

Personal savings are very high in Japan, as will be seen in Table 17-9, which provides an international comparison. Such high personal saving would appear to be the product of a tradition of frugality and certain unusual institutional arrangements, as well as the fact that family enterprise is included in the statistics of the household sector, thus resulting in the inclusion of some business savings.

In Japan frugality is not an expedient; it is a way of life. Stemming from the ethic of the warrior, the *bushi*, frugality has permeated all sectors of Japanese society. Moral strength has been and still is believed to be derived from spartan living, though Japanese consumers, like consumers elsewhere in the world, when tempted by modern conveniences have found it difficult to forego them. The tradition of frugality has been perpetuated under a strong government policy that only meager resources should be diverted to home building and in the absence of durable consumer goods. The tradition has not been perpetuated in circumstances where such items were easily purchased.

There are certain unusual institutional arrangements on the Japanese scene which affect savings. Japanese wages are in the form of weekly or monthly payments, plus substantial semiannual bonuses. In large enterprises, bonuses run as high as 30% or more of annual wages.[28] Receiving a substantial portion of one's income in lump-sum payments would appear to be conducive to saving. The fact that installment buying has barely gotten underway in Japan also affects savings. An additional factor which would seem to have inescapable influence on saving is the virtual absence of fire protection on homes. Japanese houses are lightly built and often only inches apart. The lack of fire insurance probably induces larger savings.

The inclusion of family enterprise in statistics of the household sector adds a portion of business savings to personal savings. As was noted in Chapter 1, small business is a significant element in virtually all sectors of manufacturing. It is, of course, ubiquitous in the service trades. Although without question, saving is at an exceptionally high rate in the Japanese economy, a portion of the very high figures would appear to be the product of the way the statistics are compiled.

The consequence of the foregoing, if one takes the statistics at face value, is, as is seen in Table 17-9, a saving rate in Japan roughly double that of West Germany and three times the level in the United States. A study of Table 17-9 suggests a possible additional factor in the exceptionally high Japanese level, namely the low level of taxation. Without the burden of armaments, the Japanese are under less tax pressure than are the citizens of the other leading powers. Low taxes, however, do not always cause higher savings, as is dramatically seen in the case of the Philippines.

In Table 17-10, it is seen that savings in Japan take the form of bank deposits, and, as will be observed, a large proportion of these bank deposits are time deposits. These are for the most part in commercial banks, for there are no longer any savings banks as such in Japan. The Japan Savings Bank, increased by wartime mergers to a near monopoly position, became in the postwar period a commercial bank, the Kyowa Bank. That commercial banks have such a large proportion of personal deposits in the form of time deposits is a major factor in leading Japanese banks to act so differently from commercial

[28] Ministry of Labor, *1964 Year Book of Labor Statistics*, Tokyo, 1965, Table 44, pp. 60-67.

TABLE 17-9: AN INTERNATIONAL COMPARISON OF PERSONAL INCOME EXPENDITURES AND SOURCES OF INCOME, 1962

(per cent)

| | Japan | U.S. | Canada | U.K. | France | W.Ger. | Holland | Sweden | Bel. | Greece | Philip-pines |
|---|---|---|---|---|---|---|---|---|---|---|---|
| | *Expenditure* | | | | | | | | | | |
| Personal consumption | 74.2 | 76.1 | 81.4 | 79.0 | 74.8 | 68.3 | 68.6 | 67.1 | 75.9 | 82.0 | 93.6 |
| Personal tax | 6.7 | 17.5 | 10.4 | 16.0 | 18.7 | 21.4 | 22.2 | 24.6 | 14.8 | 9.9 | 2.5 |
| Net income sent abroad | -0.1 | 0.1 | 0.2 | 0.0 | - | 0.4 | -0.2 | 0.0 | -0.1 | -3.4 | -1.0 |
| Individual saving | 19.2 | 6.3 | 8.0 | 5.0 | 6.5 | 9.9 | 9.3 | 8.3 | 9.4 | 11.5 | 4.9 |
| Total | 100 | 100 | 100 | 100 | 100 | 100 | 100 | 100 | 100 | 100 | 100 |
| | *Income* | | | | | | | | | | |
| Labor income | 58.8 | 70.7 | 66.2 | 73.3 | 53.3 | 58.4 | 59.2 | 71.6 | 52.6 | 38.3 | 43.7 |
| Individual enterprise income; personal property | 36.5[a] | 24.2 | 22.8 | 18.1 | 29.8 | 26.6 | 28.3 | 18.2 | 35.3 | 53.6 | 55.6 |
| Consumers' interest | 0.4 | 1.6 | 0.5 | | 0.1 | | | | | | |
| Transfer | 5.7 | 6.7 | 11.5 | 8.6 | 17.0 | 15.0 | 12.5 | 10.2 | 12.1 | 8.1 | 0.7 |
| Total | 100[b] | 100[c] | 100 | 100 | 100 | 100 | 100 | 100 | 100 | 100 | 100 |

Source: Economic Planning Agency, *1963 National Income White Paper*, pp. 18-19.

[a]Individual enterprise income, 26.6%, and personal property income, 9.9%.

[b]In the source table, the column for Japan and only Japan shows, in the income portion of the table, an additional entry, "net income from abroad." The entry is -0.6%. It is not clear to me how there could be a double entry for "*net* income sent (from) abroad."

[c]The figures entered for the United States add to 103.2%. Certain of the other totals are slightly over 100% due to rounding.

banks elsewhere—this circumstance and the knowledge, if a city bank, that the Bank of Japan will rescue them if caught short of funds. This is background to the situation wherein, as was seen in Chapter 12, bank financing accounts for 40 to 50% of total corporate funds and up to 70 to 80% if comparison is to external sources only. Here we have come full circle to bank-industrial ties, to the *kinyu keiretsu* groupings.

That the capital market plays such a much smaller role in corporate financing in Japan than in most other countries is probably the result of both historical and institutional factors. Although major businesses were predominantly of corporate form by World War I, "blue chip" securities were not put on the market. They were closely held in *zaibatsu* circles. The genius of the corporate form lies in its ability to build huge aggregates of capital from small pieces. Although the form was adopted, the spirit was not, so that, broadly speaking, it was

TABLE 17-10: FORMS OF PERSONAL SAVING, DECEMBER 31, 1963
(expressed as a percentage of total)

| | |
|---|---|
| Cash | 6 |
| Bank deposits | 57.5 |
| Current deposits | 0.6 |
| Short-term dep. | 13.5 |
| Time and saving dep. | 43.4 |
| Trust accounts | 4.0 |
| Insurance | 10.4 |
| Securities | 21.3 |

Source: Bank of Japan, *1964 Economic Statistics of Japan*, Table 9 p. 20. Percentages calculated from absolute figures under section, "Main Financial Asset and Liability Balances."

not until the thirties, during large capital expansion, that corporations welcomed outside capital. One cannot build a capital market when blue chip issues are withheld for the privileged. The fact that in Japan these issues were withheld for so long affects popular attitudes toward the stock exchanges even today.

Certain institutional factors have a bearing on the smaller reliance on equity financing. First the supply side. As has been noted under Japanese practice, auditors are corporate officials, a circumstance not designed to enhance the confidence of outsiders in the quality of financial statements. During the Occupation a Securities Exchange Law (Shoken Torihiki Ho) was adopted in 1948, and, as amended by Law 31 of 1950, requires that financial statements of corporations listed on the exchanges or registered with the Finance Ministry (required of corporations with a capital of Y50 million and above) be checked by a certified public accountant. Other statements need not be.

On the demand side, an exceptionally inhibiting circumstance in the corporation going into additional equity financing is the fact that virtually obligatory tradition calls for making new shares available to existing shareholders at par. Imagine IBM attempting to raise funds by such means! By contrast, the overwhelmingly common Japanese explanation of the underdeveloped state of the capital market is that under corporate income tax procedures, interest is a deductible item, whereas dividends are not. Inasmuch as this is common tax practice, such reasoning is not persuasive. The historical and institutional features mentioned above seem to have more to do with the explanation.

In view of the dependence of business on the banks, it is hardly surprising to come upon observers who see in the close bank-industrial ties an explanation of Japan's headlong investment race. The Foreign Capital Research Society, headed by the governor of the Bank of Japan and housed in the Bank of Japan, represents such a point of view (and interestingly enough in contrast to prevailing *kinyu keiretsu* analysis sees industrials rather than banks in the leadership position). Commenting on the heavy reliance on the banks because "the capital market is not sufficiently advanced," the society commented: "From the short-term standpoint, this has constituted one of the major factors that brought about the rapid economic growth, but simultaneously the internal relations cultivated between bank and enterprise has made it easy for the enterprise to borrow funds from banks on the one hand and, for the banks on the other hand to make excess loans to the enterprises under the pressure of the latter's demand."[29]

But it is doubtful that the means of financing are basically contributory toward an explanation of the exceptionally high investment levels. While ties between industrials and financial institutions may be considerably closer in Japan than among most other leading nations, historically they were even closer (and investment less). After all, the Mitsubishi Bank spent many years as a mere department of the Mitsubishi top-holding company before its separate incorporation. During the period of the 1920s and 1930s under the *zaibatsu* system, relations between the bank of the combine and its mining, industrial and commercial affiliates were of the closest sort. Furthermore, in the case of a nation such as the United States, corporations are today importantly "rolling their own."[30] One cannot get a circumstance more intimate than this. Not even the officers of a related bank, much less the capital markets, pass on investment plans.

It is, nevertheless, still clear that in the absence of a developed capital market, Japan's majors could not have carried on the scale of expansion had it not been for the supportive role of the banks (i.e., toleration of their overborrowing), and further, it is perfectly clear that the city banks could not have been so supportive did not the Bank of Japan stand ready to lend them funds whenever their high lendings (overlending) resulted in a shortage of funds. It is this distinction in lending by the Bank of Japan between city and provincial banks that creates the gulf between the two types of institutions. The OECD comments that the Bank of Japan operates more "as an im-

[29] Foreign Capital Research Society, *Japanese Industry, 1965*, Tokyo, p. 33.
[30] For pertinent U.S. statistics see Table 12-10.

mediate source of bank reserves than a lender of last resort."[31] Paraphrasing, one could say that the Bank acts as a bank of first resort. In other words, both the city banks and the central bank have been deeply committed to high growth.

That city bankers, even though enjoying Bank of Japan support, consider it safe to extend such large-scale loans, many of them for plant and equipment, and that corporation officers in the face of a distinct cyclical pattern to the economy importantly shaped by balance-of-payment forces, regard it safe to have such a high proportion of their funds in the form of debt reflects several factors. Watching Japanese operations, whether personal or institutional, one gets the feeling that risks are viewed somewhat differently than in the West. Whether one looks at the Japanese attitude toward inflation (American businessmen would freeze with anxiety over the price increases that have occurred in Japan's "modern century"), or the indifference to trains run at high speed through crowded stations without guard rails, or the scale of the risk in undertaking war against the U.S. and its Allies when the nation was with only small prospect of victory in China, there is a consistently bolder attitude than one would typically find in the West. However, it is also true that the knowledge among the city banks that the Bank of Japan will rescue them in distress and the knowledge among Japan's "majors" that the government will rescue them if they are in difficulty, may make the differences in the risk assumption less striking than appears at first glance. The Japanese government believes in bankruptcy only for the small. As a popular saying about the large corporation puts it: "too big to fail."

While close bank-industrial ties are not an explanation of Japan's growth because they were quite as strong, if not stronger, earlier, they do affect the direction of credit extension, though, as previously noted, the very enormity of present borrowings makes the ties between businesses and specific banks less clear. Although the government has done little, if anything, to curb bank-industrial ties, the very fact that it is a more important lender today than yesterday is an element making for somewhat wider access to credit. The qualifying adjective *somewhat* is used inasmuch as many government officials tend to favor the established firm over the less prestigious, quite in the manner of private institutions. The changed role of the government as a supplier of investment capital is to be seen in Table 17-11.

By turning back to Table 17-5, it will be seen that Japanese corporations have been retaining an appreciably higher proportion of earnings in recent years than was the practice when ownership and

[31] OECD, *1964 Japan*, p. 19.

TABLE 17-11: SOURCE OF CORPORATE LOANS BY TYPE OF INSTITUTION

(in percent)

| | *1935* | *1955* | *1962* |
|---|---|---|---|
| All banks | 77.1 | 56.1 | 53.8 |
| Central Coop. Bank of Agriculture & Forestry, and agriculture cooperative associations | 1.2 | 4.4 | 3.8 |
| Government financial institutions | - | 11.2 | 8.9 |
| Central Bank for Commercial & Industrial Cooperatives, mutual loans and savings banks and credit associations | 1.8 | 10.8 | 14.0 |
| Trust Fund Bureau, Ministry of Finance | 6.9 | 13.6 | 12.4 |
| Insurance Companies | 5.0 | 1.6 | 3.1 |
| Others | 8.0 | 2.3 | 4.0 |
| All financial institutions | 100 | 100 | 100 |

Source and notes: Japan Development Bank, *Facts and Figures on the Japanese Economy*, 1964, p. 148, where it is indicated the material comes from the Bank of Japan. In the Bank of Japan, *1964 Economic Statistics of Japan*, Table 13, pp. 27-28, one will find the absolute figures from which these percentages are calculated. Percentages are based on balances at the end of each calendar year. "All financial institutions" does not include short-term money lenders and pawn shops. Overlapping among financial institutions has not been eliminated. "Trust Fund Bureau, Ministry of Finance" covers post office life insurance and postal annuity.

control were one. Earlier funds on the order of magnitude of 25-30% were retained; now it will be seen that the proportion is nearer to 50%. The higher rate of retained earnings has not, however, affected the relationship between internal and external supplies of capital, for expansion has been so rapid that the higher rate of retained earnings has done no more than to keep the pattern where it was. The striking change in the pattern of corporate financing then and now is not in the relationship between internal and external capital but in the sources of external capital. By referring to Table 12-8, it will be seen that in the thirties equity financing constituted a very substantial part of external sources, between two-thirds and one-half. In 1963 it constituted but 10%, with loans and discounts making up 86%.

While foreign capital has been an increasingly significant element in Japan's enormous capital expansion program it has been obliged to overcome great obstacles if it proposes to enter as equity with 51% control. As the Business International report commented:

No other advanced, industrial country confronts the foreign investor with the sort of obstacles presented by Japan. Japanese government leaders and officials have stated that they welcome foreign capital, but the experience of many international companies seeking to establish themselves there suggests just the opposite. The problem, perhaps, is that the phrase "foreign capital" does not mean to Japanese officials what it means to the western corporate executive. To the Japanese, foreign capital means technology and loans, and if it comes only in these forms it is extremely welcome. Foreign capital appears to be decidedly unwelcome, however, if it offers itself in forms that involve equity participation in ventures on Japanese soil on a scale that implies foreign management and control.[32]

The forms of foreign capital in Japan's investment program is shown in Table 17-12. For the period 1955-64, foreign capital in the form

TABLE 17-12: ANNUAL VALIDATED CAPITAL INVESTMENT INFLOW INTO JAPAN, 1950-64

(in millions U.S. dollars, fiscal years)

| | *Validated Equity Investment* | | | *Validated Debt Investment* | | | *Grand total* | *Percent of equity in grand total* | *Percent of direct equity in grand total* |
|---|---|---|---|---|---|---|---|---|---|
| | *Direct* | *Indirect* | *Total* | *Loans* | *Foreign banks* | *Total* | | | |
| 1950 | 2.6 | 0.6 | 3.2 | 0.0 | 0.0 | 0.0 | 3.2 | 100% | 81% |
| 1951 | 11.6 | 1.7 | 13.3 | 4.0 | 0.0 | 4.0 | 17.3 | 77 | 67 |
| 1952 | 7.2 | 3.0 | 10.1 | 34.5 | 0.0 | 34.6 | 44.8 | 23 | 16 |
| 1953 | 2.7 | 2.3 | 5.0 | 49.4 | 0.0 | 50.0 | 54.9 | 9 | 5 |
| 1954 | 2.5 | 1.5 | 4.0 | 15.3 | 0.0 | 15.3 | 19.3 | 21 | 13 |
| 1955 | 2.3 | 2.8 | 5.1 | 47.1 | 0.0 | 47.2 | 52.2 | 10 | 4 |
| 1956 | 5.4 | 4.2 | 9.5 | 93.7 | 0.0 | 93.8 | 103.3 | 9 | 5 |
| 1957 | 7.3 | 4.2 | 11.5 | 124.0 | 0.0 | 124.1 | 135.6 | 9 | 5 |
| 1958 | 3.7 | 7.6 | 11.4 | 231.5 | 30.0 | 261.6 | 273.6 | 4 | 1 |
| 1959 | 14.6 | 12.5 | 27.0 | 127.6 | 0.0 | 127.8 | 154.9 | 17 | 9 |
| 1960 | 31.6 | 42.6 | 74.2 | 127.1 | 9.8 | 137.5 | 211.7 | 35 | 15 |
| 1961 | 40.2 | 75.7 | 115.9 | 387.6 | 72.4 | 461.4 | 577.3 | 20 | 7 |
| 1962 | 22.6 | 142.1 | 164.7 | 358.4 | 155.0 | 514.2 | 678.8 | 24 | 3 |
| 1963 | 42.7 | 142.6 | 185.3 | 503.9 | 194.1 | 699.0 | 884.3 | 21 | 5 |
| 1964 | 30.6 | 54.2 | 84.8 | 650.8 | 174.5 | 825.3 | 910.1 | 9 | 3 |
| Total | 227.4 | 497.7 | 725.1 | 2,754.8 | 635.8 | 3,395.8 | 4,120.9 | 18 | 6 |

Source: Business International, *Japan*, Appendix C, p. 69.

Because of rounding columns and rows do not perfectly add.

[32] Business International, *Japan*, p. 9.

of equity has amounted to some 20% of the total, but distinguishing between "direct" and "indirect" equity, we find that with respect to "direct" equity the percentage amounts to only 8%. Table 17-13 provides information on the sources of foreign loans.

In summary, it seems clear that the deconcentration program did not damage the Japanese economy. In fact, it is difficult to account for the extraordinary growth of the post-1954 years without bringing in factors which are the product of the *zaibatsu*-dissolution program—the rivalry for market position and wider dissemination of outside technology and stronger executives.

TABLE 17-13: FOREIGN LOANS TO JAPAN, 1951-62
(in millions U.S. dollars)

| *Fiscal Year* | *World Bank* | *U.S. Ex.-Im.* | *U.S. Com. Banks* | *Others* | *Total* |
|---|---|---|---|---|---|
| 1951 | - | - | - | 4.0 | 4.0 |
| 1952 | - | - | 10.0 | 24.5 | 34.4 |
| 1953 | 40.2 | - | 7.0 | 2.2 | 49.4 |
| 1954 | - | - | 4.0 | 11.3 | 15.3 |
| 1955 | 13.4 | - | 20.5 | 13.2 | 47.1 |
| 1956 | 24.3 | 25.9 | 3.0 | 40.4 | 93.7 |
| 1957 | 15.0 | 80.1 | 6.6 | 22.3 | 124.0 |
| 1958 | 166.0 | 28.2 | 31.5 | 5.7 | 231.5 |
| 1959 | 84.0 | 20.2 | 7.2 | 16.2 | 127.6 |
| 1960 | 25.0 | 21.3 | 38.8 | 42.0 | 127.7 |
| 1961 | 120.0 | 98.3 | 84.7 | 84.5 | 387.6 |
| 1962 | - | 131.7 | 75.3 | 151.4 | 358.4 |
| Total | 487.9 | 405.7 | 288.7 | 417.8 | 1,600.1 |

Source: T.F.M. Adams, *Financial History of Modern Japan*, p. 318, where it is stated that the material comes from the Foreign Capital Statistical Monthly without indication of date or page. The totals are reproduced as shown. Because of rounding, the rows and columns will not in all cases perfectly add.

# 18.

## Assessment

THE effort to create competitive enterprise in the capital-intensive sector of Japan's economy has been described as the "most ambitious antitrust action in history." Twenty-four years have gone by since the program was begun, and some 20 years since the end of the reform phase of the Occupation. As one looks back with the advantage of hindsight, was the American program in Japan good public policy or was it simply misguided?

It is necessary to ask both whether the program has promoted the objectives of the United States and whether it has promoted the interests of the Japanese people. The basic U.S. objective was the promotion of a democratic society in Japan; the reorganization of business was undertaken for political, not economic, reasons. It was not believed possible to "grow" a democratic society with the economy in the hands of a few giant combines. Therefore, in the American view, the question becomes, has economic deconcentration promoted the growth of a democratic social structure? To the Japanese, the questions are not only, has the economic deconcentration program contributed to democratic values, but also, has it contributed to economic growth, broadened national-income distribution, widened participation in enterprise, and meant less concentrated business pressure on government?

History may well regard the reforms of the Occupation period as comparable to the two other great reform periods in Japan's history, Taika and Meiji.[1] To an observer today, it is evident that democratic values have taken root and are growing. Not surprisingly, there is challenge to the new, but in my judgment, Japan is and will remain a different society.

There are those who hold that a democratic society is not new to Japan, that those who assert that it is, simply ignore developments before the Manchurian venture started the country on its conversion

[1] Professor Bisson, for example, makes this parallel; cf. Bisson, *Zaibatsu Dissolution*, p. vii. Taika reforms, which date to 645, and the period immediately following, refer to various governmental changes resulting from the first great Sinization of Japanese culture, which began in the Shotoku Taishi's reign (593-621).

to a war society. But what was Japanese society like in the 1920s? Industry, finance, and commerce were under *zaibatsu* domination; tenancy and poverty were the hallmark of agriculture; by international standards there was no such thing as a labor movement; and the grant of universal suffrage extended in 1925 was coupled within days by passage of the Peace Preservation Law, giving the police added powers of surveillance and investigation. The Emperor was held to be divine and whoever gained access to his presence had the prospect of enormous power. Relative to the 1930s one could perhaps speak of the twenties as Japan's "democratic" period; but by the standard of democracy known in the West, these years were far from democratic. To assert that Japanese society had never been democratic is not to deny that there have been individuals who perceived the richness and the dignity of the democratic belief. Among such persons one might mention are Yoshida Shoin and Fukuzawa Yukichi. Such spokesmen, however, were single voices; the social structure did not reflect their views.

Even if it is granted that postwar Japan is a far more democratic society than previously, one cannot state in specific terms the role of the deconcentration program, for it was only part of the broader economic program, which included labor-reform and land-reform; and in turn, the economic reforms were only part of the still broader program that included political, social, and legal reforms. Out of this comprehensive pattern of change, it is not possible to isolate a particular program and say it was of such and such significance. One can only speak in general terms. But in general terms, however, one can say that the *zaibatsu*-dissolution has been a major contributory element to the growth of democratic forces in postwar Japan. It emphatically denied that enterprise in the modern sector of the economy belonged to a handful of families, that what was good for Mitsui and the other combines was necessarily good for Japan. The program called for allowing executives of major corporations to be executives in fact rather than mere servants of top-holding companies. The program called for building the aggregates of capital required for modern production by pooling the resources of the many rather than depending on the fortunes of a few.

The implications of the deconcentration program are more clearly seen if one turns the question into the negative and asks, "What would have been the chances of a democratic development in postwar Japan had the combines been left intact?" If a few great combines had been able to buy successive postwar elections through the enormity of resources at their disposal there could have been little meaning to the constitutional change that sovereignty lay in the people. As we noted in Japan's earlier period of party government, the two major parties were primarily only spokesmen for the two largest combines—the Seiyukai for the Mitsui and the Minseito for the Mitsubishi.

A major element in the rise of the military in the thirties was the contempt the Japanese people felt toward the political parties, which they regarded as pawns of the *zaibatsu*. The army was thought of as a purifying element. The fall of party government in the 1930s stemmed from its sham quality.

To have imagined that party government could be restored in the postwar period without changing the source of its bad name would be engaging in fanciful thinking. For the development of a viable democracy in Japan it was essential that there be a diffusion of power in the modern sector of the economy. The dissolution of the top-holding companies has resulted in diffusion, for the member companies of today's groupings are basically self-directed. In contrast to the combine period, when all political work was handled exclusively at the top-holding company level, so the weight of the entire combine could be brought into each negotiation, today's members handle their own political arrangements, including their own political contributions.

Once again there is talk of allowing holding companies, although the quotation cited earlier from the Japan Productivity Center is indicative of the popular support for their proscription as late as 10 years after the end of the "reform" phase of the Occupation: "Against the outlawing of the holding company there has been no open criticism. . . . The evil[s] of the holding company have been so deeply impressed upon the popular mind that, in spite of the significant contributions by some of them toward the advancement of the Japanese economy at large, no voice is raised openly favoring its revival. . . ."[2]

It is, however, a cardinal, unexamined belief among almost all government officials that increases in size—whether by merger, cartel agreement, or a holding company—result in gains in output. In an eagerness for continued rapid growth in the face of freer international trade, including capital movements, and in disregard of the other implications of concentration, today's government is intent on reconcentration.

The term "political economy" is seldom used nowadays; we prefer instead to speak of "politics" and "economics." But there has been loss as well as gain in the conceptual split, for fundamentally the two cannot be separated. Democracy and competitive capitalism are of one fabric. There is no such thing as democracy and concentrated business

[2] Japan Productivity Center, p. 7.

power, when concentration is at the level which existed in Japan prior to the end of World War II.

While the program of economic deconcentration was not designed to further the fortunes of the Liberal-Democratic Party (the conservative party that has controlled all postwar cabinets except one coalition government in which it participated), in the judgment of one observer, it has done just this. When in late 1965 I asked a member of the Cabinet (with economic responsibility) his views on the merits and demerits of the *zaibatsu*-dissolution program, he couched his reply entirely in political terms. As he saw the matter, *zaibatsu*-dissolution has given the Liberal-Democratic Party far greater maneuverability and freedom. No longer is it under constant attack as defender of concentrated wealth and privilege. In the light of the recent discussion of allowing use of holding companies once again, one may speculate on how much longer this may last.

With much of the world marveling at the Japanese economy's extraordinary post-1954 performance, it is impossible to conclude that the reforms injured the economy. In fact, it may well be argued that they have in fact been an integral part of the exceptional pace of recent growth. The unrestrained rivalry for market position appears to be an essential part of the explanation of the extraordinary levels of investment; the temporary breakup of the two giant trading companies has been an element in the greater diffusion of foreign technology; and it would seem that part of the vigor of these recent years comes from greater vitality in management, from allowing corporations to act on their own best judgment rather than confining decision-making to the councils of top-holding companies.

However, to fully answer the question of the economic consequences of the program, initial costs must be considered along with later achievements. It is inconceivable that such a major reorganization as was carried through in the first three years of the Occupation did not affect output. Not only were holding companies dissolved and/or reorganized, but there was wholesale reorganization of the ownership structures of the major operating companies, substantial reorganization of top personnel, and even some splits. Summarized, the actions were as seen in the table which follows.

For the 1945-48 period, when these changes were occurring, and for the next few years production was undoubtedly lessened. True, these reforms occurred at a time when defeat had left the nation psychologically shattered; territorial adjustments and disruptions of markets would in any event have meant major adjustments, but the reforms added to the uncertainties. Major businesses faced possible loss

| *holding company action* | | |
|---|---|---|
| outright dissolution | 16 | |
| dissolution with reorganization | 26. | |
| reorganization without dissolution | 11 | |
| untouched | 30 | |

| *stock dispersal program - antitrust and other* | | |
|---|---|---|
| antitrust: | | |
| HCLC | Y8.3 billion | (proceeds from sale) |
| FTC | 1.3 " | (paid-up value) |
| other: | | |
| Finance Ministry (capital levy tax) | 1.7 " | (proceeds from sale) |
| Closed Institutions Liquidation Commission | 3.1 " | (proceeds from sale) |
| | Y14.4 billion | |

| *personnel programs* | | |
|---|---|---|
| economic purge | 1,535 executives | |
| *zaibatsu* appointees | 40 | |
| | 1,575 | |

| *reorganization of "excessive concentrations"* | | |
|---|---|---|
| companies split | 11 | |
| companies with plants or shareholding in other companies affected | 8 | |
| | 19 | |

of plant and equipment through reparations decisions. The sweeping political changes had business overtones. Japan's traditional polity had been a vital support to giant business. In view of this, the propagation of the democratic ideology would certainly be unsettling to those who all their lives had operated in terms of permanent superiors and inferiors.

One can only make an analytic statement of the costs of the antitrust action, not a statistical one. There is no norm, domestic or international, against which to measure the recovery process, nor can weights be assigned to the various inhibitors of output. Recovery from war's destruction depends on a host of factors, among which are the comprehensiveness, intensity, and type of damage; the psychological state of the population; historic work patterns; and the skill of postwar management of the economy. In Table 17-2, showing GNP in real terms, 1930 to 1963, it will be noted that gains for the period 1947 to 1952 were substantial, notwithstanding the current frequent assertion that reforms were preventing recovery. Taking the average annual increase in output from 1946 (when GNP was little more than one-half of 1944) to 1952, we will find that output increased 9.7% per annum (on a compound interest basis). The one year in which output seriously fell off was in 1949 when Joseph Dodge was carrying through the painful but necessary price stabilization program.

How much higher output would have been with no business reform is impossible to tell. It is possible that it would have been sufficiently higher that American taxpayers would not have needed to provide some $1.1 billions in assistance up to 1952 nor the $2 billion in all, though this is necessarily speculation. It is noteworthy here that agreement was worked out with the Japanese government for repayment of almost one-third of the amount.[3] Such expenditures, however, should be weighed against expenditures in the prosecution of the war. As we earlier noted, the Pacific War is estimated to have cost $100 billion. To expend billions for war and then begrudge the merest fraction of such amount for programs considered to further the peace is an odd way to expend public funds.

There is much to criticize about the deconcentration program as a whole though in all fairness the American (as well as the Japanese) lack of familiarity with Japanese industrial organization made for a clumsiness in doing things. Some programs were no doubt more extreme than they needed to be, though operating through an instrumentality—the Japanese government—which balked at every proposal could only lead to a hardening of position on the part of those pushing for change.

Looking back on the operation, a good many observers may feel that the abandonment of banking reforms was unfortunate. Tolerating special ties between banks and industrials merely perpetuates partiality in credit extension. Two circumstances mitigate, somewhat, the full consequences of this failure to act. First, the very scale of present big business borrowing is so large that it obligates reliance on numerous banks, thus reducing the position of individual institutions. Second, the increase in government credit sources has increased the number of borrowing opportunities.

Nevertheless, admitting the foregoing qualifications, it can yet be asserted that impartial access to credit remains a key social problem.

[3] T.F.M. Adams typescript, "Banking in Japan," p. 66.

Repeatedly in the postwar period, the Japanese government has pledged itself to work for the elimination of duality from the economy, but duality is not likely to be eliminated until banking reform comes. In fact, continued duality is the price to be paid for banking-industrial ties.

### *The Lasting Power of the Reforms*

Have the reforms taken root? The answer is both yes and no. Business organization in Japan is different from its old form. There have been repeated efforts to push the old structures together, but they have not succeeded. It is not for lack of trying that today's business groupings are different, but they are different. Although names deceptively suggest no change, today's groupings are loose confederations, not the tight, monolithic units of yesteryear. With respect to *zaibatsu*-dissolution, there is much that has taken hold. Further, no *zaibatsu* family member is prominent in executive circles.

Not as much, however, can be said for market concentration and cartelization, which, together with the prohibition of holding companies, the Antimonopoly Law was to guard against. As we have seen, the Japanese government is doing its utmost to promote market concentration and cartelization. Via loans at highly advantageous terms and tax advantages, the government is adding its pressures to those of business in encouraging mergers. Further, through a variety of pressures the government is pushing cartelization. The main route for formation of cartels has not been through the antidepression and rationalization exceptions permitted under the 1953 amendment of the Antimonopoly Law, but rather by bypassing the entire law. Speaking of the activities of the Fair Trade Commission, the Business International 1965 report observes: "The chief activity of the Fair Trade Commission seems to be the sanctioning and registering of exceptions to the Law, rather than the enforcing of it."[4] But the problem with which the commission wrestles is that of a weak, though not nonexistent, political base.

### *American and Japanese Attitudes Toward Competitive Policy*

The Japanese government's effort to promote market concentration and cartelization reflects the different attitudes toward competitive policy in Japan, the United States, and elsewhere. When one speaks of competitive policy he is not speaking of atomistic competition but encouragement of numbers, of entry, of the denial of privilege and partiality. Competitive policy opposes extreme market con-

[4] Business International, p. 39.

centration either from merger or self-growth. It prohibits cartels or it carefully restricts the range of their purpose and activities. Currently the position of competitive policy vis-à-vis giant conglomerates is under study in the United States,[5] though Japanese experience seems to suggest the inadvisability of viewing conglomerate extensions with equanimity.

With its antitrust policy for Japan the United States believed it was exporting one of the strengths of the American economy. Undoubtedly American capitalism has given the strongest performance of any capitalist system, and most Americans see the nation's public policy of competition as integral to the performance. In contrast to capitalism in most other parts of the world, American capitalism was not built on a feudal base; the United States began its national existence in capitalism. Thus the democratic features of competitive capitalism were easier to achieve in the United States than elsewhere.

Prior to the postwar developments in Europe, one might have said that the most striking difference between capitalism in Europe and in the United States was the antitrust tradition of the United States. American businessmen in search of the mass market have thought in terms of large output at low unit profit. European businessmen for a long time thought in terms of low output at high unit profit. American business traditionally thinks in terms of a right of entry to markets; traditionally Europeans regarded entry as privileged.

An example of the support to be found among members of the American business community for a policy of competition—even from a spokesman of a much prosecuted corporation—are the remarks of Crawford H. Greenwalt, at that time chairman of the DuPont Corporation. These comments were made before the Antitrust Section of the American Bar Association meeting in Chicago in 1963:

> I should like to make it very clear that I have for many years supported the basic antitrust statutes. I firmly believe that these laws are good laws, essential laws, and that they have been the in-

[5] Cf., for example, Donald F. Turner, "Conglomerate Mergers," *Harvard Law Review*, Vol. 78, May 1965, pp. 1,313-95; C. D. Edwards, testimony before the Subcommittee on Antitrust and Monopoly of the Senate Judiciary in *Hearings on Economic Concentration*, Part 1, "Overall and Conglomerate Aspects," 88th Cong., 2nd Sess., Washington, D.C., 1964, pp. 36-56; W. Markham, *ibid.*, Part 3, "Concentration, Invention and Innovation," 89th Cong., 1st Sess., 1965, pp. 1,269-81. Cf., likewise, the guidelines released by the Department of Justice on corporate acquisitions or mergers under Section 7 of the Clayton Act released May 30, 1968, mimeog., esp. pp. 20-27.

strument of preserving within the business community the competitive environment which is the essence of a free economy.[6]

I am convinced that my own strong support of the antitrust statutes is shared by every thoughtful businessman. I think we all recognize the merits of a vigorous competitive system.[7]

The purpose of the [antitrust statutes] . . . is to referee the competitive scene in such a way as to achieve a meaningful democracy, a high level of economic prosperity and an ethical standard offensive to no man's conscience. We can all agree that these goals may be reached most directly through unimpeded access to the marketplace, through a competition unencumbered by artificial restraints.[8]

It will be recalled that at the time of the Occupation a wide-spread Japanese interpretation of the antitrust program for Japan was that the United States sought to weaken the Japanese economy. Not only is such thinking wholly outside the way in which Americans regard a policy of competition, but in addition, it would make no sense to attempt it. The Occupation was to be for a short time, after which Japan would regain full sovereignty. Given the imagination and capability of the Japanese people, it obviously would be pointless for the United States to promote policies that would turn out to be applicable only during the period of the country's immediate postwar weakness, policies that would be overturned as soon as self-direction was resumed. In the Occupation, the United States's concern was not with the threat which Japan posed in those years, for no threat was posed. It was concerned with the long-range problem, of what Japan's foreign policy would be after the country recovered. To propose the adoption of a policy that was against the basic interests of the Japanese people would merely invite undoing. Therefore the task before United States policy-makers was to propose changes which would at the same time serve to promote the basic interests of both countries. The United States believed that a program of democratization would do this. It regarded the program of economic democratization as a requisite to political democratization, but believed such a policy to be of economic advantage.

American opinion holds that in competitive markets firms will expand to the most productive scale and will operate under the most

[6] Greenwalt, "A Businessman Looks at the Antitrust Laws," a speech delivered August 13, 1963. Citations are to the printed version of the speech delivered by the DuPont Company for general distribution, page 2.

[7] *Ibid.*, p. 9.

[8] *Ibid.*, p. 10.

efficient conditions. This opinion also holds that a competitive environment is conducive to invention and innovation. It holds that competitive markets are most in keeping with the democratic philosophy, for the creed is, "Open to large numbers, let the best win." This opinion holds that competitive markets assure the best distribution of the national income, and further, that competition not only provides checks on private business power, but that strong performance makes government "interference" unnecessary. It accordingly greatly reduces the scale of bribery and other scandal which is an almost inherent circumstance when governments enter into extensive direct dealings with private business.

But it is clear that many Japanese government officials think differently of competitive policy. In their parlance, competition is always "excessive competition." Competition (i.e., excessive competition) is considered inefficient, resulting in firms too small, firms unable to cope with cyclical changes, unable to compete effectively in international trade. Competition is not regarded as conducive to technological progress. Government officials are not concerned that highly concentrated market structures shut the door to large numbers, for they don't see that any rights are involved. Neither do they worry over the consequences of concentrated markets with respect to national income distribution. They do not see dangers of a low-wage, high-profit policy. Exports are regarded as the axis of the economy. Nor are government officials concerned with the problem of private business power. And the last thing that government officials would desire would be minimization of the government's role.

### *The Postwar Trend Toward Competitive Policy*

In pursuing a policy of merger and cartelization, Japan, many observers may feel, is moving in an unwise direction, at variance to much national and international postwar thinking. While earlier the United States was distinctive among the major powers in emphasizing the strengths of a public policy of competition, the trend among most nations in the postwar period has been in this direction. The United Kingdom now has the Monopolies and Restrictive Practices Act of 1948, the Restrictive Practices Act of 1956, the 1964 legislation dealing with resale price maintenance, as well as the Monopolies and Merger Act of 1965. The Federal Republic of Germany has the 1957 Act against Restrictions of Competition with amendment in 1965, for the most part, of a strengthening character. In France there is the Price Act as amended in 1953, 1958, and 1963, which regulates cartel practices and the practices of the dominant firm. In Norway there is the 1953 legislation entitled, Act on Control of Prices, Dividends and Restrictive Business Practices, which strengthens control of cartels and monopolies. In Sweden postwar efforts climaxed in the 1956 legislation entitled An Act to Counteract Restraint of Competition, which was amended in 1962.[9] The trend of thinking in most major nations is toward prohibition or control of restrictive business practices and checks on the activities of monopolistic or dominant firms. Cartels are viewed critically.

In the international field the trend has been in the same direction, notwithstanding setbacks. Among architects of the United Nations there had been hope of a third specialized agency alongside of the IBRD and IMF, the International Trade Organization, ITO, for the promotion of international trade. Inasmuch as trade can be restricted by private arrangements as well as public policy, there was a chapter in the charter of the proposed organization dealing with private arrangements, Chapter V. The opening article of this chapter reads in part: "Each member agrees to take appropriate measures and to work with the ITO to prevent business practices which might restrain competition, limit access to local and foreign markets, or foster monopolistic control whenever such practices may be harmful to production and trade." But the ITO never came into being, largely because of the U.S. failure to ratify. Instead, the earlier, more limited provisional arrangements of the GATT became permanent.

A second try at an international agreement was made in 1951 when the United States introduced a resolution in the Economic and Social Council of the U.N., calling for a committee to make recommendations on the prevention and regulation of private combines and cartels in international trade.[10] The resolution was adopted. In 1953 the ad hoc committee created to investigate and report, submitted its report on the various types of restrictive business practices handicapping international trade and a draft agreement for international

[9] Corwin D. Edwards, Trade Regulations Overseas, *The National Laws*, Dobbs Ferry, N.Y., 1966, *passim*. Hearings before Antitrust Subcommittee of Senate Judiciary Committee, 89th Cong., 1st Sess., "Foreign Trade and the Antitrust Laws," Part 2, "Antitrust Development and Regulations of Foreign Countries," Washington, D.C., 1965, passim. Cf. likewise, D. Swann and D. L. McLachlan, *Concentration or Competition: A European Dilemma?*, a Chatham House, PEP publication, European Series No. 1, January 1967, p. 49.

[10] This brief discussion is based on Joint Economic Committee Paper No. 4, "Private Trade Barriers and the Atlantic Community," in "Economic Policies and Practices," Washington, D.C., 1964, largely prepared by Vernon Mund of the University of Washington, pp. 33-36; General Agreement on Tariffs and Trade, *Restrictive Business Practices*, Geneva, 1959, prepared by J. L'Huillier of the University of Geneva, pp. 76-80; General Agreement on Tariffs and Trade, *The Activities of GATT, 1960/61*, Geneva, 1961, pp. 29-30, p. 32.

regulation of them. The United States wanted proscription of cartels rather than regulation of them. Although the draft agreement remained under discussion for some two years differences of view were not reconciled.

A third try at international control of restrictive business practices was attempted within the GATT organization. Although the matter of restrictive business practices had come up there in 1954-55, as part of an intensive review of the General Agreement, it was not pursued at that time, in view of the fact that the subject was still under discussion in the Economic and Social Council.[11] Under the leadership of Norway and the Federal Republic of Germany, GATT did take up the subject after the collapse of ECOSOC efforts; in 1958 it was decided to appoint a group of experts to consider what role, if any GATT should play in this field.[12] The background report (submitted in 1959) from this group listed the principal types of restrictive practices, summarized the status of such practices in the legislation of member countries, and summarized the preceding international attempts to reach agreement.[13] Again, however, agreement could not be reached on the specifics, except to agree in 1960, "that any contracting party can request another party to enter into consultations on restrictive business practices which appear to have harmful effects, on a bilateral or multilateral basis as may be appropriate."[14]

Supranational and international efforts to control and limit restrictive business practices have occurred in the European Coal and Steel Community, in the European Economic Community, and in the OECD.[15] Both the 1951 Treaty of Paris, creating the European Coal and Steel Community, and the 1957 Treaty of Rome, creating the European Economic Community, had provisions dealing with restrictive business practices. (The communities took the first step toward consolidation by merging their respective councils and commissions on July 1, 1967.)

In the Treaty of Paris, which governs the European Coal and Steel Community, cartels and mergers are dealt with in Articles 65 and 66, respectively. Cartels which fix prices, restrict output, and allocate markets are forbidden, though cartels for rationalization and in certain circumstances joint buying and selling are permitted providing the High Authority finds them in the public interest (i.e., that it

[11] *GATT Activities, 1960/61*, p. 29.

[12] *Ibid.*

[13] GATT, *Restrictive Business Practices.*

[14] *GATT Activities, 1960/61*, p. 30.

[15] For convenient short summaries see Joint Economic Committee, Mund, pp. 23-36; GATT, *Restrictive Business Practices*, pp. 87-92.

does not give the interested parties "power to determine prices, or to control or limit the production or selling of a substantial part of the product in question within the Common Market, or of protecting them from effective competition by other enterprises within the Common Market").

Article 66 provides for prior authorization of mergers when such would have the effect of "bringing about a concentration." Approval from the High Authority is to be granted in cases where such does not result in the power "to determine prices, to control or restrict production or distribution, or to prevent the maintenance of effective competition in a substantial part of the market for such products."

In the Treaty of Rome, Articles 85 through 90 deal with restrictive business practices. Article 85 proscribes cartels "which have as their object or result the prevention, restriction or distortion of competition within the Common Market." In particular, it forbids price-fixing, restriction of output (technical developments and investment), market sharing, price discrimination, and tying agreements. It permits cartels which contribute to "the improvement of the production or distribution of goods or to the promotion of technical or economic progress. . . ." Article 86 deals with "improper advantage of a dominant position." Improper practices include inequitable prices, limitation of output, and tying agreements.[16]

In the OECD, there is a similar concern with restrictive business practices. At the time the OECD came into being, September 20, 1961, negotiations had been going on within the OEEC for eliminating restrictions on international trade. Cognizant that private agreements can restrict as well as governmental, the OECD established in 1961 the Group of Experts on Restrictive Business Practices:[17]

> . . . whose most important activity has been the preparation and publication of a "Guide to Legislation on Restrictive Business Practices . . . a comprehensive survey of relevant national legislation and of administrative and court decision . . . as well as the corresponding legal dispositions of the EEC and the ECSC. . . . As part of its other activities, which include the confrontation of legislation and policies and the standardization of terminology in the field of restrictive business practices,[18] the Committee is now engaged in the study of the harmful effects which certain private restraints of competition may have on international trade.

[16] For evaluative comment, see Swann and McLachlan, pp. 43-53.

[17] OECD, *The OECD at Work*, Paris, 1964, p. 49.

[18] Cf., for example, OECD, *Glossary of Terms Relating to Restrictive Business Practices*, Paris, 1965.

The Committee's terms of reference give it the following charter:[19]

> 1. To review developments in the field of restrictive business practices both in individual countries and international or regional organizations, such as new legislation, or application of existing legislation, and to summarize this information for appropriate use;
> 2. To examine and compare laws relating to competition in individual countries and the basic principles underlying them and to comment upon particular problems arising from the nature or application of such laws;
> 3. To examine and comment upon particular problems arising from the existence of monopolies and restrictive business practices;
> 4. To promote the standardization of terminology concerning restrictive business practices;
> 5. To develop agreed definitions of specific business practices which may have an adverse effect on international trade and, on the basis of such definition, review developments in this field; and
> 6. To report and make recommendations as appropriate to the council on matters within the competence of the Committee.

Thus it is clear not only in national legislation but in the treaty arrangements which govern the Coal and Steel Community and which govern the Common Market and in procedures being developed within the OECD that industrial concentration and monopolistic practices are regarded with concern. While there tends to be a difference in the treatment of cartels between European and American procedures (Europeans typically distinguish between good and bad cartels whereas Americans condemn all), it is evident that on both sides of the Atlantic concern is felt toward monopolistic situations. The Japanese approach is much in contrast. Most Japanese government officials regard the advantages of concentration as so substantial and the liabilities so small that they are enthusiastically promoting mergers and cartelization.

Fortunately, however, not the whole of the Japanese government takes this position. Commissioner Ariga of the Fair Trade Commission writes,[20]

> In the industrialization of Japan from the Meiji era to the end of World War II . . . the concept of freedom of competition had almost no chance to emerge. . . .

[19] Joint Economic Committee, Mund, p. 36.
[20] Iyori Hiroshi, *Antimonopoly Legislation in Japan*, v-vii.

The legal concept of freedom of contract did not include freedom of competition in business. Restrictive business practices were not conceived as unfair. Monopoly and cartelization were not considered as against the public interest, because they were created by contract . . . without regard to unfairness from the viewpoint of equality or disparity.

Thus, the antitrust policy based on freedom of competition introduced into Japan after World War II . . . was [totally strange] to the Japanese. . . . The very stringent Antimonopoly Act . . . antagonized many businessmen. . . . Certain scholars [however] did support the antitrust policy and philosophy and characterized this Act as "the democratic economic charter of Japan." . . . Major amendments were made in the law during the first ten years after its enactment. . . .

[With the 20th anniversary in 1967 of the enactment of the Antimonopoly Law] the Act's policy has finally taken root and is growing. During the . . . years since . . . major amendment to the Act, the Japanese economy [has] achieved a remarkable growth. . . . It has opened its market to the international competition for commodities and liberalized capital movements. Today the people are attributing this success to the system of free competition which was nurtured by the antimonopoly policy. This evaluation is significant all the more for Japanese enterprises which do business internationally in free and fair competition with enterprises of countries throughout the world. Invisible barriers to trade likely to be or built up internationally by various restrictive business practices have to be prevented or broken down so that enterprises of any country may have access to any market or resources for the total economic welfare of the world—thus leading eventually to world peace.

## APPENDIX I

# Excerpts from President Roosevelt's Message to the Congress, calling for an investigation of concentrated economic power in the United States, April 29, 1938.

*Message from the President of the United States*
*To the Congress of the United States:*

. . . the liberty of a democracy is not safe if the people tolerate the growth of private power to a point where it becomes stronger than their democratic state itself. That, in its essence, is fascism—ownership of government by an individual, by a group, or by any other controlling private power. . . . .

The danger of this centralization [of business] in a handful of huge corporations is not reduced or eliminated, as is sometimes urged, by the wide public distribution of their securities. The mere number of security holders gives little clue to the size of their individual holdings or to their actual ability to have a voice in the management. . . .

Private enterprise is ceasing to be free enterprise and is becoming a cluster of private collectivisms; masking itself as a system of free enterprise after the American model, it is in fact becoming a concealed cartel system after the European model.

We all want efficient industrial growth and the advantages of mass production. . . . But modern efficient mass production is not furthered by a central control which destroys competition between industrial plants, each capable of efficient mass production while operating as separate units. Industrial efficiency does not have to mean industrial empire building.

And industrial empire building, unfortunately, has evolved into banker control of industry. . . . .

Government can deal and should deal with blindly selfish men. But that is a comparatively small part—the easier part—of our problem. The larger, more important and more difficult part of our problem is to deal with men who are not selfish and who are good citizens, but who cannot see the social and economic consequences of their actions in a modern economically interdependent community. They fail to grasp the significance of some of our most vital social and economic problems because they see them only in the light of their own personal experience and not in perspective with the experience of other men and other industries. They therefore fail to see these problems for the Nation as a whole.

To meet the situation I have described, there should be a thorough study of the concentration of economic power in American industry. . . .

I enumerate some of the items that should be embraced in the proposed study . . . (1) improvement of antitrust procedures . . . (2) mergers and interlocking relationships . . . (3) financial controls . . . (a) investment trusts . . . (b) bank holding companies . . . (4) trade associations . . . (5) patent laws . . . (6) tax correctives. . . . .

No man of good faith will misinterpret these proposals. They derive from the oldest American traditions. . . .

Franklin D. Roosevelt
*The White House, April 29, 1938*

SOURCE: As printed in *Final Report and Recommendations*, the Temporary National Economic Committee, Senate Document #35, 77th Cong., 1st Sess., Washington, D.C., 1944, pp. 11-20.

Membership of the Temporary National Economic Committee, as taken from the *Final Report and Recommendations*

Congress:
- Senator Joseph C. O'Mahoney, Wyoming, Chairman
- Representative Hatton W. Sumners, Texas, Vice Chairman
- Senator James M. Mead, New York
- Senator Wallace H. White, Jr., Maine
- Representative Clyde Williams, Missouri
- Representative B. Carroll Reece, Tennessee

Executive Branch:
- Justice: Thurman W. Arnold, Assistant Attorney General
  - Alternate: Hugh Cox, Special Assistant to the Attorney General
- SEC: Sumner T. Pike, Commissioner
- FTC: Garland S. Ferguson, Commissioner
  - Alternate: Edwin L. Davis, Chairman
- Labor: Isador Lubin, Commissioner of Labor Statistics
  - Alternate: A. Ford Hinrichs, Acting Commissioner, BL
- Treasury: Joseph J. O'Connell, Jr., Special Assistant to the General Counsel
  - Alternate: Charles L. Kades, Special Assistant to the General Counsel
- Commerce: Wayne C. Taylor, Undersecretary of Commerce
  - Alternate: M. Joseph Meehan, Chief Statistician, Bureau of Foreign and Domestic Commerce
- Economic Coordinator: Leon Henderson
- Executive Secretary: Dewey Anderson
- Economic Advisor: Theodore J. Kreps

## APPENDIX II

# Additional Notes to Tables 3-1, 3-2, and 3-3 in Chapter 3, Showing the Position of the *Zaibatsu* in the Economy

(All references are to the data volume of HCLC, *Zaibatsu Dissolution*)

I. *Basis of Selection of the 10 Combines.*

Indicating its belief in the family nature of "*zaibatsu,*" the Commission stated that it made its designation of the 10 combines on the basis of *zaibatsu* families, those families designated under the Law for the Termination of Zaibatsu Family Control, Law No. 2, January 7, 1948. (Cf. note 2 of notes to Section 14, in effect, p. 467.) The explanation is puzzling for two reasons. Supposedly the chief action under *zaibatsu* dissolution was holding-company dissolution, yet the designation of the 83 holding companies was completed (final designation, September 1947) before passage of the Law for the Termination of Zaibatsu Family Control. Further, such a reference appears to put the national statistics on paid-in capital in the crucial war's end table two years apart from the statistics on paid-in capital for the individual *zaibatsu* companies. (In note 1 of the notes to Table 14 it is explained that the national statistics are those of 1946; in note 2, that the *zaibatsu* corporate statistics are as of the date of designation of the *zaibatsu* families under the 1948 law.)

*Possible resolution of the difficulty.* The 10 *zaibatsu* family groups were designated twice, once under amendment to the HCLC ordinance (Imperial Ordinance 592 of December 4, 1946, amending Imperial Ordinance 233), in response to the family holdings aspect of MacArthur's July 1946 directive (SCAPIN 1079); and a second time under the Law for the Termination of Zaibatsu Family Control with respect to the family appointees aspect of the July 1946 directive. The initial designation of the 10 *zaibatsu* families was made March 13, 1947. While the Commission refers to the Law rather than this Ordinance, it is probable that the Commission intended reference to the Ordinance.

Further, individual *zaibatsu* corporate statistics were not likely to have been changing appreciably in this period, inasmuch as roughly half of the companies were on the "Schedule of Restricted Concerns," which froze their capital except with SCAP permission for change. Probably almost all of the firms were "special accounting companies" under the Enterprise Reorganization and Reconstruction Law which again froze capital until reorganization plans were approved.

II. *Definition of Companies.*

Companies are defined as "kabushiki kaisha" (joint stock), "gomei kaisha" (unlimited partnership), "goshi kaisha" (limited partnership), "yugen kaisha" (a kind of limited company), "kohin yugen konsu" (Chinese limited partnership), and "yugen konsu" (Chinese joint-stock company). (See note 1 to "Preface" ["Reigen"], unnumbered page, at the beginning of the data volume. For a discussion of these business forms see, among others, *Daihyakka Jiten.*) Thus it will be seen that what is excluded from the tables is the single proprietorships.

III. *Companies outside Japan defined.*

Companies have been regarded as "outside" if their head offices were located outside of Japan proper or if they had been incorporated under foreign law; cf. note 1 to Section 12, which is in effect, p. 343.

IV. *Sectoral Problems.*

The HCLC has attempted to give the reader a picture of *zaibatsu* activity sector by sector in the economy. Problems arise, however, because of the conglomerate character of many of the firms. The difficulty is probably more acute within the breakdowns of the major headings (with the exception of finance)—heavy industry, light industry, "other"—than between major headings. For example, it will be noted in Table 3-1 that the Big Four are shown as representing 5% of capital invested in shipbuilding, when they in fact at that time accounted for about 30% of output. A study of the individual Big Four figures would suggest that this odd circumstance comes about through the Commission having entered Mitsubishi Heavy Industry under "machine tools" rather than "shipbuilding." I would guess that the Commission did not attempt to allocate the capital of conglomerate firms activity by activity, but instead entered the full capitalization under what it regarded as the principal activity.

V. *Duplicate Entry Problems.*

Where two or more holding companies *within* a single combine each had 10%-or-above holdings, duplicate entries have been eliminated by listing the company only once, under the principal holding company. Such a company is shown under the other holding companies merely in parenthesis, but its capital has not been entered into the total capital computation.

Where two or more holding companies in *different* combines each have 10% or more of the shares, duplicate entries have not been eliminated. There are 39 duplicate entries among companies "within Japan" (Table 3-1, Part A) and 4 "outside Japan" (Table 3-1, Part B). These, of course, provide overstatement to the table. For a listing of the companies see explanatory notes to Section 14 notes 3a and 3b. The Japan Metal Fabricating Co. (Nihon Kinzoku Kogyo) is illustrative of this problem. The Mitsui combine (Mitsui Honsha) and the Furukawa combine (Furukawa Denki Kogyo) each had holdings in this company within the HCLC definition of "subsidiary." The company appears twice in Table 3-1, under the Mitsui combine and under Furukawa.

VI. *Sources for Table 3-2 data.*

The determination of which companies to include as combine subsidiaries is based on Higuchi Hiroshi, *Japan's Zaibatsu* (*Nihon Zaibatsu Ron*) and Masuo Nobuzo, *The Mitsui Reader* (*Mitsui Tokuhon*). The capitalization data for the companies selected are taken from the *Oriental Economist, Corporation Yearbook, 1941* (*Kabushiki Kaisha Nenkan, Showa 16*), and the Teikoku Bank, *Corporation Directory, 1941* (Teikoku Ginko, *Kaisha Yoroku, Showa 16*), not to be confused with the Mitsui-Shibusawa Teikoku Bank which was not established until 1943; cf. note 2 to 1941 table, p. 470.

VII. *Sources for Table 3-3 data.*

Corporate statistics are taken from *Oriental Economist, Corporation Yearbook, 1937* (Toyo Keizai, *Kabushiki Kaisha Nenkan, Showa 12*). The determination of which companies to include as combine subsidiaries is based on the following sources:

(a) from the *Japanese Combine* series (*Nihon Konzern*):

| | |
|---|---|
| Wada Hidekichi | *Mitsui Konzern Reader*, 1937 |
| Iwai Ryotaro | *Mitsubishi Konzern Reader*, 1937 |
| Nishino Kiyosaku | *Sumitomo Konzern Reader*, 1937 |
| Obama Toshie | *Yasuda Konzern Reader*, 1937 |
| Wada Hidekichi | *Nissan Konzern Reader*, 1937 |
| Nishinoiri Aiichi | *Asano, Shibusawa, Okawa, Furukawa Konzern Reader*, 1937 |
| Kuribayashi Seishu | *Konzern Securities Reader*, 1937 |
| Katsuda Teiji | *Okura, Nezu Konzern Reader*, 1937 |
| Takahashi Kamekichi and Aoyama Jiro | *Nihon Zaibatsu Ron*, 1938 |

(b) Suzuki Mosaburo — *Nihon Zaibatsu Ron*, 1934

Cf. note 1 to 1937 table, p. 472.

# APPENDIX III

## The Yasuda Plan and MacArthur's Response

A. *Official Japanese Proposal for Holding Company Dissolution Incorporating the Yasuda Plan, November 4, 1945*

The firms of Mitsui Honsha, Yasuda Hozensha, Sumitomo Honsha, and Kabushiki Kaisha Mitsubishi Honsha, hereinafter referred to as the "Holding Companies," have been holding conversations with the Minister of Finance with a view to voluntary dissolution in accordance with the desires of the Supreme Commander for the Allied Powers.

The following plan is proposed for your approval to govern the dissolution of these firms and such other firms of similar character as may volunteer for dissolution:

1.a. The Holding Companies will transfer to a Holding Company Liquidation Commission all securities owned by them and all other evidences of ownership or control of any interest in any firm, corporation or other enterprise.

b. The Holding Companies will cease to exercise direction or control, either directly or indirectly, of all financial, industrial, commercial or non-commercial enterprises whose securities they own or of which they hold any other evidences of ownership or control.

c. The directors and auditors of the Holding Companies will resign all offices held by them in such Holding Companies immediately after the transfer of the securities and other evidences of ownership referred to in paragraph 1.a. of this Memorandum and cease forthwith to exercise any influence, either directly or indirectly, in the management or policies of the Holding Companies affected by this dissolution.

d. All members of the Mitsui, Yasuda, Sumitomo, and Iwasaki families will immediately resign all offices held by them in any financial, commercial, non-commercial, or industrial enterprises and cease forthwith to exercise any influence, either directly or indirectly, in the management or policies of the enterprises affected by this dissolution.

2. The Imperial Japanese Government will establish a Holding Company Liquidation Commission whose functions, among others, shall be:

a. To proceed with the liquidation of all property transferred to it by the Holding Companies as rapidly as feasible.

b. To issue receipts to the Holding Companies in exchange for such transferred property. Such receipts will be non-negotiable, non-transferable, and ineligible for use as collateral.

c. Pending the final disposition of the transferred property, to exercise the voting rights incident thereto, but only to the extent necessary to insure proper methods of accounting and reporting and to accomplish changes in management, corporate practices and such other changes as are specifically desired by the Supreme Commander for the Allied Powers.

d. To redeem such receipts, upon the final liquidation of the transferred property, by delivery to the holders thereof, bonds of the Imperial Japanese Government, which bonds shall mature not less than ten years from the date of delivery and shall be non-negotiable, non-transferable, except by inheritance, and ineligible for use as collateral, except as the Holding Company Liquidation Commission may determine. Such exceptions will be limited to such matters as payment of taxes, death duties and comparable purposes. The Holding Company Liquidation Commission will be empowered to deliver negotiable bonds to small shareholders in the Holding Companies in redemption of their proportionate interest in such receipts in the event that such action is considered desirable by the Commission. The face value of the bonds given in redemption of the receipts shall not be in excess of the net proceeds derived in liquidation of the property transferred to it by the Holding Companies.

e. To protect the interests of small shareholders.

f. Determination of operating questions arising in the normal course of business of the Holding Companies such as disposition of funds received and payment of taxes and other debts.

3. When the securities, or other property transferred to the Holding Company Liquidation Commission, are offered for sale, preference to purchase will be given to employees of the companies involved, and in case of corporate shares the number of such shares that may be purchased by any single purchaser will be limited in order to insure maximum democratization of ownership.

4. Neither the Holding Companies nor any member of the Mitsui, Yasuda, Sumitomo, or Iwasaki families will purchase or otherwise acquire title or ownership of, or any interest in, any of the transferred property when it is offered for sale by the Holding Company Liquidation Commission.

5. The books, records, accounts, and meetings of the Holding Company Liquidation Commission will be open to the Supreme Commander for the Allied Powers at all times and all acts of such Commission will be subject to his approval or review.

6. Nominees for membership on the Holding Company Liquidation Commission will be submitted to the Supreme Commander for his approval before appointment. At any time the Supreme Commander may appoint his own nominees to membership on such Commission.

7. Immediately subsequent to the time of the transfer to the Holding Company Liquidation Commission of the securities and other evidences of ownership and control, proceedings will be commenced for the dissolution of the Holding Companies.

8. The dissolution of the Holding Companies will be under the supervision of the Holding Company Liquidation Commission and the Commission, with the consent of the Supreme Commander, will be authorized to draw upon the assets of such companies in its possession to meet the debts of the com-

panies, in event such companies do not have sufficient other assets to pay their creditors.

9. With the permission of the Supreme Commander for the Allied Powers, the bonds mentioned in paragraph 2.d. hereof, or any part thereof, may be delivered directly to the shareholders of the Holding Companies by the Holding Company Liquidation Commission in amounts proportionate to their various interests therein, in event the dissolution of such Holding Companies is completed before such bonds, or any part thereof, are issued and distributed.

The foregoing plan will be declared in immediate effect upon approval of the Supreme Commander for the Allied Powers.

SOURCE: As quoted in Bisson, pp. 241-43.

B. *Directive Accepting Japanese Proposal Under Title of "Dissolution of Holding Companies,"* SCAPIN *244, November 6, 1945*

1. Receipt of the proposed plan for the dissolution of Mitsui Honsha, Yasuda Hozensha, Sumitomo Honsha, and Kabushiki Kaisha Mitsubishi Honsha is acknowledged.

2. The plan proposed therein is approved in general and the Imperial Japanese Government will immediately proceed to effectuate it. No disposition of any property transferred to the Holding Company Liquidation Commission will be made without the prior approval of the Supreme Commander. You will submit the legislation through which the Holding Company Liquidation Commission will be created to the Supreme Commander for approval. It should be clearly understood that full freedom of action is retained by the Supreme Commander for the Allied Powers to elaborate or modify the proposed plan at any time and to supervise and review its execution.

3. The Imperial Japanese Government will immediately take such steps as are necessary effectually to prohibit the sale, gift, assignment or transfer of any movable or immovable property, including securities and other evidences of ownership, indebtedness or control by Mitsui Honsha, Yasuda Hozensha, Sumitomo Honsha, and Kabushiki Kaisha Mitsubishi Honsha and the members of the Mitsui, Iwasaki, Yasuda, and Sumitomo families or by any person acting in their behalf.

4. The Imperial Japanese Government will deliver to the Supreme Commander for the Allied Powers, within fifteen days of the receipt of this memorandum, a report listing:

a. All movable or immovable property, securities, and other evidences of ownership, indebtedness, and control in which the members of the Mitsui, Iwasaki, Yasuda, and Sumitomo families had any right, title or interest as of November 1st, 1945.

b. All transactions involving movable or immovable property, including securities and other evidences of ownership, indebtedness and control by any member of the Mitsui, Iwasaki, Yasuda, and Sumitomo families since January 1st, 1945.

5. It is the intention of the Supreme Commander to dissolve the private

industrial, commercial, financial, and agricultural combines in Japan, and to eliminate undesirable interlocking directorates and undesirable intercorporate security ownership so as to:

a. Permit a wider distribution of income and ownership of the means of production and trade.

b. Encourage the development within Japan of economic ways and institutions of a type that will contribute to the growth of peaceful and democratic forces. The plan proposed by the Imperial Japanese Government in the memorandum referred to in Paragraph 1 above will be considered only as a preliminary step toward these objectives.

6. Accordingly, the Imperial Japanese Government will promptly present for approval by the Supreme Commander for the Allied Powers:

a. Plans for the dissolution of industrial, commercial, financial, and agricultural combines in addition to those mentioned in the communication acknowledged in Paragraph 1 hereof.

b. Its program to abrogate all legislative or administrative measures which create, foster or tend to strengthen private monopoly.

c. Its program for the enactment of such laws as will eliminate and prevent private monopoly and restraint of trade, undesirable interlocking directorates, undesirable intercorporate security ownership, and [assure] the segregation of banking from commerce, industry and agriculture and as will provide equal opportunity to firms and individuals to compete in industry, commerce, finance, and agriculture on a democratic basis.

7. The Imperial Japanese Government will immediately take such steps as are necessary effectually to terminate and prohibit Japanese participation in private international cartels or other restrictive private international contracts or arrangements.

8. Acknowledgement of the receipt of this memorandum is directed.

SOURCE: As quoted in Bisson, pp. 243-44.

# APPENDIX IV

## 83 Designated Holding Companies, Alphabetically Arranged by Date of Designation

(f. = formerly)

*First Designation*, September 7, 1946—5 Companies

Fuji Industrial (f. Nakajima Aircraft)
Mitsui and Company
Mitsubishi and Company
Sumitomo and Company
Yasuda Partnership

*Second Designation*, December 7, 1946—40 Companies

Asano and Company
Daiken Industrial
Dainippon Cotton Spinning
Daiwa Cotton
Fuji Cotton Spinning
Furukawa Mining
Gunze Silk Mfg.
Hitachi Mfg.
Kanegafuchi Cotton Spinning
Katakura Industrial
Kawasaki Heavy Industries
Kobe Steel Works
Kurashiki Cotton Spinning
Matsushita Electric Industries
Naigai Cotton
Nichiden Development
Nissan & Co.
Nissan Chemical Industries
Japan Nitrogenous Fertilizer
Japan Woolen Cloth
Japan Radio
Japan Iron Mfg.
Japan Soda
Japan Mail Line
Nisshin Cotton Spinning
Nomura Partnership
Oji Paper Mfg.
Oki Electric
Oki Electric Securities
Okura Mining
Osaka Commercial Line
Riken Industries
Shibusawa and Co.
Shikishima Cotton Spinning
Showa Electric Industry
Teikoku Rayon
Teikoku Mining Development
Tokyo Shibaura Electric
Toyo Cotton Spinning
Yamashita Steamship

*Third Designation*, December 29, 1946—20 Companies

Asano Trading
Furukawa Electric Industry
Fuso Light Metals Industry (f. Sumitomo Light Metals Industry)
Hokkaido Colliery and Steamship
Mitsubishi Electric
Mitusbishi Chemical Industry
Mitsubishi Mining
Mitsubishi Heavy Industries
Mitsubishi Trading
Mitsui Trading
Mitsui Chemical Industry
Mitsui Mining
Mitsui Shipping
Naigai Trading
Japan Electric (f. Sumitomo Communication)
Japan Mining

Japan Steel Pipe
Nisshin Chemical Industry (f. Sumitomo Chemical Industry)
Seika Mining (f. Sumitomo Mining)
Sumitomo Electric Industries

*Fourth Designation*, March 15, 1947—2 Companies

International Telecommunications
Japan Telephone and Telegraph

*Fifth Designation*, September 30, 1947—16 Companies

Daiwa Ltd. Partnership
Hattori Ltd. Partnership
Hayashikane Trading
Ishihara Partnership
Kanto Development
Katakura Partnership
Kyodo Development
Mitsubishi Real Estate
Ohara Ltd. Partnership
Okazaki and Co.
Tatsuma Ltd. Partnership
Teitoku Kai
Terada Partnership
Toyoda Industrial
Wakasa Development
Yamashita & Co.

SOURCE: HCLC, *Zaibatsu Dissolution*, data vol., pp. 6-21.

# Appendix V

## Designated *Zaibatsu* Family Members

(H of H = Head of House)

*Mitsui*

| Name | | Share | Name | | Share |
|---|---|---|---|---|---|
| Mitsui Takakimi | H of H | 23% | Mitsui Takakane | H of H | 3.9%[1] |
| Mitsui Takahise | H of H | 11.5 | Mitsui Takaatsu | H of H | 3.9 |
| Mitsui Takanaru | H of H | 11.5 | Mitsui Takaakira | H of H | 3.9 |
| Mitsui Takaharu | H of H | 11.5 | Mitsui Takaose | H of H | 3.9 |
| Mitsui Takahiro | H of H | 11.5 | Mitsui Takateru[2] | H of H | 3.9 |
| Mitsui Takanaga | H of H | 11.5 | | | |

*Iwasaki* (Mitsubishi)

| | | |
|---|---|---|
| Iwasaki Hisaya | H of H | Iwasaki Takako |
| Iwasaki Hikoyata | | Iwasaki Katsutaro |
| Iwasaki Takaya | | Iwasaki Yasuya |
| Iwasaki Tsuneya | | Iwasaki Teruya |
| Iwasaki Tadao | H of H | Iwasaki Yao |
| Iwasaki Yoshiko | | |

*Sumitomo*

| | | |
|---|---|---|
| Sumitomo Kichizaemon | H of H | Sumitomo Yoshiteru |
| Sumitomo Kanichi | | Sumitomo Motoo |

*Yasuda*

| | | |
|---|---|---|
| Yasuda Hajime | H of H | Yasuda Senei[3] |
| Yasuda Zengoro | | Yasuda Koichiro |
| Yasuda Kusuo | | Yasuda Hikotaro |
| Yasuda Arata | | Yasuda Ryokichi |
| Yasuda Yoriko | | Yasuda Zenhachiro |

*Aikawa* (Nissan)

Aikawa Yoshisuke H of H

*Asano*

| | | |
|---|---|---|
| Asano Soichiro[4] | H of H | Asano Hachiro |
| Asano Ryozo | | Asano Yoshio |

[1] Associate families received 3.9% of House-of-Mitsui property according to the division specified in Article 28 of the 1900 will. A typographical error resulted in the HCLC publishing 3.6% instead of 3.9% as the share of each of the associate families.

[2] Mitsui Takateru died January 8, 1944. His heir, Mitsui Takayoshi, was named November 26, 1947.

[3] Yasuda Senei died April 17, 1947. His heir, Yasuda Takeo, was named August 7, 1947.

[4] Asano Soichiro died November 29, 1947.

| | | | |
|---|---|---|---|
| *Furukawa* | | | |
| Furukawa Jujun | H of H | Nakagawa Suekichi | H of H |
| *Okura* | | | |
| Okura Kishichiro | H of H | Okura Kumema | |
| Okura Yoshio | | Okura Hikoichiro | |
| *Nakajima* (Nakajima Aircraft, renamed Fuji Industries) | | | |
| Nakajima Chikuhei[5] | H of H | Nakajima Kimihei | |
| Nakajima Kiyoichi[6] | | Nakajima Chuhei | |
| Nakajima Monkichi | | | |

[5] Nakajima Chikuhei died October 29, 1949.
[6] Nakajima Kiyoichi died July 20, 1947.

SOURCE: HCLC, *Zaibatsu Dissolution*, data vol., pp. 2-3.

# Appendix VI

## A comparison of companies listed by the HCLC as subsidiaries of the 10 designated *Zaibatsu* combines, by the Ministry of Finance as "restricted concerns," and by the HCLC as subsidiaries of the 10 *Zaibatsu* family groups

| *10 Zaibatsu Combines* | *10 Zaibatsu Combines* | *Restricted Concerns* | *Zaibatsu Family Groups* |
|---|---|---|---|
| Mitsui Honsha | 75 | 92 | |
| Trading | 49 | | |
| Mining | 29 | | |
| Chemical | 8 | | |
| Shipping | 14 | | |
| Hokkaido Colliery & Steamship | 15 | | |
| Tokyo Shibaura Electric | 104 | 31 | |
| Total | 294 | 123 | 405 |
| Mitsubishi Honsha | 41 | 38 | |
| Trading | 58 | | |
| Heavy Industries | 30 | | |
| Electric | 33 | | |
| Mining | 22 | | |
| Chemical | 23 | | |
| N.Y.K. | 34 | 30 | |
| Total | 241 | 68 | 249 |
| Sumitomo Honsha | 29 | 31 | |
| Electric Industries | 33 | | |
| Metal Industries | 43 | | |
| Japan Electric (f. Sumitomo Communications) | 27 | | |
| Chemical | 16 | | |
| Mining | 18 | | |
| OSK | | 33 | |
| Total | 166 | 64 | 239 |

| | | | |
|---|---|---|---|
| Yasuda Hozensha | 30 | 29 | |
| Oki Electric | 4 | 23 | |
| Oki Electric Securities | 26 | | |
| Total | 60 | 52 | 110 |
| Nissan, Aikawa Gikai | 5 | 5 | |
| Nissan Chemical | 34 | 33 | |
| Nippon Mining | 25 | | |
| Hitachi | 41 | 36 | |
| Manchurian Investment Sec. | 74 | 18 | |
| Total | 179 | 92 | 210 |
| Asano Honsha | 21 | 7 | |
| Trading | 24 | | |
| Nippon Kokan (Steel Pipe) | 14 | | |
| Total | 59 | 7 | 83 |
| Furukawa Mining | 16 | 13 | |
| Furukawa Electric Industries | 37 | | |
| Total | 53 | 13 | 88 |
| Okura Mining | 36 | 29 | |
| Naigai Trading | 22 | | |
| Total | 58 | 29 | 77 |
| Fuji Industries (formerly Nakajima) | 68 | 66 | 173 |
| Nomura Gomei | 19 | 19 | 48 |
| Total for 10 designated *Zaibatsu* | 1,197 | 533 | 1,682 |
| *Other Zaibatsu Combines* | | | |
| Japan Nitrogenous Fertilizer (Nippon Chisso Hiryo (Nitchitsu)) | | 30 | |
| Japan Soda (Nippon Soda (Nisso)) | | 8 | |
| Riken Industries (Okochi) | | 25 | |
| Shibusawa | | 6 | |
| Showa Electric (Mori) | | 17 | |
| Matsushita Electric (Matsushita) | | 33 | |
| Subtotal | 0 | 119 | 0 |

APPENDIX VI

| | | | |
|---|---|---|---|
| *Textile Companies* | | | |
| cotton spinning companies | | | |
| Daiken Industrial | | 48 | |
| Dainippon Cotton Spinning | | 28 | |
| Daiwa Cotton Spinning | | 11 | |
| Fuji Spinning | | 14 | |
| Kanegafuchi Cotton Spinning | | 82 | |
| Kurashiki Spinning | | 15 | |
| Naigai Cotton Spinning | | 12 | |
| Nisshin Cotton Spinning | | 12 | |
| Shikishima Cotton Spinning | | 19 | |
| Toyo Cotton Spinning | | 65 | |
| Subtotal | 0 | 306 | 0 |
| other textile companies | | | |
| Gunze Silk | | 11 | |
| Teikoku Rayon | | 5 | |
| Japan Woolen | | 17 | |
| Katakura Industrial | | 14 | |
| Subtotal | 0 | 47 | 0 |
| Total | 0 | 353 | 0 |
| *Other Companies* | | | |
| Hayashikane Trading | | 12 | |
| Japan Iron and Steel | | 34 | |
| Japan Radio | | 23 | |
| Kawasaki Heavy Industries | | 19 | |
| *Other Companies* | | | |
| Kobe Steel Works | | 7 | |
| Nichiden Industries | | 14 | |
| Oji Paper | | 42 | |
| Teikoku Mining Development | | 22 | |
| Ube Industrial | | 1 | |
| Yamashita Steamship | | 24 | |
| Total | 0 | 198 | 0 |
| Grand Total | 1,197 | 1,203 | 1,682 |

Sources and notes: Companies listed as subsidiaries of the 10 *zaibatsu* combines: HCLC, *Zaibatsu Dissolution*, data vol., pp. 346-95; companies designated as "Restricted Concerns": GHQ-SCAP, "History of the Nonmilitary Activities of the Occupation of Japan," Vol. X, *Reform of Business Enterprise*, Part A, "Elimination of *Zaibatsu* Control, 1945 through June 1950," Appendix 1-k (which, in turn, is taken from the Restricted Concerns Section, Financial Bureau, Ministry of Finance), Office of Military History, Washington, D.C. Companies designated as subsidiaries of the 10 *zaibatsu* family groups: from folder marked, "Zaibatsu Appointees Examination Section—Prime Minister's Office," World War II Records Division, National Archives, Suitland, Md. A listing by individual companies of the first four of the eight categories will be found in HCLC, *Laws, Rules, Regulations*, pp. 103-16.

# Appendix VII

## Personnel Interlocks Among the Principal Companies of the Mitsui, Mitsubishi, Sumitomo, and Yasuda Combines, 1945 and 1937

(1) For an understanding of personnel ties within the combines it is important to bear in mind that the following tables relate to company interlocks. They do not show family and other ties except as these occur in corporate interlocks. For example, in Table I, Mitsui Mining is shown with no ties through Mitsui Takaharu, a director, who was head of one of the five principal families because he was not an officer in another company. The interlocks reproduced here are those shown in the original tables. It would appear that certain omissions have occurred in the source tables.

(2) Holding Company-subsidiaries interlocks are before the double line; interlocks among subsidiaries follow it.

(3) The nomenclature of office among these companies tends to be particularistic. Effort has been made to represent offices in general terminology, maintaining distinctions of rank.

(4) In the war's end tables earlier data have in some instances been substituted on the original tables. The notes to this effect have not been reproduced.

(5) Because of the confusion of company names in the case of the Sumitomo combine arising out of postwar name changes, both names have been included in Table 5.

(6) Abbreviations employed:

(a) among companies:

f = formerly

(b) among officers:

| | |
|---|---|
| P | president |
| VP | vice president |
| Chr | chairman |
| Mgr D | managing director |
| St D | standing director |

| | |
|---|---|
| St A | standing auditor |
| D | director |
| ADV | advisor |
| A | auditor |

Source: HCLC, *Zaibatsu Dissolution*, separately published appendix, "Personnel Interlocks Among the Principal Companies of the Big Four Zaibatsu" ("Shi Dai Zaibatsu Kei Shuyo Kaisha Jinteki Koryuen").

Note: I am indebted to Kuwabara Makoto of the National Diet Library; and Fujita Fujio, director of research, and Suzuki Yasuzo, of the staff, of the Mitsubishi Economic Research Institute for major assistance on the readings of officer names. Because highly unusual readings of Chinese characters are, at times, employed in personal names, and because these tables relate to persons who were officers 25 to 30 years ago, there may be a number of inaccuracies in the transliterations I have used.

Table 1: PERSONNEL INTERLOCKS IN THE MITSUI COMBINE, 1945.

| | ← HOLDING COMPANY AND SUBSIDIARIES | | | | | | | | | | | | | | | AMONG SUBSIDIARIES → | | | |
|---|---|---|---|---|---|---|---|---|---|---|---|---|---|---|---|---|---|---|---|
| | Mitsui Takaharu | Sumii Tatsuo | Matsumoto Kisashi | Sasaki Shuichi | Naruse Yugo | Koike Masaaki | Kawashima Saburo | Wacanabe Seizo | Sohara Kazusaku | Mityazaki Kiyoshi | Sasaki Shiro | Hanawa Yutaro | Tateno Takenosuke | Nagashima Yuji | Shimada Morio | Shimada Katsunosuk | Takahashi Agebumi | Niwata Shozo | Kanai Junzo |
| Holding Company | P | Mgr D | Mgr D | Mgr D | Mgr D | D | D | D | D | D | D | D | D | A | A | | | | |
| Mitsui Life Insurance | | | | | D | | | P | | | | | | | | | | | |
| Teikoku Bank | | | | | | | | | | | | | | | | | | | |
| Mitsui Trust | | | | | | D | | | | | | | | | P | | | | |
| Mitsui Wood Fabricating | | | | | | | | | | | A | | | | | | | | |
| Mitsui Agr. & Forestry | | | | | | Chr | | | | | | | | | | | | | |
| Mitsui Mining | | | D | | | | P | | D | | | | | | | | | | |
| Japan Steel Works | | | | | | | | | | | | | | | | D | | | |
| Mitsui Real Estate | | | | | D | | | | | | P | | | | | | | | |
| Mitsui Fat & Chemical | | | | | | | | | | | | | | | | | | | |
| Sanki Engineering | | | | | | | | | | | | | | | | | | | |
| Hokkaido Colliery & SS | | | | | | | D | | | | | | | | | Chr | | | |
| Taisho Marine & Fire Ins. | | | | | A | | | | | D | | | | | | | | | |
| Mitsui Wooden Shipbldg. | | | | D | | | | | | | | | | | | | A | D | |
| Showa Aircraft | | | D | | | | | | | | | D | D | | | | | | |
| Mitsui Shipbuilding | | | | D | | | | | | | | P | | | | | | Mgr D | A |
| Mitsui Shipping | | | | Mgr D | | | | | | | | | | | | | | | A |
| Mitsui Trading | | D | | | | | | | | P | | | | | | | A | | |
| Mitsui Chemical | | | | D | | | | | P | | | | | | | | | | |
| Mitsui Warehouse | | | P | | | | | | | | | | | | | | | | |
| Toyo Menka | | | D | | | | | | | D | | | | | | | | | |
| Japan Flour Milling | | | | | | | | | | | | | | | | | | | |
| Toyo Rayon | | | | | | | | | | | | | | | | | | | |
| Mitsui Precision Mach. | | | D | | | | | | | | | | P | | | | | | |
| Positions Held | 1 | 2 | 6 | 5 | 4 | 3 | 3 | 2 | 3 | 4 | 3 | 3 | 3 | 1 | 2 | 2 | 2 | 2 | 2 |

| | Nakane Masayoshi | Miyamoto Kunio | Kami Amane | Koizumi Hidekichi | Tashiro Toshio | Imai Tominosuke | Watanabe Kojiro | Nakajima Saburo | Mitsui Takateru | Takahashi Seigo | Yamanaka Seizaburo | Joki Masanao | Mitsui Takaatsu | Mitsui Takahisa | Mitsui Takaakira | Nakamura Yonehei | Inoue Itsuro | Interlocking Officers |
|---|---|---|---|---|---|---|---|---|---|---|---|---|---|---|---|---|---|---|
| Holding Company | | | | | | | | | | | | | | | | | | |
| Mitsui Life Insurance | | | | | | | | | | | | | | | | | | 2 |
| Teikoku·Bank | | | | | | | | | | | | | | D | | | | 1 |
| Mitsui Trust | | | | | | | | | | | | | D | | A | | | 4 |
| Mitsui Wood Fabricating | | | D | D | | | | D | | A | P | D | | | | | | 7 |
| Mitsui Agr. & Forestry | | | | | | | | | | | | | | | | | | 1 |
| Mitsui Mining | | | | | Mgr<br>D | A | | | D | | | | | | | | | 6 |
| Japan Steel Works | A | | | | | | | D | | | | | | | | | | 3 |
| Mitsui Real Estate | | | A | | | | | | | | | | | | | | A | 4 |
| Mitsui Fat & Chemical | | | | | | | | | | | | | | | | | | 0 |
| Sanki Engineering | | | | | | | | | | | | | | | | | | 0 |
| Hokkaido Colliery & SS | St<br>D | | | | | | A | | | | | | | | | | | 4 |
| Taisho Marine & Fire Ins. | | | | | | | | | | | | | | | | | | 2 |
| Mitsui Wooden Shipbldg. | | A | | P | | | | | | | D | | | | | | | 6 |
| Showa Aircraft | | | | | | | | | | | | | | | | | | 3 |
| Mitsui Shipbuilding | | | | | | | | | | | | | | D | | | | 4 |
| Mitsui Shipping | D | | | D | | | | | P | D | | | | | | | | 7 |
| Mitsui Trading | | A | | | | | | | | D | | Mgr<br>D | A | | | D | | 8 |
| Mitsui Chemical | | | | | D | Mgr<br>D | | | | | | | | | | | | 4 |
| Mitsui Warehouse | | | | | | | | | | | | | | | | | | 1 |
| Toyo Menka | | | | | | | | | | | | | | | | | | 2 |
| Japan Flour Milling | | | | | | | | | | | | | | | | | | 0 |
| Toyo Rayon | | | | | | | | | | | | | | | | D | A | 2 |
| Mitsui Precision Mach. | | | | | | | A | | | | | | | | St<br>A | | | 4 |
| Positions Held | 3 | 2 | 2 | 3 | 2 | 2 | 2 | 2 | 2 | 3 | 2 | 2 | 2 | 2 | 2 | 2 | 2 | |

Table 2: PERSONNEL INTERLOCKS IN THE MITSUI COMBINE, 1937.

| | ← HOLDING COMPANY AND SUBSIDIARIES | | | | | | | | | | AMONG SUBSIDIARIES → | | | | | | | | | | | | | | |
|---|---|---|---|---|---|---|---|---|---|---|---|---|---|---|---|---|---|---|---|---|---|---|---|---|---|
| | Mitsui Takaharu | Nanjo Kaneo | Shimada Katsunosuke | Kaneko Kenjiro | Inoue Jihei | Ogata Jiro | Fukushima Kisanji | Nagashima Yuji | Mitsui Morinosuke | Mitsui Takaharu | Mikuni Shojiro | Isomura Toyotaro | Tsuji Shunichiro | Mandai Junshiro | Tajima Shigeji | Mukai Tadaharu | Sasada Akio | Mitsui Takateru | Kajio Katsumi[a] | Ota Shizuo | Ishida Reisuke | Hara Kunizo | Ohashi Shintaro | Matsui Kazumune | Interlocking Officers |
| Holding Company | P | Mgr D | Mgr D | Mgr D | St D | St D | D | D | A | A | | | | | | | | | | | | | | | |
| Mitsui Life Ins. | | | | D | | | | | | | | | | | | | | D | | | | D | | | 3 |
| Mitsui Bank | | | | D | | | | | | D | | | | Chr | | | | | | | | D | A | D | 6 |
| Mitsui Trust | | | | D | | | | | | D | | | | D | | | | | | | | | D | Chr | 5 |
| Nitto Agr. & Forestry Colonization | | | Chr | | | | | | | | | | | | | | | | | | | | | | 1 |
| Mitsui Mining | | | D | | | Chr | | | D | | | | St A | | | | | | | | | | | | 4 |
| Japan Steel Works | | D | | | | | | | | | A | Chr | | | | | | | | | | | | | 3 |
| Toyo Steel Works | | | | | | | | | | | | | | | D | | | | | | | | | | 1 |
| Hokkaido Colliery and Steamship | | | D | | | | | | | | Mgr D | Chr | A | | | | | | | | | | | | 4 |
| Mitsui Trading | | | | D | Chr | | | | | D | | | | | Mgr D | St D | A | A | St A | St D | St D | | | | 10 |
| Taisho Marine & Fire Insurance | | | | | | | | | | | | | | | | D | | | | | | | | | 1 |
| Mitsui Warehouse | | | D | | | | | | | | | | | | | | | | | Chr | | | | | 2 |
| Toyo Menka | | | | | | | | | | | | | | | | | | | | D | D | | | | 2 |
| Toyo Rayon | | | | | | | | | | | | | | | | | D | | | | D | | | | 2 |
| Japan Flour Milling | | | | | | | | | | | | | | | | D | | | A | | | | | | 2 |
| Positions Held | 1 | 2 | 5 | 5 | 2 | 2 | 1 | 1 | 2 | 4 | 2 | 2 | 2 | 2 | 2 | 3 | 2 | 2 | 2 | 3 | 3 | 2 | 2 | 2 | |

[a]The assumption is that the printed first character of the surname was intended to be "kaji," "oar," not "ne," "root."

Table 3: PERSONNEL INTERLOCKS IN THE MITSUBISHI COMBINE, 1945.

| | ← HOLDING COMPANY AND SUBSIDIARIES | | | | | | | | | | | | | | | | | AMONG → SUBSIDIARIES |
|---|---|---|---|---|---|---|---|---|---|---|---|---|---|---|---|---|---|---|
| | Iwasaki Koyata | Iwasaki Hikoyata | Funada Kazuo | Hirai Cho | Suzuki Harunosuke | Kato Takeo | Yamamuro Subun | Mihashi Shinzo | Shiba Koshiro | Ikeda Kamesaburo | Motoyoshi Shintaro | Komura Sentaro | Miyazaki Komakichi | Tanaka Kanzo | Suzuki Sachie | Maruyama Hideya | Hatano Yoshio | Ueno Fukusaburo |
| Holding Company | P | VP | Mgr D | Mgr D | Mgr D | St D | St D | St D | D | D | D | D | D | D | A | A | A | |
| Mitsubishi Heavy Ind. | D | D | D | | A | A | A | | | | P | | A | A | | | | |
| Mitsubishi Trust | D | D | | | A | D | P | | | | | | | | A | | | |
| Mitsubishi Trading | D | D | D | | A | A | | A | | | D | D | | P | | | | D |
| Mitsubishi Oil | | | | D | | | | | | D | | D | | | | | | |
| Mitsubishi Electric | D | D | D | | A | | A | | | | D | D | P | D | | | D | |
| Tokyo Marine & Fire Ins. | D | | D | | | D | A | | | | | | | | D | D | | |
| Meiji Life Insurance | | | D | | | D | | | | | | | | | D | D | | |
| M. Chemical Machinery | | | | D | | | | | | D | | | P | | | | | |
| Mitsubishi Steamship | | | | | A | | | | | | | | | D | | | | Chr |
| Mitsubishi Paper | | | | | | A | | | | | | | | | | | | |
| Japan Steel Construction | | | | | D | | | | | | D | | D | | | | | |
| Japan Aluminum | | | D | | | | | | | D | | P | | | | | | |
| Japan Optical | | | | A | | | | | Chr | | D | | D | | | | P | |
| Mitsubishi Chemical | D | | | D | A | A | A | | | P | | D | | | | | | |
| Mitsubishi Bank | | D | D | | | P | D | | | | | | | | | | | |
| Mitsubishi Mining | D | D | D | | A | A | A | | | D | | P | | A | | | | |
| Mitsubishi Steel | D | | | D | A | D | | | | | P | D | D | | | | | |
| Mitsubishi Warehouse | D | | D | | | | | | | | | | | A | | | | |
| Mitsubishi Real Estate | | | | D | | | P | | | | | | | | | | | |
| Positions Held | 10 | 7 | 10 | 7 | 10 | 11 | 9 | 2 | 2 | 6 | 7 | 8 | 7 | 7 | 4 | 3 | 3 | 2 |

(TABLE 3. CONTINUED)

| | Iwata Chu | Hazama Shiro | Suzuki Shiro | Takagi Kenkichi | Asakura Makoto | Hara Kozo | Iino Koji | Okubo Shigeo | Goto Naota | Hattori Ichiro | Horiuchi Yasakichi | Awata Yotaro | Interlocking Officers |
|---|---|---|---|---|---|---|---|---|---|---|---|---|---|
| **Holding Company** | | | | | | | | | | | | | |
| **Mitsubishi Heavy Ind.** | | | | | | Mgr D | | | St D | | | | 11 |
| **Mitsubishi Trust** | | | | | | | | | | | | St D | 7 |
| **Mitsubishi Trading** | | A | St D | | | | St D | D | | Mgr D | | | 15 |
| **Mitsubishi Oil** | | | D | A | A | | | P | D | | | | 8 |
| **Mitsubishi Electric** | | St D | | A | | | | | | | | | 12 |
| **Tokyo Marine & Fire Ins.** | D | | | | | | | | | | Mgr D | | 8 |
| **Meiji Life Insurance** | | | | | | | | | | | | | 4 |
| **M. Chemical Machinery** | | | | | | | D | | | | | | 4 |
| **Mitsubishi Steamship** | | | D | | | | | | | | | | 4 |
| **Mitsubishi Paper** | | | | | | | | | | | | | 1 |
| **Japan Steel Construction** | | D | | | A | | | | | D | | | 6 |
| **Japan Aluminum** | | | | | | | | | | | | | 3 |
| **Japan Optical** | | | | | | A | | | | | | | 6 |
| **Mitsubishi Chemical** | | | | | | | | | | | | | 7 |
| **Mitsubishi Bank** | A | | | St D | | | | | | | | | 6 |
| **Mitsubishi Mining** | | | | | | | | | | | | | 9 |
| **Mitsubishi Steel** | | | | | | A | | | | | | | 8 |
| **Mitsubishi Warehouse** | | | | | | | | | | | | A | 4 |
| **Mitsubishi Real Estate** | | | | | | | | | | | D | A | 4 |
| **Positions Held** | 2 | 3 | 3 | 3 | 2 | 3 | 2 | 2 | 2 | 2 | 2 | 3 | |

Table 4: PERSONNEL INTERLOCKS IN THE MITSUBISHI COMBINE, 1937.

| | ← HOLDING COMPANY AND SUBSIDIARIES | | | | | | AMONG SUBSIDIARIES → | | | |
|---|---|---|---|---|---|---|---|---|---|---|
| | Iwasaki Koyata | Iwasaki Hikoyata | Kushida Manzo | Miyoshi Shigeto | Nagahara Nobuo | Sato Umetaro | Ono Masakichi | Suzuki Sachie | Kameyama Shunzo | Mishima Seiichi |
| Holding Company | P | VP | Mgr D | ST D | ST D | D | | | | |
| Mitsubishi Heavy Ind. | | D | | | A | | | | | |
| Mitsubishi Trust | D | | D | | A | | | | | |
| Mitsubishi Trading | | | | | A | | | | | D |
| Mitsubishi Oil | | | | P | | | | | | |
| Tokyo Marine Fire Ins. | D | | D | | A | | | Mgr D | St D | |
| M. Marine Fire Ins. | | | D | | A | | | D | St D | |
| Meiji Life Insurance | | | Chr | | | | | | | |
| M. Chemical Machinery | | | | | | | D | | | A |
| Mitsubishi Paper | | | | | | | | | | |
| Japan Construction | | | | | | | | | | |
| Japan Aluminum | | | | | | | | | | |
| Japan Optical | | | | | | | | | | |
| Mitsubishi Bank | D | D | D | | A | | | | | |
| Mitsubishi Mining | D | | A | | | | | | | |
| Mitsubishi Warehouse | | | D | | A | | | | | |
| Mitsubishi Real Estate | | | | | D | | | | | |
| Mitsubishi Electric | | | | | A | | | | | |
| Japan Chemical | | | | | | | D | | | |
| Positions Held | 5 | 3 | 8 | 2 | 10 | 1 | 2 | 2 | 2 | 2 |

(TABLE 4. CONTINUED)

| | Kawarabayashi Junjiro | Horiuchi Yasukichi | Miyazaki Komakichi | Hara Kozo | Shiba Koshiro | Ikeda Kamezaburo | Kagami Kamakichi | Kato Takeo | Muto Matsuji | Hayakawa Mosaburo | Hirai Sumi | Kawai Gempachi | Yamashita Motomi | Seta Kiyoshi | Funada Kazuo | Kawade Suteji | Yamamuro Sobun | Awata Yotaro | Interlocking Officers |
|---|---|---|---|---|---|---|---|---|---|---|---|---|---|---|---|---|---|---|---|
| Holding Company | | | | | | | | | | | | | | | | | | | |
| Mitsubishi Heavy Ind. | | | | D | Chr | | | | A | | | D | | | | | A | | 7 |
| Mitsubishi Trust | | | | | | | D | A | | | | | | D | | | Chr | St D | 8 |
| Mitsubishi Trading | | | | | | | | | A | Mgr D | D | A | | A | Chr | A | | | 9 |
| Mitsubishi Oil | | | | | | D | | | | D | St D | | | | | | | | 4 |
| Tokyo Marine Fire Ins. | | St D | | | | | Chr | A | | | | | | | | | | | 8 |
| M. Marine Fire Ins. | | | | | | | Chr | A | | | | | | | | | | | 6 |
| Meiji Life Insurance | Mgr D | | | | | | D | D | | | | | | A | | | | | 5 |
| M. Chemical Machinery | | | D | A | | D | | | | | | | | | | | | | 5 |
| Mitsubishi Paper | | | | | | | | | | | | | | | | | | | 0 |
| Japan Construction | | | | | | | | | | | | | | | | | | | 0 |
| Japan Aluminum | | | | | | | D | | | | | | | | | | | | 1 |
| Japan Optical | | | | | Chr | | | | | | | | | | | | | | 1 |
| Mitsubishi Bank | | | | | | | A | Mgr D | | | | | | Chr | | | D | | 8 |
| Mitsubishi Mining | | | | | | Mgr D | | | | | | | St D | | D | Chr | | | 6 |
| Mitsubishi Warehouse | | | | | | | | A | | | | | | | | | | | 3 |
| Mitsubishi Real Estate | A | D | | | | | | | | | | | | | | | D | A | 5 |
| Mitsubishi Electric | | | Mgr D | | | | | | A | | | Chr | | A | D | D | | | 7 |
| Japan Chemical | | | | | | St D | | | A | | | | D | | | D | | | 5 |
| Positions Held | 2 | 2 | 2 | 2 | 2 | 4 | 6 | 5 | 4 | 2 | 2 | 3 | 2 | 5 | 3 | 4 | 4 | 2 | |

Table 5: PERSONNEL INTERLOCKS IN THE SUMITOMO COMBINE, 1945.

| | ← HOLDING COMPANY AND SUBSIDIARIES; | | | | | | | | | | | AMONG SUBSIDIARIES → | | | | | | | | |
|---|---|---|---|---|---|---|---|---|---|---|---|---|---|---|---|---|---|---|---|---|
| | Sumitomo Kichizaemon | Furuta Shunosuke | Okahashi Rin | Yoshida Sadakichi | Haruta Hiroshi | Mimura Kiichi | Kitazawa Keijiro | Kawai Shosaburo | Kajii Takeshi | Tanaka Yoshio | Oshima Kanzo | Fukuyama Zenjiro | Shoku Ko | Yabe Chuji | Ohira Kensaku | Yoshinari Muneo | Yamazaki Takeji | Matsui Takanaga | Matsumoto Osamu | Interlocking Officers |
| Holding Company | P | Mgr D | D | D | D | D | D | D | D | D | A | | | | | | | | | |
| Sumitomo Warehouse | | Chr | D | | | | D | | | | A | | | | | | | D | | 5 |
| f. Sumitomo Machinery Shikoku Machinery | | D | A | | | Chr | | | | | A | | | | | D | | | | 5 |
| Sumitomo Electric Ind. f. S. Electric Wire | | Chr | A | | | | D | A | | D | A | | | | | | | | | 6 |
| f. Sumitomo Metal Ind. Fuso Metal Ind. | | Chr | A | D | P | | | | | | A | | | | | VP | | | D | 7 |
| S. Coop. Elect. Power f. Shikoku Coop. E.P. | | Chr | | D | | | | A | | | A | | | | | | D | | | 5 |
| Japan Engineering f. Osaka North Harbor | | Chr | D | | D | | P | A | | | A | A | | | | | | | | 7 |
| f. S. Communications Japan Electric | | Chr | | | | | | A | P | D | A | | | | | | | | | 5 |
| Nippon Chemical Ind. | | Chr | | D | D | | | | | | | | A | | | | | | D | 5 |
| f. Sumitomo Mining Seika Mining | D | Chr | A | D | | P | | | | | A | | | | | | | | | 6 |
| Sumitomo Trust | D | D | D | | | | | | | | A | P | | | | | | | | 5 |
| f. Sumitomo Chemical Nisshin Chemical | | Chr | A | P | D | | | | | D | A | | Mgr D | D | | | | | | 8 |
| Sumitomo Bank | D | D | P | | | | D | | | | A | D | | | Chr | | | | | 7 |
| Sumitomo Aluminum Reduction | | D | | Chr | D | D | | | | | A | | | Mgr D | | | St D | | | 7 |
| Sumitomo Life Ins. | D | Chr | D | | | | D | | | | A | | | | | | | P | | 6 |
| Osaka S. Marine, Fire Ins. f. Fuson Marine, Fire Ins. | | | | | | | A | | | | | | | | Chr | | | | | 2 |
| Positions Held | 5 | 15 | 11 | 7 | 6 | 4 | 7 | 5 | 2 | 4 | 14 | 3 | 2 | 2 | 2 | 2 | 2 | 2 | 2 | |

Table 6: PERSONNEL INTERLOCKS IN THE SUMITOMO COMBINE, 1937.

| | ← HOLDING COMPANY AND SUBSIDIARIES | | | | | | | | | | AMONG SUBSIDIARIES → | | | | | | | | | |
|---|---|---|---|---|---|---|---|---|---|---|---|---|---|---|---|---|---|---|---|---|
| | Sumitomo Kichizaemon | Ogura Masatsune | Yashiro Norihiko | Matsumoto Junkichi | Imamura Yukio | Kokufu Seiichi | Furuta Shunnosuke | Yamamoto Nobuo | Ohira Kensaku | Okabashi Hayashi | Mimura Kiichi | Arakawa Eiji | Oya Atsushi | Yoshida Sadakichi | Yoshida Shinichi | Yazaki Soji | Yajima Tomizo | Araki Hiroshi | J. E. Fram | Interlocking Officers |
| Holding Company | P | St D | D | D | D | D | D | D | A | A | | | | | | | | | | |
| Sumitomo Warehouse | D | Chr | D | A | A | D | | | | | | | | | | | | | | 6 |
| Sumitomo Mach. Ind. | | Chr | | A | | D | | D | | | St D | A | | | | | | D | | 7 |
| Sumitomo Electric Wire | | Chr | | A | A | | | D | A | | | | | | | | | | D | 6 |
| Sumitomo Metal Ind. | | Chr | A | A | A | D | Mgr D | D | | | | | | | | | | Mgr D | | 8 |
| Shikoku Coop. Elect. Power | | Chr | | A | | A | | D | | | D | | D | St D | | | | | | 7 |
| Osaka North Harbor | | Chr | D | A | A | D | | | | | | | | | | | | | | 5 |
| Sumitomo Communications | | | | | | | | D | | | | | | | | | A | | D | 3 |
| Sumitomo Mining | D | Chr | A | A | | | | Mgr D | | | Mgr D | St D | D | D | | | | | | 9 |
| Sumitomo Chemicals | | Chr | A | A | | D | | D | | | D | | Mgr D | | | St D | | | | 8 |
| Sumitomo Bank | D | D | Chr | | D | | | | Mgr D | St D | | | | | A | | | | | 7 |
| Sumitomo Aluminum | | Chr | | A | | A | | D | | | | | | | | D | | | | 5 |
| Sumitomo Life Insurance | D | Chr | D | A | A | | | | | | | | | | | | | | | 6 |
| Fuso Marine & Fire Ins. | | Chr | | | | | | | | | | | | | | | A | | | 1 |
| Sumitomo Trust | D | Chr | D | A | Mgr D | | | | | | | | | | D | | | | | 6 |
| Positions Held | 6 | 14 | 9 | 12 | 8 | 8 | 2 | 9 | 3 | 2 | 4 | 2 | 3 | 2 | 2 | 2 | 2 | 2 | 2 | |

Table 7: PERSONNEL INTERLOCKS IN THE YASUDA COMBINE, 1945.

| | ← HOLDING COMPANY AND SUBSIDIARIES | | | | | AMONG SUBSIDIARIES → | | | | | | | | | | | |
|---|---|---|---|---|---|---|---|---|---|---|---|---|---|---|---|---|---|
| | Yasuda Hajime | Yasuda Kusuo | Yasuda Hikoshiro | Takei Daisuke | Yasuda Zengoro | Yanai Yuzo | Yasuda Hikotaro | Nakajima Aisaku | Kitagawa Keiji | Kawasaki Sugao | Sonobe Sen | Annen Seiichi | Yasuda Sadashiro | Yasuda Ryokichi | Ishige Takejiro | Tokura Sotaro | Interlocking Officers |
| Holding Company | P | D | D | D | Adv | | | | | | | | | | | | |
| Yasuda Warehouse f. Taiyo Warehouse | | | | | | | | | | | | | D | D | P | | 3 |
| Yasuda Trust | | | | | Chr | | | | | | D | P | | | | | 3 |
| Yasuda Bank | Chr | D | A | P | D | | | D | | D | | VP | | | | | 8 |
| Teikoku Sen-i | | | | | Chr | | | | | | | | | | | | 1 |
| Toyo Steamship | | | | | | A | St<br>A | | | | | | | | | | 3 |
| Yasuda Enterprise f. Daiwa Enterprise | Chr | D | D | D | | Mgr<br>D | | St<br>D | | | A | | | | | | 7 |
| Tokyo Construction | | | | | D | | | | D | | | | | | P | A | 4 |
| Yasuda Life Ins. | Chr | | | | | | D | | St<br>D | | | | | | | | 3 |
| Yasuda Marine Fire Insurance | | | | | D | | | | | A | | | A | A | | P | 6 |
| Positions Held | 5 | 3 | 3 | 4 | 6 | 2 | 2 | 2 | 2 | 2 | 2 | 2 | 2 | 2 | 2 | 2 | |

## APPENDIX VII

Table 8: PERSONNEL INTERLOCKS IN THE YASUDA COMBINE, 1937.

| | ← HOLDING COMPANY AND SUBSIDIARIES | | | | | | AMONG SUBSIDIARIES → | | | | | |
|---|---|---|---|---|---|---|---|---|---|---|---|---|
| | Yasuda Hajime | Yasuda Zengoro | Yasuda Zenshiro | Mori Hirozo | Kawasaki Sugao | Tozawa Yoshiki | Matsumoto Joji | Ohashi Shintaro | Yasuda Hikoshiro | Hamada Yuzo | Saito Junzo | Interlocking Officers |
| Holding Company | P | D | D | D | D | D | | | | | | |
| Taiyo Warehouse | | | | | | | | | D | | | 1 |
| Yasuda Trust | | P | A | D | | Mgr D | | | | A | D | 6 |
| Yasuda Bank | P | D | D | VP | D | | | | A | St D | St D | 8 |
| Teikoku Sen-i | | P | | | | | A | D | | | | 3 |
| Toyo Steamship | | | | | | | | | | | | 0 |
| Daiwa Enterprise | | A | Chr | | | | | | | | | 2 |
| Tokyo Building | | D | | | D | | | D | | | | 3 |
| Yasuda Life Ins. | P | D | D | | | | A | | | | | 4 |
| Positions Held | 3 | 7 | 5 | 3 | 3 | 2 | 2 | 2 | 2 | 2 | 2 | |

# APPENDIX VII

Table 9: CARTELS FORMED UNDER THE MAJOR INDUSTRIES CONTROL LAW

(F is Fujita data, A is Allen data)

| *Industry* | *Cartel* | *Membership* F | *Membership* A | *Outsiders* F | *Outsiders* A | *Control objectives, remarks* |
|---|---|---|---|---|---|---|
| cotton yarn | Japan Cotton Spinners' Association | 62 | 71 | 9 | 2 | production curtailment |
| silk yarn | Silk Spinning Industrial Association | 12 | 12 | 1 | 1 | production curtailment; market agreement |
| rayon yarn | Japan Rayon Yarn Manufacturers' Association | 10 | 19 | 3 | 2 | production curtailment; market agreement |
| foreign style paper | Japan Paper Manufacturers' Association | 9 | 11 | 2 | 1 | production curtailment; control of sales quantity (by joint control of products); agreement covers most classes with exception of newsprint |
| cardboard | Japan Cardboard Manufacturers' Association (yellow cardboard paper only) | 21 | 21 | 1 | 1 | production curtailment; price agreement |
| | Brown Cardboard Control Association | 15 | 15 | - | - | production curtailment; price agreement |
| carbide | National Carbide Joint Sales Association | 15 | 18 | 7 | 6 | production curtailment (by restriction of new equipment); joint sales (estimate of quotas, prices, purchase of raw materials), "joint accounts" |
| bleaching powder | Bleaching Powder Assoc. | 12 | 14 | 3 | 5 | production curtailment; joint sales |
| sulphuric acid | Kanto Sulphuric Acid Sales Co. | 5 | 5 | 3 | 21 | joint sales — these 2 joint sales companies have an agreement covering division of the market |
| | Kansai Sulphuric Acid Sales Co. | 9 | 9 | 8 | 17 | joint sales |
| oxygen | All Japan Association of Oxygen Manufacturers | 18 | 20 | 8 | 9 | price agreement; market agreement sales quota. Agreements are carried out through 6 joint agencies in Hokkaido, Tokyo, Nagoya, Osaka, Kobe and Kyushu |
| hydrogenated oil | Hydrogenated Oil Manufacturers' Assoc. Hydrogenated Oil Sales Co. | 7 | 10 | 2 | 0 | limitation of increase of production, control of sales proportions, sales prices and markets, and distribution of orders |

## APPENDIX VII

| | | | | | | |
|---|---|---|---|---|---|---|
| cement | Cement Manufacturers' Association | 16 | 18 | 5 | 6 | production curtailment; allotment of orders, sales price agreement, market agreement, sales quota, in Korea joint sales agreement |
| | Japan Cement Exporting Association | 16 | 16 | 5 | 7 | allotment of orders, sales price agreement, market agreement, sales quota |
| flour | Flour Joint Sales Association | 3 | - | 3 | 7 | joint sales, sales quota, purchase of products, fixing of price, joint account |
| carbon bisulphide | Sulphide Manufacturer's Association | 9 | 8 | 9 | 14 | control of sales proportions, sales quantities, markets and prices |
| refined sugar | Japan Sugar Refiners' Union | 5 | 5 | 1 | 1 | production restriction |
| pig iron | Pig Iron Joint Sales Association (producers with monthly production | 3 | - | 1 | 2 | control of sales quantities, and prices of imported pig iron and domestically produced pig iron |
| ferro-alloys | Ferro-Alloys Manufacturers Association | 8 | 7 | 6 | 9 | joint sales (control of sales, proportion and prices, solicitation and distribution of orders) |
| steel bars | Steel Wire Manufacturers' Association for Division of Markets | 10 | n.1. | 3 | n.1. | no agreements now in force |
| | Steel Products Union | 6 | 5 | 6 | 5 | production allotments; sales price agreements; agreements cover round and flat bars |
| | Kanto Steel Products Sales Association | 3 | 3 | 2 | 1 | joint sales (purchase and sale of products, price fixing, joint account); agreements cover round bars only |
| steel angles | Medium Size Steel Angles Joint Sales Assoc. | 4 | 4 | 4 | 4 | joint sales (control of sales quotas, quantity, price, solicitation and distribution of orders) |

| | | | | | | |
|---|---|---|---|---|---|---|
| steel plate | Japan Thick Plates Joint Sales Association | 4 | 4 | 2 | 4 | joint sales (control of sales proportions and prices, solicitation and distribution of orders) |
| | Medium Plates Joint Sales Association | 2 | 2 | 3 | 6 | joint sales (control of sales proportions, prices, solicitation and distribution of orders) |
| wire rods | Japan Wire Rods Joint Sales Association | 2 | 2 | 3 | 3 | joint sales (control of sales proportions, price and quantity, solicitation and distribution of orders) |
| copper plates and brass plates | Copper Plate Union | 9 | 0 | 7 | 15 | there is a Rolled Copper Association but this exercises no controlling functions |
| gasoline | Petroleum Refiners Union | 3 | 4 | 3 | 2 | control of sales proportions, quantities and prices and other terms relative thereto |
| beer | Beer Joint Sales Co. | 4 | 2 | - | 2 | joint sales (control of sales price and other terms relative to price, also sales proportions and markets), curtailment of increase in output |
| | Imperial Beer Exporting Association | 4 | 3 | - | 1 | control of business terms relative to market prices |
| coal mining and marketing | Union of Coal Mine operators | 27 | 25 | 4 | 6 | adjustment of coal shipments; control over import of Manchuria coal |
| | Showa Coal Company | 28 | 26 | 2 | 13 | control of sales proportions, quantities and prices, and other terms relative thereto |

Sources: The table occurs in several places. It is reproduced here from tables appearing in Fujita Keizo, "Cartels and Their Conflicts in Japan," Osaka University of Commerce *Journal*, December 1935 (information as of May 1935), pp. 77-79, and in a chapter prepared by G. C. Allen, in E. B. Schumpter, ed., *Industrialization of Japan and Manchukuo, 1930-1940*, pp. 719-22 (information as of July 1936). Because of disparities in the data, which may be explained wholly or in part by the time difference of a year and the difficulty of checking, the material from both tables is reproduced here. The table also occurs in Yoshida Jimbu, ed., *Japan's Cartels* (*Nihon no Karuteru*), Tokyo, 1964, p. 23, where the time reference is January 1938.

## APPENDIX VIII

# Companies Designated under Paragraph 11 of Appendix I of Cabinet and Home Affairs Ministry Ordinance No. 1 of 1947, Promulgated January 4, 1947

(Arranged alphabetically by Romanization of Japanese name)
(f. = formerly)

COMPANIES IN JAPAN

| *Romanized Name in Japanese* | *Name in Translation* |
|---|---|
| Amagasaki Seitetsu K.K. | Amagasaki Iron Mfg. Co. Ltd. |
| Asahi Denka Kogyo K.K. | Asahi Electrical Industrial Co. Ltd. |
| Asahi Kasei Kogyo K.K. | Asahi Chemical Ind. Co. Ltd. |
| Asano Bussan K.K. | Asano Trading Co. Ltd. |
| Asano Cement K.K. | Asano Cement Co. Ltd. |
| Asano Honsha | Asano Holding Co. |
| Chubu Haiden | Chubu District Electricity Distribution Co. |
| Chugoku Haiden | Chugoku District Electricity Distribution Co. |
| Daido Seiko | Daido Steel Mfg. |
| Daiken Sangyo | Daiken Industry Co. |
| Dai Nippon Heiki | Great Japan Arms Mfg. |
| Dai Nippon Boseki | Great Japan Spinning |
| Fuji Sangyo | Fuji Industrial, f. Nakajima Aircraft |
| Furukawa Denki Kogyo | Furukawa Electric Industry Co. |
| Furukawa Kogyo | Furukawa Mining |
| Fuso Kinzoku Kogyo | Fuso Metal Industries, f. Sumitomo Kinzoku |
| Gisei Kai | Sacrifice Assoc. (holding Co., Nissan-Mangyo Complex) |
| Hayashikane Shoten | Hayashikane Trading |
| Hitachi Keiki Seisakusho | Hitachi Arms Mfg. Co. |
| Hitachi Kokuki | Hitachi Aeroplane Co. |
| Hitachi Seiki | Hitachi Machine Mfg. |
| Hitachi Seisakusho | Hitachi Engineering |
| Hitachi Zohei | Hitachi Arms Mfg. |
| Hitachi Zosensho | Hitachi Shipbuilding |
| Hokkaido Tanko Kisen | Hokkaido Mining and Steamship |
| Hokuriku Haiden | Hokuriku Electricity District Distribution Co. |

| *Romanized Name in Japanese* | *Name in Translation* |
|---|---|
| Ishikawajima Jukogyo | Ishikawajima Heavy Industries |
| Kanegafuchi Boseki | Kanegafuchi Spinning |
| Kansai Haiden | Kansai District Electricity Distribution Co. |
| Kanto Haiden | Kanto District Electricity Distribution Co. |
| Katakura Kogyo | Katakura Industries |
| Kawanami Kogyo | Kawanami Industries |
| Kawasaki Jukogyo | Kawasaki Heavy Industries |
| Kawasaki Kisen | Kawasaki Steamship |
| Kawasaki Sangyo | Kawasaki Industry Co. |
| Kawasaki Sharyo | Kawasaki Rolling Stock Co. |
| Keihanshin Kyuko Dentetsu | Kyoto, Osaka, Kobe Rapid Transit Co. |
| Kinki Nippon Tetsudo | Kinki Japan Railway Co. |
| Kobe Seikosho | Kobe Steel Mfg. Co. |
| Kokusai Denki Tsushin | International Electric and Communication Co. |
| Kyushu Haiden | Kyushu District Electricity Distribution Co. |
| Meiji Seimei Hoken | Meiji Life Insurance |
| Minsei Sangyo | Minsei Industries |
| Mitsubishi Denki Kikai | Mitsubishi Electrical Machinery |
| Mitsubishi Ginko | Mitsubishi Bank |
| Mitsubishi Goshi | Mitsubishi Partnership Holding Co. |
| Mitsubishi Honsha | Mitsubishi Joint Stock Holding Co. |
| Mitsubishi Jukogyo | Mitsubishi Heavy Industries |
| Mitsubishi Kasei Kogyo | Mitsubishi Chemical Industries |
| Mitsubishi Kisen | Mitsubishi Steamship |
| Mitsubishi Kogyo | Mitsubishi Mining |
| Mitsubishi Sekiyu | Mitsubishi Petroleum |
| Mitsubishi Seiko | Mitsubishi Steel Mfg. |
| Mitsubishi Shintaku | Mitsubishi Trust |
| Mitsubishi Shoji | Mitsubishi Trading |
| Mitsubishi Soko | Mitsubishi Warehouse |
| Mitsui Bussan | Mitsui Trading |
| Mitsui Fudosan | Mitsui Real Estate |
| Mitsui Ginko | Mitsui Bank |
| Mitsui Gomei | Mitsui Partnership Holding Co. |
| Mitsui Honsha | Mitsui Joint Stock Holding Co. |
| Mitsui Kakaku Kogyo | Mitsui Chemical Industries |
| Mitsui Kozan | Mitsui Mining |
| Mitsui Mokuzai | Mitsui Lumber |
| Mitsui Seiki | Mitsui Precision Instruments |
| Mitsui Sempaku | Mitsui Shipping |

| *Romanized Name in Japanese* | *Name in Translation* |
|---|---|
| Mitsui Shintaku | Mitsui Trust |
| Mitsui Soko | Mitsui Warehouse |
| Mitsui Yushi | Mitsui Oil and Fat |
| Mitsui Zosen | Mitsui Shipbuilding |
| Mizuho Shagyo | Mizuho Industries Co. |
| Nichiden Kogyo | Nichiden Industries; contraction of Japan Electric Industries |
| Nichiro Gyogyo | Japan Russia Fishing Co. |
| Nikkoku Kogyo | Nikkoku Industries |
| Nippon Alumi | Japan Aluminum |
| Nippon Chisso Hiryo | Japan Nitrogenous Fertilizer Co. |
| Nippon Chochiku Ginko | Japan Savings Bank |
| Nippon Denki | Japan Electric Co. |
| Nippon Denko | Japan Electric Development Co. |
| Nippon Denshin Denwa | Japan Telegraph and Telephone Co. |
| Nippon Keikinzoku | Japan Light Metal Industries Co. |
| Nippon Kensetsu Sangyo | Japan Construction Industries |
| Nippon Kentetsu Kogyo | Japan Kentetsu Industries |
| Nippon Kogaku Kogyo | Japan Optical Industry Co. |
| Nippon Kogyo | Japan Mining |
| Nippon Kokan | Japan Steel Pipe |
| Nippon Musen | Japan Wireless |
| Nippon Seiko | Japan Precision Bearing Co. |
| Nippon Seikosho | Japan Steel Mfg. Works |
| Nippon Seimei Hoken | Japan Life Insurance Co. |
| Nippon Sekiyu | Japan Petroleum |
| Nippon Seitetsu | Japan Iron Manufacturing |
| Nippon Soda | Japan Soda |
| Nippon Suidan | Japan Marine Products |
| Nippon Yusen Kaisha | "NYK," Japan Mail Line |
| Nissan | acronym for Nippon Sangyo, Japan Industries |
| Nissan Kagaku Kogyo | Nissan Chemical Industries |
| Nissan Jukogyo | Nissan Heavy Industries |
| Nisshin Kagaku Kogyo | Nisshin Chemical Industries |
| Nitchitsu Kogyo Kaihatsu | Nitchitsu Mining Development |
| Nitchitsu Hainan Kogyo | Nitchitsu Hainan Mining |
| Nitchitsu Nenryo Kogyo | Nitchitsu Fuel Industries |
| Nitchitsu Shoken | Nitchitsu Securities |
| Nittetsu Kogyo | Nittetsu Mining |
| Nomura Ginko | Nomura Bank |
| Nomura Gomei | Nomura Partnership Holding Co. |
| Nomura Higashi Indo Shokusan | Nomura East Indies Colonization Co. |

| *Romanized Name in Japanese* | *Name in Translation* |
|---|---|
| Nomura Shintaku | Nomura Trust |
| Nomura Shoken | Nomura Securities |
| Oji Seishi | Oji Paper Co. |
| Oki Denki | Oki Electric Co. |
| Okura Doboku | Okura Engineering Co. |
| Okura Sangyo | Okura Industries Co. |
| Okura Kogyo | Okura Mining |
| Onoda Cement | Onoda Cement |
| Osaka Shosen Kaisha | "OSK," Osaka Commercial Line |
| Osaka Sumitomo Kasai Kaijo | Osaka Sumitomo Fire and Marine Insurance |
| Otani Jukogyo | Otani Heavy Industries |
| Riken Kogyo | Riken Industries |
| Sanki Kogyo | Sanki Engineering |
| Seika Kogyo | Seika Mining; f. Sumitomo Mining |
| Shibusawa Dozoku | Shibusawa Family Co. |
| Shikoku Kikai Kogyo | Shikoku Machine Industries Co. |
| Showa Denko | Showa Electric Industries Co. |
| Showa Hikoki | Showa Aeroplane |
| Showa Tsusho | Showa Trading |
| Sumitomo Alumi Seiren | Sumitomo Aluminum |
| Sumitomo Denki Kogyo | Sumitomo Electric Mfg. Co. |
| Sumitomo Ginko | Sumitomo Bank |
| Sumitomo Gomei | Sumitomo Partnership Holding Co. |
| Sumitomo Honsha | Sumitomo Joint Stock Holding Co. |
| Sumitomo Shintaku | Sumitomo Trust |
| Sumitomo Soko | Sumitomo Warehouse |
| Tachikawa Kokuki | Tachikawa Aeroplane Mfg. Co. |
| Taisho Kasai Kaijo | Taisho Fire and Marine Insurance |
| Teikoku Ginko | Imperial Bank |
| Teikoku Seimei Hoken | Imperial Life Insurance Co. |
| Teikoku Seni | Imperial Fiber Co. |
| Titan Kogyo | Titan Industries Co. |
| Toa Kaiun | East Asia Marine Transportation |
| Tohoku Haiden | Tohoku District Electricity Distribution Co. |
| Tohoku Shinko Alumi | Tohoku Development Aluminum |
| Tohoku Shinko Pulp | Tohoku Development Pulp |
| Tokyo Gas Co. | Tokyo Gas Co. |
| Tokyo Kaijo Hoken | Tokyo Maritime Insurance |
| Tokyo Kyuko Dentetsu | Tokyo Rapid Transit Co. |
| Tokyo Shibaura Denki | Tokyo Shibaura Electric |

## APPENDIX VIII

### COMPANIES OUTSIDE JAPAN

| *Romanized Name in Japanese* | *Name in Translation* |
|---|---|
| Auto Keikinzoku | Auto Light Metals |
| Asahi Keikinzoku | Asahi Light Metals |
| Banwa | Banwa Trading Co. |
| Chintao Seitetsu | Chintao Steel Mfg. |
| Chosen Chisso Kayaku | Korea Nitrate Powder |
| Chosen Dengyo | Korea Electric Enterprise Co. |
| Chosen Denko | Korea Electric and Engineering Co. |
| Chosen Jinzo Sekiyu | Korea Synthetic Oil |
| Chosen Kogyo Shinko | Korea Mining Development Co. |
| Chosen Oryokuko Suiden | Korea Oryoku Hydroelectric Co. |
| Chosen Sekiyu | Korea Petroleum |
| Chosen Shinko Kinzoku | Korea Development Metal Industries Co. |
| Chosen Sumitomo Keikinzoku | Korea Sumitomo Light Metals |
| Chuka Koku | Central China Aviation Co. |
| Chuka Rinsen | Central China Shipping Co. |
| Chuka Seitetsu | Central China Iron Mfg. Co. |
| Chuka Tabako | Central China Tobacco |
| Daido Tanko | Daido Coal Mining Co. |
| Fushin Tanko | Fushin Coal Mining Co. |
| Hokuhyo Tanko | Hokuhyo Coal Mining |
| Honkeiko Daitetsu | Honkeiko Coal and Iron Co. |
| Ishihara Sangyo | Ishihara Industries |
| Kachu Denki Tsushin | Central China Telegraph Co. |
| Kachu Suiden | Central China Hydroelectric Co. |
| Kachu Tetsudo | Central China Railway Co. |
| Kahoku Chisso Hiryo | North China Nitrogenous Fertilizer |
| Kahoku Dengyo | North China Electric Co. |
| Kahoku Denshin Denwa | North China Telegraph and Telephone |
| Kahoku Hatabako | North China Leaf Tobacco |
| Kahoku Jidosha | North China Automobile Co. |
| Kahoku Keikinzoku | North China Light Metals |
| Kahoku Kotsu | North China Railways Co. |
| Kahoku Seni | North China Fiber Co. |
| Kahoku Toa Tabako | North China and East Asia Tobacco |
| Kako Shogyo Ginko | Kako Commercial Bank |
| Kakuko Tanko | Kakuko Coal Mining |
| Kanegafuchi Kodai Jitsugyo | Kanegafuchi Kodai Industries Co. |
| Karufuto Kogyo | Sakhalien Mining Co. |
| Kinshu Pulp | Kinshu Pulp |
| Kitashina Seitetsu | North China Iron Mfg. |
| Kitsurin Jinzo Sekiyu | Kitsurin Synthetic Oil |
| Kobayashi Kogyo | Kobayashi Mining Co. |

| *Romanized Name in Japanese* | *Name in Translation* |
| --- | --- |
| Kokusai Unyu | International Transportation |
| Kono Ginko | Agriculture Development Bank |
| Manshu Dengyo | Manchurian Electric Works |
| Manshu Denki Kagaku Kogyo | Manchurian Electric Chemical Industries |
| Manshu Denshin Denwa | Manchurian Telegraph and Telephone |
| Manshu Eiga Kyokai | Manchurian Motion Pictures Assoc. |
| Manshu Enko | Manchurian Lead Mine Co. |
| Manshu Gosei Nenryo | Manchurian Synthetic Fuel Co. |
| Manshu Hikoki Seizo | Manchurian Aeroplane Mfg. |
| Manshu Hitachi Seisakusho | Manchurian Hitatchi Mfg. Works |
| Manshu Jidosha Seizo | Manchurian Automobile Mfg. Co. |
| Manshu Jinzo Sekiyu | Manchurian Synthetic Oil |
| Manshu Keikinzoku | Manchurian Light Metals Co. |
| Manshu Kogyo Kaihatsu | Manchurian Mining Development Co. |
| Manshu Koku | Manchurian Aviation Co. |
| Manshu Kosho | Manchurian Arsenal Co. |
| Manshu Kozan | Manchurian Mining |
| Manshu Magnesium | Manchurian Magnesium |
| Manshu Nochi Kaihatsu Kosha | Manchurian Agricultural Land Development |
| Manshu Oryokuko Suiryoku Hatsuden | Manchurian Yalu River Hydroelectric Co. |
| Manshu Seitetsu | Manchurian Iron Manufacturing |
| Manshu Sekitan Ekika Kenkyusho | Manchurian Coal Liquifaction Research |
| Manshu Sekiyu | Manchurian Oil |
| Manshu Sumitomo Kinzoku | Manchuria Sumitomo Light Metals |
| Manshu Tanko | Manchurian Coal Mining |
| Manshu Tokushu Tekko | Manchurian Special Steel |
| Manshu Toshi Shoken | Manchurian Investment Securities |
| Manshu Toyo Boseki | Manchurian Toyo Spinning |
| Mitsui Keikinzoku | Mitsui Light Metals |
| Mitsuzan Tanko | Mitsuzan Coal Mining |
| Mokyo Dengyo | Mongolian Electric Co. |
| Mokyo Denki Tsushin Setsubi | Mongolian Electric Communications Equipment Co. |
| Mozan Tekko Kaihatsu | Mozan Iron Development Co. |
| Naka Shina Gunpyo Kokanyo Busshi Kaikyu Kumiai | Central China Distributing Assoc. of Material for Exchange with Military Notes |
| Nichiman Shoji | Japan Manchurian Trading Co. |
| Nippon Koshuha Jukogyo | Japan High Frequency Heavy Industries |

| *Romanized Name in Japanese* | *Name in Translation* |
|---|---|
| Okura Jigyo | Okura Enterprise |
| Ryuen Tekko | Ryuen Iron Mining |
| Sansei Sangyo | Sansei Industries |
| Seian Tanko | Seian Coal Mining |
| Showa Seikosho | Showa Steel Mfg. Works |
| Taiwan Denryoku | Formosa Electric Power |
| Tohendo Kaitatsu | Tohendo Development |

Supreme Commander for the Allied Powers, Government Section, *Political Reorientation of Japan*, Sept. 1945-Sept. 1948, GPO, Washington, D.C., pp. 538-42. English translation of titles, with but minor exceptions, is that found in this source.

# Appendix IX

SWNCC 302/2
22 January 1947
Pages 26-53, incl.

State-War-Navy Coordinating Committee

*Statement of U.S. Policy with Respect to Excessive Concentrations of Economic Power in Japan*

*Note by the Secretaries*

The enclosure, a report by the State-War-Navy Coordinating Subcommittee for the Far East prepared on its own initiative, is circulated for consideration by the Committee.

H. W. Moseley
W. A. Schulgen
V. L. Lowrance
Secretariat

State-War-Navy Coordinating Committee

Decision Amending SWNCC 302/2

Statement of U.S. Policy with Respect to Excessive Concentrations of Economic Power in Japan

*Note by the Secretaries*

1. At its 56th Meeting on 29 April 1947, after further amending, the State-War-Navy Coordinating Committee approved SWNCC 302/2, as amended by SWNCC 302/3 and SWNCC 302/4.

2. Holders of SWNCC 302/2 are requested to substitute the attached revised pages 27-30, 33-38, 47, and 53 for the ones contained therein and destroy the superseded pages by burning.

H. W. Moseley
W. A. Schulgen
V. L. Lowrance
Secretariat

Statement of U.S. Policy with Respect to Excessive Concentrations of Economic Power in Japan

Report by the

State-War-Navy Coordinating Subcommittee for the Far East

*The Problem*

1. To determine United States policy with respect to excessive concentrations of economic power in Japan.

*Facts Bearing on the Problem*

2. See Appendix "A." (Not reproduced as a part of this paper—see Appendix "A," SFE 182/1.)

*Discussion*

3. See Appendix "B." (Not reproduced as a part of this paper—see Appendix "B," SFE 182/1.)

*Conclusions*

4. It is concluded that United States policy with respect to excessive concentrations of economic power in Japan should be as stated in Appendix "C."

*Recommendations*

5. It is recommended that:

a. The State-War-Navy Coordinating Committee approve this paper.

b. This paper then be distributed to the War and Navy Departments for information, and to the State Department for submittal of Appendix "C" to the United States member of the Far Eastern Commission for transmission to the Commission. The U.S. member should be authorized to accept changes which do not alter the subsance or intent of this paper.

*Conclusions*

The United States Government desires to present herewith to the Far Eastern Commission a report of its mission on Japanese combines, and concurrently to recommend for adoption by the Commission certain policies with respect to the concentration of economic power in Japanese industry, finance, and trade.

It is the belief of this Government that the existence of the Zaibatsu, and the monopolistic controls exercised by these giant combines over Japanese economic life, have been a major factor in festering and supporting Japanese aggression. The dissolution of excessive private concentrations of economic power is essential to the democratization of Japanese economic and political life. It therefore constitutes, in the United States view, one of the major objectives of the occupation.

This basic occupation policy with respect to the Zaibatsu is stated in *Basic Post-Surrender Policy for Japan* (FEC 014), and is reaffirmed in *Basic Initial Post-Surrender Directive to SCAP for the Occupation and Control of Japan* (FEC 015). Substantial steps to implement this policy have already been undertaken by the appropriate Japanese authorities, at the direction of or with the approval of SCAP, in the organization and operations of a Japanese Holding Company Liquidating Commission, in providing for an economic purge, and in initiating other measures with respect to combines, control associations and cartel arrangements.

To aid in formulation of comprehensive policies, standards, and procedures a mission headed by Corwin D. Edwards was dispatched to Japan in January 1946. Its report is submitted herewith.

On the basis of that report, the United States Government has prepared the following statement of broad policy with respect to the Zaibatsu question, which it desires to submit for approval by the Far Eastern Commission. In many respects, this statement incorporates measures which already have been or are being implemented by the appropriate Japanese authorities, at the direction of or with the approval of SCAP, in accordance with the directives referred to above.

1. *Objective*

The over-all objective of occupation policy in dealing with excessive concentrations of economic power in Japan should be to destroy such concentrations as may now exist, and to prevent the future creation of new concentrations. Especial care should be taken to avoid the futile gesture of destroying one Zaibatsu class only to create another; a drastic change in the nature as well as the identity of the groups controlling Japanese industry and finance should therefore be effected. Realization of this change will require achievement of the following specific objectives:

a. Dissolution of all excessive concentrations of economic power, unless technological considerations require their continuation (paragraphs 2, 3, 4, below).

b. Elimination of the excessive economic power of persons formerly exercising control over these concentrations, and of certain individuals close to such persons (paragraphs 5, 6, below).

c. Support for varied and diffused types of private ownership of elements of these dissolved concentrations, as well as support for government ownership of such of these concentrations as cannot be dissolved and of such elements of the dissolved concentrations as do not lend themselves to competitive operation (paragraphs 7, 8, below).

d. Elimination of financial support for excessive concentrations—through the divestiture of Zaibatsu holdings in banks and insurance companies, through an increase in the number of sources of credit, through the termination of alliances between financial and non-financial institutions, and through the elimination of government favoritism towards certain financial institutions (paragraphs 9, 10, 11, 12, below).

e. Destruction of legal support for excessive concentrations—through the termination of control legislation, through the creation of an anti-trust law, through changes in the patent law, through amendments to corporate law, and through alterations in current tax law and practices (paragraphs 13, 14, 15, 16, 17, below).

f. Strengthening of the instruments necessary to effect the above policies—through financial and technical aid to preferred types of purchasers, through the creation of public support for anti-Zaibatsu actions of the Japanese Government, and through measures to assure the independence of government personnel from Zaibatsu influences (paragraphs 18, 19, 20, below).

It is considered that the requirements of the Potsdam Declaration will not have been fulfilled until the objectives listed above have been met through the application of measures specified in succeeding paragraphs. It is also considered, however, that the means to be employed in compelling the Japanese Government to effectuate these measures, and the timing of such means, are matters for executive decision by the SCAP. In general, the Japanese Government should be required to take such administrative, legislative and judicial measures as will be consistent with its structure and constitutional powers and will accomplish the policy set out herein.

2. *Definition of an Excessive Concentration*

For purposes of the policies set forth in this paper, an excessive concentration of economic power should be defined as any private enterprise conducted for profit, or combination of such enterprises, which, by reason of its relative size in any line or the cumulative power of its position in many lines, restricts competition or impairs the opportunity for others to engage in business independently, in any important segment of business.

In applying this standard, it should be presumed, subject to refutation, that any private enterprise or combination operated for profit is an excessive concentration of economic power if its asset value is very large; or if its working force (i.e., the working force requires to operate its facilities at capacity as evidenced by its peak past employment figure) is very large; or if, though somewhat smaller in assets or working force, it is engaged in business in various unrelated fields, or if it controls substantial financial institutions and/or substantial industrial or commercial ones; or if it controls a substantial number of other corporate enterprises; or if it produces, sells or distributes a large proportion of the total supply of the products of a major industry.

Absolute size, as well as position within a given industry, is to be considered grounds for defining a specified concentration as excessive. It is desired to eliminate not only monopolies but also aggregations of capital under the control of a given enterprise which are so large as to constitute a material potential threat to competitive enterprise.

All larger Japanese enterprises should immediately be surveyed by SCAP in the light of the above standards. Uncertainty as to whether any specified enterprise is covered by these standards should be resolved in favor of coverage since it is intended that ownership of the bulk of Japanese large-scale industry should be affected by the policies set forth in this paper. It is understood that SCAP's *Schedule of Restricted Concerns*, as may be amended from time to time in accordance with the procedures provided for that purpose, comprehends the Japanese enterprises considered to be excessive concentrations within the meaning of this paper.

3. *Dissolution vs. Non-Dissolution of Excessive Concentrations*

Excessive concentrations of economic power should immediately be dissolved into as many non-related units as possible, no one of which would be covered by any of the definitions of an excessive concentration presented in paragraph 2. Such dissolution should not be effected, however, where the technological need for large scale operation is such that dissolution would clearly cause a drastic reduction in operating efficiency. It should be presumed, subject to refutation, that such a drastic reduction would not result from the dissolution of holding companies, or from the severance of ties of ownership, directorship, and officership between operating companies; or from the severance from operating companies of portions of such companies, where these portions are in unrelated industries, or where they have had a separate corporate existence within the last five years, or where they are so separated from one another physically and technologically that they do not in fact have a common operating management. Treatment of concentrations which are to be dissolved is specified in paragraph 4; treatment of concentrations which are not to be dissolved is specified in subparagraph 8a. The provisions of paragraph 5 should apply equally to persons and holdings in concentrations which are, and are not, to be dissolved.

4. *Policy with Respect to Excessive Concentrations Which are to be Dissolved*

The following measures should be undertaken with respect to excessive concentrations of economic power which are to be dissolved:

a. All concerns in these excessive concentrations which are merely holding companies should be dissolved and divested of their security and property holdings.

b. The units, other than those described under *a* above, into which these excessive concentrations are broken down should, in the case of non-financial enterprises (insurance companies being considered financial enterprises), be divested of any securities which they may hold in other concerns, including concerns not a part of any excessive concentration of economic power.

c. All officers (auditors are to be considered officers) and directors of these operating units, and of operating units in the financial field as well, should surrender all offices and directorships except those in the company in which they are principally engaged, and should be forbidden to acquire any offices and directorships outside of whatever company they may be principally engaged in, at any time in the future, except as provided in paragraph 16. This policy does not apply to persons specified in paragraph 5, who will be dealt with in accordance with the provisions of that paragraph.

d. Certain contractual and service arrangements between the units into which these excessive concentrations have been dissolved should be terminated, including arrangements for performance of central office services, inter-change of personnel, executive agency, and preferential or exclusive trading rights. Resumption of similar arrangements should be prohibited for a time sufficient to ensure bona fide severance of the arrangement.

e. The operating units into which these excessive concentrations are dissolved should grant licenses on non-discriminatory terms to all applicants under patents which they now hold and under licenses which give them rights to sub-license; should surrender any exclusive or preferential rights which they now enjoy under patent licenses granted them by others; and, during the period of transition, should make available to all comers on non-discriminatory terms any technology and patent rights which they make available to other concerns which have been a part of the same combine. Where the units in question hold license under Japanese patents owned by foreigners under terms incompatible with the sense of this paragraph, these terms should be renegotiated. Where the licensor will not agree to renegotiation, the Japanese unit should cease utilizing the license, so that the Japanese government can cancel the patent or open up the patent to licensing on non-discriminatory terms pursuant to Chapter II, Article 41 of the Patent Law.

f. Mergers of any portions of divested or dissolved concerns should be prohibited, except when permission is granted after an affirmative showing of public interest.

5. *Treatment of Personnel in Excessive Concentrations*

All individuals who have exercised controlling power in or over any excessive concentration of economic power, whether as creditors, stockholders, managers, or in any other capacity, should be:

a. divested of all corporate security holdings, liquid assets, and business properties;

b. ejected from all positions of business or governmental responsibility;

c. forbidden from purchasing corporate security holdings or from acquiring positions of business or governmental responsibility at any time during the next ten years.

All other persons likely to act on behalf of the individuals described above should be subjected to the measures specified below. In determining who such persons may be, such factors as ties by blood, marriage, adoption or past personal relationship should be taken into account. (The phrase "past personal relationship" is used in the previous sentence chiefly in reference to persons who have been placed in positions of substantial responsibility in holding companies or their subsidiaries by the Zaibatsu families, but it should also be taken to refer to persons otherwise associated with the Zaibatsu whom SCAP may consider to be acting as "fronts" for the latter.) Such persons should be:

a. divested of liquid assets and business properties, where they possess such assets or properties in amounts of any significance; and divested of all corporate security holdings in any excessive concentration of economic power and corporate security holdings representing an interest of more than 1% in any other major private enterprise;

b. ejected from all positions in business or government which might be used to favor Zaibatsu interests;

c. forbidden from purchasing corporate security holdings, or from acquiring positions in business or government which might be used to favor Zaibatsu interests, at any time during the next ten years.

Where doubt exists as to whether a given person should be covered by the above policies, that doubt should be resolved by SCAP in favor of coverage, since it is desired to divest a sufficient number of holdings to effect a thorough-going transformation of the ownership and control of large-scale Japanese industry.

6. *Compensation of Divested Holdings*

Individuals covered by the definitions in paragraph 5 above shall be indemnified, provided that such indemnification shall be made in such manner and degree as will prohibit their buying back a place of power in the Japanese economy. In order to bring this about, it is essential that certain measures be taken in the dissolution of excessive concentrations and in the sale of the assets of these persons. The measures set out below have been designed with a view to preventing the payment of excessive indemnification to the persons covered in paragraph 5, without affecting to the same degree and manner the compensation of others who have invested in enterprises considered to be excessive concentrations. The determination of what is an excessive indemnification shall be made on the basis of the objectives of these measures. Accordingly:

a. Policies which facilitate the conveyance of divested holdings to new owners should not be modified by an effort to obtain any specified degree of compensation for the former owners of these holdings. The overriding objective should be to dispose of all the holdings in question as rapidly as possible to desirable purchasers; the objective should be achieved even if it requires that holdings be disposed of at a fraction of their real value. In negotiated sales of divested holdings to desirable types of purchasers, the purchaser's ability to pay, rather than the real value of the holding, should affect the fixing of prices and terms of payment.

b. A tax of not less than 90% should be levied on any amount by which the gross sales price exceeds the August 1945 market price (in the case of securities having a market), or the book value as of the same date (in the case of other securities or property). To prevent this tax from resulting in injury to non-Zaibatsu individuals, the following priority should govern the disposition of funds secured through the sale of divested assets:

First Priority: All taxes due, other than the 90% tax referred to above, and all liabilities should be paid in full.

Second Priority: All non-Zaibatsu equity holders, where such exist should be paid up to the amount of the August 1945 market price of their holdings (or the August 1945 book value in the case of securities not having a market).

Third Priority: The 90% tax described above should be paid in full.

Fourth Priority: All Zaibatsu equity holdings should be paid up to the amount of the August 1945 market price of their holdings (or the August 1945 book value in the case of securities not having a market), and remaining funds should be distributed among all equity holders in proportion to the amount of their holdings.

To prevent observance of the priorities cited above from resulting in total expropriation of Zaibatsu shareholders, proceeds of the 90% tax should be partially refunded to Zaibatsu shareholders, where necessary to provide such shareholders with a total compensation not exceeding 15% of the August 1945 market value (or book value where no market existed) of their divested holdings.

In lieu of the 90% tax specified above, a steeply progressive tax may be specifically imposed (in addition to capital levy) on funds which are assigned to the individuals described in paragraph 5 as a result of the sale of assets divested from such individuals.

c. A 75% tax should be levied on any gain realized through resale of divested holdings within two years; and a 50% tax should be levied on any gain realized through resale within four years.

d. Sums credited to persons defined in paragraph 5 above as compensation should be invested in government bonds, whose total par value will not exceed the sum thus credited and which will pay a rate of interest no higher than the lowest rate being paid by comparable government bonds. Such bonds should not be saleable, transferable, or useable as collateral, but should be acceptable for taxes, when all other sources of liquid assets have been dissipated, for ten years from the completion of the sale of such holdings. During this period, cash payments, even of interest, should be limited to sums required for accustomed living expenses, in order that there may be no surplus for investment.

e. After the process of dissolution and liquidation has been well advanced and before the end of the ten-year freeze period, the program should be reviewed to determine whether the sums credited to persons defined in paragraph 5 above will be so large as to make probable a revival of Zaibatsu power. If it is determined that the probability of such a revival still exists, added measures appropriate to the circumstances existing at the time should be applied to remove the probability.

f. Before the freeze is terminated, succession by the owner's heirs should be required, coupled with payment of steeply graduated inheritance taxes.

7. *Liquidation of Divested Holdings*

Liquidation of divested securities and properties should be effected rapidly in a period of about two years from the organization of the Holding Company Liquidation Commission. The plan of liquidation should allow for:

a. pro-rata distribution of security holdings to individual stockholders of the holding concern other than those specified in paragraph 4 (and in some cases to financial institutions which own the holding concern's stock);

b. exchange and cancellation of securities between companies which hold each other's stock;

c. negotiated sale of securities and properties;

d. if necessary to complete the liquidation within about two years, invitation of bids upon securities from eligible purchasers, and acceptance of the highest bids however low such bids may be.

Liquidation should be effected by the Holding Company Liquidation Commission, a wholly public agency of the Japanese Government operating under the close supervision of the SCAP. Especial care should be taken not to allow representatives of large scale business, large scale trade, or large scale finance, or of political groups, sympathetic to such business, trade, or finance, to have any place on this Commission. All nominations to the Commission should be approved by SCAP, its personnel should be removable by SCAP, and it should be required that all sales effected by the Commission be revocable by SCAP. Public announcement should be made of the terms and conditions of all sales.

8. *Sale of Divested Holdings*

In the sale of divested security and property holdings, the over-riding objective should be to transfer ownership and control of these holdings to groups and individuals in such a way as to secure, in addition to the requisite managerial skill, protection against the future creation of excessive concentrations of economic power, through a wider distribution of income and of ownership of the means of production and trade. In order to achieve this objective, the following criteria are set forth as a guide to the selection of purchasers and should be given priority, in this connection, over the purchaser's present ability to pay:

a. Divested holdings in excessive concentrations of economic power which are not to be dissolved for technological reasons, and in other enterprises such as public utilities which do not lend themselves to competitive operation, may be subjected to purchase by the national and local governments of Japan, provided, such purchases are accomplished and approved through democratic processes. Where such concentrations or enterprises are not purchased by these governments, their rates and profits should be subjected to open and effective regulation by impartial public commissions. When the National Government or a local government purchases divested equity holdings in a given concern, it should also give consideration to the concomitant purchase of non-Zaibatsu equity holdings in that concern. Every effort should be made, however, to dissolve all excessive concentrations of economic power, rather than to assign them to government ownership or regulation, until and unless the democratization of the Japanese Government has proceeded sufficiently to render it a truly trustworthy instrument for economic control.

b. In connection with non-governmental purchases, sales to wealthy and economically powerful persons and corporations should be held to a minimum, in order not to lay the groundwork for the creation of a new Zaibatsu class. A decided purchase preference, and the technical and financial aid necessary to take advantage of that preference, should be furnished to such persons as small or medium entrepreneurs and investors, and to such groups as agricultural or consumer cooperatives and trade unions, whose ownership of these holdings would contribute to the democratization of the Japanese economy. Every encouragment should be given such persons and groups to purchase divested holdings, even if they only wish to buy a small proportion of the holdings offered for sale in a given enterprise. In the case of negotiated sales, prices should be fixed with special reference to such purchasers' ability to pay, as should the time period allowed for payment of these prices.

c. No single person, or enterprise, or group of allied persons or enterprises, should be allowed to purchase a number of divested holdings so large as to render probable the future creation of a concentration of economic power approaching in size or character those concentrations defined as excessive under paragraph 2.

d. The purchase of divested holdings in ex-Zaibatsu concerns by the employees of such concerns should be encouraged only if a vigorous effort is made to disperse ownership widely through the working force in question, rather than to concentrate it in a few top executives. To render such dispersion possible, provision should be made for financing these purchases at low prices over a long period of time, possibly through wage deductions. Especial care should be taken to prevent the use of groups of employees in ex-Zaibatsu concerns as purchasing screens for persons disqualified from making these purchases themselves.

e. All sales should be screened to exclude cloaks for Zaibatsu and for other groups who fall under any of the purge directives or purge paragraphs of the Basic Directive.

The criteria specified above should be adhered to regardless of the wishes of non-Zaibatsu stockholders in the enterprises concerned.

9. *Liquidation of Zaibatsu Financial Enterprises*

Divested holdings in Zaibatsu financial and insurance enterprises should be liquidated and disposed of in accordance with the principles laid down in paragraphs 5, 6, and 7 for the liquidation of non-financial enterprises. Policy-holders in Zaibatsu insurance companies should be aided in buying stock of these concerns which is now owned by the Zaibatsu, where the condition of these concerns is sufficiently strong so that the policy-holders desire to make such purchases. Purchase should be facilitated, under these circumstances, by liberal loans on policies, or payment should be permitted in the form of a reduction in the face value of policies. Zaibatsu insurance companies which are insolvent should be mutualized by cutting back the face amount of outstanding policies, where sufficient assets still exist to render this procedure practicable. In the reconstitution of insolvent financial enterprises, stock held by Zaibatsu holding companies and Zaibatsu individuals should be subordinated to that of other stockholders.

10. *Sources of Credit*

As a fundamental measure to encourage competitive operation of the Japanese economy, the number of independent sources of credit should be increased substantially, although not to the point where the individual banks would be so small as to be unable to secure the diversification of loans necessary to banking safety. The strengthening of local savings banks, and of rural and urban credit cooperatives, as well as of independent local banks, should be encouraged. To this end, the following policies, among others should be adopted:

a. Former owners of independent financial institutions which have been merged with Zaibatsu concerns should be encouraged to reestablish their old enterprises by forced divestitures. In this connection, a procedure should be set up whereby former owners of merged banks, trust companies, or insurance companies should have the opportunity, for a limited period of time, to compel the institutions into which their organizations were merged to divest themselves of assets and liabilities to the extent necessary to reconstitute the absorbed institutions in adequate size.

b. Banks over a size to be specified by SCAP should be required to split themselves into two or more independent units within a stated period, as should other banks deemed by SCAP to enjoy a monopolistic position in the field which they serve. The permissible size should be set at a level sufficiently low to force a significant number of such actions and thus greatly increase the number of independent sources of credit, but sufficiently high to guard against the dangers of financial insecurity associated with excessively small banks.

11. *Financial Alliances*

Alliances between any financial and non-financial enterprises, and alliances among any financial enterprises, should be broken. To this end:

a. Banks and trust companies should be prevented from investing more than 10% of their capital and reserves in the securities, loans, bills, advances, and overdrafts of any one company.

b. Such concerns should not be permitted to hold, either as an owner of record or as the holder of a beneficial interest, in their proper, savings, or trust accounts, the stock of any other company in an amount which exceeds 5% of the outstanding shares of that company, nor to vote any such stock which they may hold. Nor should they be permitted to own any stock in a competitor. Exemption should be made to the percentage rule for stock acquired in connection with bona-fide underwritings and to the percentage and voting rules for stock acquired in default of loans, but any such exemptions should not run longer than one year.

c. Officers and directors of any bank or trust company, and persons holding 5% or more of the stock thereof, should be ineligible to hold any office or directorship or similarly large percentage of stock in any other company. Exception should be made for part-time non-policy making employees, such as attorneys and certifying accountants, but such exceptions should be defined as narrowly as possible.

d. No bank or trust company should be allowed to redeposit more than 10% of its deposits in any one institution other than the Bank of Japan.

12. *Elimination of Financial Discrimination*

To eliminate discrimination in favor of Zaibatsu banks:

a. A system of deposit insurance should be instituted, to diminish the belief among depositors that accounts in Zaibatsu banks are safer than elsewhere. A limit (e.g., of the order of magnitude of ten billion yen) should be set to the total amount of deposits which will be insured for a single bank. A limit should also be set to the amount of deposits which will be insured for a single account.

b. The Postal Savings System should ultimately be required to deposit its funds in ordinary banks, allocating at least 90% of what it receives in any regional grouping of prefectures among the banks having head offices in that region in proportion to the assets of such banks. A bank ineligible for deposit insurance should also be ineligible to receive the redeposits of the postal savings system.

c. Legislation should be introduced to improve the standard of commercial banking and to prevent banks from undertaking business considered unwise for commercial banks. (Performance of investment banking functions by commercial banks should not be prohibited, however, until suitable alternative agents for these functions become available.) Such legislation should also assign to the Bank of Japan, or to some other suitable public agency, powers of direction and inspection over other banks, whose activities would be required to conform to statutory provisions regarding capital, reserves, investment policy, and other matters. The discretion which the laws now entrust to the Minister of Finance, in this connection, should be greatly reduced, and his functions clearly defined by law and made subject to check and review by the Diet. His powers to legislate by ordinance and regulation should be strictly curtailed and limited to genuine emergencies. Bank examinations should take place at least every two years.

d. The functions and powers of special banks should be defined and limited by law, and these banks should not be allowed to engage in ordinary banking. The need for the existence of the special banks should be reviewed, in order to determine whether certain of these banks might not revert to the status of ordinary banks.

e. All vestiges of private ownership of the Bank of Japan should be eliminated. The board of directors should be made representative of finance, trade, industry, agriculture, and of large, medium, and smaller size business.

f. Competition among banks for customers should be restored through such measures as the abolition of the designated bank system and of the financial control associations.

g. Employees performing responsible functions in the Ministry of Finance and government banks should be forbidden to hold the securities of any financial institution, and should be ineligible for employment by private financial institutions for two years after they leave government employment.

13. *Government Support of Industrial Monopolies*

Laws and practices through which the Japanese Government has favored the growth of private monopolies should be terminated; although that Government should not be deprived of its power to regulate the Japanese economy in the public interest. To this end:

a. Laws and ordinances establishing existing control associations or special companies should be generally repealed and the associations or special companies abolished. The future assumption, by non-governmental agencies, of powers formerly exercised under these laws, should be prohibited. The future assumption, by governmental agencies, of such of these powers as have no major use other than to support monopolistic bodies and practices should also be prohibited. Necessary governmental functions formerly performed by control associations or special companies should be transferred to appropriate governmental agencies, which agencies should be created where they do not now exist. In cases where SCAP is satisfied that current conditions prevent the government from effectively performing these functions, and is further satisfied that effective performance of these functions is necessary for public purposes, he may allow temporary delegation of these functions by the government to the old control associations or special companies or to similar new quasi-private bodies, provided that final decisions are made by the government and that rights of appeal to the government against abuse of powers are provided. All quasi-private bodies exercising such delegated functions should be liquidated as soon as their functions can be transferred to appropriate governmental agencies, or at such sooner time as SCAP may find the exercise of their functions to be no longer necessary. (For example, where these functions relate to allocation, or price and trade control for reconversion purposes, their performance could be terminated upon the expiration of the reconversion period.)

b. All legislation which forbids, or requires governmental approval of, the entry of any new business into an industry, or the expansion of any old business, should be terminated, except in so far as:

(1) the right to effect such a restriction is implicit in the anti-trust legislation suggested below;

(2) the right to effect such a restriction is necessary in order to comply with SCAP directives dealing with industrial disarmament and other subjects;

(3) non-discriminatory restrictions for generally accepted public purposes, such as protecting the public against fraud, and protecting the public health, are concerned;

(4) fields of business activity reserved to the national or local governments are concerned. In this connection, pre-war laws which set up clear-cut government monopolies should be left undisturbed; but, to prevent the use of this type of law to evade other portions of the anti-Zaibatsu program, the creation of new government monopolies during the period of the occupation should be permitted only in cases where they are in the public interest or where their creation is in accordance with the policy for sale of divested holdings to the national and local governments described in paragraph 7a above. The petroleum and alcohol monopolies, which were instituted for war purposes, should be terminated as soon as possible.

c. All laws and practices under which the government has favored specific private or quasi-private enterprises, to the detriment of potentially or actually competitive enterprises, should be systematically reviewed, and such of these laws and practices as do not have a demonstrable public purpose should be terminated. In so far as any subsidies are allowed to continue, or are granted in the future, they should be controlled by the legislative branch of the government, and provision should be made that hereafter their amount, purpose, and effect be disclosed in public reports.

Principles such as those set forth in the preceding sub-paragraphs should be made effective, not only by changes in substantive law, but also by provisions giving aggrieved persons the right to attack in the courts any discriminatory subsidy, preference, or other practice.

14. *Anti-Trust Law*

A Japanese anti-trust law should be enacted, prohibiting, among other things:

a. concerted business activity which burdens trade, including, but not by way of limitation to, such activities as fixing of prices, restriction of sales or output, and allocation of markets, commodities, or customers;

b. individual or concerted activity which has the purpose or effect of coercing business enterprises to conform to business policies, or participation in programs carried on by the coercing concern or group which are designed to drive selected enterprises out of any line of business, through means which include but are not limited to intimidation of a rival's customers or sale to a rival at discriminatory prices;

c. the creation of excessive concentrations of economic power, as such concentrations are defined in paragraph 2; (where considerations of structural or technological unity require the creation of large concentrations, government ownership or strict regulation of these concentrations should be provided for);

d. types of industrial growth and of intercorporate connection which are particularly likely to lead to monopoly or to excessive size, including mergers (i.e., acquisitions of any substantial portion of the capital assets) of going concerns of other than negligible size which are in competition with one another, or mergers of non-competing concerns which might lead to the creation of large scale enterprises capable of developing into an excessive concentration of economic power, where such mergers are not explicitly found to be required in the public interest.

e. types of intercorporate relations (e.g., those described in paragraph 4d) which restrain competition.

This anti-trust law should be enforced by a specialized agency operating at a high governmental level and exercising broad investigatory and remedial powers. Consideration should be given to including in this agency representatives of the groups most likely to be aggrieved by excessive corporate growth; in any event, special care should be taken not to allow representatives of large scale business, or of political groups sympathetic to large scale business to be named to this agency.

Exemption from the provisions of this law should be provided for the joint activities of cooperatives, where such activities are not coercive or monopolistic, and where they are conducted according to the democratic principles characteristic of genuine cooperatives. Similar exemption should be provided for labor activities other than those involving the restriction of commercial competition, and for natural monopolies and public utilities in so far as they are owned or closely regulated by the government.

15. *Patent Law*

The provisions and the manner of enforcing Japanese patent law should be revised to ensure that patents in Japan cannot be used to support the establishment or perpetuation of concentrations of economic power.

16. *Corporate Law*

The following changes in Japanese corporate law should be effected:

a. Disclosure of relevant facts in selling corporate securities should be required, and the fraudulent practices in connection with such sales should be prohibited.

b. Before any call to a meeting of the stockholders of a corporation, the management of the corporation shall make full disclosure of all the facts necessary for the stockholders to appraise intelligently the proposals to be placed before the meeting.

c. Misleading practices in corporate accounting should be forbidden, and minimum standards of disclosure in such accounting should be required.

d. Interlocking officerships should be prohibited, and officers of one concern should be prohibited from serving as directors of another. Interlocking directorates should be prohibited in the case of competing concerns and in the case of concerns which rent, sell, or buy goods or services to or from each other in significant amounts. In the case of other concerns, interlocking directorates should be allowed to the point where no more than one fourth of the members of any Board of Directors are at the same time directors of other corporations. No one person should, however, be allowed to serve on the Board of Directors of more than three corporations. Nothing in this paragraph should be taken as in any way modifying the provisions of paragraph 11c. Officers and directors should be prevented from having holdings of shares in competing or supplying concerns, and should be prevented from having holdings of shares in any other enterprise representing more than 5% of their liquid assets or more than 5% of such other enterprises' outstanding shares. Officers, directors, and persons having a beneficial interest in or control of any equity issue of a corporation in excess of one percent of the total issue should be required to report their holdings and transactions in all issues of the corporation, and such reports should be publicized. Profits of corporate insiders derived from short-term transactions in the corporation's securities should be subject to recapture by the corporation.

e. An ultra vires action by a corporation should be grounds for remedial action by a stockholder or punitive action by a public agency. Moreover, a corporation should be specifically prohibited from entering partnerships, either directly or indirectly, or in other respects avoiding the limitations on intercorporate relationships.

f. It should be required that all shares having par value should be fully paid, and that equal voting rights attach to all shares of the same issue. The use of no par value shares should be permitted; such shares to be offered for sale at any time at a value to be decided by the company's board of directors. All corporations should be required to adopt the principle of pre-emptive-rights in offering new shares.

g. Every effort should be made to assure the independence of Japanese auditors, who should be prevented from having direct or indirect affiliations with management and from having conflicting interests in other concerns.

h. With stated exceptions for banks, investment trusts, insurance companies, and possibly other types of financial institutions, the Japanese company law should be amended to forbid one corporation from holding the stock of another. The use of 100% owned subsidiaries should be permitted, however (subject to the restrictions on mergers outlined under paragraph 14d).

i. Stockholders should not be unduly hampered in bringing suits against management for money damages or for equitable remedies.

17. *Tax and Inheritance Laws*

In connection with current and impending revisions of Japanese tax law, every effort should be made to favor the wider distribution of income and ownership envisaged in this paper, through the following means:

a. Income and inheritance taxes should be very much more steeply graduated than they are at present.

b. Property inherited by the head of a house should be subject to the tax rates applicable to other heirs.

c. Diffusion of inherited wealth should be assured by provision for reasonably equal distribution among heirs, insofar as estates aggregating considerable wealth are concerned.

d. Members of a house should be prevented from deriving significant tax advantages from the insolvent status of other members of the house.

e. The present discretionary power of the Minister of Finance in tax matters should be greatly reduced. Tax rates should be fixed by the Diet.

18. *Policy Concerning Preferred Purchasers*

Measures specified below should be taken in order to strengthen and democratize preferred categories of purchasers of divested holdings:

a. In order to qualify Japanese cooperatives for purchase preference in connection with divested holdings, such cooperatives should be freed from governmental influence and should be relieved of public functions. They should be subject to government supervision, only insofar as such supervision is necessary to prevent fraud and to ensure compliance with the provisions of this paragraph. Membership in these cooperatives should be voluntary, and requirements for membership therein should be nondiscriminatory. (In this connection, the minimum contribution or entrance fee should be reduced to the point where it will form no obstacle to the membership of low income persons.) All participating members should have equal votes and officers should be selected by majority vote. The proceeds should be divided equally among members or in proportion to the relative volume of business, without allowance, beyond a low fixed dividend, for contributions of capital. In addition to being converted into genuinely democratic instruments through these and other changes, cooperatives should be freed from all legal restrictions which prevent them from engaging in various kinds of activities. Specifically, consumers' cooperative societies should be recognized and afforded the same type of privileges as other cooperative societies. The minimum number of members qualifying for registration under the Cooperative Societies Law should be raised from the present figure of seven to levels which will vary for different types of societies but which should be sufficiently high in each case to prevent domination by minorities. Genuine cooperative societies should receive such public financial and technical aid as may be necessary to their expansion.

b. Where the possibility exists that trade unions might purchase Zaibatsu holdings, all possible technical and financial assistance should be furnished the trade unions concerned, provided that these unions are genuine labor organizations, and are not acting as cloaks for former owners. As a means of providing for trade union ownership of divested holdings, consideration should be given to assigning ownership of divested holdings to cooperative societies organized especially for this purpose, with a membership parallel to that of trade unions.

c. Small entrepreneurs desiring to purchase divested holdings should be given all possible public assistance so that they may compete on more advantageous terms with large scale business. The Japanese Ministry of Commerce should establish a bureau specifically devoted to aiding such small business. This bureau should give special support to the performance of joint activities of an unrestrictive character by such mutual-aid organizations of small entrepreneurs as manufacturers' guilds and export guilds. Precautions should be taken, however, against domination of these guilds by the government or by the larger firms; nor should they be permitted to engage in such of their former activities as were in restraint of trade.

19. *Public Support*

Vigorous efforts should be made by SCAP to create Japanese public understanding of, and support for, the Anti-Zaibatsu program through such means as:

a. provision for access to recent literature in English about the problems of industrial organization;

b. publication of SCAP's factual findings about the Zaibatsu;

c. encouragement of the organization of a Japanese commission of inquiry, representative of a wide range of interests and opinions, to investigate the facts about the Zaibatsu and make public its recommendations;

d. attention to the problems of industrial organization, and the dangers of monopoly and excessive concentration of economic power in the revision of the Japanese educational system;

e. provision for contact between the Japanese anti-trust agency and similar bodies in other countries.

A special attempt should be made to furnish relevant data to, and to secure the support of, those groups whose economic interests are most acutely promoted by the dissolution of the Zaibatsu: consumers, small and medium-size businessmen, trade unions, and cooperatives.

20. *Japanese Government*

An attempt should be made to deprive the Japanese Government of its former pro-Zaibatsu character, and to prevent renewed alliances between the bureaucracy and business interests:

a. SCAP should make every effort to see that new public agencies established in order to carry out the anti-Zaibatsu program envisaged in this paper are staffed with individuals not previously associated with or sympathetic to large scale business or its political spokesmen. Economists and other intellectuals or technical experts hitherto debarred from government work because of their anti-imperialist or anti-Zaibatsu views would be desirable recruits.

b. In view, however, of the limited availability of such persons, and of the uncertain political complexion of the present Japanese bureaucracy, SCAP should reduce the discretionary policy-making authority of that bureaucracy in so far as the more important issues related to this program are concerned. In economic matters at least, the Japanese bureaucracy should not be left in a position to usurp the functions of the legislative branch of the government.

c. Existing government officials performing responsible functions relating to the control or regulation of private industrial, commercial, or financial enterprises should be discharged where, because of their past employment in Zaibatsu concerns or other previous private or public actions, they are believed sympathetic to Zaibatsu interests.

d. Government officials performing responsible functions relating to the control or regulation of private commercial, industrial, or financial enterprises should be prohibited from holding the securities of any one such private enterprise in an amount which would represent more than 5% of the official's total wealth, or more than 1% of the enterprise's capital value. Reports of all security holdings by such government officials should be made public. Such officials should also be prohibited within a period of two years after their leaving of government employ, from accepting private positions which involve their representing, directly or indirectly, private enterprises before the government bureaus with which they were formerly associated, or from holding positions in any private enterprise which is the object of legal action as a result of its alleged violation of any of the measures specified in this paper.

e. Special procedures should be set up to make public the names of government officials holding responsible positions relating to the control or regulation of private, commercial, industrial, or financial enterprises, so that anti-Zaibatsu groups and persons may scrutinize their past records and protest publicly against appointments which they consider unsuitable.

f. The principle of private redress for injury suffered as a result of governmental action should be recognized in Japanese law.

21. *United Nations and Neutral Interests*

In the application of measures specified in this paper, SCAP should protect the interests of nationals of members of the United Nations in Japan, in so far as this can be accomplished without limiting the effectiveness of these measures. In general, his objective should be to provide adequate, prompt and effective indemnification for property taken from such interests to the extent feasible. He should also keep full records of any change in the status of such interests which may result from the application of these measures.

22. *Non-Profit Corporations*

An exception should be made to the provisions of this paper affecting interlocking officerships and directorates insofar as these provisions concern non-profit corporations which are devoted to public, charitable and cultural purposes and which do not hold securities of other corporations.

# Appendix X

## Record of HCLC Action on the 83 Designated Holding Companies

| *Romanized Name in Japanese* | *Name in Translation* |
|---|---|
| I. Companies required to dissolve | |
| Asano Honsha | Asano and Company |
| Daiwa Shokusan | Daiwa Industrial |
| Hattori Goshi Kaisha | Hattori Ltd. Partnership |
| Ishihara Gomei Kaisha | Ishihara Partnership |
| Kanto Kogyo | Kanto Development |
| Katakura Gumi | Katakura Partnership |
| Kyodo Kogyo | Kyodo Development |
| Mitsui Honsha | Mitsui and Company |
| Nichiden Kogyo | Nichiden Development |
| Nihon Denshin Dewa | Japan Telephone and Telegraph |
| Nomura Gomei Kaisha | Nomura Partnership |
| Ohara Goshi Kaisha | Ohara Ltd. Partnership |
| Okazaki Honten | Okazaki and Company |
| Oki Denki Shoken | Oki Electric Securities |
| Shibusawa Dozoku | Shibusawa and Company |
| Tatsuma Honke Shoten | Tatsuma Ltd. Partnership |
| II. Old company dissolved, second companies (The figure in parenthesis is the number of second companies) | |
| Daiken Sangyo | Daiken Industrial (5) |
| Fuji Sangyo | Fuji Industrial (11) |
| Fuso Kinzoku Kogyo | Fuso Metal Industries (1) |
| Hayashikane Shoten | Hayashikane Trading (1) |
| Kokusai Denki Tsushin | International Telecommunication (1) |
| Mitsubishi Honsha | Mitsubishi and Company (2) |
| Mitsubishi Jukogyo | Mitsubishi Heavy Industries (3) |
| Mitsubishi Kasei Kogyo | Mitsubishi Chemical Industries (3) |
| Mitsubishi Shoji | Mitsubishi Trading (1) |
| Mitsui Bussan | Mitsui Trading (1) |
| Mitsui Kozan | Mitsui Mining (1) |
| Naigai Boseki | Naigai Spinning (2) |
| Nippon Chisso Hiryo | Japan Nitrogenous Fertilizer (1) |
| Nihon Musen | Japan Radio (4) |
| Nihon Seitetsu | Japan Iron and Steel (4) |
| Oji Seishi | Oji Paper (3) |

| *Romanized Name in Japanese* | *Name in Translation* |
|---|---|
| Oki Denki | Oki Electric (1) |
| Okura Kogyo | Okura Mining (1) |
| Riken Kogyo | Riken Industries (11) |
| Sumitomo Honsha | Sumitomo and Company (6) |
| Teikoku Kogyo Kaihatsu | Imperial Mining Development (1) |
| Teitoku Kai KK | Teitoku Assoc. (1) |
| Terada Gomei | Terada Partnership (1) |
| Toyoda Sangyo | Toyoda Industrial (1) |
| Wakasa Kogyo | Wakasa Development (1) |
| Yamashita | Yamashita Company (1) |
| Yasuda Hozensha | Yasuda and Company (1) |

III. Old company continued, second companies

| | |
|---|---|
| Daiwa Boseki | Daiwa Spining (1) |
| Kanegafuchi Boseki | Kanegafuchi Spinning (1) |
| Kawasaki Jukogyo | Kawasaki Heavy Industries (1) |
| Kobe Seikosho | Kobe Steel Mfg (2) |
| Kurashiki Boseki | Kurashiki Spinning (1) |
| Mitsubishi Kogyo | Mitsubishi Mining (1) |
| Mitsui Kozan | Mitsui Mining (1) |
| Nihon Soda | Japan Soda (3) |
| Nissan Kagaku | Nissan Chemicals (1) |
| Seika Kogyo | Seika Mining (3) |
| Tokyo Shibaura Denki | Tokyo Shibaura Electric (14) |

IV. Companies not required to make changes

| | |
|---|---|
| Asano Bussan | Asano Trading |
| Dai Nihon Boseki | (Great) Japan Spinning |
| Fuji Boseki | Fuji Cotton Spinning |
| Furukawa Denki Kogyo | Furukawa Electric Industries |
| Furukawa Kogyo | Furukawa Mining |
| Gunze Seishi | Gunze Silk Manufacturing |
| Hitachi Seisakusho | Hitachi Engineering |
| Hokkaido Tanko Kisen | Hokkaido Colliery and Steamship |
| Katakura Kogyo | Katakura Industries |
| Matsushita Denki | Matsushita Electric |
| Mitsubishi Denki | Mitsubishi Electric |
| Mitsubishi Fudosan | Mitsubishi Real Estate |
| Mitsui Kagaku Kogyo | Mitsui Chemical Industries |
| Mitsui Sempaku | Mitsui Shipping |
| Naigai Tsusho | Naigai Trading |
| Nihon Denki | Japan Electric |
| Nihon Keori | Japan Wool Weaving |
| Nihon Kogyo | Japan Mining |

| *Romanized Name in Japanese* | *Name in Translation* |
|---|---|
| Nihon Kokan | Japan Steel Pipe |
| Nippon Yusen Kaisha | Japan Mail Line |
| Nissan | Nissan |
| Nisshin Boseki | Nisshin Spinning |
| Nisshin Kagaku Kogyo | Nisshin Chemical Industries |
| Osaka Shosen Kaisha | Osaka Commercial Line |
| Shikishima Boseki | Shikishima Spinning |
| Showa Denko | Showa Electric Industry |
| Sumitomo Denki Kogyo | Sumitomo Electric Industry |
| Teikoku Jinzo Kenshi | Imperial Rayon |
| Toyo Boseki | Oriental Spinning |
| Yamashita Kisen | Yamashita Steamship |

SOURCE: HCLC, *Zaibatsu Dissolution,* data volume, pp. 6-21.

# Index